Real Lives Revealed

Recent Titles in the Libraries Unlimited Real Stories Series

Robert Burgin, Series Editor

The Inside Scoop: A Guide to Nonfiction Investigative Writing and Exposés
Sarah Statz Cords

Real Lives Revealed

A Guide to Reading Interests in Biography

Rick Roche

Real Stories
Robert Burgin, Series Editor

Libraries Unlimited
An Imprint of ABC-CLIO, LLC

A B C 🔷 C L I O

Santa Barbara, California • Denver, Colorado • Oxford, England

Library of Congress Cataloging-in-Publication Data

Roche, Rick.
  Real lives revealed : a guide to reading interests in biography / Rick Roche.
      p. cm. — (Real stories)
  Includes bibliographical references and indexes.
  ISBN 978-1-59158-664-7 (alk. paper)
  1. Biography—Bibliography. I. Title.
  Z5301.R56 2009
  [CT104]
  016.92—dc22   2009017117

13 12 11 10 9   1 2 3 4 5

This book is also available on the World Wide Web as an eBook.
Visit www.abc-clio.com for details.

ABC-CLIO, LLC
130 Cremona Drive, P.O. Box 1911
Santa Barbara, California 93116-1911

This book is printed on acid-free paper ∞

Manufactured in the United States of America

Contents

Part 1: Nonfiction Genres

Part 2: Stylistic Genres

Part 3: Nonfiction Subject Interests

Series Foreword

In my foreword to Sarah Statz Cords's *The Real Story: A Guide to Nonfiction Reading Interests*, I noted that her book provided a much-needed map to "the rich and varied world of nonfiction."

The titles in the Real Stories Series flesh out the map that Sarah drew and take us even deeper into the exciting worlds of nonfiction genres: Investigative Writing, Biography, Autobiography and Memoir, Women's Nonfiction, True Adventure, Travel Literature, Environmental Writing, True Crime, Sports Stories, and many others.

The titles in this series are designed to assist librarians and other professionals who work with readers in identifying nonfiction books that their patrons or customers will enjoy reading. These books will also help libraries evaluate and build their collections in the various nonfiction genres.

Similar to the titles in Libraries Unlimited's Genreflecting Series, each of the volumes in the Real Stories Series focuses on a popular genre in the nonfiction arena. Individual guides organize and describe hundreds of books and include definitions of each genre and its subgenres, as well as a discussion of the appeal of the genre and its subgenres. Because readers' advisory is ultimately about making connections, recommendations of other nonfiction books and fiction read-alikes are also provided for each book highlighted.

With *The Real Story*, nonfiction lovers gained the equivalent of general guidebooks to fiction genres, such as Herald's *Genreflecting* or Saricks's *Readers' Advisory Guide to Genre Fiction*. With the titles in the Real Stories Series, we now have even more specific guidebooks, similar to the fiction guides *Make Mine a Mystery* and *Hooked on Horror*.

As twentieth-century architect Mies van der Rohe reminded us, God is in the details. The titles in the Real Stories Series help us to better understand the details of nonfiction and thereby to better serve our users who read nonfiction for pleasure.

Robert Burgin

Acknowledgments

I know that many people will skip this page, but it is for me the most important page of the book. Without the many people who gave of their time and ideas, I would never have completed this book.

Many thanks go to my wife, Bonnie Reid, who not only encouraged me but also read nearly every page twice. I owe many author and title suggestions to her. Her knowledge of libraries, readers, grammar, and spelling helped immensely. I believe we will long remember some of the funnier typos that she uncovered.

Many thanks also go to my editors, Barbara Ittner and Robert Burgin, who gave me the chance to write this book, and for finding more precise words. They helped immensely with the organization of the book and suggested more books to recommend.

Thanks to Maggie Moran, who recommended me as a writer to Robert. Without that thoughtful act, I would never have submitted a book proposal.

Thanks to Sarah Statz Cords, who wrote *The Real Story: A Guide to Nonfiction Reading Interests*, creating the pattern for this book. She also answered many of my first-time author's questions.

Thanks to Joyce Saricks for inviting me to staff book discussions when I was not even a staff member at her library and for turning me on to readers' advisory.

Thanks to Maureen O'Connor, whose advice helped me decide how to organize this book.

Thanks to Kristin Schar for her encouragement and editing the proposal that won approval.

Thanks to my daughter Laura Roche for her encouragement and helping compile the biography awards lists.

Thanks to Aaron Schmidt, who showed me blogging. If I had not started a blog to be as cool as Aaron, I would never have had the opportunity to write this book.

Thanks to Anne Kozak and the staff at the Thomas Ford Memorial Library, who encouraged me, offered title suggestions, and unpacked many books from the interlibrary loan delivery.

Thanks to the staff at the Downers Grove Public Library. The book selectors stocked the biography section with many great titles, and I kept the circulation staff busy for about eight months.

Thanks to book selectors throughout the Metropolitan Library System for having purchased such a wide variety of biographies. Thanks also to all the taxpayers who paid for these books.

Thanks now to you, the librarians and readers for whom I write. Now find your own most important page in this book, one connecting you with a great book.

Introduction

Biographers must make sense of all the clutter of life—make life into art.
—Leon Edel, *Writing Lives: Principia Biographica*

My library has a handsome old oak desk that served the original librarian when the building opened in the 1930s. We now keep it in the front of the adult services area for displays. In August several years ago, when our summer reading program ended, we wanted to replace the summer books but had not prepared our next display topic. Because they were easy to select quickly, we arranged a display of biographies and put up a sign: "Lives That Mattered: Biographies and Memoirs." To our delight, readers took many of the books right away, and in the subsequent weeks we frequently needed to restock. Because it was so popular, we left our stopgap display up for three months. With this success in mind, we chose "Uncommon Lives: Biographies and Memoirs" as the theme for a summer reading campaign a couple of years later and again found that biographies circulated well when recommended by the staff in displays.

Because of its popularity, biography is the nonfiction genre most recognized by readers, librarians, booksellers, and publishers. Sales catalogs and review journals often include biography sections, and the book distributor Baker and Taylor begins its *Booking Ahead* newsletter each month with listings of forthcoming biographies. Because so many readers enjoy reading books about the lives of famous people, it is often the only nonfiction category to be given its own section in public libraries, which usually keep the rest of their true-life books shelved by Dewey numbers. In a search for the popular biography *John Adams* by David McCullough in the SWAN Catalog of the Metropolitan Library System in Illinois, I found that forty of the sixty-seven libraries owning the book keep it in a separate biography section. Similarly, the call number for *Kate Remembered* by A. Scott Berg in thirty-eight of sixty-eight libraries was "B," "Bio," or "Biography." I imagine that the libraries that integrate their biographies with Dewey nonfiction often hear, "Where are the biographies?" from readers who prefer browsing shelves to searching through catalogs. Bookstores, which are often more attuned than libraries to marketing their merchandise, almost always have easy to locate biography sections.

Readers learn to enjoy biographies as children. They are usually introduced to this literary form during their elementary school years, when school and public libraries offer them books about the historical figures that they study and the contemporary figures that they recognize from entertainment, sports, and the news. These libraries invariably have shelves loaded with thin, illustrated books about the lives of explorers, pioneers, presidents, inventors, scientists, artists, writers, composers, athletes, and actors. Librarians thoughtfully select and acquire titles to reflect the diversity of world culture, including women, people of color, followers of various religions, and people with physical handicaps. Because the demand is strong, publishers of children's books offer large series of biographies written for varying reading levels. In looking through our library catalog for biographies, I discovered many children's titles about the same famous people covered in the books for adult readers that I include in this guide. When they grow up, young people will expect to find more biographies.

What Is Biography?

In his article "Biography" in *The New Dictionary of the History of Ideas*, Frederic Liers credits the ancient Greeks for establishing the literary form of biography. The Greek term *bios* (life) was combined with *graphein* (writing) to form the concept known as "life writing." Simply put, biography is a written account of the life of an individual, a person who lived and can be identified (Liers 2005, 217). Widely understood throughout society, the literature of life stories includes several forms, including the third-person account of a life, which is commonly called "biography." Other forms of life writing are autobiographies, memoirs, letters, and diaries. In this guide we focus only on biography written by a third person, because another volume in the Real Story Series will examine the first-person writings of autobiography and memoir.

> This book, *Real Lives Revealed: A Reader's Guide to Biography*, focuses on third-person accounts of the lives of individual persons. Most of the books reviewed are single-subject biographies. Autobiography and memoir will be the focus of another guide in the Real Story Series.

Most of the biographies in this book recount the lives of single individuals; the lengthy and detailed single-subject biography is the modern standard. According to Frederic Liers, however, the ancient Greeks began biography by writing short character sketches. The earliest examples are profiles of Pericles and Sophocles written by Ion of Chios (ca. 490–421 BCE). Four centuries later, the influential Greek author Plutarch wrote forty-six profiles pairing Greek and Roman figures, which are collected together as *Parallel Lives* or *Plutarch's Lives* (Liers 2005, 218). During the Italian Renaissance Giorgio Vasari, who had traveled widely and seen most of the great Renaissance art, wrote the collective biography *Lives of the Artists*, which pioneered art scholarship (Bondanella and Bondanella 1991, vii–viii). As late as the eighteenth century, English author Samuel Johnson wrote his *Lives of the Poets*, which Carl Rollyson in his *Biography: A User's Guide* claims pioneered the instructive "lessons for private life" approach to biography (2008, 161–162). Following in the tradition of Plutarch, Vasari, and Johnson, this guide also includes modern collective biographies with short profiles of numerous individuals.

Ironically, the rise of the single-subject biography is also linked to Samuel Johnson, the subject of the critically acclaimed and widely read *The Life of Samuel Johnson*, written by his friend, James Boswell. According to Adam Sisman in *Boswell's Presumptuous Task: The Making of the Life of Dr. Johnson*, Boswell was not the only British author to memorialize the life of Johnson in a book. Several biographies were quickly published after the English writer's death, long before Boswell completed his book; the thinking of the time was that Boswell had missed his opportunity to sell his book when public interest in the deceased Johnson was still high. Seven years had passed, but

Boswell surpassed all of the other biographers by artfully using evidence, such as letters, diaries, and interviews, to portray Johnson in great depth, setting a new standard for biography. The biographies in this guide are literary descendants of Boswell's book.

Pure Biography

Many more years passed before good modern biographies based on Boswell's model became numerous. Carl Rollyson, in *Biography: A User's Guide*, describes the British biographies of the nineteenth century as merely memorials and tributes, and he says that Americans of the period used biography as a tool for nation building, not for honestly portraying lives. In both countries, biographers lauded their subjects and avoided criticism, until 1918, when Lytton Strachey published *Eminent Victorians*, his sensationally unflattering profiles of four highly respected British figures (Rollyson 2008, 220–221). In 1928, in a series of lectures collected in *The Development of the English Biography*, Harold Nicolson decried the fact that throughout history biographers writing to glorify their subjects had fabricated stories to support their biased views. He proposed "pure biography." To qualify, a biography had to be factual, accurate, and verifiable; portray an individual; and have artistic purpose. He also asked that biographers aim to be neutral in their narratives and skeptical of laudatory stories (Rollyson 2008, 132).

Beyond Nicolson's three tenets of accuracy, a character, and a focus, there are no hard and fast rules about what has to be included in a good biography. A biography may or may not cite a subject's birth, the influence of parents, the education, the first steps in a career, the decline, and, ultimately, the death of the subject. These elements are often incorporated in recounting a life, but their importance can vary with the story that the biographer wants to tell. What the biographer must do is take the central events of a life and construct a story that appeals to readers.

In *How to Do Biography: A Primer*, Nigel Hamilton argues that a good biography is one that never forgets the reader. The problem with many academically written biographies is that scholarship gets far more attention than narration. Biographers have to remember to tell readers what they want to know—how their subjects lived and why their lives mattered—in a manner that readers can understand. To do so, authors must find the balance between too much and too little detail, making the life seem real but never becoming tedious. They must also learn to balance the gratitude that they may have to living subjects, interviewees, and literary executors with their obligation to give readers a full and accurate story. If a biographer's first loyalty is not to the reader, then the resulting book is flawed and probably unsatisfying (Hamilton 2008, 51).

> "When biographies fail to spark interest, become tedious or unsatisfying, it is usually because the biographer has lost his commitment to the reader and is taking the audience for granted, by getting too self-absorbed in the life he is depicting. Never forget or neglect the reader!"—Nigel Hamilton, *How to Do Biography: A Primer*, p. 51

Why Do People Like Biography?:
The Appeal Factors

Upon the death of actor Heath Ledger in January 2008, *Chicago Tribune* book editor Julia Keller, who was not particularly a fan of his acting, suddenly found herself wanting to know much more about his life. In her article "So You Like Biographies? Don't Hate Yourself" in the January 27, 2008, issue of the newspaper, she described her curiosity. What kind of childhood did he have in Australia? Why did he become an actor? How had he endured the separation from his daughter when he parted with her mother? These questions seemed to her personal and almost invasive, yet she recognized that they were normal human interest. She realized that she had a similar desire for knowledge when Pakistani presidential candidate Benazir Bhutto was assassinated. In her thoughtful article, she defends the rights of readers to seek intimate knowledge of the lives of public figures. She admits to loving biography, with all of its revealing and sometimes unflattering details, for bringing celebrities "down to earth" where we all share joy and sorrow.

For readers such as Keller, interest in biography is strong because character and narrative appeal are consistently high. By definition biographies, being books about the lives of individuals, have identifiable characters that readers may follow through the narrative from beginning to end, something that other nonfiction genres often lack. Titles or subtitles of biographies almost always include the name of the subject, and most narratives recount a detailed birth to death sequence of events from the life of the profiled individual. From the standpoint of predictability, biographies are perceived by some readers as safe reading. Examining the books included in this guide, I found that there is actually more variety in biography than the reading public realizes. Some authors rearrange the sequence of events to put a key incident in the first chapter; other biographers focus only on a subject's career or segments of a life; while a few writers turn to topical essays to build their biographies. Still, no matter what the narrative arrangement, biography delivers a story focused on a person whose life can be admired, lamented, or a bit of both.

The story lines in biographies are as varied as they are in novels, offering many possibilities to readers with differing tastes. Elements of adventure, romance, tragedy, mystery, suspense, horror, science, sports, and war may all be found in life stories. Settings are also quite varied. With historical subjects from many lands and centuries, the reading possibilities are seemingly endless. Most people who enjoy reading should be able to find a biography that will entertain them. And if pleasure of reading is not enough, some people can enjoy biographies for their educational qualities. All lives take place in a context of time and place; many biographies describe setting thoroughly, aligning biography with the discipline of history. The advantage that biography has over history is that biography focuses on an individual with whom the reader may identify and empathize, making the study of the past through biography more understandable and appealing to many readers.

The Truth of Biography

Biography is accepted as nonfiction, as it is certain that the subjects about whom biographies are written actually lived. Still, that does not mean that biographies always tell the whole story or present it with absolute objectivity. In his examination of the genre of biography, *Writing Lives: Principia Biographica*, Leon Edel calls the biographer "an artist under oath." Fabricating facts and stories is a violation of the biographer's ethic that an author should never commit; authors who are exposed for dishonest reporting are forever distrusted (Edel 1984, 16). Even if the facts are correct in a biography, however, characterization of the subject may be unsound. Biographers fashion lives by "organization, observation, insight, structure, composition, form, and style" (Edel 1984, 65). What they omit or never discover may also be critical to fair depiction.

In his introduction to *Extraordinary Lives: The Art and Craft of American Biography*, editor William Zinsser claims that many famous people, knowing that their lives are to be subjects of biographies, tell lies to mislead biographers (1986, 10–13). Leon Edel adds that some people also destroy documentary evidence to hamper those who would write about them (1984, 20–21). Throughout *Adventures of a Biographer*, Catherine Drinker Bowen (1959) describes the difficulties that she faced getting true stories from living subjects and obtaining access to revealing documents from the literary executors of deceased subjects. When Ian Hamilton wrote his first book about the reclusive author J. D. Salinger, Salinger sued to stop publication until all quotes from his publicly available papers were removed; to the shock of all biographers, Salinger won the court case, greatly reducing the fair use principle for quotations. Hamilton tells the story in *In Search of J. D. Salinger*. Readers of these books may begin to wonder how reliable biographies are ever written.

A phrase that is sometimes applied by book reviewers lauding new books, especially long ones, about famous people is "definitive biography." The idea is that the biographer has discovered the indisputable truth about a subject and told the full story so that the biography need never be replaced. Some authors or publishers even try to claim the distinction in their titles, such as *Jules Verne: The Definitive Biography* by William Butcher or *Kerouac: The Definitive Biography* by Paul Maher Jr. In his handbook to the genre, *Biography: A User's Guide*, Carl Rollyson objects strenuously to the term. He explains that every biographer is simply telling the story as he or she sees it, limited by the available evidence and personal prejudices (Rollyson 2008, 70–80). In *The Passions of Andrew Jackson*, Andrew Burstein (2003) also points out the limitations of biography, calling every work "a construction." Both Rollyson and Burstein would appreciate author John Man, who claims in *Gutenberg: How One Man Remade the World with Words* that he is only using the remaining evidence to issue a credible story.

> "Biography is never a faithful record. It is a construction, a clandestine effort to refashion memory, to create a new tradition, or sanction yet another myth about what is past. In the interest of writing an exciting or inspiring book, too many popular biographers refuse to confront the problems of their own pretense and ideology, the problems inherent in how they relate to their subject."—Andrew Burstein, *The Passions of Andrew Jackson*, p. xix

How the Books in This Reading Guide Were Chosen

My first task after committing to write this guide to biographies was to find the biographies to include. This was the easiest part of the entire process, as I examined over a thousand books. I began with my own reading lists and those from the Thomas Ford Memorial Library in Western Springs, Illinois, and from the Downers Grove (Illinois) Public Library. I also browsed the biography sections in the two libraries from A to Z, looking for titles that I remembered and for unknown but promising titles to consider. As I combed through these two collections representing small and medium-sized libraries, I read through many lists of award-winning books (see appendix A) and identified biographical titles included in *The Real Story: A Guide to Nonfiction Reading Interests* by Sarah Cords, *The Reader's Advisory Guide to Nonfiction* by Neal Wyatt, and recent editions of *Public Library Catalog*. I watched for new titles in *Publishers Weekly, Library Journal, Booklist, Baker and Taylor Forecast,* and *Booking Ahead,* the monthly e-mail alert from Baker and Taylor. I also noted the starred review lists at the Web site Overbooked.com and checked a selection of book reviewing blogs from libraries and librarians. Borrowing the titles that I requested kept interlibrary loan and delivery services in my area busy for much of a year.

Choosing from so many worthy books was a more difficult task. My first test for every book was, "Would any of the readers who come in my library want to read this book?" That might sound a bit limiting, but my library in a Chicago suburb has a diverse, if well-educated, clientele. Though the educational attainment is higher than average, the readers still indulge in reading what might be considered low reading by the literati. We stock books by and about movie stars, radio talk show hosts, professional wrestlers, and political candidates, like almost any other public library in the country. Many of the biographies, of course, did pass this fairly easy test, so I also considered the following:

- Interesting subjects—Interesting people with interesting stories make the best biographies.

- Readability—Lively and engaging narration is in; dry and academic text is out.

- Interesting titles—An author who identifies an element of the story with the title may tell a livelier story than one who simply states the subject's name.

- Attractiveness of the physical book—A bit of wear and tear is expected. What matters are fonts that are easy to read, generous line spacing, and pleasing cover design. People do judge books by the covers.

- Recent publishing dates—Because newer books have the latest biographical discoveries, are more likely to be in print, are more likely to still be in libraries, and are less likely to have already been read by prospective readers, I have chosen newer titles over older ones in many cases. More than 70 percent of the books date from the years 2000 to 2008, with many from 2006 and 2007. A few classics, such as *The Lives of the Artists* by Giorgio Vasari (1550) and *Eminent Victorians* by Lytton Strachey (1918), are included.

- Length of book—Shorter is better than longer, because 600-page biographies may intimidate readers and often sit unread on library shelves.

- Balance of collection—I have chosen books to represent the diversity of subjects found in biography. I have also included books from authors with a wide range of political and social viewpoints. Most authors do admire their subjects, but there is a good selection of critical biographies included.

- Availability in libraries—Every book reviewed in this guide is owned by at least three libraries in the Metropolitan Library System. Most are in at least 500 libraries, according to OCLC WorldCat, the international library catalog. (Some of the most recent titles have not yet reached the latter number.)

My method for selection was thoughtful but not scientific, as I created no formula for inclusion and exclusion. In the end I chose to add some older, longer, and less available books with simple titles when other qualities recommended them. Also, some wonderful books did not make the cut because they resembled other books that I had already included. Many of these latter books became "Now Try" recommendations. The result is annotations of about 600 titles representing a broad range of biographies that include books to suit many reading tastes.

My selection of "Now Try" recommendations to accompany each of the book reviews draws from some extra sources. The idea behind "Now Try" is to find another book that a reader will enjoy, which may or may not be another biography. Although a majority of the recommendations are biographies, others are memoirs, letters, diaries, poetry, histories, other nonfiction, and even some novels and collections of short stories. Among the extra sources, *The Biography Book: A Reader's Guide to Nonfiction, Fictional, and Film Biographies of More Than 500 of the Most Fascinating Individuals of All Time* by Daniel S. Burt was particularly helpful for identifying memoirs, letters, diaries, and some novels that include biographical subjects as characters. *Thematic Guide to Popular Nonfiction* by Lynda G. Adamson identified a few nonfiction titles. I turned to *Genreflecting* by Diana Tixier Herald, *The Encyclopedia of World Biography*, and the *NoveList*, *Readers' Advisor Online*, and *MagillOnLiterature* databases to identify other titles to consider as "Now Trys."

How to Use This Book

Organization of the Book

In this book are twelve chapters that group biographies according to genres, writing styles, and popular subject interests. Following these chapters are three appendixes that identify award winning books, top biographers, and biographical series. The book concludes with author/title, subject, and chronological indexes.

In Part 1 "Nonfiction Genres," readers will find chapters titled "Adventure Biography," "True Crime Biography," and "War Biography." The biographies in each of these three "genres" share story elements and appeal factors with similarly named popular fiction and nonfiction genres. Part 2, "Stylistic Genres" follows. This section includes "Inspirational Biography," "Investigative Biography," and "Coming-of-Age Biography." In each of these three chapters readers will find biographies grouped more by literary similarities than by common topics. Strong author attitudes toward the subjects will be found in many of these biographies. The final grouping of chapters is Part 3, "Nonfiction Subject Interests." These six chapters organize biographies around topics of great interest to many readers, including "Cultural Biography," "Celebrity Biography," "Historical Biography," "Political Biography," "Science Biography," and "Sports Biography." Biographical subjects' roles within their historical and professional settings are important in all of the chapters.

Although there is some appearance of occupational arrangement, for example, "Sports Biography" and "Science Biography," the overall intent is to help readers find books with similar appeal factors that they will enjoy. As a result, a number of sports books are together in a chapter because they all include the stories of people training for and competing in athletic events; these books invariably share other story factors, such as the physical and mental challenges of sports, the excitement and strain that competition brings to personal relations, the rewards of success, and the disappointment of failure. Similar types of people become athletes, and their biographies have similar appeal. Biographies of sports figures with different story and character elements appear in other chapters, such as "Coming-of-Age Biography" (chapter 6) "Historical Biography" (chapter 9), and "Inspirational Biography" (chapter 4) which include a number of titles about characters from many fields and eras.

In the back of the book are several extra sources for identifying biographies worth reading. The first is "Appendix A: Biography Awards," which lists books that have been honored as ALA Notable Books and Best Books for Young Adults, as well as winners of the Los Angeles Times Book Prize for Biography, National Book Critics Circle Award for Biography, the Pulitzer Prize for Biography and Autobiography, and other prizes. "Appendix B: Top Biographers" identifies authors who have proven track records in biography and lists their books. "Appendix C: Biography Series" identifies sets of biographical books issued over time on specific themes or sharing narrative formats. The book concludes with author/title, subject, and chronological indexes.

The Annotations and the "Now Try" Recommendations

There are two types of reading recommendations in each chapter. The main entries annotated in the sections of the chapters are the first level; a reader who enjoys one title should consider the others surrounding it, as they share appeal factors and story elements. Second-level recommendations are found at the end of each annotation; these "Now Try" recommendations identify biographies and other books that may be outside the scope of the chapter or section but still share some character, story, setting, or other appeal factors. These recommendations are listed starting with titles that are closely associated with the biographical subject, such as memoirs or other books that the subject wrote or other biographies about the same person. These are followed by books that feature characters who were contemporaries of the biographical subject or whose lives were similar. The final recommendations are often books about people with similar characteristics from different ages, or books that follow similar story lines or have similar settings or language. If a recommended title is reviewed elsewhere in the guide, a "see" reference to its chapter is included; the reader should use the author/title index to find the exact page.

The annotations in this guide are mostly descriptive, but some evaluative comments are offered as well. I have included enough detail so that the reader or the librarian helping the reader may understand the type of character, story line, setting, and pacing of each book. I have checked verifiable facts in the annotations when possible, but I rely heavily on the books themselves for the story lines. I have attempted to depict the characters as the biographers do. Any mistakes in this regard are my own.

The symbol 🏆 identifies titles that have won awards, and the **Awards** are listed after the **Subjects** following the annotation. Detailed lists of biographies that have won awards are found in appendix A.

The availability of unabridged audiobooks and large print editions of the books included is noted in the bibliographic statement after the ISBN. OCLC's *WorldCat* is the most complete source of information on these editions and identifies libraries from which these items may be borrowed.

I also identify "Quick Reads," "Teen Reads," and "Group Discussion Books" in the **Subject** listings. Quick Reads are usually under 250 pages and must be easy reading. Teen Reads are also shorter works that must have a topic that would interest high school students; of course teens are a diverse group, so any individual teen reader may have broader interests. I do not recommend shielding older teens from controversial topics, for those are the ones to which they are drawn. Group Discussion Books are titles with elements of controversy or mystery; knowing the difficulty of getting a group to read longer works, I have mostly chosen books under 400 pages. Turn to the subject index to find complete lists of these titles.

My Vision for Biography

I enjoy a biography that takes me to another time and place quickly, tells me interesting stories about the biographical subject, and lets me know why the author thought the life in question mattered. That is why I have read so many of the Penguin Lives series titles, quick read biographies written by noted novelists, historians, and even humorists. Novelist Bobbie Ann Mason's very personal account of why Elvis Presley mattered to her caused me to reconsider some of my opinions about the singer. Novelist Jane Smiley's biography of Charles Dickens helped me understand both his books and his life. Historian Karen Armstrong showed me that the time of the Buddha was more like the modern age than I could have imagined. I would like to see the Penguin Lives series revived. Luckily, I also still have titles in the Eminent Lives, American Presidents, and Lives and Legacies series to read.

Here are some of my other wishes for biography:

- *More biographies to be available as audiobooks.* Narrative nonfiction audiobooks are a frequent request that my library struggles to satisfy. My library's readers would welcome more entertaining biographies in audio format. Let me modify this wish—more biographies as audiobooks at affordable prices.

- *More biographies on lesser known figures.* The market for memoirs has already shown that people will read about unknown figures when characters are strong and stories compelling. Alexandra Fuller's *The Legend of Colton H. Bryant* is a step in this direction. The biography market might draw more readers if it were less dependent on works about Lincoln, the Kennedys, the Roosevelts, and other overexposed biographical subjects.

- *More biographers should turn their massive birth-to-death biographies into trilogies.* Trilogies and recurring character series work very well in many fiction genres, and biographies are often said to share narrative appeal with fiction, so sequential titles could work for biographies. An author who can please readers with a well-written first volume will have readers for the second and third.

- *More collective biographies.* There are many notable people who might be better profiled in 50 to 80 pages than in 200 or 300 pages. Several interesting short pieces together in one volume might entice readers. Good writing is, of course, essential.

- *More libraries realizing that creating a biography section is just the first step toward good public service.* Book displays, finding tools, and staff recommendations are needed to put biographies into the hands of readers.

Mostly, I hope that more readers discover the joy of reading well-written, thoroughly researched, compelling biographies. I offer this book as a tool to bring readers and biographies together.

References

Adamson, Lynda G. 2006. *Thematic Guide to Popular Nonfiction.* Westport, CT: Greenwood Press.

Bondanella, Julia Conway, and Peter Bondanella. 1991. "Introduction," in *The Lives of the Artists,* by Giorgio Vasari. Oxford: Oxford University Press.

Bowen, Catherine Drinker. 1959. *Adventures of a Biographer.* Boston: Little, Brown.

Burstein, Andrew. 2003. *The Passions of Andrew Jackson.* New York: Alfred A. Knopf.

Burt, Daniel S. 2001. *The Biography Book: A Reader's Guide to Nonfiction, Fictional, and Film Biographies of More Than 500 of the Most Fascinating Individuals of All Time.* Phoenix: Oryx Press.

Cords, Sarah. 2006. *The Real Story: A Guide to Nonfiction Reading Interests.* Westport, CT: Libraries Unlimited.

Edel, Leon. 1984. *Writing Lives: Principia Biographica.* New York: W. W. Norton.

Hamilton, Nigel. 2008. *How to Do Biography: A Primer.* Cambridge: Harvard University Press.

Keller, Julia. 2008. "So You Like Biographies? Don't Hate Yourself." *Chicago Tribune,* January 27, sec. 7, p. 8.

Lazar, David, ed. 2008. *Truth in Nonfiction: Essays.* Iowa City: University of Iowa Press.

Liers, Frederic. 2005. "Biography," in *The New Dictionary of the History of Ideas,* edited by Maryanne Cline Horowitz, vol. 1, 217–220. New York: Charles Scribner's Sons.

Nicolson, Harold. 1928. *The Development of English Biography*. New York: Harcourt, Brace.

Rollyson, Carl. 2008. *Biography: A User's Guide*. Chicago: Ivan R. Dee.

Sisman, Adam. 2000. *Boswell's Presumptuous Task: The Making of the Life of Dr. Johnson*. New York: Farrar, Straus & Giroux.

Wyatt, Neal. 2007. *The Reader's Advisory Guide to Nonfiction*. Chicago: American Library Association.

Zinsser, William, ed. 1986. *Extraordinary Lives: The Art and Craft of American Biography*. New York: American Heritage.

History of Biography

The history of biography is confusing. Every book and article about the subject begins with a different date and cites different events as significant in the development of the literature. In *Writing Lives: Principia Biographica*, Leon Edel begins in 1750, when Samuel Johnson described principles for writing biography in *The Rambler*, his literary magazine. Johnson urged writers to include personal detail to depict private life and then applied the principles that he espoused in writing *Life of Savage* and *Lives of the Poets* (Edel 1984, 59–60). In *The Nature of Biography*, Robert Gittings begins with medieval biographies of saints, identifying these tributes that were written from firsthand knowledge or oral traditions as the models for later biographies (1977, 19). In his article "Biography" in *The New Dictionary of the History of Ideas*, Frederick Liers points to hieroglyphic inscriptions on Egyptian monuments of 1300 BCE. as the earliest known biographical writings. Liers then identifies similar works in Assyria (720 BCE), Persia (520 BCE), and China (145 BCE). The author asserts that the first indisputable biographies were character profiles of the Athenian statesman Pericles and the playwright Sophocles, written by Greek poet Ion of Chios in the fifth century BCE (Liers 2005, 217–218).

> In 1750, Samuel Johnson laid out rules for the writing of biography that emphasized candor and depiction of everyday life in *The Rambler*, his literary magazine.

In *Biography: A Brief History*, Nigel Hamilton rues the fact that there is no good introduction to the history of biography for the general reader (2007, 1). Ironically, biographer Carl Rollyson states in *Biography: A User's Guide* that he thinks Hamilton's wide-ranging book on biography comes close to being that good introduction (2008, 137). The reader will find the literature of biography defined broadly in Hamilton's book, in which he includes primitive cave paintings, the plays of Shakespeare, sculpture, magazine articles, and reality television as forms of biography. He foresees biography becoming even broader in the age of the Internet, when intimate personal details become common on personal Web logs or blogs (Hamilton 2007, 279). Hamilton focuses on specific biographical issues and the innovations that changed the course of the literature. The inclusion of psychological analysis in biography after the publishing of Sigmund Freud's case studies (Hamilton 2007, 130–132), and the censorship of biography in totalitarian societies (Hamilton 2007, 69–74) are just two of the topics in this fascinating book. What the reader will not find, however, is an old-fashioned chronological history of the genre.

Just as any biography is only a construction of a life, as Andrew Burstein says in *The Passions of Andrew Jackson* (2003, xix), any history of biography is also just a creation from which to study but never gain a full understanding of the genre's past, which predates the identification of the discipline by scholars. Much of the ancient record of biography has been lost, and for many centuries biography was simply thought to be a form of history. It was not until 1683, when John Dryden coined the word *biography*, that the study of the literature began (Hamilton 2007, 81).

Despite the complaints from Hamilton that there is no good history of biography and the varied definitions of biography among historians, there is some agreement among historians about the progress of biography through time. The first point of agreement is that biography in the Dark and Middle Ages in Europe was limited to lives of saints. Because the rate of literacy was low in society as a whole, only the Roman Catholic Church had the talent and resources to write biography, which it used for the spreading of religious faith. Paul Murray Kendall, in his *Art of Biography*, points to the *Confessions of St. Augustine*, with its descriptions of sin and salvation through repentance, as the standard against which biography and autobiography were written for a thousand years (1965, 41). Frederick Liers agrees with Kendall about the nature of the biographical literature of the time, but he thinks the biographies by Plutarch, Suetonius, and St. Jerome were the models for hagiographic biography (Liers 2005, 218).

Hagiography is the biography of saints.

Historians of biography almost universally agree that *The Life of Johnson* by his friend James Boswell, published in 1791, was the book that raised the standard for all biographies that followed. Carl Rollyson explains that Boswell broke from the tradition of emphasizing the accomplishments of a man and instead used intimate details from Johnson's life to slow the pace of the book, making the life a thing to contemplate and examine. The reader discovers Johnson through his character instead of through his résumé (Rollyson 2008, 56).

Biographies in nineteenth-century America and Great Britain were written to tell sanctioned accounts of history through the lives of their leaders. According to Scott Casper (2006), founding fathers, military leaders, and industrialists were the men most likely to be held up as symbols of the expanding United States and worthy of being portrayed in biography. The "can-do" attitude of *The Autobiography of Benjamin Franklin*, the most venerated book in the country, was copied in countless biographies and autobiographies (Casper 2006, 116–117). In Great Britain, biographies were written to lift the "moral welfare of the reading public" (Rollyson 2008, 211). The most frequent subjects of British biography were royalty, nobility, and clergy (Kendall 1965, 104–105). Most historians agree that critical analysis of subjects was absent from biographies of the nineteenth century.

Although Sigmund Freud began publishing his frank psychiatric profiles of patients in 1895, and muckraking journalists in American began attacking the legacies of American public figures in the 1890s, popular biography remained adulatory until the publishing of *Eminent Victorians* by Lytton Strachey in 1918. Strachey shocked the book world and cultured society with unflattering profiles of celebrated British figures, including the revered Crimean War nurse Florence Nightingale and the martyred General Charles George Gordon, who had captured Beijing and died in battle in the Sudan. Historians uniformly agree that Strachey's rebellion against Victorian strictures freed biographers to tell unvarnished truth, as Samuel Johnson had urged back in 1750.

According to all accounts, the twentieth century was the golden age of biography, a time when the writing of biography truly became a profession. In 1928 Harold Nicolson announced new standards in *The Development of English Biography*. He defined "pure biography" as writing that was factual, accurate, and verifiable; portrayed an individual; and had artistic purpose (Rollyson 2008, 132). Writers responded, and as a result a community of biography grew, which included for the first time numerous women and minorities. These new biographers expanded the literature by writing about a wider variety of subjects, including women, minorities, and the working class (Liers 2005, 219). In the twenty-first century these trends continue, and biography has spread to television and the Internet (Hamilton 2008, 4).

Chronology of Biographical History

I did not find a chronology of biographical history in my research, so I have created one, including events mentioned in the various histories of biography that I read. The titles upon which I base this chronology are listed in the "References" section.

- **Tenth century BCE:** Ancient Greeks wrote funeral elegies praising the departed.

- **Fifth century BCE:** Greek poet Ion of Chios wrote sketches lionizing Athenian statesman Pericles and the playwright Sophocles.

- **Fourth century BCE:** Greek historian Xenophon wrote a tribute to Cyrus the Great, king of Persia.

- **Fourth century BCE:** Greek philosopher Plato wrote about his mentor, Socrates, in the *Apology* and the *Phaedo*.

- **First century BCE:** Roman biographer Cornelius Nepos wrote a series of biographies, collected as *On Illustrious Men* (*De Viris Illustribus*). Several future collections would use the same title.

- **ca. 85–110 CE:** The story of Jesus of Nazareth was written in gospels by Matthew, Mark, Luke, John, and other Christian writers.

- **ca. 105–115 CE:** Greek biographer Plutarch described the moral character of forty-six Greek and Roman figures in his *Parallel Lives*.

- **ca. 110 CE:** Roman bureaucrat Gaius Suetonius Tranquillus recounted the lives of Julius Caesar and eleven successors in *The Twelve Caesars*. He also wrote about scholars, poets, and historians in *On Illustrious Men* (*De Viris Illustribus*).

- **ca. 200 CE:** In *Lives of Eminent Philosophers* (*Vitae Philosophorum*), Diogenes Laertius described the lives and teachings of Greek philosophers.

- **ca. 392:** St. Jerome wrote *On Illustrious Men* (*De Viris Illustribus*), profiling 135 Christian authors, beginning with St. Peter and ending with himself.

- **ca. 397:** In his memoir *Confessions*, St. Augustine set the tone for a thousand years of faith-based writing, both biography and autobiography, about the struggle with sin.

- **ca. 690:** Irish abbot Adomnán of Iona wrote *Life of St. Columba* (*Vita Columbae*) to support his canonization. The English monk Bede's *Life of St. Cuthbert* (ca. 731) is another example of hagiographic biography from the period when lives of the saints dominated biographical writing.

- **ca. 829–836:** Einhard, a royal counselor to French king Charlemagne, wrote *Life of Charlemagne* (*Vita Karoli Magni*), a biased but highly detailed account of the king and his reign.

- **1354:** Giovanni Boccaccio's *Life of Dante* (*Trattello in Laude di Dante*) briefly revived the secular single-life biography, a form that had been dormant for about 500 years.

- **1405:** French poet Christine de Pisan wrote the collective biography *The Book of the City of Ladies*, often considered the first feminist biography.

- **1513–1518:** Sir Thomas More wrote *History of King Richard III* for Henry VIII, an early example of politically motivated biography.

- **1550:** Giorgio Vasari wrote about Renaissance artists, basing the profiles on his memory of seeing their works and his conversations with the artists. *Lives of the Painters, Sculptors, and Architects* is still a primary resource for art scholarship.

- **1577:** Raphael Holinshed published the jointly written *Chronicles of England, Scotland, and England*. William Shakespeare and other playwrights drew the characters and stories for many of their plays from Holinshed's account.

- **1590–1613:** William Shakespeare, adhering to politically sensitive views about English history and the legitimacy of its rulers, wrote fictional plays about historical kings of England that perpetuated myths that modern biographers still have to debunk.

- **1669–1696:** John Aubrey wrote candid, anecdotal observations and opinions about the prominent British men of his day, which he never published. These were discovered in the nineteenth century and published in 1813 as *Brief Lives*.

- **1670:** Izaak Walton completed a series of eloquent biographies of authors and clergymen, including the poet John Donne. Although these pieces were first used as prefaces to collections of writings by their subjects, they proved so popular that they were republished together.

- **1683:** The English word *biography* was first used by John Dryden in a translation of *Plutarch's Lives*, which he edited.

- **1742–1744:** Roger North wrote about his family in *Lives of the Norths*, an early example of biographical writings about prominent but not especially famous people.

- **1750:** Samuel Johnson set forth the aims of biography in his twice-weekly journal *The Rambler*. Between 1779 and 1781 he published a series of essays that became known as *Lives of the Poets*, a seminal work of literary biography.

- **1771:** Benjamin Franklin wrote his *Autobiography*, which became the model for the American self-made man stories (biographical and autobiographical) popular in the United States between the early 1820s and mid-1860s.

- **1791:** James Boswell completes his *Life of Samuel Johnson*, which has long been admired as a model biography, sympathetic but frank about the subject's shortcomings. It is also admired for its clever use of letters, diaries, and recollections of friends, including Boswell himself.

- **1804–1807:** In *The Life of George Washington*, John Marshall told the history of the young American republic through the life of its most famous leader.

- **1825:** William Hazlitt wrote *The Spirit of the Age*, a collective biography featuring profiles of literary figures of his time, including William Wordsworth and Samuel Coleridge. He followed with a multivolume biography of Napoleon Bonaparte.

- **1834–1848:** Editor Jared Sparks published the twenty-five-volume series <u>The Library of American Biography</u>, which told admiring stories of early colonists, revolutionary leaders, political figures, and pioneers of westward expansion.

- **1837–1838:** In the introduction to *Memoirs of the Life of Sir Walter Scott*, John Lockhart condemned Boswell's quoting from private conversations with Samuel Johnson and advised biographers to avoid revealing what was told them in confidence.

- **1848–1850:** Elizabeth F. Ellet elevated the role of women in the history of the United States with her collective biography *Women of the American Revolution*.

- **1851:** Thomas Carlyle published *The Life of John Sterling*, which focused more on the poet's character and not on his career and writings. Most previous author biographies were more literary criticism than life story.

- **1857:** William Makepeace Thayer wrote *The Poor Boy and the Merchant Prince*, a biography of manufacturer Amos Lawrence intended to inspire young readers to be industrious. Thayer followed with *The Bobbin Boy*, about Massachusetts governor Nathanial Banks, and *The Printer Boy*, about Benjamin Franklin. His *The Pioneer Boy, and How He Became President* is one of the first youth-oriented books about Abraham Lincoln, about whom very many books have been written.

- **1857:** In her *Life of Charlotte Brontë*, Elizabeth Gaskell recounted intimate incidents in the writer's life that provided insight into the heroines of her novels.

- **1860:** James Parton was the first American writer to be acknowledged as a biographer, upon the publication of his three-volume *Life of Andrew Jackson*, which followed his works about Horace Greeley and Aaron Burr.

- **1882–1884:** After Thomas Carlyle gave his letters and diaries to his friend James Anthony Froude, stipulating that they should be used for a biography, Froude did as he was asked and wrote a candid biography that was condemned by members of the Carlyle family, Alfred Lord Tennyson, and other prominent Victorians.

- **1878–1884:** A series called <u>English Men of Letters</u>, which included titles about English and American authors, pioneered the publishing of compact, affordable, and well-written biography series.

- **1881–1904:** Modeled after <u>English Men of Letters</u>, twenty-two volumes of the <u>American Men of Letters</u> series were published. Editor Charles Dudley Warner insisted that authors base their texts on research of verifiable records, not on reminiscences by contemporaries.

- **1885–1901:** The first edition of the British *Dictionary of National Biography*, with its alphabetical collection of short profiles of eminent British figures, was published.

- **1890:** Lincoln secretaries John G. Nicolay and John Hay completed their ten-volume *Abraham Lincoln: A History*, basing their account on documentary evidence and avoiding personal information, unlike Lincoln law partner William H. Herndon, who told many personal stories in *Herndon's Lincoln: The True Story of a Great Life*.

- **ca. 1895:** Sigmund Freud began publishing case studies, which introduced psychological assessment to biography.

- **1895:** With *Types of American Character*, Gamaliel Bradford began a series of collective biographies that applied Marxist, Darwinian, and Freudian theories to the writing of biographical profiles, which Bradford called "psychographs."

- **1901:** In *The Real Lincoln*, Charles L. C. Minor portrayed Abraham Lincoln as a hypocrite and political manipulator. The book was the most critical to date in a wave of biographies debunking the myths surrounding revered American figures, beginning with the benign *The True George Washington* by Paul Leicester Ford in 1890.

- **1917:** The Pulitzer Prize for Biography was established. *Julia Ward Howe* by Laura E. Richards and Maude Howe Elliott was the first winner.

- **1918:** In *Eminent Victorians*, Lytton Strachey broke with Victorian tradition to write critical, unflattering biographies of beloved public figures, including British nurse Florence Nightingale and General Charles George Gordon.

- **1919:** In *Theodore Roosevelt: An Intimate Biography*, William Roscoe Thayer sought a balance between idolatry and muckraking in biography, recounting Roosevelt's failings to emphasize the scope of his accomplishments.

- **1928:** The *Dictionary of American Biography* was begun.

- **1928:** Harold Nicolson lectured on the "pure biography," stating that biography had to be factual, accurate, and verifiable; portray an individual; and have artistic purpose.

- **1932:** Childhood of Famous Americans Series, biographies for young readers, was begun by Bobbs-Merrill Company. *Abe Lincoln, Frontier Boy* by Augusta Stevenson was the first series book. Stevenson went on to write twenty-nine books in the series.

- **1941–1945:** Photo essays in *Life* and *Look* magazines during World War II featured many common people supporting the war effort, democratizing biography and increasing reader interest in the genre.

- **1964:** In *New York Times v. Sullivan*, the United States Supreme Court ruled that actual malice had to be proved before public officials and public figures could sue reporters for defamation and libel. Biographers were thus free to write more critically.

- **1966:** With *In Cold Blood*, Truman Capote revolutionized the writing of nonfiction by applying narrative elements from fiction.

- **1967:** *Lytton Strachey* by Michael Holroyd was the first English biography to discuss in detail homosexual relationships of a biographical subject. It was published after Parliament passed the Sexual Offenses Act of 1967, which decriminalized homosexual acts in Great Britain.

- **1982:** Thomas Keneally novelized the true story of German industrialist Oscar Schindler, who saved many lives during the Jewish Holocaust, in *Schindler's List*.

- **1986:** In *J. D. Salinger v. Random House,* a federal court ruled that biographer Ian Hamilton could not quote extensively from Salinger's publicly available papers without express permission from Salinger, restricting all biographers working from letters and diaries still under copyright.

- **1994:** In *The Silent Woman,* Janet Malcolm challenged the invasiveness of biographers, sympathizing with Ted Hughes, husband of Sylvia Plath, whose life she depicted as ruined by writers who violated his privacy.

- **1999:** Edmund Morris was highly criticized for including himself as a fictional observer in *Dutch*, his biography of Ronald Reagan.

- **1999:** Lipper/Viking started the <u>Penguin Lives</u> series, concise biographies written by eminent novels, historians, and essayists. *Crazy Horse* by Larry McMurtry was the first title in the series.

References

Critical notes on many of these and other histories of biography can be found in *Biography: A User's Guide* by Carl Rollyson.

Altick, Richard D. 1996. *Lives and Letters: A History of Literary Biography in England and America.* New York: Alfred A. Knopf.

Burstein, Andrew. 2003. *The Passions of Andrew Jackson.* New York: Alfred A. Knopf.

Casper, Scott. 2006. "Biography," in *American History Through Literature 1820–1870,* edited by Janet Gabler-Hover and Robert Sattelmeyer, vol. 1, 116–121. New York: Charles Scribner's Sons.

Dunn, Waldo H. 1916. *English Biography.* New York: E. P. Dutton.

Edel, Leon. 1984. *Writing Lives: Principia Biographica.* New York: W. W. Norton.

Garrity, John. 1957. *The Nature of Biography.* New York: Alfred A. Knopf.

Gittings, Robert. 1977. *The Nature of Biography.* Seattle: University of Washington Press.

Hamilton, Nigel. 2007. *Biography: A Brief History.* Cambridge: Harvard University Press.

Hamilton, Nigel. 2008. *How to Do Biography: A Primer.* Cambridge: Harvard University Press.

Kendall, Paul Murray. 1965. *The Art of Biography.* New York: W. W. Norton.

Liers, Frederic. 2005. "Biography," in *The New Dictionary of the History of Ideas*, edited by Maryanne Cline Horowitz, vol. 1, 217–220. New York: Charles Scribner's Sons.

Maurois, André. 1929. *Aspects of Biography*. New York: D. Appleton.

Nicolson, Harold. 1928. *The Development of English Biography*. New York: Harcourt, Brace.

Novarr, David. 1986. *The Lines of Life: Theories of Biography, 1880–1970*. West Lafayette, IN: Purdue University Press.

O'Neill, Edward H. 1935. *A History of American Biography 1800–1935*. Philadelphia: University of Pennsylvania Press.

Pannapacker, William. 2006. "Biography," in *American History Through Literature 1870–1920*, edited by Tom Quirk and Gary Scharnhorst, vol 1, 150–158. New York: Charles Scribner's Sons.

Rollyson, Carl. 2008. *Biography: A User's Guide*. Chicago: Ivan R. Dee.

Thayer, William Roscoe. 1920. *The Art of Biography*. New York: Charles Scribner's Sons.

Whittemore, Reed. 1988. *Pure Lives: The Early Biographers*. Baltimore, MD: Johns Hopkins University Press.

Whittemore, Reed. 1989. *Whole Lives: Shapers of Modern Biography*. Baltimore, MD: Johns Hopkins University Press.

Part 1

Nonfiction Genres

Chapter 1

Adventure Biography

Definition of Adventure Biography

What is adventure? According to the fourth edition of the *American Heritage Dictionary*, adventure is "an undertaking or enterprise of a hazardous nature." A second definition is "an unusual or exciting experience." In various definitions of the verb form, the words "danger," "risk," and "hazard" are repeated, as are "uncommon" and "extraordinary." Other words often associated with adventure are "thrilling," "hair-raising," "action-packed," "challenging," and "fun," which may be used in advertisements for amusement parks, state fairs, vacations, video games, blockbuster movies, or any products that appeal to the consumer's desire for stimulating experiences. Publishers and reviewers also employ these alluring words to entice prospective readers to books.

An Adventure Biography is the story of an individual who at key points in his or her life forgoes safety and/or comfort to venture out into wild or unknown places. Such a story may involve actual danger, such as is experienced when flying experimental aircraft or climbing steep mountains, or it may simply thrill readers with the discoveries found in exploring nature or exotic places. Explorers, naturalists, and travelers are frequently subjects of Adventure Biography.

As in an adventure novel, there must be action in an Adventure Biography, and the subject has to take on a heroic role, doing something extraordinary, but the genres are not the same. In *The Readers' Advisory Guide to Genre Fiction*, Joyce G. Saricks describes adventure fiction as entertainment often featuring cardboard characters who bravely face exciting challenges time after time. Exciting action is the primary concern, and character development is minimal. More character development, however, is required of a true adventure narrative for it to truly be biography; the spirit of the biographical subject has to be made real. Through stories and descriptions that may be entertaining, the author must make the reader understand the motivations and the inner strength that allow the subject to overcome difficulties. Super powers and nerves of steel are not adequate explanations of character in the Adventure Biography.

> *Adventure Biographies* are stories of people who at key points in their lives forgo safety and/or comfort to venture out into wild or unknown places. Although authors of these biographies may describe entire lives (birth to death), recounting adventure is key to understanding characters. Explorers, naturalists, and travelers are profiled in these books.

Appeal of the Genre

At an early age, children are introduced to elements of adventure in the stories that they are told. Little Red Riding Hood has a dark forest path to follow and a dangerous wolf pursuing her. Jack in the Beanstalk, who traded the family cow for magic beans, has a tall bean stalk that reaches into the clouds to climb and an angry giant to flee. In Beatrix Potter's *Peter Rabbit*, Peter is in danger of being caught and put into a pie by Mr. McGregor every time he enters the garden. In *Babar*, the young elephant Babar sees his mother killed, escapes from the jungle, and travels to Paris before returning home to become king; in sequels to the first story by Laurent de Brunhoff, Babar sails boats and flies in a balloon. Even in Robert McCloskey's *Make Way for Ducklings*, there are dangerous bicycles and cars threatening the ducklings' safety until the policeman intervenes. The presence of danger and hope for safety compels children to keep listening to these and other children's stories.

Adults retain the love of adventure stories featuring new, exotic, and dangerous experiences. They find these in Adventure Biographies, in which traveling to remote places or taking spectacular risks is often involved in the plot. Although there is uncertainty and danger in everyday experience, the Adventure Biography requires its subject to leave comfort behind and move, if not into harm's way, at least into a precarious position. To reach a destination or return home, he or she must act courageously, solve problems, and negotiate unknown paths.

In Adventure Biography, the depiction of the central character is as important as the exciting story. For example, in *The Sound of Wings: The Life of Amelia Earhart*, biographer Mary S. Lovell tells about Earhart's aerial accomplishments and tragic disappearance on her around-the-world flight, but the author focuses her book on the pilot's character. Readers learn why Earhart was drawn to flying airplanes, how she felt about being a celebrity, whom she loved, and how she found the strength to overcome her fears. In a similar manner, in *The Man Who Loved China: The Fantastic Story of the Eccentric Scientist Who Unlocked the Mysteries of the Middle Kingdom*, Simon Winchester examines the character of biochemist Joseph Needham, describing his upbringing, education, values, and personal relationships to show why he traveled to dangerous, war-torn areas to discover science history.

Adventure biographies feature many exotic settings. Every continent, the depths of the oceans, and even the moon are explored by the characters in these books. Although many, such as seafaring Captain James Cook and African explorer Henry Morton Stanley, traveled to places that were unmapped, others, including ornithological artist Roger Tory Peterson and journalist Nellie Bly, went to known places to find what others had failed to see. Whether remote or well-known, the locations themselves test the character's resourcefulness and resolve.

Adventure novels, often telling stories that take place over several days, are known for their brisk pace, even when the books are long. Adventure biographies often take a more leisurely pace as they retell entire lives. Authors blend accounts of action with extensive background information about the character, the immediate setting, and the historical context of the story. At over 600 pages, *First Man: The Life of Neil A. Armstrong* by James R. Hansen, *A Rage to Live: A Biography of Richard & Isabel Burton* by Mary S. Lovell, and *A River Running West: The Life of John Wesley Powell* by Donald Worster each will provide many evenings of reading. Still, some quick reads are available, including *Amerigo: The Man Who Gave His Name to America* by Felipe Fernández-Armesto and *The Last American Man* by Elizabeth Gilbert.

Learning is not generally a strong appeal factor in Adventure Biographies. Most people borrowing or buying these books are seeking to read really good stories that let them vicariously experience the excitement of the adventure.

Organization of the Chapter

The first section in this chapter, "Exploration Stories," includes biographies of adventurous individuals who discovered new lands and natural wonders, found unknown people, and tested the technologies of travel. The explorers, sea captains, and test pilots in this section are historical figures, with astronaut Neil Armstrong the only subject still living at the time of this writing.

"Nature Adventure" is the second section. These biographies examine the characters of men and women who spent their lives in the outdoors, enduring weather, insects, and rugged terrain. The naturalists described lingered in wild places to gain greater understanding of flora, fauna, or other natural features, while the sportsmen tested their abilities to survive.

The final section is "Travel Stories," biographies of men and women who habitually left their homes to seek out new places to experience. These books profile curiosity-driven individuals who could negotiate difficult journeys to exotic places and then adapt to new cultures when they arrived.

Distinguishing among these categories is often a matter of emphasis, for what explorer does not travel, and what traveler doesn't admire natural phenomena? For the purpose of this guide, an Exploration Adventure is one in which readers find an emphasis on character and story; in Nature Adventure and Travel Stories, there is more focus on environment and setting—the former generally including more flora and fauna; and the latter focusing on other aspects of the environment, as well as the process of the journey itself.

Exploration Stories

Pioneering is a concept often associated with adventure. When William Clark and Meriwether Lewis led their band of explorers west on the Missouri River, they heard conflicting reports about the Native Americans, wildlife, and lands that they would find. What was really there was unknown to them.

When astronaut Neil Armstrong stepped onto the surface of the moon, no one had ever done so. Being first in any endeavor, whether it be the first student to read an oral report in class, the first farmer to try a new crop, or the first person to step on the moon, takes some courage and initiative that is admired by contemporaries. When truly great risks are taken to be first, people remember for generations.

In this section are biographies of people remembered for their bold explorations. Some traveled by land. In *Marco Polo: From Venice to Xanadu*, Laurence Bergreen recounts the twenty-four-year journey of Marco Polo across Asia to China and back. Some adventurers flew. H. Paul Jeffers describes the life of a World War I fighter pilot who later became a stunt pilot, race car driver, airline executive, and military advisor in *Ace of Aces: The Life of Capt. Eddie Rickenbacker*. Some went where they were not supposed to go. Ben MacIntyre tells the story of American Josiah Harlan, who became involved in the tribal wars of nineteenth-century Afghanistan in *The Man Who Would Be King: The First American in Afghanistan*. Wanting to be first is an obsession that sometimes kills. Mary S. Lovell tells how Amelia Earhart disappeared over the Pacific Ocean on her attempt to fly around the earth in *The Sound of Wings: The Life of Amelia Earhart*, and David Crane recounts how Antarctic explorer Robert Fulton Scott died trying to be the first man to the South Pole in *Scott of the Antarctic: A Life of Courage and Tragedy*.

The promise of incredible adventure attracts readers to exploration stories. People expect these biographies to be exciting reading, and keeping these readers' attention requires strong characterization and lively narration. Tests of endurance and threats of death contribute to narrative tension, while exotic settings give them interesting context. Many of these biographies are over 400 pages long, perfect for readers who enjoy leisurely reading. A few quick reads are also included in this section.

Exploration Stories are biographies of adventurous individuals who discovered new lands and natural wonders, contacted unknown people, and tested the technologies of travel. Explorers, sea captains, and test pilots are among the strong characters found in these books. Most of these books are 400 or more pages long; only a few are quick reads.

Berg, A. Scott

🌟 *Lindbergh.* G. P. Putnam, 1998. 628p. ISBN 0399144498. Audiobook available.

After Charles Lindbergh (1902–1974) flew solo across the Atlantic in the *Spirit of St. Louis* in 1927, he was a hero whom the entire world wanted to see. As celebrities, he and his young wife Anne satisfied this demand and led a fairy tale life of travel and high society until 1932, when their son was kidnapped and murdered. After the harsh spotlight of the trial, the couple retreated to rural England. According to popular biographer A. Scott Berg, when Lindbergh resurfaced in the news, his outlook had turned bitter, and he lost public sympathy by praising Adolf Hitler, criticizing President Roosevelt, and uttering racist remarks. In this frank and full account, Berg recounts the forgotten episodes of the Lindbergh story for readers who enjoy adventure and in-depth character study.

Subjects: Kidnapping; Lindbergh, Charles; Pilots

Awards: ALA Notable Books; Pulitzer Prize for Biography; Los Angeles Times Book Prize for Biography; Pulitzer Prize for Biography

Now Try: Readers wanting to learn more about the Lindberghs should try *Under a Wing: A Memoir* by Reeve Lindbergh, the couple's daughter, as well as *War Within and Without: Diaries and Letters of Anne Morrow Lindbergh, 1939–1944* by Anne Morrow Lindbergh. President Franklin Roosevelt was an equally compelling figure of the 1920s to 1940s. *FDR* by Jean Edward Smith (see chapter 10) will appeal to readers who enjoyed the intimate detail and epic quality of Berg's Lindbergh title. In a previous era, Henry Ward Beecher was the most influential man in America outside of government. Debby Applegate recounts how he fell from favor in *The Most Famous Man in America: The Biography of Henry Ward Beecher.* For another story about a temperamental airman, try *Howard Hughes: The Secret Life* by Charles Higham (see chapter 5).

Bergreen, Laurence

Marco Polo: From Venice to Xanadu. Alfred A. Knopf, 2007. 415p. ISBN 97814-00043453.

Marco Polo (1254–1324) spent twenty-four years with his father and uncle traveling to and around the Orient in the thirteenth century. Much of their time was spent in China in service of the Mongol emperor Kublai Khan, from whom they received great riches. Because the Khan demanded total devotion, they nearly lost their lives when plotting their return to Europe. When they returned to Venice dressed in resplendent caftans, loaded with jewelry and furs, Polo began telling his incredible tales, which revolutionized the European view of Asia. In this account of the merchant/explorer's life, biographer Laurence Bergreen takes the reader back to an ancient empire to test his classic story against documentary evidence. This compelling book will appeal to historical fiction readers, among others.

Subjects: Asia; Explorers; Italy; Merchants; Mongol Empire; Polo, Marco

Now Try: Polo's own writings are still readily found, under the title *Travels of Marco Polo*. Like Marco Polo, ship's pilot William Adams spent many years in the court of an oriental ruler. Giles Milton describes his at times dangerous life in service of a Japanese shogun in *Samurai William: The Englishman Who Opened Japan* (see this chapter). Thomas More did not have to travel far from his home in London to find a monarch who both loved him like a brother and constantly threatened his life. Bergreen's book on Marco Polo and Peter Ackroyd's *The Life of Thomas More* (see chapter 4) share a similar narrative tension. Giacomo Casanova is another historical figure whose legend was spread by his own writings. Lydia Flem looks for the truth in those memoirs in *Casanova: The Man Who Really Loved Women* (see chapter 5).

Crane, David

Scott of the Antarctic: A Life of Courage and Tragedy. Alfred A. Knopf, 2006. 572p. ISBN 0375415270.

In most biographies of Antarctic explorer Robert Falcon Scott (1868–1912), he is portrayed either as a brave hero or a tragic fool with a goal from which he could not be diverted. Historian David Crane finds a balance between these extremes in his detailed account of the ambitious Royal Navy captain who wanted to be the first man to reach the South Pole. Quoting heavily from Scott's eloquent letters and diaries, the author shows that he was not oblivious to the needs and feelings of his family and associates. Instead, he was a sane man who weighed risks and tragically erred. History readers who like epic tales with fantastic settings will enjoy this reassessment of the famous explorer.

> **Subjects:** Antarctica; Explorers; Scott, Robert Falcon

> **Now Try:** Scott's journals from his expedition are reprinted in *Scott's Last Journey.* In the dual biography *Scott and Amundsen,* Roland Huntford rejects the idolization of Scott at the expense of Norwegian explorer Roald Amundsen, who beat Scott to the South Pole and survived to return to his homeland. Readers who enjoy stories about icy landscapes will also appreciate *Ernest Shackleton* by George Plimpton (see this chapter). *Jean-Jacques Rousseau: Restless Genius* by Leo Damrosch (see chapter 10) is another epic tale that incorporates the letters and other writings of the subject. In *Too Close to the Sun: The Audacious Life and Times of Denys Finch Hatton* (see chapter 6), Sara Wheeler tells about the English settler in Kenya who shared Scott's lack of fear.

Dugard, Martin

Farther Than Any Man: The Rise and Fall of Captain James Cook. Pocket Books, 2001. 287p. ISBN 0743400682.

Captain James Cook (1728–1779) spent most of the last twelve years of his life at sea, circling the globe, claiming new lands for the British Empire, and seeking scientific wonders. The fantastic accounts of his exploits in tropical lands made him a hero, but he resisted enjoying the fame. He continued exploring dangerous places, which eventually led to his death. After telling about the explorer's modest origins on a farm and early maritime career, Martin Dugard analyzes the captain and his three great global expeditions, during which he identified Australia, Hawaii, and many South Pacific islands.

> **Subjects:** British Empire; Cook, James; Explorers; Oceania

> **Now Try:** Novelist Hammond Innes creates a private diary for the British captain in his speculative novel *The Last Voyage: Captain Cook's Lost Diary.* Cook was not the first explorer to die violently on a tropical island. Laurence Bergreen chronicles the final quest of Ferdinand Magellan in *Over the Edge of the World: Magellan's Terrifying Circumnavigation of the Globe.* Two hundred years before Cook explored the Pacific, Sir Francis Drake sailed its waters in the service of his queen. A title from the British Library Historic Lives series, *Sir Francis Drake* by Peter Whitfield profiles the swashbuckling British captain. In the same vein as this tragic story about Cook, Dian Fossey's relentless pursuit of science led to her tragic death, which can be read in *The Dark Romance of Dian Fossey* by Harold T. P. Hayes (see chapter 2).

Fernández-Armesto, Felipe

Amerigo: The Man Who Gave His Name to America. Random House, 2007. 231p. ISBN 9781400062812. Audiobook available.

Because Amerigo Vespucci (1454–1512) was a younger son of a Florentine family, he had few career prospects. Although his older brothers were given legal and ecclesiastical positions, Amerigo had to fend for himself. Always ready to change his loyalties to Spain or Portugal, he rose from a simple merchant to become a commissioning agent dealing in jewels and then a cosmographer and transatlantic explorer. Few facts about Vespucci are certain. Historians even question the num-

ber of voyages that he made to the continents that now bear his name! In this richly historical biography, Felipe Fernández-Armesto sifts through the conflicting stories of a man who may have been second only to Christopher Columbus as the most persuasive champion of exploration.

Subjects: Explorers; Italy; Quick Reads; Vespucci, Amerigo

Now Try: *The Worlds of Christopher Columbus* by William D. Phillips and Carla R. Phillips depicts Vespucci's contemporary and the world that they both knew. In the century before Vespucci, Prince Henry of Portugal sent many expeditions down and around the coast of Africa, looking for a path to the Orient. P. E. Russell profiles the first of the Iberian sponsors of exploration in *Prince Henry "The Navigator": A Life*. Vespucci came from Florence when the Medici family was still in the wool trade. Christopher Hibbert tells the family history in *The Rise and Fall of the House of Medici*. Pontius Pilate, the Roman governor who ruled over Judea, is another mysterious son of the Italian peninsula about whom little is really known but much is told. Ann Wroe examines the often told legends in *Pontius Pilate* (see chapter 5).

Fuson, Robert H.

Juan Ponce de Leon and the Spanish Discovery of Puerto Rico and Florida. McDonald & Woodward Publishing, 2000. 268p. ISBN 093992384X.

Contrary to many school textbooks, Juan Ponce de Leon (1460–1512) did not discover Florida while seeking the Fountain of Youth; other Spanish explorers had already found the peninsula. King Ferdinand of Aragon had only a casual interest in the rejuvenating water if it existed, as his primary concerns were claiming more land and setting up Juan Ponce, whom he trusted, as a rival to Governor Diego Columbus of Puerto Rico, whom he did not trust. According to geographer Robert H. Fuson, Juan Ponce was a loyal and honorable man in a time dominated by bloodthirsty men who lusted for gold and glory. Attractive, informative illustrations enhance this explorer's biography.

Subjects: Explorers; Florida; Ponce de Leon, Juan; Spain

Now Try: While Ponce de Leon was in the New World, the Old World was in flames. James Reston tells about the turmoil in Spain during the years of Ferdinand and Isabella in *Dogs of War: Columbus, the Inquisition, and the Defeat of the Moors*. Hernán Cortés, Ponce de Leon's contemporary, exceeded his orders in the conquest of Mexico. Richard L. Marks describes the conquistador and his campaign in *Cortés: The Great Adventurer and the Fate of Aztec Mexico*. In the history *Brutal Journey: The Epic Story of the First Crossing of North America*, Paul Schneider compares the legends of the disastrous 1527 Narváez Spanish expedition to Florida with recent archeological evidence, tracing how the four survivors arrived in Mexico eight years later. Like Ponce de Leon, General Nathanael Greene was another historical figure who was an honorable man trusted with a difficult assignment by his superior. His story is found in *Washington's General: Nathanael Greene and the Triumph of the American Revolution* by Terry Golway (see chapter 3).

Hansen, James R.

First Man: The Life of Neil A. Armstrong. Simon & Schuster, 2005. 769p. ISBN 978074-3256315.

According to historian James R. Hansen, Neil A. Armstrong (1930–) is a common man with uncommon experiences. The first man to walk on the moon is the descendant of immigrants, a son of Ohio, a good student, and a quiet, respectable man with whom many readers can identify. What distinguished Armstrong from his peers in the military was his cool response in emergency situations. When his reconnaissance flight in the Korean War was hit and later when his test aircraft failed, he was able to improvise to save himself and his crews. His talent and courage were just what the NASA space team needed. Hansen's book on Armstrong will please readers who enjoy in-depth biography.

> **Subjects:** Armstrong, Neil A.; Astronauts; NASA; Ohio; Project Apollo

> **Now Try:** After they returned to Earth, the *Apollo 11* crew collaborated on the joint *First Man on the Moon: A Voyage with Neil Armstrong, Michael Collins, and Edwin E. Aldrin, Jr.* Tom Wolfe describes the early astronauts who led the way for *Apollo 11* in his celebrated account *The Right Stuff.* Though the space race was fueled by the Cold War, space exploration eventually brought like-minded astronauts from different countries together. Russian Aleksei Arkhipovich and American David Scott tell their stories in *Two Sides of the Moon: Our Story of the Cold War Space Race.* Like Armstrong, Dwight D. Eisenhower also rose from humble beginnings to serve his country in war and peace. *Ike: An American Hero* by Michael Korda (see chapter 3) is an equally pleasing epic about a common life transformed by circumstance.

Jeal, Tim

🏺 *Stanley: The Impossible Life of Africa's Greatest Explorer.* Yale University Press, 2007. 570p. ISBN 9780300126259.

Leopoldville is now Kinshasa, and its statue of the Welsh-turned-American explorer Henry Morton Stanley (1841–1904) has been knocked down and discarded. Once celebrated for his adventures and for locating the missionary David Livingstone, Stanley is now reviled as a pawn of or collaborator with evil with Belgium King Leopold II, who used the explorer's travels to claim and enslave regions for his empire of rubber plantations. Using newly available diaries and letters, Tim Jeal argues that Stanley was less racist than most explorers and that his deadly battles with natives were not premeditated. In this biography he portrays Stanley as a contrite man who later questioned whether he had the right to travel the African continent uninvited.

> **Subjects:** Africa; Explorers; Group Discussion Books; Stanley, Henry Morton

> **Awards:** National Book Critics Circle Award for Biography

> **Now Try:** Stanley described his adventures in *How I Found Livingstone* and *Through the Dark Continent.* Peter Forbath dramatizes Stanley's 1888 Congo explorations in his well-researched novel *The Last Hero.* Another biography about an intrepid British explorer is *Captain Sir Richard Francis Burton: The Secret Agent Who Made the Pilgrimage to Mecca, Discovered the Kama Sutra, and Brought the Arabian Nights to the West* by Edward Rice. In *The White Nile* and *The Blue Nile,* Alan Moorehead brings together many fantastic stories of African explorers, including Stanley, Livingstone, Burton, and their predecessors. Like Stanley, Samuel Sewall of Salem has a historically tarnished

image. He later regretted his disastrous actions, which are told in *Salem Witch Judge* by Eve LaPlante (see chapter 4).

Jeffers, H. Paul

Ace of Aces: The Life of Capt. Eddie Rickenbacker. Ballantine Books, 2003. 343p. ISBN 0891417915.

The life of Eddie Rickenbacker (1890–1973) reads like episodes of a 1940s movie serial. He raced early automobiles, became a World War I flying ace, barnstormed America in aerial circuses, founded Eastern Airlines, bought the Indianapolis Speedway, and served as a military consultant in World War II. He met presidents and movie stars, survived several plane crashes, and was once lost at sea for twenty-four days. According to novelist and biographer H. Paul Jeffers, Rickenbacker was a handsome, optimistic daredevil who stayed in the news for decades. Suggest *Ace of Aces* to readers who want fast-paced, action-filled stories and old-fashioned heroes.

> **Subjects:** Pilots; Race Car Drivers; Rickenbacker, Eddie
>
> **Now Try:** Rickenbacker's memoirs emphasize the dangerous episodes in his life. *Fighting the Flying Circus* describes his fighting against German fighter pilots in World War I, and *Seven Came Through* tells his story of survival at sea during World War II. In *Richthofen: Beyond the Legend of the Red Baron*, Peter Kilduff recounts the war experiences of Rickenbacker's arch foe, Baron Manfred von Richthofen. Another American dime novel hero who became an entertainer and businessman was Buffalo Bill Cody. Robert A. Carter chronicles the Western hero's life in *Buffalo Bill Cody: The Man Behind the Legend* (see chapter 5). Rickenbacker shared a can-do attitude with businessman Frank Phillips, who is the subject of *Oil Man: The Story of Frank Phillips and the Birth of Phillips Petroleum* by Michael Wallis (see chapter 9). Both books tell quick-paced stories of men of industry who moved easily in high society.

Jones, Landon Y.

William Clark and the Shaping of the West. Hill and Wang, 2004. 394p. ISBN 9780809030415.

To say that William Clark (1770–1831) led an adventurous life is an understatement. When he was only fourteen, his family left its tired plot of Virginia farmland to settle in frontier Kentucky, where he grew up to become a soldier and backwoodsman. In 1803 he joined Meriwether Lewis on the famed Lewis and Clark Expedition across the North American continent, commanding the crew, drawing maps, and negotiating with unknown Indian tribes. Outliving his famous partner, he spent his remaining thirty years opening and developing the lands just west of the Mississippi, signing many of the Indian treaties and becoming governor of Missouri. In this admiring biography, Landon Y. Jones contends that Clark was the most knowledgeable and influential player in the development of the Midwest.

> **Subjects:** Clark, William; Explorers; Frontier Life; Indian Wars
>
> **Now Try:** The journals of Meriwether Lewis and William Clark can be found in many editions. The 2002 edition of *Journals of Lewis and Clark* from National Geographic is a handsome abridged edition. Stephen Ambrose tells

their epic story well in *Undaunted Courage: Meriwether Lewis, Thomas Jefferson, and the Opening of the American West*. Many novelists have also taken on the Lewis and Clark Expedition, notably Brian Hall in *I Should Be Extremely Happy in Your Company* and Anna Lee Waldo in *Sacajewea*. Lewis and Clark were not really the first people of European decent to head west from St. Louis. Shirley Christian reveals that much was already known by the French and Spanish settlers in St. Louis in her family biography, *Before Lewis and Clark: The Story of the Chouteaus, the French Dynasty That Ruled America's Frontier* (see chapter 9). In a sense, Clark continued the work of Daniel Boone, whom he followed into Kentucky and Missouri. Both ventured into unmapped areas and returned to direct the building of settlements. How the legendary pioneer shaped the West is described in *Boone: A Biography* by Robert Morgan (see chapter 5).

Lovell, Mary S.

A Rage to Live: A Biography of Richard & Isabel Burton. Norton, 1998. 910p. ISBN 0393046729.

Isabel Burton (1831–1896) did not burn all of her husband Sir Richard Burton's (1821–1890) diaries, letters, and unpublished manuscripts after his death in 1890. Mary S. Lovell found seven boxes of them in the Wiltshire Record Office in Trowbridge, England. With these and Isabel's own papers, the author has written a new dual biography of the famed explorer who sought the source of the Nile and the wife whom he left in England. In this new account, Richard is not a deviant or a misogynist, as he is sometimes portrayed, and Isabel is a strong, supporting partner to the man who crossed the African continent, visited forbidden Arabian cities, and translated many ancient texts.

> **Subjects:** Anthropologists; Burton, Isabel; Burton, Richard Francis, Sir; Explorers; Marriage

> **Now Try:** Burton wrote accounts of many of his travels, such as *First Footsteps in East Africa*, but his most known book is his translation of stories called either *A Thousand and One Nights* or *Tales from Arabian Nights*. The life of poet Arthur Rimbaud is also portrayed rather darkly. In *Somebody Else: Arthur Rimbaud in Africa, 1880–91* (see this chapter), Charles Nicholl tells how Rimbaud donned Arab clothes and became a wanderer in the Middle East. T. E. Lawrence was another Englishman who immersed himself in Arab culture. Lawrence James tells how Lawrence supported an Arab revolt and became widely known for his account of the affair in *The Golden Warrior: The Life and Legend of Lawrence of Arabia* (see chapter 3). Before Burton went to Africa, Olaudah Equiano left Africa as a slave; both adapted well to foreign cultures. Vincent Carretta tells how Equiano became a symbol for the abolitionist movement in *Equiano, the African: Biography of a Self-Made Man* (see chapter 9). William and Catherine Booth, founders of the Salvation Army, were contemporaries of the Burtons. Roy Hattersley recounts their working and personal relationships in *Blood and Fire: William and Catherine Booth and Their Salvation Army* (see chapter 4).

Lovell, Mary S.

The Sound of Wings: The Life of Amelia Earhart. St. Martin's Press, 1989. 420p. ISBN 0312034318.

Amelia Earhart's (1897–1937) disappearance during her attempt to fly around the world in 1937 has become the most famous episode of her life. Her many aviation accomplishments are almost forgotten. Based on the pilot's papers and contemporary accounts, Mary S. Lovell tells about Earhart's fascination with flight and her romance with the explorer and publisher G. P. Putnam, whom she married. Several chapters are devoted to Putnam, whom other biographers impugn. The story of her disappearance is told, but Lowell puts more effort into describing Earhart's character and the events that made her a celebrity in her time.

> **Subjects:** Earhart, Amelia; Love Affairs; Pilots; Putnam, George Palmer; Women
>
> **Now Try:** Earhart published a collection of essays, *The Fun of It: Random Research on My Own Flying and of Women of Aviation*. In the biography *Straight on Till Morning*, Lovell tells about another adventurous woman, the pilot Beryl Markham, who began flying in British East Africa and toured the world. Markham tells her own story in the classic memoir *West with the Night*. In *Bugatti Queen: In Search of a French Racing Legend* by Miranda Seymour (see chapter 12) tells the tragic story of a reckless woman who sought the thrill of driving fast cars. Nikki Nichols recounts a time when American hopes for athletic glory ended in an air accident in *Frozen in Time: The Enduring Legacy of the 1961 U. S. Figure Skating Team*.

MacIntyre, Ben

The Man Who Would Be King: The First American in Afghanistan. Farrar, Straus & Giroux, 2004. 351p. ISBN 0374201781.

Before Rudyard Kipling wrote his short story "The Man Who Would Be King," and 177 years before U.S. troops fought the Taliban in the twenty-first century, a lone American slipped into Afghanistan. Born a Quaker in Chester County, Pennsylvania, Josiah Harlan (1799–1871) read many books on history and adventure as a child, and he later followed his older brothers to sea. While in Calcutta he received a letter from a brother telling him his fiancée had married another man. Distraught, Harlan vowed never to return to America. Feeling he had nothing to lose, he wandered into the unknown lands of Afghanistan, where he entered the service of an Afghan prince. Through ambitiously realigning himself with a series of increasing powerful rulers, he was appointed Governor of Gujrat and proclaimed Prince of Ghor. Readers who enjoy tales in exotic lands will likely enjoy this book.

> **Subjects:** Afghanistan; Harlan, Josiah; Mercenaries
>
> **Now Try:** Kipling's *The Man Who Would Be King and Other Stories* is available in numerous editions. Like Harlan, Frenchwoman Alexandra David-Neel went somewhere she was not supposed to be able to go when she entered Tibet in 1923. Her memoir, *My Journey to Lhasa: The Classic Story of the Only Western Woman Who Succeeded in Entering the Forbidden City*, takes readers back to a time when parts of the world were virtually unknown to Western society. The restless author Zane Grey also sought to escape to obscure places when he was unhappy with his life. In *Zane Grey: His Life, His Adventures, His Women* (see chapter 7), Thomas H. Pauly portrays Grey as a man caught between the past and the present, enjoying but regretting his contemporary world. Afghanistan and other isolated countries are as dangerous today as they were in the days of Harlan and Kipling. Reporter Yaroslav Trofimov tells of recent travels through the lands of Islam in *Faith at War: A Journey on the Frontlines of Islam, from Baghdad to Timbuktu*.

Milton, Giles

Samurai William: The Englishman Who Opened Japan. Farrar, Straus & Giroux, 2002. 352p. ISBN 0374253854.

Ship's pilot William Adams (1564–1620) arrived in Japan in 1600 in bad shape. After nineteen months, he was one of only twenty-four sickly men in the lone surviving ship of a Dutch trading fleet to reach its destination, and he was in danger of being crucified as a pirate. Adams, however, impressed Shogun Tokugawa Ieyasu with his knowledge of ships and geography, delaying his threatened execution. In this adventurous tale, Giles Milton portrays Adams as a wily Englishman who transformed himself into a Japanese citizen and helped open the country to international trade. Readers with interest in the Orient will enjoy this true story.

Subjects: Adams, William; Japan; Sea Stories

Now Try: Nearly 300 years later, Commodore Matthew Calbraith Perry of the U.S. Navy forced Japanese officials to let an American ship dock in Japanese harbors, changing American–Japanese relations. Peter Booth Wiley portrays Perry as a commander not following his directions in *Yankees in the Land of the Gods: Commodore Perry and the Opening of Japan*. Adams essentially became a foreign relations advisor for the shogun. In the United States, two secretaries of state have been foreign born. Ann Blackman tells how Madeleine Albright escaped both the German Nazis and the Soviet Communists to eventually become the leading foreign policy advisor to President Clinton in *Seasons of Her Life: A Biography of Madeleine Korbel Albright* (see chapter 10). Nixon administration foreign policy leader Secretary of State Henry Kissinger was also German-born. Award-winning author Walter Isaacson recounts the life and career of the controversial bureaucrat in *Kissinger: A Biography*. For another great story of a man who transformed his life completely as he moved to a new society, read *The Librettist of Venice: The Remarkable Life of Lorenzo da Ponte* by Rodney Bolt (see chapter 7).

Plimpton, George

Ernest Shackleton. DK Publishing, 2003. 160p. A&E Biography series. ISBN 0789493152.

Polar explorer Ernest Shackleton (1874–1922) was a man celebrated for his great spirit of adventure. His Nimrod Expedition (1907–1909) went farther south than any Antarctic expeditions prior to Roald Amundsen's conquest of the South Pole in 1911. His greatest accomplishment was keeping twenty-eight crew members alive for twenty-two months when their ship *The Endurance* (1914–1916 expedition) stuck in Ross Sea ice. In this photographic biography, critic and essayist George Plimpton describes the life of a man who caught the imagination of his age. Geography readers will enjoy this attractive book.

Subjects: Antarctica; Explorers; Shackleton, Ernest

Now Try: Shackleton's accounts of his final expedition are included in another illustrated book *South: The Story of Shackleton's Last Expedition 1914–17*. Another British sailor was the first European to see the Arctic Ocean from the North American continent. Ken McGoogan tells how Royal Navy seaman Samuel Hearn sought wealth in unknown lands in *Ancient Mariner: The Arctic Adventures of Samuel Hearne, the Sailor Who Inspired Coleridge's Masterpiece*. In 1953 Charles H. Houston and Robert H. Bates tested their endurance against the steep and icy cliff of the world's second highest peak. In *K2, the Savage Mountain*, they tell how, in a less technical time, fewer preparations were made and greater risks were taken. *Ulysses S. Grant: An Album* by William S. McFeely (see chapter 10) is another successful mixture of text and illustrations celebrating the life of a greatly challenged leader.

Preston, Diana, and Michael Preston

A Pirate of Exquisite Mind: Explorer, Naturalist, and Buccaneer: The Life of William Dampier. Walker, 2004. 372p. ISBN 0802714250.

When is a pirate not a pirate? When he writes best-selling travel books and hangs around with eminent British scientists and philosophers, so that his crimes are overlooked, especially when his piracy is aimed at his nation's enemies. The hydrologist and naturalist William Dampier (1651–1715) was such a man, a charming buccaneer who charted ocean currents and described exotic birds when not attacking Spanish treasure ships. Diana and Michael Preston read all of Dampier's writings, suspicious of artifice, but concluded that his life was worth the admiration that he received from Sir Walter Scott and Samuel Taylor Coleridge.

Subjects: Dampier, William; Explorers; Great Britain; Hydrologists; Naturalists; Sea Stories

Now Try: Dampier recounted his adventures in *A New Voyage Round the World,* published in 1697. Like Dampier, Captain James Cook was responsible for the gathering of botanical samples and drawings. Martin Dugard describes the ill-fated captain in *Farther Than Any Man: The Rise and Fall of Captain James Cook* (see this chapter). British mineralogist James Smithson was another adventurous scientist; he fought in the French Revolution and rode in early hot-air balloons. Heather Ewing presents letters, legal documents, bank accounts, and other papers to dramatically recount his story in *The Lost World of James Smithson: Science, Revolution, and the Birth of the Smithsonian* (see chapter 11). *Butch Cassidy: A Biography* (see chapter 2) has similar appeal to the story of Dampier, as its author, Richard Patterson, sympathetically chronicles the criminal career of the well-traveled rogue.

Rich, Doris L.

Jackie Cochran: Pilot in the Fastest Lane. University of Florida Press, 2007. 279p. ISBN 9780813030432.

Bessie Pittman was born into a poor Florida panhandle family. When she fled to New York to enter the cosmetics industry in 1929, she chose to become Jacqueline "Jackie" Cochran (1906–1980). Within three years she was so successful that she could afford to learn to fly small planes to support her business. The world of flight opened another world to her: she met Amelia Earhart, earned over 200 aviation records, became an Air Force test pilot, and became friends with Presidents Eisenhower and Johnson. In this rags to riches story, Doris Rich describes Cochran as a persistent, sometimes abrasive woman of great achievement.

Subjects: Cochran, Jacqueline; Pilots; Women

Now Try: Cochran first told her own story in *The Stars at Noon* in 1954 and left *Jackie Cochran: An Autobiography* to be published posthumously after she died in 1980. In contrast to Cochran, Pancho Barnes was a cheerful woman who ran a bar for test pilots and sued the U.S. government to protect her land from becoming part of Edwards Air Force Base. In *The Happy Bottom Riding Club: The Life and Times of Pancho Barnes*, Lauren Kessler tells how she left her husband and son to become a barnstorming pilot in the late 1920s. Like young Bessie Pittman, Sarah Breedlove left her Southern home for New York, a new name, and the world of cosmetics. Beverly Lowry recounts how a black woman became a millionaire in *Her Dream of Dreams: The Rise and Triumph of Madam C. J. Walker* (see chapter 9). Mary Pickford also used her wits to become successful, in her case as a movie studio owner after her career as an actress. Scott Eyman tells the story of her life and career in *Mary Pickford: America's Sweetheart*.

Whitaker, Robert

The Mapmaker's Wife: A True Tale of Love, Murder, and Survival in the Amazon. Basic Books, 2004. 352p. ISBN 0738208086.

Cartographer Jean Godin arrived in Peru with the French Academy of Sciences 1736–1744 expedition to study astrophysical phenomena from the peaks of the Andes Mountains. While there he married local beauty Isabelle Grameson (1728–1792), a thirteen-year-old of Spanish descent. In 1749 he crossed the South American continent to attend to his failing finances from French Guinea, where he was imprisoned for twenty years. When released, he wrote Isabelle to join him so they could move to France. In this adventure narrative, Robert Whitaker describes her terrible journey over the Andes and through the Amazon Basin, which only she survived, losing her brothers and all of her servants to deadly accidents or desertion. An exciting story, this book is perfect for readers who enjoy epic journey stories.

> **Subjects:** Amazon River Region; Dual Biography; Ecuador; Godin des Odonais, Isabelle; Godin des Odonais, Jean; Group Discussion Books; Scientific Expeditions; Teen Reads; Women
>
> **Now Try:** About fifty years later, Alexander von Humboldt and his companion, Aimé Bolpland, traversed the Amazon and the Andes in search of plants and other wonders. Gerald Helferich recounts five rugged years traveling through jungle and over mountains in *Humboldt's Cosmos: Alexander Von Humboldt and the Latin American Journey That Changed the Way We See the World*. Centuries after Godin's dangerous expedition, the Amazonian jungle is still a treacherous place. Journalist Marc Herman describes the lives of poor miners eking out lives in *Searching for El Dorado: A Journey into the South American Rainforest on the Tail of the World's Largest Gold Rush*. For another romantic story about a man and a woman often separated by his frequent remote explorations, read *A Rage to Live: A Biography of Richard & Isabel Burton* by Mary S. Lovell (see this chapter). In his novel set along the Magdalena River in Columbia, *Love in the Time of Cholera*, Gabriel García Márquez tells another epic love story.

Nature Adventure

Almost everyone enjoys a walk in the woods or along a beach. An escape from the pressures of modern life is often cited as refreshing, and witnessing the processes of nature gives vacationers or weekend naturalists a more thoughtful perspective on the meaning of life. For some people, however, the woods, mountains, and seas are their primary habitat, and it is not escape that they seek. Their relationship with nature is far more active, and they endure unpleasant climates and storms to be in the wild, where they learn about the natural world and test their ability to survive.

1

2

3

4

5

6

7

8

9

10

11

12

Gathered in this section are biographies of men and women who dedicated their lives to the study and appreciation of wild places and the creatures that inhabit them. Douglas Carlson recounts the decades that Roger Tory Peterson spent drawing birds and working for environmental protection in *Roger Tory Peterson: A Biography*. Vicki Constantine Croke tells how Ruth Harkness traveled deep into the interior of China looking for the giant panda, when many scientists disputed whether such an animal really existed, in *The Lady and the Panda: The True Adventures of the First American Explorer to Bring Back China's Most Exotic Animal*. Naturalist and broadcaster William Beebe took an experimental submarine half a mile under the ocean to report live on his discovery of deep-sea fishes. Carol Grant Gould describes Beebe's life in *The Remarkable Life of William Beebe: Explorer and Naturalist*.

Good stories and strong characters typify Nature Adventure biographies. Although some of these books are gentler than the titles in the "Exploration Stories" section, others have just as much drama. For example, British painter J. M. W. Turner was rarely endangered by his setting, but John Wesley Powell risked his life entering the dangerous gorges of the Grand Canyon. With many of the stories taking place in woods, in meadows, on mountains, and at sea, settings are more wild than exotic. These books tend to be shorter than those about explorers. Several quick reads are available.

> *Nature Adventure* stories include biographies of people who dedicated their lives to the study and enjoyment of the natural world. Strong characters and lively stories fill these books that are set in the wild. Quick reads are available.

Carlson, Douglas

Roger Tory Peterson: A Biography. University of Texas Press, 2007. 296p. ISBN 9780292716803.

The best times for nature artist Roger Tory Peterson (1908–1996) were when he was alone in the wild, watching and listening for birds. With his sketch pad and camera, he sought the birds that he illustrated in his many editions of *A Field Guide to the Birds*. His work took him all over the world and introduced him to eminent scientists and artists, some of whom disagreed with his methods and conclusions. In time he evolved from being an artist mostly interested in the beauty of his birds into an environmental activist determined to protect their habitats. In this admiring biography, Douglas Carlson tells about Peterson sacrificing his comfort for his passion.

Subjects: Artists; Ornithologists; Peterson, Roger Tory

Now Try: *All Things Reconsidered: My Birding Adventures* brings together an entertaining selection of essays and articles written by Peterson. His *How to Know the Birds* is a good introduction to birding for anyone inspired by the biography. Children's author and illustrator Beatrix Potter also retained a lifelong love of nature and wildlife. Linda Lear chronicles her gentle life in *Beatrix Potter: A Life in Nature* (see chapter 7). Englishman Thomas Bewick spent much of his time in meadows and woods. In *Nature's Engraver: A Life of Thomas Bewick* (see this chapter), Jenny Uglow has written a gentle, loving account of the artist, which is illustrated with his own woodcuts. David McCullough recounts the lives of historical and contemporary naturalists in his collection of short pieces from magazines, *Brave Companions: Portraits in History*.

Croke, Vicki Constantine

The Lady and the Panda: The True Adventures of the First American Explorer to Bring Back China's Most Exotic Animal. New York: Random House, 2005. 372p. ISBN 0375507833. Audiobook and large print available.

By the time Ruth Harkness (1900–1947) arrived in China to take over her late husband's expedition in 1936, several big game hunters had sent giant panda skins to museums, proving that the black and white mammals did exist, but no one had succeeded in bringing a live specimen out of the country. Her husband had tried but died of cancer in a Shanghai hospital without ever seeing one. No one thought that the former dressmaker and New York socialite could succeed where seasoned hunters had failed. In this admiring biography, Vicki Constantine Croke tells the story of Harkness, the international acclaim that she received for bringing two pandas to the Brookfield Zoo, and her change of heart about the wisdom of capturing rare animals. Armchair travelers and animal lovers will relish this story.

Subjects: China; Group Discussion Books; Harkness, Ruth; Pandas; Women

Now Try: Harkness told her own story in *The Lady and the Panda: An Adventure*. English traveler Mary Kingsley is another woman who ventured into unknown parts of the world with little travel experience. Katherine Frank describes Kingsley's African travels in *A Voyager Out: The Life of Mary Kingsley*. Biochemist Joseph Needham traveled to the remotest parts of China looking for evidence that ancient Chinese engineers had developed the first compass, the suspension bridge, and other technologies. Simon Winchester profiles the eccentric professor in *The Man Who Loved China: The Fantastic Story of the Eccentric Scientist Who Unlocked the Mysteries of the Middle Kingdom* (see this chapter). Mary Shelley was another strong woman who carried on a mission after her young husband died. Novelist Muriel Sparks recounts Shelley's work to publish her husband's posthumous books and survive as a single mother in *Mary Shelley: A Biography* (see chapter 7).

Douglas, Ed

Tenzing: Hero of Everest: A Biography of Tenzing Norgay. National Geographic, 2003. 299p. ISBN 0792269837.

Tenzing Norgay (1914–1986) was the most famous Himalayan sherpa of all. In May 1953 he led Sir Edmund Hillary to the summit of Mount Everest and became internationally famous. He would reach the summit six more times. Born into poverty, the son of a yak herder, he was never spoiled by fame, but his accomplishments did let him escape from his caste to become a prominent figure in his region. In his years as a guide he met many prominent climbers, journalists, and the political leaders of the Indian subcontinent. In this tribute, journalist and mountaineer Ed Douglas describes the inspiring journey of a sweet but determined man. *Tenzing* is an appropriate choice for sensitive readers who want wholesome characters.

Subjects: India; Mountaineers; Nepal; Quick Reads; Sherpas; Tenzing Norgay

Now Try: Norgay's son Jamling Tenzing Norgay recounts his father's adventures and one of his own in *Touching My Father's Soul: A Sherpa's Journey to the Top of Everest*. For more about the life of mountaineers, read *View from the Summit* by Sir Edmund Hillary. Another book about a humble Third World figure with inborn intelligence and charity is *Nisa: The Life and Words of a !Kung Woman* by Marjorie Shostak (see chapter 4). Like sherpas, golf caddies assist and advise competitive people. John Feinstein describes the life and death of PGA golfer Tom Watson's longtime caddy in *Caddy for Life: The Bruce Edwards Story* (see chapter 12).

Ehrlich, Gretel

John Muir: Nature's Visionary. National Geographic, 2000. 240p. ISBN 079227-9549.

John Muir (1838–1914) was a wanderer and a truant. His first long journey began in 1849, when his father announced that he would not have to do his homework because they were leaving Scotland for America in the morning. Muir and his brother David spent most of the trip on the deck with the sailors. Muir would spend most of his life outdoors, examining rocks, plants, and wildlife, and writing about his love of nature. In this beautifully illustrated book, poet Gretel Ehrlich tracks the first president of the Sierra Club through the woods and mountains of California and on voyages around the world.

> **Subjects:** Activists; California; Muir, John; Naturalists; Photographic Biography; Quick Reads; Sierra Club; Teen Reads

> **Now Try:** The Library of America has collected Muir's most popular writings in *Nature Writings: The Story of My Boyhood and Youth; My First Summer in the Sierra; The Mountains of California; Stickeen; Selected Essays*. In the coffee table book *Sierra Club: 100 Years of Protecting Nature*, Tom Turner chronicles the work of the organization that Muir helped found. Though he led a much more settled life, Aldo Leopold's love of the wilderness was as great as Muir's. Marybeth Lorbiecki retells the story of his life of dedication for a cause in her photobiography *Aldo Leopold: A Fierce Green Fire* by (see chapter 4). *Last Stand: George Bird Grinnell, the Battle to Save the Buffalo, and the Birth of the New West* by Michael Punke is another book about a pioneering conservationist and his work to preserve wilderness.

Gilbert, Elizabeth

The Last American Man. Viking, 2002. 271p. ISBN 0670030864. Audiobook available.

Eustace Conway (1961–) is a modern-day frontiersman and adventurer. At age seventeen he left a comfortable suburban home to live alone in the woods, and a year later he paddled down the Mississippi River in his handmade wooden canoe. Since then he has traveled to remote villages in Central America and ridden across the United States in record time on a horse. Elizabeth Gilbert portrays Conway as a self-reliant, resourceful individual who embodies old-time pioneering spirit. Readers who dream of their own adventures will enjoy this book.

Subjects: Conway, Eustace; Outdoor Life; Quick Reads; Teen Reads; Wilderness Survival

Now Try: The memoir *Three Cups of Tea* by Greg Mortenson is a good follow-up book, because its author is also a fearless adventurer willing to climb any mountain and greet any villager as an equal. He is also out to save the world. Mike May was not only fearless, he was also blind until he had radical eye surgery. Yet he skied and tried other dangerous sports. Robert Kurson describes May's courageous life in *Crashing Through: A True Story of Risk, Adventure, and the Man Who Dared to See* (see chapter 11). In the classic adventure tale *Kon-Tiki: Across the Pacific by Raft*, Thor Heyerdahl recounts how he set out to prove that ancient South Americans could have crossed the Pacific to Polynesia. In middle age, journalist David Lamb decided to break away from routine and have an adventure. He recounts his coast-to-coast bicycle trip in *Over the Hills: A Midlife Escape Across America by Bicycle*.

Gould, Carol Grant

The Remarkable Life of William Beebe: Explorer and Naturalist. Island Press/Shearwater Books, 2004. 447p. ISBN 1559638583.

In 1932, long before Jacques Cousteau explored the oceans, William Beebe (1877–1962) broadcast on the radio from a bathysphere a half a mile below the ocean surface, describing fish and other creatures never before seen by humans. Long before the television age of David Attenborough, Beebe traveled to remote jungles seeking out rare and new species of animals and plants for his magazine articles and books. As the first ornithologist for the Bronx Zoo, the energetic scientist collected and studied birds from around the globe. Given access to Beebe's papers at Princeton University, Gould has written an adventure story about a now-forgotten celebrity of early twentieth century zoology that will appeal to viewers of televised nature programs as well as other readers.

Subjects: Beebe, William; Explorers; Naturalists; Zoologists

Now Try: Beebe's own books mix memoir and science. His titles include *Two Bird Lovers in Mexico*, *Half Mile Down* (about deep sea diving), and *Galapagos: World's End*. A more recent naturalist who will go anywhere to get a story is David Attenborough. He recounts his career of making nature films in *Life on Air: Memoirs of a Broadcaster*. Zoologist Gerald Durrell describes growing up with animals in his highly entertaining *My Family and Other Animals*. Carl Sagan was another enthusiastic scientist who doubled as media celebrity. *Carl Sagan: A Life in the Cosmos* by William Poundstone (see chapter 11) captures a life in the pursuit of knowledge that is free of difficult science reading. Peter Matthiessen has also traveled the world seeking to see wildlife in natural habitats. In *The Snow Leopard* he describes his attempt to see the reclusive cats on the rocky cliffs of the Himalayan Mountains.

Hamilton, James

Turner. Random House, 1997. 461p. ISBN 140006015X.

Light and color were very important to the great British painter J. M. W. Turner (1775–1851). With his sketchbook and watercolors at hand, he toured the British Isles extensively, capturing rural and maritime scenes that are now valuable for their historical content as well as their beauty. When there was peace, the restless artist also toured the European continent, filling his portfolio with works that he would sell at high prices. In this attractive book, with its maps and color plates of a

few of Turner's masterpieces, art historian James Hamilton portrays him as a solitary man, who was most at ease when alone in the countryside.

Subjects: Great Britain; Painters; Turner, J. M. W.

Now Try: *Turner on Tour* by Inge Herold is an attractive illustrated book focusing just on Turner's travels to the locations that he depicted in his art. By the time Claude Monet became a painter, the Industrial Revolution was changing the countryside that had been so isolated in Turner's time. In *Claude Monet: Life and Work*, Virginia Spate tells how Monet turned from modern society looking for the unspoiled setting in his later work. Spending most of his life in the woods and fields, nature artist and ornithologist Roger Tory Peterson led a life that was very Turneresque. Douglas Carlson chronicles the travels and art of a dedicated environmentalist in *Roger Tory Peterson: A Biography* (see this chapter). Turner's character, arrogant and ill-tempered, resembles that of French author Gustave Flaubert. Frederick Brown describes the life of the author of *Madame Bovary* in *Flaubert: A Biography* (see chapter 7).

Jago, Lucy

The Northern Lights. Alfred A. Knopf, 2001. 297p. ISBN 0375409807.

Geophysicist Kristian Birkeland (1867–1917) sought danger and isolation. In 1899 he led a team of observers up Haldde Mountain in northern Norway during a blizzard to test his theories about the aurora borealis. Subsequently he endured extreme weather to visit stations in the Arctic Ocean and in the Egyptian desert to witness other celestial events. These difficult explorations and his obsessive studies of electromagnetism led to his invention of the hearing aid, the cathode ray for rocket propulsion, and the mass accelerator. His success, however, cost him his marriage and his health. In this candid biography, Lucy Jago tells a classic tale of a man seduced by science and obsessed with finding answers.

Subjects: Auroras; Birkeland, Kristian; Geophysicists; Norway; Quick Reads

Now Try: Birkeland is seen as a real "mad scientist." Whether physicist Edward Teller was mad, evil, or simply pursuing knowledge is a question Peter Goodchild explores in *Edward Teller: The Real Dr. Strangelove* (see chapter 11). Chemists and physicists Marie and Pierre Curie never fully realized the dangers of handling radioactive materials nor the opposition they would face for their political ideas. Denis Brian examines their hot-tempered lives in *The Curies: A Biography of the Most Controversial Family in Science* (see chapter 11). Lieutenant Colonel George Armstrong Custer of the U.S. Cavalry disregarded danger for himself and his men in military action even before the Battle of the Little Big Horn. In *Son of the Morning Star,* Evan S. Connell tells the story of a man who personified American bravado in the time of westward expansion. Franz Kafka was as dysfunctional as Birkeland. His obsession with dark literature is told in the compact biography *Franz Kafka* by Jeremy Adler (see chapter 7).

Rhodes, Richard

John James Audubon: The Making of an American. Knopf, 2004. 514p. ISBN 03754-14126.

John James Audubon's (1785–1851) entry into the United States in 1803 was difficult. Fleeing the draft for Napoleon's army, the young Frenchman knew no English and immediately contracted yellow fever in New York. He survived to become his adopted nation's most famous ornithologist and painter of birds. For nearly half a century, he crossed the expanding country, observing birds and painting them, and starting businesses that quickly failed. Using lengthy quotations throughout, the author Richard Rhodes focuses on Audubon's private and family life in this visually descriptive book for readers who like in-depth biography.

Subjects: Audubon, John James; Ornithologists; Painters; Wilderness

Now Try: Audubon's journals and letters include many stories about how his paintings were conceived. These are matched with reproductions in *Selected Journals and Other Writings*. Daniel Boone was a woodsman who traveled much of the Ohio Valley on foot. Robert Morgan portrays him as an early environmentalist in *Daniel Boone: A Biography* (see chapter 5). John Jacob Astor also arrived in America as a poor immigrant. Biographer Axel Madsen tells how Astor staked himself in the fur trade and shipping, controlled New York real estate, and even built a glamorous hotel in *John Jacob Astor: America's First Multimillionaire* (see chapter 9). In some ways, Jane Goodall's life provides a sharp contrast to that of Audubon. She did not kill her subjects to study them or seek personal wealth through business schemes. However, *Jane Goodall: The Woman Who Redefined Man* by Dale Peterson (see chapter 4) is another epic story of a naturalist inspiring millions to take action to preserve the environment. According to his nurse and aide, Mary Street Alinder, photographer Ansel Adams was another artistic figure unable to manage daily life well. She recounts his difficult life in *Ansel Adams: A Biography*.

Todd, Kim

Chrysalis: Maria Sibylla Merian and the Secrets of Metamorphosis. Harcourt, 2007. 328p. ISBN 9780151011087.

Maria Sibylla Merian (1647–1717) was the mother of lepidopterology. As a child in mid-seventeenth-century Frankfort, she loved insects, especially moths and butterflies, and was encouraged by her stepfather, the still life painter Jacob Marrel, to draw and paint them. This was the start of an obsession that would slowly lead her away from the traditional roles as wife and mother and toward the company of amateur naturalists. At age thirty-eight she left her husband to join a quiet religious community, and in 1699 at age fifty-two she sailed to Surinam, where she spent two years studying and illustrating flora and fauna of the South American rain forest. According to author Kim Todd, Merian's contributions to entomology and scientific illustration have been overlooked. She offers this tribute to readers of the history of science.

Subjects: Butterflies; Entomologists; Merian, Maria Sibylla; Moths; Surinam; Women

Now Try: *Beatrix Potter: A Life in Nature* by Linda Lear (see chapter 7) is a similar story about a woman who never outgrew her love of the tiny creatures of nature. Like Merian, Gregor Mendel studied the natural in isolation of a religious community. Robin Marantz Henig intimately recounts the monk's education, experiments, correspondence, daily routine, and legacy in *The Monk in the Garden: The Lost and Found*

Genius of Gregor Mendel, the Father of Genetics (see chapter 11). The naturalist who wrote *Origin of Species* and *Descent of Man* spent most of his time in isolation. David Quammen tells how Charles Darwin studied and formulated his theory of evolution for many years before announcing it to the public in *The Reluctant Mr. Darwin: An Intimate Portrait of Charles Darwin and the Making of His Theory of Evolution* (see chapter 11).

Uglow, Jenny

Nature's Engraver: A Life of Thomas Bewick. Farrar, Straus & Giroux, 2006. 458p. ISBN 9780374112363.

English engraver Thomas Bewick (1753–1828) personified three trends of the late eighteenth century: the revival of the woodcut illustration, the boom in the publishing of children's books, and the rising interest in natural history. As a youth he struggled with academics but exhibited a natural ability to draw without formal training. He was apprenticed to an engraver in Newcastle and began illustrating scientific papers. As his illustrations gained fame, he won book commissions and his own publishing opportunities. His volume on birds is recognized as the original nature field guide. Jenny Uglow has written a gentle, loving account of the naturalist, illustrated with his own woodcuts, that general readers will enjoy.

Subjects: Bewick, Thomas; Illustrators; Naturalists; Wood Engravers

Now Try: *Aesop's Fables* with Bewick's illustrations are still available in many libraries. Outdoorsman Izaak Walton preceded Bewick as an advocate for the English countryside. James Prosek describes his own journey across England in search of Walton sights in *The Complete Angler: A Connecticut Yankee Follows in the Footsteps of Walton*. Artist Roger Tory Peterson was another outstanding figure in the history of birding. Douglas Carlson tells about Peterson illustrating guide books, traveling to remote sanctuaries, and advocating conservation in the tribute *Roger Tory Peterson: A Biography* (see this chapter). Readers who like books set in the English countryside will enjoy *Tennyson: An Illustrated Life* by Norman Page, the story of a poet who celebrated nature.

Worster, Donald

A River Running West: The Life of John Wesley Powell. Oxford University Press, 2001. 673p. ISBN 0195099915. Audiobook available.

As a youth, John Wesley Powell (1834–1902) often paused to look at rocks, shells, and plants. By the time he was seriously injured in the battle at Shiloh in the Civil War, he had explored the river beds of the Midwest United States and planned a scientific career. The central event of his life was the bold exploration of the Colorado River and Grand Canyon, a dangerous adventure that featured scientific discovery, scarce supplies, and mutiny. In his admiring biography of a brave and determined man, Donald Worster chronicles the evolution of a conservationist who was important in the American parks movement. Readers of natural history books will appreciate this biography.

Subjects: Conservationists; Naturalists; Powell, John Wesley

Now Try: Powell's *The Exploration of the Colorado River and Its Canyons* is an exciting tale that was ranked fourth by *Adventure Magazine* in its list of 100 classic books. Eighteenth-century Scottish gentleman farmer James Hutton was another man who enjoyed looking at rocks. Jack Repcheck tells why he is called "The Father of Geology" in *The Man Who Found Time: James Hutton and the Discovery of the Earth's Antiquity* (see chapter 11). Theodore Roosevelt was an equally determined character who through experiences in the West gained a love of wilderness. In *The Rise of Theodore Roosevelt*, Edmund Morris recounts the maturing of an awkward youth into a rugged individual. With her "Make America Beautiful" campaign, first lady Lady Bird Johnson helped start the environmental movement of the second half of the twentieth century. Jane Jarboe Russell recounts the life of a tough and resourceful woman worthy of admiration in *Lady Bird: A Biography of Mrs. Johnson* (see chapter 10).

Travel Stories

Throughout most of human history, most people spent their entire lives close to the place of their birth. Few people ever left for other lands, and, if they did, they rarely returned to their origins. People only left their homelands when hunting or agriculture failed to feed the population. Migrations may have been dramatic, but most were never documented for future readers. In such a world, travel was always an exciting topic for a story.

Though travel is available to many more people living in the modern world, readers still dream of traveling to distant, unfamiliar places and enjoy books about people who have been to places that readers have never visited. In this section are biographies of individuals who made a habit of traveling to foreign lands. Simon Winchester examines the life of Joseph Needham, a biochemist who ventured deep into the Chinese interior to discover the roots of Chinese science, in *The Man Who Loved China: The Fantastic Story of the Eccentric Scientist Who Unlocked the Mysteries of the Middle Kingdom*. Martha Gellhorn traveled the world as a reporter seeking stories for hew newspapers. Caroline Moorehead describes her vagabond life in *Gellhorn: A Twentieth Century Life.* Early in the nineteenth century former Royal Navy lieutenant James Holman traveled across Europe without companions despite being blind. Jason Roberts recounts how Holman toured remote locations and wrote a popular series of travel books, in *A Sense of the World: How a Blind Man Became History's Greatest Traveler*.

Like other Adventure Biographies, travel story biographies mix strong historical characters with incredible stories. The subjects suffered through many hardships to go to places that their contemporaries never visited, witnessing natural wonders and meeting people from foreign cultures. Settings with exotic details are very important to these narratives. The books in this section tend to be long and leisurely. Readers will enjoy these books for their eloquent descriptions of places that they may never see.

Travel Story biographies mix strong characters with incredible stories. Authors include vivid descriptions of the settings in their leisurely books aimed at letting readers experience exotic locations. Most of these books are suitable for leisurely reading.

Brogan, Hugh

Alexis de Tocqueville: A Life. Yale University Press, 2006. 724p. ISBN 9780300-108033.

In 1831 traveler and political philosopher Alexis de Tocqueville (1805–1859) wanted to escape from France as much as he wanted to visit America. Unable to foresee a safe way to survive another revolution, he wanted to distance himself from both friends and enemies. He had taken other adventurous trips, and America sounded interesting. So he left his fiancée for the New World, where he found a society struggling to offer both equality and liberty. When he returned to France, he wrote a best-selling account of American political society. In this sympathetic work, Hugh Brogan describes an emotionally complicated man who left an important historical record for generations of readers.

> **Subjects:** France; Politics and Government; Tocqueville, Alexis de; Travelers

> **Now Try:** *Democracy in America* is de Tocqueville's classic book about 1830s America. Entries from his notebooks are also in print as *Journey to America*. Two noted British authors also toured the United States and published accounts: *American Notes* by Charles Dickens and *American Notes* by Rudyard Kipling. Before de Tocqueville, the most famous French visitor to America was the Marquis de Lafayette, who fought for the colonists in the American Revolution. Harlow G. Unger assesses the Frenchman's life and legacy on both sides of the Atlantic Ocean in *Lafayette*. Walt Whitman saw a different America than Alexis de Tocqueville saw during his journey, and the American reported through poetry instead of through essays, but both lived complicated romantic and political lives. *Walt Whitman's America: A Cultural Biography* by Davis S. Reynolds (see chapter 7) serves as an ideal sequel to Brogan's book for the historical reader.

Colley, Linda

🌶 *The Ordeal of Elizabeth Marsh: A Woman in World History.* Pantheon Books, 2007. 363p. ISBN 9780375421532.

Elizabeth Marsh (1735–1785) was an observer with a keen eye and the good fortune to travel around many continents when most women were left behind by their seafaring men. Born in England in 1735, Marsh lived in Minorca, Gibraltar, Morocco, and India at a time when Great Britain was colonizing the world. As a child of an officer in the Royal Navy and the wife of a British merchant, she wrote books about her experiences, which she sold by subscription to British readers. In them she reported on military conquest, slavery, piracy, and places that most people would never see. Linda Colley includes many maps and fine illustrations in her account of an adventurous woman and her family, which will please readers of geography and history.

> **Subjects:** British Empire; Marsh, Elizabeth; Travelers; Women

> **Awards:** New York Times 10 Best Books of 2007

> **Now Try:** Martha Ballard, a midwife in Hallowell, Maine, is another woman who wrote about her experiences. Laurel Thatcher Ulrich recounts how Ballard kept a diary on folded half-sheets of paper in *A Midwife's Tale: The Life of Martha Ballard, Based on Her Diary, 1785–1812* (see chapter 4). Read-

ers wanting to read about another woman who saw and reported on the world's most unfortunate people should try *Pearl S. Buck: A Cultural Biography* by Peter Coon (see chapter 4). In the twentieth century, women made their mark in journalism by reporting on wars. *Gellhorn: A Twentieth Century Life* by Caroline Moorehead (see this chapter), *Lee Miller: A Life* by Carolyn Burke, and *Margaret Bourke-White* by Vicki Goldberg are biographies telling the women's stories of being war correspondents.

Howell, Georgina

🌂 *Gertrude Bell: Queen of the Desert, Shaper of Nations.* Farrar, Straus & Giroux, 2007. 481p. ISBN 9780374161620.

T. E. Lawrence complained that Gertrude Bell (1868–1926) was "born too gifted." She accomplished far more than he ever did in the Arab lands of the Middle East. The talented Bell, a traveler, archeologist, mountaineer, photographer, cartographer, linguist, and spy, is credited with forming the government of Iraq, negotiating its borders, and arranging the government of King Faisel in 1921. By drawing up antiquities laws for the country, she stopped outsiders from taking artifacts to the West and started the Museum of Iraq. She also formed the Baghdad Public Library. According to author Georgina Howell, Bell ranks high in the list of British colonial officials, someone who always worked for the good of the peoples that she loved. Offer this book to readers who enjoy stories about the British Empire.

Subjects: Archeologists; Bell, Gertrude; British Foreign Service; Group Discussion Books; Middle East; Mountaineers; Travelers; Women

Awards: ALA Notable Books, 2008

Now Try: Three detailed notebooks and a collection of Bell's love letters are published in *Gertrude Bell: The Arabian Diaries, 1913–1914*. T. E. Lawrence was a Bell contemporary who sought to effect the boundaries and governance of Arab countries. In *The Golden Warrior: The Life and Legend of Lawrence of Arabia* (see chapter 3), Lawrence James tells how Lawrence willingly played the role of media hero and embellished it in his own writings Like Bell, Jane Goodall has spent much of her life away from England and European comforts. Dale Peterson recounts her life among the chimpanzees and speaking for the environment in *Jane Goodall: The Woman Who Redefined Man* (see chapter 4). To learn about a talented woman who traveled to the Near East to dabble in archeology and find story lines for her mystery novels, read the entertaining *Agatha Christie: A Biography* by Janet Morgan. Many such women are profiled in *Women of Discovery: A Celebration of Intrepid Women Who Explored the World* by Milbry Polk and Mary Tiegreen.

Kroeger, Brooke

Nellie Bly: Daredevil, Reporter, Feminist. Times Books, 1994. 631p. ISBN 0812919734.

According to Brooke Kroeger, Nellie Bly (1864–1922) invented investigative journalism. She faked insanity to get into an asylum to get firsthand information for a sensational article. She later faked migraine headaches to learn how various doctors would treat her. Not content to report "women's news," she witnessed political fighting in Mexico, visited the front in World War I, and took a trip around the world. Readers who enjoy stories of adventurous women who have to fight hard to succeed will enjoy this admiring book.

Subjects: Bly, Nellie; Journalists; Women

Now Try: Bly's sensational investigative report *Ten Days in a Mad House* is difficult to find in print but is easily found in digital formats on the Internet. Like Bly, journalist Ida B. Wells risked her life by going after dangerous stories. Her adventurous story is told in *They Say: Ida B. Wells and the Reconstruction of Race* by James West Davidson (see chapter 6). Another female investigative journalist had a profound effect on the regulation of corporations. Steve Weinberg recounts a battle between a journalist and tycoon in *Taking on the Trust: The Epic Battle of Ida Tarbell and John D. Rockefeller*. Photographer Henri Cartier-Bresson took considerable risks to witness world events as they unfolded. Some of his best images are included in the admiring account of his life by Pierre Assouline, *Henri Cartier-Bresson: A Biography* (see chapter 7). Many journalists have followed Bly's examples and published damaging information about public figures, corporations, and government institutions. Longtime journalist Jack Anderson described his life in journalism in *Confessions of a Muckraker: The Inside Story of Life in Washington During the Truman, Eisenhower, Kennedy and Johnson Years*.

Moorehead, Caroline

Gellhorn: A Twentieth Century Life. Henry Holt, 2003. 463p. ISBN 0805065539.

Terminally ill, ninety-year-old Martha Gellhorn (1908–1998) took her own life. It was another experiment to see whether she still had the courage to break the rules. Born in St. Louis and educated at Bryn Mawr, the reporter traveled the world and befriended misfits. Gellhorn, who had love affairs with the philosopher Bertrand Russell and author Ernest Hemingway, especially enjoyed dangerous tropical assignments, until she retired to London. In this intimate biography, Caroline Moorehead tells the story of an unconventional woman who would not honor boundaries. The tone of scandal and gossip makes this book particularly delectable to readers with rebellious streaks.

Subjects: Gellhorn, Martha; Journalists; Women

Now Try: Gellhorn's memoirs include *The Face of War* and *Travels with Myself and Another: A Memoir*. A sampling of her short fiction can be found in *The Novellas of Martha Gellhorn*. She is one of the brave women described in the collective biography *The Women Who Wrote the War* by Nancy Caldwell Sorel (see chapter 3). Gellhorn's name is also often associated with Ernest Hemingway, whom she married. Bernice Kert includes stories about her relationship with the novelist in *The Hemingway Women*. Gellhorn and poet Dorothy Parker were both known for their tough personae. In the cautionary tale *Dorothy Parker: What Fresh Hell Is This?*, Marion Meade candidly describes a desperate woman who never finds happiness. In *Art Lover: A Biography of Peggy Guggenheim* (see chapter 8), Anton Gill describes another self-assured twentieth-century woman who collected husbands and lovers as she traveled the world.

Morgan, Susan

Bombay Anna: The Real Story and Remarkable Adventures of the King and I Governess. University of California Press, 2008. 274p. ISBN 9780520252264.

Governess Anna Leonowens (1831–1915) did not have the credentials that she claimed when she agreed to teach English to Crown Prince Chulalongkorn, son of the king of Siam. Nevertheless she did well, taught several princes and princesses, helped the king with a bit of secretarial work, and remained in Bangkok for over five years. According to author Susan Morgan, Leonownens was successful precisely because she was not an English lady with many prejudices. In this admiring biography, Morgan continues the story past the period dramatized by the musical *The King and I* to tell about Leonowens crossing Russia just before the Bolshevik Revolution and working for women's rights in Canada.

> **Subjects:** Activists; Canada; Governesses; Leonowens, Anna; Siam; Thailand; Women

> **Now Try:** Leonowens's own account, ***The English Governess at the Siamese Court***, is more critical of the king and Siamese social conditions than the biography ***Anna and the King of Siam*** by Margaret Dorothea Landon and the musical *The King and I*. French fashion designer Coco Chanel was another woman who reinvented herself by fabricating stories about her past. French *Vogue* editor Edmonde Charles-Roux tells an intimate story of this bold businesswoman and her romantic affairs in ***Chanel: Her Life, Her World, and the Woman Behind the Legend She Herself Created*** (see chapter 8). Elizabeth Shrewsbury was asked by Elizabeth I, queen of England, to serve as warden for Mary Queen of Scots. Mary S. Lovell describes Shrewsbury as a woman who knew how to survive a dangerous royal court in ***Bess of Hardwick: Empire Builder*** (see chapter 4). Like Leonowens, actress Fanny Kemble found herself uncomfortably surrounded by slavery when she started a new life, in Fanny's case as wife of a plantation owner in the antebellum South. Catherine Clinton tells how Kemble became a supporter of abolition in ***Fanny Kemble's Civil Wars*** (see chapter 9).

Nicholl, Charles

Somebody Else: Arthur Rimbaud in Africa, 1880–91. University of Chicago Press, 1999. 333p. ISBN 0226580296.

French modernist poet Arthur Rimbaud (1854–1891) abandoned his literary career at age twenty-one to seek a new life in exotic lands. After brief stays in Cyprus and Java, he landed along the Suez Canal in 1880 and submersed himself in Arab culture. He lived most of the rest of his short, obscure life in Egypt, Ethiopia, and Yemen, only leaving to die in France. Biographer Charles Nicholl uses Rimbaud's letters and quotes from his poems to describe the travels of an ever-changing young man who became a soldier of fortune, gunrunner, and possibly slave trader. Included are stories of crossing vast deserts and rugged mountains with dangerous men that will thrill adventure readers.

> **Subjects:** Africa; Poets; Rimbaud, Arthur; Travelers

> **Now Try:** Many editions of Rimbaud's poetry are available, including ***Rimbaud: Complete Works, Selected Letters: A Bilingual Edition***, for readers wanting to study his writing in the original French. After having her collected poems praised by *Time* in 1938, Laura Riding renounced poetry and spent thirty years in seclusion in Florida. Deborah Baker sorts through conflicting accounts to discover why Riding ran away from fame in ***In Extremis: The Life of Laura Riding*** (see chapter 5). The most famous young Englishman to immerse himself in Arab affairs was T. E. Lawrence. Lawrence James recounts his adventures and death in ***The Golden Warrior: The Life and Legend of Lawrence of Arabia*** (see chapter 3). Master criminal Joseph Silver dealt in guns and slaves as part of his international crime trade. Charles Van Onselen describes a truly evil man in ***The Fox and the Flies: The Secret Life of a Grotesque Master Criminal*** (see chapter 2).

Roberts, Jason

A Sense of the World: How a Blind Man Became History's Greatest Traveler. HarperCollins, 2006. 382p. ISBN 9780007161065.

James Holman (1786–1857) was a lieutenant in the Royal Navy in 1810 when a mysterious tropical disease left him crippled and blind. After a couple of years as an invalid and a stint as a praying Naval Knight of Windsor (a position for disabled naval officers), he left England for the Mediterranean for his health alone. Discovering that his skills of echolocation were acute, he set off on a series of trips that he recounted in a series of best-selling books. Known as the Blind Traveler, he climbed volcanoes, was arrested as a spy in Russia, and circled the globe. Because he could find no modern account of Holman's life, Jason Roberts sought out the traveler's own writings and other nineteenth-century documents, which he mixes into this heroic narrative. Readers looking for inspiring stories will enjoy this book.

> **Subjects:** Blindness; Holman, James; Travelers
>
> **Now Try:** California businessman Mike May never let blindness get in the way of his entrepreneurial ambitions or his love of dangerous sports. Robert Kurson tells his incredible story in *Crashing Through: A True Story of Risk, Adventure, and the Man Who Dared to See* (see chapter 11). Popular musician Ray Charles was blind from an early age. Michael Lydon tells a candid story about a poor boy from Jellyroll, Florida, who overcame class and racial discrimination to become a giant in the world of popular music, in *Ray Charles: Man and Music* (see chapter 4). Deafness is the challenge that Ludwig van Beethoven overcame to write his latter concertos and symphonies. Edmund Morris portrays Beethoven as a courageous man relying on his music to get him through his difficult life in *Beethoven: The Universal Composer* (see chapter 4). Henry Gray is another forgotten nineteenth-century figure with an interesting medical story. His biography, *The Anatomist: A True Story of Gray's Anatomy* by Bill Hayes (see chapter 11), also relies heavily on diaries and other recently discovered documents.

Winchester, Simon

The Man Who Loved China: The Fantastic Story of the Eccentric Scientist Who Unlocked the Mysteries of the Middle Kingdom. HarperCollins, 2008. 316p. ISBN 9780060884598. Audiobook and large print available.

Biochemist Joseph Needham (1900–1995) was a professor at Cambridge University when he fell in love with a Chinese student, who convinced him that her country had a glorious scientific legacy that was unrecognized in the West. While his tolerant British wife worked in her own chemistry lab, he went to China to visit his students and verify the history of Chinese scientific firsts, such as the first magnetic compass, crossbow, and suspension bridge. Braving the Japanese invasion, the Cultural Revolution, and dangerous single-engine planes, he made many trips into remote corners of the country. According to popular science author Simon Winchester, Needham identified over 250 innovations in his seven-volume history of Chinese science. This lively biography of an enthusiastic traveler will appeal to a wide audience.

Subjects: Biochemists; China; Group Discussion Books; Needham, Joseph; Travelers

Now Try: Several of Needham's books may still be found in libraries, including the compact history *Science in Traditional China: A Comparative Perspective* and the seven-volume set *Science and Civilization in China*. (One of the volumes has ten parts in separate bindings—it is larger than it sounds!) Sir Richard Burton also traveled into remote regions of the world to gather ancient knowledge. Mary S. Lovell recounts his life and love for his wife in *A Rage to Live: A Biography of Richard & Isabel Burton* (see this chapter). Journalist Harrison Salisbury's primary interest was the Soviet Union, but he also studied and wrote extensively about the Communists in China. Salisbury tells about the time that Needham worked in China in *The New Emperors: China in the Era of Mao and Deng*. Salisbury describes his own adventurous life in *A Journey for Our Times: A Memoir*. Journalist Lowell Thomas opened up much of the world to Americans through his radio broadcasts and newsreels. He told stories from remote locations in *So Long Until Tomorrow: From Quaker Hill to Kathmandu*.

Consider Starting With . . .

With these exciting adventure books on your nightstand, you might never get any sleep.

- Berg, A. Scott. *Lindbergh.*

- Bergreen, Laurence. *Marco Polo: From Venice to Xanadu.*

- Fernández-Armesto, Felipe. *Amerigo: The Man Who Gave His Name to America.*

- Howell, Georgina. *Gertrude Bell: Queen of the Desert, Shaper of Nations.*

- Talty, Stephan. *Empire of Blue Water: Captain Morgan's Great Pirate Army, the Epic Battle for the Americas, and the Catastrophe That Ended the Outlaws' Bloody Reign.*

- Whitaker, Robert. *The Mapmaker's Wife: A True Tale of Love, Murder, and Survival in the Amazon.*

- Worster, Donald. *A River Running West: The Life of John Wesley Powell.*

Further Reading

Adamson, Lynda G.

Thematic Guide to Popular Nonfiction. Greenwood Press, 2006. 352p. ISBN 0313328552.
Adamson includes chapters about conservation, the environment, exploration, survival, and travel relations in her book about nonfiction topics. Each chapter describes a topic and then presents three lengthy reviews before suggesting other titles.

Cords, Sarah Statz

The Real Story: A Guide to Nonfiction Reading Interests. Libraries Unlimited, 2006. 460p. ISBN 1591582830.

Cords's first chapter covers true adventure and the second covers travel. That's fifty-five pages of introduction to these genres and reviews of popular adventure and travel titles.

Wyatt, Neal

The Readers' Advisory Guide to Nonfiction. American Libraries, 2007. 318p. ISBN 9780838909362.

Wyatt discusses travel in chapter 8 and adventure in chapter 9. In her discussions she identifies key authors and includes generous lists of titles to recommend to readers.

Chapter 2

True Crime Biography

Definition of True Crime Biography

A True Crime Biography is a nonfiction narrative that concentrates on the character of a criminal, law enforcement official, or victim in telling the story of the commission of a crime or crimes.

The commission of a crime is a story line at least as old as the Judeo-Christian Bible. The Old Testament includes many stories about people breaking biblical laws against murder, theft, kidnapping, adultery, prostitution, and bearing false witness. Adam and Eve stole apples. Cain murdered Abel. The people of Sodom and Gomorrah broke laws governing sexual relations. Greek mythology also includes stories about people breaking the laws decreed by the gods. Oedipus kills his father and marries his mother. Orestes kills his mother. The Furies track down murderers and punish them both in the world and forever in the underworld. Ancient authors knew that readers were drawn to such stories; and they used them to teach the consequences of sin. The writers told why their characters were tempted, how they planned and committed their crimes, how they tried to hide the evidence or flee, and how they were subsequently caught and punished. While readers shook their heads at the characters who were naïve enough to think that that they could escape unnoticed or unpunished, they also learned the rules necessary for the maintenance of society and the penalties for breaking laws. Most of the same elements in these ancient texts can be found in modern crime stories, and readers react to them in the same way. What differs is that in contemporary literature, detectives, not deities, catch criminals.

In her biography *The Suspicions of Mr. Whicher: A Shocking Murder and the Undoing of a Great Victorian Detective* (in this chapter), Kate Summerscale points to the publication in 1841 of *The Murders in the Rue Morgue* by Edgar Allan Poe as the seminal moment in detective fiction and true crime. She explains in her book how the governing officials at Scotland Yard in London were so impressed with the investigative reasoning presented in Poe's story that they hired eight men as detectives the next year and asked them to apply his methods. Reporters from London newspapers covered the new detectives' investigations, and Detective-Inspector Jonathan Whicher became quite well-known in the community. When the famous detective failed to solve a murder in 1860, readers flooded the newspapers with their own analyses and recommendations. Impressed by the public involvement in the case, Wilkie Collins wrote *The Moonstone* for those same readers.

High-profile crimes are frequently recounted in books while public memory of the cases is still fresh. The authors, often journalists, obtain interviews with the people associated with the crimes, including criminals, police officers, lawyers, and psychologists, as well as victims and their families. In this chapter you'll find books that focus to a large extent on these individuals. The chapter also includes profiles of individuals associated with historical crimes.

> *True Crime Biography* includes nonfiction narratives that concentrate on a criminal, law enforcement official, or victim in telling the story of the commission of a crime or crimes. The characters are attention grabbing and the stories are compelling. Because attention to detail is important in the recounting of crimes, settings are well defined and few true crime stories can be called quick reads. These books offer readers a chance to experience danger not found in their real lives.

Appeal of the Genre

In her chapter on true crime in the readers' advisory text *Real Story*, Sarah Statz Cords claims that true crime books often have significant character appeal. The people who commit heinous crimes worthy of books are often extraordinary individuals who attract attention. Readers want to examine the details of their lives to see if they can deduce why they committed their crimes. Did Theodore John Kaczynski become the Unabomber because he was impressed with radical politics on the University of California at Berkeley campus, or was there some traumatic event in his childhood that destabilized him? What transformed the hapless chicken thief John Dillinger into a ruthlessly efficient gangster? The key to understanding crimes is understanding the characters involved. Readers want to know what forces shaped these evil men and women.

Whenever a crime is committed in a community, many citizens want the story with all of its details. Who committed the crime? Who was the victim? How did it happen? Is the criminal still at large? Why did he or she do it? The concerns in true crime books are the same. Readers want the complete story from beginning to end. Where was *Hogan's Heroes* star Bob Crane when he was murdered? Why was he in Arizona? Who found the body? How was he killed? Who killed him? Why? Readers want answers. When some of the answers are missing or withheld, the story becomes a mystery, luring readers into subsequent chapters or even other books.

Setting is also vital in True Crime Biography. Like Sherlock Holmes before them, readers want to visit the scene of the crime and absorb the atmosphere. Although the clues, such as footprints, broken locks, bits of paper, and drops of blood, are interesting, readers really want to know more about the place and the time at which the crime occurred. Why was pickpocket George Appo able to thrive in nineteenth-century New York City? Did ethnic prejudice factor in the rise of gangs in Chicago during the Roaring Twenties? Why did medical charlatan John R. Brinkley choose to locate his clinic in Kansas in 1915?

Most True Crime Biographies are not quick reads. They are in-depth character studies that include many details and may present differing accounts of alleged crimes. *Capone: The Man and His Era* by Laurence Bergreen, *Harvard and the Unabomber: The Education of an American Terrorist* by Alston Chase, and *A Pickpocket's Tale: The Underworld of Nineteenth Century New York* by Timothy J. Gilfoyle are all more than 400 pages long. Nevertheless, readers fascinated by the criminal mind may find them hard to put down.

Readers can learn and experience a great deal in True Crime Biographies, which may also act as cautionary tales. From these books about the worst people in our society, readers may safely witness crimes, see how the criminal mind works, and take heed of the dangers in their own neighborhoods. Nonfiction books on safety may give more practical advice about locking doors, carrying purses in crowds, and protecting credit information, but True Crime Biographies go deeper into the psychology of crime and tell readers whom to avoid: the lover who wants the secret affair, the stranger who asks for unusual trust, or the merchant whose offers are too good to be true. Of course, most readers of true crime are not choosing the books for educational benefits, but the "it really happened" factor increases the subgenre's appeal.

Organization of the Chapter

This chapter is divided into four sections, the first of which is "Committing Crimes." In this section, the stories focus on individuals accused of committing notorious crimes that are profiled in descriptive narratives. Bootleggers, gangsters, serial killers, corrupt politicians, and pickpockets are a few of the professions represented in books by authors who mostly disapprove of their biographical subjects. Sympathetic accounts, such as *Hurricane: The Miraculous Journey of Rubin Carter* by James S. Hirsch and *Cries Unheard: Why Children Kill: The Story of Mary Bell* by Gitta Sereny, are the exceptions. All are detailed character studies that true crime readers will relish.

The second section is "Catching Criminals," biographies of individuals who investigate crimes and track down the criminals. As expected, the authors of these books about officers of the law admire their subjects, but they also portray them realistically as fallible people with obstacles to overcome. Readers of these biographies will enjoy the inside look at investigative methods and the challenges of capturing suspects.

The third section, "Shot, Stabbed, or Bludgeoned," focuses on stories about people who are the victims of crime. The subjects in these books were not just in the wrong place at the wrong time. As the revealing narratives show, each of these unusual individuals in some way attracted his or her death or injury. These books have an element of horror that will leave readers alert to the possibility of becoming targets of heinous crimes.

In the fourth and final section, "Criminal Profile Collections," includes many short profiles of criminal figures; each can easily be read in a single sitting. These will appeal to readers who enjoy short stories.

Committing Crimes

Stage and screen actors often prefer playing villains rather than the law officers who pursue them. Criminal roles can be more challenging, requiring actors to draw on their skills to make believable the complicated characters who defy reasonable laws. Likewise, talented crime authors often choose to focus on criminals in their books about true crime. The criminals, with their contradictions and abnormal behaviors, make interesting characters, and their actions drive many of the stories. Victims usually exit the narratives of these stories early, and law enforcement officers just do their duty, reacting to the challenges presented by their cases. Thus, most of the books in this section focus on criminals—their backgrounds, their actions, and sometimes even their thoughts.

A great variety of criminal characters can be found in these books. As portrayed by Thomas Keneally in *American Scoundrel: The Life of the Notorious Civil War General Dan Sickles*, the corrupt and violent Tammany Hall politician who arranged a commission in the Union Army was totally evil. In *Billy the Kid: The Endless Ride*, Michael Wallis makes his gunslinger a youth who has lost all sense of future prospects. Ann Rule describes a lawyer obsessed with controlling relationships in . . . *And Never Let Her Go: Thomas Capano: The Deadly Seducer*. Readers never tire of reading about the fascinating personalities who kill and steal.

The stories in these True Crime Biographies are sensational and disturbing. Each book has at least two dramatic events: the committing of the crime and the confrontation between the criminal and agents of the law. In books about serial killers, the events multiply. Between the dramatic peaks are tense periods when criminals try to elude capture. Crime story fans find these books difficult to put down.

Committing Crimes stories focus on individuals accused of committing notorious crimes. Bootleggers, gangsters, serial killers, corrupt politicians, and pickpockets are a few of the professions represented in books by authors who mostly disapprove of their biographical subjects. These titles are filled with fascinating characters and compelling stories. Readers should prepare to settle in for detailed accounts of heinous crimes.

Ackerman, Kenneth D.

Boss Tweed: The Rise and Fall of the Corrupt Pol Who Conceived the Soul of Modern New York. Carroll & Graf, 2005. 437p. ISBN 0786714352.

At the height of his power, Congressman William Marcy "Boss" Tweed (1823–1878) controlled not only New York City government, but also governors, judges, and senators from several surrounding states, and he lived an opulent life far beyond what the combined salaries from his various public offices would support. From his position at Tammy Hall, he granted favors to citizens, collected bribes, and stole public funds unchecked, while the *New York Times* and cartoonist Thomas Nast decried his crimes. When his secret accounts were finally discovered, his fall was quick. Still, according to former Washington bureaucrat Kenneth D. Ackerman, the poor and the working class continued to worship Tweed, and his imprisonment and death were mourned by many New Yorkers. History readers will relish this classic account of a corrupt politician

> **Subjects:** Congresspersons; Corruption; Group Discussion Books; New York City; Tweed, William Marcy "Boss"

> **Now Try:** As governor and then U. S. senator from Louisiana, Huey P. Long held nearly dictatorial power in his state. Like Tweed, he was immensely popular with the working class voters, who cheered his plans to redistribute wealth. His story is told candidly in *Kingfish: The Reign of Huey P. Long* by Richard D. White (see chapter 10). Rail Baron Jay Gould is another powerful figure who used crooked methods to accomplish his goals. Edward J. Renehan Jr. gives a surprisingly sympathetic account in *Dark Genius of Wall Street: The Misunderstood Life of Jay Gould, King of the Robber Barons* (see chapter 9). Modern stories of political corruption are found in *The Brothers Bulger: How They Terrorized and Corrupted Boston for a Quarter Century* by Howie Carr and *Feasting on the Spoils: The Life and Times of Randy "Duke" Cunningham, History's Most Corrupt Congressman* by Seth Hettena. Stories of corruption from every level of American government are included in *The Almanac of Political Corruption, Scandals and Dirty Politics* by Kim Long.

Bergreen, Laurence

Capone: The Man and His Era. Simon & Schuster, 1994. 701p. ISBN 0671744569. Audiobook available.

> Gangster Al Capone (1899–1947) loved the limelight. The Brooklyn native who took over the Chicago mob seemed to enjoy being scrutinized by the press and legal authorities, who often failed to prove their accusations. His reputation as a benefactor of the poor and helpless grew with each failed case against him. Behind the scenes, however, he was as violent and cruel as Eliot Ness claimed, keeping the rackets in line and ordering the murder of friends as well as enemies whenever his power was threatened. In this account of a ruthless man, Laurence Bergreen sets Capone's life within the context of American ethnic prejudice of the Roaring Twenties and the poverty of the Great Depression.

> **Subjects:** Capone, Al; Chicago; Gangsters; Organized Crime; Prohibition

> **Now Try:** In *The Gangs of Chicago: An Informal History of the Chicago Underworld*, Herbert Asbury identifies Chicago's most notorious criminal districts and the men who committed the most heinous crimes. Big Jim Colosimo, Terrible Johnny Torrio, and Al Capone are just a few of the extortionists, bootleggers, and murderers included. According to Gus Russo, Chicago's crime syndicate was run as a business after the death of Capone. He chronicles forty years of "respectable" crime that made unsuspecting partners of many legitimate businesses, in *The Outfit: The Role of Chicago's Underworld in the Shaping of Modern America*. Like Capone, Soviet dictator Joseph Stalin began his career as a gangster. Though both were brutal to their enemies, they had many supporters among the lower classes, who saw them as vengeful champions who would redress their poverty. Simon Sebag Montefiore describes Stalin's apprenticeship in brutality in *Young Stalin* (see chapter 6). Like Capone, airline and oil executive Howard Hughes sought fabulous wealth through ruthless means. Readers who enjoy complex characters about whom there are as many legends as facts will appreciate *Howard Hughes: The Secret Life* by Charles Higham (see chapter 5).

Brock, Pope

Charlatan: America's Most Dangerous Huckster, the Man Who Pursued Him, and the Age of Flimflam. Crown Publishers, 2008. 324p. ISBN 9780307339881. Audiobook available.

Of all the quacks in American medical history, John R. Brinkley (1885–1942) may have been the most famous, earning the most money and killing the most patients. He sold patent medicines, treated hair loss with an electric fez, and replaced male gonads with those from goats to treat virility disorders. The American Medical Association and state governments denounced him regularly, but by cleverly marketing his services on the radio, he kept his products in demand and his popularity high. He was even nearly elected governor of Kansas. Journalist Pope Brock tells a lively story about the exploitation of ignorance by an early twentieth-century businessman. Readers who like outrageous characters will enjoy this book.

> **Subjects:** Brinkley, John R.; Kansas; Medical Malpractice; Quackery

> **Now Try:** Brinkley is only one of the many unethical characters in the history of American medicine. In *The Health Robbers: A Close Look at Quackery in America*, Stephen Barrett and William T. Jarvis document the past and warn that many charlatans are still preying on unwary consumers. Former security guards Robert Gomez and James Nichols discovered that conning people was easy once they learned what the victims dreamed of owning. John Phillips tells how the criminals enlisted a network of churches to sell their nonexistent luxury cars in *God Wants You to Roll!: The $21 Million "Miracle Car" Scam—How Two Boys Fleeced America's Churchgoers*. Although not a criminal, Kentucky Fried Chicken founder Harlan Sanders was a self-made folk hero willing to bend the truth. Like Brinkley, he nearly became governor. John Ed Pearce tells about Sanders's rise and fall in *The Colonel: The Captivating Biography of the Dynamic Founder of a Fast Food Empire* (see chapter 9). Pablo Picasso was also an outrageous self-promoter, who could sell anything he touched as a work of art. John Richardson tells about the power that Picasso had over the art market in his third book about the artist, *A Life of Picasso: The Triumphant Years, 1917–1932* (see chapter 7).

Burrows, Jack

John Ringo: The Gunfighter Who Never Was. University of Arizona Press, 1987. 242p. ISBN 0816509751.

Western novels and B-grade films portrayed outlaw John Ringo (1850–1882) as a romantic hero, a renegade scholar from back East who defended women and befriended children in the Western territories. In some biographical accounts, the young man was reported to be the fastest gunslinger in the Southwest as well as a man with a strong sense of honor. Author Jack Burrows wondered why, if all of this were true, there were no John Ringo tourist sites or museum artifacts. In this compelling investigative biography, divided into sections on the myth and the man, Burrows uncovers the real John Ringo, who lived a short and violent life in a lawless land.

> **Subjects:** Gunslingers; Outlaws; Ringo, John

> **Now Try:** In the 1840s, members of the German community in New Orleans sued a Frenchman for the freedom of an olive-skinned woman named Sally Miller, whom they believed to be Salomé Müller, a woman kidnapped in Germany twenty-five years earlier. Müller, however, may never have existed. John Bailey examines the mysterious case in *The Lost German Slave Girl: The Extraordinary True Story of Sally Miller and Her Fight for Freedom in Old New Orleans* (see chapter 5). In the 1960s, readers and writers in the science fiction community were eager to meet the secretive best-selling

author James Tiptree Jr. In 1976, however, Alice B. Sheldon, a romance writer's daughter, revealed that she was the mysterious Tiptree. Julie Phillips describes the woman behind the deception in the award-winning *James Tiptree, Jr.: The Double Life of Alice B. Sheldon* (see chapter 5). Western readers who like books that debunk legends will enjoy *Wyatt Earp: The Life Behind the Legend* by Casey Tefertiller (see this chapter) and *Crazy Horse* by Larry McMurtry (see chapter 5).

Cesarani, David

Becoming Eichmann: Rethinking the Life, Crimes, and Trial of a "Desk Murderer". Da Capo Press, 2004. 458p. ISBN 9780306814761.

Not all soldiers serve on the field of battle. During World War II, Lieutenant Colonel Adolf Eichmann (1906–1962) worked in the German Office of Jewish Emigration directing the mass murder of Jews and other people the Nazi regime found undesirable. Because he was unknown to Allied intelligence at the end of the war, he eluded capture at that time, and was not arrested until 1960, in Argentina. Accounts at the time of his trial portrayed him as a sadistic, antisocial fanatic responsible for the transport and death of two million Jews. In his well-reasoned reassessment of the German bureaucrat, David Cesarani presents a more troubling possibility: Eichmann was just an enthusiastic and charming officer concerned with efficiency and Nazi profit, not bothered by atrocities.

> **Subjects:** Courtroom Drama; Eichmann, Adolf; Germany; Holocaust; War Criminals; World War II

> **Now Try:** For nearly a year before he was put on trial, Israeli police interrogated Eichmann. During the questioning Eichmann maintained that he was just following orders in shipping Jews to extermination camps. Excerpts from the tapes are transcribed in *Eichmann Interrogated: Transcripts from the Archives of the Israeli Police*. In his statements, Eichmann admitted his total devotion to Nazi leader Adolf Hitler. In *Hitler: 1936–1945: Nemesis,* Ian Kershaw describes how Hitler, as president and chancellor of Germany, convinced many common, decent people to support his radical agenda. Filip Muller was one of the first Jewish prisoners sent to Auschwitz in 1942. He recounts what he witnessed as an attendant of the gas chambers and crematorium in *Eyewitness Auschwitz: Three Years in the Gas Chambers*. As a young soldier, Francisco Franco was apolitical and obeyed orders. When members of the Second Spanish Republic proved corrupt, he sought first to overthrow the government and then, as victor in the Spanish Civil War, attempted to rid the country of communists and heretics. In *Franco: A Concise Biography* (see chapter 5), Gabrielle Ashford Hodges portrays Franco as a psychotic dictator who would rather destroy his country than let his enemies live.

Chase, Alston

Harvard and the Unabomber: The Education of an American Terrorist. W. W. Norton, 2003. 432p. ISBN 0393020029.

After rejecting the idea that Theodore John Kaczynski (1942–) was turned into a sociopath by the culture of radical politics on campus during his teaching years at the University of California at Berkeley, author and philosopher Alston Chase examined accounts of the future Unabomber's student days at Harvard University. For over three years Kaczynski was a paid participant in what are now considered unethical psychological experiments, involving the use of verbal abuse to belittle unsuspecting subjects. Chase proposes that the stress of these experiments in brightly lit rooms with recording equipment contributed to the already insecure student's fear of technology. In light of these experiences, the author recounts the terrorist's career in a book for readers who enjoy examining psychological motives.

> **Subjects:** Group Discussion Books; Harvard University; Kaczynski, Theodore John; Psychological Experiments; Teen Reads; Terrorists; Unabomber

> **Now Try:** The text of the Unabomber's condemnation of modern technological society that was printed in the *New York Times* and *Washington Post* in 1995 is available as *The Unabomber Manifesto: Industrial Society & Its Future.* David Gelertner was one of the Unabomber's victims, sustaining permanent injuries to his right hand and right eye at Yale University in 1993. In his memoir, *Drawing Life: Surviving the Unabomber,* he describes his rehabilitation and expresses his outrage at the liberal society that he believes encourages criminal behavior. After the bombing of the Murrah Federal Building in Oklahoma City, people wondered what kind of person could commit such a crime. In *American Terrorist: Timothy McVeigh & the Oklahoma City Bombing* (see this chapter), Lou Michel and Dan Herbeck answer the question, describing Timothy McVeigh as an average person who had somehow been transformed by the rhetoric of extremists. Crime expert Jay Robert Nash chronicles the history of international terrorism with profiles of many notorious radicals in *Terrorism in the 20th Century: A Narrative Encyclopedia from the Anarchists, Through the Weathermen, to the Unabomber.*

Cornwell, Patricia

Portrait of a Killer: Jack the Ripper Case Closed. G. P. Putnam, 2002. 387p. ISBN 0399149325. Audiobook and large print available.

British artist Walter Sickert (1860–1942), known for his violently bizarre sketches and paintings, was Jack the Ripper, according to crime novelist Patricia Cornwell. Modern analyses show that his handwriting, drawing style, and DNA match those in the teasing letters that the bold serial killer sent to newspapers and Scotland Yard. Cornwell shows that as a man known to walk the dark and foggy streets, Sickert had the opportunity and personality to commit the infamous crimes. Fans of Cornwell's novels and students of detection will be drawn to this passionate retelling of the murder of five prostitutes that identifies Sickert as the most famous serial killer of all.

> **Subjects:** Jack the Ripper; London; Serial Killers; Sickert, Walter

> **Now Try:** Several books of Sickert's paintings are available, including *Sickert* by Wendy Baron. Like Jack the Ripper, the Kansas serial killer who called himself BTK (Bind, Torture, Kill) sent letters to the police challenging them to capture him. Former FBI agent John Douglas describes the crimes and motives of Dennis Rader in *Inside the Mind of BTK: The True Story Behind the Thirty-One Year Hunt for the Notorious Wichita Serial Killer.* The shadowy underworld of 1930s Berlin was much like the foggy and bloody streets of 1880s London. An international community of criminals and foreign agents walked the streets, including Lev Nussimbaum, supposedly a Muslim prince. In *The Orientalist: Solving the Mystery of a Strange and Dangerous Life* (see chapter 5), Tom Reiss seeks to identify not only who murdered Nussimbaum but also just who he was. Patricia Cornwell is the author of the <u>Dr. Kay Scarpetta mystery series</u>, starting with *Postmortum*, and the <u>Andy Brazil mystery series</u>, starting with *Hornet's Nest.*

Fanning, Diane

Into the Water: The Story of Serial Killer Richard Marc Evonitz. St. Martin's Paperbacks, 2004. 244p. ISBN 0312985266.

When he woke to find that the child he intended to be his fourth victim had escaped, serial killer Richard Marc Evonitz (1963–2002) knew that he had to flee. His double life as good neighbor and secret sexual predator was exposed, and soon everyone, including his ever supportive family, would know. In desperation he led police on a chase across three states that ultimately ended with his suicide. In this paperback original, crime writer Diane Fanning chronicles the metamorphosis of a young man's fantasies into psychosis that left three teenaged girls dead. True crime fans will enjoy the quick pace of this frank cautionary tale.

> **Subjects:** Evonitz, Richard Marc; Quick Reads; Serial Killers; Sexual Predators

> **Now Try:** There are many gritty criminal profiles. Between 1976 and 1977 New York City was the scene of a series of shootings by the mysterious "Son of Sam." Laurence D. Klausner recounts the case in *Son of Sam: Based on the Authorized Transcription of the Tapes, Official Documents and Diaries of David Berkowitz*. Dr. Helen Morrison is a noted forensic psychiatrist who has worked with the FBI on many serial murder cases, including those of Ed Gein and John Wayne Gacy. She describes her experiences and clinical findings in *My Life Among the Serial Killers: Inside the Minds of the World's Most Notorious Murderers*. Mystery writer Harold Schechter has collected many entertaining stories and facts about serial killers in *The Serial Killer Files: The Who, What, Where, How, and Why of the World's Most Terrifying Murderers*. A look at Diane Fanning's titles show that she stays abreast of crime news. Her recent titles include *The Pastor's Wife: The True Story of a Minister and the Shocking Death That Divided a Family* and *Out There: The In-Depth Story of the Astronaut Love Triangle Case That Shocked America*.

Gilfoyle, Timothy J.

A Pickpocket's Tale: The Underworld of Nineteenth Century New York. W. W. Norton, 2006. 460p. ISBN 9780393061901.

The childhood of New York's most famous pickpocket, George Appo (1856–1930), may remind readers of Dickens's *Oliver Twist*. Born in America's most infamous ghetto, Appo's father was imprisoned and his mother died before he was three years old. Raised in a series of foster homes, he never attended school and became a newspaper boy at age twelve, when he joined a child pickpocket gang that robbed the gentlemen and women on Wall Street. Arrested and imprisoned many times, Appo turned his experiences into a profitable memoir and even appeared on Broadway. Lest the story sound too charming, historian Timothy J. Gilfoyle describes the desperate and violent life of a career criminal in a city that was dangerous to visit.

> **Subjects:** Appo, George; New York City; Orphans; Pickpockets

> **Now Try:** From Vaudeville to Las Vegas, picking pockets has been associated with live entertainment. David Avadon profiles the magicians and comedians who have made lifting wallets and underwear on stage part of their acts in *Cutting Up Touches: A Brief History of Pockets and the People Who Pick*

Them. Like Appo, Giacomo Casanova rose from a ghetto to become a legendary criminal and to charm high society. Lydia Flem tells his melodramatic story in *Casanova: The Man Who Really Loved Women* (see chapter 5). Appo's ability to survive many setbacks into old age resembles that of resilient statesman Sam Houston, whose story is told in *Sam Houston: A Biography of the Father of Texas* by John Hoyt Williams (see chapter 10). Middle-class teen James Salant became a petty criminal to support his drug habit. He recounts his horrible year in *Leaving Dirty Jersey: A Crystal Meth Memoir*. Of course, *Oliver Twist* by Charles Dickens is a classic novel that is always in print.

Girardin, G. Russell, and William J. Helmer

Dillinger: The Untold Story. Expanded ed. Indiana University Press, 2005. 377p. ISBN 0253216338.

John Dillinger's (1903–1934) career in crime started with a successful chicken theft in 1924, but when he failed in an attempt to rob a grocery, he was caught and sentenced to prison for eight and a half years. Prison transformed Dillinger. When released in May 1933, the formerly inept criminal went on a fourteen-month crime spree that shocked the nation. Dillinger and his gang robbed banks across the Midwest, escaped from two jails, and shot their way out of several FBI traps. Between crimes, the confident gangster twice took friends to the Chicago World's Fair and frequently visited busy nightclubs. G. Russell Girardin and William J. Helmer tell an action-packed story full of dialogue that is sure to interest true crime readers.

Subjects: Bank Robbers; Dillinger, John; Gangsters

Now Try: Dillinger was only one of many criminals at large in a wave of crime at the height of the Great Depression. Brian Burrough examines the social conditions that led to the lawless period and identifies the most notorious criminals in *Public Enemies: America's Greatest Crime Wave and the Birth of the FBI, 1933–34*. One of the gangsters proclaimed a public enemy was a Chicago bank robber called Baby Face Nelson. In *Baby Face Nelson: Portrait of a Public Enemy*, Steven Nickel looks beyond J. Edgar Hoover's account of the diminutive Nelson to discover why a middle-class teen would become a hardened criminal. Hoover told how his FBI agents captured or shot down Ma Barker, Baby Face Nelson, John Dillinger, Machine Gun Kelly, and other gangsters in *Persons in Hiding*. Hardly hiding, Dillinger took his friends to the World's Fair. An earlier Chicago World's Fair and the serial murderer H. H. Holmes are featured in the popular crime history *Devil in the White City: Murder, Magic, and Madness at the Fair That Changed America* by Eric Larson.

Hirsch, James S.

Hurricane: The Miraculous Journey of Rubin Carter. Houghton Mifflin, 2000. 358p. ISBN 0395979854. Large print available.

On June 17, 1966, two black men murdered three whites in a bar in Paterson, New Jersey. Though tried and convicted, boxer Rubin Carter (1937–), known as Hurricane, insisted that he was not one of the killers and refused to be a cooperative prisoner. While he studied law from death row in order to petition for a retrial, his case attracted the attention of celebrities and civil rights lawyers. Two trials and twenty-two years later, the case was dismissed. In this candid narrative for readers of court room dramas, author James S. Hirsch describes the transformation of Carter from young street tough to folk hero.

Subjects: African Americans; Boxers; Carter, Rubin; Group Discussion Books; Murder; Teen Reads

Now Try: While still in prison, Carter wrote about his life in *The 16th Round: From Number 1 Contender to #45472*. Nashville washer woman Callie House was imprisoned in 1917 for posting pamphlets in support of slave reparations through the U. S. mail. Her story of racial injustice is told by Mary Frances Berry in *My Face Is Black Is True: Callie House and the Struggle for Ex-Slave Reparations* (see chapter 9). In 1987 former minor league baseball player Ron Williamson was convicted of murder in Ada, Oklahoma, without any actual evidence. John Grisham recounts Williamson's sad life and the wrongful murder conviction, from which he was exonerated, in *The Innocent Man: Murder and Injustice in a Small Town*. The subject of wrongful conviction is more thoroughly examined in *Wrong Men: America's Epidemic of Wrongful Death Row Convictions* by Stanley Cohen.

Keneally, Thomas

American Scoundrel: The Life of the Notorious Civil War General Dan Sickles.
Nan A. Talese, 2002. 397p. ISBN 0385501390.

When Tammany Hall politician Dan Sickles (1819–1914) went to London as first secretary to U.S. Ambassador James Buchanan in 1853, he could not take his wife and young son, so he took his mistress instead. Introducing her to Queen Victoria, the charming but wicked Sickles passed her off as a debutante. Six years later, when his wife had an affair, he murdered her lover in broad daylight in front of the White House in Washington, D.C. After being acquitted, he formed a unit in the U. S. Army and became a general. When the Civil War drew to a close, he was appointed military governor of South Carolina and then ambassador to Spain. In each position, he seduced women and demanded bribes for favors. In this hard-edged biography, novelist Thomas Keneally profiles an evil man in the center ring of corruption in nineteenth-century U.S. government.

Subjects: Congresspersons; Corruption; Generals; Murder; Sickles, Daniel Edgar

Now Try: During the Warren G. Harding administration, corruption moved into the White House, and the first lady may have been a key criminal. Carl Sferrazza Anthony presents his evidence in *Florence Harding: The First Lady, the Jazz Age, and the Death of America's Most Scandalous President* (see chapter 5). The link between adultery and murder is still common. Keith Elliot Greenberg describes a lurid case from Akron, Ohio, in *Perfect Beauty: A True Story of Adultery, Murder, and Manipulation in Middle America*. Dueling, speculating on land, and contemplating treason should not be standard behaviors for elected officials. Nancy Isenberg, however, tells a surprisingly sympathetic story about Aaron Burr, an early American political figure who got away with murder, in *Fallen Founder: The Life of Aaron Burr* (see chapter 10). Tsar Ivan IV of Russia had a reputation for killing members of his court indiscriminately, including members of his family. His legend is examined in *Ivan the Terrible: First Tsar of Russia* by Isabel De Madariaga (see chapter 5). Another truly mean spirited character was cosmetics king Charles Revson, a corporate tyrant whose story is told in *Fire and Ice: The Story of Charles Revson—the Man Who Built the Revlon Empire* by Andrew Tobias (see chapter 5).

Michel, Lou, and Dan Herbeck

American Terrorist: Timothy McVeigh & the Oklahoma City Bombing. Regan Books, 2001. 426p. ISBN 0060394072.

When journalists Lou Michel and Dan Herbeck wrote this biography of right-wing extremist Timothy McVeigh (1968–2001), the bombing of the Murrah Federal Office Building in Oklahoma City was still the deadliest terrorist act ever on American soil. The two reporters spent five years interviewing neighbors, friends, family, and eventually McVeigh himself. According to the authors, the accused terrorist confessed and explained the crime to them. Aimed at general readers, the resulting book paints a disturbing portrait of an average American boy who became a mass murderer.

> **Subjects:** Group Discussion Books; Mass Murder; McVeigh, Timothy; Oklahoma City Federal Building Bombing; Teen Reads; Terrorists

> **Now Try:** In *Mass Murder in the United States*, Ronald M. Holmes and Stephen T. Holmes define various types of mass murderers. McVeigh was a "set-and-run mass murderer," according to the descriptions in their text. "School killers" is another category. Columbine massacre survivor Brooks Brown and coauthor Rob Merritt examine the motives of school killers Eric Harris and Dylan Klebold in *No Easy Answers: The Truth Behind Death at Columbine*. From the tower on the campus of the University of Texas, former marine Charles Whitman killed fourteen people and wounded thirty-one others. Gary M. Lavergne describes him as a "psychotic mass killer" in *A Sniper in the Tower: The Charles Whitman Murders*. In the Russian town of Beslan, a team of terrorists stormed the opening day of school and herded parents and children into the gymnasium for a three-day siege. Timothy S. J. Phillips describes the attack, in which at least 330 people died, in *Beslan: The Tragedy of School No. 1.*

Patterson, Richard

Butch Cassidy: A Biography. University of Nebraska Press, 1998. 362p. ISBN 0803287569.

Butch Cassidy (1866–1908) was an atypical Western outlaw. Reasonably polite, he drank in moderation, loved his parents, avoided shooting people when possible, and would do anything for a friend. If he had not been a bank and train robber, he could have been a good citizen. Did he really die with the Sundance Kid in a shootout in Argentina in 1908? The Pinkerton Agency report does not say. In this entertaining biography for general readers, historian Richard Patterson thoroughly investigates the mysteries of Cassidy's career and death.

> **Subjects:** Bank Robbers; Cassidy, Butch; Outlaws; Train Robbers

> **Now Try:** One of the greatest mysteries in the history of crime is who was D. B. Cooper, the man who hijacked an airliner in 1971 and parachuted from the plane with $200,000, and whether he survived the jump. Elwood Reid turned the still unsolved case into fiction in *D. B.: A Novel*. There are many unsolved cases in the world of art theft. Simon Houpt recounts how the high prices of paintings and sculpture have attracted Nazis, gangsters, and petty thieves in his well-illustrated *Museum of the Missing: A History of Art Theft*. Like Cassidy, Buffalo Bill Cody was a Western figure whose life has been exaggerated and romanticized by the press and motion pictures. Robert A. Carter looks for the truth of Cody's life in *Buffalo Bill Cody: The Man behind the Legend* (see chapter 5). Jack Burrows tells about another dime store novel outlaw whose career has been misrepresented by Hollywood in *John Ringo: The Gunfighter Who Never Was* (see this chapter).

Rule, Ann

. . . And Never Let Her Go: Thomas Capano: The Deadly Seducer. Simon & Schuster, 1999. 479p. ISBN 0684810484. Audiobook and large print available.

Beware of older men wanting secret relationships! Thomas Capano (1949–) was a successful lawyer and political consultant from a good family with ties to power in Wilmington, Delaware. Most people thought that his marriage was sound and that he was a good father. Few knew that he kept a separate house for his affairs with a series of lovers. For three years Anne Marie Fahey, a scheduling secretary for the governor of Delaware, never let anyone know of her affair with Capano. Only when the anorexic young woman disappeared did a friend find a suspicious note with the letterhead "From the Desk of Thomas J. Capano" in Fahey's apartment. In this highly detailed account of a murder investigation without a body, crime writer Ann Rule portrays Capano as a charming but self-promoting man with a tremendous need to control women. Readers fascinated by psychological profiles of criminals will relish this absorbing case.

Subjects: Capano, Thomas J.; Fahey, Anne Marie; Murder

Now Try: What happened between Capano and Fahey is not known with certainty, but Robert Rhodes explains what commonly occurs in such cases in *Why They Kill*. One of the most perplexing mysteries of recent history is whether Claus von Bulow attempted to murder his wife Sunny with an overdose of insulin in 1982. Harvard Law School professor Alan M. Dershowitz, who also served as an attorney for von Bülow, says the defendant was innocent, in *Reversal of Fortune: Inside the von Bülow Case*. In *The Von Bulow Affair* William Wright points toward the husband's guilt. Rule had more certain knowledge of the thoughts of a notorious killer who also happened to be her personal friend. She tells the story of Ted Bundy, whom she met as a volunteer at a crisis clinic in Seattle, in *The Stranger Beside Me*.

Sereny, Gitta

Cries Unheard: Why Children Kill: The Story of Mary Bell. Metropolitan Books, 1998. 382p. ISBN 0805060677.

On May 25, 1968, in the English city of Newcastle on Tyne, eleven-year-old Mary Flora Bell (1957–) strangled four-year-old Martin Brown. Before she was identified as Martin's murderer, she also strangled three-year-old Brian Howe. When she was caught, all of England was shocked that a child so young could commit these horrendous acts. Journalist Gitta Sereny covered the sensational story at the time of the original trial and fulfilled a personal dream by interviewing Bell as an adult. Sereny reveals that as young girl Bell had been habitually neglected and abused by her parents. The author chronicles the girl's journey through the British juvenile justice system, which never provided counseling. Eventually she was moved into an adult prison, where she honed her criminal skills to survive. Written for the general public, Sereny's dark book calls for debate on the fate of young criminals.

Subjects: Group Discussion Books; Juvenile Justice; Murder; Teen Reads; Women

Now Try: Known as the Boston Boy Fiend, Jesse Pomeroy was in reform school at age twelve and a murderer at age fourteen. Convicted by a jury in 1874, he was sent to prison, where he spent forty-one years in solitary confinement. Harold Schechter reviews his case in *Fiend: The Shocking True Story of America's Youngest Serial Killer*. Carol Anne Davis profiles Pomeroy and twelve other young criminals from various periods of history in *Children Who Kill: Profiles of Pre-Teen and Teenage Killers*. The murders committed by nineteen-year-old Charles Starkweather and his fourteen-year-old girlfriend, Caril Ann Fugate, in Nebraska and Wyoming in 1959 have inspired the films *Badlands* and *Natural Born Killers*. The story of their eight-day killing spree is retold in both *Waste Land* by Michael Newton and *Starkweather: The Story of a Mass Murderer* by William Allen. Today, the names of most juvenile offenders are screened from the public, so there are few biographies about them. Writer Mark Salzman, however, met some teenagers imprisoned for violent crimes when he visited a writing class at Los Angeles's Central Juvenile Hall. His describes the young criminals in *True Notebooks: A Writer's Year at Juvenile Hall*.

Steele, Phillip W., with Marie Barrow Scoma

The Family Story of Bonnie and Clyde. Pelican Publishing, 2000. 158p. ISBN 156554756X.

Every criminal is a son or daughter. Most are brothers or sisters. In this compact account of the short criminal careers of Clyde Barrow (1909–1934) and Bonnie Parker (1910–1934), Western outlaw writer Phillip W. Steele collaborated with Bonnie's sister Marie to include stories about the duo's family origins and relationships. The authors include numerous photographs of the pair with their parents or siblings to show that there was often contact between the criminals and their loved ones during their Great Depression–era crime sprees. The epilogue shows photos of family members at the couple's gravesites. Crime readers will be challenged to think about love of family as an indicator of good character by this unusual dual biography.

Subjects: Barrow, Clyde; Families; Gangsters; Murder; Parker, Bonnie; Quick Reads; Teen Reads; Women

Now Try: Clyde Barrow's sister-in-law Blanche Caldwell Barrow recounts her experience as an accomplice to crime in her memoir, *My Life with Bonnie & Clyde*. Without girlfriends and wives renting hideouts, buying cars, running errands, and serving as couriers, John Dillinger and his gang would never have been successful in eluding the police. The story of the Dillinger women is told in *Don't Call Us Moll: Women of the John Dillinger Gang* by Ellen Poulsen. Diane Fanning includes the story of the close relationship between a serial killer and his sisters in *Into the Water: The Story of Serial Killer Richard Marc Evonitz* (see this chapter). For readers who enjoy the Bonnie and Clyde story for its account of a dramatic pursuit of criminals, Stanley Hamilton tells about the long chase and capture of a gangster in *Machine Gun Kelly's Last Stand*.

Stiles, T. J.

Jesse James: Last Rebel of the Civil War. Knopf, 2002. 510p. ISBN 0375405836.

If Jesse James (1847–1882) were alive today, he would be labeled as a terrorist, according to author T. J. Stiles. His acts were not simply criminal. He was trained as a Missouri bushwhacker in support of the Confederate military cause during the American Civil War. After the war he and his gang continued to attack U. S. government interests, including army personnel, federal marshals, banks, post offices, and trains. At times James used sympathetic Southern newspapers to conduct public debates on white supremacy and to publish his rants against the Republican Party. In this intense biography for history readers, Stiles seeks to destroy the romantic legend and prove that James was truly an evil man.

1

> **Subjects:** Bank Robbers; Bushwhackers; Civil War; James, Jesse; Outlaws; Train Robbers

2

> **Now Try:** The life of Mexican bandit Pancho Villa has been retold in many ways, sometimes portraying him as a hero. In *The General and the Jaguar: Pershing's Hunt for Pancho Villa*, Eileen Welsome describes the brutal murder of eighteen people in Columbus, New Mexico, by Villa and his gang as part of her argument that Villa was simply an ambitious and clever criminal. Nearly a century later, the major crime along the border between the United States and Mexico is the smuggling of drugs. Terrence Poppa recounts the career and death of smuggler Pablo Acosta in *Drug Lord: The Life and Death of a Mexican Kingpin*. Like Jesse James, LSD guru Timothy Leary proclaimed his crimes and called for followers to join his cause. Robert Greenfield recounts the psychedelic life of a wayward college professor in *Timothy Leary* (see chapter 5). Time and pop culture have softened the image of German pilot Manfred von Richthofen. Peter Kilduff portrays the World War I flying ace as ruthless and egotistical in *Richthofen: Beyond the Legend of the Red Baron* (see chapter 3).

3

4

5

Talty, Stephan

6

Empire of Blue Water: Captain Morgan's Great Pirate Army, the Epic Battle for the Americas, and the Catastrophe That Ended the Outlaws' Bloody Reign. Crown, 2007. 332p. ISBN 9780307236609. Large print.

> Pirates were not just petty criminals in the seventeenth century. According to Stephan Talty, Captain Henry Morgan (1635–1688) and his cutthroat crew raided Spanish ports in the New World, torturing prisoners and amassing chests full of pieces of eight, bringing the Spanish Empire to its knees. Morgan claimed that he did it all for England and his king, Charles II, who knighted him and appointed him governor of Jamaica. Talty portrays Morgan as a sometimes cruel enemy who was offended when called "pirate." Fans of *The Pirates of the Caribbean* movies will enjoy this true pirate tale.

7

8

> **Subjects:** Caribbean Islands; Morgan, Henry; Pirates; Sea Stories; Tyrants

9

> **Now Try:** In the golden age of piracy, the pirates rivaled the navies for command of the oceans. The pirate Edward Teach, known as Blackbeard, had an entire flotilla in his command and blocked Charleston, South Carolina, to rob merchant ships in 1718. Dan Perry describes the lavish life and bloody death of the pirate in *Blackbeard: The Real Pirate of the Caribbean*. Sometimes pirates were accorded the status of hero and the favors of monarchs. For the British Library Historic Lives series, Peter Whitfield recounts the life of Sir Francis Drake, a seaman who attacked and robbed Spanish ships with the approval of Queen Elizabeth I, in *Sir Francis Drake*. Throughout history, warriors and soldiers have felt free to remove artifacts from conquered cities. *Spoils of War: World War II and Its Aftermath: The Loss, Reappearance, and Recovery of Cultural Property* is a collection of reports on the long-enduring effort to get

10

11

12

European treasures back to their rightful owners. In the modern world, corporate executives are often described as pirates for their hostile takeovers. Australian Rupert Murdoch is one of the most recognized and hated of these men. Neil Chenoweth chronicles Murdoch's life of bankrupting profitable companies and stealing from employee pension funds in *Rupert Murdoch: The Untold Story of the World's Greatest Media Wizard* (see chapter 5).

Van Onselen, Charles

The Fox and the Flies: The Secret Life of a Grotesque Master Criminal. Walker, 2007. 646p. ISBN 9780802716415.

Name any type of crime, and it was probably committed by master criminal Joseph Silver (1868–1918). In his thirty years in the alleys and on the wharves of port cities around the world, he was accused of burglary, rape, assault, murder, gun running, and trafficking in prostitution and female slavery. Charles Van Onselen even claims that Silver was responsible for the Jack the Ripper murders in London in 1888. In this thick but very readable book about a deplorable man, the biographer skillfully evokes the international criminal underworld before World War I.

> **Subjects:** Gangsters; Murder; Organized Crime; Silver, Joseph

> **Now Try:** In this biography, Van Onselen compares Joseph Silver to Professor Moriarty, the master criminal that Sir Arthur Conan Doyle introduced in the Sherlock Holmes story "The Red-Headed League." Readers and scholars have often debated over who inspired Doyle to create Moriarty, the recurring nemesis who is Holmes's equal. Ben Macintyre believes that it was the phony British aristocrat Adam Worth, who stole from his rich friends and maintained a close relationship with the Pinkerton brothers, the most celebrated detectives of their time. Macintyre presents his evidence in *The Napoleon of Crime: The Life and Times of Adam Worth, Master Thief.* Doyle himself hinted that criminal mastermind Jonathan Wild was the model. Wild is portrayed in *The Thieves' Opera*, a look at crime in Georgian-era London. In early twentieth-century New York, policeman Charles Becker headed both the vice squad and the versatile crime ring that it investigated. His diverse life of crime is frankly described in *Satan's Circus: Murder, Vice, Police Corruption, and New York's Trial of the Century* by Mike Dash. Macintyre also writes about Eddie Chapman, a small-time criminal who becomes a double agent during World War II, in *Agent Zigzag: A True Story of Nazi Espionage, Love, and Betrayal* (see chapter 3).

Wallis, Michael

Billy the Kid: The Endless Ride. Norton, 2007. 328p. ISBN 9780393060683.

Life in the New Mexico Territory in the 1880s was dangerous, to say the least—the murder rate was forty-seven times that of the nation as a whole! It was a land of crooked politicians and hired guns. With open warfare between criminal gangs, between cattlemen and rustlers, and between Anglos and Hispanics, it was just the place to find a mysterious young man, who may have been Henry McCarty (1859–1881) of New York, also known as William H. Bonney. He was dubbed Billy the Kid less than a year before he was shot by Sheriff Pat Garrett. True crime and history readers will enjoy how Michael Wallis pieces together the puzzling story of a legendary outlaw.

> **Subjects:** Billy the Kid; McCarty, Henry; Murder; New Mexico Territory; Outlaws

Now Try: In the novel *Billy the Kid* by Elizabeth Fackler, the young criminal is seen as a freedom fighter against corruption and big business in lawless New Mexico. Like Billy the Kid, the identity of Bonnie Prince Charlie, the pretender to the throne of England, has been questioned. Susan Maclean Kybett tells readers who she believes he was and why he was unworthy of his folk hero status, in *Bonnie Prince Charlie: A Biography of Charles Edward Stuart* (see chapter 5). The distinction between a knight and a gunslinger is slight when chivalry is missing. In *Malory: The Knight Who Became King Arthur's Chronicler*, Christina Hardyman exposes Sir Thomas Malory, the man credited with creating the concept of chivalry, as a rapist and ruffian. Another story of an out-of-control young man bound to die tragically is *Wired* (see chapter 6), journalist Bob Woodward's book about comic actor John Belushi.

Wambaugh, Joseph

Fire Lover: A True Story. William Morrow, 2002. 338p. ISBN 006009527X. Audiobook and large print available.

Firefighter John Orr (1949–) was a successful arson investigator credited with catching numerous arsonists. He was known for his courage in a fire and had trained many of the firemen in his department in Glendale, California. The community was therefore shocked when he was charged with setting a series of fires that took four lives. In this on-the-scene story of how fellow firefighters solved the crime that the police could not, crime novelist and former policeman Joseph Wambaugh portrays Orr as a psychopath with a desire for risk who gave away his secrets by writing the firefighting novel *Points of Origin*. Mystery readers will appreciate the process of detection by the amateur sleuths.

Subjects: Arsonists; Firefighters; Orr, John

Now Try: Orr's novel that made his colleagues suspicious is *Points of Origin*, a rare book owned by only a few libraries. Nicholas Faith also profiles Orr as an arsonist in *Blaze: The Forensics of Fire*, his popular text on the history and science of arson investigation. *Cries Unheard: Why Children Kill: The Story of Mary Bell* by Gitta Sereny (see this chapter) and *American Terrorist: Timothy McVeigh & the Oklahoma City Bombing* by Lou Michel and Dan Herbeck (see this chapter) are other crime biographies in which authors interviewed the criminal subjects extensively. Sometimes the criminal turns out to be a policeman. The double life of Indiana State Trooper David Camm is the focus of the psychological crime story *One Deadly Night: A State Trooper, Triple Homicide, and A Search for Justice* by John Glatt.

Catching Criminals

Books about the men and women who catch criminals are numerous in the realm of fiction, but scarce as True Crime Biographies. As mentioned in the previous section, many true crime authors are more interested in the criminals than in the police officers and detectives who try to catch them. Unlike fictional detectives Adam Dalglish, Jane Tennison, or Sherlock Holmes, real officers of the law often have only one notable case in a career, making them less attractive subjects. When a law officer does solve a newsworthy case and catches a notorious criminal, he or she quickly signs a lucrative contract for a memoir to be ghosted by a writer for hire, leaving little reason for a third-party author to focus a biography on that officer. (Memoirs are the subject of a forthcoming book in the Real Stories Series.)

Law enforcement figures from the past are more likely to make good subjects for biographies than contemporary figures. Many became well known as the heroes of dime novels and Hollywood movies. Correcting these fictional accounts of their lives is a major purpose of well-researched contemporary biographies. These historical treatments are great reading choices for those who appreciate the search for truth.

Catching Criminals stories include biographies of individuals who investigate crimes and track down the criminals. The authors of these books about officers of the law admire their subjects but also portray them realistically as fallible people with obstacles to overcome. Readers of these biographies will enjoy the inside look at investigative methods and the challenges of capturing suspects.

Burton, Art T.

Black Gun, Silver Star: The Life and Legend of Frontier Marshall Bass Reeves. University of Nebraska Press, 2006. 346p. Race and Ethnicity in the American West. ISBN 9780803213388.

When the U.S. government established the Indian Territory in what is now Oklahoma, it hired several African Americans as deputy marshals to apprehend men accused of murder and robbery. These men had been slaves and knew the languages of the tribes that had been displaced from Southern states. According to historian Art T. Burton, the most famous of these tough men was Bass Reeves (1838–1910). Using federal court records, newspaper accounts, and oral histories, Burton pieces together a dramatic story of what was not previously documented by the mostly white historical societies in Oklahoma. Without ever being injured, the brave and dedicated lawman captured countless criminals of various ethnic origins and killed fourteen who would not surrender. History readers will enjoy this well-documented tribute to a law enforcement pioneer.

Subjects: African Americans; Indian Territory; Oklahoma; Reeves, Bass; United States Marshals

Now Try: The racial integration of American law enforcement has been slow. Abraham Bolden was the first African American to serve in the Secret Service, an agency that protects the American president. Bolden describes his career, including the discrimination he faced, in *Echo from Dealey Plaza: The True Story of the First African American on the White House Secret Service Detail and His Quest for Justice after the Assassination of JFK*. Black narcotics agents face many dangers, according to Billy Chase, who recounts his role in the war on drugs in *Chased: Alone, Black, and Undercover*. In the late 1970s many African American children in Atlanta were frightened of a serial killer who was targeting them. Kim Reid remembers the time especially well, because her mother was one of the police inspectors trying to catch the killer. She re-creates the time in *No Place Safe: A Family Memoir*. For a story about African Americans succeeding in the wake of the Civil War, like Reeves, read *The Sweet Hell Inside: A Family History* by Edward Ball (see chapter 9).

Heimel, Paul W.

Eliot Ness: The Real Story. Knox Books, 1997. 227p. ISBN 096558240x.

Federal Prohibition Agent Eliot Ness (1903–1957) was only twenty-nine years old when he and his band of agents, who were labeled "Untouchables" because they would not take bribes, celebrated their great success: the capture, conviction, and imprisonment of Chicago gangster Al Capone. The ambitious Ness expected a long and successful career as a champion of law enforcement and good government. As Cleveland's public safety director, he quickly reformed the police department and shut down gambling, prostitution, and extortion rackets in the city, but he failed to identify a serial killer who became known as the Torso Murderer. As the number of decapitated and mutilated bodies increased, the popularity of the insular police official faltered. Unable to handle criticism, Ness turned to alcohol, eventually becoming an alcoholic. In this candid book about a short and disappointing life, Paul W. Heimel deftly portrays Ness through dialogue and action.

> **Subjects:** Chicago; Cleveland; Federal Prohibition Agents; Ness, Eliot; Police Commissioners; Quick Reads

> **Now Try:** Ness wrote his own story in *The Untouchables*. In *Torso: The Story of Eliot Ness and the Search for a Psychopathic Killer*, Steven Nickel tells more about a series of unsolved murders in Cleveland and why Ness's adherence to his old methods doomed the investigation. While Ness was catching Capone, FBI Agent Melvin Purvis was catching John Dillinger, Pretty Boy Floyd, and Baby Face Nelson. Alston W. Purvis tells his father's story in *The Vendetta: FBI Hero Melvis Purvis's War Against Crime and J. Edgar Hoover's War Against Him*. More on Hoover and corruption in the FBI can be found in *Young J. Edgar: Hoover, the Red Scare, and the Assault on Civil Liberties* by Kenneth D. Ackerman (see chapter 6). Readers interested in how detectives such as Ness and Purvis caught criminals will likely appreciate *Police Procedure & Investigation: A Writer's Guide* by Lee Lofland. According to federal prosecutor John Kroger, catching criminals is not enough; they need to be convicted. The philosophical Kroger describes his work on cases in Brooklyn in *Convictions : A Prosecutor's Battles Against Mafia Killers, Drug Kingpins, and Enron Thieves*.

Maas, Peter

Serpico. Viking, 1973. 314p. ISBN 0670634980.

New York City police officer Frank Serpico (1936–) was deeply troubled by what he witnessed daily in the 1960s and early 1970s. Police officers sworn to uphold the law were shaking down gamblers and drug dealers for bribes to look the other way instead of arresting them. After his attempts to get his superiors to investigate failed, Serpico risked his life by going public with his accusations. According to Peter Maas, he was shunned and threatened by fellow officers. When he was shot in a drug raid, his companions failed to call for medical help, and he almost died. In this novel-like biography filled with dramatic action, Maas describes Serpico as a culturally hip cop who refused to back down from his claims. This quick read will please readers drawn to bravely stoical characters.

Subjects: Corruption; New York City; Police Officers; Serpico, Frank; Teen Reads

Now Try: As a result of Serpico's allegations, Detective Bob Leuci in the Special Investigating Unit of the Narcotics Division of the New York Police Department in the 1970s went undercover to investigate corruption in the force. The story of the dangers that he faced is related in *Prince of the City: The True Story of a Cop Who Knew Too Much* by Robert Daley. Robert Cea continues the account of misdeeds in the New York police story in later decades with his memoir, *No Lights, No Sirens: The Corruption and Redemption of an Inner City Cop.* According to Robert Jackall, one of the challenges for a police detective is to live in two worlds, that of the street and that of the court to which they report crimes. Jackall describes these worlds and the compromises detectives must make in *Street Stories: The World of Police Detectives.* Far from New York, the police in Alaska have to contend with the weather while solving crimes. Journalist Tom Brennan retells some of the best police stories from the largest state in *Cold Crime: Chilling Stories from Alaska's Police Detectives.*

Summerscale, Kate

The Suspicions of Mr. Whicher: A Shocking Murder and the Undoing of a Great Victorian Detective. Walker, 2008. 360p. ISBN 9780802715357.

Detective-Inspector Jonathan Whicher (1814–1881) was one of the original eight detectives hired by Scotland Yard in 1842. By 1860, when someone at the Road Hill House in rural Wiltshire viciously slit the throat of three-year-old Saville Kent, Whicher had established a national reputation for cleverly catching criminals. The new case, however, baffled the expert and became highly debated in the London newspapers. According to Kate Summerscale, every letter to the editor about the case had its own solution to promote, and the British love of detective fiction rose in the wake of Whicher's failure. This sympathetic biography of the precedent-setting detective will especially appeal to readers of British crime novels.

Subjects: Detectives; Great Britain; Murder; Scotland Yard; Whicher, Jonathan

Now Try: Whicher and his colleagues closely adhered to the investigative methods introduced in the novel *The Murders in the Rue Morgue* by Edgar Allan Poe. One of the pioneers in crime detection in the United States was Allan Pinkerton, whose stories were followed closely by newspaper readers of his time. James A. MacKay tells an admiring story about the pioneering detective in *Allan Pinkerton: The First Private Eye.* In 1884 Pinkerton published his own recollections about his famous cases, *Thirty Years: A Detective.* After the California Gold Rush of 1849, Wells Fargo needed to protect its shipments of gold and cash in areas of the West in which there was no law enforcement. The company hired lawman James B. Hume to build a private force. According to Richard H. Dillon in *Wells Fargo Detective: The Biography of James B. Hume*, Hume built a professional service concerned with both safety and justice. Noel B. Gerson claims that professional crime detection began with Frenchman Eugène François Vidocq, a former criminal who started a private detective firm. Gerson recalls the story in *The Vidocq Dossier: The Story of the World's First Detective.*

Tefertiller, Casey

Wyatt Earp: The Life Behind the Legend. John Wiley, 1997. 403p. ISBN 0471189677.

Forget all the old movies and dime store novels. Wyatt Earp (1848–1929) was not a gunslinger who served both sides of the law. He was a serious law enforcement officer who rarely carried a gun, but would gladly punch out a ruffian. In fact, he was more likely to use a gun as a bludgeon than to shoot it. According to journalist

Casey Tefertiller, Earp fought only two shoot-outs in his life. Of course, one of those was at the O.K. Corral in Tombstone, Arizona, the most famous shoot-out in American history. Earp had to live with the memory of that bloody event all his life. In this candid biography of a legendary U.S. marshal and saloonkeeper, Tefertiller tells the story of a violent man who helped tame the West.

Subjects: Arizona; Earp, Wyatt; United States Marshals

Now Try: Earp and his associates have frequently been characters in novels, including *Trouble in Tombstone* by Richard S. Wheeler and *Gunman's Rhapsody* by Robert B. Parker. Doc Holliday only lived to age thirty-six, but there are many stories about the dentist-turned-deputy sheriff who fought with Earp at the O.K. Corral. Gary L. Roberts sorts through the myths in *Doc Holliday: The Life and the Legend*. As many as half a dozen Hollywood Westerns have included a railroad detective named Whispering Smith. Allen P. Bristow reveals that there really was such a man and separates the movie legend from the true railroad detective in *Whispering Smith: His Life and Misadventures*. Richard Zacks debunks the legends of a ship captain who has been mistakenly remembered as a pirate in *The Pirate Hunter: The True Story of Captain Kidd* (see this chapter).

Zacks, Richard

The Pirate Hunter: The True Story of Captain Kidd. Theia, 2002. 426p. ISBN 0786865334. Audiobook available.

According to Richard Zacks, 300 years of adventure fiction are in error. Captain William Kidd (1645–1701) was a merchant sailor turned pirate hunter, not a pirate himself, and his treasure was the goods that he recovered for a group of businessmen, including the governor of New York. As in any good sea tale, Kidd had an archrival, the pirate Robert Culliford, who twice convinced the captain's crew to mutiny. He also sparred with the British Royal Navy. In this pirate tale, Zacks dramatically describes a long and difficult quest by a hard-nosed sea captain looking for justice.

Subjects: Kidd, William; Pirates; Sea Stories

Now Try: Before Admiral Stephen Decatur fought the British Navy in the War of 1812, he fought against the Barbary pirates, who had been attacking American merchant ships in the Mediterranean Sea and Atlantic Ocean. Leonard F. Guttridge describes the brief career of a recklessly brave, proud, and combative naval officer in *Our Country, Right or Wrong: The Life of Stephen Decatur, the U.S. Navy's Most Illustrious Commander* (see chapter 3). Further stories about fighting the Barbary pirates are included in Zack's *The Pirate Coast: Thomas Jefferson, the First Marines, and the Secret Mission of 1805*. Like Kidd, Marco Polo was foremost a merchant who knew how to deal profitably with foreign traders. Laurence Bergreen chronicles Polo's great adventure in the Far East, where he lived for over twenty years before returning to Europe with a fortune in gold, in *Marco Polo: From Venice to Xanadu* (see chapter 1). Dime store novels of the distant past miscast Wyatt Earp as badly as they did Kidd. According to *Wyatt Earp: The Life Behind the Legend by Casey Tefertiller* (see this chapter), he was never a gunslinger in the Hollywood style.

Shot, Stabbed, or Bludgeoned

Most victims of crime do not earn biographies. They are just unfortunate people who stepped in harm's way. The few victims about whom biographies are written tend to be those who were famous before the crimes took place or those who have died mysteriously. These tend to be cases where the author cannot focus on the criminal because that character is unknown. By their behavior before the crime, the victims may also have made themselves into likely targets. Primatologist Dian Fossey clashed with local authorities and local poachers before her murder in Rwanda. Many people hated the famous atheist Madalyn Murray O'Hair. Major league first baseman Eddie Waitkus should not have visited an unknown woman in a hotel room. The crimes in these books were not random.

Many of the stories in this section have elements of mystery. Like the biographies of criminals in the first section of this chapter, they may be set in historical periods or be contemporary stories familiar to readers. Several of the books work well as quick reads. Readers may shudder when they read their graphic accounts of violent death.

> *Shot, Stabbed, or Bludgeoned* stories focus people who are the victims of crime. The biographical subjects in these books were not just in the wrong place at the wrong time. As the revealing narratives show, each of these unusual individuals in some way attracted his or her death or injury. These books have an element of horror that will leave readers alert to the possibility of becoming targets of heinous crimes.

Graysmith, Robert

The Murder of Bob Crane. Crown Publishers, 1993. 274p. ISBN 0517592096.

Life after *Hogan's Heroes* was not good for actor Bob Crane (1928–1978). Without steady television work and no prospects for movie fame, he toured the country, acting in regional theaters and living in cheap apartments. His last show opened with a leading actress who could not remember her lines. Both his estranged wife and one of his numerous lovers had recently commented on the short lifeline on his palm when he was found murdered in the Winfield Apartments in Scottsdale, Arizona. In this gritty book for readers who enjoy crime puzzles, investigative reporter Robert Graysmith critically examines the life, career, and death of the unfortunate actor.

Subjects: Actors and Actresses; Crane, Bob; Murder

Now Try: Brenda Scott Royce has written a companion guide to Crane's hit television program entitled ***Hogan's Heroes: Behind the Scenes at Stalag 13.*** Actor Sal Mineo was struggling to land roles when he was savagely murdered in the alley behind his Los Angeles apartment. His friend, H. Paul Jeffers, describes the unsolved crime in ***Sal Mineo: His Life, Murder, and Mystery.*** In 1997 serial killer Andrew Cunanan led police from Minnesota to Florida on a three-month killing spree that left five people dead, four of whom he knew. Maureen Orth recounts the search for Cunanan and the murder of fashion designer Gianni Versace in ***Vulgar Favors: Andrew Cunanan, Gianni Versace, and the Largest Failed Manhunt in U.S. History.*** Vincent Bugliosi tells the lurid story of the murder of actress Sharon Tate and six others by Charles Manson and his followers in *Helter Skelter*. The unusual deaths of many actors and actresses are described in *Cut!: Hollywood Murders, Accidents, and Other Tragedies.*

Hayes, Harold T. P.

The Dark Romance of Dian Fossey. Simon & Schuster, 1990. 351p. ISBN 067163-3392. Audiobook available.

Dian Fossey (1932–1985) was one of the most prominent and celebrated zoologists in history. So who would want to kill her? Lots of people, as it turns out. In her final years at her mountain gorilla research station in Rwanda, she had become an abrasive character who clashed with everyone, including her staff, neighbors, and the students who came to the station to conduct research. She had also made enemies among the region's poachers. As in Agatha Christie novels, there were many suspects with motives, but no Miss Marple or Hercule Poirot solved the mystery. Author Harold Hayes candidly profiles Fossey, describes her love affairs, explains why she was controversial among primate scientists, and reports on the crime that shocked the reading public around the world. Those who enjoy psychological investigations will relish this true, unsolved mystery.

> **Subjects:** Fossey, Dian; Gorillas; Primatologists; Rwanda; Women

> **Now Try:** Fossey's *Gorillas in the Mist* is a classic account of natural history research. Her colleagues, William Weber and Amy Vedder, update her study of endangered gorillas in *In the Kingdom of Gorillas: Fragile Species in a Dangerous Land*. Other independent women have ventured to remote locations to study wildlife. Maria Sibylla Merian sailed to South America in 1699 to study butterflies. Her adventurous story is told in *Chrysalis: Maria Sibylla Merian and the Secrets of Metamorphosis* by Kim Todd (see chapter 1). Ruth Harkness traveled deep into China in 1936 seeking the giant panda. Vicki Constantine Croke recounts Harkness's explorations in *The Lady and the Panda: The True Adventures of the First American Explorer to Bring Back China's Most Exotic Animal* (see chapter 1). Like Fossey, Indian Prime Minister Indira Gandhi had many enemies with whom to contend. Katherine Frank tells her tragic story in *Indira: The Life of Indira Nehru Gandhi* (see chapter 10).

Honan, Park

Christopher Marlowe: Poet & Spy. Oxford University Press, 2005. 421p. ISBN 9780198186953.

If you were writing a murder mystery and needed a victim, Christopher Marlowe (1564–1593) would be an obvious target, for he had many enemies. He often fought in taverns and did not pay his debts. He offended society with his daring and provocative plays. Being a spy, of course, also posed a risk. Park Honan has written a compelling story about the dramatist-poet that involves almost every person of import in Elizabethan England. Mystery readers and history buffs especially interested in the history of literature will enjoy this book.

> **Subjects:** London; Marlowe, Christopher; Playwrights; Poets; Spies

> **Now Try:** Marlowe's plays and poems are available in many selective and complete collections. As with the murder of Marlowe, there are questions

about the deaths of the sons of Edward IV. Most historians assume they died in the Tower of London at the command of Richard III, but the bodies were never found. Years later a young man appeared claiming to be Prince Richard, one of the dead boys. Ann Wroe reviews the case in *The Perfect Prince: The Mystery of Perkin Warbeck and His Quest for the Throne of England* (see chapter 5). Four centuries later, after a ragged feral boy in Nuremberg, Germany, was identified as the rejected son of a duchess, he was murdered by an unknown assailant. Jeffrey Moussaieff Masson describes the boy and his death in *Lost Prince: The Unsolved Mystery of Kaspar Hauser* (see chapter 5). In 1942 a mysterious Russian Jew by the name of Lev Nussimbaum was murdered in rural Italy after having spent a decade in Berlin, where he may have used the names Essad Bey and Kurban Said to write best-selling books. Tom Reiss recounts the story in *The Orientalist: Solving the Mystery of a Strange and Dangerous Life* (see chapter 5).

Jardine, Lisa

The Awful End of Prince William the Silent: The First Assassination of a Head of State with a Handgun. HarperCollins, 2005. 175p. Making History Series. ISBN 9780060838355, 0060838353.

In 1580 Philip II of Spain publicly offered a reward to any "good man" who would kill Prince William I of Orange (1533–1584), the Dutch monarch. The promise of 25,000 gold coins for the deed spread across the continent and caused the Dutch to increase the guard around their leader, a close ally of Elizabeth I of England. Known as William the Silent, he rarely uttered opinions and was respected for his moderate, negotiable approach to continental affairs. According to Lisa Jardine, William is the prototype of the peacemaker assassinated by radicals, a recurring event in history..

Subjects: Assassinations; Group Discussion Books; Netherlands; Princes; Quick Reads; William I, Prince of Orange

Now Try: The plot to kill Abraham Lincoln involved many people, including one woman, Mary Surratt. Kate Clifford Larson reviews the evidence against the first woman executed by the federal government in *Assassin's Accomplice: Mary Surratt and the Plot to Kill Abraham Lincoln*. Numerous threats were made against the life of President John F. Kennedy in the days before his visit to Dallas, Texas. David E. Kaiser chronicles the days and hours leading up to the assassination in *The Road to Dallas: The Assassination of John F. Kennedy*. In 1981 John Hinckley Jr. attempted to assassinate President Ronald Reagan. Sarah Brady, whose husband James Brady was permanently paralyzed in the assassination attempt, discusses his struggle to recover and her fight with lung cancer in *A Good Fight*. Like Prince William, Mahatma Gandhi was a peace advocate who was assassinated by those opposed to peace. Stanley Wolpert examines the life of the religious leader in *Gandhi's Passion: The Life and Legacy of Mahatma Gandhi* (see chapter 4).

LeBeau, Bryan F.

The Atheist: Madalyn Murray O'Hair. New York University Press, 2003. 387p. ISBN 0814-751717.

For thirty-five years Madalyn Murray O'Hair (1919–1995) was "the most hated woman in America." The famous atheist had succeeded in a lawsuit that led to the Supreme Court ban on school prayer in 1963 and was often in the news fighting to further eliminate connections between church and state. Her opponents charged that she was rude, vulgar, and blasphemous. Then in 1995 she, a son, and a granddaughter disappeared, as did $500,000 from the *American Atheist* accounts. In this book for fans of true crime literature, historian Bryan F. LeBeau profiles O'Hair and assembles the evidence that ultimately identified her murderer.

> **Subjects:** Atheists; Murder; O'Hair, Madalyn Murray; Religious Rights; Women

> **Now Try:** When police could not find two twelve-year-old girls who disappeared in Oregon, one of the girl's stepgrandmother, a private investigator, began her own investigation. Linda O'Neal tells how she cracked the case and identified the serial killer in *Missing: The Oregon City Girls: A Shocking True Story of Abduction and Murder*. Latanisha Carmichael's was missing for twenty years before her brother and sister found her remains in a closet in the family home. Andre Carmichael, Sabrina Carmichael-Yaw, and Aurora Mackey recount the uncovering of horrible family secrets in *Family Skeleton: A Brother and Sister's Journey from Murder to Truth*. The parallels between the lives of O'Hair and abolitionist John Brown are many. Both made many enemies by persistently pursuing their unpopular causes. Neither respected opponents' opinions. Both died violent deaths. Historian David S. Reynolds describes the abolitionist in *John Brown, Abolitionist: The Man Who Killed Slavery, Sparked the Civil War, and Seeded Civil Rights* (see chapter 9). Mexican artist Frida Kahlo is another contentious woman who was considered dangerous to polite society. Her soap opera-like story is told by Hayden Herrera in *Frida: A Biography of Frida Kahlo* (see chapter 7).

Theodore, John

Baseball's Natural: The Story of Eddie Waitkus. Southern Illinois University Press, 2003. 136p. ISBN 0809324504.

In 1949 Eddie Waitkus (1919–1972) was just a happy-go-lucky, slightly bookish first baseman with the Philadelphia Phillies. He had been a smooth-fielding National League All Star for the Chicago Cubs but was traded to the Phillies after the 1948 season. Nineteen-year-old Ruth Ann Steinhagen of Chicago, who had made a shrine of photographs and newspaper clippings about Waitkus in her bedroom, was unhappy about the trade. So when the Phillies came to town, she took a shotgun to a room that she booked in the Edgewater Beach Hotel where the visiting team stayed. She waited for Waitkus to personally answer an invitation that she sent to him and then shot him. In this short biography, journalist John Theodore tells the bittersweet story of the unfortunate man whose life was sorely altered by senseless violence. Waitkus inspired the Roy Hobbs character in Bernard Malamud's novel *The Natural* (Harcourt Brace, 1952).

> **Subjects:** Attempted Murder; Baseball Players; Chicago; Quick Reads; Waitkus, Eddie

> **Now Try:** *The Natural*, Bernard Malamud's novel about a baseball player recovering from a senseless shooting, is still widely read. *Mysterious Montague: A True Tale of Hollywood, Golf, and Armed Robbery* by Leigh Montville will please readers who like a biography combining sports and true crime. Readers who enjoy tragic sports stories may appreciate *Indian Summer: The Forgotten Story of Louis Sockalexis, the First Native American in Major League Baseball* by Brian McDonald (see chapter 12). Moe Berg was

another atypical baseball player, a scholar and a master of several languages. His sad post-baseball story is found in *The Catcher Was a Spy: The Mysterious Life of Moe Berg* by Nicholas Dawidoff (see chapter 5).

Criminal Profile Collections

The books in this section differ from others in this chapter in that they profile many criminals instead of one or two. They are to biography what short stories are to fiction—perfect for those with short periods to devote to reading or those who enjoy quick reads.

> *Criminal Profile Collections* include many short profiles of criminal figures; each can easily be read in a single sitting. These will appeal to readers who enjoy short stories.

Block, Lawrence, ed.

Gangsters, Swindlers, Killers, and Thieves: The Lives and Crimes of Fifty American Villains. Oxford University Press, 2004. 287p. ISBN 0195169522.

Most of the 18,000 figures in the <u>American National Biography</u> were included for their positive contributions to society. They led the nation, fought its battles, forged its industries, or shaped its culture. To balance the collection historically, the editors also included important American criminals whose actions defined and shaped the criminal subculture of the nation. For this volume, mystery writer Lawrence Block chose fifty of the most famous criminals and added photographs or drawings to their concise three- to six-page profiles. Because many of these bad men and women were active in the distant past, this gritty collection will especially appeal to those who enjoy reading history.

Subjects: Collective Biography; Criminals

Now Try: Criminals are generally thought of as people who break the law. In *American Monsters: 44 Rats, Blackhats, and Plutocrats,* edited by Jack Newfield and Mark Jacobson, the definition of criminal is widened to include people who may be seen as villains even though they broke no enforceable laws. Some readers may be offended by the inclusion of frank profiles of Walt Disney, Billy Graham, Henry Ford, and other generally admired figures with those of true criminals John Wilkes Booth and Charles Manson. A true classic in criminal biography is *Bloodletters and Badmen: A Narrative Encyclopedia of American Criminals from the Pilgrims to the Present* by Jay Robert Nash.

Jackman, Ian, ed.

Con Men: Fascinating Profiles of Swindlers and Rogues from the Files of the Most Successful Broadcast in Television History. Simon & Schuster, 2003. 201p. ISBN 074322-4485.

60 Minutes was an acclaimed but little-watched documentary program on CBS before it began confronting crooked businessmen, unlicensed doctors, and art forgers in the early 1970s. According to Mike Wallace, who wrote the introduction to this collection of short profiles of crooked men and one woman, there was little investigative journalism on television at the time; and the *60 Minutes* audience grew rapidly when it aired these startling stories from across the country. For fans of the program and readers wanting a compact book to take on a trip or to the beach, editor Ian Jackman has crafted entertaining stories.

Subjects: *60 Minutes* (Television Show); Collective Biography; Criminals; Quick Reads; Swindlers

Now Try: During the twentieth century, especially during the J. Edgar Hoover era at the FBI, the federal government spied on prominent Americans, noting any actions it thought might indicate criminal or treasonable offenses. Dozens of amusing profiles of possible criminals are included in *Celebrity Secrets: Government Files on the Rich and Famous* by Nick Redfern. *Playboy* magazine has been reporting on crime since its inception. *The Playboy Book of True Crime* reprints forty articles about criminals, including O. J. Simpson, Gary Gilmore, and Jimmy Hoffa. According to art critic John Richardson, most artists are drunkards, liars, or thieves. His entertaining collection of artist profiles is *Sacred Monsters, Sacred Masters: Beaton, Capote, Dalí, Picasso, Freud, Warhol, and More* (see chapter 7).

Consider Starting With . . .

These well-written True Crime Biographies of modest length will appeal to most general readers.

- Brock, Pope. *Charlatan: America's Most Dangerous Huckster, the Man Who Pursued Him, and the Age of Flimflam.*
- Cornwall, Patricia. *Portrait of a Killer: Jack the Ripper Case Closed.*
- Honan, Park. *Christopher Marlowe: Poet & Spy.*
- Keneally, Thomas. *American Scoundrel: The Life of the Notorious Civil War General Dan Sickles.*
- Maas, Peter. *Serpico.*
- Summerscale, Kate. *The Suspicions of Mr. Whicher: A Shocking Murder and the Undoing of a Great Victorian Detective.*
- Wambaugh, Joseph. *Fire Lover: A True Story.*

Further Reading

Cords, Sarah Statz

The Real Story: A Guide to Nonfiction Reading Interests. Libraries Unlimited, 2006. 460p. ISBN 1591582830.

Cords's third chapter covers true crime. She describes the genre and reviews dozens of titles, with further reading recommendations.

Wyatt, Neal

The Readers' Advisory Guide to Nonfiction. American Libraries, 2007. 318p. ISBN 9780-838909362.

Wyatt discusses the appeal factors of true crime narratives in chapter 7. In her discussions she identifies key authors and includes generous lists of titles to recommend to readers.

Chapter 3

War Biography

Definition of War Biography

War is organized violence supported by governments or revolutionary movements. A War Biography is a narrative about an individual or small group whose lives are shaped or transformed by war between armed groups. Soldiers and their commanders are often subjects of war stories, as are civilians who are caught in the path of war.

According to Movindri Reddy in *The New Dictionary of the History of Ideas*, defining war is not easy. Like pornography, we all "know it when we see it," but defining a conflict as a war is a political act that may never happen officially. For example, the involvement of American military forces in Korea and Vietnam was called a "police action," as no act declaring war was ever passed by the U.S. Congress. Likewise, no declarations of war were passed before American troops entered Afghanistan in 2001 and Iraq in 2003. The impact of these armed conflicts on participants, however, is the same as if war were declared, and biographers have chosen men and women from these confrontations as subjects for their "war" narratives.

Identifying soldiers as heroes worthy of having stories told about them goes back to ancient times. In the *Iliad*, the poet Homer tells the stories of Greek warrior Achilles and his Trojan rival, Hector, risking their lives in combat for the honor of their people. In the Old Testament stories of the Bible, young Jewish shepherd David, the future king of Israel, is honored for slaying the Philistine warrior Goliath, and Hebrew leader Joshua is praised for laying siege to the city of Jericho. In *Morte d'Arthur*, Sir Thomas Malory praises King Arthur for defeating first the independent kings of Britain and then five foreign kings to solidify his rule over the kingdom. War stories are not exclusive to the West—the ancient Indian epic *Mahabharata* includes a dramatic passage on the great battle of Kurukshetra. The tradition has continued through time to America, where countless biographies have been written about soldiers from all of its wars, from George Washington in the American Revolution to women fighting in the Iraq War. Since the publication in 1947 of *The Diary of a Young Girl* by Anne Frank, the interest of biographers and readers has widened to include stories about civilians who live through these wars.

War Biography includes narratives about individuals whose lives are shaped or transformed by war. Although authors of these biographies may describe entire lives (birth to death), the experience of war or preparing for war is the key focus in these books. Military leaders, soldiers, spies, and civilians are profiled in these books.

Appeal of the Genre

Strong character is the key appeal factor in war story biographies. Readers enjoy learning about soldiers who exhibit courage and fighting skill and about cunning civilians who survive the battles around them. The desire to read about them, however, sometimes goes beyond simple admiration. The survival of a nation sometimes depended on the actions of individuals; readers of subsequent generations are often grateful for their successful efforts. Reading about these heroes can support patriotic feelings. Biographers may also profile enemy combatants. Their stories may foster understanding of the causes of war or serve as justifications for combat.

The story of an individual in danger is another strong appeal of a war story biography. Good writers lay out the events so that dramatic tension builds to a climax, at which point the conflict is resolved. Making allies, spying, hiding, escaping, calculating risks, and fighting enemies are elements in the often action-packed narratives.

The settings of war story biographies are often complex. The battles, whether in deserts, mountains, or the streets of a village, take place in a geopolitical context. The nations involved are often fighting over land or natural resources. Political, ethnic, and religious differences also complicate conflicts, making peaceful resolutions difficult. All these elements frame the War Biography.

The pacing of war story biographies varies. Some, such as *Son of the Morning Star* by Evan S. Connell, offer novel-like narratives that allow for rapid reading. Other titles in this chapter belong to compact biographical series aimed at those who enjoy quick reads. A few lengthy and highly detailed biographies, such as *Ike: An American Hero* by Michael Korda, appeal to readers who desire a long and leisurely book.

The appeal of learning also scores high in war story biographies. Readers may commit much time to reading books to learn new facts and different viewpoints about the military leaders and conflicts that fascinate them.

Organization of the Chapter

The first section of the chapter is "Battle Stories," biographies that highlight the experience of combat in an individual's life. Front line soldiers, such as General George Custer and Manfred von Richthofen, are depicted in these books. Also included are revolutionary figures, such as Ernesto "Che" Guevara and Giuseppe Garibaldi. These biographies describe preparations for war, the dangers of combat, and the repercussions of battle.

The second section is "Military Lives," featuring biographies of individuals who make a life of serving in armed forces. Although these narratives include some battle stories, they focus on an individual's professional career, identifying assignments and promotions in rank. Julius Caesar, George Washington, and John Paul Jones are among the subjects in this section.

In the third section, "Casualties of War," civilians who struggled to survive a war are profiled. Kim Phuc, the Vietnamese napalm victim in a famous photograph, and Polish zookeepers Jan and Antonina Żabiński, who hid Jews from Nazis in their zoo, are included. Whether they are on the battle front or behind the lines, the central characters in these stories face life or death choices that demand a brave response. How they respond alters their lives and those of others around them.

"Espionage and Intrigue" is the fourth section of this chapter. These stories feature spies risking their lives to learn strategic secrets that they then pass on to the commanders plotting the course of war. *Time* correspondent Pham Xuan An, Washington socialite Rose O'Neale Greenhow, and Benedict Arnold are included here.

The final section is "War Biography Collections." Readers who enjoy short profiles of wartime figures that can easily be read in single sittings will appreciate these entertaining collections.

Battle Stories

No matter why a war is fought, whether for lofty ideals or for the enrichment of political leaders, soldiers take up weapons and seek their enemy. Although the outcome of war is greatly influenced by the wealth of the opposing nations and the tactics of their generals, the courage of soldiers to face the enemy and fight is the foundation of war. Without them, nations have no ability to invade neighbors or defend their borders.

The books in this section feature men and women who risked their lives in armed combat, including frontline soldiers, fighter pilots, field generals, admirals, and support personnel. Peter Kilduff takes readers back to World War I to learn how a cavalry officer took to the skies to become a deadly fighter pilot in *Richthofen: Beyond the Legend of the Red Baron*. Rosemary and Joseph Agonito draw from recently discovered oral histories to tell about a Cheyenne woman who fought as a warrior in several battles, including Little Big Horn, in *Buffalo Calf Road Woman*. Todd DePastino reprints military cartoons from the newspaper *Stars and Stripes* in his admiring story of a World War II cartoonist in *Bill Mauldin: A Life Up Front*. Though less known than the generals, these soldiers and their stories resonate with readers, especially veterans.

Assertive characters dominate the books in this section. They see the dangers before them, overcome their fears, and fight. To fully tell their stories, authors describe settings in detail, making these books attractive to history readers who enjoy learning about other eras and foreign lands. These books will appeal to veterans and readers contemplating military service.

Battle Stories are biographies of soldiers, warriors, and others who serve on the battle lines in war. Authors are generally interested in the traits of courage, devotion, and honor exhibited by soldiers, as well as their personal responses to combat. Settings are well developed in this collection of titles, which tend to be compelling reading.

Agonito, Rosemary, and Joseph Agonito

Buffalo Calf Road Woman. Globe Pequot Press, 2006. 242p. ISBN 9780762738175. Large print available.

> When men write history, women's stories are often not considered. Authors Rosemary and Joseph Agonito wondered why there were no book-length accounts of Buffalo Calf Road Woman (1840?–1878), a Cheyenne woman for whom a battle was named. Then the authors discovered forgotten narratives from Iron Teeth and Kate Bighead, two Cheyenne women, and from the warrior Wooden Leg. These accounts told how Buffalo Calf Road fought in several battles, including Little Big Horn, and how she had saved the life of her brother at the Battle of the Rosebud. With this novel-like biography of a forgotten warrior, the authors challenge long-held views of Cheyenne women as passive.

> > **Subjects:** Buffalo Calf Road Woman; Cheyenne Indians; Indian Wars; Little Big Horn, Battle of the; Montana; Native Americans; Teen Reads; Women

> > **Now Try:** Women who fought in battle alongside the men in the American Revolution were often ridiculed when exposed. Alfred F. Young tells the story of one female soldier who gained more respect in *Masquerade: The Life and Times of Deborah Sampson, Continental Soldier* (see chapter 5). Elizabeth D. Leonard writes about women fighters in the Civil War in *All the Daring of the Soldier: Women of the Civil War Armies*. In *The Mysterious Private Thompson: The Double Life of Sarah Emma Edmonds, Civil War Soldier*, Laura Leedy Gansler recounts how one woman remained undetected in the Union Army through many of its fiercest battles. Kirsten Holmstead tells about modern women at war in *Band of Sisters: American Women at War in Iraq* (see this chapter). In *Mother Jones: The Most Dangerous Woman in America* (see chapter 4), Elliott J. Gorn tells the story of another woman who was ready to fight, even when the cause seemed hopeless. Tennis player Althea Gibson had to fight against racial prejudice to join the all-white United States Lawn Tennis Association in 1950. Frances Clayton Gray and Yanick Rice Lamb chronicle the life of a courageous athlete in *Born to Win: The Authorized Biography of Althea Gibson* (see chapter 12).

Alexander, Larry

Biggest Brother: The Life of Major Dick Winters, the Man Who Led the Band of Brothers. NAL Caliber, 2005. 297p. ISBN 0451215109. Large print available.

> Richard D. Winters (1918–) was an untested first lieutenant when he led sixteen paratroopers, each loaded with 125 pounds of gear, behind enemy lines in Normandy on D-Day. The explosions of antiaircraft fire only hinted of the dangers ahead. He could only imagine the hellish, unrelenting battle into which they dropped and their path across Holland into Hitler's stronghold. In this admiring biography, journalist Larry Alexander first dramatically describes the events of the next year, as Winters and Easy Company from the 101st Army Airborne marched into the major battles to liberate Europe, and then tells how their story

became famous nearly forty years later when Stephen A. Ambrose wrote *Band of Brothers*, which Hollywood producers Stephen Spielberg and Tom Hanks adapted for television.

Subjects: Paratroopers; Soldiers; Winters, Richard D.; World War II

Now Try: More on Winters and his company is found in *Band of Brothers: E Company, 506th Regiment, 101st Airborne: From Normandy to Hitler's Eagle's Nest* by Stephan E. Ambrose. Joseph Beyrle's jump into Normandy on D-Day was not his first, as he had twice delivered gold to the French Resistance. Thomas H. Taylor tells how Beyrle's war record differed from all other soldiers in *The Simple Sounds of Freedom: The True Story of the Only Soldier to Fight for Both America and the Soviet Union in World War II*. Polar explorer Ernest Shackleton was an adventurer who led men into danger and guided their return. George Plimpton describes the life of a man who caught the imagination of many in the photobiography *Ernest Shackleton* (see chapter 1). Theodore Roosevelt became a national hero for leading a cavalry unit called the Rough Riders across Cuba in the Spanish–American War. Edmund Morris describes Roosevelt's years before he became president in *The Rise of Theodore Roosevelt*.

Anderson, Jon Lee

Che Guevara: A Revolutionary Life. Grove Press, 1997. 814p. ISBN 0802116000. Audiobook available.

On October 10, 1967, newspapers around the world ran photographs of Argentinean militant Ernesto "Che" Guevara (1928–1967) lying dead on gruesome public display. The Bolivian military wanted to prove that it had executed the world's most famous revolutionary, the man who led guerrilla fighters in Cuba and the Congo and who toured the globe advocating communism. In his sympathetic, epic account of the fearless Marxist, author Jon Lee Anderson portrays El Che as a person who could care for people as a doctor or as president of Cuba's National Bank, as well as lead guerrillas through the jungle.

Subjects: Argentina; Bolivia; Congo; Cuba; Guerrillas; Guevara, Ernesto "Che"; Revolutionaries

Now Try: Several books written by Guevara are available in English translations, including *Back on the Road: A Journey to Latin America* and *The African Dream: The Diaries of the Revolutionary War in the Congo*. Like Guevara, Ho Chi Minh studied abroad and toured many countries in his development as a revolutionary. His little-known story is told in *Ho Chi Minh: A Life* by William J. Duiker (see chapter 10). Unlike Guevara and Ho, United Nations negotiator Sergio Vieira de Mello toured the world trying to stop regional conflicts, until he was killed in Iraq. Samantha Power chronicles his upbringing in Brazil and work in Bangladesh, Lebanon, Cambodia, Kosovo, and East Timor in *Chasing the Flame: Sergio Vieira de Mello and the Fight to Save the World* (see chapter 4). Doors lead singer Jim Morrison was another romantically tragic figure, at times literary and at others self-destructive. Jerry Hopkins and coauthor Danny Sugerman portray Morrison as a hell-bent rebel who read the Beat poets and revolutionaries, in *No One Here Gets Out Alive* (see chapter 6).

Connell, Evan S.

Son of the Morning Star. North Point Press, 1984. 441p. ISBN 0865471606. Audiobook available.

"Hurrah, boys, we've got them!" cried General George Armstrong Custer (1839–1876) as he moved his cavalry into the Little Big Horn. Confident of victory, the golden-haired commander led his men into the most famous massacre of the Indian Wars. In this novel-like biography, novelist Evan S. Connell tells the story of a man who personified American bravado in the time of westward expansion and the Sioux who stood up against him. Connell circles around the main story with many subplots and flashbacks of Custer's life before reaching a dramatic climax, and then ends with reflections on Custer's character.

> **Subjects:** Civil War; Custer, George Armstrong; Generals; Indian Wars; Little Big Horn, Battle of the

> **Now Try:** Custer's viewpoint on the Indian Wars is presented in his own book, *My Life of the Plains*, and the softer side of the often maligned general can be seen in *The Custer Story: The Life and Intimate Letters of General George A. Custer and His Wife Elizabeth*. Custer has been the subject of several novels, including *The Court Martial of General George Armstrong Custer* by Douglas C. Jones and *Marching to Valhalla: A Novel of Custer's Last Days* by Michael Blake. Like Custer, Norwegian geophysicist Kristian Birkeland was egotistical and completely consumed by his quest for glory. The story of how he led colleagues on dangerous expeditions with no thought of consequences is told in *The Northern Lights* by Lucy Jago (see chapter 1). In *The Long Road Home: A Story of War and Family*, journalist Martha Raddatz weaves the battle story of soldiers led into a trap in the Iraq War with the home front story of their Internet-connected families. Larry McMurtry describes another charismatic but doomed fighter in *Crazy Horse* (see chapter 4).

DePastino, Todd

Bill Mauldin: A Life Up Front. W. W. Norton, 2008. 370p. ISBN 9780393061833.

With his "Up Front" cartoons running in the widely distributed military publication *Stars and Stripes* and in hundreds of newspapers across America, Bill Mauldin (1921–2003) was the most famous technician third grade sergeant of World War II. Drawing many of his cartoons close to or on the battle front, he kept his focus on the everyday experiences of common soldiers, such as his badly shaven Willie and Joe. Though General Patton did not approve of the way that he portrayed soldiers, the troops and their families enjoyed and saved the strips. In this admiring biography, author Todd DePastino tells how Mauldin survived the war and as a civilian became an editorial cartoonist despised by many politicians. Military veterans and cartoon readers will likely enjoy this well-illustrated biography.

> **Subjects:** Cartoonists; Illustrated Biography; Journalists; Mauldin, Bill; Teen Reads; World War II

> **Now Try:** Mauldin's popular collection of World War II cartoons, *Up Front*, has been issued in many editions (albeit with different introductions). The 1991 edition included an introduction by Charles Schulz, another veteran who also became a fabulously popular cartoonist. His bittersweet life is detailed in *Schulz and Peanuts* (see chapter 7). Like Mauldin, independent journalist I. F. Stone knew how to irritate generals and politicians. Read the story of his muckraking career in *"All Governments Lie": The Life and Times of Rebel Journalist I. F. Stone* by Myra MacPherson (see chapter 4). Mauldin's

cartoons were evocative because they honestly portrayed the gritty details of a soldier's life in World War II. Tim O'Brien details the soldier's life in the Vietnam War in his memoir *If I Die in a Combat Zone, Box Me Up and Send Me Home* and his memoir-like novel *The Things They Carried*.

Golway, Terry

Washington's General: Nathanael Greene and the Triumph of the American Revolution. Henry Holt, 2005. 355p. ISBN 0805070664.

Nathanael Greene (1742–1786) was a Quaker with no military experience when he took charge of the Rhode Island militia in 1775. Despite his troops losing New York to the British in the early stages of the American Revolution, George Washington admired Greene's qualities of organization and ingenuity. Over the objections of his other commanders, the future president kept Greene as an advisor and eventually gave him the Southern command. There Greene kept the British army engaged in skirmishes until the opportunity for victory came in Yorktown. Historian and journalist Terry Golway focuses on Greene's actions during the war in this admiring military biography.

> **Subjects:** American Revolution; Generals; Greene, Nathanael; Yorktown, Battle of

> **Now Try:** Greene is a character in the story of the conflict between his commander and an American general who betrayed the revolution. The story is told by Dave R. Palmer in *George Washington and Benedict Arnold: A Tale of Two Patriots* (see this chapter). *Let My Name Stand Fair* by Shirley Seifert is an older but still widely available novel about the life of Greene's wife Catharine. General Greene and General Omar Bradley were patient military leaders who won battles without taking unnecessary risks. Alan Axelrod profiles the latter in *Bradley* (see this chapter). Like Greene, President Harry Truman, a steady leader, did not seek the limelight and proved his detractors wrong. David McCullough tells the president's story in *Truman* (see chapter 10).

Guttridge, Leonard F.

Our Country, Right or Wrong: The Life of Stephen Decatur, the U.S. Navy's Most Illustrious Commander. Forge, 2006. 304p. ISBN 9780765307019.

Stephen Decatur (1779–1820), the young admiral whom the U.S. Navy sent to recapture a stolen ship from Barbary pirates, was recklessly brave, proud, and combative. He would not hesitate to attack better-armed ships, and he did not shrink from a fight when he felt his honor was questioned. Decatur's pugnacity led to both his fame and his early death when he declined to settle a minor difference before a duel. In this action-packed biography, naval historian Leonard F. Guttridge describes the brief career of a popular figure of the Barbary and 1812 wars, whose name graces over two dozen American cities.

> **Subjects:** Admirals; Decatur, Stephen; Duelists; United States Navy; War of 1812

> **Now Try:** In *John Paul Jones: Sailor, Hero, Father of the American Navy* (see this chapter), Evan Thomas tells how the other great American naval hero also died young—and much less appreciated than Decatur. Naturalist John Wesley

Powell's shooting the rapids in the Grand Canyon was as foolhardy as Decatur's attacking better-armed ships of war. Donald Worster tells an adventurous story in *A River Running West: The Life of John Wesley Powell* (see chapter 1). Author Stephen Crane was another energetic and somewhat reckless man who died tragically young after a brief period of great acclaim. Linda H. Davis tells about his bittersweet life in *Badge of Courage: The Life of Stephen Crane* (see chapter 6). Winston Churchill was a daring young man who risked life and reputation without much thought. Celia Sandys describes Churchill as a young war correspondent and adventurer in *The Young Churchill: The Early Years of Winston Churchill*.

Kilduff, Peter

Richthofen: Beyond the Legend of the Red Baron. John Wiley, 1993. 256p. ISBN 047100-877X.

When World War I began, Manfred von Richthofen (1892–1918) served in the German cavalry. Whenever he saw airplanes, he shot at them without bothering to identify their markings. Little did he know that he would soon be flying himself, joining the *Fliegertruppe* and becoming a renowned fighting ace known as the Red Baron. According to aviation historian Peter Kilduff, the daring Richthofen earned the admiration of friends and foes by shooting down eighty allied planes in the fifteen months before he too was shot down. In this biography, Kilduff chronicles aerial battles and describes Richthofen's lavish funeral.

> **Subjects:** Germany; Richthofen, Manfred von; Pilots; Quick Reads; Soldiers; World War I

> **Now Try:** American flying ace Eddie Rickenbacker survived World War I to become an aerial performer, airline executive, and military advisor. His adventurous story is told in *Ace of Aces: The Life of Capt. Eddie Rickenbacker* by H. Paul Jeffers (see chapter 1). Pilots from Tennessee recount their harrowing World War II adventures in *Missions Remembered: Recollections of the World War II Air War*. Like Richthofen, British East African colonial Denys Finch Hatton was a romantic man of the air whose death was widely mourned. Sara Wheeler tells about his bittersweet life in Kenya, including his romance with *Out of Africa* author Karen Blixen, in *Too Close to the Sun: The Audacious Life and Times of Denys Finch Hatton* (see chapter 5). Like Richthofen, American actor John Wayne became a symbol of a fighting man. Garry Wills thoughtfully examines the meaning of Wayne's life to his country in *John Wayne's America: The Politics of Celebrity* (see chapter 8).

Man, John

Attila: The Barbarian King Who Challenged Rome. Thomas Dunne Press, 2005. 324p. ISBN 9780312349394. Audiobook available.

In the fifth century, when the Roman Empire was weakening, Attila (406?–453) led his troops of Huns, Goths, and allied tribes across Europe, conquering villages and brutally changing the face of warfare. He failed, however, to overpower the cities of Rome or Constantinople and eventually isolated his forces far from their homeland and the resources that they needed. According to author John Man, Attila can be compared to Napoleon and Hitler, an evil-minded and power hungry military leader who lost his sense of mortality.

> **Subjects:** Attila; Barbarians; Warriors

Now Try: A thousand years after Attila, Tsar Ivan the Terrible killed thousands of people, including members of his own family, while expanding his empire. His brutal life is described in *Ivan the Terrible: First Tsar of Russia* by Isabel De Madariaga (see chapter 5). The reputation of Roman emperor Nero is also horrific. Historian Edward Champlin investigates whether the Roman deserved condemnation in *Nero* (see chapter 5). The ultimate failure of brutal despots can be seen in *Napoleon* by Paul Johnson (see this chapter) and *Hitler of History* by John Lukas. Cosmetics king Charles Revson was not deadly but was tremendously mean. Andrew Tobias describes how he abused employees while running his corporation in *Fire and Ice: The Story of Charles Revson—the Man Who Built the Revlon Empire* (see chapter 5).

Perry, Mark

Conceived in Liberty: Joshua Chamberlain, William Oates, and the American Civil War. Viking, 1997. 500p. ISBN 0670862258.

Joshua Chamberlain (1828–1914) of Maine and William Oates (1835–1910) of Alabama lived remarkably comparable lives. Both were farmers' sons who fought in the Civil War and survived to become prominent politicians, governors in their states. Even their wartime experiences were similar, as both rose from low rank to become commanders, fought at Gettysburg, and were hospitalized for battle injuries. Author Mark Perry describes their experiences against a richly detailed background of the Civil War and the reconstruction of the nation.

> **Subjects:** Chamberlain, Joshua; Civil War; Dual Biography; Gettysburg, Battle of; Oates, William; Soldiers

> **Now Try:** *The Civil War Soldier: A Historical Reader* collects scholarly articles and essays about common soldiers of both the Union and Confederate armies. In *The Civil War Diary of a Common Soldier: William Wiley of the 77th Illinois Infantry,* the daily struggle to find food and to overcome illness is as dramatic as the dangers of battle. Great novels about soldiers in the Civil War include *The Red Badge of Courage* by Stephen Crane and *The March* by E. L. Doctorow. Finding the similarities between two men with different reputations is also the premise of *The Same Man: George Orwell and Evelyn Waugh* by David Lebedoff.

Riall, Lucy

Garibaldi: Invention of a Hero. Yale University Press, 2007. 482p. ISBN 9780-300112122.

The life of Giuseppe Garibaldi (1807–1882) spanned the major events of the nineteenth century and eventually took him around the world. Born in Nice in 1807, Garibaldi spent his youth as a sailor, learning about many different nations and developing his political convictions. In 1834 he fought in the Young Italy movement to form a united Italian republic and was exiled to South America for twelve years, where he fought to free Brazil and to defend Uruguay. An "idealist without ideology," according to Lucy Riall, Garibaldi returned to Italy and France numerous times after his exile to fight for various causes and spent more years exiled in London and New York for his activities. Riall sorts fact from fiction in this detailed biography of a great revolutionary figure.

Subjects: Brazil; Garibaldi, Giuseppe; Generals; Italy; Revolutionaries; Uruguay

Now Try: Unlike Garibaldi, Thomas Paine did have well-formed ideals. Both joined revolts in multiple nations. Craig Nelson describes Paine's political and military activity in *Thomas Paine: Enlightenment, Revolution, and the Birth of Modern Nations* (see chapter 10). Like Garibaldi, scientist James Smithson was an adventurer. Heather Ewing includes the story of his participation in the French Revolution in *The Lost World of James Smithson: Science, Revolution, and the Birth of the Smithsonian* (see chapter 11). Argentinean revolutionary Ernesto "Che" Guevara also fought in revolts around the globe. Jon Lee Anderson chronicles his development as a militant in *Che Guevara: A Revolutionary Life* (see this chapter). Actor Sean Penn has a reputation for supporting unpopular causes. Richard Kelly examines the career of the rebellious celebrity in *Sean Penn: His Life and Times*.

Sheehan, Neil

A Bright Shining Lie: John Paul Vann and America in Vietnam. Random House, 1988. 861p. ISBN 0394484479.

The funeral of John Paul Vann (1924–1972) brought together proponents and critics of the Vietnam War, who all felt compelled to honor an outspoken soldier who died in a helicopter crash returning from a battle. Vann had fought for and alongside the attending generals and soldiers; at the same time, he had revealed to journalists and war protestors the horrors of war and incompetence of the American military. Though the contradictions of his convictions troubled Vann, he served his country valiantly and gave his life for a cause that he questioned. In this psychological biography journalist Neil Sheehan, a Vietnam War correspondent, examines the life of a soldier in what came to be seen as a pointless war.

Subjects: Soldiers; Vann, John Paul; Vietnam War

Now Try: Former marine and antiwar activist Ron Kovic recounts his patriotism and paralyzing injury in the Vietnam War in his candid memoir, *Born on the Fourth of July*. In *The New Soldier*, John Kerry (who became a senator and presidential candidate many years after the writing of this book) and members of Vietnam Veterans against the War describe the horrors of an unjust war, whereas General William Westmoreland defends the war and the honor of military service in *A Soldier Reports*. Veterans from all of the branches of the military discuss their Vietnam War experiences in *Soldiers' Story: Vietnam in Their Own Words*. Tim O'Brien captures the experience of the Vietnam soldier in his novel *The Things They Carried*. John James Audubon was another solitary and troubled character, never satisfied with his life. Richard Rhodes focuses on Audubon's wandering nature in *John James Audubon: The Making of an American* (see chapter 1).

Military Lives

Throughout history, many combatants were amateurs, drafted by their lord, king, or president to fight in a time of war. If a nation had a standing army, it was small and limited to the protection of the head of state, the seat of government, and a country's borders with other nations. Few people made a career of military service when armed conflict was not imminent. These few career soldiers, however, were very important. When the time of war did come, they took command. They made the strategic decisions that won or lost the war, asked their soldiers to go into battle, and met the press afterward to justify their actions. When they devised new tactics, other strategists noticed and the conduct of future wars changed. These career soldiers are the figures of war most studied by academics and armchair historians.

In this section are biographies of individuals who either devoted their lives to the military or were called to serve their country on several occasions. Some are the men who started the wars. All are remembered for their military leadership. Historian Paul Johnson eloquently describes the life and legacy of the French general whose campaigns of conquest reshaped the nations of nineteenth-century Europe in his concise biography *Napoleon*. Military expert Alan Axelrod tells how a cadet who attended the U.S. Military Academy only for the sports and to obtain a college degree became a great World War II strategist and a general beloved by his troops, in *Bradley*. Historian John Sugden recounts the life of a Shawnee warrior and orator with a greater understanding of the stakes of history than others of his time in *Tecumseh: A Life.*

War stories about career soldiers are filled with strong characters and lively plots. The subjects discover their vocation, train for war, and lead troops into battle. Each story is framed by a conflict between nations or by a grassroots revolution demanding rights for citizens, giving readers a sense of time and place. Readers learn the stresses of command and how history regards these leaders. These biographies range from concise profiles to detailed accounts that require many evenings of reading.

Military Lives are biographies of individuals who make a life of serving in the armed forces. Although these narratives include some battle stories, they focus on an individual's professional career, identifying assignments and promotions in rank. The authors of these books generally tell how their subjects discovered their vocation, how they trained, and how they conducted themselves in command. Whereas some concise biography series depict career soldiers, most of these books are longer, more detailed accounts for dedicated readers.

Axelrod, Alan

Bradley. Palgrave Macmillan, 2008. 204p. <u>Great Generals Series</u>. ISBN 97802-30600188. Audiobook available.

According to military historian Alan Axelrod, General Omar Bradley (1893–1981), who directed American ground troops across Northern Africa and Europe during World War II, was the least known of the high commanders of the war because he was the least interested in his reputation and legacy. Military fame was not his goal. He only chose to attend the U.S. Military Academy to play sports and get a college degree, but once there he excelled in the subject of military strategy, which led to his becoming an officer. With his concern for the safety of individual soldiers and his disavowal of bold tactics, he was the general who most influenced the tactics of heavy firepower used in the wars in Korea and Vietnam. This is a concise account of the World War II leader who Axelrod says is most revered by veterans.

Subjects: Bradley, Omar; Generals; Korean War; Quick Reads; World War I; World War II

Now Try: Bradley wrote two memoirs about his career, *A Soldier's Story* and *A General's Life*. As Commander in Chief of the U.S. Pacific Fleet, Bradley's contemporary, Admiral Chester W. Nimitz, directed the island-hopping strategy that removed the Japanese Navy from the ocean in World War II. *Nimitz* by E. B. Potter from the Naval Institute Press (a good source for naval history books) depicts the admiral as a steady and distinguished commander. Bradley's "only doing my job" attitude resembles the philosophy of Daniel Boone, who never sought glory when leading settlers into the American frontier. Robert Morgan describes the woodsman as a peaceful environmentalist in *Boone: A Biography* (see chapter 5). Just as Bradley was concerned for his soldiers, Milton S. Hershey cared for his chocolate factory workers. Michael D'Antonio tells how the candy maker built his company town in *Hershey: Milton S. Hershey's Extraordinary Life of Wealth, Empire, and Utopian Dreams* (see chapter 9).

Coram, Robert

American Patriot: The Life and Wars of Colonel Bud Day. Little, Brown, 2007. 400p. ISBN 9780316758475.

Military men live by a "code of honor and loyalty," says Robert Coram. His example is the highly decorated soldier Colonel Bud Day (1925–), who fought in three wars as a Marine Corps pilot. After flying many bombing missions, Day was shot down over North Vietnam and spent over five years as a prisoner of war along with future senator John McCain. Since the Vietnam War he has been a successful lawyer and frequent advocate for veterans. In this admiring biography, Coram portrays the colonel as a formidable enemy in war and politics.

Subjects: Colonels; Day, George E.; Soldiers; Vietnam War

Now Try: Robert Coram tells another airman's story in *Boyd: The Fighter Pilot Who Changed the Art of War*. In *Faith of My Fathers*, Senator John McCain recounts how his experience in the Vietnam War followed the war experiences of his father and grandfather. A retired officer who continued to act like a soldier in civilian life was Rick Rescorla, who, as head of security for Morgan Stanley, succeeded in getting all of the company's employees safely out of the World Trade Center but lost his own life in the terrorist attack in 2001. James B. Stewart tells Rescorla's story in *Heart of a Soldier: A Story of Love, Heroism, and September 11.* Day's personality resembles that of another famous fighter pilot, baseball star Ted Williams. The Red Sox outfielder's life on and off the field is entertainingly told by Leigh Montville in *Ted Williams: The Biography of an American Hero*.

DeYoung, Karen

Soldier: The Life of Colin Powell. Knopf, 2006. 610p. ISBN 1400041708. Audiobook available.

General Colin Powell (1937–), once called "the most trusted man in America," advanced through the ranks of the U.S. Army and served in the administrations of presidents of both political parties with his good reputation intact. Then he became entangled in the Iraq War controversy of the George W. Bush administration. Why did he continue in an administration that often did not heed his advice? In presenting his life and career, journalist Karen DeYoung admiringly portrays Powell as a loyal soldier who obeyed commands regardless of his personal beliefs, having less concern for his reputation than a career politician would, and as a man still worthy of trust.

Subjects: African Americans; Generals; Persian Gulf War; Powell, Colin L.; Statesmen; Vietnam War

Now Try: Written after he retired from the army, Powell recalls his youth and military service in the best-selling autobiography *My American Journey*. Like Powell, General H. Norman Schwarzkopf became well known during the Persian Gulf War of 1991. He describes military life and his rise through the ranks in his memoir, *It Doesn't Take a Hero*. The commander of allied air forces in the Persian Gulf War, General Chuck Horner, is profiled by popular war novelist Tom Clancy in *Every Man a Tiger*. Like Powell, football pioneer Red Grange was well liked throughout every phase of his career. He stayed in the news after his playing days ended by becoming a radio and sports executive. His mostly happy life is told through a series of essays in *Red Grange and the Rise of Modern Football* by John M. Carroll (see chapter 12).

Frank, Richard B.

MacArthur: A Biography. Palgrave Macmillan, 2007. <u>Great Generals Series</u>. 198p. ISBN 9781403976581. Audiobook available.

Like his father before him, Douglas MacArthur (1880–1964) was a highly decorated war hero who fought in several wars during a career that lasted over half a century. In this first book in the <u>Great Generals Series</u>, Richard B. Frank chronicles the controversial general's career, from graduating first in his class at West Point to his removal from Korea for his failure to act as directed by President Truman. This compact biography offers an admiring yet candid account to introduce the general to a new generation of readers.

Subjects: Generals; Korean War; MacArthur, Douglas; Quick Reads; World War I; World War II

Now Try: For those wanting more about MacArthur, William Manchester describes the career of the egotistic general in much greater detail in his prize-winning *American Caesar: Douglas MacArthur, 1880–1964*. Like many generals, MacArthur also wrote a memoir; his is titled *Reminiscences*. Architect Frank Lloyd Wright was as certain of his superiority over other men as MacArthur was. Readers who like concise biographies will enjoy *Frank Lloyd Wright* by Ada Louise Huxtable (see chapter 7). Warlike and determined to have his way, MacArthur's personality resembled that of President Andrew Jackson. In *The Passions of Andrew Jackson,* Andrew Burstein tells how as a general fighting the Seminoles Indians, Jackson exceeded President Monroe's directive to protect a border and conquered Florida. Physicist J. Robert Oppenheimer was an outspoken figure who also upset politicians with his frank assessments. Kai Bird and Martin J. Sherwin portray Oppenheimer as a man of conscience in a dark period of American history in *American Prometheus: The Triumph and Tragedy of J. Robert Oppenheimer* (see chapter 11).

Freeman, Philip

Julius Caesar. Simon & Schuster, 2008. 405p. ISBN 9780743289535.

Unlike Marc Anthony in Shakespeare's play *Julius Caesar*, Philip Freeman does intend to praise Julius Caesar (100–44 BCE) for his many glorious accomplishments. Born of a noble but impoverished family, Caesar rose through the ranks quickly to become a great general; he inspired his troops with great oratory and clever tactics during military campaigns that doubled the size of the Roman Empire. He further used his talent for persuasive speech to become a successful lawyer and politician, ultimately becoming Rome's dictator. Although the author admits that Caesar was sometimes ruthless and cruel, he praises the Roman leader's military and political savvy in this engrossing biography.

Subjects: Caesar, Julius; Dictators; Generals; Roman Empire

Now Try: Julius Caesar wrote commentaries about his battles in what is now France, Britain, and Germany in *The Battle for Gaul*. The great Roman statesman Marcus Tillius Cicero led a political coalition that held the Roman Empire together temporarily after Julius Caesar's assassination by Cicero's close friends Marcus Junius Brutus and Caius Cassius Longinus. In *Cicero: The Life and Times of Rome's Greatest Politician* (see chapter 10), Anthony Everitt examines the life of the great orator who was Rome's last republican leader. Readers who enjoy stories about the struggle for power in Rome may enjoy the fictional memoir *I, Claudius: From the Autobiography of Tiberius Claudius, Born B.C. 10, Murdered and Deified A.D. 54* by Robert Graves. In *Emperor of Japan: Meiji and His World, 1852–1912*, Donald Keene describes the life of an absolute ruler, proclaimed to be a god, who led his country to military victories over China and Russia.

Johnson, Paul

Napoleon. Lipper/Viking, 2002. 190p. <u>Penguin Lives</u>. ISBN 0670030783. Audiobook and large print available.

French military dictator Napoleon Bonaparte (1769–1821) is one of history's best examples of an individual whose will to rule overcame a society's will to be free. According to historian Paul Johnson, the native of Corsica was a great opportunist who rose through the ranks of the French army to grab control in the wake of the horrors of the French Revolution. Once in control of the army, Napoleon took over the country and set his sights on conquering Europe. Masterful at military strategy, he had no understanding of political compromise and made many enemies, which eventually led to his downfall. In this concise and intimate biography, Johnson portrays Napoleon as a man whose total trust in his own power blinded his military sense in the end.

Subjects: Bonaparte, Napoleon; France; Generals; Group Discussion Books

Now Try: Philip G. Dwyer focuses on Napoleon's early military years and rise to power in his lengthy *Napoleon: The Path to Power*. Historian David Bell Avrom claims that Napoleon's legacy is that war is no longer limited to battlefields in *The First Total War: Napoleon's Europe and the Birth of War as We Know It*. Like Napoleon, Iraqi cleric Muqtada Al-Sadr is an opportunist, who established himself as a dictator over the city of Najaf after the American invasion of his country. And like the French emperor, he aspires to rule a nation. Patrick Cockburn describes this Iraqi whom most Americans do not understand in *Muqtada: Muqtada Al-Sadr, the Shia Revival, and the Struggle for Iraq*. Napoleon has often been compared with Macedonian king Alexander the Great, who led his conquering army far across Asia. Michael Wood describes the warrior and his conquest in *In the Footsteps of Alexander the Great: A Journey from Greece to Asia*.

Korda, Michael

Ike: An American Hero. Harper, 2007. 779p. ISBN 9780060756659.

General George S. Patton thought General Dwight D. Eisenhower (1890–1969) was overly cautious in pursuing the Germans near the end of World War II. British commanders complained that Eisenhower was a poor strategist. The American public, however, saw him as a grandfatherly hero, calm and trustworthy. They even elected him president in 1952 and 1956. Author Michael Korda brings forth both military and political evidence to restore Eisenhower's reputation in this admiring account of the general's long and celebrated career.

> **Subjects:** Eisenhower, Dwight D.; Generals; Presidents; World War II

> **Now Try:** Further stories about Eisenhower are found in *15 Stars: Eisenhower, MacArthur, Marshall: Three Generals Who Saved the American Century* by Stanley Weintraub. Artist Norman Rockwell, who illustrated covers of many popular American magazines, was a contemporary of Eisenhower. How he came to gain his beloved grandfatherly image is told in *Norman Rockwell: A Life* by Laura Claridge (see chapter 7). British poet Alfred Lord Tennyson was a reserved gentleman loved by the British public. Norman Page includes many photographs, cartoons, and woodcuts with his complimentary text in *Tennyson: An Illustrated Life* (see chapter 7). Actor Jimmy Stewart had a folksy demeanor and reserve similar to Eisenhower's. Marc Eliot tells the story of a great actor, describing his military career, his political evolution away from populism to conservatism, and the family and personal relationships that shaped his life in *Jimmy Stewart: A Biography* (see chapter 8).

Lengel, Edward G.

General George Washington: A Military Life. Random House, 2005. 450p. ISBN 1400060818. Audiobook available.

According to historian Edward G. Lengel, the military reputation of George Washington (1732–1799) has risen and fallen with the mood of historical scholarship. For many years after Washington's death, biographers praised him as a dynamic, victorious general, but in the 1930s scholars began to point out his failings. Eventually the consensus became that Washington and his volunteers prevailed in the American Revolution because he made fewer mistakes than the British generals did. Lengel seeks a middle ground in this military biography, portraying Washington as an admirable citizen-soldier whose steady persistence and dedication ultimately brought victory.

> **Subjects:** American Revolution; French and Indian War; Generals; Washington, George

> **Now Try:** The general's own views of the American Revolution are included in the Library of America collection *Writings* by George Washington. Some scholars have suggested that Washington could not have held his forces together if his wife Martha had not been present at Valley Forge, charming the troops and finding them food and clothing. Patricia Brady portrays Mrs. Washington as a formidable woman in *Martha Washington: An American Life* (see chapter 10). Simon Bolivar helped free six colonies from Spanish rule in the nineteenth century, for which he is often called "The George Washington

of South America." John Lynch tells how Bolivar, like Washington, feared total democracy and preferred rule by the upper classes, in *Simon Bolivar: A Life*. James R. Hansen depicts the first astronaut to step on the moon as a steady, persistent leader who served his country both in war and in peace, in *First Man: The Life of Neil A. Armstrong* (see chapter 1).

McFeely, William S.

Ulysses S. Grant: An Album. Norton, 2004. 144p. ISBN 0393020320.

As the Union general most credited with winning the American Civil War, Ulysses S. Grant (1822–1885) was the subject of many drawings and photographs. From the moment of his fame as victorious general at the Battle of Vicksburg, through his presidency, and to his death, Grant's battles, travels, dinners, and speeches were illustrated for newspapers and magazines. In this attractive book, Pulitzer Prize–winning author William S. McFeely uses these and other pertinent images to illustrate seven essays about Grant's life, work, and legacy.

> **Subjects:** Biographical Essays; Civil War; Generals; Grant, Ulysses S.; Mexican–American War; Photographic Biography; Presidents; Teen Reads

> **Now Try:** Jean Edward Smith tells a more detailed story of the general's life in her award-winning *Grant*. The autobiographical writings of the general are available in many editions, including a volume from the Library of America, *Memoirs and Selected Letters : Personal Memoirs of U.S. Grant, Selected Letters, 1839–1865*. The Union general's name is often paired with that of the Confederate leader Robert E. Lee. Lee is deftly portrayed in a volume from the <u>Penguin Lives</u>, *Robert E. Lee* by Roy Blount Jr. President John F. Kennedy is known for using his youthful image effectively to win the office in 1960 and to garner public support while in office. Yann-Brice Dherbier and Pierre-Henri Verlhac use many familiar images to tell about his life and presidency in *John Fitzgerald Kennedy: A Life in Pictures* (see chapter 10). A Midwesterner like Grant, American author Mark Twain became a celebrity of the Gilded Age. Ron Powers chronicles the career of a humorist who identified the American spirit through his stories in *Mark Twain: A Life* (see chapter 7).

Sugden, John

Tecumseh: A Life. Henry Holt, 1997. 492p. ISBN 0805041389.

If the Native Americans had succeeded in protecting their lands from the expansion of white settlers in the early nineteenth century, Shawnee chief Tecumseh (1768?–1813) would be remembered as the essential leader who brought together all the tribes. Born in Ohio in the 1760s, Tecumseh was a grand orator who traveled from the Gulf of Mexico to Canada with his message of unity. Intertribal warfare and betrayal by British allies, however, undermined his cause, and Tecumseh died in a battle in Ontario in 1813. In this sympathetic biography, historian John Sugden portrays a courageous warrior with a greater understanding of the stakes of history than others of his time had.

> **Subjects:** Chiefs; Native Americans; Shawnees; Tecumseh; Warriors

> **Now Try:** Colin G. Calloway argues that it was not always apparent that Tecumseh and the Shawnees would lose their war, in *Shawnees and the War for America*. In a volume from the <u>American Heroes</u>, Candy Vyvey Moulton describes the life of another eloquent Native American, in *Chief Joseph: Guardian of the People*. Like Tecumseh, politician William Jennings Bryan was known for his eloquent, impassioned speeches. As a

member of the minority party and frequent candidate for president, he was usually unsuccessful in his quests. Michael Kazin chronicles his career in *A Godly Hero: The Life of William Jennings Bryan* (see chapter 10). In the first century CE, Queen Boudica of Britain also fought in vain to remove a foreign force from her land. Vanessa Collingridge examines the truth of the legends about the queen in *Boudica: The Life of Britain's Legendary Warrior Queen* (see chapter 5).

Thomas, Evan

John Paul Jones: Sailor, Hero, Father of the American Navy. Simon & Schuster, 2003. 383p. ISBN 0743205839. Audiobook and large print available.

Captain John Paul Jones (1747–1792) is a familiar name to many Americans, and he is called "The Father of the American Navy," but few remember anything more about him than his famous quotation, "I have not yet begun to fight." To resurrect his memory, *Newsweek* editor Evan Thomas wrote this tribute describing the hero's upbringing and career. Though the skillful captain defeated better-armed British ships during the American Revolution, he was left unemployed when the U.S. Navy disbanded after the war. After wandering Europe looking for a navy and then serving two years as a rear admiral in the Russian Navy, he died in Paris of what was probably scarlet fever, while waiting to become the U.S. Commissioner to Algiers. The tragedy of Jones's story will touch many readers.

> **Subjects:** American Revolution; Captains; Jones, John Paul; United States Navy

> **Now Try:** How untried Americans like Jones could defeat ships of the British Navy is ascribed to British corruption and foolishness by Barbara Tuchman in *First Salute*. Samuel Adams is another often overlooked figure from the American Revolution. Both Jones and Adams were left out of the new government after the war. Mark Puls describes how Adams led the colonial protests that caused the British Army to attack Lexington and Concord in *Samuel Adams: Father of the American Revolution*. Like Jones, Western novelist Zane Grey's time to enjoy his fame was short. Unsatisfied with book royalties and name recognition, he wandered the globe looking for adventure. His melancholy story is told by Thomas H. Pauly in *Zane Grey: His Life, His Adventures, His Women* (see chapter 7). Like Jones, Chester Himes left the United States, where the public was not buying novels written by African Americans. James Sallis tells how this well-regarded contemporary of F. Scott Fitzgerald and Ernest Hemingway finally found a reading audience in France, in *Chester Himes: A Life* (see chapter 7).

Casualties of War

It is not just military people who endure war. Throughout history civilians have suffered at the hands of invading armies. They have lost their land, homes, property, food, freedom, dignity, and lives as the rules of law were suspended or ignored. Their stories tend to be tragic unless the civilians are particularly clever.

In this section are biographies of noncombatants who survived or perished in times of war. In *House of Abraham: Lincoln and the Todds, a Family Divided by War*, Stephen Berry tells how the newly elected president saw his wife's family torn apart as siblings lined up to fight for and against the right of the Southern states to leave the Union. In *The Zookeeper's Wife: A War Story* by Diane Ackerman, the civilians outwit their military oppressors to save lives and retain dignity.

The most tragic and most inspiring stories in the chapter can be found in this section. Readers may see themselves in the characters. The settings are generally communities horribly altered by the actions of military dictators, invading armed forces, or over-zealous governments. Injustice and tragedy are common elements, as are courage and determination. The settings are charged with danger in these compelling, relatively quick reads.

Casualties of War stories are biographies of civilians who struggled to survive war. Whether they were on the battle front or behind the lines, the central characters in these stories faced life or death choices that demanded a brave response. The books in this section are compelling reads.

Ackerman, Diane

🐾 *The Zookeeper's Wife: A War Story.* W. W. Norton, 2007. 367p. ISBN 97803930-61727. Audiobook and large print available.

Jan Żabiński (1897–1974) and his wife Antonina (1908–?) were gentle people who met at Warsaw's College of Agriculture, discovered their mutual love of animals, and married. They rejoiced in 1929 when Jan won the position of keeper of the Warsaw Zoo, not knowing that the invasion of Poland by Nazi troops over a decade later would bring them terrible life-and-death choices. In her novel-like narrative, essayist and poet Diane Ackerman recounts how the Żabińskis made the zoo with its many sheds, shelters, and passages into a refuge for endangered Jews. Readers looking for profiles of courage will likely enjoy this unusual Holocaust story.

Subjects: Group Discussion Books; Holocaust; Poland; Teen Reads; World War II; Żabiński, Antonina; Żabiński, Jan; Zoos

Awards: ALA Notable Books

Now Try: In *The Heart Has Reasons: Holocaust Rescuers and Their Stories of Courage*, Mark Klempner retells the dangerous adventures of the Dutch rescuers who transported Jews out of Amsterdam to villages and farms. The novel *Suite Française* by Irène Némirovsky tells another story of people surviving Nazi occupation during World War II. Lillian Hellman relays a tragic story about a Jewish friend in Nazi Germany in her memoir, *Pentimento*. Gretchen Holbrook Gerzina shares a story of the courageous couple who faced racial prejudice in colonial Massachusetts in *Mr. and Mrs. Prince: How an Extraordinary Eighteenth-Century Family Moved out of Slavery and into Legend* (see chapter 9). Readers who enjoy reading about animals may enjoy *Shaggy Muses: The Dogs Who Inspired Virginia Woolf, Emily Dickinson, Elizabeth Barrett Browning, Edith Wharton, and Emily Brontë* by Maureen Adams.

Berry, Stephen

House of Abraham: Lincoln and the Todds, a Family Divided by War. Houghton Mifflin, 2007. 255p. ISBN 9780618420056. Audiobook available.

As an adult Abraham Lincoln (1809–1865) became a Todd, according to historian Stephen Berry. With no living close relations, he spent much of his time with his wife's family, to whom he owed the success of his law practice and political career. In appreciation, he appointed many of his Todd in-laws to political and military positions, and he always kept his home (even the White House) open to them. For the Kentucky family with roots in the state's early settlement, the Civil War became a tragedy, as five of Mary Todd Lincoln's siblings sided with the Union, and the other eight with the Confederacy. In this family biography, the author chronicles the lives of Todd family members before and throughout the course of the war, completing their story with a thoughtful epilogue.

> **Subjects:** Civil War; Family Biography; Group Discussion Books; Kentucky; Lincoln, Abraham; Presidents; Teen Reads; Todd Family

> **Now Try:** Michael A. Dreese recounts the migration of family members to the Gettysburg battlefield to find their fallen sons, husbands, and fathers in *Torn Families: Death and Kinship at the Battle of Gettysburg*. Disagreements over art, not war, divided the Clark family, heirs to the Singer Sewing Machine fortune. Nicholas Fox Weber profiles the prominent family members in his collective biography *The Clarks of Cooperstown: Their Singer Sewing Machine Fortune, Their Great and Influential Art Collections, Their Forty-Year Feud* (see chapter 8). Britain's Mitford family was torn by the political dissention among its six sisters. Mary S. Lovell tells many dramatic stories in *Sisters: The Saga of the Mitford Family* (see chapter 9). Louis B. Leakey, his wife Mary, and his son Richard were all noted anthropologists who worked in East Africa. Virginia Morell tells how the Leakeys survived field work in the Olduvai Gorge in Tanzania, attacks by conservative scientists, and even family fights, in *Ancestral Passions: The Leakey Family and the Quest for Humankind's Beginnings* (see chapter 11).

Chong, Denise

The Girl in the Picture: The Story of Kim Phuc, the Photograph, and the Vietnam War. Viking, 1999. 373p. ISBN 067088040X. Audiobook available.

Everyone knows the Vietnam War picture of Kim Phuc (1963–), a naked nine-year-old Vietnamese girl running and screaming from the pain of being burned by napalm. After this stunning photograph ran in newspapers around the world, young Kim became a pawn in a Vietnamese propaganda campaign against U.S. involvement in the war. Eventually she escaped from her country and settled in Canada, where she tried to forget her past. Author Denise Chong tells a sympathetic story about an innocent young woman who lives with nightmares and remains a symbol of the suffering of civilians in the path of war.

> **Subjects:** Group Discussion Books; Kim Phuc; Teen Reads; Vietnam War; War Victims

> **Now Try:** Another famous war picture is at the heart of *Flags of Our Fathers*, the book that James Bradley wrote about his father and the men with whom he

served at Iwo Jima. Readers who like stories behind famous photos will enjoy *Daring to Look: Dorothea Lange's Photographs and Reports from the Field* by Anne Whiston Spirn, which tells how the photographer documented the Great Depression. In *Home Before Morning: The Story of an Army Nurse in Vietnam*, Lynda Van Devanter describes the hurt that she feels when family and friends will not look at her pictures of war. Harold G. Moore and Joseph L. Galloway describe their Vietnam memories thirty years after the war in *We Are Soldiers Still: A Journey Back to the Battlefields of Vietnam*.

Lee, Carol Ann

The Hidden Life of Otto Frank. William Morrow, 2002. 411p. ISBN 0060520825.

Holocaust victim Anne Frank was not the only member of her family to keep a diary. From the time of his release at Auschwitz until his return to Amsterdam in 1945, her father, Otto Frank (1889–1980), wrote daily about his liberation and desperate search for his family. Using this diary, many letters, and recorded interviews, Carol Lee describes a heartbroken man who had willingly fought for Germany in World War I and even sold black market spices to the Nazis, but had still been expelled from his homeland and sent to a concentration camp for being Jewish. In this bittersweet tale, she also describes the difficulty that he had selling Anne's diary to publishers and uncovers the identity of the Dutch man who betrayed the family to the Nazis.

Subjects: Amsterdam; Frank, Anne; Frank, Otto; Holocaust; Jews; Netherlands; World War II

Now Try: Anne Frank's diary is available in many editions. *Diary of a Young Girl: The Definitive Edition* published by Doubleday in 1995 restores much of the text that had been suppressed in earlier editions. In *The Pianist: The Extraordinary True Story of One Man's Survival in Warsaw, 1939–1945*, concert pianist Wladyslaw Szpilman tells how he survived during the Holocaust in Poland. Former baseball player Moe Berg was mentally altered by World War II. In *The Catcher Was a Spy: The Mysterious Life of Moe Berg* (see chapter 5), Nicholas Dawidoff follows Berg's trail through the war and its aftermath to find out what transformed the self-assured man into a wanderer. Life for Mary Shelley was difficult after the death of her mother and her husband, the poet Percy B. Shelley. She was a single parent with debts and many manuscripts to edit. Her story of endurance is elegantly told by novelist Muriel Spark in *Mary Shelley: A Biography* (see chapter 7). Socialite Ruth Harkness took up her dead husband's quest to bring a live panda back from China to America. Her dramatic story is told in *The Lady and the Panda: The True Adventures of the First American Explorer to Bring Back China's Most Exotic Animal* by Vicki Constantine Croke (see chapter 1).

Espionage and Intrigue

Battles and wars are often lost when commanders have faulty information about enemy positions, numerical strength, and weapons. Trying to gain strategic advantages and avoid disasters, military leaders conscript spies to infiltrate enemy headquarters. To be successful, these agents must be unlikely spies, a scenario ripe for unusual stories.

In these biographies, wartime spies utilized a variety of interesting ruses to maintain their cover. In *The Golden Warrior: The Life and Legend of Lawrence of Arabia*, Lawrence James describes how T. E. Lawrence used the cover of an interest in archeology when sent to the Middle East to gather information that helped Britain break up the Turkish empire. Larry Berman describes Vietnamese reporter Pham Xuan An as a friendly *Time* correspondent who interviewed American military commanders in *Perfect Spy: The Incredible Double Life of Pham Xuan An*, Time *Magazine Reporter and Vietnamese Communist Agent.* Ann Blackman depicts a Washington matron who stole Union Army secrets for the Confederacy at parties within view of the White House, in *Wild Rose: Rose O'Neale Greenhow, Civil War Spy.*

The biographies in this section are the most unusual and amusing titles in this chapter. The characters are crafty, cunning, and courageous. The settings are hotspots of military espionage, including capital cities and communities along battle lines. Some read like mystery or suspense novels, tense and atmospheric. Most of the titles are of moderate length and can be described as fast reads.

Espionage and Intrigue stories include biographies of secretive figures who go into enemy territory to gain strategic information for their armed forces. Danger and intrigue are necessary elements in these stories, which tend to be unhurried so that dramatic tension may build.

Berman, Larry

Perfect Spy: The Incredible Double Life of Pham Xuan An, Time *Magazine Reporter and Vietnamese Communist Agent.* Smithsonian Books, 2007. 328p. ISBN 9780060888381.

Vietnamese spy Pham Xuan An (1927–2006) told Larry Berman that he never wrote an autobiography because he knew too many secrets that "would harm the living and the families of the dead." However, he told many revealing stories to the author about delivering classified information to the North Vietnamese. Pham, who attended Orange Coast College in California and landed a war assignment with *Time* magazine, became great friends with many American military officials who never knew of his deception until after the war. Incredibly, he was able to renew many of his friendships after the thawing of Vietnamese and American relations. Berman's book takes an unusually sympathetic look at an enemy.

Subjects: Group Discussion Books; Journalists; Pham, Xuan An; Spies; Vietnam War

Now Try: Magician Harry Houdini was never suspected of being a spy. William Kalush and Larry Sloman tell how Houdini's fame let him hide his work as a spy in *The Secret Life of Houdini: The Making of America's First Superhero* (see chapter 5). Of course there were American spies operating in Hanoi during the Vietnam War, as Richard H. Shultz recounts in *Secret War Against Hanoi: Kennedy and Johnson's Use of Spies, Saboteurs, and Covert Warriors in North Vietnam*. With his spying for the Nazis on one hand and his saving the lives of Jews on the other, it is difficult to judge German industrialist

Oskar Schindler. David M. Crowe examines the German's life in *Oskar Schindler: The Untold Account of His Life, Wartime Activities, and the True Story Behind the List* (see chapter 5). Like An, Senator Bob Kerrey of Nebraska saw and contributed to many deaths during the course of the Vietnam War. Gregory L. Vistica tells how the war record of the senator hampered his effort to become president in *The Education of Lieutenant Kerrey* (see chapter 5).

Blackman, Ann

Wild Rose: Rose O'Neale Greenhow, Civil War Spy. Random House, 2005. 377p. ISBN 1400061180.

Within view of the White House, Rose O'Neale Greenhow (1817–1864) entertained statesmen, diplomats, and other dignitaries of every political persuasion in her Washington home. A personal favorite of President James Buchanan, she was often seen at social functions about the city. Her niece married Stephen A. Douglas. Who would suspect she headed a spy ring that in the early days of the Civil War warned Southern troops of Northern movements that might have ended the conflict quickly? Her Confederate sympathies were known, however, and she was soon caught and exiled to the Southern states for the duration of the war. Ann Blackman portrays Greenhow as a resourceful woman with abhorrent racial attitudes and a disregard for danger, in this true Civil War spy story.

Subjects: Civil War; Greenhow, Rose O'Neale; Spies; Washington (DC); Women

Now Try: The Union also had a female spy under the noses of the Confederate leaders in Richmond, Virginia. Elizabeth R. Varon tells the story in *Southern Lady, Yankee Spy: The True Story of Elizabeth Van Lew, a Union Agent in the Heart of the Confederacy* (see this chapter). Catherine Allgor describes Dolley Madison's role as Washington hostess in her admiring *A Perfect Union: Dolley Madison and the Creation of the American Nation* (see chapter 10), and Stacy A. Cordery chronicles Alice Roosevelt's many years as a leading hostess in *Alice: Alice Roosevelt Longworth, from White House Princess to Washington Power Broker* (see chapter 10). As a costume designer for Hollywood stars, Edith Head had access to much confidential information. David Chiericheti portrays the private woman behind the big glasses as an astute studio politician who would never betray an actress, in *Edith Head: The Life and Times of Hollywood's Celebrated Costume Designer* (see chapter 8).

Conradi, Peter

Hitler's Piano Player: The Rise and Fall of Ernst Hanfstaengl, Confidant of Hitler, Ally of FDR. Carroll & Graf, 2004. 352p. ISBN 078671283X.

In 1923 Adolf Hitler was impressed that German art dealer Ernst Hanfstaengl (1887–1975), back from running the family gallery in New York, could play Wagner so well on his rickety old piano. Wanting more music, Hitler made him a member of his inner circle. Impressed with the great orator, Hanfstaengl went along, profiting from the relationship, even publishing a Hitler songbook. In this dramatic story, Peter Conradi tells how the pianist fled to America after an assassination attempt on the German leader, and then, after collaborating with Allied intelligence, was deported back to Germany after the war, living out his final years as a distrusted man.

Subjects: Germany; Hanfstaengl, Ernst; Hitler, Adolf; World War II

Now Try: Bernd Freytag von Loringhoven accepted an assignment as aide-de-camp to Hitler's army chief of staff in July 1944. He describes the despair of the final nine months of the Fuhrer's life in his memoir, *In the Bunker with Hitler*. Eva Braun was just a shop clerk and amateur photographer when she caught the eye of Adolf Hitler. Lambert tells the tragic story of Hitler's trusting mistress in *The Lost Life of Eva Braun* (see this chapter). In Italy, ambitious Count Galeazzo Ciano married Benito Mussolini's daughter and joined the fascist's inner circle. When Mussolini aligned his country with Hitler's Germany, Ciano objected. Ray Moseley describes how the son-in-law failed to overthrow the dictator in *Mussolini's Shadow: The Double Life of Count Galeazzo Ciano* (see this chapter). Being a poet gained Geoffrey Chaucer entry into many nobles' courts, making him a witness to the events of his time. Peter Ackroyd describes the great poet and his society in his concise *Chaucer* (see chapter 7).

James, Lawrence

The Golden Warrior: The Life and Legend of Lawrence of Arabia. Paragon House, 1993. 406p. ISBN 1557785791.

When the First World War began, Thomas Edward Lawrence (1888–1935), a restless young academic with knowledge of the Arabic language and culture, relished his intelligence assignment to the Middle East, where he helped spark the Arab revolt against Turkey. In this careful investigation into the life of the man who became Lawrence of Arabia, military historian Lawrence James asserts that the American and British public needed a heroic figure to lift spirits shocked by the brutality of the trench warfare in Europe. With a bit of artifice, journalist Lowell Thomas shaped Lawrence into a golden hero in a clean war. Lawrence willingly played the role and even embellished upon it in his own writings.

> **Subjects:** Arab Revolt; Great Britain; Lawrence, T. E. (Thomas Edward); Middle East; Soldiers; World War I

> **Now Try:** Lawrence wrote disparagingly about the Arab war in *Revolt in the Desert*. He was jealous of British archeologist and diplomat Gertrude Bell, whose work in the Middle East had a more lasting effect. Her adventurous story is told in *Gertrude Bell: Queen of the Desert, Shaper of Nations* by Georgina Howell (see chapter 1). Somerset Maugham is another adventurous yet melancholy British character who meddled in the affairs of other nations. Jeffrey Meyers chronicles his international activities in *Somerset Maugham* (see chapter 7). Like Lawrence, Japanese artist Foujita, an unsettled character, appeared to cross cultural boundaries successfully, but then retreated to his homeland. Phyllis Birnbaum tells his sad story in *Glory in a Line: A Life of Foujita, the Artist Caught between East & West* (see chapter 7).

Koch, Stephen

The Breaking Point: Hemingway, Dos Passos, and the Murder of José Robles. Counterpoint, 2005. 318p. ISBN 1582432805.

When novelists Ernest Hemingway (1899–1961) and John Dos Passos (1896–1970) met in war-torn Madrid in 1937, their long friendship was already strained by jealousy and by Hemingway's worsening alcoholism. Twenty years after meeting as ambulance drivers in World War I, they found that they viewed the disappearance of Dos Passos's close friend, Spaniard José Robles, differently. Hemingway already knew that Robles was dead but kept that fact from Dos Passos, who futilely questioned Spanish officials. In the meantime, both writers were surrounded by spies who were trying to use them to discover factional intelligence. In this compelling dual biography, novelist Stephen Koch tells the story of a failing friendship against the backdrop of a war and among a cast of international republicans, fascists, and communists.

Subjects: Dos Passos, John; Dual Biography; Hemingway, Ernest; Murder; Novelists; Spanish Civil War

Now Try: Hemingway romanticized the war in Spain in his novel *For Whom the Bell Tolls*. Dos Passos recounted his Spanish travels and the death of his friend in several pieces in *Travel Books and Other Writings*, a volume in the Library of America series. In *Homage to Catalonia*, George Orwell tells of his terrible experiences as a soldier in the war. When supposedly similar people are brought together, their differences are often revealed. Such is the case in *The Yellow House: Van Gogh, Gauguin, and Nine Turbulent Weeks in Arles* by Martin Gayford (see chapter 7). The working relationship between black separatist Elijah Muhammad and his follower, Malcolm X, soured over ideals for the Nation of Islam. Karl Evanzz questions whether the leader murdered the disciple in his exposé of Muhammad, *The Messenger: The Rise and Fall of Elijah Muhammad* (see chapter 5).

Macintyre, Ben

Agent Zigzag: A True Story of Nazi Espionage, Love, and Betrayal. Harmony Books, 2007. 364p. ISBN 9780307353405. Audiobook available.

Eddie Chapman (1914–1997) was a clever man. Also known to British police as Edward Edwards, Edward Simpson, and Arnold Thompson, he transformed himself from small-time crook to wartime double agent, whose allegiance is still doubted. Using declassified MI5 documents and Chapman's unreliable autobiography, author Ben Macintyre analyzes the actions of one of World Wars II's most unusual spies.

Subjects: Chapman, Edward Arnold; Spies; World War II

Now Try: The number of copies of the 1954 autobiography *The Eddie Chapman Story* in libraries is limited, but it can be ordered through interlibrary loan. The British have a history of their citizens spying for other countries. In *My Five Cambridge Friends : Burgess, Maclean, Philby, Blunt, and Cairncross by Their KGB Controller*, KGB agent Yuri Modin recounts the story of the Cambridge Five, who were British academics who doubled as Soviet spies. Andrew Meier tells about an American academic, Isaiah Oggins, who became a Soviet spy, in *The Lost Spy: An American in Stalin's Secret Service*. Like Chapman, pickpocket George Appo was a clever character who could turn getting caught and punished for pretty crime to his advantage. Timothy J. Gilfoyle tells about the criminal turned entertainer in *A Pickpocket's Tale: The Underworld of Nineteenth Century New York* (see True Crime Biography). Mozart's librettist Lorenzo da Ponte changed his identity several times as he adapted to many economic and political cultures in his roguish life. Rodney Bolt recounts a life full of misadventure in *The Librettist of Venice: The Remarkable Life of Lorenzo da Ponte* (see chapter 7).

Moseley, Ray

Mussolini's Shadow: The Double Life of Count Galeazzo Ciano. Yale University Press, 1999. 302p. ISBN 0300079176.

Colleagues said that Count Galeazzo Ciano (1903–1944) had insured his future in 1930 when he proposed to Edda, Benito Mussolini's daughter. At that point, many world leaders admired how Mussolini was reshaping the Italian economy, making the country one of the bright spots in an economically depressed Europe. The ambitious Ciano joined the family and became Italy's foreign minister in 1936. In this dark story of romance and treason, journalist Ray Moseley tells how Ciano split with Mussolini over the close alliance with Nazi Germany, led a conspiracy to overthrow his father-in-law, and was executed.

> **Subjects:** Ciano, Galeazzo; Fascism; Italy; Politics and Government; Treason; World War II

> **Now Try:** Deception was often necessary for survival during World War II. In *The Nazi Officer's Wife: How One Jewish Woman Survived the Holocaust*, Edith Hahn Beer tells about stealing identity papers, escaping a labor camp, and marrying a German officer who hides her identity. In *This Has Happened: An Italian Family in Auschwitz*, Piera Sonnino describes the death of her family and her own survival when Mussolini's government sent Italian Jews to the Nazi death camps. After the death of Mao Zedong, the contest for power in the Communist Chinese Party was deadly. Madame Mao was one of the principal contestants. Ross Terrill describes her downfall in *The White-Boned Demon: A Biography of Madame Mao Zedong* (see chapter 5). Even honorable men in the court of Henry VIII could lose their lives by displeasing the king. In *The Life of Thomas More* (see chapter 4), Peter Ackroyd describes how More would not bend to the king's wishes.

Palmer, Dave R.

George Washington and Benedict Arnold: A Tale of Two Patriots. Regnery Publishing, 2006. 424p. ISBN 1596980206.

George Washington (1732–1799) and Benedict Arnold (1741–1801) lived similar lives until the latter betrayed the Revolutionary Army by spying for the British. Their affluent, long-established families lost much of their wealth during their childhoods, forcing both to fend for themselves by age fifteen. Later, at the First Continental Congress in Philadelphia, they even competed for the attention of the same woman—the beautiful Peggy Shippen. Although Arnold won the romantic contest, Washington won the appointment to lead their countrymen in war. Dave R. Palmer examines the qualities of character in this psychological comparison of the hero and the traitor.

> **Subjects:** American Revolution; Arnold, Benedict; Dual Biography; Generals; Group Discussion Books; Treason; Washington, George

> **Now Try:** Benedict Arnold was not the only spy during the American Revolution. The lineup of agents for the colonials is described in *Washington's Spies: The Story of America's First Spy Ring* by Alexander Rose. One of the colonial army's most noted spies was Nathan Hale, whose life is described in *Nathan Hale: The Life and Death of America's First Spy* by M. William Phelps. Finding the similarities between two men with different reputations is also the premise

of *The Same Man: George Orwell and Evelyn Waugh* by David Lebedoff. Double agent Edward Arnold Chapman may have betrayed both sides in World War II. Ben Macintyre describes one of World War II's most unusual spies in *Agent Zigzag: A True Story of Nazi Espionage, Love, and Betrayal* (see this chapter).

Varon, Elizabeth R.

Southern Lady, Yankee Spy: The True Story of Elizabeth Van Lew, a Union Agent in the Heart of the Confederacy. Oxford University Press, 2003. 317p. 0195142284.

Before Virginia left the Union at the start of the Civil War, Richmond native Elizabeth Van Lew (1818–1900) showed signs of her disagreement with slavery. The strong-willed woman sold property to free blacks and released some of her slaves. Confederate officials suspected that she did not support their cause, but they never dreamed that a Southern lady would operate a spy ring from the heart of their capital. In this novel-like biography, historian Elizabeth R. Varon describes how Van Lew joined the Richmond underground, helped Union soldiers escape capture, and reported troop movements to Union General Benjamin Butler. Even more courageously, she remained in the city after the war, speaking out for racial justice and women's suffrage even though neighbors scorned her.

Subjects: Civil War; Group Discussion Books; Spies; Teen Reads; Van Lew, Elizabeth; Women

Now Try: Mary E. Lyons describes Van Lew's adventures from the viewpoint of a girl she freed from slavery in a novel for younger readers, *Dear Ellen B.: A Civil War Scrapbook of Two Union Spies.* Marie Jacober recounts Van Lew's life through her ghost in *Only Call Us Faithful: A Novel of the Union Underground.* The memoir *Richmond During the War: Four Years of Personal Observation* by Sallie A. Brock offers another view of the Confederate capital during the war. Actress Fanny Kemble tried to be a good plantation wife after leaving the London stage, but she found she could not tolerate slavery and the attitudes of her husband and neighbors. How she came to write her abolitionist memoir is told in *Fanny Kemble's Civil Wars* by Catherine Clinton (see chapter 9). Like Van Lew, Hull House founder Jane Addams sacrificed her comfortable life to work for social reform. Gioia Diliberto tells how Addams became committed to helping the poor in *A Useful Woman: The Early Life of Jane Addams* (see chapter 4).

War Biography Collections

The books in this section differ from others in this chapter in that they profile many wartime figures instead of one or two. They are to biography what short stories are to fiction. People with only short periods of time to devote to reading will benefit from the brief, satisfying biographical narratives; and readers who wish to sample authors or the lives of characters before committing to reading an entire book will likely also enjoy these collections.

War Biography Collections include books that gather profiles of many similar military characters into a single volume. Authors focus on the key incidents and dominant characteristics in these quick profiles. These works are ideal for more leisurely or interrupted reading.

Ambrose, Stephen E.

1

Comrades: Brothers, Fathers, Heroes, Sons, Pals. Simon & Schuster, 1999. 139p. ISBN 0684867184. Audiobook and large print available.

2

Historian Stephen E. Ambrose celebrates friendship among men in this quick reading collection of biographical essays. Ambrose fans will recognize that many of the men included were the subjects of his longer books, including Dwight Eisenhower, George Armstrong Custer, and the duo of Meriwether Lewis and William Clark. For contrast, he also includes a chapter about how Richard M. Nixon failed to make lasting friends. War figures prominently in this collection, ideal for readers who like biography in small doses.

3

Subjects: Brothers; Collective Biography; Fathers and Sons; Friends; Group Discussion Books; Soldiers

4

Now Try: *Comrades* is a good introduction to *Band of Brothers* and Ambrose's other books, including *Undaunted Courage: Meriwether Lewis, Thomas Jefferson, and the Opening of the American West* and *Crazy Horse and Custer: The Parallel Lives of Two American Warriors*. In an Iraq War memoir, *Blood Brothers: Among the Soldiers of Ward 57*, embedded journalist Michael Weisskopf tells of bonding with amputees at Walter Reed Army Medical Center after losing his own hand in Baghdad. David Halberstam's book about four members of the Boston Red Sox, *Teammates: A Portrait of Friendship* (see chapter 12), also celebrates bonding among men.

5

6

Holmstead, Kirsten

Band of Sisters: American Women at War in Iraq. Stackpole Books, 2007. 327p. ISBN 9780811702676.

7

Lance Corporals Carrie Blais and Priscilla Kispetik of the Marines search Iraqi women and children for hidden weapons. Army Captain Robin Brown pilots a Kiowa Warrior helicopter guarding a convey delivering Iraqi currency to Baghdad. Army Specialist Rachelle Spors transports wounded soldiers into field hospitals. Air Force Lieutenant Colonel Polly Montgomery carries troops and cargo in her C-130 aircraft. Using extensive interviews, Kirsten Holmstead dramatically profiles these and other American military women in daily combat in Iraq.

8

9

Subjects: Iraq War; Soldiers; Teen Reads; Women

Now Try: During World War II, women were among the elite spies serving in the U.S. Office of Strategic Services. Patrick K. O'Donnell tells their story in *Operatives, Spies, and Saboteurs: The Unknown Story of the Men and Women of World War II's OSS*. Profiles of thirty military women who served during World War II are found in *They Also Served: American Women in World War II* by Olga Gruhzit-Hoyt. For more on soldiers in the war in Iraq, try the brutally frank *Heart of War: Soldiers' Voices from the Front Lines in Iraq* by Damon DiMarco.

10

11

12

Sorel, Nancy Caldwell

The Women Who Wrote the War. Arcade Publishing, 1999. 458p. ISBN 1559704934.
Martha Gellhorn, Lee Miller, and Margaret Bourke-White are well known for their stories and photos from the battlefields of World War II, but they were not the only women journalists on the fronts. Journalist Nancy Caldwell Sorel has identified nearly a hundred women who were sent by their newspapers, magazines, wire services, or radio networks to report on the action. Sorel weaves their individual profiles into a larger group biography that tells how these female photographers and reporters followed the troops and filed their stories. Readers interested in World War II veterans may also want to read about these brave women.

> **Subjects:** Group Biography; Journalists; Photographers; Women; World War II
>
> **Now Try:** Women continue to report on wars. Kimberly Dozier recounts her experiences and injury in Iraq in *Breathing the Fire: Fighting to Report—and Survive—the War in Iraq*. Readers wanting books about famous women journalists of the war may choose from *Gellhorn: A Twentieth Century Life* by Caroline Moorehead (see chapter 1), *Lee Miller: A Life* by Carolyn Burke, and *Margaret Bourke-White* by Vicki Goldberg. In the 1950s a group of women with their newly imported sports cars began challenging men on race tracks and in cross-country races. Todd McCarthy tells about these fearless women in his group biography, *Fast Women: The Legendary Ladies of Racing* (see chapter 12). Senator Kay Bailey Hutchinson admiringly tells about more brave and industrious women (some in the military) in her collective biographies *American Heroines* and *Leading Ladies: American Trailblazers* (see chapter 4).

Consider Starting With . . .

These well-written War Biographies of modest length will appeal to general readers.

• Ackerman, Diane. *The Zookeeper's Wife: A War Story.*

• Axelrod, Alan. *Bradley.*

• Berman, Larry. *Perfect Spy: The Incredible Double Life of Pham Xuan An,* **Time Magazine Reporter and Vietnamese Communist Agent.**

• Berry, Stephen. *House of Abraham: Lincoln and the Todds, a Family Divided by War.*

• Johnson, Paul. *Napoleon.*

• Palmer, Dave R. *George Washington and Benedict Arnold: A Tale of Two Patriots.*

• Thomas, Evan. *John Paul Jones: Sailor, Hero, Father of the American Navy.*

• Varon, Elizabeth R. *Southern Lady, Yankee Spy: The True Story of Elizabeth Van Lew, a Union Agent in the Heart of the Confederacy.*

Further Reading

Adamson, Lynda G.

Thematic Guide to Popular Nonfiction. Greenwood Press, 2006. 352p. ISBN 0313-328552.
> Adamson includes chapters about Vietnam War and World War II titles in this in-depth book about nonfiction topics. Each chapter describes a topic and then presents three lengthy reviews before suggesting other titles.

Cords, Sarah Statz

The Real Story: A Guide to Nonfiction Reading Interests. Libraries Unlimited, 2006. 460p. ISBN 1591582830.
> Cords does not have a war section in her book, but there are many war-related titles that can be found using the index.

Wyatt, Neal

The Readers' Advisory Guide to Nonfiction. American Libraries, 2007. 318p. ISBN 9780838909362.
> Wyatt discusses war stories in chapters 10 and 11 of her book and includes a generous list of titles to recommend to readers.

Part 2

Stylistic Genres

Chapter 4

Inspirational Biography

Definition of Inspirational Biography

Inspirational Biography includes books about people whose lives and actions encourage readers to lead better lives. These people may be virtuous or may overcome their own failings to do good deeds. Human rights advocates, peace activists, philanthropists, and religious figures are among the subjects of these biographies.

The inspirational life story has long been a staple of the biography genre. According to Paul Murray Kendall in *Art of Biography* (W. W. Norton, 1965), after St. Augustine wrote his *Confessions* in the fourth century CE, faith-based biography became the primary form of life-writing in the Christian world of Europe and the Near East. As with the gospels before them, the mission of these biographies was to praise good lives lived and to hold them up as models for readers and for listeners who could not read. From the fifth to the fifteenth centuries, most biographies written in the West told stories of saints, people who acted bravely to keep the commandments of the Holy Bible and the Roman Catholic Church. Congregations were instructed in these stories to live faithfully just like the saints and were reassured that there would be a heavenly reward for those who did.

Our world is no longer dominated by church doctrines, but the Inspirational Biography remains popular. Bookstores and libraries feature titles honoring individuals of strong character whose lives serve as examples for readers wanting to live ethical and useful lives. While praising their subjects, biographers often also suggest that readers themselves can change the world for the better. Civil rights historian Adam Fairclough, author of *Martin Luther King, Jr.*, wants readers to be inspired by the life of this Baptist minister from Georgia to work for racial justice. In writing *Jane Goodall: The Woman Who Redefined Man*, Goodall colleague Dale Peterson advocates caring for chimpanzees and other wildlife, contributing to conservation funds, and voting for environmental causes. Senator Kay Bailey Hutchinson encourages women to aspire to be scientists, generals, business executives, and political leaders similar to the subjects in her book *Leading Ladies: American Trailblazers*. Reminiscent of the authors who told the stories of the saints, some modern biographers intend to inspire and convert their readers.

Biographical subjects no longer have to be saints to be inspiring figures. In fact, many people about whom Inspirational Biographies are written had faults that they overcame before their lives became uncommonly good or praiseworthy. Erik H.

Erikson was insecure, Bill Wilson was an alcoholic, and Jane Addams was depressed. If they had not had personal flaws to overcome, their stories would not be compelling. Their marvelous transformations are fine examples for willing readers seeking to improve themselves and the world around them.

> *Inspirational Biography* includes books about people whose lives and actions encourage readers to lead better lives. Throughout history, giving readers examples of good and brave lives to follow has been a primary reason for the writing of biography. In modern biographies, these people may be virtuous or may overcome their own failings to do good deeds. Human rights advocates, peace activists, philanthropists, and religious figures are among the subjects of these biographies.

Appeal of the Genre

Strong characters are a prerequisite for Inspirational Biographies. Without people whose acts proved their courage and moral focus, there is no reason to write these books. Their characterizations may, however, be more idealized than verifiable, as in the cases of some historical legends, such as St. Patrick of Ireland, who brought Christianity to Ireland, or *A Midwife's Tale* by Laurel Thatcher Ulrich, a book about Martha Ballard, an eighteenth-century midwife in Hallowell, Maine. Many others are world famous figures about whom much is known, such as Mahatma Gandhi and Pearl S. Buck. In any case, these individuals must have been capable of the selfless acts for which they are honored.

To be truly inspiring, these biographies must also tell good stories. In some cases, the tales include physical danger and courageous action, such as the life of Sergio Vieira de Mello, whose entire career as a United Nations negotiator consisted of a series of explosive crises. His life is told by Samantha Power in *Chasing the Flame: Sergio Vieira de Mello and the Fight to Save the World*. Other books may lack life-threatening tensions but are no less dramatic; their subjects fight against societal expectations and entrenched opinions to reform their society, such as in *Gentle Subversive: Rachel Carson, Silent Spring, and the Rise of the Environmental Movement* by Mark Hamilton Lytle. In these and other titles, the authors offer intimate views of their subjects' actions and thoughts, letting readers experience their challenges and learn moral lessons.

Setting is secondary to story in the Inspirational Biography. Of course, there must be a challenging situation for the biographical subject, but the situation of time and place does not have to be greatly detailed. The best Inspirational Biographies often do, however, describe the context of the story. In *Buddha*, Karen Armstrong tells as much about India in the sixth century BCE as she does about Gautama Buddha.

The pace of Inspirational Biography may be slower than other biographies. *Helen and Teacher: The Story of Helen Keller and Anne Sullivan Macy* by Joseph P. Lash and *An Unfinished Life: John Kennedy, 1917–1963* by Robert Dallek are among the long leisurely books that detail inspirational lives in full.

Learning and experiencing are very important appeal factors in every book in this chapter, as the authors generally intend that readers examine and alter their own lives after contemplating the actions of the role models profiled. The current field of Inspirational Biography connects with many other genres. If the books in this chapter are not shelved in biography sections of your library, they may be found in the psychology, ethics, religion, philanthropy, civil rights, science, literature, or history sections. These books attract readers interested in inspiration, moral instruction, and personal growth, as well as strong characters and stories.

Look for other stories to inspire readers in the "Human Rights and Social Justice Stories" section of chapter 9.

Organization of the Chapter

This chapter is divided into five sections. The first is "Exemplary Lives." The biographies included in this section portray characters whose lives were wholly admirable, according to their authors. Their careers and lives are exhibited as models for aspiring readers. Mahatma Gandhi, Martin Luther King Jr., Jane Addams, and Harriet Tubman are some of the more famous and obvious subjects. Lesser known subjects are philanthropists, naturalists, novelists, and midwives. They were not saints and might be depicted less favorably in other biographies, but the titles chosen for this section emphasize their positive accomplishments and exemplary qualities.

The subjects of the books in the second section, "Living for a Cause," may not have lived lives that readers want to replicate, but they can be admired for dedicating themselves to selfless causes. They might have been controversial figures, such as suffragette Victoria Woodhull or labor advocate Mother Jones, who broke societal rules and were often condemned by the public, or they might be more popular figures, such as primatologist Jane Goodall and physician Paul Farmer. The authors are often candid about their faults but praise them for their life's work. Readers are inspired by their perseverance and may learn from their methods as well.

In the third section, "Overcoming Adversity," are stories about people who were faced with challenges that threatened their happiness, livelihood, or reputations. The difficulties they overcame were sometimes external, such as fascism, racial discrimination, or poverty; and sometimes internal, such as alcoholism or self-doubt. Their stories show how individuals can meet their challenges and live remarkable lives, which will inspire readers facing their own difficulties.

The fourth section contains "Religious Stories." Like the faith-based biographies of medieval times, these more modern biographies include elements of praise and moral instruction, but are more verifiable than the devotional literature of centuries past. Founders, prophets, saints, clergy, and theologians from various world religions are among the subjects in this section.

In the final section, "Inspirational Collections," are biographical collections. These books, generally theme-based, are to biography what short story collections are to fiction. Readers who enjoy short profiles of inspiring figures that can easily be read in single sittings will appreciate these collections.

Exemplary Lives

In the sixteen biographies in this section, none of the subjects has escaped criticism from detractors, but all have withstood the test of time and are generally regarded favorably in contemporary society for the model lives that they led. For example, a minority of Americans still questions the mission, methods, and legacy of Martin Luther King Jr., but society as a whole has honored him as a hero of the civil rights movement. India is still torn by ethnic violence decades after the assassination of Mahatma Gandhi, but peace advocates around the world still study his teachings and seek to apply his nonviolent principles to resolving conflict. Though none of these leaders was perfect, all were exemplary. The authors of their biographies show why they are worthy of emulation despite their faults, although aspiring readers will find these lives of great discipline difficult to copy. Few people have the opportunity, ability, or courage to live as selflessly as these eminent people did. Still, many will read the exemplary biographies, act in small and manageable ways to improve the world, and dream of doing more.

All of these books feature great characters, yet readers may not recognize all the names in this section. The story of Father Mychal Judge only appeared in the news after his brave death at the World Trade Center on September 11, 2001. Naturalist Aldo Leopold, who devoted his life to land conservation, is well known in environmental circles but not by the public at large. Martha Ballard was a midwife in Maine over 200 years ago, and her life has only recently been rediscovered with her diaries. Students still read *The Good Earth* by Pearl Buck, but few study the author's global activism. Fortunately for readers, biographies are available so they can get to know these exemplary figures.

No person is deemed exemplary without overcoming great moral challenges. These biographies are filled with stories of courage, often set in times of conflict. Readers learn much about those times in reading about the hero's challenges. Because these books are highly descriptive and somewhat rhetorical, few can be called quick reads. However, readers will find the characters and their stories compelling. Most of these books require ample time for reading and thought.

> *Exemplary Lives* are biographies of highly moral people whose careers and lives are exhibited as models for aspiring readers. These titles are filled with strong characters and compelling stories set in detailed settings. Most of these books require unhurried reading and time for thought.

Ackroyd, Peter

The Life of Thomas More. Nan A. Talese, 1998. 447p. ISBN 0385477090.

English scholar Thomas More met England's Prince Henry when showing his friend Erasmus the royal palace at Eltham in 1499. He gave young Henry a volume of patriotic poetry, beginning a long relationship that would define his life. In time the faithful Catholic, who wore a hair shirt to mortify his soul, would become the noted author of *Utopia* and a powerful minister to Henry VIII as king. In this suspenseful story of an honorable man, Peter Ackroyd explains why the tragedy of More's beheading was inevitable.

Subjects: Authors; England; Henry VIII, King of England; More, Thomas; Scholars

Now Try: In *Utopia*, Thomas More presented his ideas for a better society. Justice Thurgood Marshall of the U.S. Supreme Court was considered by many an unbending man of principle. Juan Williams describes how Marshall clashed over objectives with other civil rights leaders in *Thurgood Marshall: American Revolutionary* (see chapter 9). When Marco Polo reached China, he became an advisor to the Mongol emperor Kublai Khan, who like Henry VIII was a dangerous employer. Laurence Bergreen chronicles Polo's long and dangerous visit to the Far East in the biography *Marco Polo: From Venice to Xanadu* (see chapter 1). Peter Ackroyd writes about another man of literature who served a British king in *Chaucer* (see chapter 7).

Ascoli, Peter M.

Julius Rosenwald: The Man Who Built Sears, Roebuck and Advanced the Cause of Black Education in the American South. Indiana University Press, 2006. 453p. Philanthropic and Nonprofit Studies. ISBN 9780253347411.

Giving money away wisely was difficult, according to philanthropist Julius Rosenwald (1862–1932), a key figure at Sears, Roebuck and Company. Before funding worthy causes, he visited charities, met their petitioners, and weighed the societal impact of his gifts. In doing so, he traveled extensively and met many of the most charismatic figures of the early twentieth century. In this admiring biography for business readers, Rosenwald's grandson Peter M. Ascoli describes his grandfather and his involvement in the causes of black education and civil rights, as well as European recovery from the First World War and Jewish settlements in Israel.

Subjects: Corporate Executives; Education; Jews; Philanthropists; Rosenwald, Julius; Sears, Roebuck and Company

Now Try: Compared with Rosenwald, Milton S. Hershey was a late bloomer as a businessman, but he did eventually make millions of dollars. Michael D'Antonio tells how he tried to share his wealth with his employees in *Hershey: Milton S. Hershey's Extraordinary Life of Wealth, Empire, and Utopian Dreams* (see chapter 9). While Rosenwald contributed to colleges for African Americans, Andrew Carnegie was funding the building of public libraries across the United States. David Nasaw describes a man who could be as generous to his causes as he could be ruthless in business in *Andrew Carnegie* (see chapter 9). Other biographies of philanthropists include *Black Titan: A. G. Gaston and the Making of a Black Millionaire* by Carol Jenkins and Elizabeth Gardner Hines (see this chapter) and *Soros: The Life and Times of a Messianic Billionaire* by Michael T. Kaufman (see this chapter).

Conn, Peter

Pearl S. Buck: A Cultural Biography. Cambridge University Press, 2006. 468p. ISBN 0521560802.

Though her novel *The Good Earth* is still frequently read by students, few people remember the life of Pearl Buck (1892–1973), according to Peter Conn. In the 1930s and 1940s, the best-selling author won the Nobel Prize for literature and was considered nearly as influential as Eleanor

Roosevelt. Her causes included world peace, international dialogue, elimination of poverty, women's rights, birth control, and the welfare of children. She even spoke out against Japanese internment when doing so was considered un-American. Although her literary reputation suffered late in her career when she published unpolished works and expressed unpopular opinions, Buck's dedication to interracial understanding and peace did not wane. She went on to establish the first international, interracial adoption agency. Since her death, most of her books have been out of print. Conn's intent is to remind readers of this twentieth-century icon.

Subjects: Activists; Buck, Pearl S.; China; Novelists; Women

Now Try: Buck's own autobiographical writings are not as readily available now as they were during her lifetime. Two that may be found that give insight into her thoughts and character are *China as I See It* and *A Bridge for Passing*. For readers interested in another outspoken activist of the mid-twentieth century, Blanche Wiesen Cook wrote two volumes about former first lady Roosevelt, starting with *Eleanor Roosevelt, 1884–1933* (see chapter 6) and continuing with *Eleanor Roosevelt: The Defining Years, 1933–1938*. Biochemist Joseph Needham was first attracted to China by his love for one of his students, but once he visited the country, he loved it, too. Simon Winchester recounts the travels of Needham into remote areas of the country in *The Man Who Loved China: The Fantastic Story of the Eccentric Scientist Who Unlocked the Mysteries of the Middle Kingdom* (see chapter 1). Traveling throughout the world with his camera, photographer Henri Cartier-Bresson witnessed key events in modern Chinese history. Pierre Assouline portrays Cartier-Bresson as a visionary who imparted knowledge through photography in *Henri Cartier-Bresson: A Biography* (see chapter 7).

Diliberto, Gioia

A Useful Woman: The Early Life of Jane Addams. Scribner, 1999. 318p. ISBN 0684853655.

Jane Addams (1860–1935) was a nervous young woman, attractive but depressed, until she dedicated her life to helping the poor. She always admitted that she did social work as much for her sense of self-worth as for the welfare of the children, women, and immigrants whom she served. In this compelling biography, Gioia Diliberto tells how the socialite transformed herself into an activist, gathered together a remarkable group of dedicated women to run her missions, and became a leading figure in the international reform movement of the Gilded Age and beyond. In the process, the author shows how the Hull House founder's life was a revolt against the conventions of nineteenth-century society, especially regarding sexuality and capitalist disregard of life. Women's studies and social history scholars, as well as general readers, will enjoy this admiring coming-of-age story.

Subjects: Activists; Addams, Jane; Group Discussion Books; Hull House; Social Reformers; Teen Reads; Women

Now Try: Addams told about her work in *Twenty Years at Hull House* and *The Second Twenty Years at Hull House*. Jean Bethke Elshtain continues the story of Addams into the twentieth century, when she shaped the public welfare movement that grew to influence President Franklin Roosevelt's New Deal, in *Jane Addams and the Dream of American Democracy*. A social activist to compare with Addams is Nancy Cunard, who was born beautiful and rich. *Nancy Cunard: Heiress, Muse, Political Idealist* by Lois Gordon (see chapter 8) tells how she tried to balance her high society life with the good she sought to do. Ethiopian widow Haregewoin Teffera did not intend to start a foster home for AIDS children when she agreed to help a teenaged orphan. Melissa Fay Greene tells how Teffera saw her calling to run a mission of mercy in *There Is No Me*

Without You: One Woman's Odyssey to Rescue Africa's Children (see this chapter). Mary Ware Dennett was an Addams contemporary, who saw suffering among poor families with many children. Constance M. Chen tells how Dennett become a suffragist, peace activist, advocate for legalizing birth control, and proponent for teaching sex education in schools and churches in the admiring biography *The Sex Side of Life: Mary Ware Dennett's Pioneering Battle for Birth Control and Sex Education* (see chapter 9).

Fairclough, Adam

Martin Luther King, Jr. University of Georgia Press, 1995. 163p. ISBN 0820316903.

Born in Atlanta, then a highly segregated city and the birthplace of the Ku Klux Klan, Martin Luther King Jr. (1929–1968) grew up in an uncommonly happy, prosperous family, where his Baptist minister father instilled in him a sense of duty to less fortunate people. Well-educated, articulate, and compassionate, King Jr. was groomed for his role as a civil rights leader. Still, he was unprepared for the Montgomery bus boycott and uncertain of his path after its successful resolution. In this short, passionate book for history readers, civil rights historian Adam Fairclough describes how King evolved from a young idealist into a seasoned leader, who knew the dangers he faced but never retreated from his mission for peace and justice.

> **Subjects:** Activists; African Americans; Civil Rights Leaders; Clergy; Group Discussion Books; King, Martin Luther, Jr.; Quick Reads; Teen Reads
>
> **Now Try:** *Stride Toward Freedom: The Montgomery Story*, *Strength to Love*, and *Why We Can't Wait* are three of King's books written during his civil rights crusade. Long before the civil rights movement of the twentieth century, former slave and pamphlet writer Richard Allen worked for black rights and welfare. Richard S. Newman recounts how Allen founded the American Methodist Episcopal Church and the Free African Society, the first organization in the American abolitionist movement, in *Freedom's Prophet: Bishop Richard Allen, the AME Church, and the Black Founding Fathers* (see chapter 9). Seamstress Rosa Parks of Montgomery, Alabama, was inspired by a sermon by Martin Luther King to act for civil rights by refusing to give up her seat on a bus. Douglas Brinkley tells of the making of a civil rights hero in *Rosa Parks* (see chapter 9). Thurgood Marshall did not see eye to eye with King, but his aim was the same. *Thurgood Marshall: American Revolutionary* by Juan Williams (see chapter 9) gives the reader another intimate view of the civil rights era. Those interested in King may also want to read *Gandhi's Passion: The Life and Legacy of Mahatma Gandhi* by Stanley Wolpert (see this chapter).

Ford, Michael

Father Mychal Judge: An Authentic American Hero. Paulist Press, 2002. 207p. ISBN 0809105527.

Franciscan brother Mychal Judge (1933–2001) was not the first person to die in the terrorist attack on the World Trade Center in New York on September 11, 2001, but because he died while ministering to victims, he was named first in the official roll of casualties. Journalist Michael Ford interviewed many of Judge's friends to discover how a Catholic monk who had weathered many of his own trials came to lead a rescue effort on that fateful morning. In this collection of biographical essays, Ford lovingly describes a warm, thoughtful spiritual leader who gave his life for others in many ways.

Subjects: Firefighters; Group Discussion Books; Judge, Mychal; Monks; New York City; Quick Reads; September 11, 2001; World Trade Center

Now Try: Rick Rescorla, head of security for Morgan Stanley, succeeded in getting all of the other company's employees safely out of the World Trade Center but lost his own life in the terrorist attack in 2001. James B. Stewart describes Rescorla as a civilian who still conducted himself as a soldier in *Heart of a Soldier: A Story of Love, Heroism, and September 11.* Like Judge, Thomas Merton felt that he was a self-destructive man before he found his religious faith. Merton describes his early life and conversion in *The Seven Storey Mountain.* Father Judge shared some traits and the fate of Roberto Clemente, the baseball player who died delivering aid to earthquake victims in Nicaragua. His life is told in *Clemente: The Passion and Grace of Baseball's Last Hero* by David Maraniss (see chapter 12). Green Bay Packers coach Vince Lombardi is often quoted by inspirational speakers at management seminars for his statements that apply to life in general. In *When Pride Still Mattered: A Life of Vince Lombardi* (see chapter 12), David Maraniss thoughtfully reconsiders the sound bites within the context of a life that had been difficult.

Hedrick, Joan D.

🌸 *Harriet Beecher Stowe: A Life.* Oxford University Press, 1994. 507p. ISBN 0195066391.

Harriet Beecher Stowe (1811–1896) was not content to watch the debates of her time from the sidelines. The member of a noted family of evangelical ministers, some of whom disapproved of the reading of novels, she began her literary career in the 1830s, writing regional sketches that pioneered the use of dialect. Her pieces became popular at a time when women authors dominated the popular book industry. The great success of *Uncle Tom's Cabin* allowed her to be one of the few women writers who survived the corporate takeover of the book industry, a situation she decried. According to historian Joan D. Hedrick, Stowe struggled with a dual life as a private wife and mother as well as a public voice for abolition, women's rights, and popular literature. For general readers, Hedrick admiringly chronicles the life and career of one of the literary leaders of her time.

Subjects: Abolitionists; Novelists; Stowe, Harriet Beecher; Women

Awards: Pulitzer Prize for Biography, 1995

Now Try: In her novels *Uncle Tom's Cabin* and *Dred: A Tale of the Great Dismal Swamp,* Stowe depicted the evils of slavery. She later turned to writing traditional romances, including *The Minister's Wooing.* Stowe's brother Henry Ward Beecher was a staunch abolitionist and most respected religious figure in America before and during the Civil War. Debby Applegate recounts how Beecher shook the country by admitting to committing adultery in *The Most Famous Man in America: The Biography of Henry Ward Beecher* (see chapter 10). In Great Britain, George Eliot wrote popular books and decried social injustice in a less dramatic fashion than Stowe but with similar impact. Kathryn Hughes describes the life of the influential novelist in *George Eliot: The Last Victorian* (see chapter 7). In a later era, reporter Nellie Bly wrote passionately about the poor and victims of injustice. Like Stowe, she was highly criticized for sensationalizing her topics. Brooke Kroeger describes the dangers that Bly faced during her international travels in *Nellie Bly: Daredevil, Reporter, Feminist* (see chapter 1).

Jenkins, Carol, and Elizabeth Gardner Hines

Black Titan: A. G. Gaston and the Making of a Black Millionaire. One World, 2004. 320p. ISBN 0345453476.

1

After serving in an all-black regiment in World War I, A. G. Gaston (1892–1996) returned to Alabama to work in a coal mine at slave wages. Instead of resigning himself to poverty, he sold lunches to other miners and later established a bank for them. By the time of his death at age 103, he had established ten companies in the fields of communications, real estate, and insurance, and he had served as an advisor to Presidents Kennedy and Johnson. Though labeled by some as an "Uncle Tom," he was honored in the black community for establishing charities and financially funding black students entering traditionally white colleges. In this compelling tribute, his niece Carol Jenkins and her daughter Elizabeth Gardner Hines portray Gaston as an astute businessman with a heart. This rags-to-riches story may please business and commerce readers.

2

3

4

> **Subjects:** African Americans; Alabama; Entrepreneurs; Gaston, A. G.; Philanthropists

> **Now Try:** Like Gaston, Sarah Breedlove was a black millionaire who returned wealth to her community. Beverly Lowry tells about the cosmetics queen in *Her Dream of Dreams: The Rise and Triumph of Madam C. J. Walker* (see chapter 9). Frank Phillips worked equally hard to escape poverty. Michael Wallis tells how a Midwestern farm boy tried many professions before becoming a tycoon in *Oil Man: The Story of Frank Phillips and the Birth of Phillips Petroleum* (see chapter 9). As a presidential advisor, Gaston preceded other African Americans who became important appointees. President Jimmy Carter appointed Andrew Young as his ambassador to the United Nations. Young tells about his role in the civil rights movement, at the United Nations, and as mayor of Atlanta in *A Way Out of No Way: The Spiritual Memoirs of Andrew Young.* As secretary of state for President George Bush, Condoleezza Rice became the highest ranking African American in the United States government. Marcus Mabry portrays Rice as a person who has worked diligently to attain her position in *Twice as Good: Condoleezza Rice and Her Path to Power* (see chapter 10).

5

6

7

8

Kaufman, Michael T.

Soros: The Life and Times of a Messianic Billionaire. Alfred A. Knopf, 2002. 344p. ISBN 0375405852.

9

Surviving the Nazi and Russian occupations of Budapest deeply affected George Soros (1930–). After nine years in London, during which he earned a degree in economics and worked at a series of low-paying jobs, he moved to New York with only a small savings. He secured a position as a trader of foreign securities, quickly earned millions of dollars, and began to care for his parents and friends, who had escaped Soviet-era Hungary. Late in his fifties, having earned a vast fortune on Wall Street, Soros began to give it all away. Journalist Michael T. Kaufman tells an unusual story of a compassionate billionaire in an admiring biography that may interest business readers looking for role models.

10

11

12

Subjects: Capitalists; Group Discussion Books; Hungary; Immigrants; Jews; Soros, George; Wall Street

Now Try: Soros is the author of numerous books on economics and international relations, including *The Bubble of American Supremacy: Correcting the Misuse of American Power* and *The New Paradigm for Financial Markets: The Credit Crisis of 2008 and What It Means*. Among the many causes that Soros has adopted are black education, continuing the work of Julius Rosenwald on an international scale. Peter M. Ascoli describes how Sears executive Rosenwald became involved in philanthropy in *Julius Rosenwald: The Man Who Built Sears, Roebuck and Advanced the Cause of Black Education in the American South* (see this chapter). Moral use of capital was a theme throughout the writings of Scottish philosopher and economist Adam Smith. James Buchan describes how Smith lived for ideas in *The Authentic Adam Smith: His Life And Ideas*. Economist Milton Friedman had the ear of various American presidents and world leaders. Lanny Ebenstein recounts the personal life and career of an economist who supported government deregulation of financial markets in *Milton Friedman* (see chapter 10).

Larson, Kate Clifford

Bound for the Promised Land: Harriet Tubman: Portrait of an American Hero. Ballantine Books, 2004. 402p. ISBN 0345456270.

Harriet Tubman (1820?–1920) is best known for her escape from slavery in 1849 and for frequently risking her life and freedom to conduct slaves out of the South on the Underground Railroad. Most of the other books written about her tell about her hard life as a slave and her courage throughout the Civil War but neglect the last fifty years of her life. Historian Kate Clifford Larson completes the story, telling how Tubman farmed, ran a brick making business, became active in the women's suffrage movement, and started a hospital for indigent blacks outside Auburn, New York. American history readers may enjoy this admiring book.

Subjects: African Americans; Fugitive Slaves; Slavery; Teen Reads; Tubman, Harriet; Underground Railroad; Women

Now Try: *A Woman Called Moses* by Marcy Heidish is a fictionalized memoir that includes many of the incidents in Tubman's life. While Tubman was working secretly as a conductor on the Underground Railroad, leading slaves from the South to freedom in the North, Sojourner Truth was speaking at abolitionist meetings across the United States. Nell Irvin Painter separates myths from facts about the ex-slave who became a leading voice for abolition in *Sojourner Truth: A Life, a Symbol*. Tubman was alleged to be a friend and supporter of abolitionist John Brown. David S. Reynolds describes Brown as a religious man who believed any methods, including terrorism, were justified in the effort to end slavery, in *John Brown, Abolitionist: The Man Who Killed Slavery, Sparked the Civil War, and Seeded Civil Rights* (see chapter 9). Richmond native Elizabeth Van Lew was Tubman's contemporary. Her story of risking her life as a spy is told in *Southern Lady, Yankee Spy: The True Story of Elizabeth Van Lew, a Union Agent in the Heart of the Confederacy* by Elizabeth R. Varon (see chapter 3).

Lash, Joseph P.

Helen and Teacher: The Story of Helen Keller and Anne Sullivan Macy. Delacourt Press/Seymour Lawrence, 1980. 811p. Radcliffe Biography Series. ISBN 0440036542.

Anne Sullivan (1866–1936) was almost twenty-one years old when she arrived in Tuscumbia, Alabama to become the eyes and ears of Helen Keller (1880–1968). Using fingers to write letters on Keller's palm, the teacher gave the deaf and blind girl the gift of language and awakened a brilliant mind. Together the pair became world famous; met scientists, authors, and presidents; promoted feminist causes; and wrote a series of remarkable books. They even appeared on vaudeville stages and in early films. Joseph P. Lash reveals that their close relationship of nearly fifty years complicated their romantic affairs, and eventually they needed to rely on others to care for Keller. This intimate biography will appeal to readers who enjoy epic stories about remarkable people.

Subjects: Blindness; Deafness; Dual Biography; Keller, Helen; Macy, Anne Sullivan; Teachers

Now Try: Keller's autobiography, *The Story of My Life*, is a moving account of her education and the blossoming of her career as an activist. Late in life, Keller wrote about her relationship with Sullivan in *Teacher: Anne Sullivan Macy: A Tribute by the Foster Child of Her Mind*. William Gibson turned the story of Keller and Sullivan into a play, *The Miracle Worker*. Mitch Albom had a teacher to whom he felt indebted. In *Tuesdays with Morrie: An Old Man, a Young Man, and Life's Greatest Lesson*, Albom recounts renewing his friendship with a college professor during the later days of the instructor's life. For Elizabeth Stone, it was a former student who gave her a gift that started a learning process. In *A Boy I Once Knew: What a Teacher Learned from Her Student*, she describes the journey of reading the diaries of a student dying from AIDS. Another remarkable story of a historical figure overcoming blindness is *A Sense of the World: How a Blind Man Became History's Greatest Traveler* by Jason Roberts (see chapter 1).

Lorbiecki, Marybeth

Aldo Leopold: A Fierce Green Fire. Falcon Publishing, 1996. 212p. ISBN 1560-444789.

Early in his privileged childhood, Aldo Leopold (1886–1948) developed a great love for the outdoors and chose to become a forest ranger. From his post at the U.S. Forest Service, he became a central figure in the movement to establish wilderness reserves, challenging government policies that favored lumber and ranching interests. According to Marybeth Lorbiecki, Leopold eventually wore out his welcome in government and struggled to make ends meet and support his family as a writer. Nature-loving readers will enjoy this admiring, photo-filled biography.

Subjects: Conservationists; Forest Rangers; Leopold, Aldo; Naturalists; Photographic Biography; Quick Reads; Wilderness

Now Try: Environmental readers will enjoy Leopold's most known book, *A Sand County Almanac*. The leading environmental writer from the generation preceding Leopold was Sierra Club cofounder John Muir. Gretel Ehrlich traces Muir's life through the woods and mountains of California and on voyages around the world in *John Muir: Nature's Visionary* (see chapter 1). A biography of another gentle naturalist is *Nature's Engraver: A Life of Thomas Bewick* by Jenny Uglow (see chapter 1). After his presidency Theodore Roosevelt, who championed American parks, traveled to many remote locations of the world, looking for hunting adventure and natural wonders. Candice Millard describes one of his explorations that was difficult and disturbing in *River of Doubt: Theodore Roosevelt's Darkest Journey*.

Lytle, Mark Hamilton

The Gentle Subversive: Rachel Carson, Silent Spring, *and the Rise of the Environmental Movement.* Oxford University Press, 2007. 277p. <u>New Narratives in American History</u>. ISBN 9780195172461.

An intensely private woman, biologist Rachel Carson (1907–1964) was not the most likely person to write a book on the dangers of the pesticide DDT. Her previous books had quietly celebrated the beauty of marine environments. Despite her lack of experience at advocacy, she challenged business, government, and scientific thinking with her carefully collected evidence about the chemical found in the tissues of birds, fish, and humans. Mark Hamilton Lytle profiles Carson while telling the story of the publishing of *Silent Spring* and the environmental movement it spawned. This laudatory biography will appeal to readers who appreciate courageous figures.

Subjects: Biologists; Carson, Rachel; Environmentalists; Group Discussion Books; Science Writers; Women

Now Try: In addition to *Silent Spring*, Carson wrote a series of books about marine habitats, including *The Sea Around Us* and *Under the Sea-Wind*. Linda Lear's *Rachel Carson: Witness for Nature* is an often-recommended and lengthier account of Carson's life found in many libraries. Lear's *Beatrix Potter: A Life in Nature* (see chapter 7) is another story about a naturalist who grew stronger and more outspoken as she aged. *The Woman Who Knew Too Much: Alice Stewart and the Secrets of Radiation* by Gayle Greene (see this chapter) is a sadder, more disturbing book about a woman warning the scientific community and being ignored. Lady Bird Johnson was able to use the prestige of her position to lobby for a clean-up of America's highways. Jane Jarboe Russell describes Lady Bird as a tough and resourceful woman worthy of admiration in *Lady Bird: A Biography of Mrs. Johnson* (see chapter 10).

McNamee, Thomas

Alice Waters & Chez Panisse: The Romantic, Impractical, Often Eccentric, Ultimately Brilliant Making of a Food Revolution. Penguin, 2007. 380p. ISBN 9781594201158.

Only in a place like Berkeley, California, could the left-wing entrepreneur Alice Waters (1944–) succeed in her dream to run a restaurant. According to R. W. Apple Jr. in the foreword to this book, she is not a chef and has questionable business skills; but she has great ideas and a genius for promotion. She opened Chez Panisse in 1971 with a very limited menu costing a flat $3.95, and after many chefs and cuisines, it is still in business. In this admiring biography that will especially appeal to cooking magazine readers, Thomas McNamee tells how Waters has championed local produce, social justice, the "Delicious Revolution," the "Slow Food Movement," and the "Edible Schoolyard."

Subjects: California; Chez Panisse; Food; Restaurateurs; Social Justice; Teen Reads; Waters, Alice; Women

Now Try: Waters includes her philosophy with recipes in *Art of Simple Food*. McNamee shares a good bit of gossip about Waters's love life. Sheila Weller does the same for three women of music who are Waters's contemporaries in *Girls Like Us: Carole King, Joni Mitchell, Carly Simon—and the Journey of a Generation* (see chapter 7). Food, women's rights, and politics merge in *Unbowed: A Memoir* by Noble Peace Prize winner Wangari Maathai. Waters's call for eating local foods is continued in *Animal, Vegetable, Miracle: A Year of Food Life* by Barbara Kingsolver, Steven L. Hopp, and Camille Kingsolver. More on the slow food movement can be found in *Slow Food Nation: Why Our Food Should be Good, Clean, and Fair* and other titles by Carlo Petrini.

Ulrich, Laurel Thatcher

🕯 *A Midwife's Tale: The Life of Martha Ballard, Based on Her Diary, 1785–1812.* Alfred A. Knopf, 1990. 444p. ISBN 0394568443.

For over twenty-seven years, Martha Ballard (1735–1812), a midwife in Hallowell, Maine, kept a diary on folded half-sheets of paper that she carried as she assisted women along the Kennebec River in giving birth. In brief entries full of abbreviations, she recorded births, deaths, family events, her own health, and the activities of daily life. In this intimate portrait, Laurel Thatcher Ulrich expands on the diary by adding period details and completing the story of Ballard's life using other documentary evidence.

Subjects: Ballard, Martha; Diaries; Group Discussion Books; Maine; Midwives; Teen Reads; Women

Awards: Bancroft Prize in American History, 1991; John H. Dunning Prize, 1990

Now Try: Like Ballard, the Powhatan Indian Pocahontas was a woman of medicine. Writers can only speculate about her, because there are few records of her life. *Pocahontas: Medicine Woman, Spy, Entrepreneur, Diplomat* by Paula Gunn Allen (see chapter 5) is another intimate portrait of a woman at the edge of wilderness and European civilization. Anne Bradstreet came to America in 1630, when the Massachusetts Bay Colony was new. Charlotte Gordon tells an engaging story of a Puritan woman concerned with both the hardships of daily life and her spiritual life in *Mistress Bradstreet: The Untold Life of America's First Poet* (see chapter 7). Elizabeth Marsh was a ship captain's wife who wrote several best-selling books about her travels around the world in the eighteenth century. Linda Colley describes an adventurous woman, with many observations about her time, in *The Ordeal of Elizabeth Marsh: A Woman in World History* (see chapter 1). As with Ballard, most of the details of the life of physician Henry Gray have been forgotten. In *The Anatomist: A True Story of Gray's Anatomy* (see chapter 11), Bill Hayes reveals the long-lost story of how Gray and his illustrator, Henry Vandyke Carter, wrote the pioneering anatomy text.

Wolpert, Stanley

Gandhi's Passion: The Life and Legacy of Mahatma Gandhi. Oxford University Press, 2001. 308p. ISBN 019513060X.

"The purer the suffering, the greater the progress," Mahatma Gandhi (1869–1948) said when asked why he had abandoned comfort and pleasure to join the poor of India in their humility. Opposed by his family and violating "the bad laws" of British colonial rule, he led a nonviolent movement to reform Indian society, was frequently imprisoned, and drew the rapt attention of the world. In this respectful account for general readers, Indian scholar Stanley Wolpert examines the life and fading legacy of the strangely heroic religious leader.

Subjects: Gandhi, Mahatma; Group Discussion Books; India; Nonviolence

Now Try: *An Autobiography: Or the Story of My Experience with Truth* is Gandhi's memoir from the 1920s. Stanley Wolpert recounts the last hours of Gandhi's life in the novel *Nine Hours to Rama*; R. K Narayan describes life in Gandhi's village in *Waiting for the Mahatm*a. Vows of poverty and creative spirits link Gandhi with the poor monk Francesco di Pietro, whose story is told in *Francis of Assisi: A Revolutionary Life* by Adrian House (see this chapter). John Allen tells about a modern follower of Gandhi's mission in *Rabble-Rouser for Peace: The Authorized Biography of Desmond Tutu*.

Living for a Cause

Within the twelve books in this section are stories of individuals who dedicated their lives to causes in which they firmly believed. Many were reviled for their unpopular work and found themselves shunned by polite society. Many were women, who were condemned for being unladylike and for supporting causes that mainstream society considered sinful. Only a few of the subjects in this section received praise for their work, from societies that supported their work in word but not in deed.

The most despised of the group was Mother Jones, for she not only radically espoused labor rights opposed by the corporations that ran newspapers and owned many politicians, but she was also an Irish immigrant at a time when that the ethnic group was looked down upon by many Americans. Victoria Woodhull might be a close second for her relentless pursuit of women's issues and refusal to behave in a convention manner. Margaret Sanger followed in the wake left by Jones and Woodhull with shocking (at the time) demands for women's reproductive rights. These women are still considered controversial, despite American society having adopted many of their viewpoints.

In contrast, the primatologist Jane Goodall and physician to the poor Paul Farmer are living advocates for causes that many in society praise but few support with more than token financial donations. They mold their lives to maximize their abilities to serve their causes, and as result live lives that comfortable readers might view as Spartan.

A common thread in all the stories in this section is the inspiring courage the subjects exhibited in the face of strong opposition. Although the books will mostly appeal to readers who long for societal change, they can be enjoyed by anyone who likes strong characters, lively stories, and lessons in perseverance.

Living for a Cause stories describe lives that readers may not want to replicate but that they may admire for their great sacrifices to selfless causes. The authors are often candid about the faults of their subjects but praise them for their life's work. Readers are inspired by their perseverance and may learn from their methods as well. These books are filled with strong characters in conflict-filled stories. Most of these detailed accounts require unhurried reading.

Chesler, Ellen

Woman of Valor: Margaret Sanger and the Birth Control Movement in America. Simon & Schuster, 1992. 639p. ISBN 0671600885.

As a visiting nurse in New York City's immigrant slums, Margaret Sanger (1879–1966) saw tremendous suffering. After several comfortable years as a wife, mother, and homemaker, family finances drove her to work and led her to the cause that she would champion for the rest of her life. According to historian Ellen Chesler, Sanger's campaign for birth control evolved over fifty years. After first aligning with radical social and labor reformers, she steadily moved toward the view that birth control was an issue that should interest business, industry, and mainstream politicians. The author tells how Sanger, who faced strong rebukes as she took her crusade around the world, lived to see her ideas finally accepted. Women's history readers may enjoy this admiring biography.

Subjects: Activists; Birth Control; Feminists; Sanger, Margaret; Women; Women's Rights

Now Try: *The Pivot of Civilization* was Sanger's popular book about reproductive rights. She recounted her life in *Margaret Sanger: An Autobiography*. Noel B. Gibson turned Sanger's story into an inspiring novel, *The Crusader: A Novel on the Life of Margaret Sanger*. Sanger's long quest of advocacy and research resembles the many years that Jonas Salk spent seeking a cure for polio. Like Sanger's story, *Splendid Solution: Jonas Salk and the Conquest of Polio* by Jeffrey Kluger (see chapter 11) begins in a New York City slum and ends in medical offices across the nation. Senator Margaret Chase Smith of New York was not a feminist, but she advanced the cause of women by hiring many for government positions and running for president. Janann Sherman offers an admiring profile of a powerful woman who lived ninety-seven years in *No Place for a Woman: A Life of Senator Margaret Chase Smith* (see chapter 10). At ninety years old, NAACP pioneer Mary Church Terrell began a personal campaign to integrate the restaurants in Washington, D.C. Dennis Brindell Fradin and Judith Bloom Fradin tell another story of a woman with a cause in *Fight On!: Mary Church Terrell's Battle for Integration*.

D'Emilio, John

Lost Prophet: The Life and Times of Bayard Rustin. Free Press, 2003. 568p. ISBN 0684827808.

Civil rights visionary Bayard Rustin (1912–1987) is a forgotten man, according to historian John D'Emilio. Though he tutored Martin Luther King Jr. in the ways of nonviolence, organized the 1963 civil rights march on Washington, and served as a strategist for the Southern Christian Leadership Conference, his name is missing from most civil rights histories. The reason, the author says, is that Rustin was gay, a former communist, and a Quaker pacifist who spent twenty-seven months in prison for refusing military service in World War II. Often spurned, he continually rose to new causes, spending his later years helping the Solidarity movement in Poland and caring for refugees in Southeast Asia. D'Emilio's admiring account will interest readers who enjoy biographies of determined optimists.

Subjects: African Americans; Civil Rights Leaders; Homosexuals; Nonviolence; Rustin, Bayard

Now Try: *Down the Line, Strategies for Freedom,* and *Time on Two Crosses* are collections of Rustin's writings on civil rights. Though abolition was the great human rights cause of his lifetime, poet Walt Whitman through his verse and the conduct of his life began a movement for sexual and labor rights. *Walt Whitman's America: A Cultural Biography* by David S. Reynolds (see chapter 7) will appeal to those who enjoy reading about irrepressible American characters who break societal rules. Like Rustin, e. e. cummings spoke out for unpopular causes, especially pacifism and socialism. Catherine Reef describes a life full of good friendships with other poets, difficult romantic relationships, and political isolation in *E. E. Cummings* (see chapter 7). After baseball player Curt Flood challenged Major League Baseball's reserve clause, he became a world traveler, meeting people from other cultures. Alex Belth describes a man who believed his cause was worth his personal suffering in *Stepping Up: The Story of Curt Flood and His Fight for Baseball Players' Rights* (see chapter 12).

Finkelstein, Norman H.

With Heroic Truth: The Life of Edward R. Murrow. Clarion Books, 1997. 175p. ISBN 0395678919.

As a senior at Washington State University, Edward R. Murrow (1908–1965) earned only a B in his radio class, not a good omen for a future broadcast legend. When he was hired by CBS Radio, the network had only two five-minute and one fifteen-minute newscasts per day. Chances that the son of a farmer from Polecat Creek, North Carolina, would become a famous journalist were slim. Then he was assigned to London to report on the rise of fascism in Europe. In this admiring biography, librarian Norman H. Finkelstein tells how Murrow captured the attention of the American public and defended the role of the news correspondent in the era of McCarthyism. Aimed at teen readers, adults will also enjoy this quick read.

Subjects: Journalists; Murrow, Edward R.; Quick Reads; Radio; Teen Reads; Television

Now Try: Murrow's radio broadcasts during World War II are collected in *This Is London.* Murrow conducted interviews with many prominent people and wrote about their views of life in *This I Believe: The Living Philosophies of One Hundred Thoughtful Men and Women in All Walks of Life.* Another quick reading book about an individual who did not seek the honors that he won is *Bradley* by Alan Axelrod (see chapter 3), a book about General Omar Bradley, an American commander in World War II. Correspondent Eric Sevareid was a Murrow contemporary who also became famous for his on-the-spot reporting during World War II. As a high school student, he and a friend canoed over 2,000 miles from Minnesota to Hudson Bay in Canada. *Canoeing with the Cree* is Sevareid's memoir of the long journey. *Peter Jennings: A Reporter's Life* expands on the role of the news correspondent as protector of democracy.

Gabriel, Mary

Notorious Victoria: The Life of Victoria Woodhull, Uncensored. Algonquin Books of Chapel Hill, 1998. 372p. ISBN 1565121325.

Suffragette Victoria Woodhull (1838–1927) was for many years forgotten and left out of conventional history books. In the years just after the American Civil War, however, Woodhull was a highly visible crusader for women, speaking at rallies, writing articles, and being arrested for a variety of disturbances, including trying to vote. By the late 1870s, she was being shunned by the women's movement for being too radical, and she lived the last fifty years of her life abroad. In her candid biography of the first woman to run for U.S. president, journalist Mary Gabriel argues that Woodhull was a reformer whose ideas were a hundred years ahead of her time. Readers who enjoy outrageous characters will enjoy this book.

> **Subjects:** Feminists; Group Discussion Books; Presidential Candidates; Suffragettes; Women; Woodhull, Victoria

> **Now Try:** Mexican artist Frida Kahlo was another irrepressible woman who said what she pleased no matter the company. Hayden Herrera portrays Kahlo as a determined woman who struggled with pain and depression, leaving a legacy of distinctive, sensual paintings in *Frida: A Biography of Frida Kahlo* (see chapter 7). Alice Roosevelt Longworth opposed the liberal political stance that Woodhull espoused, but she too was an outspoken woman. In *Alice: Alice Roosevelt Longworth, from White House Princess to Washington Power Broker*, Stacy A. Cordery portrays Longworth as an outrageous woman who became one of Washington's most influential power brokers. *Woman of Valor: Margaret Sanger and the Birth Control Movement in America* by Ellen Chesler (see this chapter) and *The Sex Side of Life: Mary Ware Dennett's Pioneering Battle for Birth Control and Sex Education* by Constance M. Chen (see chapter 9) tells similar stories of women whose ideas were rejected when they were active but were accepted by later generations.

Gorn, Elliott J.

Mother Jones: The Most Dangerous Woman in America. Hill and Wang, 2001. 408p. ISBN 0809070936.

Militant matriarch Mary Harris ("Mother") Jones (1843?–1930) maintained that she had no permanent address. Instead, she lived wherever there was a labor union fighting for decent hours and living wages. At great personal risk, the white-haired woman who purportedly exaggerated her age waded into the conflicts at mines, rail yards, and factories. In his passionate biography, historian Elliott J. Gorn tells about Jones's life, beginning with her experiences in the Irish potato famine of the 1840s, the Tennessee yellow fever epidemic of 1867, and the great Chicago fire of 1871. Readers with a liberal bent, those who support the underdog, and those who enjoy stories about strong women will appreciate this passionate book.

> **Subjects:** Activists; Feminists; Immigrants; Jones, Mother; Labor Activists; Women; Working Classes

> **Now Try:** Five years before her death, Jones published an account of her life, *The Autobiography of Mother Jones*. Much of Jones's work was aimed at improving the lives of miners. D. H. Lawrence described the world of a miner as dangerous and depressing in his socially realistic novel *Sons and Lovers*. Jones's contemporary, anarchist Emma Goldman, was imprisoned for inciting riots in support of the radical labor movement. *Emma Goldman: An Intimate Life* by Alice Wexler (see chapter 10) is a sympathetic book about a woman who was equally scandalous and more dangerous than Mother Jones. As Jones was vilified by newspapers of her time, Iraq War protestor Cindy Sheehan has been ridiculed by the media for her strong stance against the war. Sheehan defends her actions and her cause in *Peace Mom: A Mother's Journey Through Heartache to Activism*.

Greene, Gayle

The Woman Who Knew Too Much: Alice Stewart and the Secrets of Radiation. University of Michigan Press, 1999. 321p. ISBN 0472111078.

As the bearer of bad news about the health risks of radiation, British epidemiologist Alice Stewart (1906–2002) was either ignored or denounced by members of the medical establishment. After praising her clinical work during World War II and honoring her as the youngest woman ever elected to the Royal College of Physicians, in the 1950s her contemporaries criticized her for reporting the harmful effects of X-raying pregnant women. Twenty years later, industrialists and politicians attacked her for her reports on cancer in nuclear weapons workers. According to author Gayle Greene, research has in time proved Stewart right in her assertions and medical practices have changed, but the courageous scientist has never gotten the credit she deserves.

> **Subjects:** Epidemiologists; Physicians; Radiation; Stewart, Alice; Teen Reads; Women
>
> **Now Try:** Karen Silkwood warned that employees of the corporation Kerr-McGee were being exposed to harmful radiation at its plant in Crescent, Oklahoma. After making her accusations, she died in a mysterious automobile accident. Richard L. Rashke describes Silkwood and the company that she opposed in *The Killing of Karen Silkwood: The Story Behind the Kerr-McGee Plutonium Case*. Rosalind Franklin was a microbiologist who made several key findings about the nature of DNA. Brenda Maddox tells how Franklin saw her work stolen and incorporated into the work of James D. Watson and Francis Crick in *Rosalind Franklin: The Dark Lady of DNA* (see chapter 11). While British scientists discriminated against Stewart for her sex, they shunned canal engineer William Smith for his social class. Simon Winchester recounts how Smith went bankrupt while gentlemen geologists took credit for his geological maps in *The Map That Changed the World: William Smith and the Birth of Modern Geology* (see chapter 11). Exposure to radiation is blamed for the anemia that killed physicist Marie Curie. Denis Brian profiles Curie and her husband Pierre in *The Curies: A Biography of the Most Controversial Family in Science* (see chapter 11).

Greene, Melissa Fay

There Is No Me Without You: One Woman's Odyssey to Rescue Africa's Children. Bloomsbury, 2006. 472p. ISBN 1596911166.

In 1998, when an Ethiopian priest asked Haregewoin Teffera (1946–) to foster a girl he had rescued from the street, she was mourning the deaths of her husband and a daughter. Needing a focus for her life, she agreed, and he delivered Genet, a frightened fifteen-year-old who reeked from several unkempt weeks alone. She was the first of many children of AIDS victims that Teffera has cleaned, fed, and mothered until they were placed in new homes in Ethiopia, the United States, or other countries. In this firsthand account, author Melissa Fay Greene tells how Teffera struggles to foster the children, finance her home, and fight the neighbors and government officials who oppose her mission of mercy. Book groups will find much to discuss in this admiring biography of an African woman dealing with her continent's worst tragedy.

> **Subjects:** AIDS; Ethiopia; Foster Parents; Group Discussion Books; Orphans; Teen Reads; Teffera, Haregewoin
>
> **Now Try:** Stephanie Nolan describes the effects of AIDS on the people of Africa in her collective biography *28 Stories of AIDS in Africa*. In late nineteenth-century Chicago,

social activist Jane Addams saw how women, children, and immigrants were struggling with poverty. Gioia Diliberto describes how Addams started Hull House to help the city's needy population in *A Useful Woman: The Early Life of Jane Addams* (see this chapter). Mother Teresa of the Sisters of Loreto was sent to India as a teacher, but she found her vocation among the homeless. She described her life and work in the memoir *Mother Teresa: Come Be My Light*. After Wangari Maathai earned her biology and veterinary medicine degrees, she returned to her native Kenya, where she discovered that the forests were disappearing. She tells how she started an environmental movement to help bring economic prosperity to rural Kenya in *Unbowed: A Memoir*.

Kidder, Tracy

Mountains Beyond Mountains. Random House, 2003. 317p. ISBN 0375-506160. Audiobook and large print available.

Harvard Medical School graduate Paul Farmer (1959–) spends much of his time and energy caring for the health of the poor in rural Haiti, an unruly, dangerous land. He hikes over rough mountain passes, sometimes staring down criminals, to visit his sickest patients. In this admiring biography, author Tracy Kidder tells how Farmer worked his way out of Southern poverty and through college. Now he juggles serving his Haitian patients with frequent fundraising trips back to the U.S. and other countries. With a large dose of ethics discussion included, this title is popular with book groups in churches and libraries.

Subjects: Activists; Farmer, Paul; Group Discussion Books; Haiti; Missionaries; Physicians; Poor; Teen Reads.

Awards: ALA Notable Books, 2004

Now Try: Physician, theologian, and musician Albert Schweitzer gave up his comfortable life in 1913 to establish a hospital for the impoverished people of Gabon. He describes the successes and failures of his mission in *Out of My Life and Thought: An Autobiography*. George Marshall and David Polling complete the doctor's story with *Schweitzer: A Biography*. Greg Mortenson became lost coming down a mountain in Pakistan and was led to a village, where the people cared for him. Since then he has returned to Pakistan frequently to build schools. He describes his life and mission in *Three Cups of Tea: One Man's Mission to Fight Terrorism and Build Nations—One School at a Time*. Microsoft executive John Wood was on a climbing vacation in the Himalayas when he was shown a dismal village library that was under lock to prevent the "valuable" books from being stolen. He promised to send the village a library, which sparked his Room to Read foundation. He recounts the effort in *Leaving Microsoft to Change the World*.

MacPherson, Myra

"All Governments Lie": The Life and Times of Rebel Journalist I. F. Stone. Lisa Drew Book, 2006. 564p. ISBN 9780684807133, 0684807130.

J. Edgar Hoover hated the independent journalist I. F. Stone (1907–1989), who uncovered many Washington secrets during his long career, from the Great Depression to the Iran-Contra Scandal. Because the FBI director and Senator Joseph McCarthy wanted him silenced, Stone was labeled a communist and blacklisted from major news organizations. In response, he started his own four-page *I. F. Stone's Weekly* and surprisingly became rich. Moreover, he kept uncovering embarrassing stories. In this admiring biography, journalist Myra MacPherson tells the adventurous story of a journalist who was a thorn in the side of many presidential administrations.

Subjects: Journalists; Stone, I. F.; Washington (DC)

Now Try: *The Best of I. F. Stone* includes samples of his investigative reports from every decade of his career. After his tour of duty as a military cartoonist in World War II, Bill Mauldin turned to political cartooning. Todd DePastino recounts Mauldin's clashes with generals and politicians over his cartoons in *Bill Mauldin: A Life Up Front* (see chapter 3). Correspondent Helen Thomas covered presidential press conferences for United Press International from the administration of John F. Kennedy to that of George W. Bush. She describes her questions and the changing relationships of the White House to the press in *Front Row at the White House: My Life and Times*. One of Stone's primary targets throughout his career was the representative from California who became senator, vice-president, and then president, Richard M. Nixon. Anthony Summers reminds readers of the dark side of the man from San Clemente in the critical biography *The Arrogance of Power: The Secret World of Richard Nixon* (see chapter 5).

Peterson, Dale

Jane Goodall: The Woman Who Redefined Man. Houghton Mifflin, 2006. 740p. ISBN 9780395854051.

For Jane Goodall's (1934–) first birthday, her father gave the little English girl a toy chimpanzee, foreshadowing that she would become the world's most famous primatologist, regularly seen in the pages of *National Geographic*. Dale Peterson, who has also edited Goodall's letters and coauthored several books with her, intimately describes her life among the chimpanzees of Gombe and her tours of the world promoting wildlife and environmental conservation. In the story are episodes of joyous scientific discovery and horrific human and animal violence. *National Geographic* fans will appreciate this tribute.

Subjects: Activists; Chimpanzees; Gombe Stream National Park; Goodall, Jane; Primatologists; Tanzania; Women

Now Try: Goodall has written many books for readers of all ages. In *Reason for Hope: A Spiritual Journey* she describes her work and vision for a better world. The love of nature began very early for Beatrix Potter, who spent her childhood sketching rabbits and reading animal stories. Linda Lear recounts a long life of creating children's books and running a farm in *Beatrix Potter: A Life in Nature* (see chapter 7). Archeologist and diplomat Gertrude Bell was another Englishwoman who bravely settled in an exotic land. Georgina Howell describes how Bell helped define the national borders of the Middle East in *Gertrude Bell: Queen of the Desert, Shaper of Nations* (see chapter 1). Goodall was chosen to study the chimpanzees of Gombe by anthropologist Louis Leakey. Virginia Morell tells how Leakey and his family discovered fossils while they fought among themselves in *Ancestral Passions: The Leakey Family and the Quest for Humankind's Beginnings* (see chapter 11). Primatologist Dian Fossey was, like Goodall, a protégée of anthropologist Louis Leakey. Her story of gorilla research and murder in Rwanda is told in *The Dark Romance of Dian Fossey* by Harold T. P. Hayes (see chapter 2).

Power, Samantha

Chasing the Flame: Sergio Vieira de Mello and the Fight to Save the World. Penguin Press, 2008. 622p. ISBN 9781594201288.

Most Americans will not recognize the name Sergio Vieira de Mello (1948–2003). Only diligent news readers will recall that he served as a United Nations representative and observer at nearly every international crisis and conflict, from the famine in Bangladesh in 1971 to the United States invasion of Iraq, where he died in 2003. On assignments in Lebanon, Cambodia, Kosovo, and East Timor, the Brazilian peace advocate often dealt with dictators, revolutionaries, war criminals, and terrorists. In this admiring and detailed biography, Pulitzer Prize–winning journalist Samantha Power chronicles Vieira de Mello's many dangerous missions and measures their impact on world security. Readers of current events will enjoy this book.

Subjects: Diplomats; Mello, Sergio Vieira de; Peace; United Nations; War Relief

Now Try: As secretary of state, Madeleine Albright traveled the globe to conduct sensitive negations aimed at bringing peace to war-torn lands. Ann Blackman recounts how Albright escaped Nazi Germany and her education as a diplomat in *Seasons of Her Life: A Biography of Madeleine Korbel Albright* by (see chapter 10). When he became secretary of state for President George W. Bush, General Colin Powell joined a group of presidential advisors with values far different from his own. Karen DeYoung examines the importance of the individual in the conduct of world diplomacy and why the former general remained in the Bush administration doing a job he disliked in *Soldier: The Life of Colin Powell* (see chapter 3). Ernesto "Che" Guevara was another South American who took a completely different approach to international relations. Jon Lee Anderson portrays El Che as a person who could care for people as a doctor or as president of the Cuba's National Bank, but was also ready to lead guerrillas through the jungle, in *Che Guevara: A Revolutionary Life* (see chapter 3). British military expert Rupert Smith admits that war solves no problems, but he still thinks it is necessary. He describes how war should be used in *Utility of Force: The Art of War in the Modern World.*

Overcoming Adversity

Some lives become difficult because of physical, economic, cultural, or other external forces that threaten their well-being or survival. Internal or personal problems upset other lives. Although many surrender and fail, others find ways to persevere and overcome adversity, and readers may learn from their examples.

In this section readers can find a variety of dramatic stories about people who refused to surrender in difficult circumstances. Physically challenged but determined, Franklin D. Roosevelt started his presidency with the country mired in the Great Depression; he immediately stabilized the banks and started to put America's unemployed laborers back to work with executive orders that opponents thought outside his power. Beethoven continued to compose symphonies, concertos, and other orchestral pieces despite his loss of hearing. Bill Wilson admitted his alcoholism and started an international movement to help other problem drinkers. These are but a few of the many inspiring stories of people overcoming adversity.

Inner drive is a common thread among these dramatic narratives, which appeal to general readers who like good stories, characters to admire, and examples to follow.

> *Overcoming Adversity* stories include biographies of people who overcame challenges that threatened their happiness, livelihood, or reputations. Authors show how individuals met these challenges to live remarkable lives that inspire readers facing their own difficulties. These titles feature strong characters in inspiring stories of fortitude. A few shorter books are included in this section.

Alter, Jonathan

The Defining Moment: FDR's Hundred Days and the Triumph of Hope. Simon & Schuster, 2006. 414p. ISBN 9780743246002. Audiobook available.

As Franklin Delano Roosevelt (1882–1945) was being sworn in as president on March 4, 1933, the entire national banking system was collapsing. With great effort he stood at the podium without an overcoat to ask Americans to act quickly and help him save the nation, saying "the only thing we have to fear is fear itself." Eight days later he was on radio outlining the plan to save the banks. It was the first of many fireside chats that FDR used to win the support of the American public. In this slice-of-life biography, journalist Jonathan Alter tells how Roosevelt brought hope back to America in his first 100 days in the White House.

> **Subjects:** Group Discussion Books; New Deal; Presidents; Roosevelt, Franklin D.

> **Now Try:** At the beginning of his first term in office, when the economic situation of the country was bleak, Roosevelt published a book of his speeches and essays expressing his confidence in the country, *Looking Forward*. The president's son, Elliott Roosevelt, has written a mystery novel, *The President's Man*, in which the candidate works with a private investigator to prevent the election from being stolen. In 1815 French general Napoleon Bonaparte escaped from a prison in Vienna and within 100 days was on the verge of regaining his empire. Stephen Coote describes the period and the outcome of the Battle of Waterloo in *Napoleon and the Hundred Days*. Boris Dmitrievich Pankin became the Soviet Union's foreign minister in August 1991, when many Soviet politicians were calling for the union to dissolve. Pankin describes the events that followed his appointment in *The Last Hundred Days of the Soviet Union*. Another biography featuring an American president framed by the events of a short period, in this case seven days, is the dual biography *Nixon and Mao: The Week That Changed the World* by Margaret Macmillan.

Baker, William J.

Jesse Owens: An American Life. Free Press, 1986. 289p. ISBN 0029017807.

Winning four gold medals at the Berlin Olympics in 1936, showing that black athletes could excel, and refuting accusations of racial inferiority, Jesse Owens (1913–1980) should have been better rewarded. After the games, he thought he would receive numerous lucrative job offers, but he was disappointed. According to William J. Baker, the always-polite Owens made the best of the few employment offers that he received and served honorably in a series of coaching, government, and industrial jobs, but bad financial and personal decisions brought him to the edge of ruin. In this book, the author tells how Owens rescued his good reputation.

Subjects: African Americans; Group Discussion Books; Olympics; Owens, Jesse; Racial Discrimination; Teen Reads; Track and Field Athletes

Now Try: Owens expressed his disappointments and his hopes for his race while frankly recounting his life in *Blackthink: My Life as Black Man and White Man*. Forty years before Owens won medals in the Berlin Olympics, African American Marshall Taylor was winning bicycle races against white professionals. Todd Balf describes the dangers Taylor faced at a time when many blacks were being lynched by white extremists in *Major: A Black Athlete, a White Era, and the Fight to Be the World's Fastest Human Being* (see chapter 12). Native American Jim Thorpe also had Olympic dreams, which were threatened by the Indian agent who would not advance him funds to attend the games. How Thorpe was caught playing professional sports under an assumed name to support his amateur career is told in *All American: The Rise and Fall of Jim Thorpe* by Bill Crawford (see chapter 12). Paul Robeson was a star athlete and talented actor and musician in the first half of the twentieth century. How his race and politics handicapped his career is discussed in a collection of biographical essays, *Paul Robeson: Artist and Citizen* (see chapter 9).

Cheever, Susan

My Name Is Bill: Bill Wilson: His Life and the Creation of Alcoholics Anonymous. Simon & Schuster, 2004. 306p. ISBN 074320154X.

You could say Bill Wilson's (1895–1971) drinking problem started at a dinner party when he was given a beer that helped him relax and talk with friends, or you could go further back and say it started with his parents' divorce, which left him insecure. You could go even further back looking for reasons but never know why he was an alcoholic. Wilson, whose marriage and business suffered because of his addiction, discovered that acceptance and resolve, not rationalizing, were what helped people with his problem. In this novel-like biography, best-selling author Susan Cheever tells how the nice man with a weakness for drink conceived of his twelve-step process and the organization Alcoholics Anonymous.

Subjects: Alcoholics; Alcoholics Anonymous; Teen Reads; Wilson, Bill

Now Try: *Bill W: My 1st 40 Years* was Wilson's autobiography, written to help other alcoholics believe that they could also stop drinking. Like her father, the author John Cheever, Susan Cheever had a drinking problem. In *Note Found in a Bottle: My Life as a Drinker*, she describes a world in which the drinking of alcohol determined one's friends and schedule and limited the depth of relationships. *Addiction: A Personal Story* is a religiously inspired collection of 260 brief stories from people recovering from a variety of addictions. Augusten Burroughs drank more than most people could imagine before he checked into a recovery center. Being a comic writer, he tells his story of staying sober with humor and irreverence in *Dry: A Memoir*.

Dallek, Robert

An Unfinished Life: John Kennedy, 1917–1963. Little Brown, 2003. 838p. ISBN 0316172-383. Audiobook and large print available.

The rocking chair in the Oval Office offered a clue. President John F. Kennedy (1917–1963) was more troubled by health problems than the American public ever knew. Like Franklin Roosevelt, he often needed help getting around the White House and made untold numbers of visits to hospitals for unreported maladies. It was a wonder he could maintain his hectic schedule and youthful appearance, much less face foreign foes and conduct romantic affairs. According to historian Robert Dallek, Kennedy did all of the above through sheer willpower and the will to live while he could. Death was never far from his mind.

> **Subjects:** Chronic Illnesses; Kennedy, John F.; Presidents

> **Now Try:** Kennedy's life nearly ended in the Pacific Theater during World War II, when the boat under his command was struck by a Japanese destroyer. Robert J. Donovan recounts how Kennedy helped his crew reach a small island, where they hid for six days until rescued, in *PT 109: John F. Kennedy in World War II*. The photobiography *John Fitzgerald Kennedy: A Life in Pictures* by Yann-Brice Dherbier and Pierre-Henri Verlhac is a useful companion volume to Dallek's biography of Kennedy. Popular singer and actor Bobby Darin knew that he had rheumatic heart disease and should take health precautions, but he had a Kennedy-like drive for living. Al DiOrio portrays Darin as a dynamic entertainer who would not rest in *Borrowed Time: The 37 Years of Bobby Darin*. Presidential biographies *FDR* by Jean Edward Smith (see chapter 10) and *John Adams* by David McCullough (see chapter 10) have a similar intimate tone and comparable epic length to Dallek's biography of Kennedy.

Friedman, Lawrence J.

Identity's Architect: A Biography of Erik H. Erikson. Scribner, 1999. 592p. ISBN 068419-5259.

It seems almost a joke to say that psychoanalyst Erik H. Erikson (1902–1994) wondered who he was, but he did. His search to identify his father sparked his thinking about identity. Trained by Sigmund and Anna Freud in Vienna, Erikson experienced personal tragedies that he incorporated into his investigations of the mind. In this admiring biography, author Lawrence J. Friedman claims that Erikson drew both criticism and acclaim for his classic books, which continue to be read and discussed. The cast in this story includes nearly every big name in twentieth-century psychology.

> **Subjects:** Erikson, Erik H.; Identity; Psychoanalysts

> **Now Try:** Erikson wrote several classic books on child development, including *Childhood and Society*, *Identity and the Life Cycle*, and *Identity: Youth and Crisis*. He also wrote the psychological biographies *Young Man Luther* and *Gandhi's Truth*. As a teenager, Erikson's daughter Sue Erikson Bloland rebelled against her parents, whom she claims were addicted to achievement. She describes the pressures of living with unrealistic expectations in her memoir, *In the Shadow of Fame : A Memoir by the Daughter of Erik H. Erikson*. Sigmund Freud also let his personal experiences influence his psychological theories. An accessible biography is *Freud: Inventor of the Modern Mind* by Peter D. Kramer (see chapter 11). The melancholy of Erikson's life resembles that of Nelson Riddle, whose sadder story is told in *September in the Rain: The Life of Nelson Riddle* by Peter J. Levinson (see chapter 7).

Kendall, Joshua

The Man Who Made Lists: Love, Death, Madness, and the Creation of Roget's Thesaurus. G. P. Putnam's Sons, 2008. 297p. ISBN 9780399154621.

There are no synonyms, according to Peter Mark Roget (1779–1869), author of *Roget's Thesaurus*, for no two words have the exact same meaning. There are many words with near meanings from which to choose to clarify messages, and the eccentric polymath and classifier tried to organize them. According to journalist Joshua Kendall, Roget was a physician and scientist who made lists from childhood in response to the discord and chaos of his life, especially to stay free of the insanity that infected his grandmother, mother, sister, and uncle. His thesaurus was a by-product of his effective personal therapy. General readers will enjoy this biography full of vocabulary facts and famous nineteenth-century English characters.

> **Subjects:** Great Britain; Group Discussion Books; Insanity; Lexicographers; Philologists; Physicians; Roget, Peter Mark

> **Now Try:** Like Henry Gray, who wrote the original *Gray's Anatomy*, Roget's name is inserted into titles of books many years after his death. In ***The Anatomist: A True Story of Gray's Anatomy*** (see chapter 11), Bill Hayes reveals the long-lost story of how Gray and his illustrator, Henry Vandyke Carter, wrote the pioneering anatomy text. A contemporary of Roget, Thomas Young was also a polymath, physician, and linguist of great talent. Though he advanced the study of light waves, explained elasticity, and formulated the three-color theory of vision, he is mostly forgotten today. Andrew Robinson tells his amazing story in ***The Last Man Who Knew Everything: Thomas Young, the Anonymous Genius Who Proved Newton Wrong and Deciphered the Rosetta Stone, Among Other Surprising Feats.*** Poet and literary critic John Ciardi had a love of words that he shared regularly on National Public Radio. His entertaining books on vocabulary include ***A Browser's Dictionary*** and ***Good Words to You: An All-New Dictionary and Native's Guide to the Unknown American Language.*** Edward M. Cifelli describes Ciardi's life and love of precision in ***John Ciardi: A Biography.***

Lovell, Mary S.

Bess of Hardwick: Empire Builder. W. W. Norton, 2005. 555p. ISBN 9780393062212.

When Queen Elizabeth I of England decided that her cousin Mary Stuart, Queen of Scots, had to be imprisoned securely but with some comfort, she selected the Earl of Shrewsbury as Mary's custodian. Much of the work of keeping Mary, however, fell to his remarkable wife, Elizabeth Shrewsbury (1527?–1608). As warden she saw Mary daily, and the two initially became quite close, a dangerous position for a subject of Queen Elizabeth. In her admiring book about the woman known as Bess of Hardwick, Mary S. Lovell tells how the countess married at age fifteen, saw many of her relatives beheaded, survived four husbands and four monarchs, and built three great houses. Her descendants include most of the nobility in England today.

> **Subjects:** Countesses; England; Shrewsbury, Elizabeth Hardwick Talbot; Women

Now Try: More about Queen Mary's tragic story is told in *Queen of Scots: The True Life of Mary Stuart* by John Guy (see chapter 9). Edith Galt had been a widow for several years, running a prosperous jewelry business inherited from her husband, when through friends she met President Woodrow Wilson, himself a widower. A quick romance and marriage followed. In *Edith and Woodrow: The Wilson White House* (see chapter 10), Phyllis Lee Levin describes how a woman of little pretense quickly reached a position of great influence and real power. Anna Leonowens did not have all the credentials that she suggested when she applied to be governess for the crown prince of Siam. In *Bombay Anna*, Susan Morgan describes Leonownens as a woman who was successful in the employ of a monarch precisely because she was not an English lady with many prejudices. A striking example of a man able to survive through many dangerous political changes is French minister Charles Maurice de Talleyrand-Périgord. David Lawday portrays Talleyrand sympathetically, admitting that the French statesman served his own interests first, but arguing that he was also the architect of contemporary Anglo–French relations, in *Napoleon's Master: A Life of Prince Talleyrand* (see chapter 10).

Lydon, Michael

Ray Charles: Man and Music. Riverhead Books, 1998. 436p. ISBN 1573221325.

Blindness was never an excuse for Ray Charles (1930–2004). After congenital juvenile glaucoma took his sight at age six, his mother still insisted he do chores, such as fetching water and scrubbing floors. His neighbor, Mr. Pit, taught him to play boogie-woogie on the piano at age three, and the local piano teacher, Mrs. Lawrence, trained him classically at age eight. By the time his mother died, when he was fourteen, Charles was on his way to a musical career. *Rolling Stone* writer Michael Lydon tells a candid story about a poor boy from Jellyroll, Florida, who overcame class and racial discrimination to become a giant in the world of popular music.

Subjects: African Americans; Blindness; Charles, Ray; Jazz Musicians; Singers

Now Try: Charles told about his childhood and his recording career, which introduced him to musicians in many fields, in his memoir, *Brother Ray: Ray Charles' Own Story*. Charles shared many of the experiences of poverty, discrimination, and success in music with Muddy Waters, whose story is admiringly told in *Can't Be Satisfied: The Life and Times of Muddy Waters* by Robert Gordon. When Fats Domino was rescued during Hurricane Katrina in 2005, many fans were stunned to learn he was still living. Unlike Charles, his career had waned, as alcohol, bad business deals, gambling addiction, marital problems, and poor health had taken their toll on his career. Rick Coleman explains why Domino is still beloved in New Orleans and why music fans remember his innovations, in *Blue Monday: Fats Domino and the Lost Dawn of Rock and Roll*. The essential person shaping Charles in his childhood was his mother. Bonnie Angelo shows how strong mothers inspired many of the U.S. presidents in *First Mothers: The Women Who Shaped the Presidents* (see chapter 10).

Morris, Edmund

Beethoven: The Universal Composer. Atlas Books, 2005. 243p. <u>Eminent Lives</u>. ISBN 9780060759742. Audiobook available.

When Joseph Haydn died in 1809, Ludwig van Beethoven (1770–1827) became the world's most famous composer. By that time he was already deaf and had been rejected as a suitor by women of higher social class, but the proud composer hid both his handicap and his disappointment. Sympathetic biographer Edmund Morris portrays Beethoven as a courageous man relying on his music to get him through his difficult life.

Subjects: Beethoven, Ludwig van; Composers; Deafness; Germany

Now Try: Beethoven was a prolific letter writer who told about his daily life and his musical ideas. Over 400 letters to friends, family, musicians, and literary figures are included in *Beethoven's Letters*, edited by Alfred Christlieb Kalischer. The world traveler and anthropologist Sir Richard Burton has often been portrayed as a romantic but tempestuous character resembling the typical depiction of Beethoven. Mary S. Lovell portrays him sympathetically as a devoted husband whose world travels were supported by his wife, in *A Rage to Live: A Biography of Richard & Isabel Burton* (see chapter 1). Spanish artist Francisco José de Goya y Lucientes is often portrayed as insane. Robert Hughes shows that Goya's life was filled with pain and despair, but with courage like Beethoven's, he maintained his relationships and work in *Goya* (see chapter 7). Many musical composers are included in small, quick reading biography series. *Mozart* by Peter Gay (see chapter 6) is found in Penguin Lives from Viking Press, and *The Life of Mendelssohn* by Peter Mercer-Taylor (see chapter 7) is in Musical Lives from Cambridge University Press, which also includes books on Berlioz, Schubert, and Verdi.

Shostak, Marjorie

Nisa: The Life and Words of a !Kung Woman. Harvard University Press, 1981. 402p. ISBN 0674624858.

In 1971 Harvard anthropologist Marjorie Shostak visited the women of the !Kung tribe in the Kalahari Desert in Botswana. Interested in these people who still lived by hunting and gathering, she recorded interviews with many women, but she was particularly struck by one woman's story. Nisa (1920?–?), who at the time was about fifty years old, told the author about her childhood, early marriage, unassisted childbirth, divorce, lovers, and the hardships of daily life in the desert. Shostak chose to write Nina's biography to appeal to general readers, not because she was a typical !Kung woman, but because she offered insights that spanned many cultures.

Subjects: Africa; Botswana; !Kung Tribe; Nisa; Women

Now Try: Biographies of individual tribal people are rare. More available are studies of their tribes, such as *Yanomamö* by Napoleon A. Chagnon and *The Gebusi: Lives Transformed in a Rainforest* by Bruce Knauft. A book about a woman suffering many of the same hardships as Nisa but set in New York City is *A Welfare Mother* by Susan Sheehan. Margaret Mead spent a lifetime studying tribal peoples in Samoa and Papua New Guinea and publishing books that questioned the development of culture. She described her education, her work in Samoa, her marriages, and the birth of her daughter in *Blackberry Winter: My Earlier Years*. Robert Cassidy completes Mead's story in his authorized biography, *Margaret Mead: A Voice for the Century*. Paleontologist and philosopher Pierre Teilhard de Chardin's studies and writings also fueled twentieth-century debates on the role of humans in the universe. Ursala King recounts his life and highlights his major works in the illustrated biography *Spirit of Fire: The Life and Vision of Teilhard de Chardin*.

Religious Stories

The most traditional form of Inspirational Biography continues to be the religious story. According to Neal Wyatt in *The Readers' Advisory Guide to Nonfiction* (American Library Association, 2007), people read these and other religious books for personal growth, increased understanding, and comfort. In the current market, memoirs dominate sales, but the third-person biography continues to appear as well in secular and religious bookstores and in libraries. In the United States the subgenre is dominated by Christian biography because of the country's demographics, but some titles featuring the founders or followers of other faiths are also available.

A wide range of religious figures are described in this section. Many are historical, going back to the patriarch Abraham, who is claimed by the Jewish, Christian, and Islamic traditions. Buddha, Jesus of Nazareth, and Muhammad are profiled, as are more recent figures, including Mother Theresa and the Dalai Lama. Because many of the authors are not clergy and seek secular readers, the texts tend to be more candid and verifiable than the religious publications of the past. Still, the intent of the books is to praise good lives and instruct readers to live spiritually rich lives.

Because there may be little documentary evidence on which to base profiles of ancient figures, the retelling of their myths and legends is often an element of these narratives. Trying to find the most likely story, the biographers sometimes examine variations in traditional tales. The elements of research and deduction resemble those in investigative writing. Readers will enjoy the strong characters, good stories, and moral lessons.

> *Religious Stories* feature characters who call on their religious faith to help them meet life's challenges. These stories include elements of praise and moral instruction but are more verifiable than the devotional literature of centuries past. Prophets, saints, clergy, and theologians from various world religions are among the subjects in this section.

Armstrong, Karen

Buddha. Lipper/Viking, 2001. 205p. <u>Penguin Lives</u>. ISBN 0670891932. Audiobook and large print available.

Not much is really known about Gotama (Armstrong's spelling), but religious author Karen Armstrong drew from many legends as well as Indian history to craft a profile that seems very contemporary. In ancient India, a place that was becoming more urbanized, bankers and merchants were taking political control from the hereditary leaders and castes were becoming more stratified. People felt traditional values were being lost. Gotama (563?–483? BCE) showed his spiritually hungry followers that the holy life was more than escapism. This Buddha profile should resonate with many contemporary readers seeking to live worthy lives.

Subjects: Buddhism; Ethics; Group Discussion Books; Guatama Buddha; India; Monks; Religious Mystic

Now Try: Deepak Chopra has written a novel about Gotama with a question-and-answer appendix, *Buddha: A Story of Enlightenment*. In Herman Hesse's novel

Siddhartha, the title character visits Gotama in one stage of his spiritual journey, but recognizes that strict adherence to the Buddha's rule is not his path. One Karen Armstrong book may lead the reader to another. *A History of God: The 4,000-Year Quest of Judaism, Christianity, and Islam* is an almost biographical treatment of the Supreme Being and is a good follow-up to her life of Buddha. In *Buddhism in America*, Richard Hughes Seager discusses how the immigration of Asians and the adoption of Buddhism by people of European heritage have increased the Buddhist community in the United States. He also describes how Americans have adapted Buddhist philosophies to Western culture.

Armstrong, Karen

Muhammad: A Prophet for Our Time. Atlas Books/Harpercollins, 2006. 249p. Eminent Lives. ISBN 9780060598976. Audiobook available.

Before his vision of the angel Gabriel in 610, little is known of the prophet Muhammad (570?–632), but from that date on, his life is heavily documented, according to religious author Karen Armstrong. Stories about his travels, preaching, and family life are well known and often told. Although he inspired the Arabs and led them to military victories, he emphasized a message of following God's laws, showing mercy to enemies, and respecting others. In this short biography written for readers curious about Islam, Armstrong portrays Muhammad as a pious, spiritually inspired man with a message often abused by many in both the East and the West.

Subjects: Group Discussion Books; Islam; Muhammad; Prophets

Now Try: The revelations of Muhammad are collected in the **Qur'an** or **Koran**, which is available in many translations. *Muhammad: His Life Based on the Earliest Sources* by Martin Lings is a more canonical approach than Armstrong's historical treatment of the founder of Islam. *No God but God: The Origins, Evolution, and Future of Islam* by Reza Aslam is a well-written account of the prophet's legacy. In Jewish and Christian histories, the figure who accepted the revelations of law was Moses. Jonathan Kirsch recounts the stories about the leader who led the Jewish people out of Egypt in *Moses: A Life*. Joseph Smith was an American prophet who founded a new religion. Robert V. Remini chronicles a life spent responding to the confusing culture of the Jacksonian Age, when issues of westward expansion, the struggle over slavery, and religious evangelism were dividing public opinion, in *Joseph Smith*.

Cahill, Thomas

Pope John XXIII. Lipper/Viking, 2002. 240p. Penguin Lives. ISBN 0670030570. Audiobook and large print available.

Historian Thomas Cahill says that John XXIII (1881–1963) was like no other pope and that readers need background on the papacy to understand his significance. To this end, the first third of this biographical profile is a history of his predecessors. The last short section describes his legacy. Sandwiched between these sections is Cahill's loving account of the gentle man who served his flock by modernizing their church. Readers who look for spiritual role models may enjoy this book.

Subjects: John XXIII, Pope; Popes; Roman Catholic Church

Now Try: Pope John XXIII described his life and faith in *The Journal of a Soul*. Pope John Paul I promised to be very like John XXIII in his approach to modernizing the Roman Catholic Church, but he died one month into his papacy. Peter Hebblethwaite describes John Paul I, his predecessor, and his successor in *The Year of Three Popes*. A handy book for answering questions about the papacy and the men who have been pope, also interesting to browse, is *The Pope Encyclopedia: An A to Z of the Holy See*. Like John XXIII, Thomas Merton spoke to an era looking for more intimate and less rule-conscious religion. He told about his life and faith in *The Seven Storey Mountain*.

Chhaya, Mayank

Dalai Lama: An Authorized Biography. Doubleday, 2007. 342p. ISBN 9780385519458. Audiobook available.

Lhamo Thondup (1935–) was three years old when monks from the Potala Palace at Lhasa identified him as the Fourteenth Dalai Lama and less than five years old when he was installed as the temporal leader of Tibetan Buddhists. At age nineteen he met with Mao Tse-Tung to negotiate a peace with China, but he was only able to delay the Chinese invasion. In 1959, at age twenty-four, he fled Tibet to avoid imprisonment and probable death. Journalist Mayank Chhaya respectfully tells how the Dalai Lama has expanded the spiritual mission of his position to teach nonviolence to the world while seeking to return to his homeland. Current events readers and spiritual pilgrims will benefit from this admiring biography.

Subjects: Buddhists; Dalai Lama, Fourteenth; Group Discussion Books; Monks; Nonviolence; Tibet

Now Try: The Dalai Lama is the author of guides for spiritual development, including *The Art of Happiness in a Troubled World, Advice on Dying and Living a Better Life*, and *The Art of Living: A Guide to Contentment, Joy and Fulfillment*. When a Dalai Lama dies, a new reincarnation is sought by the High Lamas of the Gelugpa Tradition. The current Dalai Lama is the fourteenth. Glenn H. Mullen has collected profiles of all fourteen of the incarnations in *Fourteen Dalai Lamas: A Sacred Legacy of Reincarnation*. With his emphasis on peace negotiation and respect for all people, Archbishop Desmond Tutu of South Africa has earned the admiration of people around the globe. John Allen describes the Nobel Peace Prize–winning Tutu as a man who has saved lives and brought hope to his country, in *Rabble-Rouser for Peace: The Authorized Biography of Desmond Tutu*.

Chilton, Bruce

Mary Magdalene: A Biography. Doubleday, 2005. 220p. ISBN 0385513178.

In the wake of the *Da Vinci Code*, interest in Mary Magdalene (first century CE) has increased. In this book, religious scholar Bruce Chilton examines stories about Mary, a woman who went to Rabbi Jesus to have her seven demons removed and who later anointed his body after his crucifixion. Using the biblical Gospels, the gnostic Gospels, collected legends, and historical records, he discusses her role as a disciple and the speculation that she was "the bride of Christ." This work is scholarly but accessible to most readers interested in Mary Magdalene in fact and legend.

Subjects: Judea; Mary Magdalene; Saints; Women

Now Try: Chilton's book on Mary Magdalene is third in a series of biographies including *Rabbi Jesus: An Intimate Biography* and *Rabbi Paul: An Intellectual Biography*. There are many novels with Mary Magdalene as a character. In *Mary, Called Magdalene* by Margaret George, Mary is an early feminist, leaving her husband to follow Jesus Christ; in *The Secret Gospel of Mary Magdalene* by Michele Roberts, she is a reformed courtesan turned gospel writer. Aurelius Augustinus Hipponensis wrote about his sinful life before he became a follower of Jesus in *The Confessions of St. Augustine.* James Joseph O'Donnell continues Augustine's story with an account of his forty years as Bishop of Hippo in *Augustine: A New Biography*.

Crossan, John Dominic

Jesus: A Revolutionary Biography. HarperSanFrancisco, 1994. 209p. ISBN 0060-61661X. Audiobook available.

John Dominic Crossan is a leading scholar in the Jesus Seminar, which seeks to identify the historical Jesus of Nazareth (first century CE) in scriptures and documents, a cause often opposed by other theologians. In this short biography, Crossan draws from the four biblical Gospels as well as other early Christian gospels and Roman records to characterize Jesus as a rebel who wished to reform Jewish law and free his people from the Romans. Jesus healed on the Sabbath, broke dietary laws, and associated with sinners, all acts of defiance. Readers who enjoy reading familiar Bible stories retold to reveal new meanings will enjoy this book.

Subjects: Group Discussion Books; Jesus Christ; Judea; Roman Empire

Now Try: In *The Real Jesus: The Misguided Quest for the Historical Jesus and the Truth of the Traditional Gospels*, Luke Timothy Johnson refutes much of what Crossan says in his books about Jesus. Biographies of Jesus Christ abound. In *Jesus: An Historian's Review of the Gospels*, Michael Grant presents Jesus as a holy man with miraculous power, whereas Donald Spoto presents an argument that Jesus was both divine and human in *The Hidden Jesus*. A less partisan choice is the beautifully illustrated *Jesus Christ: The Jesus of History, the Christ of Faith* by J. R. Porter. In his novel *Joshua* and its numerous sequels, Joseph F. Girzone has Jesus return to earth in modern times as a humble man who quietly preaches and disappears before too large a crowd appears. One's interpretation of the Gospels often is affected by which Bible translation is being read. In *God's Secretaries: The Making of the King James Bible*, Adam Nicolson profiles the scholars and the process that they employed to write the beautifully worded *King James Bible.*

Downing, David C.

The Most Reluctant Convert: C. S. Lewis's Journey to Faith. InterVarsity Press, 2002. 191p. ISBN 0830823115. Audiobook available.

In the tense atmosphere of early twentieth-century Northern Ireland, young C. S. Lewis (1898–1963) found his family's church more political than devout, so when his mother died in 1908, his commitment to Christianity was weak. Returning to a wretched boarding school in Surrey, England, he rejected religion, saying that there was no proof that God existed. For over twenty years he maintained a strictly secular outlook while reading mythology, writing poetry, and fighting in the First World War.

David C. Downing focuses on this skeptical period before Lewis's stated conversion, two decades skipped over by most biographers. Downing contends that it was during this time that this famous Christian author found his faith. Lewis fans and religious readers will enjoy this spiritual coming-of-age story.

Subjects: Christianity; Lewis, C. S.; Religious Authors

Now Try: Among C. S. Lewis's many spiritual classics are several autobiographical works, including *Surprised by Joy: The Shape of My Early Life* and *A Grief Observed*. Lewis belonged to a circle of writers at Oxford University who formed a literary circle that met at the Eagle and Child Pub for dearly two decades. Humphrey Carpenter chronicles their meetings and the books and letters they wrote in *The Inklings: C.S. Lewis, J.R.R. Tolkien, Charles Williams and Their Friends*. The English poet A. H. Auden experienced a conversion much like Lewis's, which is described in *W. H. Auden: A Biography*, also by Humphrey Carpenter. Unlike Lewis and his friends, Malcolm Muggeridge was a journalist and media personality with communist leanings and agnostic beliefs before converting to Roman Catholicism. *Confessions of a Twentieth Century Pilgrim* is his memoir about his change of faith.

Freeman, Philip

St. Patrick of Ireland: A Biography. Simon & Schuster, 2004. 216p. ISBN 0743256328. Audiobook and large print available.

When Saint Patrick (373?–463?) landed in Ireland for the purpose of preaching the Gospel, it was his second time on the island. In his youth he had been kidnapped from Roman Britain by Irish raiders and sold as a slave to a shepherd. He escaped after six years, became a priest, and came back to Ireland as its first bishop. Contrary to legends, he did not chase the snakes from the island or fight Druids; instead, he established churches and gathered Christians who were already on the island, many of whom were slaves. In this short, compelling biography for general readers, classics professor Philip Freeman portrays Patrick as a resourceful, dedicated missionary who faced numerous trials in a dangerous land.

Subjects: Ireland; Missionaries; Patrick, Saint; Saints

Now Try: *The Confessions of St. Patrick* is a small collection of writing attributed to the saint. In the fantasy novel *I Am of Irelaunde: A Novel of Patrick and Osian*, Julienne Osborne-McKnight imaginatively combines the story of St. Patrick evangelizing in Ireland with the story of Osian, a poet-warrior of the Fianna, a hero from earlier in Irish history. Despite its title, *Saints Behaving Badly: The Cutthroats, Crooks, Trollops, Con Men, and Devil-Worshippers Who Became Saints* by Thomas J. Craughwell is a respectful collected biography of sinners who became saints, Saint Patrick included. Another entertaining investigation of a legend of the British Isles is *Boudica: The Life of Britain's Legendary Warrior Queen* by Vanessa Collingridge (see chapter 5).

Harrison, Kathryn

Saint Thérèse of Lisieux. Lipper/Viking Book, 2003. 227p. Penguin Lives. ISBN 0670031488. Audiobook and large print available.

Thérèse Martin (1873–1897) was a pampered child. At age eleven, because she was always attended by servants, she did not even know how to dress herself or comb her hair. Surprisingly, by age fifteen the emotional and often ill child had chosen a life of self-denial as a Carmelite nun. Under the direction of her mother superior (her elder sister, Pauline), she began to write daily confessions that later formed an autobiography, which became an international spiritual classic after her death at age twenty-four. In this compact biography for religious readers, novelist Kathryn Harrison tells how Thérèse lived, died, and was canonized as a saint.

Subjects: France; Nuns; Quick Reads; Saints; Teen Reads; Thérèse of Lisieux; Women

Now Try: Thérèse's confessions can be found in *The Autobiography of St. Thérèse of Liseaux*. The heresy trial of a young woman named Joan, who led French forces against the English in the fifteenth century, is difficult for modern readers to comprehend. In *Joan: The Mysterious Life of the Heretic Who Became a Saint* (see this chapter), Donald Spoto describes the trial and the injustice of the execution of a young woman who is now called Joan of Arc. Simone Weil was a young French woman of Jewish heritage who jettisoned her adherence to Marxism when she recognized the tyranny of bureaucracy in all Marxist governments. She studied Christian theology and wrote deeply philosophical essays about faith without ever committing to conversion before her death. Francine du Plessix Gray describes a totally sincere soul in search of truth and justice in *Simone Weil*. In the wake of the reforms of the Second Vatican Council, the experience of being a nun changed dramatically in the 1960s. Karen Armstrong describes what led her to becoming a nun in *Through the Narrow Gate* and why she left the convent in *Spiral Staircase: My Climb Out of Darkness*. For readers wanting a lighthearted look at nuns, Karol Jackowski recounts the years of her novitiate and ordination as a nun in *Forever and Ever, Amen: Becoming a Nun in the Sixties*.

Hattersley, Roy

Blood and Fire: William and Catherine Booth and Their Salvation Army. Doubleday, 1999. 471p. ISBN 0385494394.

When William and Catherine Booth started the Christian Revival Society among the poor, alcoholics, and prostitutes of London's East End in 1865, they were portrayed by polite society as crude and over-zealous. William Booth (1829–1912), who had left the Methodist church and had been evangelizing since the 1840s, struggled for years to fund his group's charity, later renamed the Salvation Army, before it became accepted and respected. Catherine's (1829–1890) role in the society rose over time, as she overcame the stigma of women preaching in public. She also raised eight children, all of whom worked for the family cause. As partners, they took their message worldwide. By the time William died in 1912, he had dined with royalty all over the world, and the Salvation Army was in fifty-eight countries. Roy Hattersley's story of the couple's life is candid about the organization's controversies and internal disagreements but is mostly admiring.

Subjects: Booth, Catherine; Booth, William; Evangelists; Family Biography; Great Britain; Salvation Army

Now Try: In *In Darkest England and the Way Out*, William Booth described the physical and spiritual poverty of industrial society and the need for Christian missions. At the time of their wedding in 1912, friends doubted that a marriage between writer Leonard Woolf and temperamental Virginia Stephens could last. George Spater and Woolf neighbor Ian Parsons retell the story of the difficult romance that did endure in *A Marriage of True Minds: An Intimate*

Portrait of Leonard and Virginia Woolf (see chapter 7). Biographers have always thought that Isabel Burton lamented Sir Richard Burton's frequent explorations to Africa and Asia, pointing to her burning of Richard's papers after his death. Mary S. Lovell, however, found seven boxes of diaries and letters in the Wiltshire Record Office in Trowbridge, England. With them, Lovell portraits the couple as more attuned to each other than previously believed, in *A Rage to Live: A Biography of Richard & Isabel Burton* (see chapter 1). John Lennon and Yoko Ono reveled in the spotlight of the rock music world of the 1960s and 1970s. The editors of *Rolling Stone* chronicled the couple's antics in a series of articles collected as *The Ballad of John and Yoko.*

House, Adrian

Francis of Assisi: A Revolutionary Life. HiddenSpring, 2001. 336p. ISBN 1587680092.
At age twenty-four, Francesco di Pietro (1182–1226) stood naked in the court of Bishop Guido of Assisi and returned his clothes and money to his angry father, vowing poverty and service to the message of Jesus Christ. For the next twenty years he led a band of followers seeking simplicity and peace, caring for the sick and poor and annoying the rich and powerful religious establishment. In this biography without most of the miracle stories of more devotional literature, Adrian House portrays Francis as a hero who preached his message to everyone who would hear, even the birds of the air and the sultan of Egypt. Readers who like historical treatments of legends will enjoy this biography.

Subjects: Francis of Assisi; Italy; Monks; Saints

Now Try: Short story readers may prefer the more devotional *Salvation: Scenes from the Life of St. Francis* by Valerie Martin, which dramatizes the saint's life through a series of tales. Nikos Kazantzakis moves Francis to the twentieth century and makes him an existentialist philosopher in *Saint Francis: A Novel*. Like Francis, Mahatma Gandhi inspired followers to join him in poverty and devotion, as told in *Gandhi's Passion: The Life and Legacy of Mahatma Gandhi* by Stanley Wolpert (see this chapter). The Indian religious leader Guatama, known as the Buddha, also took a vow of poverty. Karen Armstrong describes the life and times of Guatama in *Buddha* (see this chapter). Saint Teresa of Avila was a Spanish nun who founded a reformed house for Carmelite nuns, emphasizing poverty. Cathleen Medwick describes the spiritual woman in *Teresa of Avila: The Progress of a Soul.*

Hurley, Joanna

Mother Teresa: A Pictorial Biography. Courage Books, 1997. 120p. ISBN 0762402148.
Hearing Jesuit priests talk about their mission work when she was twelve, Mother Teresa (1910–1997) chose at age eighteen to leave Serbia to join the Sisters of Loreto for the express purpose of teaching poor children in India. After eighteen years in training in Ireland, she finally got her chance to teach in 1946, but she quickly found that feeding the poor was her true mission. In this tribute written before Mother Teresa's death, journalist Joanna Hurley tells the story of a devout woman who through much hard work created a mission in Calcutta, moved hearts worldwide, and won a Nobel Peace Prize. Readers who support religious missions will appreciate this attractive photographic book.

Subjects: India; Mother Teresa; Nuns; Photographic Biography; Women

Now Try: For readers wanting more intimate knowledge of the nun, the memoir *Mother Teresa: Come Be My Light* tells about her life of constant service and strong faith despite the absence of feeling the presence of God. Albert Schweitzer came to missionary work later in his life than Mother Teresa, but still spent many years in service of the poor. A second edition of *Albert Schweitzer: A Biography* by James Brabazon adds recently uncovered documents. William and Catherine Booth started the Salvation Army to help the downtrodden in London. Roy Hattersley tells about them in *Blood and Fire: William and Catherine Booth and Their Salvation Army* (see this chapter). In nineteenth-century Chicago, Jane Addams opened Hull House to serve the many needs of the poor who were coming to her city. Gioia Diliberto tells how the socialite transformed herself into an activist in *A Useful Woman: The Early Life of Jane Addams* (see this chapter).

Kozak, Warren

The Rabbi of 84th Street: The Extraordinary Life of Haskel Besser. HarperCollins, 2004. 200p. ISBN 006051101X.

Hasidic rabbi Haskel Besser (1923–) of Manhattan is known for his infectious smile and disarming charm. Besser claims that he has to smile because he has been blessed with good fortune, having escaped Poland before the Jewish Holocaust, lived in British Palestine before the Jewish uprising, and been welcomed to live freely in the United States. Now he works to reestablish Jewish communities in Poland and to preserve the traditions of his faith. Journalist Warren Kozak describes the origins and work of a pious man in this admiring account.

> **Subjects:** Besser, Haskel; Hasidism; Israel; Judaism; New York City; Poland; Rabbis

> **Now Try:** In the twelfth century, when Christian nations across Europe were expelling Jews, Rabbi Moses Maimonides escaped Spain, going first to Morocco, where Muslims repressed Jews, and then finally to Egypt, where he became physician to the sultan. Sherwin B. Nuland tells how the revered rabbi wrote his philosophical and spiritual texts amid turmoil in *Maimonides*. As a Hasidic Jew, Besser is a follower of the founder of Hasidism, Rabbi Baal Shem Tov, whose life is told as a series of stories in *In Praise of the Baal Shem Tov*. In a series of novels set in New York City, *The Chosen*, *The Promise*, and *My Name Is Asher Lev*, rabbi Chaim Potok examined the lives of Reformed and Orthodox Jews in America. Like Besser, Hassid rabbi Arthur Hertzberg was born in Poland in the 1920s. In his memoir, *Jew in America: My Life and a People's Struggle for Identity*, he explains how forming closed communities is now an American tradition for religious groups in a new land.

LaPlante, Eve

Salem Witch Judge: The Life and Repentance of Samuel Sewall. Harper One, 2007. 352p. ISBN 9780060786618.

Five years after the Salem witch trials, Judge Samuel Sewall (1652–1730) publicly confessed that he had sinned in condemning twenty people to death. Standing before an assembly of his church, he retold a story that most of his peers wanted forgotten. No one stood with him, and few heeded his call for community penance. It was a remarkable act that signaled an awakening in the until-then predictable Puritan minister, according to Eve LaPlante. Subsequently he wrote the first abolitionist treatise, argued for better relations with the Indians, and discussed the rights of women. LaPlante's narrative about a man who had a dramatic change of heart will resonate with modern readers.

Subjects: Clergy; Group Discussion Books; Judges; Puritans; Massachusetts Colony

Now Try: Sewall said little about the Salem witch trials in his diaries, which are available in abridged volumes, but his apology is found in *Early American Writing*, edited by Giles Gunn. Arthur Miller dramatized the witch trials in his play *The Crucible*. Puritan society of colonial Massachusetts called for conformity of purpose and adherence to rules from all its citizens. It had no room for a woman who would openly question the authority of it leaders. In *American Jezebel: The Uncommon Life of Anne Hutchinson, the Woman Who Defied the Puritans* (see chapter 9), LaPlante recounts how Anne Hutchinson was expelled from the colony after being condemned by both civil and church courts. Thomas Paine was accorded much support as he opposed British rule of the colonies, but American colonial leaders withdrew their friendship as he pushed for the end of slavery and espoused the extension of voting rights to men without property. His story is told in *Thomas Paine: Enlightenment, Revolution, and the Birth of Modern Nations* by Craig Nelson (see chapter 10). In *Wounds Not Healed by Time: The Power of Repentance and Forgiveness*, Solomon Schimmel discusses the traditions of confessing sins and healing souls in Judaism, Christianity, and Islam.

Marsden, George M.

🌻 *Jonathan Edwards: A Life.* Yale University Press, 2003. 615p. ISBN 0300096933.

Congregational minister Jonathan Edwards (1703–1758) spent his life preparing to die. His main concern was always the state of immortal souls, his as well as those of his congregations across colonial New England, New York, and New Jersey. After his own religious awakening at age eighteen and his studies at Yale College, he became the voice of reformed Puritanism, penning books and sermons, such as the still often studied *Sinners in the Hands of an Angry God*. Historian George M. Marsden regrets the tendency of recent biographers to judge their subjects by modern standards and attempts to restore Edwards to his time. Readers interested in American colonial life will enjoy this full account of the clergyman's career and spiritual journey.

Subjects: Clergy; Edwards, Jonathan; Theologians

Awards: Bancroft Prize in American History and Diplomacy, 2004

Now Try: *A Jonathan Edwards Reader* includes essays, sermons, diaries, and letters from the Puritan minister. Edwards was concerned that the scientific principles expressed by his contemporary, Sir Isaac Newton, would influence his congregations. David Berlinski explains the life and work of the eminent scientist in *Newton's Gift: How Sir Isaac Newton Unlocked the Systems of the World* (see chapter 11). Edwards's predecessor on the pulpit Cotton Mather was so interested in natural phenomena and their relationship to the divine that he became a member of London's Royal Society, a body of men interested in science. Kenneth Silverman describes a complex man who contributed to the hysteria of the Salem witch trials in *The Life and Times of Cotton Mather*. Michael Kazin is another author who thinks modern biographers deal unfairly with the religious beliefs of historical figures. He tells an admiring story of an American concerned by the moral implications of his government service in *A Godly Hero: The Life of William Jennings Bryan* (see chapter 10).

Marty, Martin

Martin Luther. Penguin Viking, 2004. 199p. <u>Penguin Lives</u>. ISBN 9780312375881.

For 450 years, biographers have portrayed religious reformer Martin Luther (1483–1546) as either the man who saved Christianity by challenging the Roman Catholic Church or the villain who led many people away from the true church. Either way, he is credited with polarizing the religious and political landscape of sixteenth-century Europe. According to theologian Martin Marty, he was an admirable but flawed character. Tacking *95 Theses* on the church doors in Wittenberg in 1517 and defying the precepts of Charles V at the Diet of Worms in 1521 were courageous acts that freed individuals to interpret the Bible themselves. His treatment of Jews, however, is difficult to defend. History and theology readers will appreciate this compact biography.

> **Subjects:** Christianity; Church History; Germany; Luther, Martin; Monks; Quick Reads; Theologians

> **Now Try:** *Faith and Freedom: An Invitation to the Writings of Martin Luther* is a collection of sermons, letters, and diaries by Martin Luther. *Out of the Storm: The Life and Legacy of Martin Luther* by novelist Derek Wilson is a highly readable biography that may please readers wanting more information about the famous clergyman. Luther's contemporary Nicolaus Copernicus was concerned with scientific truth and was just as reviled by the Roman Catholic Church as the dissenting clergyman. In *Copernicus' Secret: How the Scientific Revolution Began,* Repcheck credits Georg Joachim Rheticus, a Lutheran minister, for giving Copernicus the final mathematical data he needed to successfully challenge the church scholars. Like Luther, Abraham Lincoln was a man whose detractors vilified him, yet his actions are regarded as having changed the world. David Herbert Donald chronicles the successes and failures of the president who freed the slaves in *Lincoln* by (see chapter 10). Luther would probably despise Voltaire for his libertarianism, but they both started great social movements with philosophies. Roger Pearson recounts the entertaining life of the rowdy French philosopher in *Voltaire Almighty: A Life in Pursuit of Freedom* (see chapter 9).

Noonan, Peggy

John Paul the Great: Remembering a Spiritual Father. Viking, 2005. 238p. ISBN 0670037486. Audiobook and large print available.

According to Peggy Noonan, Pope John Paul II (1920–2005) was a modern man. Born Karol Wojtyla in Poland just after World War I, before many innovations in transportation and communications, he became a world traveler who enjoyed text-messaging and reading e-mail in his later years. He spent considerable time in Africa, Asia, and South America, where he visited the poor and sought to expand his church. In her collection of admiring biographical essays for general readers, Noonan portrays John Paul II as a hero who survived Nazism, communism, and terrorism, showing his people a better way to live.

> **Subjects:** Biographical Essays; John Paul II; Poland; Popes; Roman Catholic Church

Now Try: John Paul II was a prolific author, publishing poems, meditations, spiritual guides, and tracts on canon law. Written while Pope John Paul II was still living, *Man of the Century* by Jonathan Kwitny tells much more about the pontiff's early life in the Polish resistance and claims that he was the person most responsible for ending the Cold War. Lech Walesa credits the Polish pope, who made three key visits to his country during the Solidarity labor movement's years of struggle, with bringing down communist rule in Poland and the rest of Eastern Europe. Walesa recounts his own role in the liberation of Poland in *Struggle and the Triumph: An Autobiography.* Like John Paul II, South African bishop Desmond Tutu has sought peaceful means to solve conflicts. John Allen portrays him admiringly in *Rabble-Rouser for Peace: The Authorized Biography of Desmond Tutu.* Another Roman Catholic figure who garnered respect and devotion was Mother Teresa, the nun who helped the poor in Calcutta. In *Mother Teresa: Come Be My Light,* she told about her life of constant service and strong faith.

Spoto, Donald

Joan: The Mysterious Life of the Heretic Who Became a Saint. HarperSanFrancisco, 2007. 220p. ISBN 9780060815172. Audiobook available.

According to Donald Spoto, more is known about the short life of a young woman named Jeanne (1412–1431) than is known about Jesus of Nazareth, Buddha, and Muhammad. With her letters, contemporaries' journals, and the transcripts of her trial for heresy, the last years of Joan of Arc can be fully described. The author includes quotes from many sources in his telling of the sad story of how the French king whom Joan of Arc saved allowed her to be condemned and burned at the stake by her English captors. Throughout her ordeal, Joan remained faithful to her story that she was commanded by the voices of saints to free France from England. Readers who seek tales of selfless courage will appreciate this admiring biography.

Subjects: France; Hundred Years War; Joan of Arc; Martyrs; Saints; Teen Reads; Women

Now Try: In *Joan of Arc: In Her Own Words* Willard R. Trask arranges passages from the subject's trial and quotations from her contemporaries into a memoir. Thomas Keneally examines Joan's motives in his detail-rich novel *Blood Red, Sister Rose.* Mary Queen of Scots was the victim of a political struggle that kept her imprisoned for nineteen years. John Guy tells a tragic story with an equally dramatic death scene in *Queen of Scots: The True Life of Mary Stuart* (see chapter 9). The Greek philosopher Socrates was condemned to die for criticizing the government of Athens. Emily R. Wilson examines the philosopher and the complex power struggle that led to his drinking hemlock in *The Death of Socrates.* Like Joan, Simone Weil was an impassioned young woman who went to war and died early. Her story is sympathetically told by Francine du Plessix Gray in *Simone Weil.*

Inspirational Collections

The four books in this section differ from the others in this chapter in that they tell many life stories instead of one or two. They are to biography what short stories are to fiction. People with only short periods to devote to reading will find in them biographical narratives that they may enjoy more than longer works.

Like the other books in this chapter, these books have great character appeal. The artful women in *Alone! Alone!: Lives of Some Outsider Women* by Rosemary Dinnage defied social conventions to devote themselves to an unpopular cause. The determined people in *Carrying Jackie's Torch: The Players Who Integrated Baseball—and America* by Steve Jacobson and *Leading Ladies: American Trailblazers* by Kay Bailey Hutchinson overcame strong prejudices to pursue their careers. In *Wise Men and Their Tales: Portraits of Biblical, Talmudic, and Hasidic Masters*, Elie Wiesel tells about Jewish men who devoted themselves to advancing their faith. Readers will also enjoy these books for the quick stories and for examples worth following.

> *Inspirational Collections* are collective biographies featuring inspirational characters. These books, generally theme based, are to biography what short story collections are to fiction. Readers who enjoy short profiles of inspiring figures that can easily be read in single sittings will appreciate these collections.

Dinnage, Rosemary

Alone! Alone!: Lives of Some Outsider Women. New York Review Books, 2004. 296p. ISBN 1590170695.

Literary critic Rosemary Dinnage examines why some women must stand alone to do what they feel compelled to do. Women might write wickedly funny fiction, paint disturbing landscapes, sing morbid songs, or test the limits of unfair laws and societal strictures. In twenty-four biographical essays, the author tells the stories of distinctive women from the arts, literature, science, high society, and even brothels, all of whom have been highly criticized for their work. Dinnage's strength is in evoking sympathy for these courageously cantankerous women. Almost any reader will find someone to admire in this book.

Subjects: Activists; Artists; Authors; Collective Biography; Feminists; Solitude; Teen Reads; Women

Now Try: From early history to the modern age, women have left the comforts of the known world to explore the blank places on maps. Milbry Polk and Mary Tiegreen profile many of these women in the attractively illustrated *Women of Discovery: A Celebration of Intrepid Women Who Explored the World*. Jean H. Baker intimately profiles five outspoken feminists of the nineteenth and early twentieth centuries in *Sisters: The Lives of America's Suffragists*. With the civil rights movement, the sexual revolution, the feminist movement, and protests against the war in Vietnam, the 1960s was a decade of social upheaval. Tom Brokaw has gathered an accounts of men and women who came of age in that period in *Boom! Voices of the Sixties: Personal Reflections on the '60s and Today* (see chapter 6). Sheila Weller recounts the stories of three women who wrote and sang their personal songs about sexual liberation in the 1960s in *Girls Like Us: Carole King, Joni Mitchell, Carly Simon—and the Journey of a Generation* (see chapter 8).

Hutchinson, Kay Bailey

Leading Ladies: American Trailblazers. Harper, 2007. 396p. ISBN 9780061138249. Audiobook and large print available.

    Senator Kay Bailey Hutchinson received so many comments and requests after her first collection of biographical profiles, *American Heroines* (William Morrow, 2004), that she wrote a second book. She added chapters covering women in the military, in science, and in social crusades, such as women's suffrage and relief of poverty. Each profile is between two and ten pages long, telling quick stories of how the women overcame gender-related objections to contribute to the good of the nation and the advancement of their gender. Readers who enjoy reading short stories will enjoy this collected biography.

    Subjects: Collective Biography; Leadership; Teen Reads; Women

    Now Try: For twenty-four years Supreme Court justice Sandra Day O'Connor was in the news, often as the deciding vote in important cases before the court. Joan Biskupic tells the story of this accomplished woman from her birth in El Paso, Texas, to her retirement, with an emphasis on her Supreme Court career, in *Sandra Day O'Connor: How the First Woman on the Supreme Court Became Its Most Influential Justice* (see chapter 10). Women who excelled in the sport of tennis became symbols for both the civil rights and feminist movements. *The Match: Althea Gibson and Angel Buxton: How Two Outsiders—One Black, the Other Jewish—Forged a Friendship and Made Sports History* by Bruce Schoenfeld and *The Rivals: Chris Evert vs. Martina Navratilova: Their Epic Duels and Extraordinary Friendship* by Johnette Howard are biographies of strong women athletes. Readers who like collected biographies with brief profiles built around a theme may enjoy *Boom! Voices of the Sixties: Personal Reflections on the '60s and Today* by Tom Brokaw (see chapter 9) and *Masters of Enterprise: Giants of American Business from John Jacob Astor and J. P. Morgan to Bill Gates and Oprah Winfrey* by H. W. Brands (see chapter 9).

Jacobson, Steve

Carrying Jackie's Torch: The Players Who Integrated Baseball—and America. Lawrence Hill Books, 2007. 264 p. ISBN 9781556526398.

    The story of integrating major league baseball does not end with Jackie Robinson surviving his first year. For the next twenty years the quota of black players who followed the Dodgers' second baseman faced entrenched discrimination. Sometimes they ate in kitchens while the white players were served in dining rooms. They often were not allowed in the team hotels. Abuse from the stands and hate mail dogged them when they excelled. Veteran sports reporter Steve Jacobson profiles eighteen players and one umpire who survived the stress of discrimination to become national stars. This lively book will appeal to sports fans and general readers.

    Subjects: African Americans; Baseball Players; Collective Biography; Discrimination in Sports

    Now Try: Working as porters on Pullman cars when rail travel was at its height in the 1920s, many black men were able to raise their standard of living and foresee the lives they wanted for their descendants. Larry Tye reports on a pioneering generation in *Rising from the Rails: Pullman Porters and the Making of the Black Middle Class.* David Falkner chronicles the life of Jackie Robinson from his birth in a sharecropper's cabin in Georgia to his work with Martin Luther King Jr. in *Great Time Coming: The Life of*

Jackie Robinson from Baseball to Birmingham. St. Louis Cardinal Curt Flood was one of the first generation of blacks in the major leagues. Alex Belth tells how Flood saw the binding of a player to his team as a restriction of his rights in *Stepping Up: The Story of Curt Flood and His Fight for Baseball Players' Rights* (see chapter 12). During World War II, when the military drafted many of the able-bodied players out of the major leagues, other men who had always dreamed of being sports stars got their chance. Craig Allen Cleve profiles nine players who suited up for the game during a trying time in *Hardball on the Home Front: Major League Replacement Players of World War II.* While the replacements kept the professional game going, many players in the service continued to play baseball to entertain the troops. Steven R. Bullock reports on his research on military baseball in *Playing for Their Nation: Baseball and the American Military During World War II.*

Wiesel, Elie

Wise Men and Their Tales: Portraits of Biblical, Talmudic, and Hasidic Masters. Schocken Books, 2003. 337p. ISBN 0805241736.

Though the work of many people is necessary for the communication of religious traditions and beliefs through generations, some special individuals define and refine the tenets of faith. Jewish scholar Elie Wiesel calls these leaders "masters." In this book on the history of Jewish literature and tradition, he identifies and profiles biblical figures, Talmudic scholars, and Hassidic rabbis who shaped Judaism. Wiesel tells their stories and why they matter to current believers. Readers interested in expanding their knowledge of world religions will enjoy this eloquent collected biography.

Subjects: Collective Biography; Judaism; Prophets; Rabbis; Theologians

Now Try: Wiesel has written other collective biographies, including *Sages and Dreamers: Biblical, Talmudic, and Hasidic Portraits and Legends* and *Messengers of God: Biblical Portraits and Legends.* Wiesel tells about his childhood, surviving Auschwitz, struggles with faith, and working with world leaders in *All Rivers Run to the Sea: Memoirs* and *And the Sea Is Never Full: Memoirs, 1969– .* Before the European Renaissance, scholars from Islamic countries kept knowledge from the ancient Greeks and Romans alive. Michael Hamilton Morgan identifies the many key Islamic intellectuals in *Lost History: The Enduring Legacy of Muslim Scientists, Thinkers, Artists.* In all these works, the integrity of individuals is crucial. In *Profiles in Courage* (see chapter 10), John F. Kennedy told stories of congressmen and senators who acted according to their conscience instead of following their party's directives.

Consider Starting With . . .

These well-written Inspirational Biographies of modest length will appeal to general readers.

- Alter, Jonathan. *The Defining Moment: FDR's Hundred Days and the Triumph of Hope.*

- Armstrong, Karen. *Buddha.*

- Armstrong, Karen. *Muhammad: A Prophet for Our Time.*
- Baker, William J. *Jesse Owens: An American Life.*
- Feiler, Bruce. *Abraham: A Journey to the Heart of Three Faiths.*
- Diliberto, Gioia. *A Useful Woman: The Early Life of Jane Addams.*
- Ford, Michael. *Father Mychal Judge: An Authentic American Hero.*
- Kidder, Tracy. *Mountains Beyond Mountains.*
- LaPlante, Eve. *Salem Witch Judge: The Life and Repentance of Samuel Sewall.*
- Noonan, Peggy. *John Paul the Great: Remembering a Spiritual Father.*
- Ulrich, Laurel Thatcher. *A Midwife's Tale: The Life of Martha Ballard, Based on Her Diary, 1785–1812.*

Further Reading

Kendall, Paul Murrary

Art of Biography. New York: Norton, 1965.
   Kendall begins a discussion of medieval biography on page 41.

Wyatt, Neal

The Readers' Advisory Guide to Nonfiction. American Libraries, 2007. 318p. ISBN 9780-838909362.
   Wyatt discusses religion and spirituality in chapter 11. In her discussions she identifies key authors and includes generous lists of titles to recommend to readers.

Chapter 5

Investigative Biography

Definition of Investigative Biography

An Investigative Biography is a nonfiction narrative that questions the veracity of previous biographies and reports what has not previously been told about a biographical subject. Although all biographies are expected to retell the stories of people and offer new facts based on thorough research by their authors, not all probe as deeply or with the same intent as Investigative Biographies. Having journalistic objectives, investigative biographers set out to report solutions to mysteries, expose crimes, and reshape reputations. Their mission is to set the story straight.

The call for the finding of truth goes back to the Greek philosophers Plato and Aristotle, who defined the concept and emphasized the importance of seeing what is true. Discovering the world as it truly is was the foundation of their philosophical movement, upon which our Western civilization is based. In the Gospel of John, Jesus Christ agrees with the philosophers, saying "you will know the truth, and the truth will set you free." Since the development of the printing press by Johann Gutenberg, the debate about what is true has been democratized; so anyone who can read can follow the discussion. In our modern society, we read newspapers, magazines, and books, listen to radio and television news, and surf the Internet, seeking to find out what is happening in our world; and we get very upset when we learn our political leaders or other people in the public eye have lied.

Investigative biographers look for lies and inconsistencies by consulting original and untapped sources. Journalist Georgie Anne Geyer conducted several interviews with Cuban dictator Fidel Castro and held many meetings with his associates and critics before writing *Guerrilla Prince: The Untold Story of Fidel Castro*. Literary critic Ian Hamilton tried to interview J. D. Salinger, but the reclusive novelist would not comply, so Hamilton read old magazine articles and met with the writer's editors and colleagues to write *In Search of J. D. Salinger: A Biography*. Historian Edward Champlin reread ancient texts from the historians Tacitus, Cassius Dio, and Suetonius in the writing of *Nero*, his reassessment of the infamous Roman emperor. This chapter includes these and other biographies that question the reputations of and either revise or reaffirm the stories of legendary characters, historical figures, and current world leaders.

An *Investigative Biography* is a nonfiction narrative that questions the veracity of previous biographies and reports what has not previously been told about a biographical subject. Having journalistic objectives, investigative biographers set out to report solutions to mysteries, expose crimes, and reshape reputations. Their mission is to set the story straight. Readers will find strong characters and compelling stories in these highly discussible books.

Appeal of the Genre

Investigative biographies have high character appeal. They are written about dramatic figures with stories that need explanation. The subjects include German industrialist Oskar Schindler, who risked his life to help Jewish workers escape death in Nazi Germany; LSD advocate Timothy Leary, who praised the recreational use of drugs; and Russian Tsar Ivan the Terrible, who earned his nickname by brutally killing his son, several wives, and anyone else who displeased him. Mild mannered characters rarely draw the attention of investigative writers.

The stories in these Investigative Biographies are often sensational. The central events in the lives of the people portrayed could inspire eye-catching headlines in the tabloid press: "Feral Child Found on Streets of Nuremberg"; "Dangerous Mystic Has Ear of Russian Czar"; "Wealthy Publisher Lost at Sea Was a Spy"; and "Noted Pediatrician Neglects Own Children." Readers would want to learn the stories behind such lurid headlines. In Investigative Biography, they are treated to those stories.

The settings for Investigative Biography vary greatly. Times of crisis or social upheaval figure heavily in many of the stories. Investigative biographies exist for readers favoring any period of history. Pacing also varies among the books chosen for this chapter. Titles may be found for readers who like quick reads as well as for those who want long books to savor. All appeal to readers who relish accounts that rewrite history.

Learning is not generally the appeal factor that draws the reader to Investigative Biographies, but it may be important in making the books worth reading. Most people borrowing or buying these books are seeking to read really good stories, but they gain more understanding about the characters and the settings from which they come.

Organization of the Chapter

This chapter is divided into three sections, the first of which is "Character Investigations." In this section are biographies that profile mysterious people or show that well-known characters are not as simple as they have previously been portrayed. Biographers tell stories and present evidence based on their in-depth research to satisfy readers' curiosity about the subjects. The author's attitudes toward their subjects tend to be neutral or balanced in these titles, even when the characters are controversial.

The next section is "Exposés." These books differ from Character Investigations in that the authors intend to expose the misdeeds of profiled individuals for the purpose of discrediting them. Author neutrality is absent in these passionate narratives.

The third section is "Legends Retold." The books in this section focus on historical figures about whom undocumented stories have been told. Many of these people are familiar because they have been portrayed in novels, pulp fiction, operas, plays, and movies. These books examine the legends to show what could be true about them.

Character Investigations

With around-the-clock news coverage, an abundance of journalists seeking to cover every aspect of our culture, and amateur commentators on the Internet, finding a contemporary character about whom there is any mystery is difficult. Besides international terrorists and secretive politicians, few other people in the news are refusing to be interviewed, speak at conferences, or write memoirs. Few names stay in the news more than several days or weeks, but personal stories are archived and easily retrieved from the Internet. To find personalities to investigate, many authors are turning to historical characters.

The Investigative Biographies in this section focus on individuals who are all to varying degrees mysterious. Magician and escape artist Harry Houdini led the life of a celebrity, often performing his spectacular feats before the public. Few knew, however, that he was a spy for the U.S. Secret Service. William Kalush and Larry Sloman report on the story that they have uncovered in *The Secret Life of Houdini: The Making of America's First Superhero*. Likewise, few knew about a feral boy who was found in the streets of nineteenth-century Nuremberg, Germany until Jeffrey Moussaieff Masson retold his tragic story in *Lost Prince: The Unsolved Mystery of Kaspar Hauser*. Also included in this section are investigations of some contemporary statesmen, including Venezuelan leader Hugo Chávez and former American Vice President Dick Cheney. Though both are often in the news, their past actions confuse analysts and their future intentions are difficult to predict. As different as the individuals in this section are, their biographies share the literary purpose of character revelation.

Character investigations often lure readers with two narratives, intertwining the stories of the biographical figures with those of the investigating authors, who tell how they obtained their evidence, often lending an element of mystery and suspense to the story line. As a result, settings may alternate between recent and historical times. If the author does limit his or her own story to a preface, it is usually worth reading. Pace varies, as some of the titles in this

Character Investigations profile mysterious people or show that the stories behind well-known characters are not as they have previously been told. Biographers tell stories and present evidence based on their in-depth research to satisfy readers' curiosity about the biographical subjects. Often the author's research becomes part of the story. The authors' attitudes toward the subjects tend to be neutral or balanced in these titles, even when the characters are controversial.

1

2

3

4

5

6

7

8

9

10

11

12

section are quick reads while others require a large investment of the reader's time. Devoted nonfiction readers appreciate these books for clarifying bits of history. Leisure readers just enjoy the stories.

Anthony, Carl Sferrazza

Florence Harding: The First Lady, the Jazz Age, and the Death of America's Most Scandalous President. William Morrow, 1998. 645p. ISBN 0688077943.

Unwed teenaged mother Florence Kling (1860–1924), known as Flossie, had few prospects in 1880, but she had at least escaped her abusive father. After a decade of supporting herself as a piano teacher, she married small town newspaperman Warren G. Harding, whom she molded into an attractive local politician and later U.S. president. When Mrs. Harding brought early film stars and underworld figures into the White House, rumors of scandalous behavior spread. She is even suspected of poisoning her unfaithful husband. This speculative account by Carl Sferrazza Anthony examines the evidence for and against one of the most powerful of all first ladies.

> **Subjects:** First Ladies; Harding, Florence Kling; Women

> **Now Try:** Harding was able to hide her past more successfully than Argentinean First Lady Eva Peron, but both became very influential figures in their governments. Peron's tragic story is told in *Eva Perón: A Biography* by Alicia Dujovne Ortiz (see chapter 6). A story of a wife more openly in opposition to her husband than Harding is told by Alison Weir in *Queen Isabella: Treachery, Adultery, and Murder in Medieval England* (see chapter 9). In the court of French King Louis XV, the woman behind many intrigues was his official mistress. Evelyne Lever describes a very ambitious and dangerous woman in *Madame de Pompadour: A Life* (see chapter 9). Harding's predecessor, Edith Wilson, became a powerful first lady when President Wilson suffered a stroke. Phyllis Lee Levin describes the period during which the first lady may have run the country in *Edith and Woodrow: The Wilson White House* (see chapter 10).

Bailey, John

The Lost German Slave Girl: The Extraordinary True Story of Sally Miller and Her Fight for Freedom in Old New Orleans. Atlantic Monthly Press, 2003. 268p. ISBN 0871139219. Large print available.

As the national debate over slavery raged in the 1840s, a strange story broke in New Orleans. Members of the German community in the city sued a Frenchman for the freedom of an olive-skinned woman named Sally Miller (1813–?), whom they believed to be Salomé Müller, a woman kidnapped in Germany twenty-five years earlier. After a series of court cases that included a hearing by the U.S. Supreme Court, Sally Miller and her children were released from slavery. In this Investigative Biography, John Bailey questions the identity of the woman known by many names.

> **Subjects:** Miller, Sally; Müller, Salomé; New Orleans; Slavery; Women

> **Now Try:** As in Miller's story, Olaudah Equiano was allegedly kidnapped on one continent and sold into slavery on another. His story of buying his freedom and working to end the slave trade is told in *Equiano, the African: Biography of a Self-Made Man* by Vincent Carretta (see chapter 9). In *The Girl from Botany Bay*, Carolly Erickson tells about Mary Bryant, a young British woman convicted of petty theft and sent against

her will to a penal colony in Australia. Her bold and dangerous escape from the colony drew public sympathy, and Samuel Johnson's biographer James Boswell won the young woman a royal pardon. Salomé Müller may never have existed. The same might be said for Western gunslinger John Ringo, whose legend is questioned in *John Ringo: The Gunfighter Who Never Was* by Jack Burrows (see chapter 2). Did Sarah Breedlove, a daughter of slaves from Vicksburg, Mississippi, become Madam C. J. Walker, the manufacturer of cosmetics, who lived in an elegant mansion outside New York City? Beverly Lowry tells a story about shifting identities in *Her Dream of Dreams: The Rise and Triumph of Madam C. J. Walker* (see chapter 9).

Baker, Deborah

In Extremis: The Life of Laura Riding. Grove Press, 1993. 478p. ISBN 0802113648.

After her collected poems were praised by *Time* in 1938, Laura Riding (1901–1991) renounced poetry, broke off her long-standing relationship with British author Robert Graves, and married the *Time* reporter who had praised her poetry. Having always said that she would never marry, she moved to rural Florida with her new husband and stopped writing for thirty years, turning away any questions about her once celebrated career. Deborah Baker sorts through conflicting accounts to discover why Riding ran away from her fame. Readers who like mysteries will enjoy this Investigative Biography.

> **Subjects:** Poets; Recluses; Riding, Laura; Women

> **Now Try:** The most famous story about the literary recluse is told in *In Search of J. D. Salinger: A Biography* by Ian Hamilton (see this chapter). Like Riding, poet Arthur Rimbaud found critical acclaim unsatisfying. While Riding's hiding in Florida was thought remote, it barely compares to Rimbaud's escape to the North African countries of Egypt, Ethiopia, and Yemen, a story told in *Somebody Else: Arthur Rimbaud in Africa, 1880–91* by Charles Nicholl (see chapter 1). Harper Lee did not run away or hide, but she did stop writing after *To Kill a Mockingbird*. Charles J. Shields tells how Lee's childhood is reflected in her beloved book in *Mockingbird: A Portrait of Harper Lee* (see this chapter). In the world of sports, one figure who retired at the height of his career was Los Angeles Dodgers pitcher Sandy Koufax. Jane Leavy looks at a man who walked away from fame and a high salary in *Sandy Koufax: A Lefty's Legacy* (see chapter 12).

Bergen, Peter L.

The Osama bin Laden I Know: An Oral History of al Qaeda's Leader. Free Press, 2006. 444p. ISBN 9780743278911. Audiobook available.

Who is Osama bin Laden (1957–), and what does he want? How did a shy, polite Saudi student become an international terrorist? CNN correspondent Peter L. Bergen, who met the al Qaeda leader in Afghanistan in 1997, tries to answer these urgent questions. In this probing book he organizes and comments on transcripts from news stories, American intelligence reports, Arab language sources, and his interviews with fifty of bin Laden's associates. Bin Laden's own statements from his Al-Jazeera video- and audiotapes are included in this frightening book.

> **Subjects:** Afghanistan; Bin Laden, Osama; Saudi Arabia; Terrorists

Now Try: Serbian warlord Zeljko Raznatovic was a bank robber and hit man before forming a private army and becoming an ally of Yugoslavian President Slobodan Miloševic. Christopher S. Stewart tells how the noted war criminal eluded capture for years in *Hunting the Tiger: The Fast Life and Violent Death of the Balkans' Most Dangerous Man*. In *Jesse James: Last Rebel of the Civil War* (see chapter 2), T. J. Stiles argues that the American outlaw should be labeled a terrorist. Like bin Laden, he used statements to the media of his day (newspapers) to communicate his message of hatred to his followers, to whom he was a hero. Also like bin Laden, Adolf Hitler was a late bloomer as a fiery radical. The German dictator's rise to power is told in *Hitler, 1889–1936: Hubris* by Ian Kershaw (see chapter 6). When the Supreme Court struck down the death penalty as unconstitutional in 1972, many convicted murderers were moved into the general prison population, from which many eventually won their freedom. Joan M. Cheever interviewed 125 of these ex-cons to learn what they have made of their lives in *Back from the Dead: One Woman's Search for the Men Who Walked off America's Death Row*.

Chelminski, Rudolph

The Perfectionist: Life and Death in Haute Cuisine. Gotham Books, 2005. 354p. ISBN 1592401074.

With a shotgun given to him by his wife, French chef Bernard Loiseau (1951–2003) killed himself after hearing that the guidebook *GaultMilleu* had lowered its ranking of his Cote d'Or restaurant and an unconfirmed rumor that the *Michelin Red Guide* would follow suit. The French public was shocked. Loiseau had been the most famous of chefs and seemed to have the best of everything: a loving family, financial success, and fame. In this tragic psychological biography set in the competitive world of French cuisine, journalist Rudolph Chelminski reveals that Loiseau was bipolar and had a history of depression. Meant as a cautionary tale, this story will interest readers whose families have experienced similar tragedies.

> **Subjects:** Bipolar Disorder; Chefs; France; Loiseau, Bernard; Suicide

> **Now Try:** Kurt Cobain, lead singer of the rock group Nirvana, never seemed to truly enjoy his fame. Charles R. Cross relates how Cobain rose out of the Seattle music scene and lived in an unforgiving spotlight before committing suicide, in *Heavier Than Heaven: A Biography of Kurt Cobain* (see chapter 6). In his novel *Sophie's Choice*, William Styron makes suicide the respite from despair for a Holocaust survivor who feels guilt for the loss of a child. Russian novelist Leo Tolstoy experienced great spiritual doubt about his faith and contemplated suicide in his middle years. A. N. Wilson recounts the stages of Tolstoy's life and the germination of his influential ideas in *Tolstoy*. Jesse Livermore enjoyed high society, exotic vacations, and opulent living until the stock market crash of 1929, from which he never emotionally recovered. With novelistic style, business author Richard Smitten portrays a man whose despair led to his death in *Jesse Livermore: World's Greatest Stock Trader* (see chapter 9).

Crowe, David M.

Oskar Schindler: The Untold Account of His Life, Wartime Activities, and the True Story Behind the List. Westview Press, 2004. 766p. ISBN 081333375X.

Oskar Schindler (1908–1974) was a complicated man whose actions are difficult to assess. On the one hand, he spied for the Nazis, helping them invade Poland and Czechoslovakia; but on the other, he knowingly helped over a thousand Jewish workers escape death during the Holocaust. He may have been a criminal, as he is suspected of stealing insurance premiums from his father's company. After the war he brazenly and unsuccessfully sought to sell his story to Hollywood producers. After spending seven years researching his subject, historian David M. Crowe tells a candid story about a man who might be a hero despite many flaws.

Subjects: Holocaust; Industrialists; Schindler, Oskar; World War II

Now Try: In his novel *Schindler's List*, Thomas Keneally portrays the industrialist as a flawed man, not known for compassion, who first helps a few Jews escape from the death camps and then finds that he cannot stop helping. In Holland, a network of Holocaust rescuers risked their lives throughout the war to save Jewish people. Mark Klempner interviewed surviving rescuers to learn why they acted and how they viewed their efforts years after the war. He reports their stories in *The Heart Has Reasons: Holocaust Rescuers and Their Stories of Courage*. World War II Germany was filled with characters whose culpability is difficult to assess. Is Eva Braun to be reviled for being the mistress of Adolf Hitler? Angela Lambert seeks an answer to this question in her investigation, *The Lost Life of Eva Braun* (see chapter 6). Peter Conradi tells about another odd member of the German leader's inner circle in *Hitler's Piano Player: The Rise and Fall of Ernst Hanfstaengl, Confidant of Hitler, Ally of FDR* (see chapter 3).

Dawidoff, Nicholas

The Catcher Was a Spy: The Mysterious Life of Moe Berg. Pantheon, 1994. 453p. ISBN 0679415661.

Moe Berg (1902–1972) was never an average major league baseball player. He graduated from Princeton in 1923, attended the Sorbonne in Paris, and read many books and newspapers. A month after the Japanese attack on Pearl Harbor, the journeyman catcher left the game, joined the Office of Strategic Services, the forerunner of the CIA, and headed off to save the free world. After the war he led a strangely moody and nomadic life. In this psychological biography, Nicholas Dawidoff follows Berg's trail to find answers to questions about the mysterious man.

Subjects: Baseball Players; Berg, Moe; Spies; World War II

Now Try: Pitching ace Christy Mathewson left the New York Giants to serve in Europe in World War I, where he was exposed to poisonous gas. In *Player: Christy Mathewson, Baseball, and the American Century*, Philip M. Seib describes a model baseball player and citizen, who sacrificed his career for his country. While Berg and many of the top players were in the military in World War II, major league baseball continued with replacements, who are described in *Hardball on the Homefront: Major League Replacement Players of World War II* by Craig Allen Cleve. In *Playing with the Enemy: A Baseball Prodigy, a World at War, and a Field of Broken Dreams*, Gary W. Moore tells about his father Gene Moore's tour of duty with the U.S. Navy baseball team. Like Berg, actor Errol Flynn and his son Sean were both depressed men who tried to hide their illness. The father wanted to be a spy during World War II. Jeffrey Meyers compares the parent and child in *Inherited Risk: Errol and Sean Flynn in Hollywood and Vietnam.*

Fraser-Cavassoni, Natasia

Sam Spiegel. Simon & Schuster, 2003. 464p. ISBN 068483619X.

The origins of Hollywood producer Sam Spiegel (1901–1985) are mysterious. He told many tall tales about working on German films and dramatically escaping from the Nazis. He also claimed to have been arrested in numerous countries for various petty crimes before illegally entering the United States. Journalist Natasia Fraser-Cavassoni sorts fact from fiction in this Investigative Biography of the flamboyant producer of *On the Waterfront*, *The Bridge on the River Kwai*, and *Lawrence of Arabia*.

> **Subjects:** Immigrants; Jews; Movie Producers; Spiegel, Sam
>
> **Now Try:** T. E. Lawrence, the subject of Spiegel's film *Lawrence of Arabia*, was another man who exaggerated the stories about his past. In *The Golden Warrior: The Life and Legend of Lawrence of Arabia* (see chapter 2), Lawrence James says that British intelligence agent T. E. Lawrence gave the American and British people the heroic figure they needed to lift spirits shocked by the brutality of the trench warfare in Europe. Harry Houdini made his living being flamboyant and boasting about his talent for escape. William Kalush and Larry Sloman tell how Houdini's fame let him hide his work as a spy in *The Secret Life of Houdini: The Making of America's First Superhero* (see this chapter). Unlike Spiegel, movie director Billy Wilder only told the stories of his escape from the Nazis to close friends. Charlotte Chandler tells how he worked with actors to make classic films in *Nobody's Perfect: Billy Wilder, a Personal Biography* (see chapter 8). Artist Marc Chagall witnessed both the Russian Revolution and the rise of Nazi Germany before settling in the United States. His dramatic story is told in *Marc Chagall* by Jonathan Wilson (see chapter 7).

Geyer, Georgie Anne

Guerrilla Prince: The Untold Story of Fidel Castro. Little Brown, 1991. 445p. ISBN 0316-308935.

Although former Cuban dictator Fidel Castro (1926–) is a very public figure, he is also a very private man. According to journalist Georgie Anne Geyer, who has reported on Castro throughout her career, he has kept much personal information from the Cuban people. At the time that she wrote this book, many Cubans did not even know whether their leader was married or had children. Based on hundreds of interviews with Castro's friends and enemies, this psychological biography shows how an obscure man from a penniless nation became a threat to U.S. security while becoming a folk hero throughout much of the Third World.

> **Subjects:** Castro, Fidel; Communism; Cuba; Dictators
>
> **Now Try:** Like Castro, Oliver Cromwell swept away the previous regime with his deadly rebellion, promising reforms for the good of the people, who in the end suffered. Peter Gaunt describes a man totally in command of his island kingdom in *Oliver Cromwell* (see chapter 10). After his exile from Washington, D.C., duelist and early American statesman Aaron Burr formed a militia that may have aimed to establish the Louisiana Territory as a separate country. Biographer Nancy Isenberg shows how Burr inspired a rebel following in *Fallen Founder: The Life of Aaron Burr* (see chapter 10). Readers wondering whether Hugo Chávez is the new Castro may appreciate *Hugo Chávez: The Definitive Biography of Venezuela's Controversial President* by Christina Marcano and Alberto Barrera Tyszka (see this chapter). Like Castro, W. C. Fields was an iconic figure whose personal life was virtually unknown. Simon Louvish describes a

man who was far different off stage than on in *Man on the Flying Trapeze: The Life and Times of W. C. Fields* (see chapter 8).

Hamilton, Ian

In Search of J. D. Salinger: A Biography. Random House, 1988. 222p. ISBN 039-4534689.

J. D. Salinger (1919–) was a modestly successful author with a cult following when he stopped writing his offbeat stories in 1965. His withdrawal from the publishing scene, of course, fueled readers' desire for more books, and journalists began trying to crack the wall of silence that he had erected. Literary critic Ian Hamilton joined the Salinger search in 1983, tracking down obscure letters from the author and reading old interviews. In this entertaining account, Hamilton (who was sued by Salinger to stop publication of a previous version of this book) reveals how the mysterious and antisocial Salinger drew from his own self-absorbed life in writing *Catcher in the Rye* and his short stories.

> **Subjects:** Novelists; Recluses; Salinger, J. D.; Teen Reads

> **Now Try:** Like Salinger, Salvador Dali did not like would-be biographers. Instead of hiding from them, however, Dali confused them with false accounts to keep them from discovering that all he cared about was money and his own comfort. Ian Gibson profiles the artist in *The Shameful Life of Salvador Dalí*. In 1938 poet Laura Riding renounced her writing at the height of its popularity and went into hiding in rural Florida. Deborah Baker sorts through conflicting accounts to discover why Riding ran away from her fame in *In Extremis: The Life of Laura Riding* (see this chapter). When author Bill Hayes became interested in Henry Gray, author of *Gray's Anatomy*, the best known of all medical textbooks, only a few facts about Gray were known. Hayes describes his search and his findings in *The Anatomist: A True Story of Gray's Anatomy* (see chapter 11). African American novelist Chester Himes, a well-regarded contemporary of F. Scott Fitzgerald and Ernest Hemingway, has now almost been forgotten. Like Hamilton, James Sallis had to seek obscure sources to track the writer's path from a term in prison to self-imposed exile in France, a story that he tells in *Chester Himes: A Life* (see chapter 7).

Hayes, Stephen F.

Cheney: The Untold Story of America's Most Powerful and Controversial Vice President. HarperCollins, 2007. 578p. ISBN 9780060723460. Audiobook available.

Richard Bruce Cheney (1941–) was the least seen yet most talked about vice president ever, according to Stephen F. Hayes, a reporter for the conservative *Weekly Standard*. In this admittedly sympathetic biography, he quotes heavily from interviews that he conducted with the subject, his friends, and his enemies. The result is a narrative describing Cheney's boyhood in Nebraska and Wyoming, his college years, his tenure as CEO at Halliburton, and his many years of government service. Cheney's Vietnam draft deferments, views on homosexuality, infamous hunting accident, and insistence on government secrecy are among the topics in this forgiving account.

Subjects: Cheney, Richard Bruce; Politics and Government; Vice Presidents

Now Try: Readers wanting a more critical view of the secretive vice president will likely appreciate the exposé *Vice: Dick Cheney and the Hijacking of the American Presidency* by Lou Dubose and Jack Bernstein. Peggy Noonan is a very admiring biographer who finds little to criticize in the life of Pope John Paul II. In *John Paul the Great: Remembering a Spiritual Father* Noonan portrays the Polish pope as a hero who survived Nazism, communism, and terrorism, showing his people a better way to live. Readers who sympathize with Cheney and his stand on government secrecy might look to a sympathetic account of President Richard Nixon's attorney general, *The Strong Man: John Mitchell and the Secrets of Watergate* by James Rosen. William F. Buckley was very forthright in admitting his admiration for President Ronald Reagan. Buckley told personal stories about his meetings with his friend in *The Reagan I Knew*.

Kalush, William, and Larry Sloman

The Secret Life of Houdini: The Making of America's First Superhero. Atria Books, 2006. 592p. ISBN 9780743272070.

Though magician and escape artist Harry Houdini (1874–1926) led the life of a celebrity, he kept many secrets, including that he was a spy for the U.S. Secret Service. According to authors William Kalush and Larry Sloman, his international fame gave him liberties in foreign countries that other visitors lacked, and his magician's ability to distract and deceive helped him keep his cover. They also reveal that he was a sworn enemy of Sir Arthur Conan Doyle and his spiritualist friends, who plotted to have the magician killed. With details drawn from a newly opened Houdini archive, the admiring authors portray the magician as a hero bound for tragedy.

Subjects: Houdini, Harry; Magicians; Spies; Weiss, Ehrich

Now Try: Inventor and businessman Robert Fulton was a self-promoter with a flare for public demonstrations of his famous inventions, one of which, the steamboat, helped American westward expansion. Kirkpatrick Sale describes how, despite public acclaim the contentious inventor failed to protect his patents and died in financial distress, in *The Fire of His Genius: Robert Fulton and the American Dream* (see chapter 11). Like Houdini, the doctor, linguist, and famous writer Somerset Maugham was also able to spy while traveling the world, despite being a minor celebrity. His long and melancholy life is described in *Somerset Maugham: A Life* by Jeffrey Meyers (see chapter 7). French race car driver Hellé Nice, who wanted to be the world's fastest woman, was suspected of being an agent for the Gestapo in Vichy France during World War II. Her flamboyant story is told in *Bugatti Queen: In Search of a French Racing Legend* by Miranda Seymour (see chapter 12). Like Houdini, Alfred Lee Loomis was a high-profile figure, being a successful stock broker and frequenter of night clubs. In secret, he worked on top secret weapons development for the U.S. government. Jennet Conant tells his fascinating story in *Tuxedo Park: A Wall Street Tycoon and the Secret Palace of Science That Changed the Course of World War II* (see chapter 11).

Maier, Thomas

Dr. Spock: An American Life. Harcourt Brace & Company, 1998. 520p. ISBN 0151002037.

During the last half of the twentieth century millions of American parents trusted the advice of pediatrician Dr. Benjamin Spock (1903–1998), the child advocate who ventured into the civil rights and war protests in the 1960s. In his best-selling books and other writings, Spock stressed love and tolerance of the selfish behavior of children and said that children needed attention much more than discipline. His devoted readers, however, did not know about his marital and family problems, including his persistent neglect of his own children. In this candid and yet sympathetic biography, investigative reporter Thomas Maier discloses the disturbing contradictions of the man who greatly influenced child psychology in his time.

> **Subjects:** Activists; Child Psychology; Pediatricians; Spock, Benjamin

> **Now Try:** In *Spock on Spock: A Memoir of Growing Up with the Century*, the pediatrician lightly describes his childhood, clinical training, protests against the Vietnam War, and his run for president for the People's Party. Like Spock, Cary Grant was charming and engendered the trust of the masses, but he failed badly as a family man. Both men married very young wives late in life. Marc Eliot tells the actor's off-screen story in *Cary Grant: A Biography* (see chapter 8). Albert Einstein was another iconic figure whose personal life was filled with failed relationships. Lofty ideas, politics, and family trouble are found in *Einstein* by Walter Isaacson. Another child care expert who had difficulties with his own children is profiled in *Love at Goon Park: Harry Harlow and the Science of Affection* by Deborah Blum (see chapter 11). The perspective of the child of a psychiatrist can be found in the confessional memoir *In the Shadow of Fame: A Memoir by the Daughter of Erik H. Erikson* by Sue Erikson Bloland.

Marcano, Christina, and Alberto Barrera Tyszka

Hugo Chávez: The Definitive Biography of Venezuela's Controversial President. Random House, 2007. 327p. ISBN 9780679456667.

Journalists Christina Marcano and Alberto Barrera Tyszka have succeeded in a difficult task: writing dispassionately about a current controversial figure. In their biography of Venezuelan President Hugo Chávez (1954–), who first gained national attention by surrendering graciously during a failed coup in 1992, they report on his misdeeds as an ambitious military leader, an unfaithful husband, and a president intent on staying in office, but they also explain why he is so loved by the poor and working class of his country. Anecdotes about his passions for baseball, music, and fashionable clothes and about his love of his children fill out the portrayal of Chavez as a common man. Viewed as outrageous by U.S. officials, Hugo Chavez promises to be a Latin American leader for years to come, and a person whom readers will want to understand.

> **Subjects:** Chávez, Hugo; Group Discussion Books; Presidents; Venezuela

> **Now Try:** Like Chávez, actor Marlon Brando cared little for American public opinion and often behaved without tact. His life is eloquently and briefly profiled in *Marlon Brando* by Patricia Bosworth (see chapter 8). By directing aid to the poor and controlling every aspect of government, Senator Huey P. Long was as popular in Louisiana as Chávez is in Venezuela. His rise and fall are told in *Kingfish: The Reign of Huey P. Long* by Richard D. White (see chapter 10). Eva Perón also had a strong popular following and equally determined enemies who saw her darker side. Alicia Dujovne Ortiz tells an intimate story about the woman who inspired a musical in *Eva Perón: A Biography* (see chapter 6). Novelist Graham Greene claimed to be neutral in politics, but he spent much time in his later years visiting Latin American strongmen, including Cuban dictator Fidel Castro and Nicaraguan dictator Manuel Noriega. He

described his friendship with Panamanian leader Omar Torrijos in *Getting to Know the General: The Story of an Involvement.*

Masson, Jeffrey Moussaieff

Lost Prince: The Unsolved Mystery of Kaspar Hauser. Free Press, 1996. 254p. ISBN 0684-822962.

On an afternoon in May 1828 in Nuremberg, Germany, a ragged boy was found on the streets. Unable to speak and barely able to walk, he held a letter addressed to the captain of the local cavalry to whom he was taken. Within days it was rumored that he was Kaspar Hauser (1812–1833), the rejected son of a duchess, and that he had been isolated in a dungeon most of his life, making him a sort of feral child. As soon as he learned to speak, he mysteriously became a frequent target for inept assassins. Suggesting that Hauser was abused during his isolation, psychology writer Jeffrey Moussaieff Masson translates and comments on original case documents, seeking to establish his true identity, and discover who considered him a threat.

> **Subjects:** Child Abuse; Feral Children; Germany; Hauser, Kaspar; Princes

> **Now Try:** After the first attempt on Hauser's life, he should have been protected. The tragic case is similar to that of the Protestant Dutch monarch Prince William I of Orange. His preventable death is described in *The Awful End of Prince William the Silent: The First Assassination of a Head of State with a Handgun* by Lisa Jardine (see chapter 2). In 1491 a young man who claimed to be Prince Richard, who had been imprisoned in the Tower of London by his uncle King Richard III and who was assumed dead, appeared in England seeking the throne. Ann Wroe describes the life of a royal pretender in *The Perfect Prince: The Mystery of Perkin Warbeck and His Quest for the Throne of England* (see this chapter). According to many accounts, two daughters of Tsar Nicholas II of Russia escaped execution by Bolshevik revolutionaries in 1918. James Blair Lovell is convinced the story is true and describes the life of the woman who claimed to be a princess in *Anastasia: The Lost Princess.* Poet and playwright Christopher Marlowe frequented dangerous places during his short life. Park Honan tells an absorbing unsolved murder mystery in a historical setting in *Christopher Marlowe: Poet & Spy* (see chapter 2).

McGilligan, Patrick

Oscar Micheaux: The Great and Only: The Life of America's First Black Filmmaker. HarperCollins, 2007. 402p. ISBN 9780060731397.

Most of the work of innovative black filmmaker Oscar Micheaux (1884–1951) is gone. Of the more than forty films that he made using mostly black casts (no one knows how many there were), only fifteen exist in fragments today. Though shunned by Hollywood studios due to his race, Micheaux succeeded in making a series of films that are now praised for their frankness on subjects of race, sex, and violence. According to author Patrick McGilligan, the record of Micheaux's life is as incomplete as his portfolio. Mysteries about his birth, his whereabouts during much of his life, and his death abound. This somewhat speculative book is a good choice for readers who like stories about great American innovators.

> **Subjects:** African Americans; Micheaux, Oscar; Movie Directors; Racial Discrimination

> **Now Try:** Like Micheaux, celebrated Catalonian architect Antoni Gaudi was shunned by his contemporaries, in his case because of his radical designs and religious fervor.

Gijs Van Hensbergen candidly tells the architect's story in *Gaudi*. Another forgotten black American who excelled in a white-dominated field was bicyclist Marshall Taylor. His reconstructed story is told in *Major: A Black Athlete, a White Era, and the Fight to Be the World's Fastest Human Being* by Todd Balf (see chapter 12). More is known about the Norwegian artist Edvard Munch, whose his work is frank and disturbing. Sue Prideaux sorts through the confusing portfolio to create an understandable narrative of the tormented artist in *Edvard Munch: Behind the Scream*. Artist George Bellows was a contemporary of Micheaux. Mary Sayre Haverstock tells how the gregarious Bellows tested the limits of public tolerance with his drawings and paintings of disturbing urban scenes, in *George Bellows: An Artist in Action.*

Merida, Kevin, and Michael A. Fletcher

Supreme Discomfort: The Divided Soul of Clarence Thomas. Doubleday, 2007. 422p. ISBN 9780385510806.

In opinion polls, Clarence Thomas (1948–) usually draws very low approval ratings from other black Americans. According to the authors, these critics hold that his conservative positions and the residue of the Anita Hill controversy override all other considerations in the examination of his character. They chronicle his crude jokes and apparent disregard for victims of discrimination and poverty. His defenders counter that he is a gentleman with a right to his conservatism, adding that he is held to a higher standard because he is black. Kevin Merida and Michael A. Fletcher lay out the evidence, pro and con, in this unauthorized biography.

> **Subjects:** African Americans; Biographical Essays; Group Discussion Books; Judges; Supreme Court; Thomas, Clarence

> **Now Try:** Thomas recounts his childhood and career in *My Grandfather's Son: A Memoir*. For more on Thomas and the other members of the Supreme Court, read *The Nine: Inside the Secret World of the Supreme Court* by Jeffrey Toobin. Although the political alignments of Clarence Thomas and historical figure William Jennings Bryan are far different, both have been ridiculed at times for their intransigence. Michael Kazin tells the story of the famous populist politician in *A Godly Hero: The Life of William Jennings Bryan* (see chapter 10). Other biographies presenting arguments for and against the honor of their subjects are *Jefferson Davis, American* by William J. Cooper (see chapter 10) and *Louis Armstrong: An Extravagant Life* by Laurence Bergreen.

Oakley, Jane

Rasputin: Rascal Master. St. Martin's Press, 1989. 207p. ISBN 0312032277.

Russian Grand Duchess Militsa was the first of the Romanovs to notice Siberian mystic Grigori Rasputin (1869–1916). Hearing that he could heal and prophesy, she invited the dark monk to St. Petersburg. Once in the Russian capital, Rasputin secured royal favor by predicting the birth of Tsarevitch Alexis, whose bleeding he would later control. Though he was welcome in the palace of Nicholas and Alexandra, he was despised and feared as an agent of the devil by many nobles and bureaucrats, who plotted to assassinate him. In this beautifully illustrated biography, Jane

Oakley tells a story about the controversial "mad monk" set against the turmoil of the opening days of the Bolshevik Revolution.

Subjects: Illustrated Biography; Mystics; Rasputin, Grigori; Russia; Teen Reads

Now Try: Rasputin shared an intensity and an ability to incense enemies with the American abolitionist John Brown. Both were considered religious fanatics by some and holy men by others. Brown's dramatic life is chronicled in the epic biography *John Brown, Abolitionist: The Man Who Killed Slavery, Sparked the Civil War, and Seeded Civil Rights* by David S. Reynolds (see chapter 9). Catholic priest Girolamo Savonarola would never have been accused of ingratiating himself with Florentine princes, but he was similar to Rasputin in the scorn he has drawn from historians. His violent life is described in *Fire in the City: Savonarola and the Struggle for Renaissance Florence* by Lauro Martines. Jim Morrison, lead singer for the rock group the Doors, fashioned a darkly mystical image with his stringy hair and passionate lyrics. Jerry Hopkins and Danny Sugerman portray Morrison as a hell-bent rebel who read the Beat poets and broke decency laws in *No One Here Gets Out Alive* (see chapter 6). Like Rasputin, the Roman emperor Nero is often portrayed as evil. Edward Champlin points out that our current knowledge of Nero mostly comes from three historians, Tacitus, Cassius Dio, and Suetonius, none of whom was an eyewitness to the events about which they wrote in his revisionist biography *Nero* (see this chapter).

Phillips, Julie

🐾 *James Tiptree, Jr.: The Double Life of Alice B. Sheldon.* St. Martin's Press, 2006. 469p. ISBN 9780312203856.

Who was James Tiptree Jr.? Everyone in the science fiction community of the late 1960s and early 1970s wanted to know. He had never been seen, but his stories and novels about spaceships and aliens were sensational. He wrote to many well-known science fiction writers and had convinced them that he was a restless character fond of hunting and travel. Suggestions that Tiptree was a woman were dismissed until 1976, when Alice B. Sheldon (1915–1987) revealed herself. Julie Phillips portrays this daughter of a romance novelist as a complicated figure who will appeal to the many readers who have imagined living a secret life.

Subjects: Identity; Science Fiction Authors; Sheldon, Alice B.; Tiptree, James, Jr.

Awards: ALA Notable Book; National Book Critics Circle Award for Biography

Now Try: Sheldon's writings can be found in the science fiction novels *Brightness Falls from the Air* and *The Starry Rift* and short story collections *Her Smoke Rose Up Forever* and *Crown of Stars*. In *The Orientalist: Solving the Mystery of a Strange and Dangerous Life* (see this chapter), Tom Reiss tells the story of identifying a mysterious novelist in 1930s Berlin. Bill Bryson discusses whether Shakespeare really was the author of the plays attributed to him in his witty *Shakespeare: The World as Stage* (see chapter 7). In the entertaining *The Mysterious Montague: A True Tale of Hollywood, Golf, and Armed Robbery* by Leigh Montville, the mystery is whether the affable golfer John Montegue is really the long sought bank robber LaVerne Moore.

Reiss, Tom

🐾 *The Orientalist: Solving the Mystery of a Strange and Dangerous Life.* Random House, 2005. 433p. ISBN 1400062659. Large print available.

Who was Essad Bey, the author who wrote *Blood and Oil in the Orient*, a German best-selling book about escaping the Russian Revolution? Who was Kurban Said, who wrote *Ali and Nino*, a love story about a Jewish-Muslim romance now considered the national novel of Azerbaijan? Were they both a mysterious Russian Jew by the name of Lev Nussimbaum (1905–1942), who lived among the Nazis pretending to be a Muslim prince? How truthful is the memoir that Nussimbaum wrote? Why did he die in rural Italy in 1942? Journalist Tom Reiss takes readers through the shadowy underworld of 1930s Berlin in his Investigative Biography of an elusive figure.

Subjects: Authors; Berlin; Bey, Essad; Jews; Nussimbaum, Lev; Said, Kurban

Awards: ALA Notable Book

Now Try: The epic novel *Ali and Nino: A Love Story* by Kurban Said, one of Nussimbaum's pseudonyms, is also filled with mystery and suspense. Mystery also surrounds another shadowy character from Nussimbaum's era, criminal genius Joseph Silver. Could this man really have been responsible for murders in so many cities around the world? Silver's life is examined in *The Fox and the Flies: The Secret Life of a Grotesque Master Criminal* by Charles Van Onselen (see chapter 2). One of the longest running debates in the annals of crime has been over the identity of Jack the Ripper. Patricia Cornwell claims that she has solved the mystery in *Portrait of a Killer: Jack the Ripper Case Closed* (see chapter 2). Like Nussimbaum, French poet Arthur Rimbaud became a master of disguise, living for over a decade in the underworld of Egypt and Ethiopia. His strange story is told in *Somebody Else: Arthur Rimbaud in Africa, 1880–91* by Charles Nicholl (see chapter 1).

Shetterly, Aran

The Americano: Fighting with Castro for Cuba's Freedom. Algonquin Books of Chapel Hill, 2007. 300p. ISBN 9781565124585.

Former Toledo high school janitor William Morgan (1928–1961) remains a mysterious figure. In 1958 he snuck into the Cuban jungle to join rebel leader Eloy Gutiérrez Menoyo in support of Fidel Castro's revolution against the corrupt government of Fulgencio Batista. Though at first mistrusted, he became a key lieutenant in the rebel army and was often seen with Che Guevara and other top leaders. In interviews with the American press, he insisted that he was in Cuba to fight for freedom, and that Castro was not a communist. Why then did Castro suddenly arrest and execute the American in 1961? In this gritty Investigative Biography, Aran Shetterly examines who Morgan was and what his intentions might have been.

Subjects: Cuba; Morgan, William; Revolutionaries

Now Try: In the novel *The Last King of Scotland* by Giles Foden, a young Scottish doctor shows how little he knows about the a tropical country in turmoil when he becomes personal physician to Ugandan dictator Idi Amin. The shifting alliances within partisan forces in the Spanish Civil War were as dangerous those in the Cuban Revolution. Stephen Koch tells a tragic story involving two famous American novelists in *The Breaking Point: Hemingway, Dos Passos, and the Murder of José Robles* (see chapter 3). Dave R. Palmer investigates how a trusted lieutenant could betray his revered general in the American Revolution in *George Washington and Benedict Arnold: A Tale of Two Patriots* (see chapter 3). Ship's pilot William Adams was a common seaman who was stranded in sixteenth-century Japan. Giles Milton describes his dangerous life in service of a Japanese shogun in *Samurai William: The Englishman Who Opened Japan* (see chapter 1).

Trimborn, Jurgen

Leni Riefenstahl: A Life. Faber and Faber, 2007. 351p. ISBN 9780374184933.

Though film critics praise the artistry of German filmmaker Leni Riefenstahl (1902–2003), many people condemn her for her work for Adolf Hitler during his most powerful years. Although she admitted admiring his strong leadership, she claimed that she was apolitical and never realized the uses to which her films *Triumph of the Will* and *Olympia* would be put. For four years after World War II she was held in a French detention camp, but authorities eventually released her after she was twice exonerated by postwar courts. Biographer Jurgen Trimborn questions whether Riefenstahl was as innocent as she claimed, and whether she deserves reconsideration for the entirety of her long life as a dancer, actress, writer, and filmmaker.

> **Subjects:** Actors and Actresses; Germany; Group Discussion Books; Movie Directors; Nazi Party; Riefenstahl, Leni; Women

> **Now Try:** At age ninety, Riefenstahl defended her life in *Leni Riefenstahl: A Memoir*, which describes her work among aboriginal tribes as well as her filmmaking years. *Vanishing Africa* is a collection of her photographs from her years on the African continent. The work of Margaret Mead, Riefenstahl's contemporary in studying tribes in Third World countries, has also been criticized. Derek Freeman explains that he believes Mead was tricked by Samoan tribesman in *The Fateful Hoaxing of Margaret Mead: A Historical Analysis of Her Samoan Research*. Guilt by association with Adolf Hitler is an issue in *Hitler's Piano Player: The Rise and Fall of Ernst Hanfstaengl, Confidant of Hitler, Ally of FDR* by Peter Conradi (see chapter 3) and *The Lost Life of Eva Braun* by Angela Lambert (see chapter 6). Like Riefenstahl, artist Georgia O'Keefe continued to be a provocative character throughout her long career. Art critic Hunter Drohojowska-Philp portrays her as a contentious woman in *Full Bloom: The Art and Life of Georgia O'Keeffe* (see chapter 7).

Vistica, Gregory L.

The Education of Lieutenant Kerrey. Thomas Dunne Books, 2003. 296p. ISBN 0312285477.

Senator Bob Kerrey (1943–) of Nebraska was a promising Democratic candidate in 1992. He had received the Medal of Honor for his military service in Vietnam, he had already been governor of his state, and the public had approved of his romantic affair with actress Debra Winger. However, when his conduct in Vietnam was scrutinized, he admitted participating in an incident that left innocent women and children dead. In this critical profile of a Midwestern politician, journalist Gregory L. Vistica weighs whether Kerrey is a hero, war criminal, or something in between; and whether the public has forgiven him too easily. Book groups should consider this book full of questions about the responsibilities of soldiers and the countries that employ them.

> **Subjects:** Group Discussion Books; Kerrey, Bob; Nebraska; Senators; Soldiers; Vietnam War

> **Now Try:** In *When I Was a Young Man: A Memoir*, Kerrey tells a compelling story about growing up in Nebraska, going to college, and going to war. He does not admit to the charges that he indiscriminately killed women and children in Vietnam. In the memoir *Lieutenant Calley: His Own Story*, William Calley, the only soldier convicted in the My Lai massacre, defended his role in the event that left hundreds of Vietnamese civilians dead. In his novels *Going After Cacciato* and *The Things They Carried*, Tim

O'Brien describes the lives of American soldiers in Vietnam and the compromises they made to survive. Weighing the complicated evidence of how a man acted in wartime is also the subject of *Oskar Schindler: The Untold Account of His Life, Wartime Activities, and the True Story Behind the List* by David M. Crowe (see this chapter).

Wroe, Ann

The Perfect Prince: The Mystery of Perkin Warbeck and His Quest for the Throne of England. Random House, 2003. 610p. ISBN 1400060338. Audiobook available.

Richard Plantagenet, Duke of York, the second son of Edward IV of England (1473–?) was supposedly murdered by order of his uncle, King Richard III, in 1483 or 1484, but his body was never seen. In 1491 Irish lords swore allegiance to a young man who claimed to be Prince Richard returned from exile in Portugal. Was he really the heir of the throne of England, or a boatman's son named Perkin Warbeck (1474–1499)? Medieval historian Ann Wroe chronicles the life of a tragic figure who nearly became an English king.

Subjects: England; Identity; Pretenders to the Throne; Warbeck, Perkin

Now Try: Mary Shelley, author of *Frankenstein,* also wrote a novel, *Fortunes of Perkin Warbeck,* based on her belief that Warbeck was the prince and heir. There is always doubt in a story when the body is never found. Ann Rule describes such a case in *. . . And Never Let Her Go: Thomas Capano: The Deadly Seducer* (see chapter 2). Romantic novels and old movies have glorified the campaign of Prince Charles Edward, grandson of James II of England, to claim the British throne. In *Bonnie Prince Charlie: A Biography of Charles Edward Stuart* (see this chapter), Susan Maclean Kybett describes the prince as an alcoholic adventurer mad with ambition. Sometimes legitimate rulers lose their positions in military uprisings. Randall Robinson describes the fate of Jean-Bertrand Aristide, the elected president of Haiti, who has twice been removed from office, in *Unbroken Agony: Haiti, from Revolution to the Kidnapping of a President.*

Young, Alfred F.

Masquerade: The Life and Times of Deborah Sampson, Continental Soldier. Alfred A. Knopf, 2004. 417p. ISBN 0679441654.

Posing as a young man named Robert Shurtliff, Deborah Sampson (1760–1827) spent seventeen months as a soldier in the Continental Army late in the American Revolution. The masquerade itself was not the only remarkable part of her life. Sampson distinguished herself by making a career out of the story, becoming the famous Mrs. Gannett, a celebrated public lecturer, and even gaining a pension from the U.S. government when other women who fought in the revolution as men were denied. In this entertaining biography, Alfred F. Young tells the story of a resourceful woman who succeeded in a man's world.

Subjects: American Revolution; Gannett, Deborah Sampson; Identity; Soldiers; Women

Now Try: Elizabeth D. Leonard writes about women fighters in the Civil War in *All the Daring of the Soldier: Women of the Civil War Armies*. Laura Leedy Gansler recounts how one woman remained undetected in the Union Army through many of its fiercest battles, in *The Mysterious Private Thompson: The Double Life of Sarah Emma Edmonds, Civil War Soldier*. Kirsten Holmstead tells about modern women at war in *Band of Sisters: American Women at War in Iraq* (see chapter 3). As the wife of a general, Martha Washington took an active interest in the lives of the soldiers under her husband's command. How she can be considered a key character in the American Revolution is explained in *Martha Washington: An American Life* by Patricia Brady (see chapter 10). In World War II, some American women were reporters who followed the soldiers into battle zones. *The Women Who Wrote the War* by Nancy Caldwell Sorel (see chapter 3) is a collective biography describing the brave work of dozens of young women.

Young, Jeffrey S., and William L. Simon

iCon: Steve Jobs, the Greatest Second Act in the History of Business. John Wiley, 2005. 359p. ISBN 9780471720836.

The reputation of Steve Jobs (1955–) has fluctuated wildly. He began as a hippie geek inventing electronic gadgets with friends. When hooked to a telephone, one of their first devices allowed users to place free long distance calls, illegally circumventing telephone company controls. But he grew to be a legend in the computer and entertainment industry. In this critical biography, Jeffrey S. Young and William L. Simon show how Jobs, with his genius for innovation, drive for wealth, and disregard for laws, has resurrected a once-failing career. Business and technology readers will especially enjoy this journalistic exposé.

Subjects: Apple Computers; Computer Engineers; Corporate Executives; Jobs, Steve; Teen Reads

Now Try: What Jobs did for the personal computer, Tim Berners-Lee did for the World Wide Web. He tells his own story in his book about the Web, *Weaving the Web: The Original Design and Ultimate Destiny of the World Wide Web*. Like Jobs, physicist William Thomson, first Baron Kelvin, was at the top of his field, and he was known across Great Britain at a very early age. His reputation declined as he reached middle age, but unlike Jobs, he did not rebound. David Lindley describes how a scientific innovator becomes a reactionary unwilling to consider new ideas in *Degrees Kelvin: A Tale of Genius, Invention, and Tragedy* (see chapter 11). Whereas Jobs moved from electronic genius to entertainment mogul, animator and movie maker Walt Disney started in entertainment and then became technical innovator. Disney's personal and corporate affairs are described in the epic biography *Walt Disney: The Triumph of the American Imagination* by Neal Gabler (see chapter 9).

Exposés

Ideally, biographers attempt to write balanced accounts of their subjects. Trying to convey the truth, authors dispassionately tell what their subjects did and what their reasons were, if known. Their feelings about the people about whom they write are supposed to be restrained. In the real world, however, biographers do not necessarily follow this code, and they often let their admiration or disdain color their accounts, making the books more compelling and less academic. When investigative writers abandon their neutrality and aim to discredit their biographical subjects, the results are Exposés, books that blame and condemn.

In the books in this section, the authors aim to sully their subjects' reputations by exposing their misdeeds and proving the validity of their censure. In *Rupert Murdoch: The Untold Story of the World's Greatest Media Wizard*, Neil Chenoweth portrays the newspaper mogul as solely concerned with his own power and wealth, with no regard for employees or stockholders of the companies he ruins. In *Malory: The Knight Who Became King Arthur's Chronicler*, Christina Hardyman aims to expose Sir Thomas Malory, the man credited with founding the concept of chivalry, as a rapist and ruffian. In the classic exposé *Boss: Richard J. Daley of Chicago*, journalist Mike Royko chronicles the corruption of one of the most powerful mayors in the United States. These authors want readers to know the dark sides of these men and women.

Character is central to these stories. Many readers find evil characters fascinating, and they read exposés to learn every sordid detail of their stories. The importance of the setting varies in these books, as does pacing. The atmosphere of outrage, however, remains constant in these compelling books.

Exposés are biographies that are intended by their authors to expose the misdeeds of profiled individuals for the purpose of discrediting them. As in a court of law, authors tell what the subjects did and present the evidence. They also explain why the misdeeds mattered. These detailed accounts require unhurried reading. Author neutrality is absent in these passionate narratives, which aim to rouse readers' feelings.

Chang, Jung, and Jon Halliday

Mao: The Unknown Story. Alfred A. Knopf, 2005. 814p. ISBN 0679422714. Audiobook available.

Mao Zedong (1893–1976) oversaw the deaths of seventy million Chinese peasants, intellectuals, dissidents, and party members during the twenty-seven years that he was the communist dictator of China. As horrible as his reign of terror was, it was often argued by apologists that he was pursuing a dream, trying to construct a model workers' society. In this epic biography, Jung Chang and Jon Halliday expose the fallacy of Mao's reported idealism and ideology. They contend that from birth he was a misfit, rebuked by his severe father and pampered by his mother. Always ruthless, he used Stalin as a sponsor to gain power in the Chinese Communist Party, and ultimately he outdid the Soviet leader in murder.

Subjects: China; Communists; Dictators; Mao Zedong

Now Try: Before Joseph Stalin became a close aide to Vladimir Ilyich Lenin during the Bolshevik Revolution, he was a gangster involved in robbery, arson, and murder. His obscure Georgian origins are described in *Young Stalin* by Simon Sebag Montefiore (see chapter 6). Unlike Mao and Stalin, Cecil Rhodes, who became a diamond magnate and prime minister of the Cape

Colony, was seen as a charming and gregarious young man who mixed well with people of many races when he first went to South Africa. Antony Thomas tells how the lust for wealth and political power transformed him into a tyrant in *Rhodes: Race for Africa*. General Francisco Franco began his military career with seemingly good intentions, but he became a tyrant in reaction to the Spanish Civil War. The story of his harsh rule of Spain is told in *Franco: A Concise Biography* by Gabrielle Ashford Hodges (see this chapter). Mohammad Rezâ Shâh Pahlavi, known as the Shah of Iran, used imprisonment and torture to punish dissidents in his country. Marvin Zonis offers a psychological profile of the Shah in *Majestic Failure: The Fall of the Shah*.

Chenoweth, Neil

Rupert Murdoch: The Untold Story of the World's Greatest Media Wizard. Crown Business, 2001. 398p. ISBN 0609610384.

Australian Rupert Murdoch (1931–) is the most hated man in the news and entertainment industry. For decades he has bought newspapers, radio and television stations, cable systems, and movie studios to add to his multinational company, the News Corporation, which he grew from the purchase of the *Daily Mirror* in Sydney in 1960. After the acquisitions, longtime employees lose their jobs and pensions, editors lose their independence, and media markets lose diversity. According to business journalist Neil Chenoweth, Murdoch often loses billions of dollars in reckless deals, but he always recovers. In this critical biography, the author focuses on the media mogul's relations with his family, his stockholders, and his many enemies, including Ted Turner, Michael Eisner, Bill Gates, and Pat Robertson. Readers who savor a good exposé will likely enjoy this stinging account.

> **Subjects:** Billionaires; Mass Media; Murdoch, Rupert; Newspaper Publishers
>
> **Now Try:** Few would argue that Steve Jobs is as internationally menacing as Murdoch, but he has broken laws and tried to corner markets. Jeffrey S. Young and William L. Simon describe his shady dealings in *iCon: Steve Jobs, the Greatest Second Act in the History of Business* (see this chapter). The railroad tycoon Jay Gould controlled his industry in the nineteenth century much in the way Murdoch does today. Edward J. Renehan Jr. tells a surprisingly lenient story in *Dark Genius of Wall Street: The Misunderstood Life of Jay Gould, King of the Robber Barons* (see chapter 9). Elizabeth Drew portrays Richard Nixon as a ruthless and egocentric politician in the concise *Richard M. Nixon*. George Steinbrenner, chairman of American Shipbuilding Company and owner of the New York Yankees, has distinguished himself as a ruthless man. Maury Allen describes the team owner's egocentric rule over the Yankees in *All Roads Lead to October: Boss Steinbrenner's 25-Year Reign over the New York Yankees*.

Evanzz, Karl

The Messenger: The Rise and Fall of Elijah Muhammad. Pantheon Books, 1999. 667p. ISBN 067944260X.

Black separatist Elijah Muhammad (1897–1975) was accused of many crimes during his life. The FBI kept a file on him that included 127 aliases and suggested that he was an agent of the Japanese empire during World War II. He was suspected of misusing Nation of Islam funds and of arranging the assassination of Malcolm X. Nevertheless, he inspired millions of African Americans to join his self-empowerment movement and was even praised by Chicago Mayor Richard J. Daley. In this Investigative Biography, journalist Karl Evanzz shows how the son of a Georgia sharecropper came to be one of the most notorious men in America. Readers interested in conspiracy stories will undoubtedly relish this meaty exposé.

Subjects: African Americans; Black Muslims; Elijah Muhammad

Now Try: *Message to the Blackman in America* is Elijah Muhammad's most famous follower was Malcolm X, who told about his break with the religious leader in *The Autobiography of Malcolm X*. Since Sun Myung Moon brought the Unification church to America in the 1970s, it has found followers throughout the country from many ethnic backgrounds. John Gorenfeld reports on Moon's secret financial dealings and political influence in *Bad Moon Rising: How Reverend Moon Created the Washington Times, Seduced the Religious Right and Built an American Kingdom*. Kenneth D. Ackermann tells a story of a man becoming popular and rich while inspiring the downtrodden in *Boss Tweed: The Rise and Fall of the Corrupt Pol Who Conceived the Soul of Modern New York* (see chapter 2). Another epic biography of a complicated figure whose reputation was tarnished by his involvement in conspiracies is *Fallen Founder: The Life of Aaron Burr* by Nancy Isenberg (see chapter 10).

Fellman, Michael

The Making of Robert E. Lee. Random House, 2000. 360p. ISBN 0679456503.

The common image of Confederate General Robert E. Lee (1807–1870) is of a proud, honorable military leader facing overwhelming odds with courage. According to historian Michael Fellman, this legend has replaced the true man, who was often troubled by his responsibilities and filled with prejudices. He loved his family better from afar, sent many soldiers to their deaths needlessly, and believed that both poor whites and former slaves were inferior to the Southern aristocracy. Fellman even questions Lee's leadership skills. This biography of a "grudge-bearing" man is bound to upset many Lee sympathizers.

Subjects: Confederate States of America; Generals; Lee, Robert E.; Virginia

Now Try: *Robert E. Lee: A Penguin Life* by Roy Blount Jr. and *Robert E. Lee: A Life* by Emory M. Thomas are dispassionate, giving more balanced accounts of the general's successes and failures. It is difficult to imagine another biographer belittling his subject as much as Fellman does Lee, but Ben Proctor comes close in *William Randolph Hearst: Final Edition, 1911–1951* (see chapter 9), in which he tells the story of a man obsessed with power who lost his moral values. *Joan Crawford: The Last Word* by Fred Lawrence Guiles (see chapter 8) and *More Than a Woman: An Intimate Biography of Bette Davis* by James Spada (see chapter 8) also describe their subjects as devoid of admirable traits. Along the same lines, *Son of the Morning Star* by Evan S. Connell (see chapter 3) portrays General George Armstrong Custer as a military leader blinded by self-conceit, incapable of seeing the danger of underestimating the enemy. President James Buchanan, who failed to stop the country's slide toward the Civil War, is held by some historians to be the worst American president. Jean H. Baker presents the evidence in *James Buchanan* (see chapter 10).

Greenfield, Robert

Timothy Leary: A Biography. Harcourt, 2006. 689p. ISBN 9780151005000. Audiobook available.

Fame and controversy were Timothy Leary's (1920–1996) true addictions, and rejection of authority was this rebel's mission from an early age. Being assigned as an intern in a psychological unit, combined with being a patient in the infirmary at judiciously chosen times, he was able to get through military training in World War II without ever firing a gun. After the war he landed prestigious academic positions at the University of California at Berkeley and at Harvard University, from which he became an advocate for recreational drug experimentation. In this candid account of the Pied Piper of LSD, Robert Greenfield places Leary at the center of the cultural revolution that included Allen Ginsberg, the Grateful Dead, Jefferson Airplane, and the Weather Underground.

> **Subjects:** Drug Culture; Leary, Timothy; Psychologists
>
> **Now Try:** Leary's account of his life with drugs is *Flashbacks: A Personal and Cultural History of an Era*. Journalist Hunter S. Thompson lived a life devoted to drugs, alcohol, guns, and culture shock. His articles portrayed figures on the fringe of society acting abnormally. *Rolling Stone* editor Jann S. Wenner celebrates his life in *Gonzo: The Life of Hunter Thompson* (see chapter 7). Like Leary, Jack Nicholson has become an icon of hedonism and rebellion. His career of pleasure seeking is chronicled in *Jack: The Great Seducer: The Life and Many Loves of Jack Nicholson* by Edward Douglas (see chapter 8). Poet Allen Ginsberg, whose advocacy of freedom of speech and sexual orientation is viewed as more acceptable than Leary's campaign for LSD, was another character involved with the West Coast cultural revolution. Bill Morgan portrays Ginsberg as a creative and affable dissenter in *I Celebrate Myself: The Somewhat Private Life of Allen Ginsberg* (see chapter 7).

Hardyman, Christina

Malory: The Knight Who Became King Arthur's Chronicler. HarperCollins, 2005. 634p. ISBN 9780066209814.

Known today for *Le Morte D'Arthur*, the source for many Arthurian legends, Sir Thomas Malory (1405–1471) remains a mysterious figure who witnessed many historical events during his long life. In Normandy as an aide to Richard Beauchamp, Earl of Warwick, he may have met Joan of Arc and seen her execution. With the Knights Hospitaller he fought the Turks in Rhodes. As a member of Parliament he knew the courts of Henry VI and Edward IV. He was imprisoned and then pardoned for rape, murder, and theft several times during the War of the Roses. In this richly historical biography, Christina Hardyman questions the character of the man known for championing chivalry.

> **Subjects:** Arthurian Romances; England; Knights; Malory, Sir Thomas; War of the Roses
>
> **Now Try:** English translations of Malory's tales of King Arthur are still usually entitled *Le Morte d'Arthur*. Writing was a second job for Italian diplomat Niccolo di Bernardo dei Machiavelli, who wrote the classic political treatise *The Prince*. Ross King concisely describes his life of corruption in *Machiavelli: Philosopher of Power* (see chapter 10). Historical depictions of Oliver Cromwell, who led the Puritan Revolution in Great Britain, are often critical. Peter Gaunt lays out the historical evidence for and against Cromwell in *Oliver Cromwell* (see chapter 10). Fourteenth-century English poet Geoffrey

Chaucer was witness to many historic events as a royal accountant and court entertainer. His struggle to stay in royal favor and out of bankruptcy is told in *Chaucer* by Peter Ackroyd (see chapter 7). Nearly as shocking as the proponent of chivalry being a violent criminal is the idea that a children's book author did not care for children. Jen Anderson describes Hans Christian Andersen as a complicated man who wanted to be seen as a man of literature in *Hans Christian Andersen: A New Life* (see this chapter).

Higham, Charles

Howard Hughes: The Secret Life. G. P. Putnam's Sons, 1993. 368p. ISBN 0399-138595.

Howard Hughes (1905–1976) was among the most mysterious figures of the twentieth century. After his initial success as a businessman in the oil and aeronautical industries and his public affairs with many of Hollywood's most attractive women, he became a recluse, always in the background of corporate affairs, American politics, and foreign relations. Though he did not smoke or drink alcohol, the hypochondriac developed serious pharmaceutical addictions and disturbing behaviors that kept him isolated from society. Celebrity biography Charles Higham recounts many bizarre tales in this fast-paced exposé that is sure to please readers who enjoy gossip about the rich and famous.

Subjects: Hughes, Howard; Industrialists; Mental Illness; Millionaires

Now Try: Newspaper publisher William Randolph Hearst courted actresses and political figures, using his money to buy many favors. Ben Proctor tells how Hearst tried to run the country but eventually lost his political clout in *William Randolph Hearst: Final Edition, 1911–1951* (see chapter 9). Hughes inherited a company selling tools to oil companies, but Frank Phillips made his original fortune as a banker financing oil wells. In *Oil Man: The Story of Frank Phillips and the Birth of Phillips Petroleum* (see chapter 9), Michael Wallis tells about a fabulously rich man who demanded the attention of celebrities and politicians, but who in the end gave most of his money away. Charles Lindbergh was another secretive character with extreme political ideas who figures in the history of American aviation. His story is more sympathetically told by A. Scott Berg in *Lindbergh* (see chapter 1). Like Hughes, Wernher von Braun, who understood aviation engineering and design, was a private man with skeletons in his closet, namely his use of concentration camp labor in the manufacture of his missiles in Germany. Michael J. Neufeld weighs the Jekyll and Hyde aspects of von Braun's life in *Von Braun: Dreamer of Space, Engineer of War* (see chapter 11).

Hodges, Gabrielle Ashford

Franco: A Concise Biography. Thomas Dunne Books, 2000. 290p. ISBN 031228-2850.

General Francisco Franco (1892–1975) was shocked when his beloved King Alfonso VIII fled Spain after the Republican elections of 1931. As a young man, Franco had distinguished himself in the Foreign Legion and had received medals from the king. Now his country was controlled by people whom he considered heretics. In response, he sought revenge and then total power. In this psychological biography, Gabrielle Ashford

Hodges portrays Franco as a psychotic dictator who would rather destroy his country than let his enemies live.

Subjects: Dictators; Franco, Francisco; Generals; Spain

Now Try: Like Franco, Lieutenant Colonel Adolf Eichmann, who worked in the German Office of Jewish Emigration directing the mass murder of Jews and other minorities, found the idea of ethnic cleansing admirable. David Cesarani describes Eichmann as an enthusiastic and charming officer concerned with efficiency and Nazi profit, never bothered by atrocities, in *Becoming Eichmann: Rethinking the Life, Crimes, and Trial of a "Desk Murderer"* (see chapter 2). Robert Mugabe became president of Zimbabwe after a bloody civil war. Initially he promised tolerance and opportunity for all, but his rule has become progressively more dictatorial. Martin Meredith recounts the life and evolving personality of Mugabe in *Mugabe: Power, Plunder, and the Struggle for Zimbabwe*. Benito Mussolini came to power in Italy after World War I, promising to restore economic prosperity. Ray Moseley describes the transformation from benign dictatorship to ruthless suppression from the viewpoint of the dictator's son-in-law in *Mussolini's Shadow: The Double Life of Count Galeazzo Ciano* (see this chapter). Like Franco, Soviet leader Nikita Khrushchev's life is a key story in the history of his country. William Taubman uses Krushchev's memoirs as well as newly available documents and interviews to reexamine the long career of a former metalworker turned world statesman in *Khrushchev: The Man and His Era* (see chapter 10).

Kybett, Susan Maclean

Bonnie Prince Charlie: A Biography of Charles Edward Stuart. Dodd, Mead & Company, 1988. 343p. ISBN 0396084966.

Romantic novels and old movies often portray Prince Charles Edward Stuart (1720–1788), grandson of James II of England, as a tragic hero who led a valiant fight to restore his family to the British throne. Historians have long wondered why Scottish Highlanders would follow him to certain doom at the Battle of Culloden, from which the prince escaped. Having spent years studying rare documents, Susan Maclean Kybett strips away the legends and tells the tale of an alcoholic adventurer mad with ambition. British history buffs will likely appreciate this investigative account.

Subjects: Charles Edward, Prince; Great Britain; Jacobite Rebellion; Scotland

Now Try: When the Jacobite Rebellion failed in 1746, Charles Edward Stuart had to flee across the Scottish Highlands. In *The Flight of Bonnie Prince Charlie*, biographer Hugh Douglas and landscape photographer Michael J. Stead have produced a photographic look at the locations that harbored the prince while he eluded British troops. James II's great-grandmother Mary, Queen of Scots, also had designs on the British throne. Her tragic story is told in *Queen of Scots: The True Life of Mary Stuart* by John Guy (see chapter 9). Adventurer Josiah Harlan, a Quaker in Chester County, Pennsylvania, went into Afghanistan in the mid-nineteenth century with no right to be there and amazingly for a time became a monarch. In *The Man Who Would Be King: The First American in Afghanistan,* Ben MacIntyre recounts the life of a world traveler whose story inspired Rudyard Kipling's short story "The Man Who Would Be King." The reputation of British adventurer T. E. Lawrence has been greatly bolstered by good press and fiction. A more realistic account of his career is presented in *The Golden Warrior: The Life and Legend of Lawrence of Arabia* by Lawrence James (see chapter 3).

Pollak, Richard

The Creation of Dr. B: A Biography of Bruno Bettelheim. Simon & Schuster, 1997. 478p. ISBN 0684809389.

From the confusion of Nazi-torn Europe, just released from the Buchenwald concentration camp where he had been "a Jew incarcerated for his own protection," Bruno Bettelheim (1903–1990) arrived in the United States and claimed that he was a degreed psychoanalyst and an associate of Sigmund Freud. He soon attached himself to the University of Chicago and began a celebrated career as a psychological researcher and author. After his suicide in 1990, critics claimed that Bettelheim had faked his credentials and much of his research and charged that he had abused some of the children under his care. In this detailed exposé, Richard Pollak chronicles how a depressed, insecure Bettelheim fooled the popular press and academic world alike.

Subjects: Bettelheim, Bruno; Fraud; Psychoanalysts

Now Try: Among Bettelheim's influential books that are still available are *The Good Enough Parent* and *The Uses of Enchantment*. Like the work of Bettelheim, the findings of anthropologist Margaret Mead, who studied tribes in Third World countries, are being reexamined. Derek Freeman explains that he believes Mead was tricked by Samoan tribesman in *The Fateful Hoaxing of Margaret Mead: A Historical Analysis of Her Samoan Research*. Werner von Braun, a rocket specialist who designed missiles for the German Army in World War II, surrendered to U.S. troops at the end of the war. Michael J. Neufeld describes how von Braun soon became a key figure in the American space effort of the 1950s and 1960s despite his shadowy past, in *Von Braun: Dreamer of Space, Engineer of War* (see chapter 11). In the early twentieth century, John R. Brinkley offered alternative medical treatments and patent medicines to anyone willing to pay, to the chagrin of health authorities, who lacked the power to shut down his clinic in Kansas. Pope Brock tells how Brinkley killed patients with suspect remedies in *Charlatan: America's Most Dangerous Huckster, the Man Who Pursued Him, and the Age of Flimflam* (see chapter 2). The problem for behavioral scientist B. F. Skinner was not that his research data were faked; rather, conservative academics and religious leaders objected to his conclusion that humans behave no differently than apes and lower life forms. Daniel W. Bjork tells the story of a scientist under siege in *B. F. Skinner: A Life* (see chapter 11).

Roston, Aram

The Man Who Pushed America to War: The Extraordinary Life, Adventures, and Obsessions of Ahmad Chalabi. Nation Books, 2008. 369p. ISBN 978156-8583532.

Businessman and former deputy prime minister in the initial post–Saddam Hussein Iraqi government Ahmad Chalabi (1944–) is a charming and persuasive man, according to journalist Aram Roston. Allies and enemies alike agree that without his lobbying of the Bush administration and key members of the U.S. Congress, there would have been no U.S. invasion of Iraq in 2003. He was a primary source of intelligence, claiming that Hussein had stockpiled weapons of mass destruction. In this exposé, Roston reports on how Chalabi, whom he suspects of bank embezzlement, has spent most of his life in exile plotting his return to his homeland. A solid choice for readers who closely follow political news.

> **Subjects:** Bankers; Chalabi, Ahmad; Embezzlers; Iraq War

> **Now Try:** Had his plan worked, Ahmad Chalabi hoped to become head of the Iraqi government with generous support from the U.S. government, reminiscent of the support given Philippine President Ferdinand Marcos in a previous era. James Hamilton-Paterson recounts the life of the Philippine leader who robbed his country's treasury in *America's Boy: A Century of Colonialism in the Philippines*. Fox Network News also pushed heavily for the U.S. invasion of Iraq. Neil Chenoweth profiles the powerful man behind the cable news network in *Rupert Murdoch: The Untold Story of the World's Greatest Media Wizard* (see this chapter). In the 1980s Lieutenant Colonel Oliver North secretly arranged for weapons shipments to Iran in exchange for guns that went to the Contra rebels in Nicaragua, bypassing all oversight of American military aid. Ben Bradlee profiles this staff assistant to the National Security Council in *Guts and Glory: The Rise and Fall of Oliver North*. President James Buchanan is known as the man who did nothing to stop the American Civil War. The story of his contentious presidency is told in the compact biography *James Buchanan* by Jean H. Baker (see chapter 10).

Royko, Mike

Boss: Richard J. Daley of Chicago. Dutton, 1971. 215p. ISBN 0525070001.

Newspaper columnist Mike Royko thanked but did not name his sources for this book. He did not want them to be run out of town or dropped in the lake for the things that they told him about longtime Chicago mayor Richard J. Daley (1902–1976). According to Royko, Daley was born in a small Irish village, which just happened to also be on the South Side of Chicago, the center of the city's political power. By being a good party soldier and earning favors, he rose to control the city through his loyal ward bosses. Written while Daley was still in power, this behind-the-scenes story of the mayor who ordered his police to "shoot to kill" during the 1968 race riots is a classic American tale.

> **Subjects:** Chicago; Corruption; Daley, Richard J.; Mayors; Politics and Government

> **Now Try:** *American Pharaoh: Mayor Richard J. Daley: His Battle for Chicago and the Nation* by Adam Cohen and Elizabeth Taylor completes and expands Royko's account of Mayor Daley's life and discusses the enduring legacy of his administration.. The other twentieth-century Chicago icon with similar clout was mobster Al Capone. Laurence Bergreen sets Capone's life within the context of American ethnic prejudice of the Roaring Twenties and poverty of the Great Depression in *Capone: The Man and His Era* (see chapter 2). Senator Huey P. Long of Louisiana was in control of nearly every political job in the state in the 1920s and 1930s. Richard D. White depicts Long as a canny politician whose longing for power threatened the entire democratic process in *Kingfish: The Reign of Huey P. Long* (see chapter 10). In *The Path to Power: The Years of Lyndon Johnson* (see chapter 6), Robert A. Caro tells how a young Texas politician carefully bent the law, knowing that he wanted to win higher office someday. In *The Lady Upstairs: Dorothy Schiff and the New York Post* (see chapter 10), Marilyn Nissenson tells how the editor of a major city newspaper used the power of endorsements and favorable stories to control politicians.

Summers, Anthony

The Arrogance of Power: The Secret World of Richard Nixon. Viking, 2000. 640p. ISBN 0670871516.

In the wake of former president Richard Nixon's (1913–1991) death in 1994, politicians and journalists publicly praised his service to his country, hardly mentioning Watergate and other controversies. Anthony Summers responded with this lively biography to remind readers of the dark side of the man from San Clemente. Within this chronicle of a frequently disgraced life, he exposes many lies that Nixon told about his own accomplishments and about his many enemies. The book especially appeals to readers who enjoy polemics.

Subjects: Corruption; Nixon, Richard M.; Politics and Government; Presidents

Now Try: Nixon defended his part in the Watergate Scandal in *In the Arena: A Memoir of Victory, Defeat, and Renewal.* Muriel Spark took the Nixon White House and moved the story to a fictional abbey in Great Britain in her wickedly funny novel *The Abbess of Crewe.* Margaret Macmillan provides a more positive view of Richard Nixon in her dual profile *Nixon and Mao: The Week That Changed the World.* Like Nixon, J. Edgar Hoover kept secret records and had no qualms about breaking the law for his own purposes. Kenneth D. Ackerman reveals how the secretive Hoover perfected his clandestine methods between 1919 and 1924 in *Young J. Edgar: Hoover, the Red Scare, and the Assault on Civil Liberties* (see chapter 6). In *"All Governments Lie": The Life and Times of Rebel Journalist I. F. Stone,* Myra MacPherson tells how an independent journalist led the attack on crooked politicians from the McCarthy Era to the Iran-Contra scandal.

Terrill, Ross

The White-Boned Demon: A Biography of Madame Mao Zedong. William Morrow, 1984. 446p. ISBN 0688024610.

Jiang Qing (1914–1991), widow of Mao Zedong, was defiant at her trial for plotting to install herself as China's supreme leader. After the courtroom antics, she stood silently when her death sentence was read, a punishment that was never administered. Chinese historian Ross Terrill tells the dramatic story of a woman who left two husbands, starred as an actress, joined Mao's Long March across China during the revolution, married Mao when he exiled his wife, and helped plan the bloody Cultural Revolution. A study in evil for those who enjoy reading about the darker side of humanity.

Subjects: Chiang, Ch'ing; China; Communists; Jiang, Qing; Revolutionaries; Women

Now Try: In fiction, Jiang Qing's equal is Livia Drusilla, the ruthless wife of the Roman emperor Augustus, who is portrayed as exceedingly wicked in *I, Claudius* by Robert Graves. When Mary Tudor took the throne of England after the early death of her younger brother, she sought to return the country to Roman Catholicism by suppressing Protestant sects. Jasper Godwin Ripley recounts the beheading and burning of Mary's enemies in *Bloody Mary's Martyrs: The Story of England's Terror.* The defrocked bishop Charles Maurice de Talleyrand-Périgord only survived by knowing when to be ruthless with his enemies. David Lawday tells a story of intrigue in France in *Napoleon's Master: A Life of Prince Talleyrand* (see chapter 10). Communist Party leader Vladimir Ilyich Lenin abandoned his Marxist principles when consolidating his power over the postrevolutionary Soviet Union. The story of his ruthless reign is told in *Lenin: A Biography* by Robert Service (see chapter 10).

Thomas, Gordon, and Martin Dillon

Robert Maxwell, Israel's Superspy: The Life and Murder of a Media Mogul. Carroll and Graf, 2002. 448p. ISBN 0786710780.

Telephones rang in capitals around the world when British publisher Robert Maxwell (1923–1991) disappeared from his yacht in the Atlantic Ocean. To most newspaper readers he appeared to be a fabulously rich and powerful businessman, but his clandestine job was as an agent for Israel's Mossad, a powerful and somewhat ruthless spy organization akin to the CIA. With his financial empire secretly crumbling, Maxwell had been trying to use his knowledge of sensitive information to extort funds from his intelligence associates. According to Gordon Thomas and Martin Dillon, Maxwell's death was not an accident. They describe his rise from poverty and fall from grace in this thrilling account.

> **Subjects:** Israel; Maxwell, Robert; Mossad; Newspaper Publishers; Spies
>
> **Now Try:** The murder of playwright Christopher Marlowe was a highly likely end to his violent life story, which is told in *Christopher Marlowe: Poet & Spy* by Park Honan (see chapter 2). Another murder with international political ramifications was the assassination of a Dutch monarch. Lisa Jardine recounts the sad case in *The Awful End of Prince William the Silent: The First Assassination of a Head of State with a Handgun* (see chapter 2). In 1942 a mysterious Russian Jew by the name of Lev Nussimbaum was murdered in rural Italy after having spent a decade in Berlin, where he may have used the names Essad Bey and Kurban Said to write best-selling books. Tom Reiss recounts the story in *The Orientalist: Solving the Mystery of a Strange and Dangerous Life* (see this chapter). When Amelia Earhart disappeared, there was an international search to learn her fate. Mary S. Lovell tells about Earhart's fascination with flight, her romance with the explorer and publisher G. P. Putnam, and her final flight in *The Sound of Wings: The Life of Amelia Earhart* (see chapter 1).

Tobias, Andrew

Fire and Ice: The Story of Charles Revson—the Man Who Built the Revlon Empire. Morrow, 1976. 282p. ISBN 0688030238.

Cosmetics king Charles Revson (1906-1975) had no real friends, according to Andrew Tobias. Instead, he sought short, intense relationships with employees and lovers, controlling the outcome and then moving on. At Revlon he managed every aspect of his company, even spending one day a week in the new products lab. He was especially active in sales and promotions and is credited for creating some of Revlon's famous cosmetics ad campaigns. In this exposé Tobias portrays Revson as a corporate tyrant who controlled not only those who worked for him, but ultimately the look of the American woman. This is juicy historical gossip for exposé fans.

> **Subjects:** Cosmetics Industry; Revlon, Inc.; Revson, Charles
>
> **Now Try:** The world of fashion is a breeding ground for sensational stories. Edmonde Charles-Roux tells how a poor French girl became the head of an international perfume and fashion corporation in *Chanel: Her Life, Her World, and the Woman Behind the*

Legend She Herself Created (see chapter 8). French queen Marie Antoinette was known for the extravagance of her clothes at a time when many of the French were starving. Caroline Weber takes readers back to the French court of Louis XVI in her story of fashion and disdain for the poor, *Queen of Fashion: What Marie Antoinette Wore to the Revolution* (see chapter 9). Samuel F. B. Morse, the inventor of the telegraph, was an unpleasant person who was forever losing partners, fighting patent claims, and staving off bankruptcy. Kenneth Silverman portrays Morse as an advocate of technical progress who exhibited all that was good and bad about society during the Industrial Revolution in *Lightning Man: The Accursed Life of Samuel F. B. Morse* (see chapter 11). Tammany Hall politician Dan Sickles was a brash man who took his mistress to meet Queen Victoria and shot his wife's lover in front of the White House. Thomas Keneally profiles an evil man in the center ring of corruption in nineteenth-century U.S. government in *American Scoundrel: The Life of the Notorious Civil War General Dan Sickles* (see chapter 2).

Legends Retold

The rise of investigative journalism and its culture of disbelief have turned the world of legends upside down. Writers and readers expect the stories told about heroes and heroines that have come down through time to include inaccurate data and even fabrications. With the ability to travel and visit great libraries and archives around the world, scholars today can track down original sources and transcriptions to study legendary characters, with the aim of discovering the truth behind the often-told tales.

To become the subject of Legends Retold does not require great antiquity. What is required is that the character's story inspire admirers to tell it enough times for discrepancies in the narrative to appear. Stories about nineteenth-century figures such as Davy Crockett, Buffalo Bill Cody, and Crazy Horse, who inspired cheaply produced popular literature, have nearly as many errant details as those about ancient figures like Tutankhamen and Cleopatra.

In all of the books in this section, the point of the biographer's quest is finding the true character of the subject. Not all truly succeed in making the central figure verifiable, leaving the appeal of mystery to compensate for the lack of a well-defined character. In the absence of character detail and narrative, some biographers instead turn to describing the environmental factors that must have shaped the personalities of their subjects. As in the works in the other sections of this chapter, the pace at which the narrative unfolds varies, though there are more quick reads than epic tales here. Readers who enjoy rethinking history will likely appreciate these biographical puzzles.

Legends Retold focus on historical figures about whom undocumented stories have been told. Many of these people are familiar because they have been portrayed in novels, pulp fiction, operas, plays, and movies. These books examine the legends to show what could be true about them. These biographies tend to be shorter than character investigations and exposés.

Allen, Paula Gunn

Pocahontas: Medicine Woman, Spy, Entrepreneur, Diplomat. HarperSanFrancisco, 2003. 350p. ISBN 006053687X.

In her investigative account of Pocahontas (1596–1617), the Powhatan princess who may have saved the life of Captain John Smith in early Virginia, historian Paula Gunn Allen tells the story from a Native viewpoint, integrating the spirit beliefs and love of earth of the indigenous people. As a result, myths and hearsay mingle with the known facts. Included are a surprising number of stories about a young woman who died around the age of twenty-one. As an important member of her tribe, she crossed a racial bridge, became a tobacco farmer's wife, and met the king and queen of England. This expansive look at an American legend will please most history readers.

Subjects: Native Americans; Pocahontas; Powhatan Indians; Virginia Colony; Women

Now Try: Scott O'Dell wrote about Pocahontas for young adults in *The Serpent Never Sleeps: A Novel of Jamestown and Pocahontas*, which adults may also enjoy. Unlike Pocahontas, Buffalo Calf Road Woman became a warrior who fought the loss of her tribe's lands. Her story is told in the novel-like biography *Buffalo Calf Road Woman* by Rosemary Agonito and Joseph Agonito (see chapter 3). Thérèse Martin was a quiet young woman who left a legacy despite dying in her early twenties. Kathryn Harrison tells about the writings of this humble nun in *Saint Thérèse of Lisieux* (see chapter 4). Like Pocahontas, young Princess Isabella of France, sent to England to be the bride of King Edward II early in the fourteenth century, married for diplomacy. In Isabella's case, the relationship went sour. Alison Weir recounts how Isabella deposed her uninterested husband and may have had him murdered, in *Queen Isabella: Treachery, Adultery, and Murder in Medieval England* (see chapter 9).

Andersen, Jens

Hans Christian Andersen: A New Life. Overlook Duckworth, 2005. 624p. ISBN 15856-7642X.

When Hans Christian Andersen (1805–1875) was a child in Odense, Denmark, the penalty for rumor telling was wearing a yoke hung with a foxtail and bells. This threatened punishment did not, however, stop the eloquent Dane from inventing stories about his childhood, including that he was of royal birth. He enjoyed a long career as a storyteller, travel writer, poet, novelist, playwright, and celebrity. According to Jen Andersen (no relation), many legends grew about the unconventional author of fairy tales who, ironically, did not want any noisy children at his readings. A detailed account for those who enjoy the analysis of complex characters.

Subjects: Andersen, Hans Christian; Children's Authors; Denmark; Fairy Tales

Now Try: Danish author Stig Dalager portrays Andersen more sympathetically in *Journey in Blue: A Novel About Hans Christian Andersen*. Like Andersen, author Margaret Wise Brown is remembered for her classic children's books. Leonard S. Marcus tells about an insecure but prolific young woman who died tragically young in *Margaret Wise Brown* (see chapter 7). Scholars have long debated how Jacob and Wilhelm Grimm collected the stories that they retold in their fairy tale collections. Valerie Paradiz argues that they heard most of them from young women who were collecting them to preserve German culture. The author identifies the women in *Clever Maids: The Secret History of the Grimm Fairy Tales*. Like Andersen, Yiddish storyteller Isaac

B. Singer, who won a Nobel Prize for Literature, was a complicated character who embodied contradictions. Biographer Florence Noiville pieces together his story from his autobiographies and interviews with family and friends in *Isaac B. Singer: A Life*.

Bell, Madison Smartt

Toussaint Louverture: A Biography. Pantheon Books, 2007. 333p. ISBN 9780-375423376.

Like the English colonists along the eastern coast of North America, French subject Toussaint Louverture (1743–1803) did not intend to rebel against the empire to which he belonged. Born on All Saints' Day on a plantation in Saint Domingue (now Haiti), he was given his freedom at age thirty-three by his owner. After earning the trust of the white landed class, he became an overseer and leader of the militia, sworn to protect their lives and property from rebel slaves. Ironically, he later led the only successful slave rebellion in the Americas. In this sympathetic biography, novelist Madison Smartt Bell sorts through many conflicting stories to assemble a believable history of a little understood, legendary figure who achieved victories over Spanish, British, and French troops.

> **Subjects:** African Americans; Generals; Haiti; Louverture, Toussaint; Revolutionaries

> **Now Try:** Madison Smartt Bell also wrote a fictional trilogy about Toussaint Louverture, starting with the novel *All Souls' Rising*. After the Haitian Revolution, plantation owners in the South watched for signs of uprisings among their slaves. In 1822 a rebellion planned by freeman Denmark Vesey in South Carolina was exposed, and Vesey and seventy-six followers were executed. David Robertson attempts to describe the little-known rebel leader in *Denmark Vesey*. The largest American slave revolt took place in Virginia in 1831. William Styron tells the story in his novel *The Confessions of Nat Turner*. Slavery was not just an institution in the American South. In the eighteenth century, black farmers in New England found the need to defend themselves from the aggressions of their white neighbors. In *Mr. and Mrs. Prince: How an Extraordinary Eighteenth-Century Family Moved out of Slavery and into Legend* (see chapter 9), Gretchen Holbrook Gerzina tells the story of freed slaves in Massachusetts taking their neighbors to court and winning. Like Louverture, Nelson Mandela was the key figure in the liberation of a country. His story is attractively told through photographs, interviews, and commentaries in *Mandela: The Authorized Portrait* (see chapter 10).

Carter, Robert A.

Buffalo Bill Cody: The Man Behind the Legend. John Wiley, 2000. 496p. ISBN 0471319961.

The life of Buffalo Bill Cody (1846–1917) bridged the period between westward expansion of the United States and the country's entry into the First World War. Though dime novels exaggerated and romanticized his life, he really was a Pony Express rider, buffalo hunter, army scout, and Indian fighter. He used his storybook fame to become a popular entertainer on the stage and to head spectacular Wild West shows. According to Robert A. Carter, Cody was a pragmatic man who did what he needed to survive personal tragedies, financial difficulties, and changing national attitudes. Carter sorts fact from myth in this detailed story of a flamboyant life.

> **Subjects:** Buffalo Bill; Cody, William Frederick; Frontiersmen; Scouts; Wild West Shows

> **Now Try:** Cody is still being written into fiction, including Matt Braun's Western *Hickok & Cody*. Legends misinform readers about many figures from the American West. Wyatt Earp was not a gunslinger who served both sides of the law. He was a serious law enforcement officer who rarely carried a gun. Casey Tefertiller explains that the shootout at the OK Corral was an unusual event that bothered Earp for the rest of his life in *Wyatt Earp: The Life Behind the Legend* (see chapter 2). Jack Burrows had to search to find the source of the John Ringo legends and identifies the real John Ringo, who lived a short and violent life in a lawless land, in *John Ringo: The Gunfighter Who Never Was* (see chapter 2). Friend of royalty and the peer of criminals, Giacomo Casanova also lived a flamboyant life. Lydia Flem corrects many of the fictionalized stories in *Casanova: The Man Who Really Loved Women* (see this chapter). Like Cody, Benjamin Franklin mastered many trades and became an American icon. His epic story is told in *Benjamin Franklin: An American Life* by Walter Isaacson (see chapter 10).

Champlin, Edward

Nero. Belknap Press, 2003. 346p. ISBN 0674011929.

Many historians describe the Roman emperor Nero Claudius Caesar Augustus Germanicus (37–68 CE), who ruled from 54 to 68 CE, as a tyrant guilty of murder, incest, brutality, and arson. He may have also committed suicide, and, if so, he died at age thirty-one to forever be remembered as purely evil. Skeptical historian Edward Champlin points out that our current knowledge of Nero mostly comes from three historians, Tacitus, Cassius Dio, and Suetonius, none of whom was an eyewitness to the events about which he wrote. In this collection of well-argued biographical essays, full of maps and quotations, Champlin examines other records and retells the story of Nero in the context of Roman life in his time. A contrary account for readers interested in revisionist history.

> **Subjects:** Emperors; Nero; Roman Empire

> **Now Try:** Nero appears in many historical novels about Rome, including *Quo Vadis: A Narrative of the Time of Nero* by Henryk Sienkiewicz. Ivan IV, Tsar of Russia, has a similar reputation for killing members of his court indiscriminately. His legend is examined in *Ivan the Terrible: First Tsar of Russia* by Isabel De Madariaga (see this chapter). In 1975 Pol Pot and the Khmer Rouge, a militant communist organization, violently took control of Cambodia. Philip Short describes his search for information and his findings about Pol Pot, the mysterious village boy who became a tyrant, in *Pol Pot: Anatomy of a Nightmare*. In Uganda in 1971, General Idi Amin deposed dictator Milton Obote, his former ally. Over the next ten years Amin and his military killed more than 300,000 Ugandan citizens. Giles Foden depicts Amin as a deranged and barbaric mass murderer in the suspenseful novel *The Last King of Scotland*.

Collingridge, Vanessa

Boudica: The Life of Britain's Legendary Warrior Queen. Overlook Press, 2005. 390p. ISBN 1585677787.

Queen Boudica of the Iceni (d. 60 or 61 CE), whose name means "victory," was described by Greek historian Cassius Dio as a tall woman with fierce eyes who wore a golden necklace and a multicolored cloak. Recent archeological evidence has found that her early Anglican tribe in the first century (CE) was more advanced than scholars had previously thought, and that she was a Roman citizen who spoke Latin. The allegations of mass murder during her burning of London to expel the Romans have also been refuted. Vanessa Collingridge describes a strong queen with a sense of destiny in this collection of speculative biographical essays.

1

2

> **Subjects:** Biographical Essays; Boadicea, Queen of the Britons; Britain; Queens; Roman Empire; Women

> **Now Try:** *Dreaming the Eagle* by Manda Scott is the first book in the fictional trilogy The Boudica Saga, which chronicles the revolt against the Roman Empire led by the Celtic queen in the first century CE. British historian Michael Wood has written a series of books investigating the true stories behind legends, including **In Search of the Dark Ages,** which examines the origins of the King Arthur stories, the discovery of Anglo-Saxon artifacts at Sutton Hoo, and the events at the Battle of Hastings. Novelist Mary Renault recounts the life and legends of the Greek warrior king Alexander the Great in her illustrated *The Nature of Alexander.* Rodrigo Diaz, who freed Spain from the Moors in the eleventh century, is the subject of many legends. R. A. Fletcher reveals that Diaz was a mercenary who switched sides in the long fought war in *The Quest for El Cid.* Although Vanessa Collingridge removes the barbarian label from Boudica, author John Man retains it for Attila the Hun. How the brutal chieftain led Huns and Goths across Europe is told in *Attila: The Barbarian King Who Challenged Rome* (see chapter 3).

3

4

5

De Madariaga, Isabel

6

Ivan the Terrible: First Tsar of Russia. Yale University Press, 2005. 484p. ISBN 0300097573.

7

Modern readers may think Ivan the Terrible (1530–1588) a fictional character, but he did exist, and he earned his name. As the first true tsar of Russia, he spared no lives in his conquest of an empire, even murdering his own son. Like European monarchs of the time, he used marriage to acquire land and allies, but unlike most other kings, he then killed his wives. Using Russian histories as her sources, Isabel de Madariaga presents Ivan as a ruthless man who modernized warfare while impoverishing his country.

8

> **Subjects:** Ivan IV, Tsar of Russia; Russia; Tsars

9

> **Now Try:** Ivan IV appears as an evil character in the vampire fantasy *Darker Jewels* by Chelsea Quinn Yarbro. In *The Ringed Castle*, the fifth volume of the Lymond Chronicles, Dorothy Dunnett portrays Ivan IV as a capricious and violent tsar. Soviet dictator Joseph Stalin was also known for killing off his opponents. How he began his career as a ruthless gangster is told in *Young Stalin* by Simon Sebag Montefiore (see chapter 6). Whether Englishman Oliver Cromwell, leader of the Puritan Revolution, was a murderous tyrant or a justified reformer is the topic of the biography *Oliver Cromwell* by Peter Gaunt (see chapter 10). The Roman emperor Gaius Germanicus Caesar, known as Caligula, is commonly depicted as a violent and depraved tyrant who murdered associates indiscriminately. Anthony A. Barrett reexamines the historical sources and finds minimal exaggeration in *Caligula: The Corruption of Power.*

10

11

12

El Mahdy, Christine

Tutankhamen: The Life and Death of a Boy-King. St. Martin's Press, 1999. 341p. ISBN 0312262418.

Because of the 1922 discovery of his tomb filled with golden artifacts, which captured newspaper headlines around the world, Tutankhamen (1358–1340 BCE) is the most famous of all Egyptian pharaohs. Because there are few verifiable facts about the pharaoh's life, the public desire for stories about the young king, who died at about age sixteen, was fulfilled with many legends and speculation. Egyptologist Christine El Mahdy discounts many of the fantasies and sets forth a reasonable yet still dramatic story in her well-illustrated book for lovers of ancient history.

Subjects: Egypt; Pharaohs; Tutankhamen

Now Try: Lynda S. Robinson uses Tutankhamen as a continuing character in her series of murder mysteries set in ancient Egypt, starting with *Murder in the Place of Anubis.* Another ancient figure about whom very little is known is Roman governor Pontius Pilate. Ann Wroe examines the records and describes his era in *Pontius Pilate* (see this chapter). Similarly, little is known about Guatama, known as the Buddha, but religious author Karen Armstrong drew from many legends as well as Indian history to craft a profile that seems very contemporary in *Buddha* (see chapter 4). Edward VI of England was only ten when he became king. Chris Skidmore sympathetically describes the promising but short reign of the son of Henry VIII in *Edward VI: The Lost King of England* (see chapter 9).

Flem, Lydia

Casanova: The Man Who Really Loved Women. Farrar, Straus & Giroux, 1997. 256p. ISBN 0374119570.

In old age Giacomo Casanova (1725–1798) wrote an autobiography about his pleasure-seeking life. Born the child of poor entertainers, the famous Venetian gentleman roamed the European continent as the friend of royalty and the peer of criminals. Lydia Flem corrects and expands Casanova's slanted account, telling about his short career as a monk, his many love affairs, his frequent scrapes with the law, and his late-life interest in writing.

Subjects: Casanova, Giacomo; Love Affairs; Philanderers; Venice

Now Try: Andrei Codrescu focuses on Casanova's later years, when the Venetian was writing his book and remembering his many adventures, in *Casanova in Bohemia: A Novel.* Lorenzo da Ponte, Mozart's librettist, grew up in a Jewish ghetto in Venice and later mingled with high society as a wandering priest with his close friend Giacomo Casanova. Rodney Bolt profiles da Ponte in a lighthearted biography, *The Librettist of Venice: The Remarkable Life of Lorenzo da Ponte* (see chapter 7). Like Casanova, Marco Polo spread the news of his adventures himself through his books. Laurence Bergreen examines the veracity of Polo's tales against documentary evidence in *Marco Polo: From Venice to Xanadu* (see chapter 1). Actor Jack Nicholson has had a series of romantic involvements with women who are much younger than he. Edward Douglas chronicles the affairs for movie fans in *Jack: The Great Seducer: The Life and Many Loves of Jack Nicholson* (see chapter 8).

Groneman, William, III

David Crockett: Hero of the Common Man. Forge, 2005. 207p. <u>American Heroes</u>. ISBN 9780765310675. Audiobook available.

As a congressman from Tennessee in the 1820s, David Crockett (1786–1836) was already known as a teller of tall tales, many about himself. Dime novel authors of the nineteenth century then embellished the obviously false legends. In recent times historians have belittled Crockett and his death at the Alamo, but in his fast-paced book from the <u>American Heroes</u> series, William Groneman III tells an admiring story about a frontiersman who was a friend of the common man. He concludes with an account of how the popular Davy Crockett legend grew.

> **Subjects:** Congresspersons; Crockett, David; Frontiersmen; Tennessee; Texas

> **Now Try:** David Thompson focuses on Crockett in his paperback fiction series <u>Davy Crockett</u>, beginning with *Homecoming*. Like Crockett, frontiersman Sam Houston was a failed politician in need of a new start when he went to join the rebellion in Texas. John Hoyt Williams tells how Houston followed success with failure throughout his life in *Sam Houston: A Biography of the Father of Texas* (see chapter 10). Kit Carson, a cavalry scout during the Indian Wars, was once another dime store novel hero, but now his reputation as a cruel and racist expansionist prevails. Thomas W. Dunlay cautions against applying twenty-first-century standards to a nineteenth-century man and shows a better side of the frontiersman in *Kit Carson and the Indians*. Like Crockett, Nathan Hale is honored as a martyr for his heroic death, at which he may have said, "I only regret that I have but one life to give my country." M. William Phelps draws from Hale's letters and diaries to portray him as a common man who made a great sacrifice in *Nathan Hale: The Life and Death of America's First Spy*.

Holmes, Rachel

African Queen: The Real Life of the Hottentot Venus. Random House, 2007. 161p. ISBN 9781400061365.

The British Parliament abolished the slave trade in the British Empire in 1807. Yet a young Khoisan woman from the Cape Colony was kidnapped and brought to London as a scientific curiosity in 1810. Known to Europeans as Saartjie Baartman (ca. 1775–1815), this young woman with large buttocks was put on display mostly nude—first in private showings and later to paying audiences. The promoters, who were mostly dance hall men, prospered from exploiting British attitudes toward race and colonial subjects while subjecting Baartman to a miserable existence. Abolitionists lost their court case to free her, and she performed at country fairs and exhibitions in England and France until she died in 1815. Rachel Holmes tells a dark, disturbing tale that ended in 2002 when Baartman's remains were removed from the Museum of Natural History in Paris and returned to South Africa for burial.

> **Subjects:** Africans; Baartman, Saartjie; Colonial Exploitation; Group Discussion Books; Hottentot Venus; London; Racial Discrimination; Teen Reads; Women

Now Try: Barbara Chase-Riboud retells Baartman's tragic story in *Hottentot Venus: A Novel*. Like Baartman, two-foot-tall Jeffrey Hudson was treated as a freak, in his case for the entertainment of Queen Henrietta Marie of England. His adventurous story is told in *Lord Minimus: The Extraordinary Life of Britain's Smallest Man* by Nick Page (see this chapter). African slave Olaudah Equiano secured his freedom and helped the abolitionist movement in Great Britain by writing a popular narrative of his life. Vincent Carretta chronicles his adventurous life in *Equiano, the African: Biography of a Self-Made Man* (see chapter 9). The enslavement of women in harems lasted in Turkey until 1909. Using letters and diaries from harem women, Aley Lytle Courtier reveals the complicated social structure within these closed societies in *Harem: The World Behind the Veil*.

Hughes-Hallett, Lucy

Cleopatra: Histories, Dreams and Distortions. Harper & Row, 1990. 338p. ISBN 006016-2163.

The tragedy of Cleopatra VII's (69–30 BCE) life is one of the most repeated stories of all time. The mysterious queen of the Nile appears in countless books, plays, movies, and paintings. Although these stories all end with her dying from the bite of the asp, the portrayals vary widely; many reflect more about their authors and readers than about the real last queen of Egypt. In this collection of biographical essays, Lucy Hughes-Hallett sorts through ancient documentary sources, seeking the person behind the legends and explaining why Cleopatra matters to modern women.

Subjects: Biographical Essays; Cleopatra VII of Egypt; Egypt; Queens; Women

Now Try: Karen Essex speculates on how a young Egyptian woman became queen in her novel *Kleopatra*. More is known about the life of Joan of Arc than about Cleopatra, but her pride amid desperation was similar. She died abandoned by the king to whom she had pledged allegiance. Donald Spoto uses the transcript of her heresy trial dramatically in *Joan: The Mysterious Life of the Heretic Who Became a Saint* (see chapter 4). Like Cleopatra, soprano Maria Callas lived a passionate life worthy of opera heroines. Robert Levine includes stories of her stormy relationships in *Maria Callas: A Musical Biography*. Marilyn Monroe died of a drug overdose after a series of high-profile marriages and affairs. In the racy celebrity biography *Goddess: The Secret Lives of Marilyn Monroe* (see chapter 8), which suggests that Monroe might have been murdered, Anthony Summers portrays the beautiful actress as a fragile, frequently suicidal woman.

Man, John

Gutenberg: How One Man Remade the World with Words. John Wiley, 2002. 312p. ISBN 0471218235.

A book about Johann Gutenberg (1398–1468), the fifteenth-century inventor of the printing press, should have a classy typeface. It should also tell how Gutenberg's press was built, including the failed experiments and technical breakthroughs. Moreover, it should tell about the man who envisioned what a press could do to revolutionize the spread of knowledge. John Man delivers on all these counts in this profile of the printer. Much of what is known about Gutenberg comes from thirdhand copies of court depositions related to business disputes, supplemented by church and tax records. With his vast knowledge of Germany in the fifteenth century, Man weaves these together to create a credible profile of this important historical figure.

Subjects: Germany; Gutenberg, Johann; Inventors; Printers

Now Try: Blake Morrison portrays Gutenberg as a man who knew that he had unleashed a possibly demonic technology in the novel *The Justification of Johann Gutenberg*. Like Gutenberg, Josiah Wedgwood combined practical knowledge and curiosity with good business sense. *Wedgwood: The First Tycoon* by Brian Dolan tells an early rags to riches story to inspire would-be entrepreneurs. Johannes Vermeer, whose paintings are now considered masterpieces, was a shrewd businessman. Anthony Bailey comes to this conclusion from studying Vermeer's accounts in *Vermeer: A View of Delft* (see chapter 7). Samuel F. B. Morse had the inventive streak found in Gutenberg and Wedgwood but lacked their business acumen. Kenneth Silverman describes Morse's tendency to fail in *Lightning Man: The Accursed Life of Samuel F. B. Morse* (see chapter 11). Bill Bryson states that little is really known about William Shakespeare, but he tells a good story, following Shakespeare from his childhood in Stratford to his career as an actor and playwright in London and on tour around the country in *Shakespeare: The World as Stage* (see chapter 7).

McCalman, Iain

The Last Alchemist: Count Cagliostro, Master of Magic in the Age of Reason. HarperCollins, 2003. 272p. ISBN 0060006900.

Born in poverty in Palermo, Sicily, Giuseppe Balsamo (1743–1795) transformed himself into the world-famous magician Count Cagliostro, the inspiration for Sarastro in Mozart's *The Magic Flute,* and the subject of Johann Strauss's operetta *Cagliostro in Wein*. He performed his magic before royalty, posed as a faith healer, pretended to be an African, and founded branches of the Egyptian Masonic movement. Making many enemies, including Catherine the Great and Casanova, Cagliostro was tried as a heretic by the Roman Inquisitor and died in prison. Through seven episodes of the Count's life, Iain McCalman recounts the strange tale of a romantic charlatan who charmed much of Europe. This novel-like biography will especially appeal to readers who love historical fiction.

Subjects: Biographical Essays; Cagliostro, Alessandro, Count; Magicians; Occultists

Now Try: Isabelle Grameson crossed the Andes and the Amazon to reach her husband, who had been imprisoned for twenty years. *The Mapmaker's Wife: A True Tale of Love, Murder, and Survival in the Amazon* (see chapter 1), Robert Whitaker's account of an impassioned and fearless woman, reads like a great adventure novel. Like Cogliostro, Spanish artist Francisco José de Goya y Lucientes relied on the goodwill of the royal court by which he was employed. Art critic Robert Hughes tells how Goya's depression after his wife's death brought him close to madness in *Goya* (see chapter 7). Wolfgang Amadeus Mozart was inspired by Cagliostro to create the character of Sarastro in *The Magic Flute*. Peter Gay describes Mozart as a basically happy man who lived mostly as he pleased in his compact *Mozart* (see chapter 6). John R. Brinkley entertained the public with radio shows while he sold them patent medicines and useless medical treatments. Pope Brock tells a lively story about the exploitation of ignorance by an early twentieth-century businessman in *Charlatan: America's Most Dangerous Huckster, the Man Who Pursued Him, and the Age of Flimflam* (see chapter 2). Sir Walter Raleigh was an engaging man who, like Cagliostro, died in prison. Raleigh Trevelyan reveals that behind the charming exterior, Raleigh was a ruthless entrepreneur, in *Sir Walter Raleigh*.

McMurtry, Larry

Crazy Horse. Lipper/Viking, 1999. 148p. <u>Penguin Lives</u>. ISBN 0670882348. Audiobook and large print available.

According to popular Western novelist Larry McMurtry, less is known about the Lakota warrior Crazy Horse than is known about ancient Greek warrior Alexander the Great. Still, because of his role in central events of the American Indian Wars of the nineteenth century and the legends that have grown up around him, he is an intriguing figure. In this short book McMurtry distills essential information and the best stories about the chief into a moving portrait of an important American character.

Subjects: Biographical Essays; Chiefs; Crazy Horse; Lakota Sioux Indians; Native Americans; Quick Reads; Warriors

Now Try: In *Crazy Horse: A Lakota Life*, Kingsley M. Bray emphasizes the warrior's sense of obligation and destiny. In *Stone Song: A Novel of the Life of Crazy Horse*, Winfred Blevins focuses on the psychological and spiritual sides of the Lakota chief. Named to "Best Books for Young Adults" by the Young Adult Library Services Association, *Sitting Bull and His World* by Albert Marrin provides an illustrated and detailed account of the life of one of the last Lakota chiefs. Adults can enjoy this 246-page biography as much as teens. Like Crazy Horse, Joan of Arc believed fully in her cause and never faltered against overwhelming odds, according to Donald Spoto in *Joan* (see chapter 4). Likewise, the abolitionist John Brown did not measure the odds he faced. David S. Reynolds recounts his life in *John Brown, Abolitionist: The Man Who Killed Slavery, Sparked the Civil War, and Seeded Civil Rights* (see chapter 9).

Morgan, Robert

Boone: A Biography. Algonquin Books of Chapel Hill, 2007. 538p. ISBN 9781565124554.

Daniel Boone (1734–1820) was a woodsman, pioneer, and family man who sought good land for building settlements. Although he took up arms when necessary, he was a reluctant soldier and Indian fighter. Contrary to legend, he never wore a coonskin cap and was not the first white man in Kentucky. However, he was a leading figure in the settling of the American West. Portraying Boone as an early environmentalist and advocate for wilderness, poet and novelist Robert Morgan admiringly chronicles the career of an early American who helped his country mature from colony to nation.

Subjects: Boone, Daniel; Explorers; Kentucky; Missouri; Pioneers

Now Try: Daniel Boone is still the focus of pulp fiction as the hero in Dodge Tyler's series <u>Dan'l Boone: The Lost Wilderness Tales</u>, starting with *A River Runs Red*. Like Boone, John James Audubon was most comfortable away from settlements and cities, but his art and other business enterprises called him back frequently. Richard Rhodes tells the story of the great zoologist but poor businessman in *John James Audubon: The Making of an American* (see chapter 1). Another unsettled American who loved wandering in the woods was John Muir. Gretel Ehrlich includes historical photographs in her illustrated *John Muir: Nature's Visionary* (see chapter 1). Both Boone and founding father Benjamin Franklin are icons of American history. Walter Isaacson's *Benjamin Franklin: An American Life* (see chapter 10) is an expansive biography that shows his subject as key figure in his era. Author Wallace Stegner was seen as a man of both literature and the environment. His friends and family wrote appreciative pieces for the collection of essays *Geography of Hope: A Tribute to Wallace Stegner*.

Page, Nick

Lord Minimus: The Extraordinary Life of Britain's Smallest Man. St. Martin's Press, 2001. 261p. ISBN 0312291612.

Over four centuries, the story of tiny Jeffrey Hudson (1619–1682), who was given to Queen Henrietta Marie by the Duke of Buckingham in a pie, has become muddied by fiction. Sir Walter Scott used Hudson as a character in *Peveril of the Peak* (Houghton Mifflin, 1923), inventing many tales about the dwarf that have since been told as true by careless historians. Nick Page returned to the original accounts and documents to find that the true story of the twenty-four-inch tall man is sensational and needs no embellishing. He fought a duel, took part in the English Civil War, was captured by pirates, and died a mostly forgotten man.

> **Subjects:** Dwarfs; England; Hudson, Jeffrey

> **Now Try:** Hudson is a comic but courageous character who says, "fear is a thing unknown to me" in his last scene in *Peveril of the Peak* by Sir Walter Scott. James Holman was a lieutenant in the Royal Navy in 1810 when a mysterious tropical disease left him crippled and blind. When he discovered he could navigate by echolocation, he set off alone on a series of trips across Europe. Jason Roberts describes a brave, determined man in *A Sense of the World: How a Blind Man Became History's Greatest Traveler* (see chapter 1). Readers who enjoyed Hudson's bold tale may also enjoy the pirate story *Empire of Blue Water: Captain Morgan's Great Pirate Army, the Epic Battle for the Americas, and the Catastrophe That Ended the Outlaws' Bloody Reign* by Stephan Talty (see chapter 2). Like Hudson, who wanted to prove with swashbuckling action that he could contend with larger people, Errol Flynn wanted to prove he was more than a movie image by helping the Allies during war. Tony Thomas tells how he failed in *Errol Flynn: The Spy That Never Was* (see chapter 8).

Wroe, Ann

Pontius Pilate. Random House, 1999. 412p. ISBN 0375503056.

The physical evidence of the life of Pontius Pilate, the Roman governor of Judaea from the year 26 to the year 36, famous for his role in the Gospels of the Christian Bible, consists of one inscribed stone and a handful of coins. He is also briefly mentioned in the writings of Josephus, Philo of Alexandria, and Tacitus. From this scant information many writers have created full biographies speculating on his origins, sense of guilt, and subsequent conversion to the Christian cause. In this collection of biographical episodes, Ann Wroe closely examines the literary legends about Pilate in the context of Roman and Christian history. Who was the real Pilate? History readers will pursue the answer in this readable exploration.

> **Subjects:** Governors; Judea; Pilate, Pontius; Roman Empire

> **Now Try:** Pontius Pilate can be found as a character in many novels, including *Pilate's Wife: A Novel of the Roman Empire* by Antoinette May. With few existing records, looking for Pilate is like looking for the historical Jesus of Nazareth. John Dominic Crossan uses the Gospels with Roman records to portray Jesus as a rebel fighting the Jewish establishment and the occupying Romans in *Jesus: A Revolutionary Biography* (see chapter 4). Like Pilate, there are few records remaining about the explorer Amerigo Vespucci, for whom the Ameri-

can continents are named. Felipe Fernández-Armesto sifts through the conflicting stories to find the real Vespucci in *Amerigo: The Man Who Gave His Name to America* (see chapter 1). Another story about a bureaucrat just doing his job, this time in Nazi Germany, is *Becoming Eichmann: Rethinking the Life, Crimes, and Trial of a "Desk Murderer"* by David Cesarani (see chapter 2).

Consider Starting With . . .

These well-written Investigative Biographies of modest length will appeal to general readers.

- Bailey, John. *The Lost German Slave Girl: The Extraordinary True Story of Sally Miller and Her Fight for Freedom in Old New Orleans.*
- Bell, Madison Smartt. *Toussaint Louverture: A Biography.*
- Collingridge, Vanessa. *Boudica: The Life of Britain's Legendary Warrior Queen.*
- Higham, Charles. *Howard Hughes: The Secret Life.*
- Holmes, Rachel. *African Queen: The Real Life of the Hottentot Venus.*
- Macintyre, Ben. *Agent Zigzag: A True Story of Nazi Espionage, Love, and Betrayal.*
- McMurtry, Larry. *Crazy Horse.*
- Phillips, Julie. *James Tiptree, Jr.: The Double Life of Alice B. Sheldon.*
- Royko, Mike. *Boss: Richard J. Daley of Chicago.*
- Terrill, Ross. *The White-Boned Demon: A Biography of Madame Mao Zedong.*
- Wroe, Ann. *The Perfect Prince: The Mystery of Perkin Warbeck and His Quest for the Throne of England.*

Further Reading

Cords, Sarah Statz

The Real Story: A Guide to Nonfiction Reading Interests. Libraries Unlimited, 2006. 460p. ISBN 1591582830.

Cords's tenth chapter covers investigative writing, including exposés. She describes the genre and reviews dozens of titles, with further reading recommendations.

New Dictionary of the History of Ideas. Charles Scribner's Sons, 2005. 6 vols. ISBN 0684-313774.

The essay "Truth" by Frederick F. Schmidtt tells about the development of the concept of truth.

Chapter 6

Coming-of-Age Biography

Definition of Biography

A Coming-of-Age Biography is a true story about the childhood, adolescence, education, emotional development, and maturation of an individual. Furthermore, it may describe the transition from novice to expert in a given field or profession. Unlike biographies that portray subjects from birth to death, Coming-of-Age Biography stops near the point at which a subject attains maturity. For this chapter, the boundaries of age are broadened well past adolescence to include biographies of adults who have not yet reached their prime years, people who still have developmental lessons to learn.

We were all young once. Some of us still are. Either way, the stories of young people struggling to assert themselves in the culture of adults interest us. Reading stories of past transformations when we are young may help us mature, or help us understand our own lives if we are older. The attraction of these stories, however, is more than simply reader identity. According to Kenneth Millard in *Coming of Age in Contemporary American Fiction* (Edinburgh University Press, 2007), "Adolescents are important because of the ways in which they are at the forefront of social change, even while they are simultaneously the products of an adult social culture that shapes their development." Understanding youthful motivations helps us foresee the new world into which we are headed.

Coming-of-age is a familiar theme in novels from many periods, including *Portrait of an Artist as a Young Man* by James Joyce, *A Separate Peace* by John Hershey, and *The Absolute True Diary of a Part-Time Indian* by Sherman Alexie. It is also an especially important theme in memoirs and autobiographies. Many famous people have taken time late in life to write about their early years, when they were poor, misguided, threatened, or simply untested. In these books they identify how they survived, triumphed, and changed. *The Education of Henry Adams* by Henry Adams and *Running with Scissors* by Augusten Burroughs offer us examples from different eras.

Coming-of-Age Biographies written by authors who researched instead of witnessed the early years of famous people are less common than fictional or autobiographical accounts. Most biographers writing for adults construct complete life stories, which contain coming-of-age sections but continue through maturity to retirement, old age, and/or death. Rare are biographies such as *King of the World: Muhammad Ali and the Rise of an American Hero* by David Remnick, which tells the story of young boxer

Cassius Clay (later to be known as Muhammad Ali) up to the day he beat Sonny Liston for the world boxing title, or *Young Hickory: The Making of Andrew Jackson* by Hendrik Booraem, which describes how future president Andrew Jackson developed the important traits of his character by age twenty-one.

A *Coming-of-Age Biography* is a true story about the childhood, adolescence, education, emotional development, and maturation of an individual. Unlike biographies that portray subjects from birth to death, Coming-of-Age biography stops near the point at which a subject attains maturity. The subjects of these books are famous people whose lives are heavily documented or people who die at an early age. Because there are books of various lengths and pacing available, most readers will find appealing books in this chapter.

Appeal of the Genre

Many biography readers of the baby boom generation grew up reading books from the Childhood of Famous Americans Series, coming-of-age stories about early settlers, founding fathers, soldiers, athletes, inventors, businessmen, and civic leaders written for young readers. The first volumes were published in the 1930s, and by the 1950s and 1960s there were over a hundred titles that were commonly found in school and public libraries. These popular books, full of dialogue and memorable stories, described famous Americans as bright, curious children bound to grow into good citizens. Designed by educators, the fast-paced stories taught idealized versions of American history to enthusiastic readers. Appeal factors in contemporary Coming-of-Age Biographies for adult readers are remarkably similar to these books that were created for children.

Coming-of-Age Biographies tend to be written about the most famous characters from history, the people about whom there are already many books. Because there are often many documents to study and many readers wanting more books about these men and women, biographers can profitably focus on the early years of figures like George Washington, Abraham Lincoln, Eleanor Roosevelt, C. S. Lewis, and J. Edgar Hoover. Tragic figures who die young are also popular subjects with readers. Popular biographies describing lives that barely matured before they ended have been written about figures such as author Stephen Crane, singer Janis Joplin, and actor John Belushi.

As in coming-of-age novels and memoirs, story plays an important role in these books. They must include compelling accounts of youths being transformed for good or bad by the influences of their lives. For example, *They Say: Ida B. Wells and the Reconstruction of Race* by James West Davidson describes how witnessing racist acts against blacks inspired a young teacher to become a crusading journalist. Another example is *No One Here Gets Out Alive* by Jerry Hopkins and Danny Sugerman, which chronicles the life of drug and alcohol addiction leading to the early death of the Doors' lead singer, Jim Morrison.

Settings may also come to the forefront in Coming-of-Age Biographies. All of the young characters described in this chapter are products of their age. Andrew Jackson formed many of his beliefs and was introduced to war as a teenager during the American

Revolution. As a teen, Pete Maravich surrendered to his domineering father's wishes, attending the college his father chose. Joseph Stalin learned to terrorize and control people as a young member of criminal gangs during the final desperate years of tsarist Russia.

Pacing in these books varies. *The Education of a Coach* by David Halberstam and *I've Got Things to Do with My Life: Pat Tillman: The Making of an American Hero* by Mike Towle are short books that quickly tell intimate stories. On the other hand, *The Path to Power: The Years of Lyndon Johnson* by Robert A. Caro and *W. E. B. Du Bois: Biography of Race, 1868–1919* by David Levering Lewis offer lengthy and detailed accounts that will appeal to epic readers. Learning is not generally a strong appeal factor in Coming-of-Age Biographies. Most people borrowing or buying these books are seeking to read really good stories that let them vicariously experience the excitement of coming-of-age.

Organization of the Chapter

The first section of this chapter, "Learning Lessons," includes biographies that describe their subjects' childhoods, adolescence, and early adulthood. Readers learn about the influences of parents or other guardians, the schools that they attended, and the societies from which they came. Stories usually end at a point of maturation when the subjects' characters are formed or proved by an event.

The second section, "Lives Cut Short," includes biographies of people who died relatively young. These books are coming-of-age accounts by default, for there are no prime-of-life or mature-years stories to tell. Singer Kurt Cobain and actor John Belushi are among the tragic figures in this section.

The next section, "Life, Chapter One," identifies the first volume of prestigious multivolume biographies of major historical figures. The initial volumes in these sets deal with the youth and education of well-researched lives, including those of Eleanor Roosevelt, Lyndon Johnson, and Adolf Hitler.

In the final section, "Group Biography," the adolescent and young adult protagonists are often strongly influenced by the company they keep and sometimes mature and earn fame together. Group biographies of writers, musicians, and athletes are found in this section.

Learning Lessons

The origins of people in the news are always of interest to the public. Readers look for newspaper and magazine articles to tell them certain things about people who are profiled. How old are they? Where do they live? How did they learn to do whatever it is that they do? The articles comply. The age of a newly discovered pop singer is noted. A candidate for president is described as being from a specific state. The college that a professional football player attended is cited. Terrorists are identified by nationality. The deprived or depraved childhood of the criminal is described.

Biographies include the same "where did they come from" elements that are found in other media, and the stories of origin are often told in an opening chapter. Describing the childhood and education of an individual is essential for understanding the resulting adult. What distinguishes Coming-of-Age Biography from other forms of biography is the focus on the shaping of the individual, while leaving the subsequent career of the famous person to other books. For example, *Becoming Victoria* by Lynne Vallone tells how Princess Victoria was trained to be the queen of England, and it stops the story near the time of her coronation. Likewise, in *The Education of a Coach* David Halberstam tells much more about the childhood and apprenticeship of football coach Bill Belichick than about his years with the New England Patriots. The biographies in this section essentially stop the story when the individuals' characters are formed.

Formation of character provides the central focus of these books. The narratives are mostly chronological, though some biographers start with chapters describing critical points in their subjects' lives and then proceed from birth to a point of maturation. Because youths are molded by their environments, settings are well defined. Pace varies as the biographers include varying levels of detail. Revisiting the universal trials of youth and learning that individuals can respond so differently to their situations is the primary learning/experiencing element in these books.

Learning Lessons stories include biographies that describe childhood, adolescence, and early adulthood. Readers learn about the influences of parents or other guardians, the schools that subjects attended, and the societies from which they came. Stories usually end at a point of maturation when the subjects' characters are formed or proved by an event. Story, character, and setting are well developed in these books.

Ackerman, Kenneth D.

Young J. Edgar: Hoover, the Red Scare, and the Assault on Civil Liberties. Carroll & Graf, 2007. 472p. ISBN 9780786717750.

When twenty-eight-year-old J. Edgar Hoover (1895–1972) was chosen by new Attorney General Harlan Fiske Stone as temporary head of the Bureau of Investigation, the Justice Department was in disarray. The Teapot Dome Scandal had revealed many of the bureau's agents to be guilty of corruption. As a young law clerk, Hoover had escaped being linked to the scandal and was thought to be morally spotless. Fiske did not know that Hoover had been a key player in the arrest, without charges, of thousand of anarchists and their sympathizers; nor did he realize that Hoover had already begun keeping secret files. Kenneth D. Ackerman reveals how the secretive Hoover perfected his methods between 1919 and 1924 in this book for crime and espionage readers.

Subjects: Abuse of Power; Corruption; Federal Bureau of Investigation; Hoover, J. Edgar

Now Try: In *Persons in Hiding*, Hoover tells how his FBI agents captured or shot down Ma Barker, Baby Face Nelson, John Dillinger, Machine Gun Kelly, and other gangsters in the 1920s and 1930s. According to some accounts, Hoover became jealous of the fame that some of his agents earned. Alston W. Purvis tells how his father, FBI agent Melvin Purvis was punished for stealing the spotlight from his boss in *The Vendetta: FBI Hero*

Melvis Purvis's War Against Crime and J. Edgar Hoover's War Against Him. Hoover probably had a file on Florence Harding, wife of President Warren G. Harding. The secrets of her illegitimate child and the possibility that she killed the president are discussed in *Florence Harding: The First Lady, the Jazz Age, and the Death of America's Most Scandalous President* by Carl Sferrazza Anthony (see chapter 5). Anthony Summers tells about a secretive president breaking laws during Hoover's final years in *The Arrogance of Power: The Secret World of Richard Nixon* (see chapter 5).

Beauman, Nicola

E. M. Forster: A Biography. Knopf, 1994. 404p. ISBN 0394583817.

British author E. M. Forster (1879–1970) wrote six great novels before the age of forty-five and then never wrote fiction again, though he lived to age ninety-one. In her literary biography of Forster, Nicola Beauman chronicles his stressful childhood and novel-writing years and says little about his later years. Instead, she highlights personal incidents that reappear slightly fictionalized in his celebrated novels. Her analytical narrative of a lonely man will interest readers of Forster novels.

> **Subjects:** Forster, E. M.; Great Britain; Novelists

> **Now Try:** Of Forster's six novels, *The Longest Journey* and *Maurice* seem the two that most reflect his own experiences. While many readers wish that Forster had written fiction again, they really wish that Harper Lee had not stopped writing after *To Kill a Mockingbird,* her only novel. Charles J. Shields tells how Lee's childhood is reflected in her beloved book in *Mockingbird: A Portrait of Harper Lee* (see this chapter). Although the stories in Franz Kafka's books are bizarre, incidents in his life were the source of ideas for his writings. Jeremy Adler tells how Kafka fantasized his experiences in *Franz Kafka* (see chapter 7). In the world of sports, a figure who retired at the height of his career was Los Angeles Dodgers pitcher Sandy Koufax. Jane Leavy looks at a man who walked away from fame and a high salary in *Sandy Koufax: A Lefty's Legacy* (see chapter 12).

Booraem, Hendrik

Young Hickory: The Making of Andrew Jackson. Taylor Trade Publishing, 2001. 318p. ISBN 0878332634.

Andrew Jackson (1767–1845) was only eight years old and living in backwoods South Carolina when the American colonies began their rebellion against Great Britain. By the time the war ended, his family had fled British troops several times and he had taken up arms, been arrested, and nearly died of the smallpox that killed both his mother and brother. In this coming-of-age story for history readers, Hendrik Booraem shows how the future president's character was forged by the dire circumstances of his early life.

> **Subjects:** American Revolution; Group Discussion Books; Jackson, Andrew; Presidents; South Carolina

> **Now Try:** The rise of Jackson to political power signaled the growing strength of the Western states and the longing to expand the country. Arthur M. Schlesinger Jr. describes the era in *The Age of Jackson.* Elizabeth Van Lew of

Richmond, Virginia, was also transformed by living in the vicinity of war. Readers sense the danger of her being arrested in *Southern Lady, Yankee Spy: The True Story of Elizabeth Van Lew, a Union Agent in the Heart of the Confederacy* by Elizabeth R. Varon (see chapter 3). Like Jackson, naval officer Stephen Decatur was infected early with the thrill of battle. His life is described in *Our Country, Right or Wrong: The Life of Stephen Decatur, the U.S. Navy's Most Illustrious Commander* by Leonard F. Guttridge (see chapter 3). Once he gained the presidency, Jackson closed the national bank, changing the way business was conducted in the United States. Maury Klein tells how other strong and determined individuals have shaped the economy in *The Change Makers: From Carnegie to Gates, How the Great Entrepreneurs Transformed Ideas into Industries.*

Davidson, James West

They Say: Ida B. Wells and the Reconstruction of Race. Oxford University Press, 2007. 242p. New Narratives in American History series. ISBN 9780195160208.

Born during the American Civil War, about the time of Abraham Lincoln's Emancipation Proclamation, Ida B. Wells (1862–1931) witnessed the initial promise and subsequent failure of the Reconstruction era. Her earliest memories were of her father, a local black activist in Holly Springs, Mississippi, and her mother, a woman determined to see her children live better lives. When she was sixteen years old, both died from yellow fever, leaving Wells to support her siblings. Historian James West Davidson tells how the young Wells met her obligations, held off several suitors, and began a career as a journalist crusading for civil rights.

Subjects: African Americans; Journalists; Racial Discrimination; Wells, Ida B.; Teen Reads; Women

Now Try: Much of Wells's writing appeared in her newspaper, *The Free Press*, or in pamphlets, some of which have been collected in *On Lynchings: Southern Horrors*. She recounted her life in *Crusader for Justice: The Autobiography of Ida B. Wells*. Like Wells, journalist Nellie Bly risked her safety by going after dangerous stories. Her adventurous story is told in *Nellie Bly: Daredevil, Reporter, Feminist* by Brooke Kroeger (see chapter 1). Outspoken colonial religious leader Anne Hutchinson was the first American woman to risk her own well-being for social reform. Eve LaPlante tells her story in *American Jezebel: The Uncommon Life of Anne Hutchinson, the Woman Who Defied the Puritans* (see chapter 9). Unlike Wells, black entertainer Josephine Baker came to social activism late. As a young woman she danced, sang, and lived the high life, but she joined the French Resistance during World War II and adopted children from around the world during the 1950s. Phyllis Rose portrays Baker as a courageous, free-spirited woman in *Jazz Cleopatra: Josephine Baker in Her Time.*

Halberstam, David

The Education of a Coach. Hyperion, 2005. 277p. ISBN 1401301541. Audiobook and large print available.

New England Patriots head coach Bill Belichick (1952–) learned football from his father, Steve Belichick, a longtime assistant coach and scout for the U.S. Naval Academy. From an early age, Bill went to all the academy's games and later watched his father analyze the game films. Without ever starring as a player or coaching in a major college football program, he apprenticed himself to the great minds of professional football and became the head coach of the New England Patriots, leading them to three Super Bowl victories. Halberstam profiles Belichick as a dedicated, serious coach, who shuns celebrity, insists that his players subsume their egos to the team, and remains close to his father. Success consultants will want to read this book as much as sports fans.

1

> **Subjects:** Belichick, Bill; Belichick, Steve; Fathers and Sons; Football Coaches; Success

> **Now Try:** General Douglas MacArthur learned about military affairs from his father, who was also a general. He described his career in *Courage Was the Rule: General Douglas MacArthur's Own Story*. Readers who like compact biographies that emphasize the development of moral character will enjoy *Father Mychal Judge: An Authentic American Hero* by Michael Ford (see chapter 4). Green Bay Packers coach Vince Lombardi is often quoted by inspirational speakers at management seminars. In *When Pride Still Mattered: A Life of Vince Lombardi* (see chapter 12), David Maraniss thoughtfully reconsiders the sound bites within the context of Lombardi's difficult life. Belichick has not written about his life, but former NFL head coach George Allen did, describing his career in *Merry Christmas, You're Fired*.

2

3

4

Hamilton, Nigel

JFK, Reckless Youth. Random House, 1992. 898p. ISBN 0679412166. Audiobook available.

5

> Young John F. Kennedy (1917–1963) brashly took advantage of every perk offered to the son of a powerful Boston politician and U.S. ambassador. He attended prestigious boarding schools; entered Harvard after failing at Princeton; traveled internationally; and mixed with socialites in Boston, New York, and Hollywood. He charmed his way into dangerous assignments in the U.S. Navy despite health problems that should have excused him from service. Moreover, he used his connections to promote himself as an author and political candidate. In this intimate account of the rise of a visionary political figure, Nigel Hamilton portrays the future president as an unstoppable character determined to overcome all barriers. Students of political power will appreciate this lengthy coming-of-age story.

6

7

> **Subjects:** Kennedy, John F.; Politics and Government; Presidents

8

> **Now Try:** Before Kennedy was president, he was a biographer, addressing the issue of personal integrity in Congress in his collective biography *Profiles in Courage*. Peter the Great of Russia was another charismatic young leader. Becoming tsar at the age of ten, he sought to enrich his country's culture, science, and industry as well as extend its boundaries. Robert K. Massie describes the tsar's life and the Russian court in *Peter the Great: His Life and World* (see chapter 9). Like Kennedy, Henri Cartier-Bresson was a man of high society. The artful photographer often ventured into dangerous regions to capture images for the world press. Pierre Assouline tells about his risky and stylish life in *Henri Cartier-Bresson: A Biography* (see chapter 7). Quarterback Johnny Unitas was a working-class character, unlike Kennedy, but he too ignored pain in order to do his job. Tom Callahan describes Unitas as a persuasive on-the-field leader quickly able to assess his opponents in *Johnny U: The Life & Times of Johnny Unitas* (see chapter 12).

9

10

11

12

Heymann, C. David

American Legacy: The Story of John & Caroline Kennedy. Atria Books, 2007. 592p. ISBN 9780743497381. Large print available.

> Being the children of the president and members of the most famous political family in America, Carolyn and John Kennedy led highly documented childhoods. Hardly a moment is missing from the record before their father was killed. After that, their mother tried to seclude them, with little success. They matured with reporters always nearby to tell their news. Until John's death in an airplane crash, the siblings lived public lives, free from the addictions that marked their cousins; and John was always regarded as a future political candidate. C. David Heymann's melancholic dual biography, permeated with the feeling of accumulated doom, appeals to celebrity story readers.

> **Subjects:** Brothers and Sisters; Children of Presidents; Dual Biography; Kennedy, Caroline; Kennedy, John, Jr.

> **Now Try:** Tragedy has been a frequent visitor of the Kennedy family. Edward Klein chronicles the assassinations, plane crashes, diseases, and other misfortunes in *The Kennedy Curse: Why Tragedy Has Haunted America's First Family for 150 Years.* Historian Doris Kearns Goodwin expands the focus to chronicle the lives of the related Fitzgerald clan, as well as the Kennedys, in *The Fitzgeralds and the Kennedys.* Because the Concord circle of authors wrote copious letters and diaries, the relationship between novelist Louisa May Alcott and her father is well documented. John Matteson tells how Bronson Alcott tried to dictate his philosophy to his daughter, who had ideas of her own, in *Eden's Outcasts: The Story of Louisa May Alcott and Her Father* (see chapter 9). Wolfgang Amadeus Mozart was close to his sister. Their relationship is part of the story in *Mozart's Women: His Family, His Friends, His Music* by Jane Glover (see chapter 7).

Levin, Gail

Becoming Judy Chicago: A Biography of the Artist. Harmony Book, 2007. 485p. ISBN 9781400054121.

> Artist Judy Chicago (1939–) is tough but not mean. She also thinks big, intending to make the world a better place, according to Gail Levin. Having thrown off her married name to reject male social dominance, she worked with other women throughout the 1970s to create *The Dinner Party*, a symbolic triangular table with dinner settings that celebrate the lives of thirty-nine women. The piece traveled to many museums before it found a home in the Brooklyn Museum of Art. Like her most famous piece, Chicago has had difficulty being accepted in the male-dominated art world. Levin's admiring account of Chicago's development will please feminist readers.

> **Subjects:** Artists; Chicago, Judy; Feminists; Women

> **Now Try:** Chicago has written two autobiographies, *Through the Flower: My Struggle as a Woman Artist* and *Beyond the Flower: The Autobiography of a Feminine Artist.* Another independent feminine spirit who loved to stir up controversy with her symbolic art is described in *Frida: A Biography of Frida Kahlo* by Hayden Herrera (see chapter 7). Mary Cassatt was far more private than Chicago or Kahlo, but she was as concerned with modern feminist issues and found getting her art into galleries difficult. Her life and work are concisely described in *Mary Cassatt* by Nancy Mowll Mathews. The most radical of the women's rights activists of the nineteenth century

was Victoria Woodhall. She ran for president when she could not even vote. Mary Gabriel argues that Woodhull was a reformer whose ideas were a hundred years ahead of her time in *Notorious Victoria: The Life of Victoria Woodhull, Uncensored* (see chapter 4).

Montefiore, Simon Sebag

🌳 *Young Stalin.* Alfred A. Knopf, 2007. 460p. ISBN 9781400044658. Audiobook available.

During his violent and oppressive rule over the Soviet Union, a nation that he helped found, the West knew little about the obscure origins of the Georgian Joseph Stalin (1879–1953). His debut in international news was as a henchman of Vladimir Ilyich Lenin during the Bolshevik Revolution. Given access to newly opened archives in Russia and Georgia, historian Simon Sebag Montefiore discovered that before Stalin became a leading revolutionary, he had been a notorious gangster whose crimes involved bank robbery, arson, and murder. What distinguished him from other criminals and attracted Lenin to him was his love of poetry and fiery rhetoric. Aimed at history readers, Montefiore chronicles the education of a tyrant in this dramatic account of the final days of tsarist Russia.

Subjects: Dictators; Russia; Soviet Union; Stalin, Joseph

Awards: Los Angeles Times Book Prize for Biography

Now Try: World War II letters between Stalin and President Franklin Roosevelt are collected in *My Dear Mr. Stalin: The Complete Correspondence of Franklin D. Roosevelt and Joseph V. Stalin*. Chinese communist leader Mao Zedong was also a misfit as a youth. In their exposé *Mao: The Unknown Story* (see chapter 5), Jung Chang and Jon Halliday aim to dispel any ideas about the brutal dictator being a revolutionary with good intentions. Like Stalin, Arthur Rimbaud was a tough poet and criminal. Charles Nicholl recounts Rimbaud's disappearance into the Arab culture of Egypt, Ethiopia, and Yemen in *Somebody Else: Arthur Rimbaud in Africa, 1880–91* (see chapter 1). Like Stalin, Al Capone, though brutal to his enemies, had many supporters among the lower classes, who saw him as a vengeful champion who would redress their poverty. His story is told in *Capone: The Man and His Era* by Laurence Bergreen (see chapter 2).

Remnick, David

🌳 *King of the World: Muhammad Ali and the Rise of an American Hero.* Random House, 1998. 326p. ISBN 0375500650. Audiobook available.

To understand boxer Muhammad Ali (1942–), you must know Floyd Patterson and Sonny Liston, the" "Good Negro" and the" "Bad Negro" of boxing in the early 1960s. According to David Remnick, young Cassius Clay, a star of the 1960 Olympics, had been slighted by both and was determined to mold a new character. After winning the heavyweight championship, he proclaimed his dominance and took a new name. In this book Remnick tells how Ali, who is now seen as a hero of the civil rights movement, upset boxing fans and the NAACP with his remarks and behavior. Sports fans and history readers will enjoy this lively book.

Subjects: African Americans; Ali, Muhammad; Boxers; Clay, Cassius; Teen Reads

Award: ALA Notable Books

Now Try: Ali was boastful in his first memoir *The Greatest, My Own Story*, but was more spiritual in his book about life with Parkinson's disease, *Soul of a Butterfly: Reflections on Life's Journey*. Bicyclist Marshall Taylor may have been the first nationally known black athlete. Like Ali, he upset many whites with his refusal to behave as if he were inferior. His inspiring story is told in *Major: A Black Athlete, a White Era, and the Fight to Be the World's Fastest Human Being* by Todd Balf (see chapter 12). Ali's contemporary, baseball player Curt Flood, challenged the sports establishment with a lawsuit to end the reserve clause, an agreement among team owners that kept players tied to their teams. Like Ali, his enemies attacked him personally. His melancholy story is told in *Stepping Up: The Story of Curt Flood and His Fight for Baseball Players' Rights* by Alex Belth (see chapter 12). Like Ali, novelist James Joyce cared little about the controversy and condemnation that he attracted with his provocative statements. John McCourt describes the life of a man who enjoyed being an exile in the photobiography *James Joyce: A Passionate Life*.

Shields, Charles J.

Mockingbird: A Portrait of Harper Lee. Henry Holt, 2006. 337p. ISBN 9780805079197. Large print available.

Novelist Nelle Harper Lee (1926–) is a very private person whom friends in Monroeville, Alabama, call" "Nail." She is reported to have once said that she wanted to be" "the Jane Austen of south Alabama." If so, why has she never written another novel, leaving readers with only *To Kill a Mockingbird*? How did she come to write the book? Did press treatment of her friend Truman Capote influence her to stop writing? Using hundreds of interviews with her friends and old articles from newspapers and magazines, English teacher Charles J. Shields attempts to answer these questions in this respectful biography of a woman who was just trying to lead a normal life.

Subjects: Alabama; Group Discussion Books; Lee, Nelle Harper; Novelists; Women

Now Try: Lee's *To Kill a Mockingbird* is closely drawn from her own life. Truman Capote based the character Idabel Thompkins in his novel *Other Voices, Other Rooms* on Harper Lee. Humorist Russell Baker led a poor but mostly happy childhood. He describes his upbringing and the way that his family survived poverty in his memoir, *Growing Up*. Right after *Time* praised her collection of poems, poet Laura Riding stopped writing and hid in rural Florida. Deborah Baker investigates the story behind Riding's disappearance in *In Extremis: The Life of Laura Riding* by (see chapter 5). Like Lee, British novelist Barbara Pym drew heavily from her own experiences in writing her perceptive fiction. Her life is told sympathetically by a friend in *A Lot to Ask: A Life of Barbara Pym* by Hazel Holt.

Starkey, David

Elizabeth: The Struggle for the Throne. HarperCollins, 2001. 363p. ISBN 0060184973.

The first twenty-five years in the life of Elizabeth I of England (1533–1603) were filled with dangers. She was neglected by her father, Henry VIII, after her mother, Anne Boleyn, was beheaded; sexually harassed by her stepfather, Thomas Seymour; and imprisoned for treason during the reign of her half-sister, Mary. Luckily she had tutors and friends who steered her through the troubles and helped her gain political insights that would serve her well once she became queen. In dramatic fashion, historian David Starkey tells the coming-of-age story of one of the most renowned of all English monarchs.

Subjects: Elizabeth I, Queen of England; England; Queens; Women

Now Try: Although there are no autobiographies from Elizabeth I, two novels pretend to be such: *I Elizabeth: The Word of a Queen* by Rosalind Miles and *Queen of This Realm: The Story of Queen Elizabeth I* by Jean Plaidy. Like Elizabeth, the heroine of the novel *Ellen Foster* by Kaye Gibbons finds shelter from her negligent father in a foster family after her mother has died. Young Charles II of Great Britain was endangered by the civil war that dethroned and beheaded his father, Charles I. Stephen Coote portrays Charles II as an astute and ambitious man in *Royal Survivor: A Life of Charles II* (see chapter 9). As the child of Indian Prime Minister Jawaharlal Nehru, Indira Gandhi was bred and tutored on the responsibilities of leadership. Katherine Frank sympathetically depicts how the most powerful woman in India used her political talents to survive many tragedies, only to be assassinated by her bodyguard in 1984, in *Indira: The Life of Indira Nehru Gandhi* (see chapter 10). Even when women were constitutionally prohibited from voting and holding office, they influenced government. Catherine Allgor describes Dolley Madison as one of the most powerful people in Washington in *A Perfect Union: Dolley Madison and the Creation of the American Nation* (see chapter 9).

Uruburu, Paula

American Eve: Evelyn Nesbit, Stanford White, the Birth of the "It" Girl, and the Crime of the Century. Riverhead Books, 2008. 386p. ISBN 9781594489938.

Evelyn Nesbit (1884–1967) was only fifteen when she arrived in New York City in 1900. Within a year she was America's top model, with her seductive image on postcards and in national magazines. For several years she lived an elegant life in high society while newspaper reporters, entertainment moguls, and attractive men sought her time and company. She married millionaire Harry Thaw, who then murdered her lover, architect Stanford White, in public, leading to two highly publicized trials, the loss of her social standing, and the loss of her access to the Thaw family fortune. In this biography focusing on Nesbit's early life, Paula Uruburu portrays her as a young woman who threw off Victorian morals without any concern for her future. General readers cannot help but compare her directionless life with those of contemporary celebrities.

Subjects: Models; Murder; Nesbit, Evelyn; New York City; Teen Reads; Women

Now Try: Fiction readers may remember that the Nesbit-Thaw-White triangle was a subplot of the novel *Ragtime* by E. L. Doctorow. *A Pickpocket's Tale: The Underworld of Nineteenth Century New York* by Timothy J. Gilfoyle (see chapter 2) is a lively biography of crime and fame in New York. High society and crime led to another celebrated court case. Amateur golfer John Montague, who frequently played golf with Hollywood stars, admitted in court that he really was LaVerne Moore of Syracuse, New York, but he denied that he was a robber in the entertaining book *The Mysterious Montague: A True Tale of Hollywood, Golf, and Armed Robbery* by Leigh Montville. In France, young dancer and model Hellé Nice coaxed a car manufacturer into letting her drive his race cars. Miranda Seymour tells the story of a reckless woman who broke the rules of sport and society in *Bugatti Queen: In Search of a French Racing Legend* (see chapter 12).

Vallone, Lynne

Becoming Victoria. Yale University Press, 2001. 256p. ISBN 0300089503.

When Edward, Duke of Kent, died in 1820, his eight-month- old daughter Victoria (1819–1901) became a possible successor to the British throne. With the nation and empire relying on" "the Rose of England," her mother and government advisors began training her in womanly arts and social graces, a curriculum that included many books and much personal instruction, for Victoria would have to be the perfect wife and mother, as well as being queen. Historian Lynne Vallone claims that many biographies of Victoria have disregarded the importance of her childhood. In this book for general readers, she shows how early influences on her character made Victoria into a memorable monarch.

Subjects: Great Britain; Queens; Victoria, Queen of Great Britain; Women

Now Try: *Queen Victoria in Her Letters and Journals: A Selection*, edited by Christopher Hibbert, reveals more humor and compassion than most accounts of the long-reigning queen. Jean Plaidy wrote six novels about Victoria, including one fictional autobiography, *Victoria Victorious*. Stories about the succession to the throne of England abound. In *The Perfect Prince: The Mystery of Perkin Warbeck and His Quest for the Throne of England* (see chapter 5), Ann Wroe tells how one of the princes thought to have been murdered by the order of Richard III may have survived. The continuation of the monarchy was a hot topic of debate during the reign of Charles II ,who is profiled as a savior of tradition in *Royal Survivor: A Life of Charles II* by Stephen Coote (see chapter 9). Like Queen Victoria, Salvation Army cofounder Catherine Booth was known for her faith and high morals. Roy Hattersley recounts the lives and good works of advocates for the physical and spiritual care of England's poor in *Blood and Fire: William and Catherine Booth and Their Salvation Army* (see chapter 4).

Lives Cut Short

Some biographies become Coming-of-age Biographies by default because their subjects die young, depriving them of the prime years of their careers and the lessons of aging. In some cases they may not have even fully matured. These are the stories collected in this section.

Lives may end too soon for a number of reasons. Novelist Stephen Crane died of consumption (tuberculosis) at age twenty-nine. A heart attack killed basketball star Pete Maravich at age forty-one. Wyoming roughneck Colton H. Bryant fell through an oil rig drilling platform. Nirvana lead singer Kurt Cobain committed suicide. These deaths were all relatively quick, ending the character and career development of these individuals, but not ending reader interest in them. In fact, stories of early death generate reader interest.

Readers enjoy these books for their sometimes puzzling, highly discussable characters, whose lives could have been better and whose deaths were often preventable. The stories of their childhood and early adulthood are filled with foreboding, and the accounts of their deaths are compelling. The settings for the stories include danger from which the subjects do not escape. Because the biographers offer varying levels of detail, pacing varies. Through these stories young readers experience tragedies that no one should suffer, while older readers recognize their own good fortune and safer paths in life.

Lives Cut Short stories include biographies of people who died relatively young. These books are coming-of-age accounts by default, for there are no prime-of-life or mature-years stories to tell. These books tend to be highly discussable and appeal to teen readers.

Buck, Rinker

Shane Comes Home. William Morrow, 2005. 272p. ISBN 0060593253.

Marine Lieutenant Shane Childers (1972–2003) was the first American soldier killed in the Iraq War. Son of a Vietnam veteran, he was a career Marine who had served in the Gulf War and at American embassies around the globe. In this psychological biography based on interviews with family and close associates, Rinker Buck describes Childers's youth, his military education, and his nine-year career. The author also explains military protocols for notifying next of kin and the impact that Childers's death had on his family, friends, and hometown of Powell, Wyoming. Readers concerned with the personal costs of war will appreciate this thoughtful biography.

Subjects: Childers, Shane; Group Discussion Books; Iraq War; Marines; Soldiers

Now Try: *I've Got Things to Do with My Life: Pat Tillman: The Making of an American Hero* by Mike Towle (see this chapter) is another story set in Iraq. Towle recounts NFL football star Tillman's troubled adolescence and decision to fight in Iraq. At the start of World War II, the first American forces to engage the Japanese were soldiers already stationed in the Philippines. Although many soldiers surrendered and went to prison camps, others escaped to the jungle. In *Bataan Diary: An American Family In World War II, 1941–1945,* Chris Schaefer tells how families waited through the entire war to learn who had lived and died. Young people who survive war are often emotionally troubled for the rest of their lives. In a famous photograph from the Vietnam War, Kim Phuc was the naked nine-year-old Vietnamese girl running and screaming from the pain of being burned by napalm. Denise Chong tells how Kim Phuc, who lives with nightmares, remains a symbol of the suffering of civilians in the path of war in *The Girl in the Picture: The Story of Kim Phuc, the Photograph, and the Vietnam War* (see chapter 3). Like Buck, Alexandra Fuller tells about the family's reaction to the sudden death of a young man in *The Legend of Colton H. Bryant* (see this chapter).

Cross, Charles R.

Heavier Than Heaven: A Biography of Kurt Cobain. Hyperion, 2001. 381p. ISBN 0786865059. Audiobook available.

A screamer at eighteen months, by age fourteen Kurt Cobain (1967–1994) was making violent super 8 films and talking indifferently about suicide.

Unhappy, he already dreamed about playing his music on *Saturday Night Live*, thinking that if he could be a rock star, he would find peace. By the time he did play on the show with his band, Nirvana, in 1992, his heroin habit prevented him from enjoying the acclaim. In this candid but sympathetic biography, music journalist Charles R. Cross relates how Cobain rose out of the Seattle music scene and lived in an unforgiving spotlight with singer Courtney Love. This cautionary tale will attract older teens and alternative rock fans.

> **Subjects:** Cobain, Kurt; Drug Abuse; Rock Musicians; Seattle; Suicide; Teen Reads
>
> **Now Try:** *Dirty Blonde: The Diaries of Courtney Love* is more of a scrapbook than an autobiography, but it offers glimpses into Cobain's character. French chef Bernard Loiseau seemed to be enjoying his success when two food magazines downgraded his restaurant's rating. In the biography *The Perfectionist: Life and Death in Haute Cuisine* (see chapter 5), Rudolph Chelminski tells how family and friends failed to see the desperation that led him to commit suicide. Novelist Ernest Hemingway had been a troubled man for decades by the time he committed suicide in 1961. Valerie Hemingway, who was the novelist's secretary and later married his son, describes the tragedy in *Running with the Bulls: My Years with the Hemingways*. Salvador Dali was not suicidal, but he was self-destructive. Ian Gibson tells about the artist's out-of-control life in *The Shameful Life of Salvador Dalí*.

Davis, Linda H.

Badge of Courage: The Life of Stephen Crane. Houghton Mifflin, 1998. 414p. ISBN 0899199348. Audiobook available.

Charming, handsome, and fearless, author Stephen Crane (1871–1900) lived a contrary life. His Methodist minister father condemned fiction, so he became a novelist. Known for his antiwar novel *Red Badge of Courage*, he sought the experience of battle and reported from wars in Cuba and Greece. Appearing healthy and energetic to others, he died at age twenty-eight of consumption (tuberculosis). According to Linda H. Davis, he left a substantial legacy of five novels, two books of poetry, three short story collections, and numerous essays, all written in the last four years of his life. During this time he also befriended most of the leading literary figures in the United States and England, offended Theodore Roosevelt, and left his common-law wife Cora deeply in debt.

> **Subjects:** Crane, Stephen; Journalists; Novelists
>
> **Now Try:** After *The Red Badge of Courage*, readers may try *The Complete Poems of Stephen Crane* and *The Complete Short Stories & Sketches* by Stephen Crane. Western novelist Zane Grey was dissatisfied with his literary success. Always seeking but never finding happiness, he lived a nomadic life of desperation, which is described in *Zane Grey: His Life, His Adventures, His Women* by Thomas H. Pauly (see chapter 7). Like Crane, British author and adventurer T. E. Lawrence sought out dangerous locations for adventure and to embellish his own story. His melancholy story is told in *The Golden Warrior: The Life and Legend of Lawrence of Arabia* by Lawrence James (see chapter 3). Crane admired Theodore Roosevelt, whose early life is vividly described in *Mornings on Horseback: The Story of an Extraordinary Family, a Vanished Way of Life and the Unique Child Who Became Theodore Roosevelt* by David McCullough.

Echols, Alice

Scars of Sweet Paradise: The Life and Times of Janis Joplin. Metropolitan Books, 1999. 408p. ISBN 0805053875.

Singer Janis Joplin (1943–1970) never cared about respectability. She was a strange, artsy girl in high school who later dropped out of college and hung around record stores listening to the blues. In San Francisco she sang and recorded with future rock stars, but her drug and alcohol addictions forced her back home to Texas after a couple of years. After one sober year her music friends charmed her back into a psychedelic life that she could not control. According to Alice Echols, the singer may have shone among the boys of rock and roll, but she was always lonely and insecure. In this sympathetic biography, the author portrays the ill-fated Joplin as a rule breaker who led the way for later women of rock and roll.

> **Subjects:** Drug Abuse; Joplin, Janis; Rock Musicians; Singers; Teen Reads; Women

> **Now Try:** Lady Caroline Blackwood entered the male-dominated world of novel writing and literary criticism after being an artist's and photographer's model. Nancy Schoenberger tells how alcohol, drugs, and depression shortened her career and life in *Dangerous Muse: The Life of Lady Caroline Blackwood* (see chapter 7). When Jimi Hendrix died of an overdose of drugs, there was a question whether it was suicide. In *Room Full of Mirrors: A Biography of Jimi Hendrix*, Charles R. Cross describes the rock guitarist Jimi Hendrix as an insecure young man without self-discipline, worn out by the world of rock music, but not suicidal. Poet Dorothy Parker lived the rock star life of alcohol, drugs, and sex long before the advent of rock music. Her self-destructive and surprisingly long life is described in *Dorothy Parker: What Fresh Hell Is This?* by Marion Meade (see chapter 7). Miranda Seymour profiles another small-town girl who went wild in high society in *Bugatti Queen: In Search of a French Racing Legend* (see chapter 12).

Fuller, Alexandra

The Legend of Colton H. Bryant. Penguin Press, 2008. 202p. ISBN 978159420-1837. Audiobook available.

Like his father and grandfather before him, Colton H. Bryant (1980–2006) dreamed of being a cowboy but settled for roughnecking in the Upper Green River Valley of Wyoming. Having been an accident prone boy who was well known in the emergency room of the local hospital, the reckless young man who lived on Mountain Dew and hamburgers claimed that he would not live to see his twenty-fifth birthday. Though he exceeded his prediction by eight months, he still died tragically young in an easily avoidable oilfield drilling accident. In her intimate biography of the ill-fated Bryant, Alexandra Fuller portrays a working-class character who would do anything for his friends and family, including dangerous work. General readers will enjoy this novelistic biography.

> **Subjects:** Bryant, Colton H.; Cowboys; Group Discussion Books; Roughnecks; Teen Reads; Wyoming

Now Try: *Chopin's Funeral* by Benita Eisler (see chapter 7) is another compelling novelistic biography that readers know will end sadly before they open the book. Although Kenyan colonial settler Denys Finch Hatton was definitely better educated than Bryant, he shared a lack of ambition and love of idleness with the roughneck. His story is sympathetically told in ***Too Close to the Sun: The Audacious Life and Times of Denys Finch Hatton*** by Sara Wheeler (see this chapter). Addicted to drugs, the Beach Boys' Brian Wilson lost his ambition and spent years resigned to depression, watching one brother die in a drowning accident and another from cancer. Peter Ames Carlin weaves together stories of Wilson and his family and friends, from early childhood to the release of the long-lost album *Smile* in 2005, in his sympathetic psychological biography, ***Catch a Wave: The Rise, Fall & Redemption of the Beach Boy's Brian Wilson***. Witnessing suicide and insanity, Edvard Munch had little hope for happiness in his life. Sue Prideaux sorts through the painter's confusing portfolio to create an understandable narrative of his depression in ***Edvard Munch: Behind the Scream***.

Gay, Peter

Mozart. Viking, 1999. 177p. <u>Penguin Lives</u>. ISBN 0670882380. Audiobook available.

Composer Wolfgang Amadeus Mozart (1756–1791) died too soon. He was still young and at the height of his artistic achievement when he mysteriously died of an undetermined illness. Most novelists, dramatists, and filmmakers have emphasized the tragedy of the loss of the great composer. Peter Gay, however, insists that the composer enjoyed most of his life, despite his overbearing father, poverty, and failure to gain high appointments. His peers admired him and his poverty was mostly self-induced. Gay's Mozart was a man who lived mostly as he pleased and would have lived a little richer with just a little more luck.

Subjects: Biographical Essays; Composers; Mozart, Wolfgang Amadeus; Prodigies; Quick Reads; Vienna

Now Try: ***Mozart Speaks: Views on Music, Musicians, and the World*** is a collection of Mozart's writings. Composer Felix Mendelssohn was another prodigy who died at a young age. Peter Mercer-Taylor reveals that the composer's seemingly idyllic life was complicated by fears of anti-Semitism, the demands of royal patrons, and ill-health, in *The Life of Mendelssohn*. Eighteenth-century magician Giuseppe Balsamo was the inspiration for Sarastro in Mozart's *The Magic Flute*. In ***The Last Alchemist: Count Cagliostro, Master of Magic in the Age of Reason*** (see chapter 5), Iain McCalman describes seven episodes of Cagliostro's life inside and outside of the courts of Europe, a world that Mozart knew well. Like Mozart, the theatrical couple Alfred Lunt and Lynn Fontanne were creatively prolific and entertaining on and off the stage. Margot Peters describes their charmed life in ***Design for Living: Alfred Lunt and Lynn Fontanne: A Biography*** (see chapter 8).

Hopkins, Jerry, and Danny Sugerman

No One Here Gets Out Alive. Warner Books, 1980. 387p. ISBN 0446939218.

Over thirty publishers rejected this biography before it was published and became a best seller. Rock journalist Jerry Hopkins and coauthor Danny Sugerman portray Doors lead singer Jim Morrison (1943–1971) as a hell-bent rebel who read the Beat poets and broke many laws of decent behavior. Though explosive with anger and often vulgar, he had a rough charm that attracted worshippers. To some fans, he was a god. In the final chapter of this book—often stolen from libraries in the 1980s—the authors question whether the rock idol really died in Paris in 1971.

Subjects: Alcoholics; Doors, Musical Group; Drug Abuse; Morrison, Jim; Rock Musicians; Singers; Teen Reads

Now Try: Morrison's devoted fans will want to update the story with *The Lizard King: The Essential Jim Morrison* by Jerry Hopkins, in which the author presents further discoveries, reproduces many photos and interviews, and relates the love story between Morrison and Pamela Courson. As a writer, Morrison was inspired by a volume of Arthur Rimbaud's poetry that he kept nearby. Charles Nicholl describes the French modernist poet as a soldier of fortune and master of disguise in *Somebody Else: Arthur Rimbaud in Africa, 1880–91* (see chapter 1). Like Morrison, the iconic face of communist rebel Ernesto" "Che" Guevara has adorned millions of T-shirts. Jon Lee Anderson tells why the hard-living Argentinean soldier garnered great respect from the poor of Latin America in *Che Guevara: A Revolutionary Life* (see chapter 3). Though James Dean clearly died in an automobile accident, his death still has a bit of the mystery associated with Morrison's death. Warren Newton Beath provides an hour-by-hour account of the events leading up to the accident in *The Death of James Dean*.

Kriegel, Mark

Pistol: The Life of Pete Maravich. Free Press, 2007. 381p. ISBN 9780743284974. Audiobook available.

Like father, like son. Basketball coach Press Maravich (1947–1988) was determined to make a basketball star out of his son Pete. From an early age, he drilled Pete in basketball skills and tested him against older players. Each time Press took a new coaching position, Pete moved to a new school, where he became the team's star. Major colleges noticed and recruited the teen, but his father took the head coaching job at Louisiana State University, promising to deliver his son to the team. Pete nearly rebelled but reluctantly surrendered to his father's demand. Kriegel portrays the long-haired Maravich, who died of a heart attack at age forty-one, as a great athlete whose victories on the court were never more to him than just what his father expected.

Subjects: Basketball Players; Fathers and Sons; Maravich, Pete; Teen Reads

Now Try: Maravich praises his father for his patience and devotion in *Heir to a Dream*, his memoir about overcoming alcoholism and finding Christian faith. Like Maravich, Elvis Presley's maturation was arrested by a demanding parental figure, in his case Colonel Tom Parker. Peter Guralnick describes the singer's youth in *The Last Train to Memphis: The Rise of Elvis Presley*. A story with both the father and the son dying tragically young as a result of immature recklessness is *Inherited Risk: Errol and Sean Flynn in Hollywood and Vietnam* by Jeffrey Meyers. Actor Peter Fonda recounts the strained relationship that he had with his father, actor Henry Fonda, in *Don't Tell Dad: A Memoir*.

Lambert, Angela

The Lost Life of Eva Braun. St. Martin's Press, 2007. 495p. ISBN 9780312-366544, 031236654X.

In October 1929, when Eva Braun (1912–1945) had worked at Heinrich Hoffmann's camera shop only a few weeks, her employer entered with his best client, Adolf Hitler. Later the young shop assistant and amateur photographer told her sister Ilse that the man in the light-colored overcoat had a funny moustache. According to Angela Lambert, the shop owner used the unsuspecting Braun as bait to continue his very profitable contract. In this sympathetic biography, Lambert tells the tragic story of how an ordinary German girl became the loving mistress of the murderous dictator.

> **Subjects:** Braun, Eva; Germany; Hitler, Adolf; Mistresses; Women

> **Now Try:** In *The Murder of Adolf Hitler: The Truth About the Bodies in the Berlin Bunker*, forensic scientist W. Hugh Thomas proves that German leader Adolf Hitler was killed in his bunker in 1945 but claims that Eva Braun escaped. Braun was not the only young woman drawn to Adolf Hitler's power. In *The Sisters: The Saga of the Mitford Family*, Mary S. Lovell tells how Unity Mitford joined Hitler's inner circle and tried to commit suicide when war was declared between her homeland and Germany. Cult leader and murderer Charles Manson drew women to his commune, including Lynette Alice" "Squeaky" Fromme. Jess Bravin describes Fromme's attraction to Los Angeles counterculture, joining the Manson sect, and attempt to kill President Gerald Ford in *Squeaky: The Life and Times of Lynette Alice Fromme*. A young Algerian woman named Nadia did not count on becoming associated with international terrorism when she married a petty criminal. Journalist Baya Gacemi recounts Nadia's story about becoming the slave for a terror cell in *I, Nadia, Wife of a Terrorist*.

Ortiz, Alicia Dujovne

Eva Perón: A Biography. St. Martin's Press, 1995. 325p. ISBN 0312145993.

As an illegitimate child, Eva Perón (1919–1952) was shunned at school by the daughters of merchants and bureaucrats. As soon as she was able, she escaped her village to become a film and radio actress in Buenos Aires. How she attracted the attention of future dictator Juan Perón is still debated, as is the question of whether she was a Nazi spy. The story of the short life of Eva Peron, the glamorous first lady whose speeches won the hearts of Argentineans, is filled with mysteries. Given access to Perón archives, journalist Alicia Dujovne Ortiz tells an intimate story of the life and death of the woman who inspired the musical *Evita*.

> **Subjects:** Actors and Actresses; Argentina; First Ladies; Perón, Eva; Women

> **Now Try:** The authenticity of *Evita: In My Own Words*, a deathbed memoir by Perón published thirty-five years after her death, has been questioned. *My Mission in Life*, translated into English just after Perón's death, is accepted as hers, but historians agree that it is filled with factual errors. Like Perón, Empress Josephine of France, consort of Napoleon, was living in poverty before she attracted the eye of the nation's most powerful man. Andrea Stuart tells a sympathetic story of a woman often betrayed in *The Rose of Martinique: A Life of Napoleon's Josephine* (see chapter 9). Because Florence Harding, wife of President Warren G. Harding, brought scandalous entertainers and underworld figures into the White House for her dinners and other social functions, she was suspected of selling political favors. Carl Sferrazza Anthony examines the evidence for and against one of the most powerful of all first ladies in *Florence Harding: The First Lady, the Jazz Age, and the Death of America's Most Scandalous President* (see chapter 5). Mary, Queen of Scots was only twenty-five when she was imprisoned by her cousin, Elizabeth I of England, who suspected Mary of being a party to conspiracies. According to John Guy, the young woman was certainly capable and connected to Elizabeth's enemies. He describes Mary as an astute politician, a powerful woman, and a person to admire in *Queen of Scots: The True Life of Mary Stuart* (see chapter 9).

Savigneau, Josyane

Carson McCullers: A Life. Houghton Mifflin, 2001. 370p. ISBN 0395878209.

Novelist Carson McCullers (1917–1967) lived a short and difficult life. Her comfortable childhood was interrupted at age fifteen by an undiagnosed case of rheumatic fever, the first of many debilitating illnesses. Using a typewriter given to her by her father, she began composing stories, and at age twenty-three her novel *The Heart Is a Lonely Hunter* was a surprising best seller. In this admiring biography for literature fans, *Le Monde* editor Josyane Savigneau tells how the author drew upon her small-town experiences, her troubled marriage, and her psychiatric sessions to write poignant novels, stories, and plays that always kept a fresh and adolescent perspective.

> **Subjects:** Georgia; McCullers, Carson; Novelists; Women
>
> **Now Try:** *The Heart Is a Lonely Hunter, The Ballad of the Sad Café,* and *Collected Stories* are McCullers's most known titles. The inability of a young woman to find happiness with a husband or satisfaction through literary success is at the heart of the tragic biography *Her Husband: Hughes and Plath—A Marriage* by Diane Middlebrook. Country music singer Patsy Cline was an ill-fated woman beset by many tragedies. Mark Bego chronicles Cline's critically acclaimed but unlucky career in *I Fall to Pieces: The Music and the Life of Patsy Cline.* As an antidote to these tragedies, readers who enjoy stories about literary women may read the happier *Elizabeth Barrett Browning: A Biography* by Margaret Forster (see chapter 7), the story of a woman who did find love.

Towle, Mike

I've Got Things to Do with My Life: Pat Tillman: The Making of an American Hero. Triumph Books, 2004. 190p. ISBN 1572437081.

The death in Iraq of Pat Tillman (1976–2004), NFL football player turned Army Ranger, was front page news that later became a scandal as the U.S. military lied about the circumstances of his death to his family and the public. Focusing on the young man's life instead of his death, this book is the tale of the making of a soldier. Sportswriter Mike Towle profiles Tillman, an overachieving, loyal-to-the-team athlete whose felony assault of a student in high school had landed him in jail but who had learned to curb his temper to adhere to sports and military discipline. This journalistic-style profile will likely appeal to sports fans and military readers.

> **Subjects:** Football Players; Iraq War; Quick Reads; Soldiers; Tillman, Pat
>
> **Now Try:** One of the most famous American soldiers to die in battle was General George Armstrong Custer. Like Tillman, he had a violent temper and an excess of bravado. Evan S. Connell tells of Custer's lifelong journey to the Little Big Horn battle in *Son of the Morning Star* (see chapter 3). In *At the Altar of Speed: The Fast Life and Tragic Death of Dale Earnhardt* by Leigh Montville (see chapter 12), stock car racing is the setting for the death of a fearless character. The death of actor Bob Crane from the television series *Hogan's Heroes* was also misreported by the government officials responsible for the investigation. Robert Graysmith reexamines the evidence in the unsolved case in *The Murder*

of Bob Crane (see chapter 2). The merits of the investigation following the assassination of President John F. Kennedy have been debated since the tragedy. Vincent Bugliosi recounts the many conspiracy theories in his defense of the *Warren Commission Report*, entitled *Reclaiming History: The Assassination of President John F. Kennedy*.

Wheeler, Sara

Too Close to the Sun: The Audacious Life and Times of Denys Finch Hatton. Random House, 2006. 292p. ISBN 9781400060696.

Denys Finch Hatton (1887–1931), son of a socially declining English family, lacked ambition and focus, but he was handsome and charming. After service on the remote East African front of World War I, he stayed on the continent to try his hand at farming, big game hunting, land speculation, and aerial delivery services. Because of his prominent friends in East Africa, especially his lover, Karen Blixen, author of *Out of Africa*, he has become a romantic figure and a symbol of British colonialism. Sara Wheeler sifts through the fact and fiction in this melancholy biography.

   Subjects: Africa; British Empire; Finch Hatton, Denys; Pilots

   Now Try: Finch-Hatton is the hero of *Out of Africa*, a memoir by Karen Blixen written under her pseudonym, Isak Dinesen; his companionship and good cheer made living on the coffee plantation in Kenya tolerable for Blixen. Like Finch-Hatton, composer Felix Mendelssohn seemed to live an idyllic life but died tragically young. Peter Mercer-Taylor chronicles the life of the romantic young man in *The Life of Mendelssohn* (see chapter 7). Antarctic explorer Robert Falcon Scott was another tragic British figure who died far from the motherland. Robert Crane portrays Scott as a sane but overly optimistic man who tragically erred in his preparations for the conquest of the South Pole in *Scott of the Antarctic: A Life of Courage and Tragedy* (see chapter 1). German fighter pilot Manfred von Richthofen died after his airplane was shot down in battle in World War I. Peter Kilduff tells how the daring Richthofen, who shot down eighty allied planes in battle, earned the admiration of friends and foes, in *Richthofen: Beyond the Legend of the Red Baron* (see chapter 3).

Woodward, Bob

Wired: The Short Life & Fast Times of John Belushi. Simon & Schuster, 1984. 432p. ISBN 0671473204.

Comedy fans were shocked in 1982 when they heard that John Belushi (1949–1982) had died of a drug overdose. So young and funny, his crazy, irreverent characters on *Saturday Night Live* and in the movies *Animal House* and *The Blues Brothers* had become cultural icons. What fans did not see was Belushi's constant use of alcohol and cocaine to energize his daily life. Investigative journalist Bob Woodward candidly reports on the out-of-control life of a comic genius and the friends who could not or would not help. This classic tragedy continues to appeal to pop culture readers.

   Subjects: Actors and Actresses; Belushi, John; Comedians; Drug Abuse; Television; Teen Reads

   Now Try: Belushi's wife Judith Jacklin Belushi wrote about her life with the comedian and adjusting to life after his death in *Samurai Widow*. She also published a tribute with photos and testimonials entitle *Belushi: A Biography*. Other comedians have died tragically young. Martin Knelman looks beyond" "the funny stuff" in his book *Laughing on the Outside: The Life of John Candy*, and Tom Farley describes his brother's immoderate life in *Chris Farley Show: A Biography in Three Acts*. Drug addiction stories do not always have tragic endings. In the memoir *Beautiful Boy: A Father's Journey Through His Son's Meth Addiction*, David Sheff describes how a family can heal even when the addict's prognosis is still in doubt.

Life, Chapter One

The lives of some prominent historical figures are very well documented and lend themselves to being retold in multiple-volume biographies. The initial volumes in these sets focus on early years in which personalities are shaped, and thus serve well as Coming-of-Age Biography. This section identifies some of these biographies.

Only the most famous of lives are worthy of multiple-volume biographies that are issued over a number of years or even decades. The subjects tend to be long-lived in fame and popularity and are often in the public eye for decades. Presidents and other heads of state who led their countries during crises, such as Abraham Lincoln and Adolf Hitler, are the most frequent subjects of these detailed biographical treatments.

Defining the character of these very important historical figures provides the focal point of these epic works. So much detail is presented and scrutinized that the narrative sometimes get lost, although the better biographers keep the stories moving. Settings too are often well defined, sometimes even more than some readers want. The pace is usually unhurried. Only readers very interested in the subject attempt to read the entire set. More are apt to try the first volume, as childhood stories tend to be less complicated and more universal.

> *Life, Chapter One* stories identify the first volume of prestigious multivolume biographies of major historical figures. The initial volumes in these sets deal with the youth and education of well-researched lives. Detail is rich in these books meant for leisurely reading. Readers who enjoy these books may wish to read the later volumes.

Caro, Robert A.

❀ *The Path to Power: The Years of Lyndon Johnson.* Random House, 1981. 786p. ISBN 0394499735. Audiobook available.

Future president Lyndon Johnson's father died penniless, despite being a six-term member of the Texas State Legislature. Anxious not to repeat his father's failure, Johnson (1908–1973) sought ways to cash in on his political power profitably without endangering his future, for even as a young congressman in Roosevelt's New Deal Washington, he aimed for high national office. In the first of a series of books on the thirty-seventh president, Robert A. Caro tells the fascinating story of political maturation, beginning with the politician's birth in the Texas Hill Country and ending with the death of President Franklin D. Roosevelt. Readers who enjoy epic tales about the quest for political power will enjoy all three volumes in this candid series.

Subjects: Group Discussion Books; Johnson, Lyndon Baines; Politics and Government; Presidents; Texas

Awards: National Book Critics Circle Award for Nonfiction

Now Try: Johnson recounted his years in the White House in his memoir, *The Vantage Point: Perspectives of the Presidency, 1963–1969*. Many readers who enjoyed LBJ's story will also enjoy *Mornings on Horseback* by David McCullough. McCullough tells how a young and often ill Theodore Roosevelt transformed himself into a person of consequence, destined to become an American president. Harland Sanders, the founder of Kentucky Fried Chicken, also rose from difficult beginnings. John Ed Pearce tells how a sixth-grade dropout became a fabulously rich chicken chef with a secret spices recipe in *The Colonel: The Captivating Biography of the Dynamic Founder of a Fast Food Empire* (see chapter 9). Like Johnson, Pablo Picasso was an ambitious and profane man who could alternately be generous or mean. His coming-of-age story is told in *A Life of Picasso: Prodigy, 1881–1906* by John Richardson.

Cook, Blanche Wiesen

🐾 *Eleanor Roosevelt: Volume One, 1884–1933*. Viking, 1992. 587p. ISBN 067080-486X. Audiobook available.

Former first lady Eleanor Roosevelt (1884–1962) was admired or despised by Americans according to their political philosophies. Though a peacemaker and arbitrator, she was never neutral in her opinions and feelings, and she was cast into the spotlight by FDR's campaign for president. According to Blanche Wiesen Cook, Roosevelt lived according to a rule of her teacher Marie Souvestre," "Never be bored and you will never be boring." She took on the causes of civil rights, fair labor practices, and the end of poverty—liberal causes that pitted her against powerful conservatives of her time. In this first volume of an expansive biography, the author chronicles Eleanor's privileged childhood, romances, life as a mother, and years caring for the health of her polio-stricken husband.

Subjects: First Ladies; Roosevelt, Eleanor; Women

Awards: ALA Notable Books, Los Angeles Times Book Prize for Biography

Now Try: Living a long and active life, Roosevelt wrote her memoirs several times, the last being *Autobiography of Eleanor Roosevelt*, published in the year before her death. She told of her life with Franklin Roosevelt, her years as first lady, and her travels around the world. Roosevelt's contemporary, Helen Keller, met many world luminaries in her quest to advance liberal causes. How she could do this while deaf and blind is told in *Helen and Teacher: The Story of Helen Keller and Anne Sullivan Macy* by Joseph P. Lash (see chapter 4). Like Roosevelt, Pearl Buck used newspaper columns and radio commentary to spread her message of international dialogue and world peace. Peter Conn recounts the life of the woman who loved China in *Pearl S. Buck: A Cultural Biography* (see chapter 4). *Martha Washington: An American Life* by Patricia Brady (see chapter 9) and *A Perfect Union: Dolley Madison and the Creation of the American Nation* by Catherine Allgor (see chapter 9) are stories of first ladies whose efforts contributed much to the success of their husbands.

Edel, Leon

Henry James: The Untried Years, 1843–1870. J. B. Lippincott, 1953. 350p. No ISBN.

1

Many biographers writing about their profession point to Leon Edel's biography of the American novelist Henry James (1843–1916) as a model for the genre. In the first volume of five, Edel tells about James's ancestry, childhood, education, and early European travels. The book ends with the novelist returning to America from his first extended European stay without his family, a test of his adaptability to the expatriate's life. Readers will appreciate Edel's ability to incorporate many details and incidents from James's life without sounding overly academic.

2

3

Subjects: Expatriates; James, Henry; Novelists

Now Try: Henry James wrote three volumes of his memoirs before he died in 1916: *A Small Boy and Others, Notes of a Son and Brother,* and *The Middle Years.* When James settled in England in the 1870s, Alfred Lord Tennyson was a leading figure in the world of English literature. Norman Page tells how the English people loved Tennyson as much for the simple and generous life that he led as for his poetry in *Tennyson: An Illustrated Life.* James's contemporary, Edward the Prince of Wales, was still many years away from becoming king. Stanley Weintraub chronicles the social life, romantic affairs, and world travels of the gregarious prince in *Edward the Caresser: The Playboy Prince Who Became Edward VII* (see chapter 9). James became the one person that every aspiring writer went to see. In the world of architecture, the person to see was Frank Lloyd Wright, who was in the prime of his career before James died. Ada Louise Huxtable describes Wright as charming, usually in debt, and absolutely certain of his place in history as the most influential architect who ever lived, in *Frank Lloyd Wright* (see chapter 7).

4

5

6

Freeman, Douglas Southall

7

🌿 *George Washington: A Biography: Volume One, Young Washington.* Charles Scribner's Sons, 1948. 549p. No ISBN.

Noted biographer Douglas Southall Freeman included many details with supporting footnotes in his seven-volume biography of George Washington (1732–1799), a tome that was completed by his assistants after his death in 1953. In the first volume he describes the youth of the first American president within the context of the history of the Washington family as leaders in the Virginia colony. Having a journalist's concern for the reader, Freeman keeps the narrative lively with stories of the daily life of a child on the plantation and of the work of a young land surveyor. Readers interested in the early years of historical figures will appreciate this account of the first twenty-two years of Washington's life.

8

9

10

Subjects: Land Surveyors; Presidents; Virginia; Washington, George

Awards: Pulitzer Prize for Biography

Now Try: Washington was a prolific writer of letters, diaries, and speeches. The Library of America has put together a compilation of his important pieces, *Washington: Writings.* Like Douglas Southall Freeman, David Herbert Donald writes clear, direct prose. Donald recounts the key events in the life of Abraham Lincoln, from his birth in Kentucky to his death in the Ford Theater

11

12

in Washington, D.C., in *Lincoln* (see chapter 10). Readers who like detailed founding fathers' stories will enjoy Walter Isaacson's storytelling in his epic biography, *Benjamin Franklin: An American Life* (see chapter 10). Stephen Ambrose was another great story-teller, whose *Undaunted Courage: Meriwether Lewis, Thomas Jefferson, and the Opening of the American West* practically puts the reader in the boats with the explorers crossing the continent.

Kershaw, Ian

Hitler, 1889–1936: Hubris. W. W. Norton, 1998. 845p. ISBN 0393-046710.

German dictator Adolf Hitler (1889–1945) was a strange, poorly educated dreamer as a youth with unrealistic expectations for his life. As a student, he saw himself as a renowned artist or architect, though he had little aptitude for either profession. As he lived through lean, disappointing years and the first World War, he grew angrier about German political conditions and joined radical nationalist groups, where he discovered that his fellow members listened to his impassioned speeches against Jews and minorities in society. According to historian Ian Kershaw, Hitler became the" "indispensable fulcrum and inspiration" of the rise of the Nazi Party and the militarization of his country. Readers who enjoy epic stories will enjoy this story about the rise of the dominant villain of the twentieth century.

> **Subjects:** Austria; Dictators; Germany; Hitler, Adolf; Nazi Party

> **Now Try:** The book that Hitler wrote from prison, *Mein Kampf* or *My Struggle*, revealed his racial hatred and his belief that strong people should subjugate the weak. In *Hitler's Second Book: The Unpublished Sequel to* **Mein Kampf**, Hitler laid out plans for German prosperity through constant aggression against neighboring countries. In Japan, Emperor Hirohito was a key voice in the Japanese wartime government, not just a puppet of his generals, as is sometimes suggested. In the epic biography *Hirohito and the Making of Modern Japan* (see chapter 10), Herbert P. Bix explains how the sly emperor became an American ally against the Chinese after the war, avoiding World Court prosecution for war crimes. Jesse James used newspaper columns to spread racial hatred in much the same way as Hitler used media to spread anti-Semitism. T. J. Stiles dispels any notion of James as a folk hero in *Jesse James: Last Rebel of the Civil War* (see chapter 2). CNN correspondent Peter L. Bergen examines the character and aspirations of Osama bin Laden in *The Osama bin Laden I Know: An Oral History of al Qaeda's Leader* (see chapter 5).

Lewis, David Levering

W. E. B. Du Bois: Biography of Race, 1868–1919. John Macrae Book, 1993. 735p. ISBN 0805026215.

Education saved William Edward Burghardt Du Bois (1868–1963) from poverty. Foreseeing education as the key to black prosperity and the end of discrimination, he dedicated his life to black scholarship, establishing the study of African American sociology with his series of well-regarded books refuting the idea of the natural inferiority of the Negro race. According to historian David Levering Lewis, Du Bois also laid the foundation of the civil rights movement in the United States, creating the National Association for the Advancement of Colored People and publishing *The Crisis*, a journal of opinion about race in America. In this sprawling biography for readers of epics, Levering covers just the first half of Du Bois's long and active life.

Subjects: Activists; African Americans; Civil Rights Leaders; Du Bois, William Edward Burghardt; Scholars

Awards: Bancroft Prize in American History; Pulitzer Prize for Biography

Now Try: In the posthumously published *The Autobiography of W. E. B. DuBois,* the scholar and activist recounted his career and the formation of the NAACP. *Darkwater: Voices from Within the Veil* is a collection of Du Bois's essays and poetry from the time when he was the leading voice calling for civil rights. Like Du Bois, Marcus Garvey was a high-profile black activist of the early twentieth century who published his own national magazine. Both men went to prison for their activism. The two, however, had very different plans for their race. Garvey's "back to Africa" story is fully told in *Negro with a Hat: The Rise and Fall of Marcus Garvey* by Colin Grant. The philosopher and psychologist William James has been compared by some scholars with Plato and Aristotle. An epic account of his long and influential academic career is *William James: In the Maelstrom of American Modernism* by Robert D. Richardson (see chapter 7). Noam Chomsky is a contemporary social critic who has made as many enemies as Du Bois made in his time. Robert F. Barsky recounts Chomsky's career and controversies in *Noam Chomsky: A Life of Dissent.*

Sandburg, Carl

Abraham Lincoln: The Prairie Years. Blue Ribbon Books, 1926. 604p. No ISBN. Audiobook available.

Poet and folksinger Carl Sandburg was inspired to write this first volume (of six) about Abraham Lincoln (1809–1865) by the stories his neighbors told about the future president visiting Galesburg, Illinois. They told Sandburg about meeting a country lawyer who rode the court circuit of the state and later campaigned to become the nation's leader when the issue of slavery was dividing its citizens. Using these cherished folk stories and personal anecdotes as his foundation, Sandburg wrote a lively, entertaining biography, praised for its readability, and criticized for its factual errors. According to Sandburg, Lincoln was an ordinary man who rose to greatness, just trying to do what was right for his family and state.

Subjects: Illinois; Lawyers; Lincoln, Abraham; Presidents

Now Try: Numerous collections of Lincoln's letters and speeches are available, including *The Essential Abraham Lincoln* and the Library of America's two-volume *Abraham Lincoln: Speeches and Writings.* Like Lincoln, Mark Twain was the subject of many legends. *Mark Twain: A Life* by Ron Powers (see chapter 7) dispels many of the rumors that Twain himself fostered. Daniel Boone was another major American historical character. In *Boone: A Biography* (see chapter 5), Robert Morgan strips away unreliable legends about Daniel Boone but retains a Sandburg-like sense of biography as a statement of character. In times of financial crisis, the leadership of Franklin D. Roosevelt during the Great Depression is remembered. Jean Edward Smith chronicles the life of the New Deal president in great detail in *FDR* (see chapter 10).

Group Biography

Teens and young adults are thought to be influenced by their peers more than other age groups. They are more likely to belong to clubs, teams, bands, or gangs and to congregate to trade ideas and try out new behaviors. With the outcome of their lives yet to be determined, they tend to feel uncertain and pressured to succeed at school and other endeavors. Belonging to a group gives young people social standing and confidence but also may demand conformity. With positive group support, individuals mature.

This section profiles groups of peers who distinguish themselves as such. With numerous individuals to follow, the narratives include multiple story lines, making them particularly complex and engrossing. The books have well-defined settings and somewhat deliberate pacing as the focus moves among various individuals profiled. Readers may remember their own group experiences and enjoy reading about the many relationships within the groups.

> Group Biography portrays peers together, showing how adolescents and young adults are often strongly influenced by the company they keep. These subjects mature and earn fame together. Group biographies of writers, musicians, and athletes are found in this section.

Carpenter, Humphrey

The Brideshead Generation: Evelyn Waugh and His Friends. Houghton Mifflin, 1990. 523p. ISBN 0395441420.

In England, everyone in the upper classes seems to meet in school. Between the world wars, the hot spots were Eton and Oxford, where young scholars dedicated themselves to publishing literary broadsheets, listening to the gramophone, writing sketches, drinking tea, dressing up, and preparing to become novelists. While they fought among themselves over the issues of communism, fascism, Catholicism, homosexuality, and poetics, they drank plenty of cocktails and smoked many cigars. According to Humphrey Carpenter, Evelyn Waugh (1903–1966) became the central figure of a literary community that included Harold Acton, Nancy Mitford, Cyril Connolly, and Graham Greene. Readers who are fond of English literature will undoubtedly enjoy learning how these authors' lives intersected.

Subjects: Friends; Great Britain; Novelists; Waugh, Evelyn

Now Try: *Brideshead Revisited* is Evelyn Waugh's evocative novel about the period before World War II when young men could be optimistic and philosophical before they learned the realities of life. In contrast, Graham Greene's *Brighton Rock* depicts the hopelessness of characters among that period's lower classes. The circle of writers that surrounded nineteenth-century poet and essayist Ralph Waldo Emerson defined American literature. Susan Cheever tells their peer group story in *American Bloomsbury: Louisa May Alcott, Ralph Waldo Emerson, Margaret Fuller, Nathaniel Hawthorne, and Henry David Thoreau: Their Lives, Their Loves, Their Work* (see this chapter). Nancy Caldwell Sorel tells the story of the sorority of brave women who followed the troops around the theaters of the Second World War in *The Women Who Wrote the War* (see chapter 3).

Art critic John Richardson describes the late twentieth-century community of art and culture in *Sacred Monsters, Sacred Masters: Beaton, Capote, Dalí, Picasso, Freud, Warhol, and More* (see chapter 7).

Cheever, Susan

American Bloomsbury: Louisa May Alcott, Ralph Waldo Emerson, Margaret Fuller, Nathaniel Hawthorne, and Henry David Thoreau: Their Lives, Their Loves, Their Work. Simon & Schuster, 2006. 223p. ISBN 9780743264617.

In the 1840s and 1850s outside Boston, in a village called Concord, where the first shots of the American Revolution were fired, Ralph Waldo Emerson nursed a literary community from which came numerous American classics, including *The Scarlet Letter*, *Walden*, and *Little Women*. Bronson Alcott and his family, Nathaniel Hawthorne, and Henry David Thoreau lived at times in houses near the bridge upon which the Americans and British fought. Emerson often paid the bills. Their visitors included novelist Herman Melville, the abolitionist John Brown, and early feminist Margaret Fuller. In this fast-reading account, novelist Susan Cheever captures the tension of an exciting time in a remarkable place.

Subjects: Authors; Massachusetts; Transcendental Movement

Now Try: Readers will have no problem finding books to read after this book, as the subjects wrote many classic books. Emerson's essays, *The Scarlet Letter* by Nathaniel Hawthorne, *Walden* by Henry David Thoreau, and *Little Women* by Louisa May Alcott are just a start. *American Transcendentalism* by Philip F. Gura goes into more depth about the philosophical glue of the group and similarly minded people in America and Europe. In *The London Yankees: Portraits of American Writers and Artists in England 1894–1914*, Stanley Weintraub describes the expatriate literary community that gathered around Henry James in late Victorian and early Edwardian times. *Eudora: A Writer's Life* by Ann Waldron (see chapter 7) recounts the life of Eudora Welty, an American writer whose literary friends were seldom seen but often heard from by mail.

Hajdu, David

Positively 4th Street: The Lives and Times of Joan Baez, Bob Dylan, Mimi Baez Fariña, and Richard Fariña. Farrar, Straus & Giroux, 2001. 328p. ISBN 0374-281998. Audiobook available.

Before the invasion of the Beatles, Rolling Stones, and other British bands, folk music dominated the music charts in the United States. Joan Baez (1941–) and her sister Mimi Baez Fariña (1945–2001) were leaders among the talented young women, playing their guitars and singing at coffee houses and folk festivals across the country. Bob Dylan (1941–) played the part of a musician with literary aspirations, and unpublished novelist Richard Fariña (1937–1966) hung out with the others, attracted to music. According to critic David Hajdu, the four formed a complicated bond that sparked their careers and defined the Bohemian lifestyle of the 1960s. Suggest this title to baby boomers who enjoy remembering their youth.

Subjects: Baez, Joan; Dylan, Bob; Fariña, Mimi Baez; Fariña, Richard; Folk Singers; Group Biography; Novelists; Teen Reads

Now Try: *And a Voice to Sing With: A Memoir* is Joan Baez's look back at her childhood and the early days of her career. For an early look at Bob Dylan, see *Forever Young: Photographs of Bob Dylan* by Douglas Gilbert. The collected biography *Girls Like Us: Carole King, Joni Mitchell, Carly Simon—and the Journey of a Generation* by Sheila Weller (see chapter 8) tells stories about a trio of musical women who inspired young listeners in the 1960s and 1970s. A generation before Bob Dylan and Joan Baez, the Carter Family defined country music and the role of musicians in popular culture. Their bittersweet story is told by Mark Zwonitzer in *Will You Miss Me When I'm Gone: The Carter Family and Their Legacy in American Music*. Martin Gayford recounts how two painters spent nine tense weeks in collaboration in *The Yellow House: Van Gogh, Gauguin, and Nine Turbulent Weeks in Arles* (see chapter 7).

Sokolove, Michael

🎗 *The Ticket Out: Darryl Strawberry and the Boys of Crenshaw.* Simon & Schuster, 2004. 291p. ISBN 0743226739.

In the bad neighborhoods of Los Angeles, sports are often seen as the best escape from poverty, drugs, and gangs. In 1979 fifteen talented black teenagers on the Crenshaw High School Cougars baseball team, hoping baseball would save them, drew the attention of numerous professional scouts. Several players received minor league contracts, but only Chris Brown (1961–2006) and Darryl Strawberry (1962–) made it to the major leagues. In a story about many broken promises, journalist Michael Sokolove relates what became of the young men and their grave disappointment in Strawberry, the one who got more than his fair share of chances.

Subjects: Baseball Players; Brown, Chris; Chenshaw High School; Group Biography; Los Angeles; Strawberry, Darryl; Teen Reads

Awards: ALA Notable Books

Now Try: Charisse and Darryl Strawberry write about the baseball player's recovery from drug addiction in *Recovering Life*. Strawberry was not the only highly talented New York Met to let his career slip away. Bob Klapisch pairs his story with that of a promising pitcher in *High and Tight: The Rise and Fall of Dwight Gooden and Darryl Strawberry*. When East St. Louis High School football coach Bob Shannon drilled his players, there was more at stake than winning and losing games. He was preparing his students for life and helping them get football scholarships so they could attend college. Kevin Horrigan pays tribute to a remarkably successful teacher in a poverty stricken community in *The Right Kind of Heroes: Coach Bob Shannon and the East St. Louis Flyers*. Similarly, at St. Anthony's High School in Jersey City, New Jersey, Bob Hurley is coaching basketball with the intention of saving directionless boys from misfortune. Adrian Wojnarowski describes how the tough but compassionate coach trains his players in *The Miracle of St. Anthony: A Season with Coach Bob Hurley and Basketball's Most Improbable Dynasty*.

Spitz, Bob

The Beatles: The Biography. Little, Brown, 2005. 983p. ISBN 0316803529. Audiobook available.

According to Bob Spitz, Beatlemania might never have happened if not for a few lucky breaks. The group threatened to fall apart many times, as each of the Fab Four tried to leave the group at a stressful point, but the music, money, and insane experience of being a Beatle drew them back. And from Liverpool through Hamburg to London and beyond, the Beatles rocked the world. The author has filled this sympathetic group biography with fan-pleasing stories describing how the group evolved, lingered in obscurity, learned from mistakes, and enjoyed the high life of success. At the end, readers may feel both relief and regret at the breakup.

Subjects: Beatles; Harrison, George; Lennon, John; Liverpool; McCartney, Paul; Rock Musicians; Starr, Ringo

Now Try: *In His Own Write* is John Lennon's collection of eccentric stories, poems, and drawings. In 1971 Jann S. Wenner republished a *Rolling Stone* interview with Lennon as *Lennon Remembers,* a small book about the singer's life. *I, Me, Mine* is a memoir from George Harrison. Ringo Starr has reproduced fifty-one postcards that he received from former Beatles in *Postcards from the Boys. Simon and Garfunkel: Old Friends* by Joseph Morella and Patricia Barey (see chapter 8) tells how artistic differences divided two young musicians struggling to maintain their friendship. *The Rolling Stones: In the Beginning* by Bent Rej (Firefly Books, 2006) is a photographic coming-of-age story about the band that has lasted nearly three decades after the Beatles broke up.

Consider Starting With . . .

These well-written Coming-of-Age Biographies of modest length will appeal to general readers.

- Buck, Rinker. *Shane Comes Home.*
- Fuller, Alexandra. *The Legend of Colton H. Bryant.*
- Gay, Peter. *Mozart.*
- Hajdu, David. *Positively 4th Street: The Lives and Times of Joan Baez, Bob Dylan, Mimi Baez Fariña , and Richard Fariña.*
- Remnick, David. *King of the World: Muhammad Ali and the Rise of an American Hero.*
- Shields, Charles J. *Mockingbird: A Portrait of Harper Lee.*
- Uruburu, Paula. *American Eve: Evelyn Nesbit, Stanford White, the Birth of the" "It" Girl, and the Crime of the Century.*
- Woodward, Bob. *Wired: The Short Life & Fast Times of John Belushi.*

Further Reading

Adamson, Lynda G.

Thematic Guide to Popular Nonfiction. Greenwood Press, 2006. 352p. ISBN 0313328552.

Adamson includes a short chapter on adolescent females. Each chapter in her book discusses themes and identifies titles to recommend.

Millard, Kenneth

Coming of Age in Contemporary American Fiction. Edinburgh University Press, 2007. 191p. ISBN 9780748621743.

> Though Millard is interested in fiction and not biography, he identifies the themes and appeals of contemporary coming-of-age stories.

Part 3

Nonfiction Subject Interests

Chapter 7

Cultural Biography

Definition of Cultural Biography

According to *The American Heritage Dictionary of the English Language*, fourth edition, *culture* is "intellectual and artistic activity and the works produced by it." This is the meaning of culture used by newspapers and magazines when they include cultural sections covering art, architecture, literature, the theater, music, and dance. Likewise, a community's cultural calendar will list concerts, ballets, plays, poetry readings, and exhibitions at art galleries and museums. Using this sense of the term, Cultural Biography refers to books about the lives of people who create culture with their writings, musical compositions, art, and architecture.

The history of culture is long, reaching into the foggy past. One may imagine a cave dweller inviting another over to see his wall paintings as the beginning of culture, but prehistoric hunters probably had more practical or religious intentions when they depicted their prey. These paintings might still be considered cultural works, according to T. S. Eliot, who in *Notes Toward the Definition of Culture* suggests that the idea of culture arose from religion. By the time of the ancient Greeks, society had embraced cultural works, as palaces were decorated with fresco paintings and citizens attended the plays of Aeschylus, Sophocles, Euripides, Aristophanes, and Menander. This tradition has continued in Western civilization, as art, music, and literature have helped define human experience, and the shared enjoyment of creative works has intellectually and emotionally bound individuals to their society. Cultural enterprise is now big business, as most Americans, Europeans, and economically developed countries enjoy reading, watching movies, listening to music, and seeing art.

Cultural Biography refers to books about the lives of artists, architects, composers, dancers, writers, and other figures whose creative works have endured and become important pieces of our cultural heritage. These books recount the lives of unique, generally familiar figures who devote their lives to their careers, often overcoming hardships to become known as historical representatives of their times. Readers learn about their works and the societies that they reflect. Quick reads and longer biographies are included in this chapter.

Appeal of the Genre

People love to create. For some it is a hobby, such as knitting, arranging flowers, painting landscapes, taking photographs, or writing personal Web logs that they post on the Internet. Some people become quite serious about their compulsions to build their own furniture, landscape their gardens, design their dream house, or sell their creations at local or regional craft fairs. Many people even study art, dance, music, and writing, wanting to better their skills, dreaming of careers that are rarely realized. From these dreamers come the people who enjoy reading about artists, writers, and composers who struggled and succeeded at becoming professionals and whose works contribute to our culture.

The books in this chapter feature distinctive characters whose talents and accomplishments set them apart from others in their fields. Most also exhibited unusual personalities that made them people to remember, and some, such as playwright William Shakespeare and artist Andy Warhol, became iconic symbols of their times. All contributed creative works that endure in the cultural life of our society, and readers remain interested in learning about these remarkable people.

Many compelling stories reside in these books. A few individuals were child prodigies, such as composer Felix Mendelssohn and the pianist Mary Lou Williams, but many struggled as adults to create their works and earn recognition as artists or writers. Some, including diarist Samuel Pepys and folksinger Woody Guthrie, witnessed pivotal historical events about which they wrote books or songs. Others, such as painter Francisco José de Goya and novelists Charles Dickens and Sinclair Lewis, used their works to call attention to society's woes. Several, including the poet Anne Sexton and journalist Hunter Thompson, ended their lives when their work no longer protected them from their own destructive personalities. All succeeded in creating meaningful works that have been preserved in the cultural record.

Settings can be especially important in works of Cultural Biography. The societies into which the subjects were born to some extent formed them, but they in turn reshaped their societies. Readers learn about the geographical places, social classes, emotional milieus, and political events to which the subjects responded. The authors of these biographies often conclude by showing the impact the subjects had on society.

Cultural Biographies may be concise or expansive. Some quick reads are available for readers who enjoy shorter books. Length of narrative matters less than compelling text to readers who seek information about the characters and want to read good stories.

Organization of the Chapter

The first section of this chapter is "Masters of Art," a collection of biographies about cultural figures who excelled in their work and have been recognized for it. Readers will easily recognize most of the figures in this section, which includes biographies of William Shakespeare, Michelangelo, Frank Lloyd Wright, and Dr. Seuss. Jazz fans know Thelonious Monk; readers familiar with ballet know Rudolf Nureyev and George Balanchine.

"Witnesses of an Era" is the next section. The cultural figures about whom these biographies are written captured the essence of their times in their creative works, making them spokespeople to succeeding generations. The photographer Henri Cartier-Bresson, the painter Norman Rockwell, children's author Margaret Wise Brown, and poet Walt Whitman are among the individuals in these biographies.

The next section is "Struggling Artists," biographies about writers, composers, and artists who suffered social, economic, health, or mental difficulties while creating the works for which they are remembered. Biographies of novelist Franz Kafka, poet Elizabeth Barrett Browning, artist Vincent Van Gogh, and musical arranger Nelson Riddle are included in this section.

"Eccentrics, Rebels, Rule-Breakers, and Other Unconventional Characters" is the next section of the chapter. These biographers recount the lives of artists who challenged the strictures of society with their works and the conduct of their lives. Playwright Oscar Wilde, cartoonist Charles Addams, poet Dorothy Parker, and artist Georgia O'Keeffe are included in these biographies.

The chapter ends with "Cultural Collections," collective biographies that profile numerous cultural individuals in one volume.

Masters of Art

Masterpieces of art, music, and literature, being open to interpretation, manage to stay fresh and relevant for generations. The images, melodies, and words remain fixed and unaltered, but they take on new meanings as succeeding students of culture apply their own perspectives based on the realities of their lives. Likewise, there always seem to be unverified stories and discrepancies in the documentary records about the masters who created these works, leaving their life stories open to reinterpretation. Each generation wants to solve the mysteries in the lives of the master artists and generate new biographies trying to do so.

In this section are biographies of some of the most critically acclaimed cultural figures in history, people about whom countless books have been written. Humorist Bill Bryson makes an attempt to define the essence of playwright William Shakespeare in his serious but cheery account, *Shakespeare: The World as Stage*. Novelist Jane Smiley sympathetically describes how the great novels by Charles Dickens were drawn from his life and interests in *Charles Dickens*. The section also includes some more recent figures whose works have been cited by cultural forecasters as those that will survive over time. Though the records of their lives may be readily available, mysteries about character and actions persist. Judith Morgan and Neil Morgan recount the puzzling life of a children's author who is readily recognized but hardly understood in *Dr. Seuss & Mr. Geisel*. Michael Schumacher recounts stories from the movie sets of *The Godfather* and *Apocalypse Now* in *Francis Ford Coppola: A Filmmaker's Life*, her biography of the eminent film director.

Characters larger than life populate these biographies, which are mostly written about deceased cultural figures. (At the time of this writing, only film director Francis Ford Coppola is living.) Their names and stories, however, are still familiar and relevant, as their works endure. Authors describe their careers, seek to answer lingering questions about their lives, and explain their legacies. The settings range from the fourteenth century, when poet Geoffrey Chaucer wrote about pilgrims to Canterbury, to more recent times, when Soviet defector Rudolf Nureyev danced in ballets. Both quick reads and biographies requiring more of the reader's time are included in this section.

> *Masters of Art* stories are biographies of the most renowned cultural figures in history, whose works persist over time and whose lives continue to interest readers. Authors retell these lives with the aim to explain their cultural importance and enduring legacy. Readers can learn much about the eras in which the artists, writers, and other cultural figures lived. Quick reads, as well as books requiring more of the reader's time, are included in this section.

Ackroyd, Peter

Chaucer. Nan A. Talese, 2005. 188p. <u>Ackroyd's Brief Lives</u>. ISBN 0385507976. Audiobook available.

Being a poet gained Geoffrey Chaucer (1343?–1400?) entry into many nobles' courts, but it did not pay the rent. To afford his apartment above Aldgate, where he could see everyone entering and leaving London to the east, this son of a wine merchant worked as the royal comptroller of customs for the port of London and represented the British crown on missions abroad. While in Italy and France Chaucer listened to the poets, noting their cadences, voices, and storytelling. In London, when he was not working for the king, he wrote and recited his poems. According to Peter Ackroyd, Chaucer was not the first British poet, but with *Troilus and Criseyde* and *Canterbury Tales*, he established the rules for the next seven centuries of English verse.

Subjects: Chaucer, Geoffrey; Diplomats; England; Poets; Quick Reads

Now Try: Readers having difficulty with original Chaucer texts may want to try *Canterbury Tales in Modern Verse*, translated by Joseph Glaser, or *The Canterbury Tales: A Prose Version in Modern English*, rewritten by David Wright. Several editions of *Troilus and Criseyde* are also available. The mystery writer P. C. Doherty has adapted the stories into a series of novels, beginning with *Ancient Evil: The Knight's Tale of Mystery and Murder as He Goes on Pilgrimage from London to Canterbury*. Peter Ackroyd describes a member of a later royal court in his story about an honorable man, *The Life of Thomas More* (see chapter 4). John Man recounts the life of another astute man concerned with both business and literature in *Gutenberg: How One Man Remade the World with Words* (see chapter 5).

Bryson, Bill

Shakespeare: The World as Stage. Atlas Books, 2007. 199p. <u>Eminent Lives</u>. ISBN 9780060740221. Audiobook available.

Humorist Bill Bryson turns to biography with this book on William Shakespeare (1564–1616). Though he frequently states that little is really known about the Bard, Bryson tells a good story, following Shakespeare from his childhood in Stratford to his career as an actor and playwright in London and on tour around the country. He also includes many curious details about daily life in Elizabethan England, describes Shakespeare's friends, and reports on the grave political dangers for actors who displeased the queen. Readers do not have to enjoy Shakespeare's plays to enjoy this lively biography.

> **Subjects:** England; Group Discussion Books; London; Playwrights; Quick Reads; Shakespeare, William; Teen Reads

> **Now Try:** There are many entertaining books about the playwright, including *Will in the World: How Shakespeare Became Shakespeare* by Stephen Greenblatt, which examines the literary development of the playwright in the context of his dangerous world. In *The Lodger Shakespeare*, Charles Nicholl turns the playwright's life into a dark and compelling mystery story. Simon Hawke has written a series of mysteries with Shakespeare and his friend Symington Smythe as sleuths, starting with *Mystery of Errors*. Readers who enjoy Elizabethan-era stories will like *Christopher Marlowe: Poet & Spy* by Park Honan (see chapter 2). *Beethoven's Hair: An Extraordinary Odyssey and a Scientific Mystery Solved* by Russell Martin (see chapter 11) is another biography filled with curiously entertaining details about life in the past.

De Wilde, Laurent

Monk. Marlowe, 1997. 214p. ISBN 1569247404.

In his collection of insightful biographical essays, jazz pianist and music critic Laurent de Wilde describes the life, world, and impact of composer Thelonious Monk (1917–1982) in a way that only a jazz musician can. Using the language of the jazz culture, he details how Monk learned and perfected his technique, identifies the pianist's contemporaries, describes his important performances and recordings, and explains the silence of the musician's last ten years. Though acclaimed by critics, Monk struggled financially throughout his career and with mental illness in later years. This quick read will please Monk fans and general readers wanting to understand jazz culture.

> **Subjects:** African Americans; Biographical Essays; Composers; Jazz Musicians; Monk, Thelonious; Quick Reads

> **Now Try:** Thirty-nine essays about Monk and his legacy, written by music critics over the course of half a century, can be found in *The Thelonious Monk Reader*. Unlike Monk, Louis Armstrong made a fortune as the popular face of jazz music. In *Louis Armstrong: An Extravagant Life*, Laurence Bergreen fuels the debate over the innovative trumpeter's place in black history. When Alan Lomax from the Library of Congress found McKinley Morganfield on a sharecropping plantation in the Mississippi Delta in 1941, the farmer was supplementing his cotton crop income by selling moonshine and playing guitar at fish fries. Robert Gordon tells how the guitarist became known as the "Father of Chicago Blues" in *Can't Be Satisfied: The Life and Times of Muddy Waters*. From his teenaged big band years through bebop, cool, and funk, photographers captured Miles Davis with his horn on stage, in studios, and at bars. Richard Williams offers a look at the world of jazz musicians in his photobiography, *The Man in the Green Shirt: Miles Davis*.

Huxtable, Ada Louise

Frank Lloyd Wright. Lipper/Viking, 2004. 251p. <u>Penguin Lives</u>. ISBN 0670033421. Audiobook and large print available.

Ada Louise Huxtable tries to be even handed in assessing the many contradictory stories told by influential architect Frank Lloyd Wright (1867–1959) in his books and interviews. In her concise biography she examines each of the major stories from several viewpoints, revealing that often the truth is not really known. Even his birth date and birthplace are still debated by Wright scholars. Wright was charming, usually in debt, and absolutely certain of his place in history as the most influential architect ever. A choice read for those who like outrageous characters.

> **Subjects:** Architects; Quick Reads; Wright, Frank Lloyd

> **Now Try:** Wright described his work, explained his philosophy, and discussed incidents in his life in *An Autobiography*. With so many mysteries still unresolved, Wright's life is ripe for fictional accounts, such as *Loving Frank* by Nancy Horan, *Murder in Perspective* by Keith Miles, and *The Architect* by Levin Meyer. Ayn Rand's novel *The Fountainhead* includes a character reputed to be modeled after Wright, a claim that both Rand and Wright disputed. Wright's ideas about organic architecture came from his mentor and boss, Louis Sullivan, a famous architect in his own right. Robert C. Twombly describes the rise and fall of Sullivan's career in *Louis Sullivan: His Life and Work*. Poet Robert Frost, a contemporary of Wright, was a self-assured genius who reportedly disparaged all other poets. In *Robert Frost: A Biography*, Jeffrey Meyers counters harsh portrayals of the poet and argues that he was the most influential poet of his time.

Hyland, William G.

George Gershwin: A New Biography. Praeger, 2003. 279p. ISBN 0275981118.

The piano hoisted up to the second floor apartment was for Ira Gershwin, who had asked to take music lessons. According to the family story, without benefit of any instruction, Ira's twelve-year-old brother George Gershwin (1898–1937) immediately sat down and played a tune that he had learned from watching a player piano. Growing up in New York City, the country's musical capital, the brothers shared an interest in the lively songs of vaudeville and Tin Pan Alley. George absorbed it all effortlessly, began composing, and quickly moved beyond popular song to opera and orchestral composition. In this collection of biographical essays, admiring scholar William G. Hyland describes the brilliant and tragically brief life of a musical genius.

> **Subjects:** Biographical Essays; Brothers; Composers; Gershwin, George; New York City

> **Now Try:** George's brother Ira was a quieter, more deliberate artist who worked with many of the composers on Broadway. Philip Furia examines Ira's career in *Ira Gershwin: The Art of the Lyricist*. Though he never learned to read music, Irving Berlin wrote more than 1,500 songs and is celebrated as the master of the Broadway musical. Edward Jablonski describes the long career of the composer of "Cheek to Cheek," "There's No Business like Show Business," and "White Christmas" in *Irving Berlin: American Troubadour*. Novelist Jerome Charyn describes a later and different New York in three memoirs: *The Dark Lady from Belorusse; The Black Swan: A Memoir;* and *Bronx Boy: A Memoir*. Stephen Crane was a young writer with apparently limitless talent. Linda H. Davis recounts how Crane's short but well-traveled life as reporter and

novelist was ended by tuberculosis at age twenty-eight in *Badge of Courage: The Life of Stephen Crane* (see chapter 6).

Kavanagh, Julie

Nureyev: The Life. Pantheon Books, 2007. 782p. ISBN 9780375405136.

Born on a train that was skirting the coast of Lake Baikal, with his mother and family uprooted to join his military father on the Soviet–Manchurian border, the life of ballet dancer Rudolf Nureyev (1938–1993) begins with a scene reminiscent of a Russian novel. While the newborn was carried in a train car for military families, farther back were "enemies of the nation" on their way to eastern gulags. Throughout his somewhat privileged early life, protected by his talent, the dancer would often sidestep the dangers of Soviet society, but in 1961 he dramatically defected to the West. Dancer Julie Kavanagh completes the story with a full account of Nureyev's acclaimed ballet career in Paris, London, and New York, and of his secret life as a homosexual.

> **Subjects:** Ballet Dancers; Homosexuals; Nureyev, Rudolf; Soviet Union

> **Now Try:** Capitalizing on his notoriety, Nureyev published his own account of his young life soon after his defection. Richard Avedon contributed the photographs to *Nureyev: An Autobiography*. Prima ballerina Margot Fonteyn was one of Nureyev's principal partners after his defection. Her life is told in *Margot Fonteyn: A Life* by Meredith Daneman. The second great Russian dancer to defect from the Soviet Union was Mikhail Baryshnikov. Gennady Smakov focuses on the dancer's years in Russia, the defection, and his immediate success in the United States in *Baryshnikov: From Russia to the West*. Painter Marc Chagall left Belarus for life on an Israeli kibbutz and later escaped the Nazis in Vichy France. Jonathan Wilson recounts his dramatic life and the development of his art in *Marc Chagall* (see this chapter). Willem de Kooning was a Dutch artist who made a dramatic escape to America in 1926. Mark Stevens and Annalyn Swan describe the notorious life of the modern artist in *de Kooning: An American Master* (see this chapter).

King, Ross

Michelangelo & the Pope's Ceiling. Walker, 2003. 373p. ISBN 0802713955. Large print available.

Michelangelo Buonarroti (1475–1564) was a rude, scruffy-looking sculptor who accepted many commissions but completed few. What he completed, however, was exquisite. That's why Pope Julius II insisted in 1508 that the artist paint the ceiling of the Vatican's Sistine Chapel. The work took four stress-filled years, during which Michelangelo juggled the family finances and oversaw his shiftless brothers while designing scaffolding and inventing new pigments and methods to apply them. Ross King tells the story of the artist against a backdrop of Italian wars, plague, and the religious fanaticism of Savonarola. Ross's effortless storytelling will especially please readers interested in art and history, as well as those who enjoy a good story.

> **Subjects:** Architects; Buonarroti, Michelangelo; Group Discussion Books; Italy; Julius II, Pope; Painters; Renaissance; Rome; Sculptors; Sistine Chapel

Now Try: Michelangelo never wrote about himself, but the novelist Irving Stone and his wife Jean constructed an "autobiography" from the sculpture's letters, *I, Michelangelo, Sculptor* after Stone had published *The Agony and the Ecstasy*, his popular novel about the Italian's life. Michelangelo also wrote poetry, which has most recently been translated in *Complete Poems and Selected Letters of Michelangelo* by Creighton E. Gilbert. Although Pope Julius II succeeded in persuading Michelangelo to complete the Sistine Chapel ceiling, he failed in dictating the marriage partners for his daughter. Caroline P. Murphy describes a woman with as great a love of wealth and power as her father in *The Pope's Daughter: The Extraordinary Life of Felice della Rovere*. Ross King has written several popular histories of art and architecture, including *Brunelleschi's Dome: How a Renaissance Genius Reinvented Architecture* and *The Judgment of Paris: The Revolutionary Decade That Gave the World Impressionism*.

Lear, Linda

Beatrix Potter: A Life in Nature. St. Martin's Press, 2007. 583p. ISBN 9780312369347.

The rabbits that she kept as pets were always Beatrix Potter's (1866–1843) favorite subjects for drawing. Raised in a comfortable family, being told many folk and fairy tales, and given time to draw, Beatrix developed into a talented scientific illustrator before she turned to writing children's books. In this admiring biography, Linda Lear continues Potter's story well beyond her success in publishing and the tragic death of her first fiancé, telling how the artist became a successful farmer and an important leader in the movement to conserve the Lake District of England.

> **Subjects:** Children's Authors; Farmers; Great Britain; Illustrators; Naturalists; Potter, Beatrix; Women

> **Now Try:** Susan Wittag Albert has written a series of mysteries with Potter and her talking animals as sleuths, starting with *Tale of Hill Top Farm: The Cottage Tales of Beatrix Potter*. Like Potter, Maria Sibylla Merian enjoyed drawing from nature at an early age, her interest being butterflies and moths. Kim Todd recounts how Merian broke away from her marriage and the comforts of England to become an illustrator of tropical butterflies in *Chrysalis: Maria Sibylla Merian and the Secrets of Metamorphosis* (see chapter 1). Jane Goodall's childhood love was a toy chimpanzee. Dale Peterson describes the zoological studies and environmental work of the world's most famous primatologist in *Jane Goodall: The Woman Who Redefined Man* (see chapter 4).

Morgan, Judith, and Neil Morgan

Dr. Seuss & Mr. Geisel: A Biography. Random House, 1995. 345p. ISBN 0679416862.

If you have read *The Cat in the Cat*, you will not be surprised to learn that Theodor Geisel (1904–1991), better known as Dr. Seuss, was a mischievous, fun-loving spirit. What you might not expect is that the writer of outlandishly funny verse was shy and uncomfortable around children. Though his best-selling children's books brought him unexpected fame and financial security, he never truly overcame his self-doubt, and preferred to spend most of his time alone or with close friends and family. Judith Morgan and Neil Morgan describe Geisel's long career, with frequent periods of writer's block broken by moments of great inspiration, and chronicle the history of his wildly popular books.

> **Subjects:** Children's Authors; Dr. Seuss; Geisel, Theodor; Group Discussion Books; Illustrators

Now Try: Richard H. Minear shows Geisel's work before he became a children's author in *Dr. Seuss Goes to War: The World War II Editorial Cartoons of Theodor Seuss Geisel*. Maurice Sendak wrote the introduction, and Geisel's wife Helen wrote notes, for *The Secret Art of Dr. Seuss*, a collection of whimsical illustrations that were never used in his books. Geisel contemporary Benjamin Spock was a real doctor, the most trusted child psychologist in the middle years of the twentieth century. Thomas Maier examines Spock's professional career and family relationships in *Dr. Spock: An American Life* (see chapter 5). Children's authors Margret Rey and H. A. Rey were directly affected by the German invasion of France in World War II. *The Journey That Saved Curious George: The True Wartime Escape of Margret and H.A. Rey* by Louise Borden is an illustrated biography that will please children's literature fans.

Porter, Carolyn

William Faulkner. Oxford University Press, 2007. 199p. <u>Lives and Legacies</u>. ISBN 9780195310498.

William Faulkner (1897–1962) grew up in a family of storytellers in Oxford, Mississippi. His grandfather, his aunts, and his uncles entertained him with tall tales about their ancestors and neighbors. After failing to become a pilot during World War I and struggling as a poet, it was natural that William turned to writing fiction. He spent years under the tutelage of Sherwood Anderson in New Orleans and with other American expatriates in Paris, before he impressed critics with *The Sound and the Fury*. In this concise literary biography, Carolyn Porter deftly describes Faulkner's career, his books, and the impact he made on American literature.

Subjects: Faulkner, William; Mississippi; Novelists; Quick Reads

Now Try: The key to reading William Faulkner's novels, such as *The Sound and the Fury* and *As I Lay Dying*, is recognizing when the narrative voice changes. Faulkner wrote no autobiography, but several collections of his letters are available, as is *My Brother Bill: An Affectionate Reminiscence* by John Faulkner. In *Tom: The Unknown Tennessee Williams*, Lyle Leverich describes another complicated writer from Mississippi. In another title from the <u>Lives and Legacies</u> series from Oxford University Press, Craig Raine deftly clarifies the life and writing of an often misunderstood poet in *T. S. Eliot*.

Schumacher, Michael

Francis Ford Coppola: A Filmmaker's Life. Crown Publishers, 1999. 536p. ISBN 0517704455.

After taking many financial and artistic risks, Francis Ford Coppola (1939–) established himself as Hollywood's preeminent director in 1972 with his wildly successful film *The Godfather*. Then, with the long shooting of *Apocalypse Now* in the steamy jungle of the Philippines, beset by foul weather, Communist rebels, and the ill health of his cast, he almost lost everything—industry reputation, investments, and even his life. In this candid and analytical biography, Michael Schumacher tells many "on the set" stories to show how the former UCLA film student steered a dangerous course through many failures to ultimately be recognized as a master of his art.

Subjects: Coppola, Francis Ford; Movie Directors

Now Try: Coppola is one of a number of filmmakers who rose to prominence in the 1970s. Readers may also enjoy *Steven Spielberg: A Biography* by Joseph McBride and the updated edition of *Skywalking: The Life and Films of George Lucas*. John Huston took many risks in the making of his films, especially the 1951 box office hit *The African Queen*. He describes his life and career in his memoir, *An Open Book*. Director Billy Wilder spent over sixty years in film after escaping from Nazi Germany. Charlotte Chandler recounts his acclaimed career in *Nobody's Perfect: Billy Wilder, a Personal Biography* (see chapter 8).

Smiley, Jane

Charles Dickens. Lipper/Viking, 2002. 212p. Penguin Lives. ISBN 0670030775. Audiobook and large print available.

Charles Dickens (1812–1870) may have been the first international celebrity author. His serialized novels sold many newspapers in Britain, his lecture tour of American cities was wildly successful, and readers around the world bought his books. The social commentary in his novels and other writings even affected public policy. His family life, however, was unhappy: he separated from his wife, neglected his ten children, and conducted several romantic affairs. In this eloquently written and compact biography, novelist Jane Smiley mixes the details of Dickens's daily life with analysis of his famous novels.

Subjects: Dickens, Charles; Great Britain; Group Discussion Books; Novelists; Quick Reads

Now Try: Almost any public library will have at least one shelf of Dickens novels, including *David Copperfield, Great Expectations, Oliver Twist*, and *A Tale of Two Cities*. Mystery writer William J. Palmer has taken the liberty of making Dickens himself a character in his series of Victorian stories, beginning with *Detective and Mr. Dickens: Being an Account of the Macbeth Murders and the Strange Events Surrounding Them*. In America, Mark Twain became a favorite of the lecture circuit in the nineteenth century. Andrew Hoffman reveals the insecure and conflicted man behind the public figure that he became in *Inventing Mark Twain: The Lives of Samuel Langhorne Clemens*. While Dickens was exposing social ills in Great Britain, Henry Ward Beecher was arguing for abolition in America. Debby Applegate recounts his career and its controversies in *The Most Famous Man in America: The Biography of Henry Ward Beecher* (see chapter 10).

Teachout, Terry

All in the Dances: A Brief Life of George Balanchine. Harcourt, 2004. 185p. ISBN 0151-010889.

George Balanchine (1904–1983) is remembered for his ballets without plots, in which movement to music replaces story, and for founding the New York City Ballet and the School of American Ballet. This alone would be enough to ensure his reputation, but there is more. He was a demanding director who drove ballerinas, such as Vera Zorina, Maria Tallchief, and Suzanne Farrell, into either stardom or destruction, and was the central figure in the rise of modern ballet. Terry Teachout explains the importance of Balanchine in the world of dance in this biographical essay intended for new fans of ballet.

Subjects: Balanchine, George; Ballet; Biographical Essays; Choreographers; Quick Reads

Now Try: Balanchine included a review of his career and the ballets that he staged in his history of ballet, *Balanchine's Complete Stories of the Great Ballets*. Maria Tallchief danced for Balanchine's company for twenty years and was his wife for six. Her memoir is entitled *Maria Tallchief: America's Prima Ballerina*. Ballerina Suzanne Farrell also describes her professional and romantic relationships with Balanchine in her memoir, *Holding on to the Air: An Autobiography*. The Impressionist painter Edgar Degas was taken by the color and motion of ballet. Over half of his paintings depict dancers. *Degas: The Man and His Art* by Henri Loyrette is an attractively illustrated biography that describes his work among dancers.

Waldron, Ann

Eudora: A Writer's Life. Doubleday, 1998. 398p. ISBN 0385476477.

Because her mother was from West Virginia and her father was from Ohio, the opinions expressed in Eudora Welty's (1909–2001) home differed somewhat from the rest of Jackson, Mississippi, society. Of necessity Welty learned early that every story has many sides, according to Ann Waldron. Her book about the novelist and short story writer is a large collection of brief topical essays, each revealing a personal trait, identifying a friend, or telling a story. Welty's childhood, life in college, brief tenure in New York, and long residence in Mississippi are all lovingly described.

Subjects: Biographical Essays; Mississippi; Novelists; Welty, Eudora; Women

Now Try: Welty told a bit of her own life story in the slim volume *One Writer's Beginnings* and displayed her photography in *One Time, One Place: Mississippi in the Depression: A Snapshot Album*. Welty's novel *Delta Wedding* and *The Collected Stories of Eudora Welty* are enjoyable reading. A fuller account of Welty's life supported by quotes from letters is found in *Eudora Welty: A Biography* by Suzanne Marrs, a friend who overcame Welty's opposition to a biography and gained access to all her papers. In *The Habit of Being: Letters*, Southern novelist and short story author Flannery O'Connor's short life is described through her own correspondence with writers, editors, and friends. Novelist Mary Gordon recounts the influences on her life and writing in *Seeing Through Places: Reflections on Geography and Identity*.

Wilson, Jonathan

Marc Chagall. Nextbook/Schocken, 2007. 237p. Jewish Encounters. ISBN 9780-805242010.

By the time Marc Chagall (1887–1985) died at age ninety-seven, he had witnessed most of the events of twentieth-century history. He grew up in a poor Jewish neighborhood in Belarus; attended school in St. Petersburg, where he lived illegally; served as a Soviet art commissar; met the Dadaists and Surrealists in Paris in the 1920s; lived on early Jewish kibbutzim in Palestine; escaped from Vichy France in 1941; and helped decorate the United Nations headquarters in New York. He also created some of the century's most spiritually inspiring art. In this illustrated biography, Jonathan Wilson focuses on the artist's career, major works, and legacy.

Subjects: Artists; Chagall, Marc; Illustrated Biography; Jews; Painters; Russia

Now Try: To learn more about the artist's early life, read his memoir, *My Life*, written at age thirty-five. Several of the artists who lead the American modernist movement emigrated from Europe. Willem de Kooning stowed away on a steamer ship to reach the United States. Mark Stevens and Annalyn Swan describe his difficult career in *de Kooning: An American Master* (see this chapter). Like Chagall, Mozart's librettist, Lorenzo da Ponte, adapted to many economic and political cultures in his roguish life. Rodney Bolt recounts a life full of misadventure in *The Librettist of Venice: The Remarkable Life of Lorenzo da Ponte* (see this chapter). The Jewish Encounters series is a growing collection of books on Jewish topics, including *Benjamin Disraeli* by Adam Kirsch and *Maimonides* by Sherwin B. Nuland.

Wroe, Ann

Being Shelley: The Poet's Search for Himself. Pantheon Books, 2007. 452p. ISBN 9780-375424939.

Poet Percy Bysshe Shelley (1792–1822), living before atomic theory and a modern understanding of matter, wrote about the fusion of earth, water, air, and fire. While to Shelley's thinking all these elements governed daily life, man's spiritual nature reigned supreme, and his physical being was only its shadow. Assuming that what he thought meant more than his daily movements, Ann Wroe has written an elegantly inventive biography of Shelley, incorporating his poetry, prose, and drawings.

Subjects: Great Britain; Poets; Shelley, Percy Bysshe

Now Try: An attractive collection of Shelley's poetry with notes by his wife Mary Shelley is the Modern Library edition *The Complete Poems of Percy Bysshe Shelley*. Muriel Spark recounts the difficult life that Shelley's wife Mary led after his death in *Mary Shelley* (see this chapter). According to Catherine M. Andronik, Shelley and the other young men who wrote romantic poetry in the early 1800s were the rock stars of their time. She recounts stories of subversive behavior in *Wildly Romantic: The English Romantic Poets: The Mad, the Bad, and the Dangerous*. Like Shelley, Keats, and Byron, many rock stars died young. The Jim Morrison biography *No One Here Gets Out Alive* by Jerry Hopkins and Danny Sugerman (see chapter 6), *Scars of Sweet Paradise: The Life and Times of Janis Joplin* by Alice Echols (see chapter 6), and *Catch a Fire: The Life of Bob Marley* by Timothy White are modern tragedies aimed at fans of popular music.

Witnesses of an Era

A witness is a person who was present at an event or saw an incident as it unfolded. In a court of law, a witness is sworn to tell the truth before the court about a disputed matter of which he or she has firsthand knowledge; violating the trust of the court with false reports brings condemnation upon the eyewitness. The artists, writers, and other cultural figures in this section expressed their firsthand knowledge of life in their times through their paintings, novels, songs, and other works. The perceived truth of their works makes them valued pieces of cultural heritage that endure when other insincere and dishonest works fade from societal memory.

The subjects in the biographies in this section witnessed not only dramatic historical events, but also mundane moments of daily living. In *Samuel Pepys*, Stephen Coote recounts the life of a British diarist who witnessed the return to England of King

Charles II and survived the Great Fire of London. Miles Harvey describes the experiences of French botanical artist Jacques Le Moyne de Morgues, who survived the failure of a French colony in Florida in the sixteenth century, in *Painter in a Savage Land*. Pierre Assouline chronicles the world travels of an influential photographer who captured many dramatic moments on film in *Henri Cartier-Bresson: A Biography*. Douglas M. Parker tells how a gentle observer of life created many funny poems in *Ogden Nash: The Life and Work of America's Laureate of Light Verse*.

Rich descriptions of place and time fill these Cultural Biographies. The subjects were people of their times, and their important action was to create artistic works reflecting their environs and experiences. In these stories, biographers describe how societies shaped artists, composers, and musicians, who in turn shaped their cultures. These are compelling texts of different lengths that will especially appeal to readers interested in history.

Witnesses of an Era stories includes biographies of cultural figures whose works especially reflect the eras in which they lived. The settings of these books are richly detailed, and the stories explain how the subjects incorporated their knowledge of the times into their works. These works are especially appealing to readers interested in history.

Assouline, Pierre

Henri Cartier-Bresson: A Biography. Thames & Hudson, 2005. 280p. ISBN 9780500512234.

French photographer Henri Cartier-Bresson (1908–2004) had a knack for being on the spot to witness pivotal events and capture the climactic moment on film. After focusing on the creation of surrealistic images early in his career, he turned to photojournalism. In his still photographs and documentary films, he captured the horrors of the Spanish Civil War, the joy at the Liberation of Paris from the Nazis, the quiet of Mahatma Gandhi just before his assassination, and the unstoppable birth of the Communist government in China. He was also known for his evocative portraits of Jean Paul Sartre and Albert Camus. In this admiring biography, Pierre Assouline portrays Cartier-Bresson as a visionary, who imparted knowledge through photography to make us see our world as it is.

Subjects: Cartier-Bresson, Henri; Group Discussion Books; Photographers; Teen Reads

Now Try: Evocative collections of Cartier-Bresson's photography include *America in Passing, The Face of Asia*, and *Scrapbook*. His occasional essays have been collected in *The Mind's Eye: Writings on Photography and Photographers*. Like Cartier-Bresson, newspaper reporter Nellie Bly traveled the world to witness dramatic events as they unfolded. Brooke Kroeger recounts Bly's adventures in *Nellie Bly: Daredevil, Reporter, Feminist* (see chapter 1). Rather than witnessing events, Giuseppi Garibaldi sought out revolutions to join. Lucy Riall recounts the career of the international activist in *Garibaldi: Invention of a Hero* (see chapter 3).

Bailey, Anthony

Vermeer: A View of Delft. Henry Holt, 2001. 272p. ISBN 0805067183.

Johannes Vermeer (1632–1675) remains as much a mystery as his paintings. Anthony Bailey, who often writes for *The New Yorker*, used the few remaining documents about the artist in constructing this story about a man who occasionally painted and constantly struggled with debt. Despite his small portfolio, Vermeer became well known among his peers as a master of color and light. This well-illustrated biography with descriptions of Delft and its art community will likely attract readers interested in art and culture.

> **Subjects:** Delft; Painters; Vermeer, Johannes

> **Now Try:** The scarcity of verifiable information on Vermeer's life and personality works to the benefit of novelists. Two popular works incorporating Vermeer as a character are *Girl with a Pearl Earring* by Tracy Chevalier and *Girl in Hyacinth Blue* by Susan Vreeland. The details of the life of Johann Gutenberg, the fifteenth-century inventor of the printing press, are also sparse. As reconstructed by John Man in *Gutenberg: How One Man Remade the World with Words* (see chapter 5), the printer lived the life of a small businessman concerned both with his product and the possibility of expanding his market. Vermeer's paintings of women inspired painter Mary Cassatt, who focused on feminine portraits. Griselda Pollock describes the career of an American artist, spent mostly in France, in *Mary Cassatt: Painter of Modern Women.*

Burstein, Andrew

The Original Knickerbocker: The Life of Washington Irving. Basic Books, 2007. 420p. ISBN 9780465008537.

Washington Irving's life (1783–1859) was, as he put it in a letter to his niece, "full of shifting scenes and sudden transformations." Born in 1783 and named for the hero of the American Revolution, he grew up in then provincial New York, where he read adventure novels by candle light. Joining his politically active older brothers, he became a writer for Aaron Burr's short-lived newspaper *Morning Chronicle*, and then, for his health, went on a series of travels in Europe, during which he wrote diaries. Returning to the United States, he became a lawyer, soldier, diplomat, and writer of essays, biography, and fiction. Andrew Burstein profiles Irving as an energetic man attuned to the industry and expansion of his era.

> **Subjects:** Humorists; Irving, Washington; Novelists; Travelers

> **Now Try:** Irving was too busy writing fictional work and biographies to bother with autobiography. Even his travel pieces are more journalistic and tend to slip into fiction. The Library of America has published two volumes collecting his writings: *Washington Irving: Bracebridge Hall—Tales of a Traveller—the Alhambra; Washington Irving: History, Tales, and Sketches*; and *Washington Irving: Three Western Narratives*. Irving began his writing career working for New York statesman Aaron Burr, whose notorious life is assessed in *Fallen Founder: The Life of Aaron Burr* by Nancy Isenberg (see chapter 10). Like Irving, Nathaniel Hawthorne moved in both literary circles and the world of politics. Brenda Wineapple portrays the author of *The Scarlet Letter* as a maddeningly complex man filled with conflicting values, much like the age in which he lived, in *Hawthorne: A Life* (see this chapter). Mark Twain expanded the travel genre

that Washington Irving pioneered. Ron Powers chronicles the career of the humorist in *Mark Twain* (see this chapter).

Claridge, Laura

Norman Rockwell: A Life. Random House, 2001. 544p. ISBN 0375504532.

The public image of Norman Rockwell (1894–1978) is of an all-American grandfather winking at the sly mischief of a couple of kids. Through his drawings in *Boy's Life* and covers on *The Saturday Evening Post*, his name became known nationally, a sort of trademark for wholesomeness. According to Laura Claridge, few knew about the complicated life and feelings of the sensitive man behind the art. In this sympathetic biography, she vividly recounts stories about his family, bouts of depression, and the creation of his most famous paintings.

> **Subjects:** Illustrators; Mental Depression; Painters; Rockwell, Norman

> **Now Try:** Rockwell recounted the stories behind some of his most important works in *Norman Rockwell: My Adventures as an Illustrator*. Both children and adults enjoyed reading daily *Peanuts* cartoons in the newspaper. None suspected the deep depression and unhappy marriage that tormented its creator. David Michaelis reveals the troubled life of Charles Schulz in *Schulz and Peanuts: A Biography* (see this chapter). A. A. Milne was a successful humorist and playwright before he published his children's stories. Ann Thwaite tells how Milne began to regret the fame of his children's stories because they overshadowed his adult work, in *A. A. Milne: The Man Behind Winnie-the-Pooh*. Farmer and amateur geologist James Hutton was a gentlemanly character, well respected in eighteenth-century England. Jack Repcheck tells how Hutton laid the groundwork for Charles Darwin's theories of evolution in *The Man Who Found Time: James Hutton and the Discovery of the Earth's Antiquity* (see chapter 11).

Coote, Stephen

🏵 *Samuel Pepys: A Life.* Palgrave, 2000. 386p. ISBN 0312239297.

Samuel Pepys (1633–1703) is best known as a witness to a volatile era of British history. He saw Charles I beheaded, sailed with the fleet that brought Charles II back from Holland, and survived the Great Fire of London. As a diarist, he wrote about these events, as well as war, science, the theater, and plague. What he did not reveal in his diaries were intimate details of his own life, including his neglect of his family and his association with powerful political allies. In this admiring book, Stephen Coote establishes Pepys as a savvy survivor of a tumultuous time and an able bureaucrat who rose to become a member of Parliament and secretary to the admiral of the Royal Navy.

> **Subjects:** Bureaucrats; Diarists; England; Pepys, Samuel

> **Awards:** Whitbread Biography Award

> **Now Try:** The University of California Press has published a ten-volume, complete text of *The Diary of Samuel Pepys*, but most readers may choose a one-volume selection of entries, such as that from Modern Library. Niccolo Machiavelli wrote the book on political power, but he did not have the survival skills of Pepys. Ross King describes the rise and fall of the

Italian bureaucrat in *Machiavelli: Philosopher of Power* (see chapter 10). Like Pepys, Marie Tussaud witnessed an epic human tragedy. Kate Berridge tells how Tussaud re-created incidents from the French Revolution and crime scenes in her museum of wax figures in *Madame Tussaud: A Life in Wax* (see chapter 9). Many readers have read selections from William Clark's diary in books about the Lewis and Clark Expedition across North America. Landon Y. Jones continues the story in *William Clark and the Shaping of the West* (see chapter 1).

Elledge, Scott

E. B. White: A Biography. W. W. Norton, 1984. 400p. ISBN 0393017710.

Not many subjects have the opportunity to proofread their own biographies. E. B. White (1899–1985), author of the beloved children's book *Charlotte's Web* and staff writer for *The New Yorker*, said that Scott Elledge's book about his life was too long. White, who was the joint author of the writers' handbook *The Elements of Style*, found misspellings and a few factual errors as well. Overall, however, he approved of the mostly complimentary account of his long life, featuring his relationship with *New Yorker* founder Harold Ross, his romance with his wife Katharine Angell White, and his friendship with the comic genius James Thurber. These stories about the nature-loving man whose friends called him Andy will charm his fans and win new readers to his children's books, essays, and letters.

Subjects: Children's Authors; Essayists; *New Yorker, The* (magazine); White, E. B.

Now Try: An *E. B. White Reader* is a good introduction to the author, as it includes samples from his many writings. For deeper insight into the author's thoughts, readers may try *The Letters of E. B. White*. At *The New Yorker* and later in his career, White was associated with the humorist James Thurber. Thurber tells of his childhood in *My Life and Hard Times*, while Neil A. Grauer sympathetically chronicles the writer's career in *Remember Laughter: A Life of James Thurber*. Like the Whites, Queen Elizabeth II of England and Prince Philip have also maintained a long marriage. Gyles Brandreth tells family stories to interest and encourage readers in *Philip and Elizabeth: Portrait of a Royal Marriage* (see chapter 8).

Gordon, Charlotte

Mistress Bradstreet: The Untold Life of America's First Poet. New York: Little, Brown, 2005. 337p. ISBN 0316169048.

Anne Bradstreet (1612–1672) came to America in 1630, arriving on the *Arbella* with her husband, Simon;, her parents, Thomas and Dorothy Dudley; and her three sisters and one brother. She was only eighteen at the time, but had been married for two years, and she was unhappy about coming to the wilderness of Massachusetts Bay Colony. Able to get parchment from her father, who had taught her the mechanics of poetry as a child in England, she began to write verse for her family and learned friends. She never expected her work to be published. Charlotte Gordon tells an engaging story of a Puritan woman who obeyed the rules of her patriarchal religion yet still advanced the idea of gender equality.

Subjects: Bradstreet, Anne; Massachusetts Bay Colony; Poets; Women

Now Try: Bradstreet's more personal poems have been collected in a small volume, *To My Husband and Other Poems*. The life of women was difficult in the early colonies. A taste of the hardships and toil can be found in *A Midwife's Tale: The Life of Martha Ballard, Based on Her Diary, 1785–1812* by Laurel Thatcher Ulrich (see chapter 4). One hundred years after Bradstreet, it was still rare for a woman, much less an African American, to write poetry. Henry Louis Gates tells how the genuineness of Phyllis Wheatley's poetry was debated among learned men in *Trials of Phillis Wheatley: America's First Black Poet and Her Encounters with the Founding Fathers*. In the twentieth century, Sylvia Plath's poetry and that of her husband led to jealousy, bitterness, and suicide. Diane Middlebrook recounts the poetry-driven relationship of Sylvia Plath and Ted Hughes in *Her Husband: Hughes and Plath—A Marriage*.

Harvey, Miles

Painter in a Savage Land: The Strange Saga of the First European Artist in North America. Random House, 2008. 338p. ISBN 9781400061204.

In 1564, French botanical artist Jacques Le Moyne de Morgues (1533–1588) arrived in Florida with 300 other hopeful colonists. By the next year he was one of only a few who had survived famine and attacks by the unfriendly Timucau Indians and was able to return to France. While in Florida he painted numerous small canvases with images of the flora and fauna, the settlement, and the peninsula's native people. These pictures have been rediscovered in the twenty-first century and now garner interest from archeologists and art museums. Miles Harvey includes dozens of Le Moyne's drawings in this investigative biography of an adventurous artist.

Subjects: Botanical Artists; Famines; Florida; Native Americans; Le Moyne de Morgues, Jacques; Timucau Indians

Now Try: Young scientist Charles Darwin served as the naturalist and illustrator on board the HMS *Beagle* during its five-year exploratory journey. David Quammen recounts how Darwin spent the rest of his life studying his observations from that voyage in *The Reluctant Mr. Darwin: An Intimate Portrait of Charles Darwin* (see chapter 11). In the 1830s painter George Catlin made four tours of the American frontier to record the life of the Native Americans. The Smithsonian American Art Museum profiled the artist in the illustrated *George Catlin and His Indian Gallery*. About seventy years later, photographer Edward S. Curtis began his thirty-year effort to photograph the native tribes of the United States. In *Sacred Legacy: Edward S. Curtis and the North American Indian*, the National Geographic Society has reproduced more than 200 images with commentary about Curtis and the tribes that he visited. Another European settlement that failed to take root in America was the English colony of Roanoke. Lee Miller speculates why the settlers disappeared in *Roanoke: Solving the Mystery of the Lost Colony*.

Hughes, Kathryn

George Eliot: The Last Victorian. Farrar, Straus & Giroux, 1998. 383p. ISBN 0374161380. Audiobook available.

Mary Ann Evans (1819–1880) was born in an age when women had few prospects for self-determination. She was expected to marry, obey a husband, raise children, and be satisfied with the praise that she might be given if she did these things well. Like Queen Victoria, her contemporary, she was unable to vote, yet she rose beyond her assigned role to become an important figure in nineteenth-century England. In this psychological account, Kathryn Hughes describes how Evans became the author George Eliot and found happiness outside the constrictions of Victorian society. Eliot withstood criticism from the British public for living unmarried with her lover, for which Hughes portrays her to be as brave as the unconventional heroines of her novels.

> **Subjects:** Eliot, George; Evans, Mary Ann; Great Britain; Group Discussion Books; Novelists; Women
>
> **Now Try:** Eliot was the author of novels set in the English countryside, including *Adam Bede, Mill on the Floss, Middlemarch,* and *Silas Marner.* French novelist George Sand was much more public than Eliot with her political opinions and sexuality. Benita Eisler's *Naked in the Marketplace: The Lives of George Sand* is a novel-like account of Sand and her relationships with three lovers and her mother. In *The Sex Side of Life: Mary Ware Dennett's Pioneering Battle for Birth Control and Sex Education* (see chapter 9), Constance M. Chen recounts how Dennett overcame her Victorian upbringing to work for birth control, sex education, and the rights of women. Richmond, Virginia, native Elizabeth Van Lew was another courageous woman who stood against society. Historian Elizabeth R. Varon tells how Van Lew worked for the abolition of slavery and the victory of the Union from the capital of the Confederacy in *Southern Lady, Yankee Spy: The True Story of Elizabeth Van Lew, a Union Agent in the Heart of the Confederacy* (see chapter 3).

Lingeman, Richard

Sinclair Lewis: Rebel from Main Street. Random House, 2002. 659p. ISBN 0679438238.
When Sinclair Lewis (1885–1951) died in Rome, most of his friends, critics, and readers were surprised to learn that he wanted to be buried back in Sauk Center, Minnesota. His novels had satirized small-town life, and he had spent his later years far from his roots. Why would the author of *Main Street* and *Babbitt* want to go home? In his sympathetic book, Richard Lingeman presents the Nobel Prize winner as a caring man, a friend to populist causes, and a key figure in American literature. Living the high life, however, did not save him from loneliness.

> **Subjects:** Lewis, Sinclair; Minnesota; Novelists
>
> **Now Try:** Lewis decries the hypocrisy in town and city life in his famous novels *Main Street, Babbitt, Arrowsmith,* and *Elmer Gantry.* Saul Bellow was an astute observer of life in the city of Chicago, noting characters of high and low class. James Atlas connects the events of Bellow's life with the themes and characters in his many stories and novels in *Bellow: A Biography.* Literary critic Alfred Kazin was a leading voice in the intellectual world of New York City, yet he was unable to maintain good relations with his wife and children. Richard M. Cook chronicles the literary career of a lonely man in *Alfred Kazin: A Biography* (see this chapter). Like Lewis, Russian author Alexander Solzhenitsyn was very critical of his birthplace, but ultimately he wanted to return to it. D. M. Thomas chronicles the difficult life of a dissident in *Alexander Solzhenitsyn: A Century in His Life* (see chapter 9).

Marcus, Leonard S.

Margaret Wise Brown. Beacon Press, 1992. 337p. ISBN 0807070483.
Margaret Wise Brown (1910–1952), a struggling poet and short story author, became a student teacher at Bank Street School in Greenwich Village. She later said that she learned honesty from the second graders at the school, which helped her

write picture books for young children, including the classic *Goodnight Moon*. Enjoying companionship and recognition, she sought artists to collaborate with her on her many books, became an editor and mentor to other children's book authors, and attended countless parties. Independent, she never married, though she had lovers and was engaged when she suddenly died from an embolism. According to Leonard S. Marcus, who writes intimately about his subject, the highly creative Brown is now viewed as a key author in the golden age of the American picture book.

Subjects: Brown, Margaret Wise; Children's Authors; Women

Now Try: Marcus also wrote *The Making of Good Night Moon: A 50th Anniversary Retrospective*, describing Brown's ideas and showing the objects that she used as models for her classic children's picture book. Like Brown, actress Katherine Hepburn was an independent woman. Scott Berg describes her life in *Kate Remembered* (see chapter 8). Novelist George Eliot defied Victorian strictures to live with a lover. In her psychological account, Kathryn Hughes chronicles the life and career of the author of *Middlemarch* in *George Eliot: The Last Victorian* (see this chapter). Country music singer Patsy Cline also died suddenly in an airplane crash. Her soap opera-like life is described in *I Fall to Pieces: The Music and Life of Patsy Cline* by Mark Bego.

Mercer-Taylor, Peter

The Life of Mendelssohn. Cambridge University Press, 2000. 238p. Musical Lives. ISBN 0521630258.

Felix Mendelssohn (1809–1847) was a model nineteenth-century musical gentleman. The son of a wealthy banker from Berlin, he received early training in violin and composition and had written several polished pieces by age ten. During adolescence he performed with his sister Fanny for audiences across Europe; wrote music criticism; and championed the forgotten works of Bach, Mozart, and Beethoven. In this admiring biography, Mendelssohn scholar Peter Mercer-Taylor reveals that the composer's seemingly idyllic life was complicated by fears of anti-Semitism, the demands of royal patrons, and the ill health that shortened his life.

Subjects: Composers; Jews; Mendelssohn-Bartholdy, Felix; Prodigies

Now Try: Mercer-Taylor's book on Mendelssohn is part of the Musical Lives series from Cambridge University Press, a series of concise illustrated biographies that describe the lives and works of composers without use of technical language. *The Life of Bellini* by John Rosselli and *The Life of Schubert* by Christopher H. Gibbs are also included in the series. Wolfgang Amadeus Mozart was another child prodigy whose life was cut short by ill health. Peter Gay succinctly profiles the Austrian composer in *Mozart* (see chapter 6), a title in the Penguin Lives series. Denys Finch Hatton, a romantic figure, was living a seemingly idyllic life in East Africa when he met Karen Blixen, known as the author Isak Dinesen. Sara Wheeler tells a more modern story about untimely death in *Too Close to the Sun: The Audacious Life and Times of Denys Finch Hatton* (see chapter 6).

Parker, Douglas M.

Ogden Nash: The Life and Work of America's Laureate of Light Verse. Ivan R. Dee, 2005. 316p. ISBN 156663637X

Poet Ogden Nash (1902–1971) shone as a bright spot in the dark time of the Great Depression. He became popular when his humorous verse began to appear regularly in *The New Yorker, Saturday Evening Post,* and other magazines. Based in New York, Nash became very involved in the literary scene of the 1920s and 1930s. He knew Dorothy Parker, F. Scott Fitzgerald, E. B. White, and many other writers. Douglas M. Parker describes this world and Nash's family life and tells much about mid-twentieth-century publishing in this serious biography filled with lighthearted stories.

> **Subjects:** Humorists; Nash, Ogden; Poets
>
> **Now Try:** Nash's letters to his wife and daughters include many funny verses and serious concerns. A selection of these entertaining dispatches are found in *Loving Letters from Ogden Nash: A Family Album.* Comic Groucho Marx was at the height of his popularity during the Great Depression. Like Parker, Stefan Kanfer has included many humorous quips and stories in his otherwise bittersweet book, *Groucho: The Life and Times of Julius Henry Marx* (see chapter 8). French chef Julia Child was a very funny lady. Laura Shapiro reveals the great effort Child made to get her culinary training against a background of her husband's diplomatic work in *Julia Child.* Readers who enjoy the silliness of Nash's verses often also enjoy the humorous essays by newspaper columnist Art Buchwald. Buchwald revealed his difficult childhood in *Leaving Home: A Memoir.*

Partridge, Elizabeth

This Land Was Made for You and Me: The Life and Songs of Woody Guthrie. Viking, 2002. 216p. ISBN 0670035351.

Wandering troubadour Woody Guthrie (1912–1967) was the model for twentieth-century folksingers. Caring little for comfort or wealth, he followed the never-ending stream of American crises, writing songs about the Great Depression, the Dust Bowl, labor unrest, McCarthyism, and civil rights. Though Huntington's disease struck him in his late forties, and he died relatively young, many of his songs and his legend inspired the next generation of singers/songwriters. In this admiring illustrated biography, Elizabeth Partridge chronicles the constant movement of a man who would not sit still when there was a reason to sing.

> **Subjects:** Activists; Folksingers; Guthrie, Woody; Photographic Biography; Quick Reads; Teen Reads
>
> **Now Try:** Guthrie wrote about wandering the country in the company of hobos during the Great Depression in his autobiography, *Bound for Glory.* James Agee and Walker Evans depicted the same era in their photodocumentary *Let Us Now Praise Famous Men,* as did John Steinbeck in his novel *The Grapes of Wrath.* Folksinger Pete Seeger first met Woody Guthrie in 1940 at a benefit for the Dust Bowl refugees. Seeger describes his association with Guthrie and his life as an activist in *The Incompleat Folksinger.* Another wandering troubadour and free spirit is profiled in *A Boy Named Shel: The Life and Times of Shel Silverstein* by Lisa Rogak (see chapter 8). With his work for Farm Aid, John Mellancamp has become a musical folk hero of rural America. Heather Johnson tells about his life and work in *Born in a Small Town: The John Mellencamp Story.*

Powers, Ron

Mark Twain: A Life. Free Press, 2005. 722p. ISBN 9780743248990.

Samuel Clemens's (1835–1910) first complaint in life was that, unlike cats and dogs, he did not have a tail. His amused uncle John cut out a paper tail for the toddler, who was just learning to speak, rewarding his humorous remark. Later, as the author Mark Twain, he would make a career of such surprisingly humorous remarks, often satirizing culture and society. He began by writing entertaining reports for newspapers in Nevada and California, then moved to the East Coast to capitalize on the lecture circuit, and there caught the attention of William Dean Howells of *The Atlantic* magazine, whose favorable review increased sales of Twain's *Innocents Abroad*. In this epic biography, historian Ron Powers focuses on Twain's friendships, family life, and struggles to live within his means in the opulence of the Gilded Age.

Subjects: Clemens, Samuel; Humorists; Journalists; Novelists; Twain, Mark

Now Try: Twain is a character in his travel books, such as *Innocents Abroad* and *Life on the Mississippi*, which stray heavily into fiction; and he drew heavily from his experiences to write his novels *The Adventures of Tom Sawyer* and *The Adventures of Huckleberry Finn*. Groucho Marx was another American humorist with a knack for great one-liners. In the candid *Groucho: The Life and Times of Julius Henry Marx* (see chapter 8), Stefan Kanfer celebrates the brilliance of Marx's comedy, which includes many jokes and dialogue from vaudeville, radio, and movie routines. Like Twain, his contemporary Ulysses S. Grant turned to writing to pay his debts, accumulated while he was living the good life. William S. McFeely describes Grant's life, career, and retirement in the illustrated *Ulysses S. Grant: An Album* (see chapter 3). Like Twain in his prime on the lecture circuit, Buffalo Bill Cody was a pioneering entertainer who knew how to please the public. Robert A. Carter describes a life spanning the time between the opening of the American frontier and the modern age in *Buffalo Bill Cody: The Man Behind the Legend* (see chapter 5).

Rampersad, Arnold

Ralph Ellison: A Biography. Alfred A. Knopf, 2007. 657p. ISBN 9780375408274.

Ralph Ellison (1914–1994) never finished his second novel. Although some critics cite this failure to depict him as a disappointing figure, Arnold Rampersad considers the writer's life an unqualified success. Though criticized by some blacks as an "Uncle Tom," his novel *Invisible Man* is considered by many to be one of the masterpieces of the twentieth century, and his essays and short stories were published in distinguished journals and magazines. After growing up in Oklahoma, he briefly rode the rails like a hobo; attended the Tuskegee Institute (but did not graduate); and befriended many artists, musicians, and writers. Dabbling in photography, traveling the world, and doing what he pleased, Ellison's life proved intellectually stimulating, not a tragedy to be regretted.

Subjects: African Americans; Ellison, Ralph Waldo; Novelists; Oklahoma

Now Try: In addition to *Invisible Man*, several books by Ellison are available, including *The Collected Essays of Ralph Ellison* and *Flying Home and Other*

Stories. Like Ellison, black author Ernest J. Gaines has published a few highly acclaimed books. In *Mozart and Leadbelly: Stories And Essays*, he combines memorable short fiction with autobiographical pieces. Ellison is often compared to his contemporary, James Baldwin. James Campbell concentrates on Baldwin's writings and public causes, only mentioning his private affairs when they illuminate the career, in his admiring biography *Talking at the Gates: A Life of James Baldwin*. Black novelist Chester Himes wrote many books, but he found American readers reluctant to buy them. James Sallis describes the life of an author who found more success as an expatriate in *Chester Himes: A Life* (see this section).

Reynolds, David S.

🏵 *Walt Whitman's America: A Cultural Biography*. Alfred A. Knopf, 1995. 671p. ISBN 0394580230.

Everything that Walt Whitman (1819–1892) experienced went into his poems. He celebrated all the affairs of nature and humankind in *Leaves of Grass*, his great collection of poetry, which he rewrote and expanded many times. The power of storms, the horror of war, the march of industry, and sexual relations of all sorts fill his poetry, which was sometimes denounced by political and religious leaders. According to David S. Reynolds in his collection of essays on the poet, Whitman tried to live simply, but misfortune and distrust complicated his uncommon life.

Subjects: Biographical Essays; Poets; Whitman, Walt

Awards: Bancroft Prize in American History

Now Try: Of the many editions of *Leaves of Grass*, the 1891 "Deathbed Edition" (which Whitman claimed was complete) is now the most commonly used. A much shorter first edition is also in print. The Library of America has combined all the poetry with selected prose pieces in *Walt Whitman: Complete Poetry and Collected Prose*. Whitman wrote his book to answer a call by Ralph Waldo Emerson for Americans to create their own form of poetry. *Emerson: The Mind on Fire* by Robert D. Richardson clarifies the sequence of influential ideas as they developed in Emerson's thoughts. Susan Cheever puts Whitman's nineteenth-century contemporaries into the context of their collective society in *American Bloomsbury: Louisa May Alcott, Ralph Waldo Emerson, Margaret Fuller, Nathaniel Hawthorne, and Henry David Thoreau: Their Lives, Their Loves, Their Work* (see chapter 6). In the twentieth century, poet Alan Ginsberg enjoyed personal freedoms of which Whitman only dreamed. Bill Morgan tells how Ginsberg strove to protect civil liberties in *I Celebrate Myself: The Somewhat Private Life of Allen Ginsberg* (see this chapter).

Richardson, Robert D.

🏵 *William James: In the Maelstrom of American Modernism*. Houghton Mifflin, 2006. 622p. ISBN 9780618433254.

There was nothing William James (1842–1910) could not do. As a member of one of America's most brilliant families, James started his academic life studying drawing, painting, chemistry, medicine, and comparative anatomy. From there he became a key figure in the fields of psychology, philosophy, religious studies, educational theory, and literature. He is still frequently quoted in scholarly circles. In this detailed account of a great mind, Robert D. Richardson states that James can be compared to Plato and Aristotle.

Subjects: Harvard University; James, William; James Family; Philosophers; Psychologists; Scholars

Awards: Bancroft Prize

Now Try: Basic texts for James readers are *The Principles of Psychology, The Philosophy of William James: Selected from His Chief Works,* and *The Varieties of Religious Experience: A Study in Human Nature.* William James's brother (the novelist Henry James) and sister (the feminist Alice James) were also well-known intellectuals. Paul Fisher recounts their childhoods and careers within the context of family and friends in *House of Wits: An Intimate Portrait of the James Family.* Paul Robeson was another multitalented individual. *Paul Robeson: Artist and Citizen* (see chapter 9) includes a collection of essays from several Robeson experts about the intellectual, artistic, and athletic legacies of an African American who was active before the rise of the civil rights movement. *Einstein* by Walter Isaacson and *W. E. B. DuBois: Biography of Race, 1868–1919* by David Levering Lewis are other in-depth biographies of great thinkers with scholarly legacies.

Tomalin, Claire

Thomas Hardy. Penguin Press, 2007. 486p. ISBN 9781594201189. Audiobook and large print available.

Born in a cottage in rural England, young Thomas Hardy (1840–1928) loved the outdoors, reading books, and pretending that he was a country parson. The innocent boy, however, later became an architect, read radical French literature, and wrote an unpublished novel attacking the British class structure. In his subsequent books he tempered his criticism, depicting tragic characters in rural landscapes, and was embraced by the British reading public until he published *Jude the Obscure,* which was perceived as having an anti-Christian message. He then gave up novels and wrote poetry for the last thirty years of his life. In this compelling epic biography, Claire Tomalin describes Hardy as a complex man who loved his first wife more in death than in life, and who transformed himself from a Victorian novelist into a modern poet.

Subjects: Great Britain; Hardy, Thomas; Novelists; Poets

Now Try: *Far from the Madding Crowd, Jude the Obscure, The Mayor of Casterbridge, Return of the Native,* and *Tess of the d'Urbervilles* are Hardy's better known novels. After his death in 1928, his second wife Florence compiled *The Life and Work of Thomas Hardy,* a selection of his notes, letters, diaries, and interviews. While a student, Hardy's thinking was greatly influenced by the writings of John Stuart Mill. The most accessible work about the influential philosopher is *The Autobiography of John Stuart Mill.* Like Hardy, E. M. Forster retired from writing novels early in his career. Nicola Beauman recounts the experiences that influenced Forster's novels and what led to his switch to journalism in *E. M. Forster: A Biography* (see chapter 6). Whereas Hardy rejected the tenets of his faith and traditional English society, Rudyard Kipling tried to preserve the rule of the upper classes and the British Empire. Harry Ricketts examines Kipling's literature and prejudices in *Rudyard Kipling: A Life.*

Wineapple, Brenda

Hawthorne: A Life. Alfred A. Knopf, 2003. 509p. ISBN 0375400443.

Early stories and novels by Nathaniel Hawthorne (1804–1864) were highly praised, but he was never satisfied with his situation. The native of Salem, Massachusetts, always seemed to want something that he did not have: business success, political appointments, and new experiences. He tried communal life with the transcendentalists of Concord and traveled through Europe when his finances allowed, but he felt restricted by insufficient income and family obligations. In this sympathetic but critical account, Brenda Wineapple portrays the author of *The Scarlet Letter* as a maddeningly complex man filled with conflicting values, much like the age in which he lived.

> **Subjects:** Hawthorne, Nathaniel; Massachusetts; Novelists
>
> **Now Try:** *The Complete Short Stories* is the best introduction to Hawthorne's writings before the novels *The Scarlet Letter* and *The House of Seven Gables*. Like Hawthorne, Herman Melville knew the Concord transcendentalists but never really fit into the group. Elizabeth Hardwick describes the temperamental novelist in her entry in the Penguin Lives series, *Herman Melville*. Like Hawthorne, Washington Irving sought political appointments, enjoyed European travels, and wrote popular books. Andrew Burstein describes the life of a happier individual in *The Original Knickerbocker: The Life of Washington Irving* (see this section). Statesman Sam Houston was a Hawthorne contemporary with a tendency to depression. John Hoyt Williams portrays the statesman as a flawed man with a remarkable ability to rebound from personal problems and scandal in *Sam Houston: A Biography of the Father of Texas* (see chapter 10).

Struggling Artists

The lives of artists, composers, and writers are often filled with hardships that help shape their work. Rarely is a creative person healthy, wealthy, brilliant, and untroubled; such a person usually has no compulsion toward art or little insight into the experiences of the less fortunate. Instead, those who become successful artists, composers, and writers are people who have lived through difficult experiences, such as economic setbacks, broken hearts, physical ailments, and grave self-doubt.

In this section are stories of cultural figures who struggled with their work and their lives. In *Franz Kafka*, Jeremy Adler recounts the tragic story of an insecure and disturbed writer of short stories and novellas, who published very little before his death. Robert Hughes shows how insanity was really a mask for Spanish artist Francisco José de Goya y Lucientes in his in-depth biography *Goya*. Ill health and a domineering father were the difficulties that faced the poet who is the subject of *Elizabeth Barrett Browning* by Margaret Forster. Adam Sisman tells how James Boswell overcame alcoholism, laziness, and a bad reputation to deliver a contracted book in *Boswell's Presumptuous Task: The Making of the Life of Dr. Johnson*. David Michaelis describes the depression and unhappy life from which cartoonist Charles Schulz drew his inspiration in *Schulz and Peanuts*.

Compelling stories about human suffering dominate these Cultural Biographies. Authors depict their subjects as victims of either circumstance or their own vices in tales that relate how major cultural works were created. As in other Cultural Biographies, the authors here include many details about the eras in which their subjects lived. Some quick reads and longer works are included.

Struggling Artists biographies are about writers, composers, and artists who suffered social, economic, health, or mental difficulties while creating the works for which they are remembered. The well-being of the individual is often sacrificed to career and creative projects. Compelling, unpredictable stories are found in these narratives with well-developed settings.

Adler, Jeremy

Franz Kafka. Overlook, 2001. 164p. <u>Overlook Illustrated Lives</u>. ISBN 158567-267X.

Franz Kafka (1883–1924) was a difficult, unhappy child, already prone to dark moods long before he wrote his intensely modern horror stories. Growing up privileged on the edge of a ghetto, he discovered his passion for writing as a schoolboy in Prague. After graduating from school with a law degree, he worked for an insurance firm and wrote in secret. As he lost interest in his work, viewed World War I with dread, and failed at love, Kafka's depression deepened. To worsen the situation, he contracted tuberculosis. In this compact, well-illustrated biography, Kafka scholar Jeremy Adler chronicles a series of unfortunate events in the life of an author whose major works were published after his death.

Subjects: Authors; Illustrated Biography; Jews; Kafka, Franz; Mental Depression; Prague; Quick Reads

Now Try: Readers wanting to sample Kafka's writings can begin with the novella *The Metamorphosis* or the Modern Library's *Selected Short Stories.* Nahum M. Glatzer collected pieces from Kafka's letters and diaries to form *I Am a Memory Come Alive: Autobiographical Writings by Franz Kafka.* American poet and short story writer Edgar Allan Poe's life was also short and unhappy. Kenneth Silverman resists being sensational in depicting the writer of dark, disturbing pieces in *Edgar A. Poe: Mournful and Never-Ending Remembrance.* Norwegian artist Edvard Munch expressed pain and despair in his paintings. In *Edvard Munch: Behind the Scream*, art historian Sue Prideaux sorts through the confusing portfolio of self-portraits to create an understandable narrative about the tormented artist. The comic actor Peter Sellers was another dark, unstable character. Ed Sikov recounts his frenzied career in *Mr. Strangelove: A Biography of Peter Sellers* (see chapter 8).

Birnbaum, Phyllis

Glory in a Line: A Life of Foujita, the Artist Caught Between East & West. Faber & Faber, 2006. 331p. ISBN 9780571211791.

Japanese artist Tsugouharu Foujita (1886–1968), painter of portraits, cats, and nudes, was a very fashionable person in 1920s Paris society, where he knew Modigliani and Picasso. For a time French ladies lined up to sit for the man with the funny moustache in the crazy clothes, but he quickly spent what money he earned on luxuries. Initially praised, his art drifted between brilliant and hackneyed, and he left the third of his five wives to tour America seeking patrons. When World War II began, Foujita returned to Japan to support his emperor's cause, after which he was shunned by Western galleries. In this melancholy biography, Phyllis Birnbaum portrays the forgotten Foujita as a drifter, never certain of his life or art.

Subjects: Foujita, Tsugouharu; Japan; Painters

Now Try: Foujita contemporary Pablo Picasso was certain of his artistic talent. Art critic John Richardson has written three volumes of a continuing biography of the Spanish artist, including *A Life of Picasso: The Triumphant Years, 1917–1932* (see this chapter), the time during which he knew Foujita. Comic actor Buster Keaton displayed brilliance early on and then drifted through the rest of his life. Edward McPherson describes the madcap comedy that made Keaton a legend and the quiet despair of his life off the screen in his tribute, *Buster Keaton: Tempest in a Flat Hat* (see chapter 8). Like Foujita, Beatles drummer Ringo Starr is a character who is difficult to judge. Alan Clayson describes his career before, during, and after his Beatle years in *Ringo Starr: Straight Man or Joker* (see chapter 8).

Cook, Richard M.

Alfred Kazin: A Biography. Yale University Press, 2007. 452p. ISBN 9780300115055.

Literary critic and memoirist Alfred Kazin (1915–1998) rose from the poverty of his brownstone section of Brooklyn to become one of the leading intellectuals of twentieth-century New York. His writings in *Atlantic Monthly, Commentary, New York Review of Books*, and other journals and newspapers, which spoke to urban and Jewish audiences, brought him fame and the company of novelists, but his work allowed little time for his resentful family. In this sympathetic biography, literary historian Richard M. Cook describes a life that illustrates the dangers of being too dependent on literary success.

Subjects: Critics; Essayists; Jews; Kazin, Alfred; New York City

Now Try: Kazin was prolific at autobiographical writing, publishing *Starting Out in the Thirties, New York Jew*, and *Writing Was Everything*. He identified heavily with the short-lived author Stephen Crane, editing and writing an introduction for *Maggie: A Girl of the Streets and Selected Stories*. Jane Smiley, in her compact biography *Charles Dickens* (see this chapter), tells how the English author was successful at the bookstore but despondent at home. Ironically, another man who neglected his family was pediatrician Dr. Benjamin Spock, famous for his child-rearing books. Thomas Maier uncovers the contradictions in the man who most influenced child psychology in his time in *Dr. Spock: An American Life* (see chapter 5). Susan Sontag was another urban intellectual whose books and articles drew heavy criticism from conservative political commentators. Carl Rollyson and Lisa Paddock recount her provocative career in *Susan Sontag: The Making of an Icon*.

Dahl, Linda

Morning Glory: A Biography of Mary Lou Williams. Pantheon Books, 1999. 463p. ISBN 0375408991.

"Jazz [is] created through suffering," Mary Lou Williams (1910–1981) wrote in her notes for an autobiography. It was a seemingly atypical statement, because she refused to be labeled as a jazz musician and composer and her outlook was usually optimistic. She had survived playing piano for both Pittsburgh society teas and brothels at age seven and a rough early career to claim a spot in the musical world of Duke Ellington, Benny Goodman, and Louis Armstrong. She could not, however, hold her place. Marijuana, gambling, and jealous lovers distracted her from her art. In this candid biography, Linda Dahl tells her story, one of dignity reclaimed in later life.

> **Subjects:** African Americans; Composers; Jazz; Musicians; Williams, Mary Lou; Women
>
> **Now Try:** Further insight into Williams's life can be gained by listening to the compact disc *Marian McPartland's Piano Jazz with Guest Mary Lou Williams: Conversation & Music as Heard on National Public Radio.* Singer Peggy Lee also had a long dry spell in her career before celebrating a personal comeback. Peter Richmond recounts the singer's life on the stage and in high society in *Fever: The Life and Music of Miss Peggy Lee.* Abuse of drugs and alcohol shortened the career of Billie Holiday. David Margolis describes Holiday's life and association with a song about the lynching of blacks in *Strange Fruit: The Biography of a Song.* Louis Armstrong's career was never hampered by his addictions. Laurence Bergreen tells how Armstrong's musical success and public cheer hid his connections to underworld figures, in *Louis Armstrong: An Extravagant Life.*

Eisler, Benita

Chopin's Funeral. Knopf, 2003. 230p. ISBN 0375409459.

Beginning her biography of Frédéric Chopin (1810–1849) with his funeral, Benita Eisler tells the composer's story like a movie with cinematic flashback. Alhough there are scenes from all periods of his life, the central focus is the romantic relationship between Chopin and the French novelist George Sand, set in Paris just before the Second Republic. Franz Liszt, Eugene Delacroix, and a host of other luminaries in Parisian society are included in this tragic story. This deftly told story, which leaves readers wanting to learn more, is an excellent candidate for discussion groups.

> **Subjects:** Chopin, Frédéric; Composers; Group Discussion Books; Paris; Quick Reads; Sand, George; Teen Reads
>
> **Now Try:** In the novel *Lucrezia Floriana*, George Sand exaggerates the Chopin/Sand relationship through fiction, with an obvious bias toward the heroine. Benita Eisler has written more about George Sand in her novel-like *Naked in the Marketplace: The Lives of George Sand.* Eisler has examined the troubled relationship between painter Georgia O'Keeffe and photographer Alfred Stieglitz in *O'Keeffe and Stieglitz: An American Romance.* Russell Martin also breaks away from the usual chronological model of biography in *Beethoven's Hair: An Extraordinary Odyssey and a Scientific Mystery Solved* (see chapter 11). Like Chopin, C. S. Lewis was a conservative man who reluctantly fell in love with a woman with children. Lewis tells about his bereavement after his wife, Joy Gresham, died in *A Grief Observed.*

Forster, Margaret

Elizabeth Barrett Browning: A Biography. Doubleday, 1988. 400p. 0385249594. Audiobook available.

This story about Elizabeth Barrett Browning (1806–1861) reads like a Dickens novel. A young woman spends many years confined to her parents' house as an invalid. Her father's inheritance from his grandfather languishes in chancery court for thirty-six years. Her mother bears a child every eighteen months. The family settles in a house called Hope End. Margaret Forster drew from family documents and Elizabeth's letters, many discovered in the late 1950s and early 1960s, in writing this book, which tells much more about the poet's childhood and early adult years than previous biographies. She completes the story with Elizabeth's elopement with Robert Browning and her happy, although short, final years.

> **Subjects:** Browning, Elizabeth Barrett; Group Discussion Books; Poets; Women

> **Now Try:** *Elizabeth Barrett Browning: Selected Poems,* selected and edited by Forster, is a handy companion volume for this biography. Forster also wrote a novel about the poet from the perspective of her maid, *Lady's Maid.* Julia Markus dramatizes the relationship of Elizabeth, the invalid poet, and Robert, her suitor, in the fiction-like dual biography, *Dared and Done: The Marriage of Elizabeth Barrett and Robert Browning.* Poetry, music, and art brought John Lennon and Yoko Ono together. The staff of *Rolling Stone* wrote many articles on the couple, which the editors compiled in *The Ballad of John and Yoko.* The Brownings were both poets; William and Catherine Booth were both evangelists who worked among the poor in London. Roy Hattersley describes how they shared the duties of organizing aid for the needy in *Blood and Fire: William and Catherine Booth and Their Salvation Army* (see chapter 4).

Gayford, Martin

The Yellow House: Van Gogh, Gauguin, and Nine Turbulent Weeks in Arles. Little, Brown, 2006. 339p. ISBN 9780316769013.

In 1888 Vincent Van Gogh (1853–1890) and Paul Gauguin (1848–1903) were little-known artists trying to change the direction of French painting. Van Gogh was especially excited about creating an artist's colony, but was only able to attract one artist, Gauguin, to join him. In *The Yellow House,* Martin Gayford recounts how the two painters spent nine tense weeks in collaboration, during which Van Gogh became increasingly psychotic. Gayford quotes from many letters between the artists as well as from their family and friends in this sympathetic dual biography.

> **Subjects:** Dual Biography; France; Gauguin, Paul; Gogh, Vincent Van; Group Discussion Books; Impressionism; Painters; Teen Reads

> **Now Try:** Readers wanting to learn about Vincent's other important relationship should try *Vincent and Theo van Gogh: A Dual Biography* by Jan Hulsker. Irving Stone recounted Van Gogh's life in his novel *Lust for Life* and in his selection of the artist's letters to his brother, *Dear Theo.* Letters can be illuminating tools for biographers. In *Lovingly, Georgia: The Complete Correspondence of Georgia O'Keeffe and Anita Pollitzer,* Clive Giboire documents a short, intense artistic friendship and reveals O'Keeffe's thoughts about her first contact with Alfred Stieglitz. Like Van Gogh, poet Stanley Kunitz saw both the beauty and the despair in life. Approaching his one hundredth birthday, he wrote about the joy of having a garden in *The Wild Braid: A Poet Reflects on a Century in the Garden.* Mathematician John Forbes Nash Jr. was another brilliant and unstable character. Sylvia Nasar recounts the course of his malady in *A Beautiful Mind: A Biography of John Forbes Nash, Jr., Winner of the Nobel Prize in Economics, 1994* (see chapter 11).

Hughes, Robert

Goya. Alfred A. Knopf, 2003. 429p. ISBN 0394580281.

Spanish artist Francisco José de Goya y Lucientes (1746–1828) is often described as a link between classical master painters and rule-breaking modern artists. He could please the members of the Spanish court with stately portraits and fulfill his commissions from the Catholic Church for devotional works, but in private, after the death of his wife and the onset of his deafness, his works turned dark, especially his carnival etchings filled with demons and fantastic creatures. According to art critic Robert Hughes, Goya's life was filled with pain and despair, but he did not truly go insane. The artist saw clearly and depicted life's injustice and violence, foreshadowing even greater tragedies to come. Hughes's beautifully illustrated biography of Goya pleases readers who enjoy challenging books about complicated characters.

Subjects: Goya, Francisco; Group Discussion Books; Mental Depression; Painters; Spain

Now Try: Russian novelist Leo Tolstoy experienced great spiritual doubt about his faith and even contemplated suicide in his middle years. A. N. Wilson recounts the stages of Tolstoy's life and the germination of his influential ideas in *Tolstoy*. Sir Arthur Conan Doyle reportedly despaired at seeing the horrors of World War I and rejected rationalism for spiritualism. Andrew Lycett examines the transformation in *Man Who Created Sherlock Holmes: The Life and Times of Sir Arthur Conan Doyle*. French chef Bernard Loiseau killed himself when ratings of his restaurant were lowered. Rudolph Chelminski reveals that Loiseau was bipolar and had a history of depression in *The Perfectionist: Life and Death in Haute Cuisine* (see chapter 5).

Levinson, Peter J.

September in the Rain: The Life of Nelson Riddle. Billboard Books, 2001. 320p. ISBN 0823076725.

Like Frank Sinatra, for whom he arranged many songs, Nelson Riddle (1921–1985) was a lonely soul from New Jersey. Both had learned their crafts under band leader Tommy Dorsey, but unlike the spotlight-driven Sinatra, the musical arranger and orchestra leader stayed in the background, letting the singers take all the bows. Though he was the genius behind many popular songs of the 1950s, fan magazines did not report on his broken marriage, sad affairs, and loss of direction in the wake of the rock revolution of the mid-1960s. The man who established Nat King Cole was pretty much forgotten until Linda Ronstadt asked him to arrange songs and tour with her. In his sympathetic biography, Peter J. Levinson portrays Riddle as an insecure man who never knew his own talent and who deserved more critical acclaim.

Subjects: Band Leaders; Musical Arrangers; Riddle, Nelson

Now Try: Composer Irving Berlin also felt lost in the age of rock and roll, and he withdrew from the world of entertainment in his later years. Edward Jablonski recounts the celebrated career of a songwriter who could not read music in *Irving Berlin: American Troubadour*. Playwright Moss Hart also suffered from severe self-doubt. Steven Bach recounts how Hart overcame his social class, education, and insecurity to become a Broadway success in *Dazzler: The Life and Times of Moss Hart* (see chapter 4). Actor David Niven portrayed himself as a mostly happy survivor of British schoolboy life in his own memoirs. Graham Lord reveals that Niven actually suffered from self-doubt and depression, especially after the death of his first wife, in *Niv: The Authorized Biography of David Niven* (see chapter 8).

Meyers, Jeffrey

Somerset Maugham: A Life. Knopf, 2004. 411p. ISBN 0375414754.

Somerset Maugham (1874–1965) was more than just a popular writer of novels, stories, plays, screenplays, essays, and travel books. Active for over sixty years, he was also a doctor, spy, Red Cross volunteer, art collector, and contract bridge player, who went everywhere and knew many important and famous people, including Winston Churchill and Queen Elizabeth II. Despite the appearance of perfection that he cultivated, he was an unhappy man with low self-esteem, torn between homosexual and heterosexual relationships. Jeffrey Meyers combines elements of the adventure story with celebrity reporting and psychological insight in this profile of a major literary figure of the first half of the twentieth century.

> **Subjects:** Homosexuals; Maugham, Somerset; Novelists; Spies; Travelers

> **Now Try:** *The Complete Short Stories of W. Somerset Maugham* is available in many editions, as are his most popular novels, *Of Human Bondage* and *The Razor's Edge*. In his autobiographies, *The Summing Up* and *A Writer's Notebook*, Maugham told much about his literary beliefs and little about the events of his life. Like Maugham, magician and escape artist Harry Houdini used his fame when he traveled to hide the fact that he was a spy. William Kalush and Larry Sloman detail Houdini's clandestine operations in *The Secret Life of Houdini: The Making of America's First Superhero* (see chapter 5). British agent T. E. Lawrence traveled under assumed names and met with Arab rebels working to overthrow Turkish rule. Lawrence James tells how Lawrence played up his hero's role to the press and in his memoir in *The Golden Warrior: The Life and Legend of Lawrence of Arabia* (see chapter 3).

Michaelis, David

Schulz and Peanuts: A Biography. Harper, 2007. 655p. ISBN 9780066213934.

Millions of daily readers did not know that Charles M. Schulz (1922–2000) put much of his personal life into his comic strip *Peanuts*. He had an attractive family, a large home, millions of fans, a high income, and the best job in America. He was not Charlie Brown, was he? Surely he had escaped all the troubles of his childhood. Not so, according to David Michaelis, who claims that *Peanuts* was almost an open diary, recording Schulz's doubts, fears, and the heartbreak of his unhappy marriage. Like Charlie Brown, he knew the pain of unrequited love for a little redheaded girl.

> **Subjects:** Cartoonists; Mental Depression; Schulz, Charles M.

> **Now Try:** Schulz told about his life and work in his memoir, *Charlie Brown, Snoopy and Me: And All the Other Peanuts Characters*. Like Schulz, cartoonist Bill Mauldin was a soldier in World War II. In fact, his job was to draw cartoons for *Stars and Stripes*, the military newspaper. Todd DePastino recounts his cartooning career during and after the war in *Bill Mauldin: A Life Up Front* (see chapter 3). Peanuts cartoons were popular with children and adults, as was comic actor Danny Kaye. Like Schulz, Kaye was not the happy man he pretended to be in public. Martin Gottfried reveals the actor's darker side in *Nobody's Fool: The Lives of Danny Kaye* (see chapter 8). The popular painter of happy American scenes Norman Rockwell also was unhappy. Laura Claridge sympathetically recounts Rockwell's career as an illustrator in *Norman Rockwell: A Life* (see this chapter).

Middlebrook, Diane Wood

Anne Sexton: A Biography. Houghton Mifflin, 1991. 488p. ISBN 0395353629.
Anne Sexton (1928–1974) seemed to be an attractive but unremarkable woman with a good marriage and a nice house until she became suicidal after the birth of her second child. Her therapist prescribed writing poetry, and she joined a writers' group that included Maxine Kumin. Sexton soon also met Robert Lowell and Sylvia Plath and began publishing her acclaimed poems in journals, magazines, and books. But her mental state wavered, and she went into temporary trances and attempted suicide several times. In this sympathetic account, poet Diane Wood Middlebrook chronicles the tortured life of a poetic genius who died too soon.

> **Subjects:** Mental Depression; Poets; Sexton, Anne; Suicide; Women
>
> **Now Try:** *To Bedlam and Part Way Back* and other poetry collections by Sexton include many autobiographical verses. Selected letters to her family, friends, and colleagues were used to create *Anne Sexton: A Self-Portrait in Letters*. Sexton's friend Sylvia Plath committed suicide. Diane Wood Middlebrook examines Plath's husband Ted Hughes to assess his role in the tragedy in *Her Husband: Hughes and Plath—A Marriage*. Carson McCullers did not commit suicide, but her life was filled with romantic heartbreak and ill health. Josyane Savigneau praises McCullers for her accomplished writing in the face of hardships in *Carson McCullers: A Life* (see chapter 6). Facing blindness and church opposition to some of his ideas, John Milton's life could have been grim, as some readers imagine from his descriptions of Hell. Anne R. Beer shows him as a man who overcame depression and was politically and socially active in *Milton: Poet, Pamphleteer, and Patriot*.

Pauly, Thomas H.

Zane Grey: His Life, His Adventures, His Women. University of Illinois Press, 2005. 385p. ISBN 9780252030444.
Zane Grey (1872–1939) was a best-selling author in the 1920s, and his Western novels, although not the first of their type, established the genre as a major part of the book market of the time. A failed dentist, he dreamed of being a baseball player, but found he could sell stories to magazines. With his new income, he often left his loving family to travel the world seeking sport, adventure, and authentic settings for his fiction. Prone to depression and stung by Eastern critics, Grey sought comfort in the company of attractive women and solace in the great outdoors. In his sympathetic psychobiography, English professor Thomas H. Pauly portrays Grey as a man caught between the past and the present, enjoying but regretting his contemporary world.

> **Subjects:** Grey, Zane; Mental Depression; Novelists; Travelers
>
> **Now Try:** Grey's most popular Western novels are *Riders of the Purple Sage*, *The U.P. Trail*, and *The Vanishing American*. His son, Loren Grey, put together a tribute to his father with pictures from his travels and sporting adventures, *Zane Grey: A Photographic Odyssey*. Adventurer Josiah Harlan wandered the globe after having his heart broken. Ben MacIntyre tells how Harlan became a subject for a Rudyard Kipling story by becoming involved in

tribal wars in Afghanistan in *The Man Who Would Be King: The First American in Afghanistan* (see chapter 1). Stephen Crane traveled to nations involved in regional wars to report for newspapers and gather topics for his books. Linda H. Davis describes his short but adventurous life in *Badge of Courage: The Life of Stephen Crane* (see chapter 6). American naval captain John Paul Jones was an unsettled man who wandered Europe in his later years looking for a navy to join. Evan Thomas tells his tragic story in *John Paul Jones: Sailor, Hero, Father of the American Navy* (see chapter 3).

Sallis, James

Chester Himes: A Life. Walker, 2000. 368p. ISBN 0802713629.

When novelist Chester Himes (1909–1984) wrote his Harlem crime stories in the 1950s, the cardboard covered books were priced at thirty-five cents. Although few sold in the United States, the books were hits in France, where Himes was living the expatriate's life with other blacks. Through research on the now forgotten author, whose later genre fiction has been compared with that of Dashiell Hammett and Raymond Chandler, novelist James Sallis discovered that Himes was a well-regarded contemporary of F. Scott Fitzgerald and Ernest Hemingway in the 1930s, when he wrote for *Esquire* from prison, where he served a sentence for armed robbery. In this admiring biography, Sallis seeks to restore the reputation of a great American author.

> **Subjects:** African Americans; France; Group Discussion Books; Himes, Chester; Novelists

> **Now Try:** *If Trouble Was Money, Cotton Comes to Harlem,* and *The Heat's On* are some of Himes's novels. He wrote two volumes about himself, *The Quality of Hurt* and *My Life of Absurdity*. Alexander Solzhenitsyn is another author who found sanctuary and a more appreciative audience in a foreign country. D. M. Thomas recounts the Russian author's life as a Soviet dissident in *Alexander Solzhenitsyn: A Century in His Life* (see chapter 9). Like Himes, the life of J. D. Salinger has been obscured by rumors. Ian Hamilton describes the difficulty of writing about Salinger in *In Search of J. D. Salinger: A Biography* (see chapter 5). Baseball player Curt Flood moved to France after he challenged baseball's reserve clause and lost. Alex Belth recounts Flood's career and his fight for player's rights in *Stepping Up: The Story of Curt Flood and His Fight for Baseball Players' Rights* (see chapter 12).

Schoenberger, Nancy

Dangerous Muse: The Life of Lady Caroline Blackwood. Nan A. Talese/Doubleday, 2001. 377p. ISBN 038548979X.

A muse is an artist's inspiration. Lady Caroline Blackwood (1931–1996), beautiful and sensual heiress to the Guinness fortune, was muse to her three husbands, painter Lucian Freud, composer Israel Citkowitz, and poet Robert Lowell. Living with them in Soho or Greenwich Village, she socialized with photographer Walker Evans, writer Cyril Connelley, and poet Andrew Harvey. Unsatisfied to be just a muse, she eventually became a novelist, book reviewer, and film critic, but alcohol, drugs, depression, and guilt over family tragedies undermined her spirit and shortened her life. In this psychological biography, poet Nancy Schoenberger lovingly describes Blackwood as a witness to and participant in twentieth-century Bohemian culture.

> **Subjects:** Blackwood, Caroline; Drug Abuse; Novelists; Women

Now Try: Schoenberger describes another self-destructive character in *Talent for Genius: The Life and Times of Oscar Levant*. Artist Georgia O'Keeffe was a muse for her husband, photographer Alfred Stieglitz, but she eventually escaped his controlling personality. Hunter Drohojowska-Philp describes her long life in detail in *Full Bloom: The Art and Life of Georgia O'Keeffe* (see this chapter). Like Blackwood, poet Dorothy Parker was a talented member of a culturally astute circle of writers and artists. Marion Meade tells the story of her drug and alcohol abuse in *Dorothy Parker: What Fresh Hell Is This?* (see this chapter). Lois Gordon counters these sad stories with a tribute to an heiress with a moral conscience in *Nancy Cunard: Heiress, Muse, Political Idealist* (see chapter 8).

Sisman, Adam

Boswell's Presumptuous Task: The Making of the Life of Dr. Johnson. Farrar, Straus & Giroux, 2000. 351p. ISBN 0374115613.

For twenty-one years, literary sidekick James Boswell (1740–1795) kept a record of the statements of his friend, Dr. Samuel Johnson. Even before the great man of letters died, knowing that Boswell had kept journals, publishers approached him with book proposals, but he always refused to put together a quick book, saying he would honor his friend with a well-crafted work. According to Adam Sisman, the alcoholic Boswell spent seven years struggling to write his landmark book, often cited as the first modern biography. Though readers today know that Boswell succeeded, the author shows how he was expected to fail by those who knew him.

Subjects: Biographers; Boswell, James; Essayists; Great Britain; Johnson, Samuel

Now Try: Boswell's famous book may be found as *Life of Dr. Johnson* or *Life of Samuel Johnson*. A selection of his essays and journals may be found in *The Portable Johnson & Boswell*. Peter Mark Roget was a physician, mathematician, and scientist who was unhappy with his vocabulary when he started keeping lists of synonyms. Joshua Kendall explains how putting together one of the world's most popular reference books kept him sane in *The Man Who Made Lists: Love, Death, Madness, and the Creation of Roget's Thesaurus* (see chapter 4). Charles Darwin spent decades writing his famous *The Origin of the Species*. Janet Browne recounts the evolutionist's struggle to complete the book in *Darwin's Origin of the Species*. Little was known about physician Henry Gray, author of *Gray's Anatomy*, until author Bill Hayes began a search for journals and records. Hayes's research and findings are described in *The Anatomist: A True Story of Gray's Anatomy* (see chapter 11).

Spark, Muriel

Mary Shelley: A Biography. Dutton, 1987. 248p. ISBN 0525245359.

Daughter of an eminent philosopher and an early feminist, and the wife of a famous Romantic poet, Mary Shelley (1797–1851) could easily have been overshadowed by her parents' and husband's fame, but she too was a novelist, editor, and active member of a literary circle, and her tale *Frankenstein* is still frequently read today. After the drowning of her husband, Percy B. Shelley, Mary spent twenty-nine years fending off bankruptcy while compiling her mother's letters and her husband's poems for publication, raising a son, and continuing to write. This admiring biography is as compelling a read as Muriel Spark's poignant novels.

> **Subjects:** Novelists; Quick Reads; Shelley, Mary Wollstonecraft; Teen Reads; Women

> **Now Try:** *Mary Shelley: Collected Tales and Stories with Original Engravings* is available, as are her novels *Valperga: Or, the Life and Adventures of Castruccio, Prince of Lucca* and *Frankenstein: Or, the Modern Prometheus*. Muriel Spark wrote many novels, including *The Prime of Miss Jean Brody* and *Memento Mori*. Ruth Harkness took over her husband's quest for the giant panda after his death. Vicki Constantine Croke recounts her perilous adventures in *The Lady and the Panda: The True Adventures of the First American Explorer to Bring Back China's Most Exotic Animal* (see chapter 1). While Shelley was involved in the English Romantic movement, the Peabody sisters of Salem, Massachusetts, influenced the transcendental movement in America. Megan Marshall describes the sisters and their circle of suitors in *The Peabody Sisters: Three Women Who Ignited American Romanticism* (see chapter 9). Like Shelley, Holocaust survivor Otto Frank became the champion of a posthumous book. Carol Ann Lee tells how he struggled to find a publisher for his daughter Anne's *The Diary of a Young Girl* in *The Hidden Life of Otto Frank* (see chapter 3).

Spater, George, and Ian Parsons

A Marriage of True Minds: An Intimate Portrait of Leonard and Virginia Woolf. Harcourt Brace Jovanovich, 1977. 210p. ISBN 0151574499.

> After Leonard Woolf (1880–1969) returned from Ceylon in 1911, he courted and proposed to Virginia Stephen (1882–1941). Friends doubted that the relationship could last. The couple had health problems, other lovers, differing class status, and discordant temperaments, yet they remained together until Virginia Woolf's suicide in 1941. Using many photographs taken from Leonard's collection along with notes from his diaries, George Spater and Woolf neighbor Ian Parsons retell the story of the difficult romance of two great writers.

> **Subjects:** Dual Biography; Essayists; Great Britain; Group Discussion Books; Marriage; Mental Depression; Novelists; Photographic Biography; Quick Reads; Woolf, Leonard; Woolf, Virginia

> **Now Try:** Many editions of Virginia Woolf's letters and diaries are available, as are her novels, including *Mrs. Dalloway*, *To the Lighthouse*, and *Orlando: A Biography*. Many of her views are concentrated into her book on writing, *A Room of One's Own*. Leonard Woolf wrote about his marriage in *Beginning Again: An Autobiography of the Years 1911 to 1918*. Michael Cunningham includes the Woolfs in *The Hours*, his novel about three women dealing with despair. A couple with whom the Woolfs were closely involved were Harold Nicolson and Vita Sackville-West. Their son, Nigel Nicolson, recounts their lives in *Portrait of a Marriage*. Whereas Leonard Woolf remained close to care for Virginia in her depression, Richard Burton abandoned his wife for years while he explored the world. According to Mary S. Lovell, there was still a passionate and sometimes jealous connection between them. Lovell describes the relationship in *A Rage to Live: A Biography of Richard & Isabel Burton* (see chapter 1).

Stevens, Mark, and Annalyn Swan

🐾 *De Kooning: An American Master.* Knopf, 2005. 731p. ISBN 1400041759.

> Willem de Kooning (1904–1997) arrived in America in 1926 after stowing away in the engine room of a British freighter. With few prospects for employment, the radical Dutch artist painted houses and signs around Hoboken until he moved in

with the poets and artists of Greenwich Village, where he learned that artists earn even less than craftsmen. Stevens and Swan describe how the ambitious de Kooning overcame alcohol and depression to rise and then fall again in the world of contemporary art, leaving a very ambiguous reputation that is still debated.

Subjects: Artists; de Kooning, Willem; Immigrants; New York City; Painters

Awards: Los Angeles Times Book Prize for Biography; National Book Critics Circle Award for Biography; Pulitzer Prize for Biography

Now Try: *The Essential Willem de Kooning* by Catherine Morris is a compact and helpful illustrated guide to the artist. Other titles about artists from the Abrams Essential Series include *The Essential Jackson Pollack* by Justin Spring and *The Essential Mark Rothko* by Klaus Ottmann. Whereas de Kooning fled poverty, artist Marc Chagall left political repression when he fled his homeland. Jonathan Wilson chronicles a long career and describes a rich legacy in his admiring *Marc Chagall* (see this chapter). The defection from the Soviet Union by ballet dancer Rudolf Nureyev was a dramatic story of the Cold War in the 1960s. Julie Kavanagh recounts the incident and the subsequent career of the ballet star in *Nureyev: The Life* (see this chapter). Greta Garbo left Sweden for America, hoping to become a Hollywood star. Using interviews and many photographs, Raymond Daum tells a collection of intimate stories about a woman who succeeded in a new land in *Walking with Garbo: Conversations and Recollections* (see chapter 8).

Eccentrics, Rebels, Rule-Breakers, and Other Unconventional Characters

Some cultural figures test the boundaries of social convention as much with their lives as with their daring works. How society responds varies with the seriousness of the challenge to social order. Eccentricities are often forgiven or even enjoyed by a public that appreciates entertaining characters. Artistic geniuses may even be given license to flaunt the rules of polite society. However, when the public perceives that basic tenets of society are being threatened, cultural figures may be shunned or even punished for their innovative work and their unconventional behavior.

In this section are biographies of people who drew attention to themselves with their avant-garde works as well as their irregular behavior. Poet e. e. cummings did so with his refusal to use capital letters in his name. Catherine Reef chronicles the life of a gentle and cerebral poet in *E. E. Cummings*. (Note: his name is capitalized on the title page.) Hayden Herrera describes how Frida Kahlo drew both acclaim and criticism for her vivid, symbol-filled paintings and stormy relationships in *Frida: A Biography of Frida Kahlo*. London's William Blake worked with both words and images to create mysterious poems and mystical paintings. Peter Ackroyd recounts how the poet-artist lived the life of a recluse in his biography, printed in an antique font, *Blake*. Bill Morgan recounts poet Allen Ginsberg's legal challenges to restrictions on free speech in *I Celebrate Myself: The Somewhat Private Life of Allen Ginsberg*.

Strong, interesting characters and extraordinary stories draw readers to these Cultural Biographies. As in other Cultural Biographies, the settings are well developed, and readers may learn a great deal about the various historical periods. There are a couple of quick reads, but most of these books are longer than other books in this chapter.

Eccentrics, Rebels, Rule-Breakers, and Other Unconventional Characters stories are biographies of cultural figures who challenged the strictures of society with their works and the conduct of their lives. These compelling books include strong characters and uncommon stories. The longest, most detailed books in the chapter are in this section.

Ackroyd, Peter

Blake. Knopf, 1996. 399 p. ISBN 067940967x. Audiobook available.

Born in London, the son of a hosier, William Blake (1757–1827) hung up his childhood verses and drawings in his mother's room. Because his father feared young William would become unmanageable, the boy was never sent to school. From early in life, at home or on his long solitary walks, William began seeking divine visions for his poetry and paintings. Peter Ackroyd describes the strange life of the mysterious artist in this attractive book, which uses antique type and thick paper reminiscent of ancient volumes. Color plates and many drawings are included.

> **Subjects:** Blake, William; Illustrated Biography; Great Britain; Mysticism; Painters; Poets

> **Now Try:** *Songs of Innocence and of Experience* and *The Marriage of Heaven and Hell* are two collections of Blake's verse. Tracy Chevalier utilizes Blake as a character in her novel *Burning Bright.* Like Blake, Ludwig Van Beethoven was a dark and moody character. Russell Martin suggests a reason for his maladies in *Beethoven's Hair: An Extraordinary Odyssey and a Scientific Mystery Solved* (see chapter 11). Discredited psychoanalyst Bruno Bettelheim also suffered from depression. Richard Pollak sympathetically portrays the psychologist who fabricated much of his scholarly evidence in *The Creation of Dr. B: A Biography of Bruno Bettelheim* (see chapter 5). Thérèse Martin was a pampered child who became a young nun. Like Blake, she was wholly concerned with the spiritual world. Kathryn Harrison describes her life and confessional writings in *Saint Thérèse of Lisieux* (see chapter 4).

Belford, Barbara

Oscar Wilde: A Certain Genius. Random House, 2000. 381p. ISBN 0679457348.

Oscar Wilde (1854–1900) once said "one duty we owe to history is to rewrite it." He said many other witty things, too, which is one reason that he is so well remembered. His plays, poetry, and essays might not still be read if he had not been so quotable—and so outrageous. In this literary biography, which examines *The Importance of Being Earnest* and *The Picture of Dorian Gray* in the context of Wilde's life, Barbara Belford rejects the idea that the author died a broken man. She portrays him as a free spirit who lived in his own way to the end.

> **Subjects:** Great Britain; Group Discussion Books; Homosexuals; Novelists; Playwrights; Wilde, Oscar

Now Try: *The Letters of Oscar Wilde* offer an entertaining look at the flamboyant playwright and poet. *The Importance of Being Earnest* and *The Picture of Dorian Gray* are also available in many editions. Lenny Bruce's cause was freedom of speech and the right to say what others considered profane. Ronald K. L. Collins and David M. Skover portray Bruce as a principled fanatic who valued truth over social accommodation in *The Trials of Lenny Bruce: The Fall and Rise of an American Icon* (see chapter 9). Singer Michael Jackson has been vilified for pedophilia, which he denies. Margo Jefferson examines Jackson's upbringing and career in *On Michael Jackson* (see chapter 8). In a time when many African Americans were lynched by whites for speaking up for their rights, bicyclist Marshall Taylor kept insisting that he be allowed to compete in bicycle races. Todd Balf recounts the life of a fearless athlete and civil rights proponent in *Major: A Black Athlete, a White Era, and the Fight to Be the World's Fastest Human Being* (see chapter 12).

Bolt, Rodney

The Librettist of Venice: The Remarkable Life of Lorenzo da Ponte. Bloomsbury, 2006. 428p. ISBN 9781596911185.

When writers quote Mozart operas, they should attribute the words to his librettist, Lorenzo da Ponte (1749–1838), a remarkable man who grew up in a Jewish ghetto in Venice and later mingled with high society as a wandering priest with his close friend, Giacomo Casanova. Da Ponte ended life as a man about town in New York, where he was a noted author, professor of Italian at Columbia College, and opera impresario. In this gently humorous narrative, Rodney Bolt profiles da Ponte as a clever man who reinvented himself many times.

Subjects: Da Ponte, Lorenzo; Impresarios; Librettists; London; Opera; New York City; Venice; Vienna

Now Try: Da Ponte's *Memoirs* are filled with adventurous stories and encounters with historical characters. Venetian gentleman Giacomo Casanova changed his identity with each phase of his roguish life. Lydia Flem recounts how he roamed the European continent as the friend of royalty and the peer of criminals in *Casanova: The Man Who Really Loved Women* (see chapter 5). French modernist poet Arthur Rimbaud fled European society to become an underworld figure in the Middle East. Charles Nicholl describes a soldier of fortune and master of disguise in *Somebody Else: Arthur Rimbaud in Africa, 1880–91* (see chapter 1). Like da Ponte, ship's pilot William Adams transformed his life completely as he moved into a new culture. Giles Milton tells how William became a confidant of the shogun and a very wealthy man in *Samurai William: The Englishman Who Opened Japan* (see chapter 1). Born in Vienna, movie director Billy Wilder adapted to America so well that few people suspected he was an immigrant. Charlotte Chandler tells of Wilder's Austrian childhood, escape from the Nazis, and career in Hollywood in *Nobody's Perfect: Billy Wilder, a Personal Biography* (see chapter 8).

Brown, Frederick

Flaubert: A Biography. Little, Brown, 2006. 628p. ISBN: 9780316118781.

Reviewers praised Frederick Brown's account of the long life of the French novelist Gustave Flaubert (1821–1880) for sticking to the facts and not speculating about his thinking. Brown describes Flaubert's privileged youth and education, early travels, dysfunctional relationships, great literary success, and dislike for most of humanity, especially creditors. Throughout his life, he wrote many letters to his few friends, including George Sand and Ivan Turgenev, which Brown frequently uses to illustrate Flaubert's impact on the literary community and future novelists, including Franz Kafka and Willa Cather.

> **Subjects:** Flaubert, Gustave; France; Novelists

> **Now Try:** Several collections of Flaubert's letter are available, as are editions of his master work, *Madame Bovary*. Julian Barnes retells much of the reclusive novelist's life in *Flaubert's Parrot*, a novel about a struggling, antisocial Flaubert scholar. Frederick Brown tells more about the cast of the nineteenth-century French literary scene in *Zola*. Like Flaubert, the French author and philosopher Voltaire was considered notorious by much of society for satirizing the Catholic Church and French nobility. Roger Pearson chronicles the Frenchman's controversy-filled career in *Voltaire Almighty: A Life in Pursuit of Freedom* (see chapter 9). Winston Churchill was a rare politician in that, like Voltaire, he cared little what the public thought of him. Paul Addison tells how Churchill's reputation rose and fell during the course of his long public life in *Churchill: The Unexpected Hero* (see chapter 10).

Davis, Linda H.

Chas Addams: A Cartoonist's Life. Random House, 2006. 382p. ISBN 0679463259.

> *New Yorker* cartoonist Charles Addams (1912–1988) was never a person to stop rumors. He did not mind that the public believed that he slept in a coffin, owned his own guillotine, and dropped eyeballs into martinis. He cultivated his aura by wearing antique clothes, driving classic cars, and cracking morbid jokes. Linda H. Davis looks behind the legends in this entertaining biography illustrated with many photographs and classic cartoons.

> **Subjects:** Addams, Charles; Cartoonists; Illustrated Biography; *New Yorker, The* (magazine); Teen Reads

> **Now Try:** *The World of Charles Addams* includes selected Addams cartoons from his fifty-year association with *The New Yorker*. *The New Yorker's* other macabre cartoonist was Edward Gorey, who tells how he became a cartoonist and what sparked his imagination in *Ascending Peculiarity: Edward Gorey on Edward Gorey*. Unlike Addams, who sold his comics to mainstream publications, comic artist Robert Crumb illustrated many underground newspapers and magazines. In *The Life and Times of R. Crumb: Comments from Contemporaries*, figures as diverse as Monty Python's Terry Gilliam and film critic Roger Ebert tell how they view Crumb's admittedly subversive art. Comic actor W. C. Fields also enjoyed being thought to be the character that he portrayed. Simon Louvish humorously sorts through the myths and verifiable facts to construct a possible life of the private actor in *Man on the Flying Trapeze: The Life and Times of W. C. Fields* (see chapter 8).

Drohojowska-Philp, Hunter

Full Bloom: The Art and Life of Georgia O'Keeffe. Norton, 2004. 630p. ISBN 039305-8530.

> The colors and shapes in the paintings by Georgia O'Keeffe (1888–1987) are often startling and as memorable as her long life. Early in her career, she was overshadowed by her husband, Alfred Stieglitz, who photographed her both clothed and

nude for his much-discussed exhibitions. Once O'Keeffe defined her own vision, she set out to work independently, often alone in the desert. In this illustrated psychological biography of O'Keeffe, art critic Hunter Drohojowska-Philp tells the fascinating story of how a Wisconsin farm girl became a grand visionary of American modern art and lived as a hermit in New Mexico.

Subjects: Illustrated Biography; New Mexico; O'Keeffe, Georgia; Painters; Women

Now Try: *Georgia O'Keeffe: Art and Letters* combines selected correspondence with illustrations of her paintings. Like O'Keeffe, photographer Lee Miller was a muse in the Bohemian world of art before becoming an artist in her own right. Carolyn Burke portrays Miller as a passionate woman, independent yet talented at collaboration, in her admiring biography *Lee Miller: A Life.* Living 101 years, Leni Riefenstahl began as a dancer and actress before she became an acclaimed film director closely associated with the Nazi regime of Adolf Hitler. Jurgen Trimborn examines the responsibility the filmmaker bore for war crimes in *Leni Riefenstahl: A Life* (see chapter 5). Peggy Guggenheim used the small fortune that she inherited from her father to buy her way into the art business and befriend many of the luminaries of twentieth-century art. Anton Gill describes her jet setting life in *Art Lover: A Biography of Peggy Guggenheim* (see chapter 8).

Greenberg, Jan, and Sandra Jordan

🏵 *Andy Warhol: Prince of Pop.* Delacorte Press, 2004. 193p. ISBN 038573056x.

Pop artist Andy Warhol (1928–1987), famous for his paintings of consumer products and celebrities, dominated the New York contemporary art scene in the 1960s. Unlike many artists who secluded themselves to create, Warhol surrounded himself with aspiring artists, actors, musicians, and writers. At his studio, which he called the Factory, he and his assistants mass-produced paintings, films, books, and magazines. According to Greenberg and Jordan, Warhol foresaw the coming convergence of art and entertainment and the democratization of fame. Written for teens, this candid psychological profile of the anorexic artist in the silver wigs will also appeal to adults.

Subjects: Artists; New York City; Painters; Pop Art; Teen Reads; Warhol, Andy

Awards: Best Books for Young Adults

Now Try: In *Popism: The Warhol Sixties,* Warhol candidly reminisces about the people who frequented the Factory in the 1960s. *The Andy Warhol Diaries* contains selections from the personal journals that Warhol kept during the last twelve years of his life. Punk rock singer/songwriter Patti Smith was one of the aspiring musicians who frequented Warhol's Factory. Author Victor Bockris and photographer Roberta Bayley recount how Smith transformed from a poet to a musician, the company she kept, and the years when she stopped performing in *Patti Smith: An Unauthorized Biography* (see chapter 8). Like Warhol, Wolfgang Amadeus Mozart was a very social person. Mozart expert Jane Glover brings to life the community of women that surrounded the artist in eighteenth-century Salzburg and Vienna in *Mozart's Women: His Family, His Friends, His Music* (see this chapter).

Herrera, Hayden

Frida: A Biography of Frida Kahlo. Harper & Row, 1983. 507p. ISBN 0060118431.
Frida Kahlo (1907–1954) claimed that she was born in 1910 at the start of the Mexican Revolution, with which she closely identified. Weakened from childhood polio and sustaining multiple injuries in a bus accident, she lived always in pain. Her brightly colored works drew international attention and led to a stormy marriage to fellow artist Diego Rivera. Art historian Hayden Herrera portrays Kahlo as a determined woman who struggled with pain and depression, leaving us distinctive, sensual paintings.

> **Subjects:** Group Discussion Books; Kahlo, Frida; Mexico; Painters; Revolutionaries; Teen Reads; Women

> **Now Try:** *The Diary of Frida Kahlo: An Intimate Self-Portrait* reproduces illustrations and handwritten entries from Kahlo's personal diary and adds English translations, revealing the artist's mental processes and the depth of her pain. Diego Rivera married Kahlo twice. Patrick Marnham includes details about Rivera's relationships with women, including Kahlo, in his intimate biography *Dreaming with His Eyes Open: A Life of Diego Rivera*. President John F. Kennedy also hid his physical pain. From youth he suffered a series of health problems that kept him out of school, should have kept him out of the Navy, and were kept quiet during his presidency. Nigel Hamilton portrays the future president as an unstoppable character determined to overcome all barriers in *JFK, Reckless Youth* (see chapter 6). Like Kahlo, Judy Chicago fills her art with symbolic images. Gail Levin describes how Chicago has overcome the difficulty of being accepted in the male-dominated art world in *Becoming Judy Chicago: A Biography of the Artist* (see chapter 6).

Meade, Marion

Dorothy Parker: What Fresh Hell Is This? Villiard Books, 1988. 459p. ISBN 0394544404.
Audiobook available.
Dorothy Parker (1893–1967) did not deny rumors about herself because everything that was said was true. After smoking, drinking rotgut whiskey, and carrying on all night, she would still appear daily for lunch at the big round table in the Algonquin Hotel, where literary stars traded quips. By 1927 she had reached the height of fame by being the wittiest and most outrageous voice, with a book of satirical poems on the best-seller list. According to candid biographer Marion Meade, the party did not last long for Ms. Parker, as broken marriages, abortions, suicide attempts, and FBI probes plagued her. Parker survived into bitter old age. Meade portrays Parker as a complex woman with an unmet need for self-esteem.

> **Subjects:** Parker, Dorothy; Poets; Women

> **Now Try:** *Enough Rope*, Parker's first collection of clever poems, was published during her association with the Algonquin Round Table. *The Portable Dorothy Parker* and *The Penguin Dorothy Parker* offer selected plays, poems, and short stories. James R. Gaines describes the cast of New York literary figures who dined at the Algonquin in *Wit's End: Days and Nights of the Algonquin Round Table*. Like Parker, rock singer Janis Joplin never cared about respectability. Alice Echols portrays the ill-fated Joplin as a rule breaker who led the way for later women of rock and roll in *Scars of Sweet Paradise: The Life and Times of Janis Joplin* (see chapter 6). Parker contemporary and gossip columnist Louella Parsons used her newspaper columns to make or break Hollywood careers. Samantha Barbas chronicles the life of a conflicted woman who helped

establish the celebrity news industry in ***The First Lady of Hollywood: A Biography of Louella Parsons*** (see chapter 8).

Morgan, Bill

I Celebrate Myself: The Somewhat Private Life of Allen Ginsberg. Viking, 2006. 702p. ISBN 0670037966.

Allen Ginsberg (1926–1997) was a great American hero, according to Bill Morgan. Though he was often depicted by the mainstream press as a madman, the author contends that he was a calculating dissenter and central figure in the protection of American civil rights. Through his poetry and interviews in the 1940s and 1950s, he planted the seeds of the social revolution of the 1960s and 1970s. Gregarious and restless, he was constantly seeking new experiences, which took him around the world. In this intimate biography, the author tells many stories about a brave man who struggled with self-doubt and the need for acceptance.

Subjects: Beat Generation; Ginsberg, Allen; Homosexuals; Poets

Now Try: Ginsberg describes his life and work through interviews in ***Spontaneous Mind: Selected Interviews, 1958–1996***. His most popular poetry collections are ***Howl and Other Poems*** and ***Reality Sandwiches***. Ginsberg's contemporary, Timothy Leary, challenged establishment rules about drugs and speech. Robert Greenfield places Leary at the center of the cultural revolution that included Allen Ginsberg, the Grateful Dead, Jefferson Airplane, and the Weather Underground in ***Timothy Leary: A Biography*** (see chapter 5). Actor Marlon Brando tested the boundaries of pornography laws with *The Last Tango in Paris* and supported unpopular causes, such Native American restitution. Patricia Bosworth draws a psychological portrait of the actor in her Penguin Lives series biography ***Marlon Brando*** (see chapter 8).

Reef, Catherine

E. E. Cummings. Clarion Books, 2006. 149p. ISBN 9780618568499.

Poet and pacifist e. e. cummings (1894–1962) is remembered by contemporary readers more for his novel use of capitalization and punctuation than for his verses. Scattered across pages and broken up into fragments, his words are often hard to follow and their meaning difficult to grasp. In this compact, illustrated account of the revolutionary poet, Catherine Reef explains that cummings viewed his poems as bridges between language and visual art. He viewed his life as an artistic mission that should not be compromised by violence and greed. The result was a life full of good friendships with other poets (Ezra Pound and William Carlos Williams), difficult romantic relationships, and political isolation. Although the book is aimed at teenaged readers, adults will also enjoy this sympathetic portrait of a gentle but complicated man.

Subjects: cummings, e. e.; Poets; Quick Reads; Teen Reads

Awards: Best Books for Young Adults

Now Try: Cummings describes his time in a French detention center during World War I in ***The Enormous Room,*** and all of his poems are available in ***Complete Poems, 1913–1962***. Civil rights visionary Bayard Rustin was also cited as un-American for his pacifist views. John D'Emilio portrays the proponent of many unpopular causes as an irrepressible man in *Lost Prophet: The Life and Times of Bayard Rustin* (see chapter 4). Biologist Rachel Carsons was another figure a step ahead of the prevailing attitudes of her time. Mark Hamilton Lytle recounts how she began the movement to ban the use of the pesticide DDT in *The Gentle Subversive: Rachel Carson,* Silent Spring, *and the Rise of the Environmental Movement* (see chapter 4). Like cummings, Ernest Hemingway was an ambulance driver in World War I. Michael S. Reynolds describes that experience in *Hemingway's First War: The Making of a Farewell to Arms.*

Richardson, John

A Life of Picasso: The Triumphant Years, 1917–1932. Alfred A. Knopf, 2007. 592p. ISBN 9780307266651.

Spanish artist Pablo Picasso (1881–1973) enjoyed his greatest fame during the years between the world wars of the twentieth century. Although he continued to paint cubist and oddly neoclassical images, he also successfully took on theatrical design and sculpture. This work took him to Italy, Spain, and the French Riviera, where he met rich patrons and other artists. After a series of broken engagements with a variety of lovers, he married a ballerina and later began an affair with a seventeen-year-old admirer that would last several decades. In this third volume of his detailed biography of Picasso, art critic John Richardson chronicles the career and personal life of the irrepressible artist in his prime.

Subjects: Artists; Painters; Paris; Picasso, Pablo; Sculptors; Spain

Now Try: *A Life of Picasso: 1881–1906* and *A Life of Picasso: 1907–1916* are Richardson's first two volumes in his continuing biography of the artist. These engaging books can be read in any order. Picasso also wrote poetry, some of which is collected in *The Burial of the Count of Orgaz & Other Poems*. Early in his career, Spanish painter Salvador Dalí was influenced by Picasso, but he then joined the French surrealist movement. Ian Gibson describes how Dalí captured public attention and promoted himself as an intellectual jester in *The Shameful Life of Salvador Dalí*. Unlike Picasso, Catalonian architect Antoni Gaudi remained in Spain, concentrating on his one great mission, the building of the Church of the Sagrada Familia in Barcelona. In his sympathetic and well-illustrated biography *Gaudi*, Gijs Van Hensbergen portrays the designer of organic architecture as an impractical genius. Like Picasso, President Lyndon B. Johnson was known for manipulating, sometimes bullying, associates to get his way. Robert Caro recounts Johnson's early political career in *The Path to Power: The Years of Lyndon Johnson* (see chapter 6).

Wenner, Jann S.

Gonzo: The Life of Hunter Thompson. Little, Brown, 2007. 467p. ISBN 9780316005272.

After journalist Hunter Thompson (1937–2005) committed suicide, Jann S. Werner, his editor at *Rolling Stone*, began calling all of the journalist's friends and associates to collect their memories. In addition to childhood friends, family, and journalists, the list of people telling their fond recollections and tall tales included actor Johnny Depp, singer Jimmy Buffett, and former senator George McGovern. The result is this lively biography, a public wake for a man who celebrated guns, drugs, raising hell, and finding a good story to tell.

Subjects: Drug Culture; Journalists; Suicide; Thompson, Hunter S.

Now Try: *Fear and Loathing in Las Vegas* is Thompson's most famous book. Others include a collection of essays, *The Great Shark Hunt*, and *The Curse of Lono*, a report on his trip to Hawaii. More about Thompson and other figures responsible for the rise of *Rolling Stone* magazine is told in *Gone Crazy and Back Again: The Rise and Fall of the* **Rolling Stone** *Generation* by Robert Sam Anson. Thompson listed the Chicago novelist Nelson Algren as his literary inspiration. Bettina Drew depicts Algren as a free spirit who championed the poor and the addicted in her admiring biography *Nelson Algren: A Life on the Wild Side*. Timothy Leary did not like guns, getting through his military career without ever firing one, but he was perhaps even more committed to recreational drugs than Thompson. Robert Greenfield candidly recounts the career of the "Pied Piper of LSD" in *Timothy Leary: A Biography* (see chapter 5).

Cultural Collections

The books in this section differ from others in this chapter in that they profile many cultural figures instead of one or two. They are to biography what short stories are to fiction. People with only short periods to devote to reading will benefit from the brief, satisfying biographical narratives; and readers who wish to sample authors or the lives of characters before committing to reading an entire book will also enjoy these collections.

> *Cultural Collections* include books that gather profiles of many similar cultural characters into a single volume. Authors focus on the key incidents and dominant characteristics in these quick profiles. These works are ideal for more leisurely or interrupted reading.

Adams, Maureen

Shaggy Muses: The Dogs Who Inspired Virginia Woolf, Emily Dickinson, Elizabeth Barrett Browning, Edith Wharton, and Emily Bronte. Ballantine Books, 2007. ISBN 9780345484062. Audiobook available.

Known for their loyalty and freely given companionship, dogs played important roles in literary history. Without her dog Flush, Elizabeth Barrett Browning might never have eloped with Robert Browning. Emily Brontë used incidents of her life with Keeper in *Wuthering Heights*. When Virginia Woolf could not admit her own feelings, she described how Pinka felt. In this entertaining collective biography, Maureen Adams tells a mixture of sad and happy stories about five literary women and their dogs.

Subjects: Authors; Brontë, Emily; Browning, Elizabeth Barrett; Collective Biography; Dickinson, Emily; Dogs; Teen Reads; Wharton, Edith; Women; Woolf, Virginia

Now Try: Sometimes more is revealed in a photograph than the central image. Such is the case in *Hemingway's Cats: An Illustrated Biography* by Carlene Brennen, which allows readers to see Ernest Hemingway's homes, meet his friends, and intimately follow his long literary career. Biographical tidbits may be found in *Poetry for Cats: The Definitive Anthology of Distinguished Feline*

Verse by Henry Beard, a book of poems supposedly written by cats that mimic their famous literary owners. Louise Bernikow rescued a sixty-pound stray boxer in Manhattan. In her humorous memoir *Dreaming in Libro: How a Good Dog Tamed a Bad Woman*, she tells how the dog domesticated her. After her husband died, Mary Beth Crain adopted a Chihuahua for company and named him for her hero, President Harry S. Truman. She recounts how he was as reliable as the president in *A Widow, a Chihuahua, and Harry Truman: A Story of Love, Loss, and Love Again*.

Glover, Jane

Mozart's Women: His Family, His Friends, His Music. HarperCollins, 2005. 406p. ISBN 9780060563509.

Wolfgang Amadeus Mozart (1756–1791) was often found in the company of women. His mother, sister, and wife were the most important women in his life, but there were also in-laws, patrons, wives of friends, and the singers employed in his operas. He noted all of their feelings and incorporated them into the strong female characters for which his operas are known. In this clever group biography, conductor and Mozart expert Jane Glover brings to life a community of women from eighteenth-century Salzburg and Vienna.

> **Subjects:** Composers; Family Biography; Group Discussion Books; Mozart, Wolfgang Amadeus; Mozart Family; Salzburg; Vienna; Weber Family; Women

> **Now Try:** Jon Kukla profiles five women with whom Jefferson had romantic relationships in the lively collective biography *Mr. Jefferson's Women* (see chapter 9). Ernest Hemingway's life can be divided into periods according to the women in his life. Bernice Kert describes relationships of Hemingway with his mother and his four wives in *The Hemingway Women*. After years of marriage without the birth of a live son, King Henry VIII of England abandoned love for the promise of an heir to the throne. David Starkey creates the ultimate soap opera, with elements of romance, intrigue, horror, and tragedy, in *Six Wives: The Queens of Henry VIII* (see chapter 9). Actress Ava Gardner learned after two disastrous marriages to keep her relationships short. Jane Ellen Wayne chronicles Gardner's love life in *Ava's Men: The Private Life of Ava Gardner* (see chapter 8).

Richardson, John

Sacred Monsters, Sacred Masters: Beaton, Capote, Dalí, Picasso, Freud, Warhol, and More. Random House, 2001. 363p. ISBN 0679424903.

Art historian John Richardson writes biography with a poison pen, loading his accounts with gossip and criticism. The strange result is that the reader then wants to see the work of the artists that Richardson has so cheerfully described as drunkards, liars, or thieves. The reason is that Richardson praises the art while tattling on the artists, many of whom he actually likes. In this book he widens his focus to include art collectors and patrons as well. An appealing read for those who enjoy irreverent writing.

> **Subjects:** Artists; Collective Biography

> **Now Try:** Alistair Cooke met many cultural and political figures in his long literary career. In *Six Men* he describes friendships with Charlie Chaplin, the Duke of Windsor, H. L. Mencken, Adlai Stevenson, Bertrand Russell, and Humphrey Bogart. In the first half of the nineteenth century, a remarkable group of literary figures resided in the Concord, Massachusetts, area. Susan Cheever describes the culture of

the transcendentalists and their friends in *American Bloomsbury: Louisa May Alcott, Ralph Waldo Emerson, Margaret Fuller, Nathaniel Hawthorne, and Henry David Thoreau: Their Lives, Their Loves, Their Work.* Rail and shipping tycoon Cornelius Vanderbilt attracted a circle of powerful and cultured people to his mansions and estate. In *The Vanderbilt Era: Profiles of a Gilded Age* (see chapter 8), Louis Auchincloss describes through short profiles the world of privilege in late nineteenth-century America. As the twentieth century began, London was filled with American writers and artists who formed circles of companionship in various neighborhoods of the city. Stanley Weintraub shows how London changed them all in *The London Yankees: Portraits of American Writers and Artists in England 1894–1914.*

Vasari, Giorgio

The Lives of the Artists. Oxford University Press, 1991. Oxford World Classics. ISBN 019283410x. Audiobook available.

According to Julia Conway Bondanella and Peter Bondanella, translators of this edition, *The Lives of the Artists* by Giorgio Vasari is the most important secondary source for the study of Italian Renaissance art. Without modern archives and scholarly texts on which to rely, Vasari drew from his remarkable visual memory of masterpieces that he had seen and from his recollection of stories about artists to write this innovative collective biography. The author, who was himself a noted artist and architect, included some factual errors and confused some chronologies, but his clearly written profiles of thirty-four artists are still appreciated by scholars. Modern readers can best contend with the many personal and geographical names by reading this work in conjunction with an illustrated history of Italian Renaissance art.

Subjects: Architects; Artists; Collective Biography; Italy; Painters; Renaissance; Sculptures

Now Try: In *The Stones of Florence*, Mary McCarthy revisits the great Renaissance city to show that the spirit of its artists still matters. None of the figures profiled in Vasari's book is a woman. Social historian Frances Borzello reveals 500 years of feminine art in *World of Our Own: Women as Artists Since the Renaissance*. Another seminal collective biography from which scholars draw profiles of historical figures is *The Twelve Caesars* by Gaius Suetonius Tranquillas.

Consider Starting With . . .

These well-written Cultural Biographies of modest length will appeal to general readers.

- Adams, Maureen. *Shaggy Muses: The Dogs Who Inspired Virginia Woolf, Emily Dickinson, Elizabeth Barrett Browning, Edith Wharton, and Emily Bronte.*

- Assouline, Pierre. *Henri Cartier-Bresson: A Biography.*

- Bolt, Rodney. *The Librettist of Venice: The Remarkable Life of Lorenzo da Ponte.*

- Bryson, Bill. *Shakespeare: The World as Stage.*
- Davis, Linda H. *Chas Addams: A Cartoonist's Life.*
- Eisler, Benita. *Chopin's Funeral.*
- Gayford, Martin. *The Yellow House: Van Gogh, Gauguin, and Nine Turbulent Weeks in Arles.*
- Gordon, Charlotte. *Mistress Bradstreet: The Untold Life of America's First Poet.*
- King, Ross. *Michelangelo & the Pope's Ceiling.*
- Parker, Douglas M. *Ogden Nash: The Life and Work of America's Laureate of Light Verse.*
- Reef, Catherine. *E. E. Cummings.*
- Smiley, Jane. *Charles Dickens.*
- Spark, Muriel. *Mary Shelley: A Biography.*
- Stevens, Mark, and Annalyn Swan. *de Kooning: An American Master.*

Further Reading

Adamson, Lynda G.

Thematic Guide to Popular Nonfiction. Greenwood Press, 2006. 352p. ISBN 0313328-552.

> Adamson includes some memoirs from writers in the "Mavericks" and "Writers" chapters in her in-depth book about nonfiction topics. Each chapter describes a topic and then presents three lengthy reviews before suggesting other titles.

Cords, Sarah Statz

The Real Story: A Guide to Nonfiction Reading Interests. Libraries Unlimited, 2006. 460p. ISBN 1591582830.

> Cords includes a small section called "The Creative Life: Artists, Entertainers, Writers" in chapter 7, which examines biographies.

Wyatt, Neal

The Readers' Advisory Guide to Nonfiction. American Libraries, 2007. 318p. ISBN 978-0838909362.

> Wyatt discusses arts and literature in chapter 11 of her book and includes a generous list of titles to recommend to readers.

Chapter 8

Celebrity Biography

Definition of Celebrity Biography

Celebrity Biography refers to books about people famous for being famous, figures whose work becomes secondary to their image in popular culture.

Celebrity is a state of fame or renown. In the broadest sense, almost every biography is a celebrity publication aimed at readers who want to learn about famous people. Paraphrasing an old *National Enquirer* commercial, inquiring people want to know all about them. Where were our presidents, tycoons, military heroes, scientists, and other prominent people born and raised? How did they live and die? Whom did they love? Whom did they marry? How did they become famous? The litany of topics included in all biographies is very similar. In the latter part of the twentieth century, however, the concept of celebrity became narrower. According to Daniel Boorstin in *The Image: A Guide to Pseudo-Events in America* (Vantage Books, 1987), a celebrity is a person "who is known for his well-knownness." For most Americans, celebrities are the movie stars, television personalities, rock musicians, society luminaries, and other beautiful people whose faces are on the covers of *People*, *Us*, and the supermarket tabloids.

Many people read celebrity magazines and fan Web sites hoping to learn the latest news and gossip about the personalities whom they admire for their success and envy for their lifestyle. These readers may develop a one-way love/hate relationship with celebrities, whom they come to feel they know. Although they may fantasize about having a celebrity's wealth and fame, they may also draw comfort from knowing that the celebrity also has very common human faults. The books in this chapter are generally aimed at these readers.

A few of the individuals profiled here are still active, including Johnny Depp, Elizabeth Taylor, Michael Jackson, Diana Ross, Woody Allen, and Ringo Starr. All top ten female screen legends from the American Film Institute's list are here as well. Though many of the subjects are historical, not today's hot celebrities, biographers make them current with never-before-told stories. Their names and images are still commonly known by a wide variety of people. With older movies shown on cable television and available as DVDs, documentaries shown on PBS and the History Channel, old music played on radios and broadcast over the Internet, and biographies available in bookstores and libraries, these people are still famous.

Celebrity Biography includes books about people who are idolized by the general public, including movie stars, television personalities, rock musicians, and society luminaries. In these works, biographers emphasize intimate details of their personal lives, including their relationships, physical appearance, personal habits, dreams, and disappointments. These fast-paced books strive to tell stories untold by previous portrayals in books or media. Books for both quick and leisurely reading are included.

Appeal of the Genre

Celebrity Biography focuses on character even more than do other forms of biography. Authors often quote the subjects' friends, associates, and enemies to tell very personal details about their lives and careers. Appearance, personal habits, mannerisms, phobias, dreams, and disappointments are all important details in these intimate life stories written for fans who want to know everything about their favorite stars.

Story is also an important appeal factor of Celebrity Biography. Biographers weave together many incidents, telling how the subjects behaved and with whom they lived, worked, and fought. Documented or attributed gossip is a frequent element in the tales. Revealing incidents that have been kept from the public until the publication of these books is fairly standard and important for book sales. The pace of most Celebrity Biographies is quick; and few of the books are particularly large. Exceptions include some of the high society stories and biographies of some very long-lived entertainment figures. Most of the books are aimed at a general audience who want light reading.

Setting is often minimal in Celebrity Biography. Although many of the subjects travel to exotic locations by virtue of their work and wealth, readers learn much less about these places than they would in adventure or historical biography. Often the community of celebrities, all of whom are famous, is the main setting in many of the books.

Learning and experiencing is a factor in the most successful Celebrity Biographies. A good author uses the intimate details to communicate to the reader what it feels like to be a celebrity, which is an appealing fantasy for many fans.

Organization of the Chapter

This chapter is divided into four sections, the first of which is "Tell-All Tales." These fast-paced, sometimes gossipy books focus on the lives of famous figures in popular culture, mostly entertainers. Their authors tell in great detail how these men and women became famous, how they conducted their careers, and what they did with their spare time. These biographies may or may not be complimentary in tone, but they all discuss the private affairs of well-known individuals at a very intimate level. Sources for the stories may or may not be noted.

The second section is "Tributes to the Stars." These books differ from Tell-All Tales in emphasis and tone. They focus more on celebrating the careers and accomplishments of the subjects and less on revealing their struggles and failings. They are complimentary, and readers are meant to admire the celebrities.

The people portrayed in the third section, "High Society Stories," enjoyed the privilege of living extravagant lives in the company of other members of the social elite. They may have been born into the upper levels of society or have risen from the lower levels by the accumulation of wealth. With their names and portraits frequently in newspapers or other media, they are or were well-known, admired, and discussed. Like other Celebrity Biographies, the conduct of their private lives is the focus.

The books in the final section, "Celebrity Collections," differ from the others in this chapter by telling many life stories instead of one ore two. Often the collections are organized around themes or career types. They are to biography what short stories are to fiction. People who enjoy short pieces will enjoy these books.

Tell-All Tales

Once people become popular entertainers known for their movies, television shows, or hit music, they surrender much of their privacy, as writers and photographers begin following them to examine the details of their lives. In the first stage of their fame, their stories appear in newspapers and magazines, on Web sites, and on television celebrity programs. Many of these initial stories are introductory and less critical, as the new celebrities' flaws have not been revealed. If they can sustain their fame long enough, they reach a second stage during which the level of gossip rises. In this phase opportunistic authors may write either approved or unauthorized mass market biographies. To attract willing readers, the biographers include intimate stories that allow fans to witness the celebrities' lives "up close and personal." If the celebrities dominate their fields and their careers span decades, they reach a third stage, in which the books become more substantial, more objective, and lasting.

In this section are third-stage Celebrity Biographies that retain the author-sees-all tone. They take readers back to subjects' origins and chronicle their careers, emphasizing all the hardships and setbacks. The results include admiring biographies, such as *Marlon Brando* by Patricia Bosworth and *Enchantment: The Life of Audrey Hepburn* by Donald Spoto, along with unflattering accounts, such as *Jack: The Great Seducer: The Life and Many Loves of Jack Nicholson* by Edward Douglas and *Errol Flynn: The Spy That Never Was* by Tony Thomas. Most of the books fall between these extremes of admiration and revulsion. They all claim to reveal private thoughts and actions and to show their subjects as few people were allowed to see them.

Readers enjoy these books for their strong characters and intimate stories. Ironically, although the readers want the characters to be well-known, they want new, fresh stories that have never before been told. The most common criticism in reviews of Celebrity Biographies is "nothing new is revealed." The setting is generally of little real importance. The pace of these books is generally lively; though some of the books are relatively long, they may not take long to read.

Tell-All Tales are fast-paced, often gossipy books that focus on the lives of famous figures in popular culture, mostly entertainers. Biographers tell how these men and women became famous, how they conducted their careers, and with whom they had relationships. These books make for lively reading.

Barbas, Samantha

The First Lady of Hollywood: A Biography of Louella Parsons. University of California Press, 2005. 417p. ISBN 0520242130.

Hollywood gossip columnist Louella Parsons (1881–1972) was the original "most famous person from Dixon, Illinois" before she helped promote the acting career of Ronald Reagan, another Dixon native. Between 1915 and 1960 her chatty scoops on the stars ran in Hearst newspapers across the country, as well as in magazines and on radio. Parsons could sell millions of movie tickets with a good review, but she could also kill a film by panning it, giving her power she sometimes abused. She could also ruin careers with her innuendos. In this candid biography, film historian Samantha Barbas chronicles the life of a conflicted woman who helped establish the celebrity news industry.

Subjects: Gossip Columnists; Parsons, Louella O.; Women

Now Try: Parsons wrote a memoir late in her career titled *Tell It to Louella*. Her archrival in the gossip industry was former friend Hedda Hopper, who wrote two memoirs, *From Under My Hat* and *The Whole Truth and Nothing But*. George Eells wrote about their rivalry in *Hedda and Louella*. Marion Meade describes another woman with the power to sting people with her words in *Dorothy Parker: What Fresh Hell Is This?* (see chapter 7). Another entertaining Hollywood exposé about a mean-spirited woman is *More Than a Woman: An Intimate Biography of Bette Davis* by James Spada (see this chapter).

Baxter, John

Woody Allen: A Biography. Carroll & Graf, 1998. 492p. ISBN 078670666x.

Woody Allen (1935–) is the least American of American film directors. Like his idol, French director Francois Truffaut, the Brooklyn native has circumvented the Hollywood studio system to become the writer, director, and star of many of his films. Europeans love the former stand-up comic for his films, but in America he is known more for the scandal of his marrying the adopted daughter of his former lover. John Baxter features stories from the sets of all his films up to *Deconstructing Harry* in this candid biography. Fans wondering how much of Allen's life is in his films will want to read this book.

Subjects: Actors and Actresses; Allen, Woody; Comedians; Movie Directors; New York City

Now Try: Allen has written several volumes of essays, which have been collected in *The Complete Prose of Woody Allen*. Like Allen, Francis Ford Coppola broke many rules in the making of his award-winning films. His life and career are expansively told in *Francis Ford Coppola: A Filmmaker's Life* by Michael Schumacher (see chapter 7). *Charlie Chaplin: Genius of the Cinema* by Jeffrey Vance is a handsome and intimate book about one of Allen's idols. Whereas Allen has chosen to remain outside the Hollywood studio system, early filmmaker Oscar Micheaux was excluded because of his race. Patrick McGilligan describes his search for information about this forgotten director in *Oscar Micheaux: The Great and Only: The Life of America's First Black Filmmaker* (see chapter 5).

Bockris, Victor, and Roberta Bayley

Patti Smith: An Unauthorized Biography. Simon & Schuster, 1999. 336p. ISBN 0684823632.

The life of punk rock musician Patti Smith (1946–) as told by poet Victor Bockris and photographer Roberta Bayley seems almost wholesome, despite the abundance of drugs, sex, and violence. Smith grew up in a poor but mostly happy family in Chicago and Philadelphia and started her rock career at a celebrated poetry reading in New York. After about eight years of falling off stages stoned or drunk and hanging out with Robert Mapplethorpe, Andy Warhol, Sam Shepard, and other controversial figures, she dropped out of music to raise a family. This rebel's tale with a happy ending is great entertainment for rock music readers.

Subjects: Drug Abuse; Poets; Rock Musicians; Smith, Patti; Women

Now Try: *Patti Smith Complete, 1975–2006* is a collection of her lyrics and artwork. Her poetry is found in *Auguries of Innocence, Babel, Coral Sea*, and *Early Works*. Readers wanting more behind-the-scenes rock and roll stories can try the sympathetic biography *Iggy Pop: Open Up and Bleed* by Paul Trynka or the tell-all memoir *Scar Tissue* by Anthony Kiedis, vocalist for the Red Hot Chili Peppers. Jan Greenberg and Sandra Jordan describe the community that surrounded Andy Warhol in their candid psychological biography *Andy Warhol: Prince of Pop* (see chapter 7). Smith claims that one of her strongest influences was the poet Arthur Rimbaud, whose story is told in *Somebody Else: Arthur Rimbaud in Africa, 1880–91* by Charles Nicholl (see chapter 7).

Bosworth, Patricia

Marlon Brando. Viking, 2001. 228p. Penguin Lives. ISBN 0670882364. Audiobook and large print available.

Was Marlon Brando (1924–2004) the greatest actor of his time? His psychological approach revolutionized acting, and he was probably the first actor to turn stuttering and mumbling into an asset. According to *Vanity Fair* editor Patricia Bosworth, Brando mesmerized the American public both with his film performances and his publicized participation in social protests. In this compact chronicle of his acting career and private life, the author points to the actor's talented but tormented mother as the source of his creative inspiration and personal dysfunction. This candid biography of the actor who declined an Academy Award is destined to fascinate readers.

Subjects: Actors and Actresses; Brando, Marlon; Quick Reads; Teen Reads

Now Try: In *Brando: Songs My Mother Taught Me*, Brando discusses his childhood, career, and political activism. Brando was a follower of Russian director Konstantin Stanislavski's methods of acting, which the director described in *An Actor Prepares*. Actress Jane Fonda upset even more people with her political statements than Brando did. She presents her side of the story in her autobiography, *My Life So Far*. Another prominent American dissenter of Brando's time is described in *I Celebrate Myself: The Somewhat Private Life of Allen Ginsberg* by Bill Morgan (see chapter 7). In an earlier era, the novelist Sinclair Lewis was a leading American critic. Richard Lingeman recounts his melancholy story in *Sinclair Lewis: Rebel from Main Street* (see chapter 7).

Clayson, Alan

Ringo Starr: Straight Man or Joker? Paragon Books, 1991. 292p. ISBN 1557785759. Audiobook available.

Drummer Ringo Starr (1940–) is sometimes considered the luckiest rock musician, for he became a Beatle just before the bloom of their popularity. Did he really earn his fame? According to music journalist Alan Clayson, he did, because he added the last element the group needed to succeed. In this candid biography, Clayson celebrates the work of the famed rock musician before, during, and after his Beatle years, portraying Starr as a great collaborator who was nearly ruined by drugs and alcohol. An intimate look at Starr and his unfocused life, this is a great reading choice for baby boomers.

> **Subjects:** Beatles; Drug Abuse; Rock Musicians; Starr, Ringo

> **Now Try:** Starr has reproduced fifty-one postcards that he received from former Beatles in *Postcards from the Boys*. Beatles fans will also enjoy *Behind Sad Eyes: The Life of George Harrison* by Marc Shapiro (see this chapter) and *The Beatles: The Biography* by Bob Spitz (see chapter 6). Michael Streissguth tells about another musical star who struggled with drug addiction in *Johnny Cash: The Biography*. Elton John is a flamboyant performer who says that he refuses to grow up. Elizabeth J. Rosenthal shows how the rock star has risen above drug and alcohol abuse in *His Song: The Musical Journey of Elton John*.

Douglas, Edward

Jack: The Great Seducer: The Life and Many Loves of Jack Nicholson. Harper-Entertainment, 2004. 438p. ISBN 0060520477.

As Jack Nicholson (1937–) gets older, his on-screen and off-screen women get younger. Although he stayed with lover Anjelica Huston, who is fourteen years younger, for seventeen years, his relationships have been shorter and the gaps greater since then. "I haven't fallen in love since Anjelica" is one of Nicholson's frequently used pick-up lines, reports Edward Douglas. Although there are movie tidbits in this Celebrity Biography, the focus is on his romantic relationships. Celebrity magazine readers will enjoy this gossip-filled narrative.

> **Subjects:** Actors and Actresses; Love Affairs; Nicholson, Jack

> **Now Try:** Written during Nicholson's relationship with Huston, Martha Harris's *Anjelica Huston: The Lady and the Legacy* describes the actress's life and career. In number of lovers, Nicholson falls far short of Giacomo Casanova, whose biography, *Casanova: The Man Who Really Loved Women*, by Lydia Flem (see chapter 5) provides a historical perspective on many of the celebrities in this chapter. For readers who enjoy Hollywood gossip, J. Randy Taraborrelli tells about the often married Elizabeth Taylor in a book titled simply *Elizabeth* (see this chapter), and Marc Eliot tells a similar story in *Cary Grant: A Biography* (see this chapter). The pickpocket George Appo was, like Nicholson, an audacious character. Timothy J. Gilfoyle describes a criminal who enjoyed his notoriety in *A Pickpocket's Tale: The Underworld of Nineteenth Century New York* (see chapter 2).

Edwards, Anne

Streisand: A Biography. Little, Brown, 1997. 600p. ISBN 0316211389. Audiobook available.

As the caption below a photo of Streisand (1942–) at age eighteen states, her dream has always been to be a star. She overcame the early death of her father, stage fright, and extreme vulnerability to become an icon of stage and screen, successful as a singer, actor, writer, and director. In the process, she sacrificed many romantic relationships for her career. Celebrity biographer Anne Edwards interviewed more than 140 friends, relatives, and associates to compile this big book full of stories about the diva. Her love life and psychiatric history are featured in this candid biography.

> **Subjects:** Actors and Actresses; Singers; Streisand, Barbra

> **Now Try:** Soprano Maria Callas was a stormy character whose romances and tantrums were featured in newspaper celebrity columns as often as Streisand's were. Robert Levine tells about her tragic career in *Maria Callas: A Musical Biography*. Another moody singer who has also starred in movies is profiled in *Diana Ross: A Biography* by J. Randy Taraborrelli (see this chapter). Both Streisand and Julie Andrews, who began in musical theater, have enjoyed long, productive careers in film and on stage. Andrews recounts her childhood and early career in *Home: A Memoir of My Early Years*. Streisand can be found in the richly illustrated history *Broadway: The American Musical* by Laurence Maslon.

Eliot, Marc

Cary Grant: A Biography. Harmony Books, 2004. 435p. ISBN 140005026X. Audiobook available.

After signing a long-term contact with Paramount Studios in 1931, the eternally handsome Cary Grant (1904–1986) spent thirty-five years as Hollywood's leading man, paired with the most desirable actresses of each decade. Like most actors who spend time in the limelight, he saw his life chronicled in the daily newspapers. His five marriages and an unusually close relationship with Randolph Scott provided abundant fuel for gossip about his fidelity and sexual orientation. Grant often reacted by snapping at reporters, who seemed to enjoy finding his touchy spots. In this sympathetic biography of the usually debonair Grant, author Marc Eliot mixes accounts of relationship problems with stories from movie sets, giving fans much to ponder.

> **Subjects:** Actors and Actresses; Grant, Cary

> **Now Try:** Family friend Nancy Nelson collected many quotations from and about Grant into a memoir-like volume, *Evenings with Cary Grant: Recollections in His Own Words and by Those Who Knew Him Best*. Grant lived with Maureen Donaldson for four years, who recounts their relationship in *An Affair to Remember: My Life with Cary Grant*. David Niven was never a matinee idol like Grant, but they shared the ability to charm and entertain moviegoers. Like Grant, Niven was not as happy as he pretended to be in interviews and his own memoirs. Graham Lord tells about his life in *Niv: The Authorized Biography of David Niven* (see this chapter). Another debonair Englishman who kept many secrets can be found in *Somerset Maugham: A Life* by Jeffrey

Meyers (see chapter 7). The light poetry of Ogden Nash and the comic acting of Cary Grant were popular entertainments during the Great Depression. Douglas M. Parker recounts Nash's personal and celebrity life in *Ogden Nash: The Life and Work of America's Laureate of Light Verse* (see chapter 7).

Finstad, Suzanne

Natasha: The Biography of Natalie Wood. Harmony Books, 2001. 454p. ISBN 0609603590. Audiobook available.

A fortune teller told Natalie Wood's mother that her second child would be world famous. When she held the beautiful child, whom she named Natasha, she vowed to make the fortune come true. By the time she was six, Wood (1938–1981) was on the set for a movie and slated for more. Movie fans saw her mature from child actor in *Miracle on 34th Street* to adult actress in *Bob and Carol and Ted and Alice*, always glamorous, vivacious, and vulnerable. According to Suzanne Finstad in this intimate biography, Wood's mother was always near, directing her career and interfering with her husbands and lovers.

Subjects: Actors and Actresses; Teen Reads; Women; Wood, Natalie

Now Try: In *Heart to Heart with Robert Wagner,* Diana Maychick and L. Avon Borgo recount Wagner's marriage to Wood. Wagner describes his career and relationships in his memoir, *Pieces of My Heart: A Life.* Actress Linda Darnell also died tragically at an early age. Ronald L. Davis tells how Darnell's mother pushed her into acting in *Hollywood Beauty: Linda Darnell and the American Dream.* Other troubled actresses pushed into their careers by their mothers are described in *Elizabeth* by J. Randy Taraborrelli (see this chapter) and *Judy Garland: World's Greatest Entertainer* by John Fricke (see this chapter). The history of child actors in the film industry is the subject of *Hollywood Kids: Child Stars of the Silver Screen from 1903 to the Present* by Thomas G. Aylesworth.

Gottfried, Martin

Nobody's Fool: The Lives of Danny Kaye. Simon & Schuster, 1994. 352p. ISBN 06718-64947. Audiobook available.

Danny Kaye (1913–1987) was loved by fans for his wacky comedy routines. Known for his joyful versatility, he would act childish one moment and become philosophical the next. Although the audience laughed, his fellow entertainers sometimes cursed him for stealing their lines and shamelessly upstaging them. Unknown to the fans, Kaye was involved in a complicated love triangle with his wife, Sylvie Fine, and actress Eve Arden. In this frank biography, drama critic Martin Gottfried portrays Kaye as an unhappy actor who disliked the label of comedian but needed the attention that comedy brought him.

Subjects: Actors and Actresses; Comedians; Kaye, Danny

Now Try: Eve Arden discreetly remembered her career and relationships in her memoir, *Three Phases of Eve.* Gene Kelly was a Kaye contemporary who sometimes used his dance talents for comic effect. Alvin Yudkoff celebrates his stage and film career in *Gene Kelly: A Life of Dance and Dreams.* Peter Sellers was another outrageous comedian with many personal problems. Ed Sikov tells about his career and failed marriages in *Mr. Strangelove: A Biography of Peter Sellers* (see this chapter). Other sad men who made people laugh are profiled in *Schulz and Peanuts: A Biography* by David Michaelis (see chapter 7) and *Dr. Seuss & Mr. Geisel: A Biography* by Judith Morgan and Neil Morgan (see chapter 7).

Guiles, Fred Lawrence

Joan Crawford: The Last Word. Birch Lane Press, 1995. 233p. ISBN 155972269X. Large print available.

1

Since the publication of *Mommie Dearist* after her death, Joan Crawford (1905–1977) has often been viewed as a monster. Fred Lawrence Guiles argues that this portrayal is unfair. Crawford, who came from a family that was severe in its discipline, had a long and glorious career and many friends. He admits that the fashionable actress made many enemies, including Bette Davis; was an alcoholic; and was often harsh to her adoptive children, but he counters that she could also be warm and generous to her fans and friends. Readers must decide whether the fallen star deserves her bad reputation.

2

3

> **Subjects:** Actors and Actresses; Adoption; Crawford, Joan; Women

> **Now Try:** The famous tell-all memoir *Mommie Dearest* by her adopted daughter Christina Crawford is still available in many public libraries. Crawford's own books, *A Portrait of Joan* and *My Way of Life*, told much about her makeup and clothing and little about her life and relationships. Many books about her archrival Bette Davis are also available, including *More Than a Woman: An Intimate Biography of Bette Davis* by James Spada (see this chapter). Jane Ellen Wayne profiles fifteen movie actresses from Crawford's era in her gossipy collective biography, *Golden Girls of MGM: Greta Garbo, Joan Crawford, Lana Turner, Judy Garland, Ava Gardner, Grace Kelly and Others*. Another sympathetic book about an often vilified woman is *Eva Perón: A Biography* by Alicia Dujovne Ortiz (see chapter 6).

4

5

6

Haygood, Wil

In Black and White: The Life of Sammy Davis, Jr. Knopf, 2003. 516p. ISBN 037540354X. Audiobook available.

7

Sammy Davis Jr. (1925–1990) did not really like sleeping. There was always another job to win, another person to meet, or another dollar to earn. And at times the singer's worries about racial discrimination and death threats kept him awake. From age five, when he debuted on the vaudeville stage, until his death, Davis lived at a frantic pace. In this Celebrity Biography, author Wil Haygood portrays the sole black man in Frank Sinatra's Rat Pack as an energetic, insecure man who liked everyone he met, from Richard Nixon to Martin Luther King Jr.

8

9

> **Subjects:** African Americans; Davis, Sammy, Jr.; Singers

> **Now Try:** Davis published a series of memoirs, including *Yes, I Can* and *Hollywood in a Suitcase. Photo by Sammy Davis, Jr.*, a collection of his personal photographs of his friends and home was published in 2007. Long before Davis, the top black entertainer was vaudeville star Bert Williams. Eric Ledell Smith describes the singer/comedian's twenty-year career in the days of severe racial prejudice in *Bert Williams: A Biography of the Pioneer Black Comedian*. Janis Joplin may have had a different approach to life than Davis, but she was just as alone and insecure as a woman among the men of her band. Alice Echols tells her tragic story in *Scars of Sweet Paradise: The Life and Times of Janis Joplin* (see chapter 6). Davis's peer group is described by Bill Zehme in

10

11

12

The Way You Wear Your Hat: Frank Sinatra and the Lost Art of Livin' (see this chapter).

Jefferson, Margo

On Michael Jackson. Pantheon, 2006. 146p. ISBN 0375423265. Audiobook available.

When Michael Jackson (1958–) read a biography of P. T. Barnum, he told his friends that he wanted his career to be "the greatest show on earth." In the first of five essays on the life and mind of the pop singer, critic Margo Jefferson discusses how Jackson's career fits into the carnival show tradition. In subsequent essays she examines his family life, the child star phenomenon, his image transformation, and his trial for various offenses against children. Although her tone is often critical of Jackson, she also admonishes the celebrity press for its treatment of him. Serious students of popular culture will find much food for thought in this critical biography.

Subjects: African Americans; Child Abuse; Jackson, Michael; Quick Reads; Singers

Now Try: In 1988, before the worst of the controversies, Jackson offered an account of his life in the autobiography *Moonwalk*. Jackson's life as an adored and then ridiculed pop star can be compared with that of Elvis Presley. Bobbie Ann Mason examines the meaning of the latter's life in her compact *Elvis Presley* (see this chapter). Singer Elton John has also made a spectacle of his life. Elizabeth J. Rosenthal looks behind the headlines and music in *His Song: The Musical Journey of Elton John*. Like Jackson, Woody Allen has been reviled for his relationship with a minor. John Baxter discusses how much of Allen's life has reappeared in his films in *Woody Allen: A Biography* (see this chapter).

Leamer, Laurence

As Time Goes By: The Life of Ingrid Bergman. Harper & Row, 1986. 423p. ISBN 0060154853. Audiobook available.

Before she left her daughter and husband for another man in 1949, Ingrid Bergman (1915–1982) had nine very successful years in Hollywood, starring in films with many popular leading men. Because she had kept her love affairs private and played mostly virtuous characters, she had an untarnished, Cinderella-like public image. However, her stormy affair and marriage to Roberto Rossellini upset her fans and damaged her career, and it was seven years before she made another American film. Using many quotations from newspaper articles, interviews, and Bergman's autobiography, Laurence Leamer tells an emotion-filled story for Celebrity Biography readers.

Subjects: Actors and Actresses; Bergman, Ingrid; Love Affairs

Now Try: *Ingrid: Ingrid Bergman, a Personal Biography* by Charlotte Chandler is filled with quotations from the subject. The author says "Ingrid told me" so often that it almost reads like a memoir. Bergman's actual memoir is titled *Ingrid Bergman: My Story*. Tad Gallagher chronicles the career and life of Bergman's Italian lover in *Adventures of Roberto Rossellini*. Patricia Neal was a Bergman contemporary whose career was interrupted by a massive stroke in 1965. Stephen Michael Shearer chronicles her career and her return to the screen in *Patricia Neal: An Unquiet Life*. Tallulah Bankhead was a rowdy, undisciplined actress, a complete contrast to Bergman. Her story of her flamboyant life is told in *Tallulah!: The Life and Times of a Leading Lady* by Joel Lobenthal.

Another Cinderella story turned sour is told about Diana, the Princess of Wales, in *The Diana Chronicles* by Tina Brown (see chapter 9).

Lord, Graham

Niv: The Authorized Biography of David Niven. T. Dunne Books, 2004. 370p. ISBN 031232863X. Large print available.

On the surface, David Niven (1910–1983) seemed to have lived a rather ideal English gentleman's life. He went off to school, joined the rugby and cricket teams, played drums in the school band, enlisted in the Highland Light Infantry, and became a highly sought actor in Hollywood. His first marriage was a joy that only ended with his beloved wife's accidental death. Unknown to many fans, however, he suffered from emotional problems, which increased during his second marriage. In this authorized but sometimes critical biography, novelist Graham Lord tells the story of an insecure man who was never sure of his parentage or whether his relationships would last.

> **Subjects:** Actors and Actresses; Great Britain; Niven, David

> **Now Try:** Niven's memoirs *The Moon's a Balloon* and *Bring on the Empty Horses*, which Lord describes as exaggerated, are lively, entertaining accounts that were very popular when published. British actor Peter Ustinov, who was also witty and a bit more intellectual than Niven, wrote *Dear Me*, an autobiography in the form of an interview with himself. Terry Coleman describes the life of Sir Laurence Olivier, another debonair but insecure British actor, in *Olivier*. Michael Caine has used his persona of the sophisticated British gentleman to land far more starring roles than Niven, who tended to get supporting roles. Caine describes his career in *What's It All About?: An Autobiography*.

Maguire, James

Impresario: The Life and Times of Ed Sullivan. Billboard Books, 2006. 344p. ISBN 9780823079629.

Ed Sullivan (1901–1974) was an unlikely television star. The upbeat sports reporter turned himself into a gossipy celebrity columnist for a series of newspapers in New York. Although his radio and film careers failed, because he was well-connected to the entertainment world, he succeeded greatly in staging variety benefits. He adapted this skill into producing a popular television show that featured almost every big star of stage and screen of the 1950s and 1960s. Though his production company was ultimately successful, he was always insecure and jealous of other television personalities, especially Jack Paar. This in-depth profile of an early television icon will especially appeal to readers who remember the 1950s and before.

> **Subjects:** Newspaper Columnists; Sullivan, Ed; Television Producers

> **Now Try:** Steve Allen was another television pioneer whose programs brought together celebrities from many fields. His cheerful story is told in *Inventing Late Night: Steve Allen and the Original* **Tonight Show** by Ben Alba. *When Television Was Young* by Ed McMahon and *Backstage at the* **Tonight Show** by Don Sweeney also include many entertaining and sometimes humorous stories about early television. Sullivan's entertainment roots were in celebrity news. His great rival was the newspaper and radio columnist Walter

Winchell. Neal Gabler describes Winchell as slang-spewing, hot-headed, and insecure in *Winchell: Gossip, Power and the Culture of Celebrity*.

Morella, Joseph, and Patricia Barey

Simon and Garfunkel: Old Friends. Birch Lane Press, 1991. 261p. ISBN 1559720891.

As an old song says, "Breaking up is hard to do." For baby boomers, Paul Simon (1941–) and Art Garfunkel (1941–) will always be linked, despite the fact that their act ended in 1970 and each went on to a successful solo career. In this dual biography, Joseph Morella and Patricia Barry tell the story of how two teenagers from the Forest Hills neighborhood in Queens, New York, recorded some mildly successful pop songs as the duo Tom and Jerry, drifted apart, and then tried again as serious folk singers. They had broken up again when radio stations began playing their record "The Sound of Silence." They reunited for a concert tour, and several successful recordings followed. Ultimately, artistic differences and jealousy tore them apart. The authors give the reader a sad look at what fame can do to friendship.

> **Subjects:** Dual Biography; Friends; Garfunkel, Art; Simon, Paul; Singers
>
> **Now Try:** Art Garfunkel has published a collection of poetry called *Still Water: Prose Poems*. All the song lyrics from Paul Simon's career are collected in the illustrated *Lyrics 1964–2008*. Like Simon and Garfunkel, the Beatles tried other names for their act, split several times, and might have never have made it in music if not for a little luck. Their in-depth story is told by Bob Spitz in his long book, *The Beatles: The Biography* (see chapter 6). With romantic desire complicating musical collaboration, Joan Baez and Bob Dylan had a difficult relationship early in their careers, which is chronicled by David Hajdu in *Positively 4th Street: The Lives and Times of Joan Baez, Bob Dylan, Mimi Baez Fariña, and Richard Fariña* (see chapter 6). The musical team of W. S. Gilbert and Arthur Sullivan stuck together through their terrible disagreement to produce many beloved operettas. Michael Angier describes their working relationship in *Gilbert and Sullivan: A Dual Biography*.

Robb, Brian J.

Johnny Depp: A Modern Rebel. Revised and updated. Plexus, 2006. 208p. ISBN 97808-59653855.

Photos abound in this fan-pleasing biography of Johnny Depp (1963–). He has made a lot of movies and had many girlfriends in the last two decades without losing his youthful image. Although the death of actor River Phoenix outside Depp's club The Viper Room and Depp's out of control behavior brought him early criticism, in his forties he has become a widely admired celebrity. The author maintains that Depp's acting is almost always the best part of a movie. Readers may be initially attracted to the book by the photos, but will find they want to read the text.

> **Subjects:** Actors and Actresses; Depp, Johnny; Photographic Biography; Teen Reads
>
> **Now Try:** Readers who like the offbeat sense that Depp brings to his characters may want to check out the dual biography *The Coen Brothers* by Ronald Bergan, which tells about the directors' efforts to make their often controversial films, including *Blood Simple*, *Fargo*, and *O Brother, Where Art Thou?* Readers who like stories about handsome leading men will enjoy Brian J. Robb's *Brad Pitt* and *Leonardo Dicaprio*. Older readers may enjoy an illustrated biography about a leading man from another era, *Paul*

Newman: A Life in Pictures. Readers who think of Depp as a pirate may enjoy a real pirate story, *A Pirate of Exquisite Mind: Explorer, Naturalist, and Buccaneer: The Life of William Dampier* by Diane Preston and Michael Preston.

Rogak, Lisa

A Boy Named Shel: The Life and Times of Shel Silverstein. St. Martin's Press, 2007. 239p. ISBN 9780312353599.

Most people recognize the bald and bearded Shel Silverstein (1930–1999) as the author of a series of delightful children's books, including *The Giving Tree* and *Where the Sidewalk Ends.* Few know that he was a free spirit who drew cartoons for *Playboy,* a singer-songwriter whose works were recorded by the Irish Rovers and Johnny Cash, and the author of over 100 one-act plays. He knew everyone from David Mamet to Kris Kristofferson. According to Lisa Rogak, Silverstein was a very private, energetic, and creative person whose next work was always a departure from his previous work. This intimate biography of a wanderer who never let success or wealth change his approach to life will appeal to a broad spectrum of readers.

> **Subjects:** Cartoonists; Playwrights; Poets; Silverstein, Shel; Songwriters
>
> **Now Try:** *Different Dances* is a collection of Silverstein's cartoons for adults. *Where the Sidewalk Ends: The Poems and Drawings of Shel Silverstein* and *The Giving Tree* are his best known books for children. Like Silverstein, Jim Henson was a creative man with many interests who never slowed down. *Jim Henson: The Works* by Christopher Finch (see this chapter) is an illustrated biography that celebrates the muppeteer's many accomplishments. James Thurber was a talented cartoonist for *The New Yorker* who expanded into prose. Harrison Kinney portrays him as an energetic and ambitious man who worked even when he went blind in *James Thurber: His Life and Times.* Another musician who took risks with his projects was Miles Davis, whose life and career are described by Richard Williams in *The Man in the Green Shirt: Miles Davis.*

Shapiro, Marc

Behind Sad Eyes: The Life of George Harrison. St. Martin's Press, 2002. 235p. ISBN 031230109X.

The story of guitarist George Harrison (1943–2001) may be well known, but it is still compelling as told in this quick read by rock journalist Marc Shapiro. The author focuses on Harrison's changing moods, including his initial joy during the time of Beatlemania, his lingering hurt that few of his songs were recorded by the group, his confidence after *All Things Must Pass* became a top-selling album, and his despair when his popularity slumped. The "Serious Beatle" sought confirmation through music, drugs, Eastern religions, and relationships. Written just after Harrison's death, this sympathetic account is a good choice for fans of rock music.

> **Subjects:** Beatles; Harrison, George; Rock Musicians
>
> **Now Try:** *I, Me, Mine: An Autobiography* contains Harrison's recollections of his musical career and spiritual awakening. Former wife Pattie Boyd tells about the circle of friends who formed around the Beatles in *Wonderful To-*

night: George Harrison, Eric Clapton, and Me. Harrison's post-Beatles success is associated with his collaborations with Bob Dylan, whose early career is compellingly told in *Bob Dylan* by Anthony Scaduto. Beatle fans will also enjoy *Ringo Starr: Straight Man or Joker?* by Alan Clayson (see this chapter) and *The Beatles: The Biography* by Bob Spitz (see chapter 6). The Canadian guitarist Neil Young has led a stormier life than Harrison, but in later life has developed a similar legacy of music and activism. Jimmy McDonough recounts Young's life in *Shakey: Neil Young's Biography*.

Sikov, Ed

Mr. Strangelove: A Biography of Peter Sellers. Hyperion, 2002. 433p. ISBN 0786866640.
Peter Sellers (1925–1980) was descended from burglars, boxers, and scam artists—a good resume for a comic actor who plays criminal roles. On the surface, everything was funny to Sellers, who worked his way up from smoky nightclub comedy to starring in radio's *The Goon Show* and from there to hit movies such as *The Ladykillers* and *The Pink Panther*. Behind the comedy, however, were paranoia, perfectionism, and four failed marriages. Using interviews with Sellers's friends as the basis of the book, film historian Ed Sikov tells how the troubled actor stumbled through his career, making many friends but remaining somehow very lonely. British comedy fans will especially appreciate this work.

> **Subjects:** Actors and Actresses; Comedians; Great Britain; Sellers, Peter
>
> **Now Try:** Everyone was a joke to American comedian John Belushi, who rode a wave of success in the 1970s and early 1980s. Behind the scenes, he was addicted to alcohol and cocaine. Bob Woodward reveals the comedian's out of control life in *Wired: The Short Life & Fast Times of John Belushi* (see chapter 6). Groucho Marx was another very funny man whose life off screen was a mess. Stefan Kanfer tallies the tragedies in *Groucho: The Life and Times of Julius Henry Marx* (see this chapter). Sellers was a contemporary of the "Prophet of LSD," Timothy Leary. Robert Greenfield describes Leary as a man addicted to fame and controversy in *Timothy Leary: A Biography* (see chapter 5). *Niv: The Authorized Biography of David Niven* by Graham Lord and *Nobody's Fool: The Lives of Danny Kaye* by Martin Gottfried (both in this chapter) are equally sad stories.

Spada, James

More Than a Woman: An Intimate Biography of Bette Davis. Bantam Books, 1993. 514p. ISBN 0553095129. Audiobook available.
The real Bette Davis (1908–1981) was as short-tempered and vicious as many of the evil characters that she played on stage, in the movies, and on television. Some of her contemporaries were actually frightened of the award-winning actress. In this psychological biography, James Spada says that Davis lived a soap opera life full of desertion, betrayal, and infidelity. From the day her father told her that she was insignificant, to the day of her death with cancer, she was an unhappy, unsatisfied soul. Supermarket tabloid readers and other star watchers will undoubtedly enjoy this strangely sympathetic exposé.

> **Subjects:** Actors and Actresses; Davis, Bette; Mental Illness
>
> **Now Try:** Like Joan Crawford, Davis had a daughter vilify her in a memoir, *My Mother's Keeper* by B. D. Hyman. Davis's second memoir, *This 'N' That*, is a rebuttal of her daughter's accusations against her. Ed Sikov portrays Davis as more accomplished and proud in his candid biography, *Dark Victory: The Life of Bette Davis*. Film fans

will enjoy reading about Davis's nemesis in *Joan Crawford: The Last Word* by Fred Lawrence Guiles (see this chapter). Whether these women were really evil is debatable. A stronger case can be made for Madame Mao Zedong. Ross Terrill recounts her life in the Communist Party of China in *The White-Boned Demon: A Biography of Madame Mao Zedong* (see chapter 5).

Spoto, Donald

Enchantment: The Life of Audrey Hepburn. Harmony Books, 2006. 352p. ISBN 9780307237583. Audiobook and large print available

Audrey Hepburn (1929–1993) still has many fans, including Donald Spoto. Born in Belgium as Audrey Kathleen Ruston, she changed her name to escape association with her fascist parents, who once dined with Hitler. When her father abandoned the family, the six-year-old was sent to an English boarding school, where she stayed until the outbreak of World War II, during which she lived with her grandparents in Nazi-occupied Holland. Spoto chronicles her subsequent acting career, her many flirtations and multiple marriages, and her dedication to humanitarian causes worldwide. This book for general readers may even gain the late actress more fans.

> **Subjects:** Actors and Actresses; Hepburn, Audrey; Teen Reads; Women

> **Now Try:** *When in Rome* by Gemma Townley is a lightly comic novel with a Hepburn-like protagonist. *Natasha: The Biography of Natalie Wood* by Suzanne Finstad (see this chapter) has the same sadly romantic tone and bit of gossip as Donald Spoto's book on Hepburn. *Nancy Cunard: Heiress, Muse, Political Idealist* by Lois Gordon (see this chapter) portrays another celebrity who toured the world to visit the poor. Jane Addams was another young daughter of society without much direction until she discovered her vocation for helping the poor. Gioia Diliberto tells how Addams transformed herself into an activist, gathered together a remarkable group of dedicated women, and became a leading figure in the international reform movement of the Gilded Age in *A Useful Woman: The Early Life of Jane Addams* (see chapter 4).

Summers, Anthony

Goddess: The Secret Lives of Marilyn Monroe. Macmillan Publishing, 1985. 415p. ISBN 0026154609. Audiobook and large print available.

Actress Marilyn Monroe (1926–1962) is the subject of many biographies, each claiming to reveal something new. *Goddess* may be the most lurid. Through interviews with many friends and associates, journalist Anthony Summers discovered a secret marriage to writer Robert Slatzer, wedged between her first arranged wedding at age sixteen to merchant marine James Dougherty (her foster parents wanted her out of the house) and her highly reported union with baseball star Joe DiMaggio. With a fourth marriage to dramatist Arthur Miller and many affairs during her marriages, Monroe was never free of romantic entanglements. Summers portrays the beautiful actress as a fragile, frequently suicidal woman who may have been murdered to preserve the secrets that she knew about John Kennedy and Robert Kennedy. This racy Celebrity Biography will especially appeal to readers interested in conspiracy theories.

Subjects: Actors and Actresses; Conspiracies; Monroe, Marilyn

Now Try: Monroe's memoir *My Story* was published posthumously in 1974. Joyce Carol Oates describes the rise of Monroe to stardom in *Blonde: A Novel*. According to Norman Mailer in his highly illustrated *Marilyn, a Biography* (Grosset and Dunlap, 1973), Monroe was a pioneer and martyr of the sexual revolution. Richard Ben Cramer tells how Monroe's second husband lived a mostly solitary life in *Joe DiMaggio: The Hero's Life* (see chapter 12). Mary Queen of Scots seems to have been an equally doomed woman. In *Queen of Scots: The True Life of Mary Stuart* (see chapter 9), however, John Guy portrays Mary as an astute politician and powerful woman, a person to be admired, not the helpless pawn she is sometimes portrayed as being. Patsy Cline's life reads like a soap opera plot, with a husband who beat her, a record company that cheated her, an auto accident, and finally an airplane crash that took her life. Mark Bego compares her tragic life with those of Monroe and Judy Garland in *I Fall to Pieces: The Music and the Life of Patsy Cline*.

Taraborrelli, J. Randy

Diana Ross: A Biography. Citadel Press, 2007. 539p. ISBN 9780806528496.

According to the author, former Supremes singer Diana Ross (1944–) is talented, ambitious, and misunderstood. Unfairly portrayed as the villain who broke up the successful act, the spoiled starlet who wanted all of the headlines, and a diva with an ego to match, she did what she had to do to protect her business interests and personal sanity. Taraborrelli tells Ross's story of growing up in Detroit, singing for Motown Records, and starring in the movie *Lady Sings the Blues*. Fans who think Ross has been treated unfairly will appreciate this sympathetic biography.

Subjects: Actors and Actresses; African Americans; Motown Records; Ross, Diana; Singers; Supremes; Women

Now Try: In her book *Secrets of a Sparrow: Memoirs*, Ross remembers the successes of her career, omitting most of the conflicts in her life. *The Lost Supreme: The Life of Dreamgirl Florence Ballard* by Peter Benjaminson recounts the sad story of Ross's colleague Florence Ballard, who was expelled from the Supremes, failed as a solo act, and died of a heart attack at age thirty-two. An even sadder, more gossip-filled look at the Motown scene is Raynoma Gordy Singleton's memoir *Berry, Me, and Motown: The Untold Story*. Ross's movie *Lady Sings the Blues* links her with the tragic jazz singer Billie Holiday. Julia Blackburn candidly recounts Holiday's difficult career, broken family, and drug addiction in *With Billie*. Like Ross, Edith Piaf's rise to fame was mercurial. Margaret Crosland chronicles the stormy singer's career and early death in *Piaf*.

Taraborrelli, J. Randy

Elizabeth. Warner Books, 2006. 548p. ISBN 9780446532549. Audiobook and large print available.

Elizabeth Taylor (1932–) was born beautiful. Her mother began training her as an actress at age two, and by age nine she was in front of the cameras at Universal Studios. According to J. Randy Taraborrelli, her mother's insistence on perfection succeeded in making Liz into a star but eventually led her to subconsciously embrace failure in her personal life as a form of release. Married eight times to a total of seven men, she has often been on the front pages of tabloids, overshadowing her sometimes outstanding work in serious films. Longtime celebrity magazine readers will enjoy this book which puts today's bad girl stories into perspective.

Subjects: Actors and Actresses; Divorce; Marriage; Taylor, Elizabeth

Now Try: Taylor offers a glimpse into her life by showing her jewelry collection and telling stories about the pieces in *Elizabeth Taylor: My Love Affair with Jewelry*. In the 1950s and early 1960s, Taylor shared the tabloid headlines with Marilyn Monroe, whose tragic story is told in *Goddess: The Secret Lives of Marilyn Monroe* by Anthony Summers (see this chapter). Nancy Schoenberger tells about the often-married Caroline Blackwood, who sought to write and be considered for more than her physical beauty, in *Dangerous Muse: The Life of Lady Caroline Blackwood* (see chapter 7). Marie Antoinette was also very concerned with her clothing. Caroline Weber describes the rise and fall of Antoinette's popularity, highlighting the tact or lack thereof she showed in selecting her wardrobe, in *Queen of Fashion: What Marie Antoinette Wore to the Revolution* (see chapter 9).

Thomas, Tony

Errol Flynn: The Spy That Never Was. Citadel Press Books, 1990. 186p. ISBN 080651180X.

Errol Flynn (1909–1959) was denied a position in U.S. intelligence work during World War II. His idea was that he could hang out in Ireland and watch for enemy activity. Could he have become a Nazi spy after being rejected by the Americans, as suggested by Charles Higham in his 1979 book *Errol Flynn: The Untold Story*? Tony Thomas says "no" and refutes Higham's interpretation of Flynn's passport and visa documents. In this biography of the actor from Tasmania, he portrays Flynn as a handsome, charming man who wasted his life with drink and useless pursuits and was totally incapable of committing espionage.

Subjects: Actors and Actresses; Flynn, Errol; Spies; World War II

Now Try: Flynn admitted his own failings and lack of principles in his often-republished memoir *My Wicked, Wicked Ways*. In *Inherited Risk: Errol and Sean Flynn in Hollywood and Vietnam*, Jeffrey Meyers compares the lives of Flynn and his son Sean, a wild pot-smoking youth who appeared in eight movies, went to Vietnam as a war photographer, and was dead at age twenty-nine. An equally sad story about a baseball player who became a spy in World War II but wandered without purpose after the war is *The Catcher Was a Spy: The Mysterious Life of Moe Berg* by Nicholas Dawidoff (see chapter 5). The failings of inventor and artist Samuel F. B. Morse included not controlling his volatile temper and the inability to compromise in negotiations. Kenneth Silverman portrays Morse as a terrible businessman and unhappy soul in *Lightning Man: The Accursed Life of Samuel F. B. Morse* (see chapter 9).

Wayne, Jane Ellen

Ava's Men: The Private Life of Ava Gardner. St. Martin's Press, 1990. 268p. ISBN 0312037945. Large print available.

After marrying boyish actor Mickey Rooney, who was more interested in golf than love, little of actress Ava Gardner's life was ever private again. Her name was often paired in the Hollywood gossip columns with men such as Howard Hughes, Clark Gable, and several of the top bullfighters in Spain. After Gardner (1922–1990) married and divorced conceited bandleader Artie Shaw and jealous singer/actor Frank Sinatra, the sultry seductress stuck to short-term relationships with leading men. In this frank and gossip-filled volume, Jane Ellen Wayne focuses on the brunette bombshell and her romantic affairs. This book is a great bit of gossip history for celebrity tabloid readers.

> **Subjects:** Actors and Actresses; Gardner, Ava; Love Affairs; Women

> **Now Try:** Ava Gardner described her three marriages and how she avoided a relationship with billionaire Howard Hughes in the posthumously published *Ava: My Story*. Gardner's first husband Mickey Rooney is careful in describing his relationships but frank about his problems with alcohol and gambling in his memoir *Life Is Too Short*. Actress Elizabeth Taylor has married eight times. J. Randy Taraborrelli portrays Taylor as a woman suffering from her mother pushing her into acting and never getting a chance to mature emotionally in *Elizabeth* (see this chapter). Jane Ellen Wayne has written similar titles about other Hollywood idols, including *Marilyn's Men*, *Grace Kelly's Men*, and *Gable's Women*.

Weller, Sheila

Girls Like Us: Carole King, Joni Mitchell, Carly Simon—and the Journey of a Generation. Atria Books, 2008. 584p. ISBN 9780743491471. Audiobook available.

During the rise of women's liberation and the sexual revolution of the 1960s and early 1970s, three female singers/songwriters rose to the top of the pop music charts with their songs about being new women. Carole King (1942–), Joni Mitchell (1943–), and Carly Simon (1945–) became spokeswomen for a social movement and magnets for the attention of men from the entertainment industry. Constantly in the spotlight, their romantic relationships publicly failed as they strove to live up to their lyrics proclaiming their independence. *Vanity Fair* contributor Sheila Weller weaves together their three stories into a lively account about music, romance, and heartbreak.

> **Subjects:** Group Biography; Group Discussion Books; King, Carole; Mitchell, Joni; Simon, Carly; Singers; Women

> **Now Try:** A collection of Joni Mitchell's drawings are collected with her writings in *Joni Mitchell: The Complete Poems and Lyrics*. Carly Simon has written several children's books, including *Amy the Dancing Bear* and *The Midnight Farm*. The group biography *Positively 4th Street: The Lives and Times of Joan Baez, Bob Dylan, Mimi Baez Fariña, and Richard Fariña* by David Hajdu (see chapter 6) describes four young musical artists beginning their careers in the 1960s. Tom Brokaw profiles eighty-five individuals coming of age in the same period in his collective biography *Boom! Voices of the Sixties: Personal Reflections on the '60s and Today* (see chapter 9). Another book focusing on women who suffer for their art is *Alone! Alone!: Lives of Some Outsider Women* by Rosemary Dinnage (see chapter 4).

Tributes to the Stars

When entertainers reach the stage of their careers where they begin receiving lifetime achievement awards, they also start being honored with celebrity books that are mostly complimentary. These tributes look back on their careers, highlighting their successes more than revisiting their failures. More honest biographers will examine the troubled periods in their subjects' lives, but the overall tone of their books is admiration or sympathy.

Of all the books in this section, at the time of this writing, only two profile living individuals, Martha Stewart and Doris Day. All of the subjects attained legendary status in their fields, and photographs of most are instantly recognized by the general public. *Kate Remembered* by A. Scott Berg and *Nobody's Perfect: Billy Wilder, a Personal Biography* by Charlotte Chandler recounts the lives of recently deceased celebrities. *Man on the Flying Trapeze: The Life and Times of W. C. Fields* by Simon Louvish and *Design for Living: Alfred Lunt and Lynn Fontanne: A Biography* by Margot Peters profile legendary stars from the past who are still popular culture icons. John Wayne, Greta Garbo, and Elvis Presley are other celebrities included.

In the real world of biography writing, the intention of the author is not always clear cut. The line between the Tell-All Tales and Tributes to the Stars may be fine. Readers may not always notice the difference, as both have strong characters and compelling stories to attract them to the books. Readers who regret our cultural obsession with gossip may prefer the positive tone of the books in this section.

Tributes to the Stars biographies focus on celebrating the careers and accomplishments of entertainers. Biographers may include some candid details, but readers are meant to admire their biographical subjects. Books for quick and leisurely reading are included.

Affron, Charles

Lillian Gish: Her Legend, Her Life. Scribner, 2001. 445p. ISBN 0684855143.

During the shooting of an early silent film, actress Lillian Gish (1893–1993) was nearly swept over a waterfall. In some ways her life in the employ of director D. W. Griffith was as perilous and dramatic as the lives of the heroines she played. Beginning her acting career at age nine in 1902, Gish starred in plays, movies, and television dramas for eighty-five years. In this candid account of Gish's long career and personal life, during which she was often engaged but never married, Charles Affron reveals the strengths and weaknesses of a very independent and determined actress who pioneered cinematic acting.

Subjects: Actors and Actresses; Gish, Lillian; Women

Now Try: Gish remembered her early movie experiences in *Lillian Gish: The Movies, Mr. Griffith, and Me* and wrote about her relationship with her sister in *Dorothy and Lillian Gish.* From her days as the highest paid actress in silent films to her years as a Hollywood producer, Gish's friend Mary Pickford tried to maintain a pristine image, but failed as her marriage to Douglas Fairbanks unraveled in public. Scott Eyman tells the story of her life and career in *Mary Pickford: America's Sweetheart.* Actress Helen Hayes was also a close friend of Gish. She wrote three memoirs, *A Gift of Joy, On Reflection,* and *My Life in Three Acts.* Agatha Christie was another independent and industrious woman from Gish's era. Janet Morgan recounts the personal life and literary career of the first lady of mystery in *Agatha Christie: A Biography.* Sarah Breedlove was born in Mississippi to former slaves. Beverly Lowry tells how Breedlove became Madame C. J. Walker, the first American woman to make a million dollars, in *Her Dream of Dreams: The Rise and Triumph of Madam C. J. Walker* (see chapter 9).

Allen, Lloyd

Being Martha: The Inside Story of Martha Stewart and Her Amazing Life. John Wiley, 2006. 230p. ISBN 9780471771012. Audiobook and large print available.

A friend reported that when she and media celebrity Martha Stewart (1941–) flew to Japan, the home economist brought homemade applesauce and organic yogurt for a snack on the plane. According to entertainment writer Lloyd Allen, Stewart is that kind of woman: not a success-driven control freak, but a good neighbor and friend. In this defense of the battered image of the model turned stockbroker turned media star, Allen provides an intimate look at Stewart's childhood, family life, and business career and tells how she rebounded from her imprisonment.

Subjects: Entrepreneurs; Home Economists; Insider Trading; Quick Reads; Stewart, Martha: Teen Reads; Women

Now Try: Decorating and entertaining books by Stewart abound in libraries and at bookstores. Although they all reflect Stewart's personality, they aren't autobiographical. *The Martha Rules: 10 Essentials for Achieving Success as You Start, Build, or Manage a Business* may be the most revealing. With numerous restaurants, packaged foods, and cookbooks, chef Emeril Lagasse has become as much a business executive as celebrity. Marcia Layton Turner tells his success story in *Emeril! Inside the Amazing Success of Today's Most Popular Chef* (see this chapter). Laura Shapiro tells how Julia Child overcame sexual and national stereotyping to enter the world of French cuisine, sell her cookbook, and become a television star in the quick read *Julia Child*. Like Stewart, Arnold Palmer transcended his occupation to become an American icon. Besides his golf career, he markets golf equipment and his own line of clothes and has spent many years as a sports broadcaster. Thomas Hauser illustrates his life in the admiring photobiography *Arnold Palmer: A Personal Journey* (see chapter 12).

Berg, A. Scott

Kate Remembered. Putnam, 2003. 370p. ISBN 0399151648. Audiobook and large print available.

For over twenty years, Katherine Hepburn (1907–2003) and A. Scott Berg were friends. Because she knew everyone in Hollywood and on Broadway, the actress had many useful stories for the author, helping him with *Goldwyn: A Biography*, his book about a movie mogul. When attending dinners and plays, Hepburn always said something amusing. Being an author, Berg, of course, kept notes. In this fond and touching biography, the author portrays the actress as a lively and thoughtful witness to a golden age of entertainment. Readers will find themselves wishing that they too could have met Hepburn.

Subjects: Actors and Actresses; Broadway; Hepburn, Katherine

Now Try: More about Hepburn can be learned in her chatty autobiography *Me: Stories of My Life*. Like Hepburn, novelist Eudora Welty was an independent woman who lived a long life and charmed many fans with her accent. Ann Waldron examines the Mississippi native's career, literary friendships, and outlook on life in *Eudora: A Writer's Life* (see chapter 7). Children's author Margaret Wise Brown was a warm, optimistic woman who loved to collaborate with other authors and artists to produce children's books. Leonard S. Marcus recounts her fruitful career in *Margaret Wise Brown* (see chapter 7). In Washington, D.C., President Theordore Roosevelt's daughter Alice married a congressman and remained in the city the rest of her life. Stacy A. Cordery recounts the power Roosevelt obtained as an independent Washington hostess in *Alice: Alice Roosevelt Longworth, from White House Princess to Washington Power Broker.*

Chandler, Charlotte

Nobody's Perfect: Billy Wilder, A Personal Biography. Simon & Schuster, 2002. 352p. ISBN 0743217098.

Groucho Marx introduced Charlotte Chandler to Billy Wilder (1906–2002). Because the famous movie director was a very helpful interviewee, giving her great stories for a Marx biography, she consulted him on subsequent books. She always found him warm and humorous, even when he had very serious criticisms to make about Hollywood and the world at large. She also discovered that, though he seemed very American, he was born and raised in Vienna, Austria, in a Jewish neighborhood. In this admiring biography, she recounts stories that he told about Nazis killing his family, fleeing to America, and directing some of Hollywood's greatest stars.

Subjects: Immigrants; Movie Directors; Wilder, Billy

Now Try: Wilder and director Cameron Crowe collaborated on a book-length interview entitled *Conversations with Wilder.* Chandler wrote a similar book about famed British director Alfred Hitchcock, *It's Only a Movie: Alfred Hitchcock, a Personal Biography.* Like Wilder, Hollywood producer Sam Spiegel was an immigrant who, after fleeing the Nazi takeover of Europe, made many award-winning films. Not all of his stories about his escape, however, were true. Natasia Fraser-Cavassoni sorts fact from fiction in *Sam Spiegel* (see chapter 5). Another lively biography about an immigrant to America who did well in the world of entertainment is *The Librettist of Venice: The Remarkable Life of Lorenzo da Ponte* by Rodney Bolt (see chapter 7).

Chierichetti, David

Edith Head: The Life and Times of Hollywood's Celebrated Costume Designer. HarperCollins, 2003. 251p. ISBN 0060194286.

Satisfying movie producers, directors, and the actresses for whom she designed costumes was always a challenge for Edith Head (1897–1981), winner of ten Oscars from the Academy of Motion Pictures Arts and Sciences. "Give them what they want" was her advice to interns, but that was easier said than done. In this biography full of costume photos, film historian David Chiericheti uses his interviews with Head and many of her colleagues to portray the private woman behind the big glasses as an astute studio politician who would never betray an actress.

Subjects: Costume Designers; Head, Edith; Women

Now Try: In *Edith Head's Hollywood,* Head was discreet in telling stories about the actors and actresses that she dressed. Margaret J. Bailey tells more about Head and other costume designers in *Those Glorious Glamour Years.* Screenwriter Frederica Sagor Maas tells many behind the scenes stories about working in Hollywood and about movie personalities in her memoir, *The Shocking Miss Pilgrim: A Writer in Early Hollywood*. Another story about life as a studio employee is screenwriter Francis Marion's *Off with Their Heads: A Serio-Comic Tale of Hollywood*.

Daum, Raymond

Walking with Garbo: Conversations and Recollections. HarperCollins, 1991. 222p. ISBN 0060164921.

Ready to run, Greta Garbo (1905–1990) leaned away from the MGM lion in a 1925 publicity photo. Though the film studio was already hailing the Swedish actress as a great star, it was still involving her in attention-getting stunts. With the screening of *The Temptress* in 1926, she captured critical acclaim and established her film persona as a glamorous, sensual woman. For fifteen years she starred in major Hollywood films, and then she retired to New York, where for nearly fifty years, fans and photographers tried to spot her out walking. Using interviews and many photographs, friend Raymond Daum tells a collection of intimate stories about the career of a very private woman.

Subjects: Actors and Actresses; Garbo, Greta

Now Try: *Mary Pickford Rediscovered* by Kevin Brownlow also has a great collection of photographs chronicling an actress throughout her career. The other Swedish actress who became a Hollywood leading lady was Ingrid Bergman. Laurence Leamer tells an up-close story about her rocky career in *As Time Goes By: The Life of Ingrid Bergman* (see this chapter). When he died at age 101, Irving Berlin had spent several decades in seclusion. In *Irving Berlin: American Troubadour*, admiring author Edward Jablonski recounts the glorious career of one of America's most prolific songwriters. J. D. Salinger stopped writing short stories and meeting with journalists and scholars in the 1960s. In *In Search of J. D. Salinger*, Ian Hamilton describes his legal quarrel with Salinger over Hamilton's writing Salinger's biography.

Eliot, Marc

Jimmy Stewart: A Biography. Harmony Books, 2006. 463p. ISBN 1400052211. Large print available.

Controlling his emotions was the key to Jimmy Stewart's success (1908–1997), according to celebrity biographer Marc Eliot. The author tells how unsettled the actor was as a youth, never able to satisfy his father and always turning to his mother for comfort. His first performances in Hollywood movies were panned, but then drawing on his inner control, he was able to shape complex and memorable characters that are still loved by moviegoers today. In this psychological biography, Eliot tells the story of the life of a great actor, describing his military career, his political evolution away from populism to conservatism, and the family and personal relationships that shaped his life.

Subjects: Actors and Actresses; Stewart, Jimmy

Now Try: Stewart remembered his life in light verse in the autobiographical *Jimmy Stewart and His Poems*. Stewart's name is often associated with director Frank Capra, who directed the actor in *It's a Wonderful Life*, *Mr. Smith Goes to Washington*, and *You Can't Take It with You*. Capra recounted his career and fight for artistic control of his films in *Name Above the Title: An Autobiography*. Like Stewart, the humorous poet Ogden Nash entertained Americans with dry wit during the Great Depression and middle years of the twentieth century. Douglas M. Parker describes Nash as a thoughtful man who found great success in bringing joy to readers in *Ogden Nash: The Life and Work of America's Laureate of Light Verse* (see chapter 7). Another lanky folk hero with a big following is golfer Arnold Palmer. Thomas Hauser portrays Palmer as a gentleman on and off the golf course in *Arnold Palmer: A Personal Journey* (see chapter 12).

Finch, Christopher

Jim Henson: The Works. Random House, 1993. 251p. ISBN 0679412034.

A biography about Jim Henson (1936–1990) cannot be about just Jim Henson. It is also about Kermit the Frog, the La Choy Dragon, Cookie Monster, Bert and Ernie, Big Bird, and countless other Muppets. All these characters came from the minds of Henson and his team, from which he also cannot be separated. From the early days creating the TV show *Sam and Friends* with Jane Nebel, through *Sesame Street*, *The Muppet Show*, and beyond, Henson was always a collaborator who found friends to help him to realize his dreams. Christopher Finch includes many colorful sidebars in this heavily illustrated tribute to genius.

Subjects: Henson, Jim; Leadership; Muppets; Photographic Biography; Puppeteers; *Sesame Street*; Television

Now Try: Henson never wrote a memoir, but his friends collected quotations—some spoken by his characters—in *It's Not Easy Being Green: And Other Things to Consider*. Henson's imagination is often compared with that of Walt Disney, who began as an animator and became the head of an entertainment empire. Neal Gabler argues that Disney's work has greatly changed the American way of life in his detailed account of the animator's life, *Walt Disney: The Triumph of the American Imagination* (see chapter 9). Although Henson had many ideas on his own, he relied on Frank Oz, Carroll Spinney, and the other members of his creative team for collaboration. Children's book author Margaret Wise Brown was also a great collaborator, who cowrote over 100 books. Leonard S. Marcus chronicles her life in *Margaret Wise Brown* (see chapter 7). Like Henson, the cartoonist Charles Addams created an identifiable world filled with unusual characters. Linda H. Davis describes that world in her entertaining biography *Chas Addams: A Cartoonist's Life* (see chapter 7).

Fricke, John

Judy Garland: World's Greatest Entertainer. Henry Holt, 1992. 255p. ISBN 0805017380.

In her public singing debut, two-and-a-half-year-old Frances Ethyl Gumm sang "When My Sugar Walks Down the Street" with her sisters on the stage of the New Grand Theater in Grand Rapids, Minnesota. Later known as singing sensation Judy Garland (1922–1969), she spent the next forty-five years on stage, in the movies, on radio, and on television. Whereas most books about Garland focus on her alcoholism and bad behavior, this photobiography with admiring text by John Fricke celebrates her career and explains why fans loved her. Hundreds of photos show Garland at work and play with many other stars. A good book for Garland fans and readers tired of tell-all tales.

Subjects: Actors and Actresses; Garland, Judy; Photographic Biography; Singers

Now Try: Garland's first husband, Vincente Minnelli, wrote about her roles in his musicals in his memoir *I Remember It Well*. Like Garland, actress Grace Kelly was often photographed for publicity for her movies. *Grace Kelly: A Life in Pictures* (see this chapter) combines studio photos with family snapshots from every period of her life, showing her as child, actress, and princess. *Frank Sinatra: The Family Album* by Charles Pignone is a selective illustrated biography, presenting only the happy moments of his life. Fans of Hollywood photobiographies will also enjoy a tribute to John Wayne, *The Duke: A Life in Pictures* by Rob L. Wagner.

Giddins, Gary

Bing Crosby: A Pocketful of Dreams, the Early Years, 1903–1940. Little, Brown, 2001. 728p. ISBN 0316881880. Audiobook available.

Who takes Bing Crosby (1903–1977) seriously today? The singer/actor became just part of the background of twentieth-century culture for many born after World War II. Few realize today how successful he was in vaudeville, radio, movies, and early television. Some 368 of his recordings appeared on music charts, 300 more than the Beatles and 159 more than Frank Sinatra! His vocal innovations were copied by many singers, and he even invented the celebrity pro-am golf tournament. In this book for general readers, Gary Giddins tells an intimate story of an energetic, popular entertainer loved by his fans.

Subjects: Actors and Actresses; Crosby, Bing; Singers

Now Try: Crosby's happy memoir telling about his music and film career is titled *Call Me Lucky*. Crosby fans will also enjoy a book about his movie partner, Bob Hope. *Bob Hope: The Road Well-Traveled* by Lawrence J. Quirk is an entertaining look at the popular twentieth-century comedian. Irving Berlin is another American musical icon whose accomplishments are now mostly forgotten. Edward Jablonski tells an upbeat story about the composer's great success in *Irving Berlin: American Troubadour*. According to Laurence Bergreen, Louis Armstrong's role in music and racial history is hotly debated. In *Louis Armstrong: An Extravagant Life*, he argues that the trumpeter and band leader defined the sound of American jazz in the 1920s and 1930s.

Gourse, Leslie

Unforgettable: The Life and Mystique of Nat King Cole. St. Martin's Press, 1991. 309p. ISBN 0312059825.

Nat King Cole (1919–1965) epitomized sophistication. Always well-dressed, pleasant, and smooth, the talented jazz pianist and singer charmed national audiences at a time when other black performers were rarely seen on television or the stage. He was always discreet, and few knew that his family had left Alabama for the south side of Chicago to escape poverty. When he was ten, his family only had Thanksgiving dinner because Cole won a turkey at a talent contest. In this life of a quiet man who died young, Leslie Gourse celebrates his musical talent and defends him against the claims that he ignored the civil rights movement.

Subjects: African Americans; Cole, Nat King; Jazz Musicians; Singers

Now Try: Cole's daughter Natalie is also a popular singer. In her candid book, *Angel on My Shoulder: An Autobiography*, she credits her father's spirit with saving her from drug addiction. Singer Charley Pride grew up poor in rural Mississippi. He tells how he struggled with prejudice as the sole black singer on country music tour in his memoir *Pride: The Charley Pride Story*. Cole's success resembled that of Ray Charles, who is profiled in *Ray Charles: Man and Music* by Michael Lydon (see chapter 4). Like Cole, baseball star Roberto Clemente rose from poverty to become a quiet advocate for his race and died tragically young. David Maraniss tells his inspiring story in *Clemente: The Passion and Grace of Baseball's Last Hero* (see chapter 12).

Grace Kelly: A Life in Pictures. Pavilion, 2006. 208p. ISBN 1862057613.

After only five years, Grace Kelly (1929–1982) walked away from a successful career as a leading lady in Hollywood at age twenty-six to become the princess of Monaco. Some critics at the time argued that she did not realize what she was giving up and that she would regret the move. They obviously did not know how her parents opposed her acting career and constantly urged her to become "respectable." Always the model of perfect behavior, she never publicly complained about the demands of her parents or husband. Celebrity magazine readers will relish this photobiography, with shots of her leading movie roles, her storybook wedding, and scenes with her family in Monaco.

> **Subjects:** Actors and Actresses; Kelly, Grace; Monaco; Photographic Biography; Princesses

> **Now Try:** *My Book of Flowers* is Kelly's book about the history and arrangement of flowers. Kelly is one of the few celebrities to truly become royal. Readers who enjoyed this illustrated biography will also enjoy *Elizabeth: Fifty Glorious Years* by Jennie Bond (see chapter 9), a book celebrating half a century of Elizabeth II as monarch of Great Britain. Charles Higham tells of an earlier American beauty who joined British nobility through marriage in *Dark Lady: Winston Churchill's Mother and Her World* (see this chapter). Lady Bird Johnson also loved flowers, and her husband became the head of state. Jane Jarboe Russell portrays Lady Bird as a tough and resourceful woman worthy of admiration in *Lady Bird: A Biography of Mrs. Johnson* (see chapter 10).

Kanfer, Stefan

Ball of Fire: The Tumultuous Life and Comic Art of Lucille Ball. Knopf, 2003. 361p. ISBN 0375413154.

Working as a soda jerk in 1928, Lucille Ball (1911–1989) forgot to put a banana in a banana split and was fired. How appropriately goofy for an actress who would one day play the role of Lucy Ricardo on the hit television comedy *I Love Lucy*! In this story-filled biography, Stefan Kanter tells how Ball struggled to get good parts on stage and in movies before becoming one of America's favorite television stars. She also grew in confidence and became a top television producer after her divorce from Desi Arnaz. This admiring look at the slapstick queen is a great reading choice for television comedy fans.

> **Subjects:** Actors and Actresses; Ball, Lucille; Comedians; Television Executives; Women

> **Now Try:** In her memoir *Love, Lucy*, Ball focuses on the early years, her marriage to Desi Arnaz, and the making of *I Love Lucy*. Desi Arnaz recounted his life in a memoir titled simply *A Book*. Lucille Ball's close associate and televi-

sion star Carol Burnett remembers her own difficult childhood and her early years in television in her memoir *One More Time*. Like Ball, actress Mary Tyler Moore starred on a long-running television comedy and became a television producer. She remembers her career in her memoir *After All*. Chef Julia Child was a humorous woman who worked in her field for years before starring on a highly successful television program. Laura Shapiro tells an admiring story in *Julia Child*.

Kanfer, Stefan

Groucho: The Life and Times of Julius Henry Marx. Knopf, 2000. 465p. ISBN 0375-402187.

The funniest men lead the saddest lives. Groucho Marx (1890–1977) saw his mother die, his investments evaporate in the 1929 stock market crash, many relationships fail, his family act break up, and a dry period last through his middle years. His jokes were at times cynical and irreverent, suggesting an unhappy soul. Only near the end of his life did he reconcile with his children. Stefan Kanfer acknowledges Marx's failures but also celebrates the brilliance of Marx's comedy in this candid biography, which includes many jokes and dialogue from Marx's vaudeville, radio, and movie routines.

> **Subjects:** Comedians; Families; Marx Brothers; Marx, Groucho

> **Now Try:** Marx turned to autobiography frequently during his life. Among his books are *Groucho and Me*, *The Secret Word Is Groucho*, and *Memoirs of a Mangy Lover*. He also is credited with a book about the Marx Brothers comedy team called *The Marx Brothers Scrapbook*. Like Marx, W. C. Fields was an iconic star of vaudeville and early films and a far different person on stage than off. Simon Louvish recounts many of Field's classic sketches in his admiring biography *Man on the Flying Trapeze: The Life and Times of W. C. Fields* (see this chapter). Architect Frank Lloyd Wright, who sometimes wore capes or eye-catching apparel, was also a man who could be charming or overbearing. Ada Louise Huxtable sorts through the myths about this iconic figure in *Frank Lloyd Wright* (see chapter 7). In later years Marx became very isolated, much like Gustave Flaubert, whose life is recounted in *Flaubert: A Biography* by Frederick Brown (see chapter 7).

Louvish, Simon

Man on the Flying Trapeze: The Life and Times of W. C. Fields. Norton, 1997. 564p. ISBN 0393041271.

The rotund, sour-faced comedian W. C. Fields (1880–1946), the original mass media grouch, started his career in vaudeville in 1905. The former cigar store clerk and newsboy perfected his comic act and pool shark image in silent films, the Ziegfeld Follies, the talkies, and radio. Along the way, he told many lies about his childhood and career. In this book filled with classic comic sketches to make readers groan, novelist Simon Louvish humorously sorts through the myths and verifiable facts to construct a possible life of one of early film's most recognized characters.

> **Subjects:** Actors and Actresses; Comedians; Fields, W. C.

> **Now Try:** *Fields for President* is a collection of essays by the comic actor, and *W. C. Fields by Himself: His Intended Autobiography* is a posthumously published collection of his letters and scripts. Like Fields, Groucho Marx was famous for his quick wit. Stefan Kanfer includes many one-liners and short sketches in *Groucho: The Life and*

Times of Julius Henry Marx (see this chapter). Another humorous biography is *Chas Addams: A Cartoonist's Life* by Linda H. Davis (see chapter 7), which includes many famous Addams cartoons. Fields told journalists that he most admired the author Charles Dickens. Jane Smiley explains the life and novels of the British author in *Charles Dickens* (see chapter 7).

Mason, Bobbie Ann

Elvis Presley. Lipper/Viking, 2003. 178p. Penguin Lives. ISBN 0670031747. Audiobook and large print available.

Although there are many biographies of Elvis Presley (1935–1977), this small book stands out because novelist Bobbie Ann Mason tells readers who were not fans of the King why his music and acting careers mattered to her and millions of other fans. All the major events of his life are included: the Sun Record sessions, appearing on Ed Sullivan, his movies, his military service, meeting the Beatles and Richard Nixon, his marriage, and his death. Mason also examines his relationships with his mother, his manager Colonel Parker, and his wife Priscilla, and describes his addictions and decline. This title in the Penguin Lives series will appeal to reluctant readers of any age.

> **Subjects:** Actors and Actresses; Group Discussion Books; Memphis; Presley, Elvis; Rock Musicians; Teen Reads

> **Now Try:** No Presley memoirs have surfaced, but he is credited as an alternate author of the cookbook *Are You Hungry Tonight?: Elvis' Favorite Recipes* by Brenda Arlene Butler. Priscilla Presley wrote about her romance and marriage to the singer in *Elvis and Me.* Presley has appeared as a character in several novels, notably *Elvis Presley Calls His Mother After the Ed Sullivan Show* by Samuel B. Charters. In the music world, Johnny Cash shared some of the same fame and pain as Presley. Michael Streissguth tells a sympathetic but candid story about the musician in *Johnny Cash: The Biography.* Presley, Cash, Jerry Lee Lewis, Roy Orbison, and Carl Perkins all started recording at Sun Records in Memphis, Tennessee. Colin Escott recounts the seminal days of rock music in *Good Rockin' Tonight: Sun Records and the Birth of Rock 'N' Roll.* Like Presley, John Lennon's fame has continued well past his death. Lennon friend Ray Coleman describes the life of the ex-Beatle in *John Lennon: The Definitive Biography.*

McPherson, Edward

Buster Keaton: Tempest in a Flat Hat. Newmarket Press, 2004. 289p. ISBN 155-7046654.

Joseph Frank Keaton (1895–1966) fell down the stairs at eighteen months old, his first pratfall, witnessed by a hotel guest who proclaimed him a "buster." The name stuck with this son of vaudeville entertainers, who grew up to be a master of physical comedy and star in silent films of the 1920s. After many lean years and unhappy marriages, Keaton revived his career in television in the 1950s. In this sympathetic, sometimes witty biography, film fan Edward McPherson focuses on the madcap comedy that made Keaton a legend. Film historians will enjoy this nostalgic look at the comedian.

Subjects: Actors and Actresses; Comedians; Keaton, Buster

Now Try: Keaton titled his memoir *My Wonderful World of Slapstick*. Zane Grey, a similarly melancholy character, could not feel the joy that he brought to others. Thomas H. Pauly tells his sad story in *Zane Grey: His Life, His Adventures, His Women* (see chapter 7). The saddest of all comedians may have been Peter Sellers, whose story is told by Ed Sikov in *Mr. Strangelove: A Biography of Peter Sellers* (see this chapter). Jane Scovell describes the life of a comedian's wife in *Oona: Living in the Shadows: A Biography of Oona O'Neill Chaplin*. An ALA Notable Book about early film comedians is *The Silent Clowns* by Walter Kerr.

Naudet, Jean-Jacques, comp.

Marlene Dietrich: Photographs and Memories, from the Marlene Dietrich Collection of the FilmMuseum Berlin. Knopf, 2001. 262p. ISBN 0375405348.

Marlene Dietrich (1901–1992) kept everything, including letters, telegrams, playbills, and photographs. The actress claimed that she had every dress, blouse, cape, shoe, hat, and accessory that she used on stage or in a film. When she died, her executor opened six storage units in London, Paris, New York, and California and donated the items to the Film Museum in Berlin. Through family photos, movie stills, displays of artifacts, and comments from her friends, this big museum book gives fans an intimate look at the life and career of the legendary actress.

Subjects: Actors and Actresses; Costumes; Dietrich, Marlene; Photographic Biography; Women

Now Try: Dietrich's 1989 autobiography *Marlene* is praised for its insight and criticized for its many factual errors. *Jacqueline Kennedy: The White House Years: Selections from the John F. Kennedy Library and Museum* is a fascinating exhibit catalog that shows readers the care the first lady took with her wardrobe. Photographs show the gowns, dresses, coats, hats, gloves, and purses both as artifacts and in use by Mrs. Kennedy as she entertained dignitaries. Elizabeth Taylor has written a memoir full of museum-quality photographs to celebrate her jewelry collection, *Elizabeth Taylor: My Love Affair with Jewelry*. Caroline Weber describes the clothes worn by French queen Marie Antoinette that impressed nobility and insulted the poor in *Queen of Fashion: What Marie Antoinette Wore to the Revolution* (see chapter 9).

Peters, Margot

Design for Living: Alfred Lunt and Lynn Fontanne: A Biography. Knopf, 2003. 394p. ISBN 0375411178.

The Fabulous Lunts are a Broadway legend. For four decades, married actors Alfred Lunt (1892–1977) and Lynn Fontanne (1887–1983) entertained theatergoers in a series of comedies and dramas, many from the pen of their good friend Noël Coward. Rarely separated and totally devoted to each other, they fought tooth and nail in rehearsals, inspiring the musical *Kiss Me, Kate*. They were known for their sophistication and urbanity and rejected many Hollywood offers to stay on the stage. In this lively dual biography for theater fans, Margot Peters chronicles the escapades of this witty couple and their circle of friends.

Subjects: Actors and Actresses; Broadway; Dual Biography; Fontanne, Lynn; Lunt, Alfred

Now Try: A sweeter celebrity romance story is found in *Say Good Night, Gracie! The Story of Burns & Allen* by Cheryl Blythe and Susan Sackett. Paul Newman and Joanne

Woodward had a long and apparently happy marriage despite all the pressures of Hollywood. Joe Morella and Edward Z. Epstein chronicle the major events in the couple's careers and marriage in *Paul and Joanne: A Biography of Paul Newman and Joanne Woodward*. One of Hollywood's most famous couples never married. Christopher P. Andersen describes the famous relationship in *Affair to Remember: The Remarkable Love Story of Katharine Hepburn and Spencer Tracy*. In the world of science, a story about a devoted couple and their children is told in *The Curies: A Biography of the Most Controversial Family in Science* by Denis Brian (see chapter 11).

Santopietro, Tom

Considering Doris Day. Thomas Dunne Books, 2007. 388p. ISBN 9780312362638.

Between 1939 and 1975, Doris Day (1924–) could be seen or heard everywhere. Her big band and jazz recordings played on the radio and sold like hotcakes. Moviegoers saw her paired up with many of the most romantic men in Hollywood. Eventually she had several television comedy series and variety specials. Then she retired, to be seen only when advocating for animal rights. According to Tom Santopietro, Day's performances seemed so effortless that her talents were underappreciated. In this collection of essays for movie fans, he tells how Day worked hard for her success, sometimes at the expense of her marriages.

> **Subjects:** Actors and Actresses; Day, Doris; Singers

> **Now Try:** In *Doris Day: Her Own Story*, Day describes her first three failed marriages and her son's suicide. Movie studios often matched Day with actor Rock Hudson. Jerry Oppenheimer chronicles Hudson's career, personal life, and death from AIDS in *Idol, Rock Hudson: The True Story of an American Film Hero*. Like Day, Peggy Lee has now been forgotten by many people. In *Fever: The Life and Music of Miss Peggy Lee*, Peter Richmond argues that she was as prominent as Bing Crosby and Louis Armstrong in her prime. Bing Crosby was as comfortable as Day in the worlds of both music and film. Gary Giddins chronicles his early accomplishments in *Bing Crosby: A Pocketful of Dreams, the Early Years, 1903–1940* (see this chapter).

Turner, Marcia Layton

Emeril! Inside the Amazing Success of Today's Most Popular Chef. John Wiley, 2004. 248p. ISBN 0471656267.

Emeril Lagasse (1959–) never let child labor laws stop him. He got a part-time job in a restaurant as a dishwasher at age ten and had a full-time evening shift at age twelve. By age twenty-three he was an executive chef. By age forty-four he owned nine restaurants and his own food company, had written eight cookbooks, and starred in two television shows. According to small business expert Marcia Layton Turner, Emeril has the personality and drive to success in today's highly competitive food industry. In this book she explains how he built his empire and helps his community.

> **Subjects:** Chefs; Entrepreneurs; Lagasse, Emeril; New Orleans; Quick Reads; Restaurateurs; Television

Now Try: In *Chef's Tale: A Memoir of Food, France and America*, Pierre Franey charmingly tells about becoming a successful chef and food critic in a less hurried time. Julia Child also got her start as a chef and cookbook author in Paris, which she tells about in *My Life in France*. American journalist Bill Buford went to Babbo, a chic restaurant in New York, to learn if a competent home cook could become a four-star chef. He recounts his experiences and the story of his boss, chef Mario Batali, in the memoir *Heat*. Another young laborer, Judy Garland, was on the vaudeville stage at age two and a half. John Fricke focuses on the singer's achievements and the happier episodes in her life in the photobiography *Judy Garland: World's Greatest Entertainer* (see this chapter). Wall Street legend Jesse Livermore was a stock trader by age fifteen and wealthy before he was twenty. Richard Smitten tells the story of a driven man in *Jesse Livermore: World's Greatest Stock Trader* (see chapter 9).

Wills, Garry

John Wayne's America: The Politics of Celebrity. Simon & Schuster, 1997. 380p. ISBN 0684808234. Audiobook available.

Like the Western characters that he often portrayed, John Wayne (1907–1979) seemed to come from out of nowhere. Although Hollywood publicists celebrated the small-town roots of many other actors, they never spoke about Wayne's origins. The tactic worked better than planned, as moviegoers believed the masculine Wayne to be the tough, self-reliant champion for justice that they saw on the screen. As the years passed, Wayne grew to believe it himself. In this meditation on the meaning of the life of John Wayne, Garry Wills admiringly recounts the childhood, career, and private life of an icon of American film. General readers will be attracted to this book by a prolific author.

Subjects: Actors and Actresses; Biographical Essays; Group Discussion Books; Wayne, John

Now Try: Pilar Wayne, his third wife, describes his three marriages and his battle with cancer in *John Wayne: My Life with the Duke*. Wayne's name is often associated with movie director John Ford. Scott Eyman chronicles the celebrated career of the director of *The Grapes of Wrath, The Quiet Man*, and *Stagecoach* in *Print the Legend: The Life and Times of John Ford*. Jimmy Stewart turned to the Western movie late in his career, starring with Wayne in John Ford's *The Man Who Shot Liberty Valance*. Marc Eliot describes Stewart's long and varied career in *Jimmy Stewart: A Biography* (see this chapter).Elvis Presley is another iconic American entertainment figure. Novelist Bobbie Ann Mason explains the importance of Presley's life to fans in her compact book *Elvis Presley* (see this section).

Zehme, Bill

The Way You Wear Your Hat: Frank Sinatra and the Lost Art of Livin'. HarperCollins, 1997. 245p. ISBN 006018289X. Audiobook and large print available.

The cocked hat, nice suits, sharp ties, and spiffy shoes were very important to Frank Sinatra (1915–1998). He had an image to maintain, as did his friends. He saw to it that they too dressed and behaved according to his standards. Drinking, smoking, and flirting (even if married) were permitted, but no one was supposed to cuss in front of a woman. Everyone in the Rat Pack had to live with style—Sinatra style. In this collection of entertaining essays on clothes, friends, women, family, and performing, journalist Bill Zehme gives readers a look at the life of the Chairman of the Board by describing the way he lived his daily life. Sinatra fans will appreciate this detailed "how to be like Frank" guide.

Subjects: Actors and Actresses; Biographical Essays; Photographic Biography; Sinatra, Frank; Singers

Now Try: Although definitely biased, Nancy Sinatra calmly addressed most of the controversies in her father's life in *Frank Sinatra, My Father*. Many photos from early in Sinatra's life can be found in *Frank Sinatra: The Family Album* by Charles Pignone. Biographical essays have been used to tell the lives of other prominent people in many fields. Gretchen Craft Rubin uses short essays and even quizzes in her creative biographies of historical figures, *Forty Ways to Look at JFK* and *Forty Ways to Look at Winston Churchill*. John M. Carroll uses essays to describe the importance of Red Grange in the history of sports in *Red Grange and the Rise of Modern Football* (see chapter 12). Terry Teachout also uses essays to describe the life and career of ballet master George Balanchine in *All in the Dances* (see chapter 7).

High Society Stories

Before the public became fixated on entertainers, it followed the lives of high society figures, most of whom were rich. These people may have been born into wealthy families or attained their affluence through successful business or marriage. By virtue of their wealth, they were invited into the parlors of other wealthy people and attended balls, operas, and other exclusive functions. In summer they went to comfortable vacation retreats together. Society pages in newspapers reported who was engaged to whom, who was visiting whom, who was abroad, and what all the women wore. Like entertainers, the figures of high society sometimes misbehaved, and reports of the scandals spread through all levels of society.

In this section are biographies of people famous for their positions in society. Most lived their luxurious lives in New York, London, or Paris. Readers who enjoy British history will recognize Lady Harriet Spencer, Lady Randolph Churchill, and Alice Kipling and her sisters. Art lovers will know Peggy Guggenheim and Isabella Stewart Gardner. From the jet set of the 1960s come Coco Chanel and Jacqueline Kennedy Onassis.

Like other Celebrity Biographies, the portrayal of character is the primary concern, closely followed by the telling of stories involving the characters and their high society friends. Friendly and intimate relationships are more important than the businesses that made these people wealthy. Settings tend to be more detailed in these biographies than in those of entertainers. High society figures frequent mansions, exclusive clubs, art galleries, and exotic vacation locations. Some quick reads are included.

High Society Stories portray privileged people who lived extravagantly in the company of other members of the social elite. With their names and pictures frequently in newspapers or other media, they were well-known, admired, and discussed. As in other Celebrity Biographies, the conduct of their private lives is the focus. Some quick reads are included.

Brandreth, Gyles

Philip and Elizabeth: Portrait of a Royal Marriage. Norton, 2005. 413p. ISBN 039306-1132.

> As is often the case among royals, Princess Elizabeth of Great Britain (1926–) married a distant cousin, Prince Philip of Greece (1921–), in 1947. Unlike many other royal marriages throughout history, their relationship has worked well for over sixty years. There have been a few problems with the children and the children's spouses, but the couple has remained steady through the hard times. In this intimate portrait of the royal couple, Gyles Brandreth tells family stories bound to interest royalty fans.
>
> > **Subjects:** Dual Biography; Elizabeth II, Queen of Great Britain; Great Britain; Marriage; Philip, Prince of Great Britain; Princes; Queens
> >
> > **Now Try:** Jennie Bond tells much more about the long-reigning queen in *Elizabeth: Fifty Glorious Years*, an attractive photobiography. *Debrett's Queen Elizabeth, the Queen Mother, 1900–2002* by Valerie Garner is harder to find but will please royal family fans who followed the long life of the mother of the queen. Like the royal couple, Ronald and Nancy Reagan enjoyed a warm, supportive relation amid the troubles of politics and errant children. Celebrity biographer Anne Edwards examines their relationship closely in *The Reagans: Portrait of a Marriage*. In the admiring *E. B. White: A Biography* (see chapter 7), Scott Elledge tells about the long, warm relationship between *The New Yorker* editor and his wife, Katharine.

Charles-Roux, Edmonde

Chanel: Her Life, Her World, and the Woman Behind the Legend She Herself Created. Translated from the French by Nancy Amphoux. Knopf, 1975. 380p. ISBN 0394476131.

> Why has there been no television miniseries about fashion designer Coco Chanel (1883–1971)? Her life reads like a racy French novel. After her childhood in an orphanage, she rose in society, meeting royalty and knowing all of Europe's most famous designers. Her accomplishments were many. She not only created perfumes, the first modern woman's bathing suit, and the first little black dress, she also convinced women to throw away their corsets, shorten their skirts, and wear costume jewelry without apology. Edmonde Charles-Roux, the former editor of *French Vogue*, tells an intimate story of this bold businesswoman and her romantic affairs in this book that will please general readers.
>
> > **Subjects:** Chanel, Coco; Fashion Designers; France; Women
> >
> > **Now Try:** Like Chanel, Dorothy Schiff was a woman of great financial power who held her own with the men in her industry. Marilyn Nissenson tells about her rise to fame and her personal life in *The Lady Upstairs: Dorothy Schiff and the New York Post* (see chapter 10). Cosmetics entrepreneur Charles Revson was Chanel's contemporary. Andrew Tobias tells how the overbearing man changed the look of the fashionable woman in *Fire and Ice: The Story of Charles Revson—the Man Who Built the Revlon Empire* (see chapter 5). Jackie Cochran made a quick fortune in cosmetics, which she used to finance a career as a test pilot. Doris L. Rich recounts how Cochran set many aviation records and met many people in society and politics in *Jackie Cochran: Pilot in the Fastest Lane* (see chapter 1). Like Chanel, Anna Leonowens left one country for another, where she joined a higher social class based on false credentials. Susan Morgan recounts Leonowens's life in the court of Siam and her years in Canada in *Bombay*

Anna: The Real Story and Remarkable Adventures of the King and I Governess (see chapter 1).

Flaherty, Tina Santi

What Jackie Taught Us: Lessons from the Remarkable Life of Jacqueline Kennedy Onassis. Perigee, 2004. 237p. ISBN 0399529888.

Jacqueline Bouvier married an ambitious Bostonian who became the youngest elected president of the United States. Initially, the first lady was perceived as just a fashionable wife from whom not much was expected, but as the spotlight caught her more frequently, Americans discovered she was a woman of substance with a mission. According to Tina Santi Flaherty, Jacqueline Kennedy Onassis (1929–1994), who was an avid reader and became a book editor, transformed the image of the intelligent woman, making smart acceptable. In this book Flaherty tells what Jackie did right in each phase of her life.

Subjects: Biographical Essays; First Ladies; Group Discussion Books; Onassis, Jacqueline Kennedy; Quick Reads; Teen Reads; Women

Now Try: Editor Bill Adler has collected quotations from Onassis's letters, speeches, and magazine articles to form a memoir, *The Eloquent Jacqueline Kennedy Onassis: A Portrait in Her Own Words.* C. David Heymann describes the lives of the first lady's children in *American Legacy: The Story of John & Caroline Kennedy* (see chapter 6). Extended family relations and their husband's extramarital affairs are the focus of *Jackie, Ethyl, Joan: Women of Camelot* by J. Randy Taraborrelli. Martha Stewart has also been praised for her contributions to the art of entertaining and women's fashion and criticized for other aspects of her life. Lloyd Allen defends the home economist in *Being Martha: The Inside Story of Martha Stewart and Her Amazing Life* (see chapter 9). *Founding Mothers* by Cokie Roberts (see chapter 9) will interest readers who wish to compare this first lady with other historical American women.

Flanders, Judith

Circle of Sisters: Alice Kipling, Georgiana Burne-Jones, Agnes Poynter and Louisa Baldwin. Norton, 2005. 392p. 0393052109.

George Browne Macdonald (1805–1868) was a modest Methodist minister in rural England who married Hannah Jones, the daughter of a grocer, in 1833. The couple had eleven children, including four daughters who married into Britain's upper classes. One married a famous artist, another married the president of the Royal Academy, a third gave birth to a prime minister, and the fourth was the mother of a world famous poet and storyteller. For history readers and those interested in British high society, Judith Flanders tells the remarkable story of the Macdonald family, following the daughters into their varied lives of success and distress.

Subjects: Baldwin, Louisa; Burne-Jones, Georgiana; Great Britain; Kipling, Alice; Poynter, Agnes; Sisters

Now Try: David Grafton tells about a remarkable group of American siblings in *The Sisters: Babe Mortimer Pauley, Betsey Roosevelt Whitney, Minnie Astor Fosburgh: The Lives and Times of the Fabulous Cushing Sisters* (see this chapter). The six Mitford sisters stirred controversy with their flamboyant behavior and unpopular causes. Two of the sisters even befriended Adolf Hitler. Mary S. Lovell chronicles the sisters' exploits in *The Sisters: The Saga of the Mitford Family* (see chapter 9). In 1920s China, sisters Amy Ling Chen and Ling Shuhua chose different lives. One emigrated to America to become a doctor; the other became a noted writer and artist in Beijing. Sasha Su-Ling Welland evokes two vastly different worlds in her accounts of the women in *A Thousand Miles of Dreams: The Journeys of Two Chinese Sisters*.

Gill, Anton

Art Lover: A Biography of Peggy Guggenheim. HarperCollins, 2002. 480p. ISBN 0060-196971.

With a small fortune inherited from her father, who died on the *Titanic*, flamboyant art patron Peggy Guggenheim (1898–1979) roamed Europe between the world wars, attending parties, meeting modern artists, and buying their paintings and sculptures. She also collected numerous husbands and lovers while neglecting her children. As cash-strapped artists fled the Nazis, she bought up their works, which she sold for great profit from her gallery in London. Back in the United States after fleeing Vichy France, she discovered the abstract expressionists, including Jackson Pollock. In this intimate biography, Anton Gill shows Guggenheim as an ambitious woman and essential player in the world of twentieth-century art.

Subjects: Art Collectors; Guggenheim, Peggy; Women

Now Try: Guggenheim discussed her art business and love life in her candid memoir, *Confessions of an Art Addict*. Her love life resembled that of Ava Gardner. Jane Ellen Wayne recounts the actress's many marriages and affairs in *Ava's Men* (see this chapter). Guggenheim supported struggling artist Jackson Pollack through financial and mental difficulties by loaning a cabin to him and his wife and buying some of his works. Steven Naifeh and Gregory White Smith portray the painter as a brilliant but suicidal character in *Jackson Pollock: An American Saga*. Ian Gibson tells another story of bad behavior by a Guggenheim associate in *The Shameful Life of Salvador Dalí*.

Gleeson, Janet

Privilege and Scandal: The Remarkable Life of Harriet Spencer, Sister of Georgiana. Crown Publishers, 2006. 419p. ISBN 9780307381972.

After her death, the sons of Lady Harriet Spencer (1761–1821) tried to burn all her letters to destroy evidence of many family indiscretions and her love affairs. The contents of her desk and the special box that she took everywhere were burned, but the effort was useless. Many of her letters were in the hands of other people, and the scandalous stories were told anyway. Janet Gleeson tells stories about Harriet and her well-connected friends in British and French society during the time of King George III that will attract romance readers and Anglophiles.

Subjects: Bessborough, Henrietta Frances Spencer Ponsonby, Countess of; Great Britain; Love Affairs; Nobility; Scandals

Now Try: The Spencer family story continues with *The Diana Chronicles* by Tina Brown (see chapter 9) among many books about the Princess of Wales. *Improper Pursuits: The Scandalous Life of an Earlier Lady Diana Spencer* by Carola Hicks tells of another mischievous Spencer. This Diana left her husband for another man, took up

High Society Stories   287

painting, and socialized with the artist Joshua Reynolds and the author Samuel Johnson. In France, Gabrielle Emilie le Tonnelier de Breteuil, the marquise Du Chatelet, left her husband to frolic with Voltaire and write texts on physics and mathematics. Judith Zinsser recounts the exciting life of an unconventional woman in *La Dame d'Esprit: A Biography of the Marquise Du Chatelet* (see chapter 11). Art patron Isabella Stewart Gardner burned her scandalous letters herself. Douglass Shand-Tucci tells her story in *The Art of Scandal: The Life and Times of Isabella Stewart Gardner* (see this chapter).

Gordon, Lois

Nancy Cunard: Heiress, Muse, Political Idealist. Columbia University Press, 2007. 447p. ISBN 9780231139380.

Nancy Cunard (1896–1965) inspired photographers, artists, novelists, and poets with her beauty and character. She posed for photos for Man Ray and Cecil Beaton. She sat for painters Oskar Kokoschka, Alvaro Guevara, and Wyndham Lewis. Ezra Pound, T. S. Eliot, Ernest Hemingway, Pablo Neruda, and other writers based characters on the idealistic socialite. In this book for general readers, Lois Gordon tells an admiring tale about a shipping heiress who became a model, poet, publisher, advocate for racial justice, reporter in the Spanish Civil War, and humanitarian aid worker in post–World War II Europe.

> **Subjects:** Cunard, Nancy; Humanitarians; Journalists; Poets; Publishers; Teen Reads; Women

> **Now Try:** Cunard told about her life among the literary expatriates in Paris in the late 1920s in *These Were the Hours: Memories of My Hours Press, Reanville and Paris, 1928–1931*. Like Cunard, Lady Caroline Blackwood posed for artists and conversed with writers, but her life lacked the idealism of her contemporary. Her tragic story is told by Nancy Schoenberger in *Dangerous Muse: The Life of Lady Caroline Blackwood* (see chapter 7). Cunard's humanitarian work resembles that of Audrey Hepburn, whose story is told in *Enchantment: The Life of Audrey Hepburn* by Donald Spoto (see this chapter). Supreme Court Justice Sandra Day O'Connor is a woman who with maturity became more concerned with the societal implications of legal decisions. Joan Biskupic recounts O'Connor's story from her birth in El Paso, Texas, to her retirement, with an emphasis on her Supreme Court career, in *Sandra Day O'Connor: How the First Woman on the Supreme Court Became Its Most Influential Justice* (see chapter 10).

Grafton, David

The Sisters: Babe Mortimer Pauley, Betsey Roosevelt Whitney, Minnie Astor Fosburgh: the Lives and Times of the Fabulous Cushing Sisters. Villard Books, 1992. 316p. ISBN 0394584163.

The three Cushing sisters, born into comfort, married into wealth and influence. Minnie (1906–1978), Betsey (1908–1998), and Babe (1915–1978) had two husbands each, industrious men who topped the power structures in Boston, New York, and Washington, D.C., and for forty years the sisters' names frequently appeared in newspaper society pages. In this nostalgic narrative, David Grafton takes general readers into the world of the rich and famous during a charmed period in American cultural history.

> **Subjects:** Cushing Family; Family Biography; Fosburgh, Minnie Astor; Paley, Babe Mortimer; Sisters; Whitney, Betsey Cushing Roosevelt; Women
>
> **Now Try:** The five Langhorne sisters of Virginia may have exceeded the achievements of the Cushing sisters. In the wake of the Civil War, Reconstruction had tarnished their proud family, but the beautiful and charming girls moved to Northern states and across the ocean to England to find wealthy husbands. One even claimed a seat in Parliament. Their story is told in *Five Sisters: The Langhornes of Virginia* by James Fox. In eighteenth-century New England, Elizabeth, Mary, and Sophia Peabody held social functions that drew all the writers of the transcendental movement, including Ralph Waldo Emerson and Nathaniel Hawthorne. Megan Marshall tells how they married well in *The Peabody Sisters: Three Women Who Ignited American Romanticism* (see chapter 9). Margaret Chase was a society woman until her husband died and she took his seat in Congress. Janann Sherman offers an admiring profile of a powerful woman who lived ninety-seven years, *No Place for a Woman: A Life of Senator Margaret Chase Smith* (see chapter 10). India's Indira Gandhi lived a very public life from childhood, groomed for national leadership. Katherine Frank sympathetically depicts how the most powerful woman in India used her political talents to survive many tragedies, only to be assassinated by her bodyguard in 1984, in *Indira: The Life of Indira Nehru Gandhi* (see chapter 10).

Higham, Charles

Dark Lady: Winston Churchill's Mother and Her World. Carroll & Graf, 2006. 250p. ISBN 9780786718894.

> Born Jeanette Jerome in mid-nineteenth-century Brooklyn, Lady Randolph Churchill (1854–1921) was always well-connected to wealth and political power. Her father was a ruthless financier who profited from government contracts during the American Civil War, and her first husband, from whom she got her title, was in the English prime minister's cabinet. According to Charles Higham, Winston Churchill's mother was never happy in the 200 rooms of Blenheim Palace, so she traveled frequently. Also unhappy with her husband, she often took lovers. Higham's candid biography will please readers who enjoy dramatic romance stories.

> **Subjects:** Churchill, Lady Randolph; Churchill, Winston; Jerome, Jeanette; Mothers; Women

> **Now Try:** An entertaining book about Lady Randolph's son is *Forty Ways to Look at Winston Churchill: A Brief Account of a Long Life* by Gretchen Rubin. Winston had a far better marital experience than his mother. *Winston and Clementine: The Personal Letters of the Churchills* is a collection of letters spanning fifty-seven years of their happy marriage. Like Lady Randolph, Empress Josephine of France rose from a childhood of mere privilege to social prominence through marriage. Andrea Stuart recounts her rise and fall as the consort of Emperor Napoleon Bonaparte in *The Rose of Martinique: A Life of Napoleon's Josephine* (see chapter 9). Judith Zinsser tells the story of another very intelligent woman bored with marriage who turned to love affairs and physics to lift her spirits in *La Dame d'Esprit: A Biography of the Marquise Du Chatelet* (see chapter 11).

Shand-Tucci, Douglass

The Art of Scandal: The Life and Times of Isabella Stewart Gardner.
HarperCollins, 1997. 351p. ISBN 0060186437.

At the end of her life, art patron Isabella Stewart Gardner (1840–1924) burned her vast collection of letters, denying scholars many stories about her friendships, travels, and the provenance of the art that she collected. Among her friends were artists, merchants, authors, and the cream of society, and in those letters were radical ideas and accounts of indiscreet behavior. According to Douglass Shand-Tucci, Gardner failed in her effort to edit her legacy and leave only her museum with its strict rules of preservation as an enduring statement of her life. In this intimate biography the author portrays Gardner for general readers, recounting many stories about the complex woman and worthy subject of Henry James's novels and John Singer Sargent's paintings.

Subjects: Art Collectors; Boston; Gardner, Isabella Stewart; Travelers; Women

Now Try: Patricia Vigderman looks at the Gardner Museum and the woman who built it in the illustrated *The Memory Palace of Isabella Stewart Gardner*. Gardner was a patron and friend of painter John Singer Sargent. Deborah Davis tells about the scandal he sparked with a painting in *Strapless: John Singer Sargent and the Fall of Madame X*. Mystery author Agatha Christie was another unconventional woman who sought unsuccessfully to keep her personal affairs from the public. Janet Morgan describes her adventurous life in *Agatha Christie: A Biography*. Marilyn Nissenson tells about a strong woman who sought to dominate the political world through her newspaper in *The Lady Upstairs: Dorothy Schiff and the* **New York Post** (see chapter 10).

Celebrity Collections

Instead of telling about one or two celebrities, the books in this section cover numerous famous people in separate entries or chapters. Although some of the books are more historical than other books in this chapter, the emphasis is still on telling about people famous for the positions they reached in their cultures.

> *Celebrity Collections* include books that gather profiles of many similar celebrity characters into a single volume. Authors focus on the key incidents and dominant characteristics in these quick profiles. These works are ideal for more leisurely or interrupted reading.

Aubrey, John

Brief Lives. Boydell Press, 2004. (1813). 332p. ISBN 1843831120. Audiobook available.

In this collection of biographical sketches of prominent seventeenth-century Englishmen, it is the accounts and not the lives themselves that are brief. John Aubrey (1626–1697) knew many of the men from meetings in coffeehouses and at the Royal Society, of which he was a member. He kept notes about the scientists, mathematicians, writers, and gentlemen of London society, including many tidbits of gossip and scandal as well as basic facts and his personal opinions about their character. Probably never meant for publication, these entertaining biographical sketches were discovered and published in 1813, adding much to our knowledge of gentlemen's lives of their time.

> **Subjects:** Collective Biography; England; London

> **Now Try:** In the biography *John Aubrey and His Friends,* Anthony Powell recounts how the papers of Aubrey were discovered and their importance to scholars. *Life of Johnson* by James Boswell is another classic that students of the biography genre must read. Johnson and Boswell also knew and commented on the world of the London coffeehouse. Humphrey Carpenter brings the London literary scene forward 300 years in *The Brideshead Generation: Evelyn Waugh and His Friends* (see chapter 6). Art historian John Richardson writes very candidly about the people he knew in *Sacred Monsters, Sacred Masters: Beaton, Capote, Dalí, Picasso, Freud, Warhol, and More* (see chapter 7).

Auchincloss, Louis

The Vanderbilt Era: Profiles of a Gilded Age. Charles Scribner's Sons, 1989. 214p. ISBN 0684191121.

In New York society of the nineteenth century, Cornelius Vanderbilt (1794–1877) was at first shunned because he earned rather than inherited his great wealth. The rail and shipping tycoon could have cared less, for old families mattered less to him than his sense of merit in the new order of business and industry. His progeny and their friends, however, were more sensitive to societal opinions and cared more for their reputations. In this insightful collection of short profiles of Gilded Age individuals, novelist Louis Auchincloss describes how characters as diverse as the commodore's sons and their friends Jay Gould, Edith Wharton, and Louis Tiffany fit into the Vanderbilt world.

> **Subjects:** Gilded Age; New York City; Vanderbilt Family

> **Now Try:** Vanderbilt friend Edith Wharton described the world of Old New York in her novels *The Buccaneers, The House of Mirth*, and *The Age of Innocence.* Because of his ruthless financial dealings, Jay Gould was the most notorious of the Vanderbilt friends. Edward J. Renehan Jr. contends that Gould was the model for contemporary financiers in *Dark Genius of Wall Street: The Misunderstood Life of Jay Gould, King of the Robber Barons* (see chapter 9). Stanley Weintraub profiles a similar and slightly overlapping group in his collection of witty profiles, *The London Yankees: Portraits of American Writers and Artists in England 1894–1914.* The children of industrialist Edward Cabot Clark also become high society figures. Their story is told in *The Clarks of Cooperstown: Their Singer Sewing Machine Fortune, Their Great and Influential Art Collections, Their Forty-Year Feud* by Nicholas Fox Weber (see this section).

Remnick, David, ed.

Life Stories: Profiles from **The New Yorker**. Random House, 2000. 530p. ISBN 0375-503552. Audiobook available.

According to magazine editor David Remnick, a profile is a combination of "anecdote, incident, interview, and description" that gives readers an intimate look at a person in the news, arts, sports, or society. *The New Yorker* has been running these biographical sketches since the magazine began publishing in 1925. For the seventy-fifth anniversary of the publication, twenty-five of its best examples from well-known writers, including Calvin Trillin, John McPhee, Truman Capote, and Roger Angell, were collected in this volume. These elegantly written celebrity profiles should appeal to a wide range of readers.

Subjects: Artists; Athletes; Authors; Collective Biography

Now Try: A good follow-up book for this collection is *E. B. White: A Biography* by Scott Elledge (see chapter 7), giving the reader a look behind the scenes at *The New Yorker* and the literary world it represented during White's life. Another collection from *The New Yorker* featuring a diverse group of biographical profiles is **Character Studies: Encounters with the Curiously Obsessed** by Mark Singer. Writer and television commentator Alistair Cooke befriended a diverse group of characters during his long career, including Charlie Chaplin, the Duke of Windsor, H. L. Mencken, Adlai Stevenson, Bertrand Russell, and Humphrey Bogart. He elegantly profiled them in his collective biography *Six Men*.

Strachey, Lytton

Eminent Victorians. Oxford University Press, 2003 (1918). 300p. ISBN 0192801-589. Audiobook available.

Every book on the history of biography points to this book, first published in 1918, as the first modern work of biography. Strachey shocked the book world and cultured society with these unflattering profiles of prominent English characters. He is credited with giving biographers the charge to sketch out characters instead of simply chronicling all their deeds and to tell the unvarnished truth. Ironically, accuracy was a problem for Strachey, and his research methods and exclusions have been questioned. Historians agree that he changed the form and tone of biography. Written during World War I, its chapter "The End of General Gordon" works as biography as well as a criticism of British military ethics. Strachey also portrays three other seemingly random British citizens of the Victorian era. In his introduction Strachey indicates that they were just people who interested him. Readers wanting perspective on the traditions of Celebrity Biography will appreciate this classic.

Subjects: Arnold, Thomas; Collective Biography; Gordon, Charles George; Great Britain; Manning, Henry Edward; Nightingale, Florence; Victorian Era

Now Try: More on Strachey is found in *The Bloomsbury Group: A Collection of Memoirs and Commentary*, edited by S. P. Rosenbaum. Strachey was a member of this group with Virginia and Leonard Woolf, Vanessa and Clive Bell, E. M. Forster, Roger Fry, John Maynard Keynes, and others. Readers interested in the author can also try *Lytton Strachey: A Biography* by Michael Holroyd, from which the movie *Carrington* was adapted. A more balanced view of Florence Nightingale is provided in the collective biography *Three Victorian Women Who Changed Their World* by Nancy Boyd. According to historian A. N. Wilson, the Victorian era was a time of great change and radical thought hidden behind social conservatism. He gives a decade by decade account in *The Victorians*.

Weber, Nicholas Fox

The Clarks of Cooperstown: Their Singer Sewing Machine Fortune, Their Great and Influential Art Collections, Their Forty-Year Feud. Alfred A. Knopf, 2007. 420p. ISBN 9780307263476.

When a man becomes fabulously rich, his descendants often benefit from his success. Such was the case with the Clark family of Cooperstown, New York. In the nineteenth century Edward Cabot Clark (1811-1882) made his first fortune wisely investing in real estate. Then, as the lawyer for Isaac M. Singer, he became the majority stockholder in the Singer Manufacturing Company. His son Alfred, never feeling the need to work, spent his youth wandering around Europe, where he visited all the major museums. Alfred's sons Sterling and Stephen became very competitive art collectors and had serious disagreements about the merits of various art movements. In this intimate collective biography that gives readers a glimpse of the world of early twentieth-century art and philanthropy, curator Nicholas Fox Weber separately profiles the prominent members of the Clark family. Readers who enjoy family sagas will enjoy this book.

Subjects: Art Collectors; Clark Family; Collective Biography; Family Biography; Philanthropists

Now Try: The descendants of wildly successful capitalists often fight over an inheritance, which they then spend conspicuously. Elizabeth Candler Graham and Ralph Roberts tell a conflict-filled story in *The Real Ones: Four Generations of the First Family of Coca-Cola* (see chapter 9). Ron Chernow has written biographies of eminent business families who are also active in philanthropic causes in his family biographies, *The House of Morgan: An American Banking Dynasty and the Rise of Modern Finance* and *The Warburgs: The Twentieth Century Odyssey of a Remarkable Jewish Family* (see chapter 9). Stephen Berry tells about another feuding family in *House of Abraham: Lincoln and the Todds, a Family Divided by War* (see chapter 3).

Consider Starting With . . .

These well-written Celebrity Biographies of modest length will appeal to general readers.

- Berg, A. Scott. *Kate Remembered.*

- Bosworth, Patricia. *Marlon Brando.*

- Charles-Roux, Edmonde. *Chanel: Her Life, Her World, and the Woman Behind the Legend She Herself Created.*

- Eliot, Marc. *Jimmy Stewart: A Biography.*

- Higham, Charles. *Dark Lady: Winston Churchill's Mother and Her World.*

- Mason, Bobbie Ann. *Elvis Presley.*

- Spoto, Donald. *Enchantment: The Life of Audrey Hepburn.*

- Summers, Anthony. *Goddess: The Secret Lives of Marilyn Monroe.*

- Taraborrelli, J. Randy. *Elizabeth.*

• Zehme, Bill. *The Way You Wear Your Hat: Frank Sinatra and the Lost Art of Livin'.*

Further Reading

Boorstin, Daniel

The Image: A Guide to Pseudo-Events in America. Vintage, 1992. 336p. ISBN 0679741801.

> Many celebrity studies quote Boorstin. This seminal works was first published as *The Image or What Happened to the American Dream* in 1962.

Fitzgerald, Terence J., ed.

Celebrity Culture in the United States. H. W. Wilson, 2008. 181p. The Reference Shelf, vol. 80, no. 1. ISBN 9780824210786.

> Editor Fitzgerald collected essays on the history and meaning of celebrity culture in the United States. "Celebrity Culture" by Joseph Epstein examines the psychological aspects of relationships between celebrities and their fans.

Marshall, P. David

Celebrity and Power: Fame in Contemporary Culture. University of Minnesota Press, 1997. 290p. ISBN 0816627258.

> Marshall describes the workings behind the celebrity industry and its impact on society. Some of the celebrities named in this book are now forgotten, but the points made by the author are still relevant.

1
2
3
4
5
6
7
8
9
10
11
12

Chapter 9

Historical Biography

Definition of Historical Biography

History is a record of events from the past. Historical Biographies are stories about individual lives in the context of recorded events. Indeed, it may be argued that all biographies are to some extent historical, even when the subject is still living, but for the sake of this chapter, a narrower definition is used. To be a Historical Biography, a book must (1) recount the life of a deceased person; (2) fully describe the time, place, and events of the subject's life; and (3) help explain the era in which the subject lived.

According to Scott Casper in "Biography" in *American History Through Literature, 1820–1870*, the nineteenth century was a time when the writing of biography increased in the United States, as it "became a significant vehicle for narrating and interpreting the nation's history and particularly for contesting who merited inclusion in that history." Biographies of people of high morals and good actions were intended to inspire their readers to be moral and good and to engender love of country. According to Casper, the ever popular *Autobiography* by Benjamin Franklin became a model for other books about men building the nation, especially through commerce and industry. In 1839 Henry How published *Memoirs of the Most Eminent American Mechanics*, and *Merchant's Magazine* began to regularly profile successful men of business. By 1849 there was even a book called *Lives of Distinguished Shoemakers*. Although these titles may not have sold as well as modern biographies aimed at national audiences, they helped advance the American biographical tradition.

In the twenty-first century, the idea that biography can be a tool of history remains. Ron Chernow tells the story of John D. Rockefeller in *Titan: The Life of John D. Rockefeller, Sr.* not only because the oil tycoon was a fascinating and important character, but also because Rockefeller's attitudes reflected the prevailing philosophy of men of commerce in his time. In *My Face Is Black Is True: Callie House and the Struggle for Ex-Slave Reparations*, Mary Frances Berry describes the difficult life of Callie House, a washerwoman with five children from Nashville, Tennessee, because millions of black Americans faced the same hardships and dangers as House. Stephen Coote explains in *Royal Survivor: A Life of Charles II* how King Charles II of Great Britain saved the monarchy, an accomplishment that has affected the life of every British subject since the seventeenth century.

Historical Biographies are stories about the lives of individuals set in the context of time, place, and events of their era. The authors of these books fully describe the circumstances of their biographical subjects' lives, because those circumstances are important in depicting the era. People of any social class or occupation may be profiled in a Historical Biography.

Appeal of the Genre

Setting is especially important in Historical Biography, because explaining historical circumstances is a primary objective of the author and often the deciding factor in the reader's choice of a book. Biographical subjects are famous for their actions in the context of the history of a place or time. Readers wanting to learn historical details and understand the events of an era often choose to read these books.

To keep the reader's interest, these books must present good stories. In most, authors lay out the events of a subject's life in chronological order. The most common variation of this pattern is for the author to tell about a key event or a turning point in a person's life in the first chapter, and then start the birth-to-death life story in the second chapter. Final chapters may explain the legacy of a historical figure's life.

Likewise, the prospect of reading about a specific character may not always be the factor that drew a reader to a Historical Biography, but strong character development is necessary to keep the reader's interest. Some of the biographical subjects in this character are not well-known by twenty-first-century American readers, including stock trader Jesse Livermore, the fur trading Chouteau family of St. Louis, or welfare mother Rosa Lee, but their biographers bring them to life for readers.

Some of these stories are fast-paced and full of action, while others require unhurried reading to understand the sequence of events and the motivations of the characters. The appeal of learning is high in Historical Biographies. Readers with great interest in particular eras, places, or events will commit the time needed to read big books to learn new facts and different viewpoints about popular topics.

Organization of the Chapter

The sections of this chapter focus on historical themes. The first is "Success Stories," a topic that was popular with American readers as early as the 1830s, as described at the beginning of this chapter. Chocolate manufacturer Milton S. Hershey, multimillionaire John Jacob Astor, and movie producer and theme park builder Walt Disney are among the subjects in this section.

The second section, "Historical Families," focuses on families who through generations played important roles in history. Many of the family names will be very familiar to readers, such as Jefferson, Lee, and Ford, but others will be less so, including Hairston, Candler, and Chouteau.

The third section is "Human Rights and Social Justice Stories." These stories tell about individuals who proclaimed and fought for equal rights and humane treatment of people regardless of nationality, race, sex, or religion. Puritan minister Anne Hutchinson,

NAACP activist Rosa Parks, and French philosopher Voltaire are among the subjects.

"Royal Lives" is the fourth section. The lives of monarchs and members of royal families are told in these biographies set in several nations. Charlemagne of France, Catherine the Great of Russian, and Mary, Queen of Scots are among the monarchs included.

The chapter ends with "Historical Biography Collections." In this section are collective biographies that profile numerous historical individuals in one volume.

Success Stories

The Puritan work ethic, the belief that it is virtuous to work diligently to earn wealth and status, is a foundation of the American national character, and books that tell how individuals achieved their wealth and simultaneously contributed to economic development are appealing to many readers. The books in this section profile individuals who excelled at their trades or professions, earning riches beyond the modest expectations of most members of society.

Among the titles in this chapter, several could be classified as rags-to-riches stories, books that tell how individuals through self-initiative pulled themselves out of poverty and became rich. To readers wishing to improve their own financial situations, these books are evidence that prosperity is possible in the capitalist world. In *Wedgwood: The First Tycoon,* Brian Dolan tells how Englishman Josiah Wedgwood, a poor potter's son, became a wealthy and important industrialist by developing and selling better glazes for pottery. David Nasaw recounts how a poor Scottish immigrant became a steel manufacturer and philanthropist in America in *Andrew Carnegie.* Beverly Lowry accounts for the missing years in the life of Sarah Breedlove, the poor daughter of a former slave in Mississippi who became a cosmetics mogul, in *Her Dream of Dreams: The Rise and Triumph of Madam C. J. Walker.* Other titles, including *Dark Genius of Wall Street: The Misunderstood Life of Jay Gould, King of the Robber Barons* by Edward J. Renehan Jr. and *Titan: The Life of John D. Rockefeller, Sr.* by Ron Chernow, focus more on the character of business individuals and the roles they played in the economic development of their country.

The settings of these titles are rich with details about the economic conditions of their times. Readers learn about the formation of businesses, the development of industries, and the rise of national economies. The narratives describe the ingenuity and hustle of individuals and the struggle to beat competitors to markets. Only the strongest characters survive in the cutthroat world of business, where profit motives often justify any means taken to finance the company, develop the product, and make the sale. Readers wishing that they too were industrious and wealthy, or conversely those appalled by business ethics, will find these biographies fascinating.

> *Success Stories* include biographies of businesspeople whose lives contributed to the development of national economies. Authors generally tell how their subjects attained and benefited from their wealth. Readers enjoy these books for their depictions of economic history, compelling stories, and strong characters. Although many of these titles are lengthy, several quick reads are included.

Berridge, Kate

Madame Tussaud: A Life in Wax. William Morrow, 2006. 352p. ISBN 9780060528478.
When the heads of her friends fell from the guillotine during the French Revolution, wax museum entrepreneur Madame Tussaud (1761–1850) was there to pick them up and cast death masks. At least, she wanted her customers to believe that she was there, because it made a good story. According to British journalist Kate Berridge, Madame Tussaud was a master of publicity and often bent the truth in the interest of entertainment. The author reports that this daughter of a cook was already in Paris during the revolution, exhibiting wax reenactments in a house where she catered to the masses who could not read the daily broadsides. From this unsavory beginning, she created an entertainment empire and a brand name that is still known today.

> **Subjects:** Entrepreneurs; France; French Revolution; Rags to Riches Stories; Tussaud, Marie; Wax Modelers; Women

> **Now Try:** Like Tussaud, P. T. Barnum became fabulously rich by offering exotic and sensational entertainment to willing customers. In *P.T. Barnum: America's Greatest Showman*, Philip B. Kunhardt portrays the circus master as a master of deception and marketing. Television host and producer Ed Sullivan was a hustler who aimed to capture a wide audience with his variety shows. James Maguire tells how Sullivan adapted to his times in *Impresario: The Life and Times of Ed Sullivan* (see chapter 8). French fashion designer Coco Chanel prospered by marketing her name and products. Edmonde Charles-Roux tells her rags to riches story in *Chanel: Her Life, Her World, and the Woman Behind the Legend She Herself Created* (see chapter 8). French neoclassical painter Jacques-Louis David survived both the French Revolution and the years of Napoleon's reign. Anita Brookner recounts his dangerous life and renowned work in *Jacques-Louis David*.

Chernow, Ron

🌢 *Titan: The Life of John D. Rockefeller, Sr.* Random House, 1998. 774p. ISBN 0679438084. Audiobook available.
Oil tycoon John D. Rockefeller (1839–1937) felt that he had a God-given right to make as much money as he could. He believed that the end would justify any means that he used because his company strengthened the nation. Many cheered while others opposed his heavy-handed tactics, which created a world of corporate politics, laid the foundation for industrial America, and allowed the nation to become a world power in the twentieth century. In this in-depth study, Ron Chernow avoids praising or condemning the mogul. Instead, he describes Rockefeller's grand schemes, management fights, family affairs, philanthropy, rivalry with Andrew Carnegie, and legal struggles with President Theodore Roosevelt.

Subjects: Industrialists; Philanthropists; Rockefeller, John D., Sr.; Standard Oil Company

Awards: ALA Notable Book

Now Try: Rockefeller and Andrew Carnegie came from the same mold. David Nasaw tells an epic story in *Andrew Carnegie* (see this chapter). Like Rockefeller, rail and shipping tycoon Cornelius Vanderbilt spawned a large family and a circle of followers. Novelist Louis Auchincloss describes the society of millionaires in *The Vanderbilt Era: Profiles of a Gilded Age* (see chapter 8). Chernow has written biographies of eminent business families, including *The House of Morgan: An American Banking Dynasty and the Rise of Modern Finance* and *The Warburgs: The Twentieth Century Odyssey of a Remarkable Jewish Family* (see this chapter).

D'Antonio, Michael

Hershey: Milton S. Hershey's Extraordinary Life of Wealth, Empire, and Utopian Dreams. Simon & Schuster, 2006. 305p. ISBN 9780743264099.

Before he built his chocolate company and his model community with its streetlights shaped like candy kisses, Milton S. Hershey (1857–1945) failed at selling candy in Denver, Chicago, and New York. Like his father before him, his business sense had been mostly dreams, until a caramel recipe and a bit of luck came his way in Lancaster, Pennsylvania. Then after an eye-opening visit to the Columbian Exposition in Chicago in 1893, he turned his attention to chocolate. In this admiring biography, Michael D'Antonio tells the story of a businessman with a sense of responsibility for his employees and their families.

Subjects: Candy Manufacturers; Chocolate Industry; Hershey, Milton S.; Industrialists; Teen Reads

Now Try: Marcia Morton includes a chapter on Hershey and his company in her artful *Chocolate: An Illustrated History*. A bit of a competitor's history, with recipes, can be found in *Ghirardelli Chocolate Cookbook: Recipes and History from America's Premier Chocolate Maker*. Philip Kotler examines the idea that companies must give back to their communities in *Corporate Social Responsibility: Doing the Most Good for Your Company and Your Cause*. George Soros is held up as a model of social responsibility. Michael T. Kaufman tells how the Hungarian immigrant made and then gave away his money in *Soros: The Life and Times of a Messianic Billionaire* (see chapter 4). Like Hershey, golfer Ben Hogan struggled for years before he succeeded in his profession. How practice and persistence also helped the athlete overcome later challenges is told in *Ben Hogan: An American Life* by James Dodson (see chapter 12).

Dolan, Brian

Wedgwood: The First Tycoon. Viking, 2004. 396p. ISBN 0670033464.

Though as a poor potter's son, Josiah Wedgwood's (1730–1795) prospects were not promising, he was naturally curious. Experimenting with ceramic glazes, he discovered how to get a purer white, attracting business partners to bankroll a new line of pottery. He eventually started an innovative factory and sold specially commissioned pieces to the crowned heads across Europe. According to Brian Dole, the remarkable aspect of Wedgwood's life was the way he used his hard-won wealth to become a leading citizen, join reading societies, and keep company with eminent scientists of his day.

Subjects: Great Britain; Industrialists; Potters; Rags to Riches Stories; Wedgwood, Josiah

Now Try: More about Wedgwood's pottery can be learned from *Story of Wedgwood* by Alison Kelly. In *Bishop's Boys: A Life of Wilbur and Orville Wright*, James Tobin tells how after their successful early flights, the Wright Brothers became successful businessmen. Carpenter and clockmaker John Harrison had a tougher time than Wedgwood getting upper class Englishmen to accept his great invention, the maritime chronometer. Dava Sobel tells Harrison's story of persistence in *Longitude: The True Story of a Lone Genius Who Solved the Greatest Scientific Problem of His Time* (see chapter 11). Like Wedgwood, German printer Johann Gutenberg had good business sense to go along with his inventive mind. John Man re-creates the printer's life and times in *Gutenberg: How One Man Remade the World with Words* (see chapter 5).

Gabler, Neal

🌷 *Walt Disney: The Triumph of the American Imagination.* Knopf, 2006. 851p. ISBN 067943822X. Audiobook available.

Neal Gabler claims that movie producer Walt Disney (1901–1966) was the man who most reshaped American culture after World War II. Critics say that he homogenized and vulgarized culture and that he was a symbol of prejudiced America focusing on the suburban dream. Gabler counters that Disney was a popular pioneer in the areas of film animation, nature cinematography, and the building of amusement parks. Moreover, he popularized forecasting the future of technology, which he was able to do while marketing nostalgia for the past. At the same time, Gabler is candid about Disney's absorption in work, neglect of his family, and abysmal labor relations. Students of popular culture and general readers will likely enjoy this detailed account of an American icon.

Subjects: Animators; Disney, Walt; Movie Producers; Popular Culture; Theme Parks

Awards: Los Angeles Times Book Prize for Biography

Now Try: In *Art of Walt Disney: From Mickey Mouse to the Magic Kingdoms*, Christopher Finch reproduces drawings, movie stills, and other illustrations from the Disney studios while chronicling the studio's history. Like Disney, puppeteer Jim Henson was able to leverage his creative skill into an entertainment empire. In the brightly illustrated photobiography *Jim Henson: The Works* (see chapter 8), Christopher Finch shows the varied achievements of an energetic man. Like Disney, Albert Einstein succeeded tremendously on the world stage but struggled with family and personal relationships. Walter Isaacson tells the physicist's epic story in his monumental biography *Einstein* (see chapter 11). Disney biographer Neal Gabler describes the lurid world of journalism in his book about Disney contemporary Walter Winchell in *Winchell: Gossip, Power and the Culture of Celebrity*.

Lowry, Beverly

Her Dream of Dreams: The Rise and Triumph of Madam C. J. Walker. Alfred A. Knopf, 2003. 481p. ISBN 0679446427.

This biography of a successful black entrepreneur is a rags to riches story with elements of mystery. Novelist Beverly Lowry sought to find out how Sarah

Breedlove (1867–1919), a daughter of slaves from Vicksburg, Mississippi, become Madam C. J. Walker, the sellers of cosmetics, who lived in an elegant mansion outside New York City. The author's problem was that no primary records of Breedlove existed and the accounts from Walker and her associates sometimes conflicted or seemed imagined. Through a series of storylike chapters, which move the narrative through different American cities, Lowry weaves a plausible biography of the first American woman to make a million dollars on her own.

> **Subjects:** African Americans; Breedlove, Sarah; Cosmetics Industry; Rags to Riches Stories; Walker, Madame C. J.; Women

> **Now Try:** Another biography concerned with shifting identity is *The Lost German Slave Girl: The Extraordinary True Story of Sally Miller and Her Fight for Freedom in Old New Orleans* by John Bailey (see chapter 5). Like Walker, Agatha Christie kept secrets about her past. Janet Morgan speculates on the missing details of Christie's life in *Agatha Christie: A Biography*. Early movie star Lillian Gish was another independent and determined woman. Charles Affron tells how the actress increased her wealth by becoming a studio executive in *Lillian Gish: Her Legend, Her Life* (see chapter 8). Like Walker, A. G. Gaston lifted himself out of poverty. Carol Jenkins and Elizabeth Gardner Hines chronicle his long and prosperous life in *Black Titan: A. G. Gaston and the Making of a Black Millionaire* (see chapter 4).

Madsen, Axel

John Jacob Astor: America's First Multimillionaire. John Wiley, 2001. 312p. ISBN 0471385034.

With a case full of flutes, butchering skills, and great ambition, John Jacob Astor (1763–1848) arrived in Baltimore after a four-month voyage across the Atlantic Ocean. The year was 1784, the American Revolution had just ended, and there was no national currency. Astor sold enough flutes to pay for a coach ticket to New York, where he eventually became the nation's richest man. Alex Madsen tells how Astor staked himself in the fur trade and shipping, controlled New York real estate, and even built a glamorous hotel. He was also a slum lord, war profiteer, and opium magnate. Madsen finishes the story with an account of Astor's descendants and legacy.

> **Subjects:** Astor, John Jacob; Entrepreneurs; New York City; Quick Reads; Rags to Riches Stories; Teen Reads

> **Now Try:** Washington Irving wrote about Astor and the fur trading community he founded in Oregon in *Astoria, or, Anecdotes of an Enterprize Beyond the Rocky Mountains*, which can be found in the Library of America collection *Three Western Narratives*. Like Astor, ornithologist and artist John James Audubon came to America with little more than the will to succeed. In *John James Audubon: The Making of an American* (see chapter 1), Richard Rhodes tells how the illustrator of bird books inspired great love of wildlife and the environment. The Chouteaus of early St. Louis made a fortune selling furs. How they then became important players in the futures markets in New York is told in *Before Lewis and Clark: The Story of the Chouteaus, the French Dynasty That Ruled America's Frontier* by Shirley Christian (see this chapter). New York was also the setting for the life of another man whose merits can be debated. In *Boss Tweed: The Rise and Fall of the Corrupt Pol Who Conceived the*

Soul of Modern New York (see chapter 2), Kenneth D. Ackermann argues that Mayor William Tweed was not totally evil, as depicted in other biographies.

Nasaw, David

Andrew Carnegie. Penguin Press, 2006. 878p. ISBN 1594201048. Audiobook available.

Steel executive Andrew Carnegie (1835–1919) was a complicated man about whom many historians disagree. According to David Nasaw, the industrialist felt no guilt about the methods he employed to accumulate wealth because he intended to give much of it away to libraries, schools, and other causes. Feeling that he had a license to become as rich as possible, he would not allow even striking workers to alter his plans. While telling how Carnegie rose from poverty to become one of the world's richest men, Nasaw tries to remain fair, neither praising nor condemning the controversial tycoon. This rich biography would be a great discussion book if it were not so long.

> **Subjects:** Carnegie, Andrew; Industrialists; Labor; Philanthropists; Pittsburgh; Rags to Riches Stories; Scotland

> **Now Try:** Carnegie tells his own story in *The Autobiography of Andrew Carnegie*. The education of young people was also a concern for Sears Roebuck executive Julius Rosenwald and African American industrialist A. G. Gaston. Peter Max Ascoli tells about Rosenwald's efforts in *Julius Rosenwald: The Man Who Built Sears, Roebuck and Advanced the Cause of Black Education in the American South* (see chapter 4). Carol Jenkins and Elizabeth Gardner Hines tell a rags to riches story set in Alabama in *Black Titan: A. G. Gaston and the Making of a Black Millionaire* (see chapter 4). Characters similar to Carnegie may be found in *Titan: The Life of John D. Rockefeller, Sr.* by Ron Chernow (see this chapter) and *Morgan: American Financier* by Jean Strouse (see this chapter).

Pearce, John Ed

The Colonel: The Captivating Biography of the Dynamic Founder of a Fast Food Empire. Doubleday, 1982. 225p. ISBN 0385181221.

When Harland Sanders (1890–1980) died, the state of Kentucky flew its flags at half-mast for its native son. Yet even while the body of the founder of Kentucky Fried Chicken waited for burial, the debate over his legacy began. Most of the obituaries praised Sanders's promotion of the state and its business and his generosity to the unfortunate, but others remembered his profanity, violent temper, manipulation of state politics, disastrous business deals, and lawsuits against franchise owners. In this entertaining biography of a man whose image became a corporate symbol, journalist John Ed Pearce tells how a sixth-grade dropout became a fabulously rich chicken chef with a secret spices recipe.

> **Subjects:** Kentucky; Kentucky Fried Chicken; Quick Reads; Rags to Riches Stories; Restaurateurs; Sanders, Harland

> **Now Try:** Sanders told his own story in *Life as I Have Known It Has Been Finger Lickin' Good*, and fast food pioneer Ray Kroc told his own success story in *Grinding It Out: The Making of McDonald's*. President Lyndon Johnson may have been better educated and more successful politically than Sanders, but both have been remembered for their regional identities and rough language in backroom conversations. How Johnson rose to national prominence is told in *The Path to Power* by Robert A. Caro (see chapter 10). Like Sanders, comic actor W. C. Fields knew how to manage an iconic image to his

benefit. Simon Louvish tells both amusing and melancholy stories about the comedian in *Man on the Flying Trapeze: The Life and Times of W. C. Fields* (see chapter 8).

Proctor, Ben

William Randolph Hearst: Final Edition, 1911–1951. Oxford University Press, 2007. 325p. ISBN 9780195325348.

At age forty-seven, publisher William Randolph Hearst (1863–1951) was already a powerful man who could sway American public opinion through his empire of sensational newspapers, which were read by one quarter of the nation. His next forty years were a very public story, full of romance, conspicuous spending of his vast wealth, international travel, and political conflict. His own newspapers told of his expulsion from France in 1930 for anti-French reporting, his love affair with actress Marion Davies, and his cordial meeting with German Chancellor Adolf Hitler. His influence began to decline when he backed Herbert Hoover in the 1932 presidential election, making an enemy of Franklin Delano Roosevelt. Historian Ben Proctor tells a fascinating story of a man obsessed with personal power.

Subjects: Hearst, William Randolph; Newspaper Publishers; Politics and Government

Now Try: David Nasaw tells how Hearst built his newspaper empire and sought to control politicians in his lengthy full-life account, *The Chief: The Life of William Randolph Hearst.* Hearst's ill-fated love affairs contributed to his downfall. Adultery was also disastrous for the reputation of abolitionist minister Henry Ward Beecher, whose life is chronicled in *The Most Famous Man in America: The Biography of Henry Ward Beecher* by Debby Applegate (see chapter 10). Howard Hughes was a powerful businessman who, like Hearst, became more temperamental and paranoid with age. Celebrity biographer Charles Higham tells his strange story in *Howard Hughes: The Secret Life* (see chapter 5). According to Neil Chenoweth, Rupert Murdoch is an updated, international version of Hearst. He tells about Murdoch's quest for control of media markets and public opinion in his exposé *Rupert Murdoch: The Untold Story of the World's Greatest Media Wizard* (see chapter 5).

Renehan, Edward J., Jr.

Dark Genius of Wall Street: The Misunderstood Life of Jay Gould, King of the Robber Barons. Basic Books, 2005. 352p. ISBN 0465068855. Audiobook available.

Railroad baron Jay Gould (1836–1892), who dominated the U.S. economy in the middle of the nineteenth century, has been unfairly demonized, according to Edward J. Renehan Jr. He may have tried to corner the gold market, which led to an economic panic, and he may have manipulated stock prices, but these were acceptable business practices of the time, according to the author. He further contends that Gould was a financial innovator whose methods are still used by corporations today. More important, his railroads helped build the country. This account of a crafty and controversial entrepreneur is a good selection for discussion groups.

Subjects: Entrepreneurs; Gould, Jay; Railroad Tycoons

Now Try: More on backroom financial manipulations that influence the American economy can be found in the company history *The Last Tycoons: The Secret History of Lazard Frères & Co.* by William D. Cohan. Like Renehan, Nancy Isenberg also objects to applying contemporary ethics to historical figures, in *Fallen Founder: The Life of Aaron Burr* (see chapter 10). Like Gould, baseball's first great hitter Ty Cobb had no sympathy for his competition. Al Stump tells how the aggressive player fought throughout life on and off the field in *Cobb: A Biography* (see chapter 12). Steve Jobs is another businessman of questionable ethics who has been credited with greatly boosting the world economy. Jeffrey S. Young recounts the computer maker's career in *iCon: Steve Jobs, the Greatest Second Act in the History of Business* (see chapter 5).

Smitten, Richard

Jesse Livermore: World's Greatest Stock Trader. John Wiley, 2001. 319p. Wiley Investment Series. ISBN 0471023264.

After running away from home at age fourteen in 1891, Jesse Livermore (1877–1940) became a chalkboard boy at Paine Webber in Boston. Within a year he was a full trader, and by age twenty he was fabulously rich. Known for radical investment strategies, he went bankrupt several times, but recovered to pay his creditors each time. Marrying a Ziegfeld showgirl, he enjoyed high society, exotic vacations, and opulent living, until the stock market crash of 1929, from which he never recovered emotionally. In novelistic style, business author Richard Smitten portrays Livermore as a flawed, tragic figure who reflected the attitudes of his time.

Subjects: Livermore, Jesse L.; Stockbrokers

Now Try: F. Scott Fitzgerald gives a glimpse into the glittery world of the fabulously rich before the stock market crash of 1929 in *The Great Gatsby*. Baseball great Babe Ruth lived the high life throughout his long, well-paid sports career, but as soon as he retired from the game his spirit declined, and he died of cancer at an early age. Leigh Montville tries to solve all the mysteries of Ruth's unusual life in *The Big Bam: The Life and Times of Babe Ruth* (see chapter 12). The loss of his income was particularly hard on artist Salvador Dalí. Ian Gibson tells how the painter ran out of benefactors to exploit in *The Shameful Life of Salvador Dalí*. Rudolph Chelminski tells how the loss of critical acclaim sparked despair in depressed French chef Bernard Loiseau in *The Perfectionist: Life and Death in Haute Cuisine* (see chapter 5).

Strouse, Jean

Morgan: American Financier. Random House, 1999. 796p. ISBN 0375501665. Audiobook available.

The financial power of banker J. Pierpont Morgan (1837–1913) cannot be overstated. When he died in 1913, the New York Stock Exchange closed for his funeral, and the Federal Reserve was established to replace a private arrangement that Morgan had controlled. Having organized large corporations and railroad empires, he was both lauded as a great man of finance and vilified as a proponent of greed and exploitation of labor, foreign countries, and natural resources. He lived a long life full of friendships and romance, built a great library of original manuscripts, and filled museums with art. In her expansive biography of the famous tycoon, Jean Strouse weighs the good and the bad sides of "America's central banker," seeking to dispel the many prevailing myths.

> **Subjects:** Art Collectors; Bankers; Capitalists; Morgan, J. Pierpont

> **Now Try:** Morgan was a central figure of his time. Depicting the age, E. L. Doctorow included the banker in his acclaimed novel *Ragtime*. Ron Chernow describes the entire Morgan family in *The House of Morgan: An American Banking Dynasty and the Rise of Modern Finance*. Chernow also wrote about Secretary of the Treasury Alexander Hamilton, who was the first man to have the power to shape the American economy to his will. Chernow describes him as a dashing but conflicted character in *Alexander Hamilton* (see chapter 10). Two centuries before the banker named Morgan amassed a great fortune, a pirate named Morgan did the same, but by bloodier means. Stephan Talty tells the adventurous story of Captain Henry Morgan in *Empire of Blue Water: Captain Morgan's Great Pirate Army, the Epic Battle for the Americas, and the Catastrophe That Ended the Outlaws' Bloody Reign* (see chapter 1).

Wallis, Michael

Oil Man: The Story of Frank Phillips and the Birth of Phillips Petroleum. Doubleday, 1988. 480p. ISBN 0385238053.

> Born on a Nebraska homestead and raised on a farm in Iowa, Frank Phillips (1873–1950) grew up all too familiar with hard work and crop failures. Dreaming of escape, he apprenticed to a barber and then left for the mining boom in Colorado, where he cut hair, sold patent medicines, married a banker's daughter, and began to invest in high-risk ventures. When oil was found in Oklahoma, he and his brothers formed a bank in Bartlesville and became oilmen. In this compelling biography, Michael Wallis describes the colorful career of a ruthless tycoon who threw great barbecues, met glamorous people, and in the end gave most of his money away.

> **Subjects:** Industrialists; Oil Industry; Oklahoma; Phillips, Frank; Rags to Riches Stories

> **Now Try:** Like Phillips, Herbert Hoover was an Iowa farm boy who made his fortune in mining and later became famous for his humanitarian work. Without ignoring the failures of the Hoover presidency, Richard Norton Smith portrays the statesman sympathetically in *An Uncommon Man: The Triumph of Herbert Hoover*. Beginning as an apprentice and then finding many opportunities to advance his wealth was the formula for success of Benjamin Franklin, who also enjoyed a good party and high society. His epic story is told by Walter Isaacson in *Benjamin Franklin: An American Life* (see chapter 10). After he earned a billion dollars, securities broker George Soros began giving the money away. His unusual story is told in *Soros: The Life and Times of a Messianic Billionaire* by Michael T. Kaufman (see chapter 4).

Historical Families

Any village, town, or city has prominent families, people who lead their community civically and politically. Being businesspeople and property owners of long standing, they often retain their social positions over several generations. Sons and daughters may succeed their parents as heads of companies, mayors, presidents of local organizations, and members of fashionable society. On a larger stage, some families are prominent in the affairs of nations over several generations and worthy of being the subjects of biographies.

Wealth and powerful alliances built over time are the most common factors keeping families in control of companies, in the halls of government, and at the top of the social ladder. Some of these families attained their position by being early settlers. Such stories are told in *Before Lewis and Clark: The Story of the Chouteaus, the French Dynasty That Ruled America's Frontier* by Shirley Christian and *The Lees of Virginia: Seven Generations of an American Family* by Paul C. Nagel. For some prominent families, the tremendous accomplishments of one generation benefit succeeding generations, as is seen in the family biographies *The Fords: An American Epic* by Peter Collier and *The Real Ones: Four Generations of the First Family of Coca-Cola* by Elizabeth Candler Graham and Ralph Roberts. A few families become prominent for their cultural accomplishments, as told by Mary S. Lovell in *The Sisters: The Saga of the Mitford Family* and by Edward Ball in *The Sweet Hell Inside: A Family History*.

When a family is prominent for generations, an important place often remains the primary setting throughout the family narrative. The place itself evolves over time, as do the personalities of the characters. For the Lees, it was the plantations of Virginia, and for the Candlers, it was Atlanta, Georgia. Familial relationships, with their inherited qualities and inevitable differences, dominate these narratives. The strength of individual characters varies, with some family members meriting larger portions of the story. Because family biographies have numerous stories to tell and characters to depict, they tend to be longer books that call for unhurried reading. Readers who enjoy fictional family sagas and celebrity biographies may also enjoy the books in this section.

Historical Families biographies depict families that remain prominent over generations. Authors profile the families and their component individuals in the context of the eras in which they lived. The interactions of parents, siblings, and children are described in these books, which sometimes resemble fictional family sagas. There are no quick reads in this section.

Ball, Edward

The Sweet Hell Inside: A Family History. William Morrow, 2001. 384p. ISBN 068816840X. Audiobook available.

The Harleston family enjoyed the privileges that wealth brought fair-skinned African Americans in Charleston, South Carolina, from the era of Reconstruction to the advent of the Great Depression. Members of the family successfully operated funeral and orphanage businesses, allowing them to live comfortably and travel internationally. However, when sons of the family tried to compete in the worlds of jazz music and serious art, they found racial barriers rise up against them. Edward Ball, who won a National Book Award for the memoir *Slaves in the Family*, illustrates the difficulties of living with the entrenched prejudice of the old South. Family saga readers will especially enjoy this richly detailed book.

Subjects: African Americans; Family Biography; Harleston Family; Racial Discrimination

Now Try: Ball's *Slaves in the Family* offers a gripping account of the author's search for the past and the present members of his black and white family. A similar book from a correspondent of the *Washington Post* is *Pearl's Secret: A Black Man's Search for His White Family* by Neil Henry. Readers wanting to step back a generation prior to the Harleston family story may enjoy *Dwelling Place: A Plantation Epic* by Erskine Clarke, which tells the story of the white Joneses and the black Joneses on a plantation in Liberty County, Georgia, from 1805 to 1869. The memoir *Another Way Home: The Tangled Roots of Race in One Chicago Family* by Ronne Hartfield is a compelling contemporary story about racial identity.

Chernow, Ron

🏵 *The Warburgs: The Twentieth Century Odyssey of a Remarkable Jewish Family.* Random House, 1993. 820p. ISBN 0679418237.

In 1559 Simon von Cassel was granted a charter by the Prince-Bishop of Paderborn to serve as a moneychanger and pawnbroker in the Westphalian town of Warburg, a role denied Catholics by their church. From this position outside Christian restrictions, generations of Warburgs amassed and gave away great wealth, joined in high society, and served the German royal class. How they represented elite German Jews through the centuries and then failed to see the danger of the Nazis in the 1930s is a great epic tale told by acclaimed financial biographer Ron Chernow.

Subjects: Bankers; Germany; Jews; Warburg Family

Awards: ALA Notable Book

Now Try: Polish Jew Haskel Besser understood the dangers that the Nazi movement posed for his country and his own life, yet he lingered in Poland and only narrowly escaped the country before the Jewish Holocaust. Warren Kozak profiles the rabbi as a grateful man in *The Rabbi of 84th Street: The Extraordinary Life of Haskel Besser*. Stanley Weintraub describes the world of Jewish banking in Great Britain in the dual biography *Charlotte and Lionel: A Rothschild Love Story*. Management consultant Peter F. Drucker wrote about the role of Jewish bankers in Austria before World War I in his wide-ranging novel *The Last of All Possible Worlds*. In the novel *The Eye of the Abyss*, Marshall Browne tells a story about a man of Jewish ancestry serving as a banker for the Nazi Party.

Christian, Shirley

Before Lewis and Clark: The Story of the Chouteaus, the French Dynasty That Ruled America's Frontier. Farrar, Straus & Giroux, 2004. 509p. ISBN 037411-0050.

Most American history is written as though nothing of significance ever happened in the territories before the English colonists or the early American frontiersmen arrived. This family biography counters that mistaken view. Historian Shirley Christian recounts the adventurous story of the French colonial Chouteau family of St. Louis, who saw the Americans headed their way. Having settled St. Louis for the French in the 1760s and staying under Spanish ownership of the Louisiana territory, the

Chouteaus greeted the newcomers, then moved east to conquer American financial markets in Boston and New York. Readers of family saga fiction will likely enjoy this story of a fascinating family dynasty.

> **Subjects:** Chouteau Family; Family Biography; Louisiana Purchase; Missouri River; Pioneers; St. Louis

> **Now Try:** William Clark was a friend of the Chouteaus and another important figure in the opening of Missouri. Landon Y. Jones chronicles his adventurous life in *William Clark and the Shaping of the West* (see chapter 1). Members of the Chouteau family explored trade routes to Indian villages that were as unknown to the French as the Orient was to the Venetians of Marco Polo's era. Laurence Bergreen tells about Polo's adventurous travels and foreign trade in *Marco Polo: From Venice to Xanadu* (see chapter 1). When they moved to New York and Boston, the Chouteau family became rivals of another fur merchant, whose story is told in *John Jacob Astor: America's First Multimillionaire* by Axel Madsen (see this chapter). Like the Chouteau family, the Vanderbilt family retained prominence through several generations. Louis Auchincloss describes the high society life of the latter family in *The Vanderbilt Era: Profiles of a Gilded Age* (see chapter 8).

Collier, Peter, and David Horowitz

The Fords: An American Epic. Summit Books, 1987. 496p. ISBN 0671540939. Large print available.

When William Ford returned from seeing the 1876 Centennial Exposition in Philadelphia, he told his son Henry about the wonders in the Mechanics Hall, sparking a love of tinkering. Twenty years later the ambitious son built his first automobile. Nearly fifty years after the invention, the pioneering automaker's un-businesslike grandson, also named Henry, took control of one of America's largest corporations, signaling a decline in the once dominant company. Writing team Peter Collier and David Horowitz focus on the flawed lives of the two Henrys in this entertaining but candid family biography.

> **Subjects:** Automobile Industry; Family Biography; Ford, Henry; Ford, Henry, II; Ford Family; Ford Motor Company; Industrialists

> **Now Try:** Collier and Horowitz have also written similar books on the Kennedy and Rockefeller families, *The Kennedys: An American Drama* and *The Rockefellers: An American Dynasty*. The life of Captain Eddie Rickenbacker fits in time between the lives of the two Henry Fords. H. Paul Jeffers describes his racing automobiles and airplanes in their early developmental periods in *Ace of Aces: The Life of Capt. Eddie Rickenbacker* (see chapter 1). Like Henry Ford, inventor and businessman Samuel F. B. Morse, a sometimes acerbic man, fought with competitors over patents. How his belligerence hampered his business life is told in *Lightning Man: The Accursed Life of Samuel F. B. Morse* by Kenneth Silverman (see chapter 11).

Fraser, Flora

Princesses: The Six Daughters of George III. Knopf, 2005. 478p. ISBN 0679451188.

Of the fifteen children of King George III and Queen Charlotte of Great Britain, six were girls, starting with Princess Charlotte, born in 1766, and ending with Princess Amelia, born in 1783. Although it was expected that these princesses would enjoy charmed lives, the king went mad and kept his daughters cooped up, refusing to marry them to European princes. The resourceful girls, however, found ways to break free from their confinement. Based on their letters and other sources, Flora Fraser tells a lurid story of clandestine romances, an illegitimate birth, and family dysfunction.

> **Subjects:** Family Biography; George III, King of Great Britain; Princesses; Teen Reads

> **Now Try:** George III was the last king to rule over the American colonies. Christopher Hibbert describes the king who underestimated the strength of his American subjects in *George III: A Personal History.* The six Mitford sisters, daughters of an English baron, stirred controversy with their flamboyant behavior and espousal of unpopular causes. Two of them even befriended Adolf Hitler. Mary S. Lovell chronicles the sisters' exploits in *The Sisters: The Saga of the Mitford Family* (see this chapter). Princess Victoria, daughter of the Duke of Kent, led a very protected and controlled life as a child. Lynne Vallone describes her childhood and how it shaped her reign in *Becoming Victoria* (see chapter 6). Seven countries in Europe still have royal families. Geoffrey Hindley recounts the history of the monarchies in *Royal Families of Europe.*

Graham, Elizabeth Candler, and Ralph Roberts

The Real Ones: Four Generations of the First Family of Coca-Cola. Barricade Books, 1992. 344p. ISBN 0942637623.

In 1888 pharmacist Asa Griggs Candler joined a struggling company trying to sell a headache remedy made of cocaine and kola nut extract in a wine base. Within a year, he had bought all the rights to Coca-Cola for a total investment of $2,300 and began marketing his medicine to a wider audience. He succeeded, and with the substantial profits he established his family as leading citizens of the quickly growing city of Atlanta, Georgia. Graham and Roberts chronicle the triumphs and losses of a colorful family full of saints and sinners in this intimate and entertaining book.

> **Subjects:** Atlanta; Candler, Asa Griggs; Candler Family; Coca-Cola; Family Biography

> **Now Try:** Like Asa Candler, Edward Cabot Clark of Cooperstown, New York, made a fortune that his descendants spent lavishly. Nicholas Fox Weber describes the troubled family in *The Clarks of Cooperstown: Their Singer Sewing Machine Fortune, Their Great and Influential Art Collections, Their Forty-Year Feud* (see chapter 8). Like the Candler family story, the story of the Dodge family is full of melodrama. As suppliers of parts for Ford Motor Company, John and Horace Dodge learned the auto trade and then built their own cars. Caroline Latham tells how their descendants fought over the company and fortune in *Dodge Dynasty: The Car and the Family That Rocked Detroit.* During the Civil War many families were torn by siblings choosing opposite sides. The Todds, in-laws of the new president, were no exception. Their story is told in *House of Abraham: Lincoln and the Todds, a Family Divided by War* by Stephen Berry (see chapter 10). Another story about a family fortune used to buy art is told in *Art Lover: A Biography of Peggy Guggenheim* by Anton Gill (see chapter 8).

Kukla, Jon

Mr. Jefferson's Women. Alfred A. Knopf, 2007. 279p. ISBN 9781400043248.

After DNA evidence proved that a child of Sally Hemings was of Jefferson family descent, historians were divided in their assumptions about Thomas Jefferson's relationships with his slaves and other women. One camp assumed the third president had honorable intentions toward the women, while the other decided that he was a misogynist. Jon Kukla, the former director of the Library of Virginia, turned to the documentary evidence to seek the truth. The result is this lively collective biography profiling five women with whom Jefferson had romantic relationships. Among the revelations is that the founding father discussed (but declined) appointing women to public office.

> **Subjects:** Collective Biography; Jefferson, Thomas; Presidents; Romance; Sex Roles; Women
>
> **Now Try:** Sally Hemings was only one member of a family that Jefferson relied upon to run his household. Annette Gordon-Reid recounts the lives of several generations in *Hemingses of Monticello: An American Family*. Like Jefferson, William Shakespeare is a historical character about whom there remains much speculation despite centuries of research. Charles Nicholl examines some of the mysteries in great detail in his highly entertaining biography, *The Lodger Shakespeare: His Life on Silver Street*. Jefferson is not the only president accused of having mistresses. Kay Summersby Morgan, in her deathbed memoir, admitted to an affair with her boss in *Past Forgetting: My Love Affair with Dwight D. Eisenhower*. Wolfgang Amadeus Mozart's relationships with the women who surrounded him are examined in *Mozart's Women: His Family, His Friends, His Music* by Jane Glover (see chapter 7).

Lovell, Mary S.

The Sisters: The Saga of the Mitford Family. Norton, 2001. 611p. ISBN 0393010430.

How could the six Mitford sisters, born in the early years of the twentieth century to minor British aristocrats, all beautiful and intelligent, have been so different? Among Nancy, Pamela, Diane, Unity, Jessica, and Deborah were a novelist, a muckraker, a communist, two fascists, and a duchess, whose friends included Winston Churchill, Adolf Hitler, the Windsors, George Bernard Shaw, and Salmon Rushdie. Between the world wars and even later in the century, the sisters behaved outrageously and sold many books. In this family chronicle, prolific biographer Mary S. Lovell shows how much trouble one group of determined sisters can generate.

> **Subjects:** Family Biography; Great Britain; Mitford Family; Sisters; Women
>
> **Now Try:** *The Mitfords: Letters Between Six Sisters* offers more fascinating details about the family. Like the Mitfords, the James family of New England wrote many books, letters, and diaries. Paul Fisher intimately profiles Henry, William, Alice, and other members of the family in *House of Wits: An Intimate Portrait of the James Family*. The Cushing sisters of Boston, Massachusetts, did not throw off the mantle of wealth as the Mitford sisters did. They sought greater riches, and each married fabulously wealthy husbands—two husbands for each sister. Their quest is described in *The Sisters: Babe Mortimer Pauley, Betsey Roosevelt Whitney, Minnie Astor Fosburgh: the Lives and Times of the Fabulous Cushing Sisters* by David Grafton (see chapter 8). At the time that Unity and Diane Mitford were frequenting the salons of German Nazi generals and flirting with Adolf Hitler, he was pursuing a relationship with a young

woman he met at a camera shop. Angela Lambert tells the tragic story of the woman who eventually married and committed suicide with the German ruler in *The Lost Life of Eva Braun* (see chapter 6).

Marshall, Megan

The Peabody Sisters: Three Women Who Ignited American Romanticism. Houghton Mifflin, 2005. 602p. ISBN 0395389925.

In Salem, Massachusetts, in the 1820s, Eliza Peabody taught her daughters Elizabeth, Mary, and Sophia that independent thought was more important than domestic tranquility. As a schoolteacher, aiming to give her offspring the advantages of private schooling that they could not afford, she gave them books and slates more often than needles and thread. The sisters bonded and vowed never to marry. However, friends and suitors, including Ralph Waldo Emerson, Horace Mann, and Nathaniel Hawthorne, swarmed their Wednesday night open houses to hotly debate transcendental issues and other topics; and eventually the promises about not marrying were broken. For this family biography, women's historian Megan Marshall read the sister's diaries, letters, and other writings. The result is a rich story of strong family feelings in a time of literary affluence.

> **Subjects:** Family Biography; Hawthorne, Sophia Peabody; Mann, Mary Tyler Peabody; Massachusetts; Peabody, Elizabeth Palmer; Peabody Family; Sisters; Women

> **Now Try:** Elisa Peabody, the mother of the three young women, was herself a formidable woman who established schools for young children. *The Letters of Elizabeth Palmer Peabody: American Renaissance Woman* chronicles her life and work. Susan Cheever profiles the main characters of the Concord transcendental movement in her collective biography *American Bloomsbury: Louisa May Alcott, Ralph Waldo Emerson, Margaret Fuller, Nathaniel Hawthorne, and Henry David Thoreau: Their Lives, Their Loves, Their Work* (see chapter 6). The MacDonald sisters, daughters of a modest Methodist minister in rural England, were successful in marrying into prominent families, as Judith Flanders relates in *Circle of Sisters: Alice Kipling, Georgiana Burne-Jones, Agnes Poynter and Louisa Baldwin* (see chapter 8). In addition to marrying an author, Mary Shelley was one herself. Novelist Muriel Spark writes admiringly of the widow who served as her husband's literary executor in *Mary Shelley: A Biography* (see chapter 7).

Matteson, John

Eden's Outcasts: The Story of Louisa May Alcott and Her Father. Norton, 2007. 497p. ISBN 9780393059649.

Bronson Alcott (1799–1888) believed in the perfectibility of the person and subsequently of society. As a matter of principle, he studied, worked his crops, and turned himself into a philosophical gentleman, who shared his thoughts through his Temple School and with his friends Emerson, Thoreau, and Hawthorne. He also raised four daughters, of which the second, Louisa May (1832–1888), challenged his authority and patience. John Masters chronicles the famous clash of father and daughter from their toughest years to their eventual understanding in this psychological biography.

Subjects: Alcott, Amos Branson; Alcott, Louisa May; Dual Biography; Fathers and Daughters; Novelists; Philosophers; Transcendental Movement

Now Try: *The Journals of Louisa May Alcott* present her views of her father and family, as does her novel *Little Women*. Gerald Brooks expands on the father's story from *Little Women* in her *March: A Novel*. Whereas Alcott's father challenged her intellectually, Beatrix Potter's parents wanted her to abandon her art and intellectual pursuits so she could be a good Victorian wife. Linda Lear tells how Potter had to break with her family in *Beatrix Potter: A Life in Nature* (see chapter 7). In *Elizabeth Barrett Browning: A Biography* (see chapter 7), Margaret Forster tells of another daughter who found her happiness only after leaving her family. The relationship between Italian scientist Galileo and his daughter Suor Maria Celeste ironically grew stronger when they were apart. Dava Sobel uses the daughter's letters to reconstruct the story in *Galileo's Daughter: A Historical Memoir of Science, Faith, and Love* (see this chapter).

Nagel, Paul C.

The Lees of Virginia: Seven Generations of an American Family. Oxford University Press, 1990. 332p. ISBN 0195053850. Audiobook available.

From Richard Lee's arrival in Jamestown around 1640 to the death of Robert E. Lee in 1870, seven generations of Lees led lives of wealth and influence in Virginia. Two Lees signed the Declaration of Independence, and several fought in the American Revolution. One of these soldiers, Light Horse Harry Lee, became governor and then was later imprisoned for bankruptcy after a shady real estate speculation. Hannah Lee Corbin, a daughter of the family, fought for widows' rights and stirred religious controversy. With insight into many of the individual characters, Virginia historian Paul C. Nagel tells a lively story of a family important to the state and the nation.

Subjects: Family Biography; Group Discussion Books; Lee Family; Virginia

Now Try: Carey Roberts and Rebecca Seely turned the Lee family history into fiction in *Tidewater Dynasty: The Lees of Stratford Hall*. The Todds of Kentucky were a slave-owning family tied by marriage to the Republican presidential candidate of 1860 who wanted to end the spread of slavery. Stephen Berry describes how the family split politically in *House of Abraham: Lincoln and the Todds, a Family Divided by War* (see chapter 3). The family and descendants of President John Adams remained important citizens of Massachusetts for generations. Jack Shepherd tells the family story in *The Adams Chronicles: Four Generations of Greatness*. The African American Madden family arrived in the state of Virginia as indentured servants of the famous Madison family and stayed there as long as the Lees. Using many documents kept by the family, descendant T. O. Madden tells their story in *We Were Always Free: The Maddens in Culpeper County, Virginia: A Two-Hundred Year Family History*.

Sobel, Dava

Galileo's Daughter: A Historical Memoir of Science, Faith, and Love. Walker, 1999. 420p. ISBN 0802713432. Audiobook and large print available.

In 1613 Galileo Galilei (1564–1642) placed his two illegitimate daughters in the Convent of San Matteo in Arcetri near Florence. When his beloved sister died in 1623, his older daughter, Suor Maria Celeste, wrote him a moving condolence letter. It was the first of 124 surviving letters from his daughter that the famed astronomer kept. These letters show how Galileo came to trust and seek the understanding of his daughter through the difficulties that he had with heresy trials, scientific discoveries, and bad health. Dava Sobel features translated letters and the scientist's drawings in this compelling family story.

> **Subjects:** Astronomers; Florence; Galilei, Galileo; Galilei, Maria Celeste; Heresy; Letters; Roman Catholic Church; Scientists; Teen Reads

> **Now Try:** The writings of a young nun named Thérèse give readers another look at life in a convent in *Saint Thérèse of Lisieux* by Kathryn Harrison. Like Sobel, Ross King tells much about the Renaissance by focusing on great individuals of the era. *Brunelleschi's Dome: How a Renaissance Genius Reinvented Architecture* and *Michelangelo and the Pope's Ceiling* portray an architect and an artist with great tasks to perform in a context of papal intrigue and artistic jealousies. *A World Lit Only by Fire: The Medieval Mind and the Renaissance: Portrait of an Age* by William Manchester and *The Renaissance: A Short History* by Paul Johnson are popular and entertaining surveys of Renaissance history covering key artists, writers, popes, and statesmen of the time.

Wiencek, Henry

🏆 *The Hairstons: An American Family in Black and White.* St. Martin's Press, 1999. 361p. ISBN 0312192770.

With several plantations in nineteenth-century North Carolina, the wealthy Hairston clan may have owned more slaves than any other family in America, many of whom were offspring of the masters. In the wake of the Civil War, the family spread across the country, entering many professions with varied success. In this sympathetic story about forgiveness and redemption, historian Henry Wiencek chronicles the rise and fall of the black and white descendants of cotton kings, judges and generals. A great choice for readers who enjoy family sagas.

> **Subjects:** African Americans; Family Biography; Hairston Family; North Carolina; Slavery

> **Awards:** National Book Critics Circle Award for Biography

> **Now Try:** When researching his ancestors, Edward Ball found that he had more family than he ever imagined. *Slaves in the Family* is his account of his quest and what he learned. Ball also wrote the compelling family biography *The Sweet Hell Inside: A Family History* (see this chapter), which tells about class stratification within the black community of Charleston, South Carolina. Race was only one of the factors used to separate people in the antebellum South. In *Life in Black and White: Family and Community in the Slave South*, Brenda E. Stevenson examines class, ethnicity, religion, and gender differences as indicators of social standing in Loudoun County, Virginia, during the period from 1730 to 1850. In *One Drop: My Father's Hidden Life: A Story of Race and Family Secrets*, Bliss Broyard tells about her difficult quest to uncover the connections between her white and black ancestors.

Human Rights and Social Justice Stories

According to Carl J. Nederman in "Human Rights: Overview" in *The New Dictionary of Ideas*, the idea that all people regardless of their circumstances (class, nationality, philosophy) or physical condition (age, sex, race) deserve respect and have basic rights began with the Greek philosophers, especially Aristotle and Zeno of Citium. The author also credits Roman statesman Cicero with elaborating a doctrine of natural law guaranteeing justice, regardless of nationality or ethnicity. Nederman points out that these early theories were incomplete and rarely practiced until more modern times. Thus, the course of Western history can be viewed as a slow movement with many setbacks toward the expansion of human rights.

In this section are stories of individuals trying to protect their own rights and extend the rights of others. In *Rosa Parks,* Douglas Brinkley describes the life of an African American seamstress who chose to test the segregation laws of Alabama by not moving to the back of a bus. Lesley Downer recounts the story of a young Japanese woman who refused to remain a geisha, defying her father and the house to which she had been indentured, in *Madame Sadayakko: The Geisha Who Bewitched the West.* In *American Jezebel: The Uncommon Life of Anne Hutchinson, the Woman Who Defied the Puritans,* Eve LaPlante depicts an intelligent, religious woman who believed that she had as much right as any man of her colony to speak at Puritan meetings. Of course, not all struggles for rights end happily. *John Brown, Abolitionist: The Man Who Killed Slavery, Sparked the Civil War, and Seeded Civil Rights* by David S. Reynolds and *The Trials of Lenny Bruce: The Fall and Rise of an American Icon* by Ronald K. L. Collins and David M. Skover tell stories of far-reaching men who died trying to win contested rights.

Character, story, and setting are all strong appeal factors in human rights stories. Only determined and resourceful characters are capable of opposing entrenched forces that restrict their rights. These tension-filled narratives describe psychological, legal, and physical struggles in which the livelihoods or even the lives of the protagonists are jeopardized by the decision to fight injustice. Set in communities divided by class, ethnicity, race, or religion, the stories share a common theme, with parties who fear losing their rights when others gain them. The pacing of the stories may be sped by lively descriptions of conflict or slowed by the background details in these Historical Biographies.

> *Human Rights and Social Justice Stories* highlight the lives of people who have struggled for their own rights and to advance the rights of others. Readers often find these books about consequential lives compelling and inspiring.

Berry, Mary Frances

My Face Is Black Is True: Callie House and the Struggle for Ex-Slave Reparations. Alfred A. Knopf, 2005. 314p. ISBN 1400040035. Audiobook available.

Callie House (1861–1928) was a washerwoman with five children in Nashville, Tennessee, when she was elected assistant secretary of the National Ex-Slave Mutual Relief, Bounty and Pension Association in 1898. At the time, she and many other ex-slaves were financially stricken and disenfranchised by the recently enacted Jim Crow laws and terrorized by the Ku Klux Klan. In the face of overwhelming odds, House led a call for the federal government to repay ex-slaves for their unpaid labor during the slave era. Fearing that her call could gain widespread support, the Justice Department declared that her lobbying was illegal and persuaded the postmaster to ban her literature, with the result that she was arrested and imprisoned for improper use of the mail. Mary Frances Berry, a former chairwoman of the United States Commission on Civil Rights, admiringly profiles a woman who fought a noble battle that she could not win.

> **Subjects:** African Americans; Civil Rights Leaders; Ex-slaves; House, Callie; Nashville; Teen Reads; Women

> **Now Try:** Berry also wrote *The Pig Farmer's Daughter and Other Tales of American Justice: Episodes of Racism and Sexism in the Courts from 1865 to the Present*, which collects eight essays about courts failing to protect individuals' rights. In *Ella Baker and the Black Freedom Movement: A Radical Democratic Vision*, Barbara Ransby tells about a black woman who fought for fifty years to ensure that women had a say in the civil rights movement. In *They Say: Ida B. Wells and the Reconstruction of Race* (see chapter 6), James West Davidson recounts how Wells witnessed injustice in her community and turned to journalism as a means to expose it. Microbiologist Rosalind Franklin was not only robbed of credit for her DNA studies by James Watson and Francis Crick, she was also slandered by Watson. Brenda Maddox tells another story of injustice in *Rosalind Franklin: The Dark Lady of DNA* (see chapter 11).

Brinkley, Douglas

Rosa Parks. Lipper/Viking Books, 2000. 246p. Penguin Lives. ISBN 0670891606. Audiobook and large print available.

In 1955 Rosa Parks (1913–2005), a seamstress, and her husband Raymond, a barber, had a decent home in the projects in segregated Montgomery, Alabama, where they quietly worked with a branch of the NAACP on local racial issues. Shocked by the Emmett Till murder and inspired by the sermons of Martin Luther King Jr., Parks wanted to do something to help her race, so she agreed to test the segregation laws by refusing to move to the back of a bus. This act and her arrest sparked the Montgomery Bus Boycott, which lasted twelve months. In his compact biography of Parks, historian Douglas Brinkley describes the making of a civil rights hero.

> **Subjects:** African Americans; Civil Rights Leaders; Parks, Rosa; Quick Reads; Teen Reads; Women

> **Now Try:** At ninety years old, NAACP pioneer Mary Church Terrell began a personal campaign to integrate the restaurants in Washington, D.C. Dennis Brindell Fradin and Judith Bloom Fradin tell Terrell's courageous story in *Fight On!: Mary Church Terrell's Battle for Integration*. Ernest J. Gaines's *The Autobiography of Miss Jane Pittman* is a novel (often mistakenly thought to be true) about an aged former slave who joined the fledgling civil rights movement of her rural community in the 1960s. Nurse Margaret Sanger was also moved to demonstrate against restrictive laws by the suffering that she saw. Her cause was birth control. Ellen Chesler describes Sanger and her work in *Woman of Valor: Margaret Sanger and the Birth Control Movement in America* (see chapter 4). Georgia Congressman John Lewis recounts the early efforts for civil rights in the South in *Walking with the Wind: A Memoir of the Movement*.

Carretta, Vincent

Equiano, the African: Biography of a Self-Made Man. University of Georgia Press, 2005. 436p. ISBN 9780820325712.

Olaudah Equiano (1745–1797) was the talented author of one of the most important eighteenth-century slave narratives. Also named Gustavus

Vassa by his Royal Navy master, he claimed that he was born in Nigeria, enslaved at eleven, and shipped across the Atlantic Ocean to the West Indies and then Virginia, where he was purchased by Captain Michael Henry Pascal. After years in the Royal Navy, back in the West Indies he purchased his freedom and became for a time a slave owner himself before moving to England and becoming an abolitionist. In this compelling investigative biography of a man who witnessed terrible cruelty, professor of English Vincent Carrett examines Equiano's story and its impact on the British abolition movement.

> **Subjects:** Abolitionists; Africans; Equiano, Olaudah; Great Britain; Slavery

> **Now Try:** Equiano's slave narrative is available in many editions with different titles, including *The Life of Olaudah Equiano, or Gustavus Vassa the African*. The release from bondage of Saartjie Baartman, an African woman exhibited as a medical anomaly, was also a celebrated cause of the nineteenth-century British abolition movement. Her tragic story is told in *African Queen: The Real Life of the Hottentot Venus* by Rachel Holmes (see chapter 5). In *Amazing Grace: William Wilberforce and the Heroic Campaign to End Slavery*, Eric Metaxas profiles the British abolitionist and member of Parliament who is credited with ending the British slave trade. Frederick Douglass wrote one of the most famous slave narratives. He describes his life as a slave and his escape to the Northern states in *Narrative of the Life of Frederick Douglass an American Slave*. More slave narratives can be found in *Classic Slave Narratives*, edited by Henry Louis Gates Jr.

Chen, Constance M.

The Sex Side of Life: Mary Ware Dennett's Pioneering Battle for Birth Control and Sex Education. New Press, 1996. 374p. ISBN 1565841328.

Mary Ware Dennett (1872–1947) was born of Puritan heritage in Massachusetts at the height of the Victorian era. A well-behaved young woman with an academic mind, she did not intend to become a suffragist, peace activist, advocate for legalizing birth control, and proponent for teaching sex education in schools and churches, but she acted according to her conscience. For writing and mailing sex education pamphlets, she was charged with breaking obscenity laws. Author Constance M. Chen has written an admiring yet candid biography of Dennett that will please many feminist readers.

> **Subjects:** Activists; Birth Control; Dennett, Mary Ware; Feminists; Sex Education; Teen Reads; Women; Women's Rights

> **Now Try:** Dennett's mission resembled those of the heroines in *Woman of Valor: Margaret Sanger and the Birth Control Movement in America* by Ellen Chesler (see chapter 4) and *Notorious Victoria: The Life of Victoria Woodhull, Uncensored* by Mary Gabriel (see chapter 4). The use of contraceptives and other means of birth control has long been a matter of public policy in the United States. Linda Gordon chronicles over 150 years of public debate over birth control in *The Moral Property of Women: A History of Birth Control Politics in America*. The battle over sex education has not ended. Kristin Luker recounts the history of the issue in *When Sex Goes to School: Warring Views on Sex and Sex Education since the Sixties*.

Clinton, Catherine

Fanny Kemble's Civil Wars. Simon & Schuster, 2000. 302p. ISBN 0684844141. Large print available.

When Fanny Kemble (1809–1893) left the British stage to marry a plantation owner from the American South, she knew that he owned slaves, but she had not seen them in the fields or kitchen. She had accepted the argument that they were well treated until she saw the situation firsthand. She recorded her observations about the plantation in a journal, whose publication and popularity doomed her marriage and contributed to the slavery debate on both sides of the Atlantic Ocean. According to Catherine Clinton, Kemble chose badly in marriage and scraped by after the divorce by writing. Readers interested in nineteenth-century culture will enjoy this book as much as those interested in slavery and abolition.

> **Subjects:** Abolitionists; Actors and Actresses; Kemble, Fanny; Marriage; Plantations; Slavery; Teen Reads; Women

> **Now Try:** *The Plantation Mistress: Woman's World in the Old South* by Catherine Clinton goes into more detail about the daily lives of women on prewar plantations. *Fanny Kemble's Journals*, edited by Clinton, which contributed to the slavery debate, are also available. While Kemble was decrying slavery, Harriet Tubman guided escapees along the Underground Railroad. Kate Clifford Larson tells Tubman's story in *Bound for the Promised Land: Harriet Tubman: Portrait of an American Hero* (see chapter 4). Like Kemble, Sojourner Truth spoke and wrote about the evils of slavery. In *Sojourner Truth: A Life, a Symbol*, Nell Irvin Painter examines the many myths about the famous abolitionist to find the true story. Like Kemble, Irene Heron Forsythe discovers that she has married a man whose values are abhorrent to her in the novel *The Forsythe Saga* by John Galsworthy.

Collins, Ronald K. L., and David M. Skover

The Trials of Lenny Bruce: The Fall and Rise of an American Icon. Sourcebooks, Inc., 2002. 562p. ISBN 1570719861.

When comedian Lenny Bruce (1925–1966) died of a heroin overdose, his legal fight for First Amendment rights ended without resolution. He had lost many of his friends and most of his public support during his unrelenting five-year campaign to say anything, no matter how obscene, in his comedy routines. Death, however, resurrected his reputation, and he became a martyr for the cause of free speech and personal liberty. In this highly detailed account of Bruce's life, court cases, and legacy, legal historians Ronald K. L. Collins and David M. Skover portray Bruce as a principled fanatic, who valued truth over social accommodation. Readers interested in rebellious figures will likely enjoy this sympathetic but candid book.

> **Subjects:** Bruce, Lenny; Comedians; First Amendment Rights; Free Speech

> **Now Try:** George Carlin continued his friend Bruce's cause with his outrageous comedy. His books include *Brain Droppings, Napalm & Silly Putty*, and *When Will Jesus Bring the Pork Chops?* Comedians can be very tragic figures. Martin Knelman looks beyond "the funny stuff" in *Laughing on the Outside: The Life of John Candy*, and Tom Farley describes his brother's immoderate life in *Chris Farley Show: A Biography in Three Acts*. Bob Woodward tells a story of alcohol and drugs destroying another comedian in *Wired: The Short Life & Fast Times of John Belushi* (see chapter 6). *Marlon Brando* by Patricia Bosworth (see chapter 8) tells about another entertainment figure who risked his career for causes.

Dash, Leon

Rosa Lee: A Mother and Her Family in Urban America. Basic Books, 1996. 279p. ISBN 0465070922.

Rosa Lee Cunningham (1936–1995) had spent fifty years in the housing projects of Washington, D.C., when journalist Leon Dash asked to shadow her. For four years he watched the difficult episodes of her life: bailing children out of jail, attending funerals, and visiting drug treatment centers. At the end of this book, Cunningham dies of AIDS. Using his observations, Dash wrote about Cunningham and the lives of the desperately poor in a series of prize-winning articles for the *Washington Post*, which he expanded into this candid biography.

> **Subjects:** African Americans; Cunningham, Rosa Lee; Drug Abuse; Group Discussion Books; Poor; Teen Reads

> **Now Try:** Frank McCourt describes the plight of poor Irish workers in the Depression era in *Angela's Ashes: A Memoir.* Susan Sheehan writes about Carmen Santana, a Puerto Rican mother whose income did not meet her expenses, in *A Welfare Mother,* an eye-opening book, which was expanded from an article in *The New Yorker.* Alex Kotlowitz shows the difficulty of escaping the slums of Chicago, even with tremendous sports talent, in his profile of two African American basketball players in *There Are No Children Here.* Beverly Lowry tells how one woman escaped poverty in *Her Dream of Dreams: The Rise and Triumph of Madam C. J. Walker* (see this chapter), and Michael Lydon describes the rural poverty of singer Ray Charles's early life in *Ray Charles: Man and Music* (see chapter 4).

Downer, Lesley

Madame Sadayakko: The Geisha Who Bewitched the West. Gotham Books, 2003. 321p. ISBN 1592400051.

Born into a declining samurai family, Sadayakko (1871–1946) was indentured by her father at an early age to become a geisha and was expected to become the mistress of an influential man. As a geisha, she was noted for her great beauty and for never fawning over her clients, enhancing her appeal to wealthy patrons. She shocked Tokyo society when she married an actor, who put her on stage as the first Japanese actress in centuries. Called the Japanese Sarah Bernhardt, Sadayakko drew crowds worldwide and inspired Giacomo Puccini's *Madame Butterfly.* In this admiring profile, Lesley Downer tells how the self-assured actress blazed a trail for women's rights in Japan. A wonderful read for opera lovers and those interested in Japanese history.

> **Subjects:** Actors and Actresses; Geishas; Japan; Kamakami, Sadayakko; Teen Reads; Women; Women's Rights

> **Now Try:** In the novel *Memoirs of a Geisha,* Arthur Golden describes the life of a geisha in Japan before World War II. *Autobiography of a Geisha* by Sayo Masuda is a true account from a pre–World War II geisha, who tells of the hardships and cruelty of being a sex-slave. Like Sadayakko, the illegitimate daughter of Pope Julius II also broke free from her father's plans for her marriage and tried to make a good life for herself. Caroline P. Murphy tells an ultimately tragic story in *The Pope's Daughter: The Extraordinary Life of Felice della Rovere.* Children are still stolen and sold into slavery in the Sudan. Mende Nazur describes her life and escape in *Slave,* and Francis Bok tells a similar story in *Escape from Slavery: The True Story of My Ten Years in Captivity.*

Gerzina, Gretchen Holbrook

Mr. and Mrs. Prince: How an Extraordinary Eighteenth-Century Family Moved out of Slavery and into Legend. Amistad, 2008. 256p. ISBN 9780060510732.

Bijah Prince (1705?–1794) was a freed slave who owned property in Massachusetts and Vermont. His young wife, Lucy Terry (1724?–1821), survived a transatlantic journey on a slave ship, learned to read, and wrote poetry. After they married in 1756, they tried to live quietly as New England farmers, selling maple syrup and helping their neighbors; but racists burned their crops and buildings and attacked their children numerous times. Instead of fleeing, they fought back with words. In this romantic and compelling account, Gretchen Holbrook Gerzina tells the story of the determined couple who persuasively used the courts to protect their rights and prevail in rural New England.

> **Subjects:** African Americans; Farmers; Hate Crimes; Prince, Bijah; Prince, Lucy Terry

> **Now Try:** While many African Americans were demonstrating on the streets and in "white only" institutions, Thurgood Marshall was taking discrimination cases to court. Juan Williams chronicles Marshall's efforts as a lawyer and Supreme Court justice in ***Thurgood Marshall: American Revolutionary*** (see this chapter). Books about free blacks like the Princes are in short supply. ***The Essence of Liberty: Free Black Women During the Slave Era*** by Wilma King, ***A Stranger and a Sojourner: Peter Caulder Free Black Frontiersman in Antebellum Arkansas*** by Billy D. Higgins, and ***Chained to the Rock of Adversity: To Be Free, Black & Female in the Old South*** are worth finding. Harriet E. Wilson's dramatic nineteenth-century novel ***Our Nig, or Sketches from the Life of a Free Black***, is available in many editions.

Johnson, Charles, and Bob Adekman

King: The Photobiography of Martin Luther King, Jr. Viking Studio, 2000. 288p. ISBN 0670892165.

Martin Luther King Jr. (1929–1968) usually wore a suit when he marched, preached, and met with religious and civil rights leaders. Though he removed his tie during the Selma to Montgomery March in 1965 and wore pajamas when hospitalized after a knife attack, he lived and died impeccably dressed. As readers can see in this photographic biography, he looked especially dignified at the Nobel Prize ceremonies. They also see a real man facing many hardships, accepting arrest, comforting the afflicted, challenging authorities, and caring for his family. Charles Johnson and Bob Adelman have created an illuminating book that chronicles the career of the great civil rights leader.

> **Subjects:** African Americans; Civil Rights Leaders; Clergy; King, Martin Luther, Jr.; Photographic Biography

> **Now Try:** More stories about Martin Luther King Jr.'s career in civil rights are found in ***To the Mountaintop: Martin Luther King Jr.'s Sacred Mission to Save America: 1955–1968*** by Stewart Burns. Dr. King also appears in the photobiography ***John Fitzgerald Kennedy: A Life in Pictures*** by Yann-Brice Dherbier and Pierre-Henri Verlhac (see chapter 10). ***Mandela: The Authorized Portrait*** (see chapter 10) lacks photographs of the South African leader during

his long prison stay, but has many from before and after that time. Like the book about King, it focuses on the major events of his life. In *This Land Was Made for You and Me: The Life and Songs of Woody Guthrie* (see chapter 7), Elizabeth Partridge illustrates the life of a folksinger/activist through photographs.

LaPlante, Eve

American Jezebel: The Uncommon Life of Anne Hutchinson, the Woman Who Defied the Puritans. HarperSanFrancisco, 2004. 312p. ISBN 0060562331.

The American fight for women's rights began in Boston in 1637 at the heresy trial of Anne Hutchinson (1591–1643). This mother of fifteen children had been arrested for the "crime" of leading women's religious discussion groups. In court she declared openly that the forty Puritan judges had no more divine insight into the word of God than she did. For this insult and for defying the law against women teaching religion, she was banished from the colony. In this admiring biography, Hutchinson descendant Eve LaPlante portrays her ancestor as an opinionated woman who set an example for later generations of women.

> **Subjects:** Group Discussion Books; Hutchinson, Anne; Massachusetts Bay Colony; Puritans; Religious Rights; Teen Reads; Women

> **Now Try:** Anarchist Emma Goldman was also deported by a court that judged her seditious. Her causes were labor reform, women's rights, birth control, free love, and pacifism. Alice Wexler describes the personal life of the outspoken woman in *Emma Goldman: An Intimate Life* (see chapter 10). Like Hutchinson, Catherine Booth was religious and felt compelled to witness her faith as a minister. Roy Hattersley describes how she helped establish an international Christian mission society in *Blood and Fire: William and Catherine Booth and Their Salvation Army* (see chapter 4). Anne Bradstreet, a colonial contemporary of Hutchinson, did not challenge male dominance of church and state, but she outshone the men in poetry, a pursuit not considered suitable for a woman in the seventeenth century. Charlotte Gordon intimately recounts Bradstreet's life in *Mistress Bradstreet: The Untold Life of America's First Poet* (see chapter 7). Karenna Gore Schiff examines the lives of twentieth-century women who dedicated themselves to justice and reform in the collective biography *Lighting the Way: Nine Women Who Changed Modern America*.

Neeley, Bill

The Last Comanche Chief: The Life and Times of Quanah Parker. John Wiley, 1995. 276p. ISBN 0471117226.

Though Comanche Chief Quanah Parker (1845?–1911) fought against white settlement longer than most other American Indians, he recognized the time for diplomacy when it came. Ironically, he was half white, the son of early Texas settler and kidnap victim Cynthia Ann Parker. Trained as a warrior and council leader, he was able to become an effective lobbyist for his tribe, securing their lands and rights. In his later years he became a wealthy cattleman. In this admiring biography, historian Bill Neeley portrays the chief as an honorable man who made the best of bad times.

> **Subjects:** Chiefs; Comanche Indians; Native Americans; Parker, Quanah; Texas

> **Now Try:** The story of Parker's mother is recounted in the family history *Frontier Blood: The Saga of the Parker Family* by Jo Ella Powell Exley and in the novel *Where the Broken Heart Still Beats: The Story of Cynthia Ann Parker* by Carolyn Meyer.

Tecumseh was a Shawnee chief of an earlier age who believed his tribe could retain their lands by fighting the European settlers. John Sugden describes the warrior as a grand orator and talented leader in *Tecumseh: A Life* (see chapter 3). Like Parker, former Pony Express rider, buffalo hunter, army scout, and Indian fighter William Cody adapted to a modernizing world. How he used his Western image to become a wealthy entertainer is told in *Buffalo Bill Cody: The Man Behind the Legend* by Robert A. Carter (see chapter 5).

Newman, Richard S.

Freedom's Prophet: Bishop Richard Allen, the AME Church, and the Black Founding Fathers. New York University Press, 2008. 357p. ISBN 9780814-758267.

Former slave and pamphlet writer Richard Allen (1760–1831) is known as the Apostle of Freedom. Thought to have been born in Philadelphia, and owned by a prominent lawyer, he spent his childhood and adolescence on Delaware plantations, where he became a passionate Methodist and secured his freedom before he was twenty. He returned to Philadelphia to found the American Methodist Episcopal Church and the Free African Society, the first organization in the American abolition movement. According to historian Richard S. Newman, the first black bishop was an eloquent speaker, early advocate of nonviolent protest, and smart businessman. Many readers will enjoy this account of a mostly forgotten founding father.

Subjects: Abolitionists; African Americans; Allen, Richard; American Methodist Episcopal Church; Clergy; Philadelphia; Slavery

Now Try: In 1791 Robert Carter III, one of Virginia's wealthiest planters, did what better-known American founding fathers never did—he freed his slaves. Andrew Levy tells how Carter came to his heartfelt decision in *The First Emancipator: The Forgotten Story of Robert Carter, the Founding Father Who Freed His Slaves.* When Allen began his abolition work, the cause seemed almost hopeless, but he persevered. The problems in Haiti are overwhelming, but Paul Farmer has tried to provide medical care and improve living conditions in the war-torn country. Tracy Kidder describes the life of the tireless doctor in *Mountains Beyond Mountains* (see chapter 4). Allen founded a tradition of black ministers leading the fight for civil rights. *Bearing the Cross: Martin Luther King, Jr., and the Southern Christian Leadership Conference* by David J. Garrow and *Partners to History: Martin Luther King, Jr., Ralph Abernathy and the Civil Rights Movement* by Donzaleigh Abernathy are books about the continuing of that tradition in the American South.

Paul Robeson: Artist and Citizen. Rutgers University Press, 1998. 331p. ISBN 0813525101.

Paul Robeson (1898–1976) did everything well. After being an All-American football player and graduating with honors from Rutgers University, he became an accomplished actor and singer whose performances in plays, musicals, movies, concerts, and recordings were highly praised. However, as an outspoken African American in a white society, he drew increasing criticism as he became involved in the civil rights and labor movements, and his defense of the Soviet Union was especially condemned. In this collection of essays with over 200 illustrations, scholars reassess the life and career of a now mostly forgotten figure of the twentieth century.

Subjects: Actors and Actresses; African Americans; Athletes; Civil Rights Leaders; Photographic Biography; Robeson, Paul; Singers

Now Try: Robeson set an example for future black leaders, including baseball player Jackie Robinson, who broke the color barrier in Major League Baseball. David Falkner portrays Robinson as a man who worked hard to succeed in *Great Time Coming: The Life of Jackie Robinson from Baseball to Birmingham* (see chapter 12). Like Robeson, folk singer Pete Seeger was criticized and blacklisted for his political statements during the 1950s and 1960s. David King Dunaway admiringly chronicles the troubadour's life in *How Can I Keep from Singing.* Comedian Dick Gregory describes his own civil rights efforts in his memoirs *Nigger: An Autobiography* and *Callus on My Soul: A Memoir.* Like Robeson, James Earl Jones is an accomplished actor, whose deep voice has won him many critically acclaimed roles in film and on the stage. Jones describes his overcoming a stuttering problem and learning the craft of acting in *James Earl Jones: Voices and Silences.*

Pearson, Roger

Voltaire Almighty: A Life in Pursuit of Freedom. Bloomsbury, 2005. 447p. ISBN 1582-346305.

French author and philosopher Voltaire's (1694–1778) life was a long series of incidents, conflicts, and controversies, much in the vein of his classic novel *Candide.* He lived with few restraints, making love to married women, working as an actor, smuggling banned books, gambling, and writing controversial plays and verse promoting personal freedom. As a result, he was jailed twice and exiled once. Roger Pearson, cognizant of Voltaire's philosophy and manners, has written a *Candide*-like biography, using clever chapter titles and subtitles to organize this entertaining "one-thing-after-another" story.

Subjects: France; Freedom; Novelists; Philosophers; Voltaire

Now Try: Voltaire's novel *Candide* is an exciting tale that satirizes the upper classes and public officials in eighteenth-century France. Voltaire was the lover of one of the most remarkable women of eighteenth-century France. Judith Zinsser includes his affair with mathematician and physicist Gabrielle Emilie le Tonnelier de Breteuil in *La Dame d'Esprit: A Biography of the Marquise Du Chatelet* (see chapter 11). Readers who enjoyed Pearson's book on Voltaire may also enjoy *Jean-Jacques Rousseau: Restless Genius* by Leo Damrosch (see chapter 10), about an equally controversial Frenchman whose philosophical writings are still widely read and quoted. French novelist George Sand lived as libertine a life as Voltaire. Benita Eisler dramatizes the life of this outspoken woman in *Naked in the Marketplace: The Lives of George Sand.*

Reynolds, David S.

🗡 *John Brown, Abolitionist: The Man Who Killed Slavery, Sparked the Civil War, and Seeded Civil Rights.* Knopf, 2005. 578p. ISBN 0375411887.

When abolitionists celebrated the Emancipation Proclamation in 1863, they held "John Brown parties" with speeches and sang the war song "John Brown's Body." They considered Brown (1800–1859), not President Lincoln, the key figure in ending slavery in the South. Yet few people now think of Brown as the prime character in the story of freeing the slaves. In this sympathetic biography, David S.

Reynolds retells the story of the man who used terrorist tactics attempting to bring about societal change.

Subjects: Abolitionists; Brown, John; Group Discussion Books

Awards: ALA Notable Books

Now Try: Russell Banks recounts John Brown's story through the memories of one of his sons in *Cloudsplitter: A Novel.* In the history *Bound for Canaan: The Underground Railroad and the War for the Soul of America*, Fergus M Bordewich includes Brown in a cast of abolitionists with conflicting ideas about how to free the slaves. Like Brown, President Andrew Jackson was formed by the dramatic experiences of his childhood. Hendrik Booraem tells of the future president surviving the dangers of the British army's sweep through Virginia during the American Revolution in *Young Hickory: The Making of Andrew Jackson* (see chapter 6). William Jennings Bryan is another mostly discounted character from American history whose religion compelled him to oppose the status quo. *A Godly Hero: The Life of William Jennings Bryan* by Michael Kazin (see chapter 10) portrays him as a sincere and persuasive populist who championed the rights of working people.

Thomas, D. M.

Alexander Solzhenitsyn: A Century in His Life. St. Martin's Press, 1998. 583p. ISBN 0312180365.

Born a year after the Bolshevik Revolution, already fatherless and at times abandoned by his mother, Alexander Solzhenitsyn (1918–2008) grew up under Soviet communism, offering his loyalty to country instead of family. Eager to write, he planned a novel praising the Soviet Revolution, but war intervened and he joined the Red Army to fight German invaders in 1942. After winning military honors in the war, he was accused of anti-Stalin statements and was sentenced to prison, where he began a long struggle to publish his dark and critical novels. In this appreciative biography, novelist D. M. Thomas tells an epic story of a man and his tragic love affair with his faithless country.

Subjects: Dissenters; Exiles; Freedom of Speech; Novelists; Russia; Solzhenitsyn, Alexander; Soviet Union

Now Try: Solzhenitsyn blends his prison experiences into a history and indictment of the Soviet penal system in *The Gulag Archipelago, 1918–1956: An Experiment in Literary Investigation.* Among the novels drawn from his experiences are *One Day in the Life of Ivan Denisovich* and *The First Circle.* Russian physicist Andrei Sakharov was kept in internal exile by the Soviet Union for his dissent. He remembers his difficult life in *Memoirs.* Like Solzhenitsyn, African American novelist Chester Himes found his writings unread in his homeland. James Sallis tells of Himes's imprisonment and life as an expatriate in *Chester Himes: A Life* (see chapter 7). Like the Russian author, Italian sculpture and artist Michelangelo Buonarroti was a severe character with few kind words for his government. Ross King tells about the artist's fight with popes, creditors, and his brothers in *Michelangelo & the Pope's Ceiling* (see chapter 7).

Williams, Juan

Thurgood Marshall: American Revolutionary. Times Books, 1998. 459p. ISBN 0812920-287.

Thurgood Marshall (1908–1993) was the architect of race relations in the United States in the latter half of the twentieth century, according to journalist Juan William. As a lawyer he argued many famous cases, including *Brown v. the Board of Education*, and as a justice of the U.S. Supreme Court he wrote decisions protecting the rights of individuals. Despite his success, he was not always appreciated, and he clashed with civil rights leaders over methods and goals. In this admiring biography, the author tells how a descendant of slaves worked to erase slavery's legacy in American society.

Subjects: African Americans; Civil Rights Leaders; Judges; Lawyers; Marshall, Thurgood; Supreme Court

Now Try: Forty of Marshall's opinions from the Supreme Court are reprinted and introduced by law professors in *Thurgood Marshall: Justice for All.* In *Simple Justice: The History of Brown v. Board of Education and Black America's Struggle for Equality*, Richard Kluger recounts the important Supreme Court case and its legacy. English lawyer and statesman Thomas More was another man of unbending principle. The example he set for people of conscience is told in *The Life of Thomas More* by Peter Ackroyd (see chapter 4). Like Marshall, Pittsburgh Pirates outfielder Roberto Clemente was a dignified man concerned for the less fortunate. David Maraniss tells how the baseball player worked for the relief of the poor in Puerto Rico and died taking emergency aid to earthquake victims in Nicaragua in *Clemente: The Passion and Grace of Baseball's Last Hero* (see chapter 12).

Royal Lives

Biographies of kings, queens, and other members of royal families have long been a sizable portion of any public library biography section. Even our study of English history and culture reflects our fascination; we identify eras by the names of monarchs. "Elizabethan," "Georgian," "Victorian," and "Edwardian" are now adjectives so common that the progenitors from which they came are often forgotten when the words are used to describe arts, architecture, fashion, and literature. The books in this section help readers reconnect the names with these historically influential characters.

Having no monarchs of their own, American readers have to turn to books about the kings and queens of other countries. Most popular are books about the rulers of Great Britain, the country from which our nation parted. Two such books are *Richard II* by Nigel Saul, which describes the short reign of a king crowned at age ten, and *Edward the Caresser: The Playboy Prince Who Became Edward VII* by Stanley Weintraub, the story of the prince whose mother, Queen Victoria, kept him waiting for the throne for many years. Kings and queens of other nations are also popular biographical subjects. Virginia Rounding describes a powerful Russian queen in *Catherine the Great: Love, Sex, and Power*; and Caroline Weber tells about a French queen who lost her head in *Queen of Fashion: What Marie Antoinette Wore to the Revolution*. Poet Robert Pinsky examines the life of a king of ancient Israel in his contemplative biography *The Life of David*.

Royal biographies have multiple appeal factors. Possessing great wealth and supreme power over a nation, monarchs are often unrestrained characters who act wisely or outrageously. The irony is that these privileged lives are sometimes horrible. Their stories often include bitter fights for royal succession, unhappy marriages, rebellions led by unhappy subjects, tense diplomatic negotiations, and foreign wars fought to extend the monarch's kingdom. The fates of the nations in which these stories are set are sometimes decided by their personal affairs. Filled with rich details, subplots, and many characters in the courts, royal biographies often require unhurried reading. Royal biography may also appeal as a variation of celebrity biography, as every intimate detail of royal lives is often publicly told.

> *Royal Lives* are biographies about monarchs and members of royal families. Authors examine the personalities and actions of these powerful people entrusted with the fates of nations. Readers may enjoy royal biography for its history of nations or for its celebrity appeal. Most of these books are lengthy, and no true quick read is included in this section.

Brown, Tina

The Diana Chronicles. Doubleday, 2007. 542p. ISBN 9780385517089. Audiobook and large print available.

Things were going from bad to worse when Princess Diana (1961–1997) suddenly died in an automobile accident. The urbane young woman so unsuited to be a member of the horse-and-hound royal family had run out of friends and had never overcome the insecurity that she felt around her mother, stepmother, and the queen. Neither Prince Charles nor Dodi Fayed had proved to be a romantic character to compare with the lovers in the Barbara Cartland novels that she often read. In this sensational best seller, former *Tatler* editor Tina Brown tells a gossip-filled story about a depressed young woman with no clear prospects for privacy, much less happiness.

Subjects: Diana, Princess of Wales; Great Britain; Princesses; Women

Now Try: *The People's Princess: Cherished Memories of Diana, Princess of Wales, from Those Who Knew Her Best*, edited by Larry King, which collects stories from fifty-three friends and acquaintances, including Pattie Boyd, Barbara Bush, Nigel Havers, Twiggy, and David Sassoon. These memories of luncheons, work for charities, and private encounters present many positive views of the princess whom everyone wanted to meet. Books about scandals in previous generations of the Spencer family, from which Diana came, include *Privilege and Scandal: The Remarkable Life of Harriet Spencer, Sister of Georgiana* (see chapter 8) by Janet Gleeson and *Improper Pursuits: The Scandalous Life of an Earlier Lady Diana Spencer* by Carola Hicks. Like Diana, Empress Josephine of France was always surrounded by controversy. Infidelity, jealousy, and divorce are among the topics in *The Rose of Martinique: A Life of Napoleon's Josephine* by Andrea Stuart (see this chapter).

Coote, Stephen

Royal Survivor: A Life of Charles II. St. Martin's Press, 2000. 396p. ISBN 031222687X.

Without Charles II of England (1630–1685), there would be no British monarchy today, according to Stephen Coote. Exiled from England when his royal father was beheaded in 1649, Charles led an army from Scotland to retake England from Oliver Cromwell, but he was unsuccessful and escaped to France to plot further attempts. After Cromwell died, Parliament invited Charles to return. Crowned in 1660, he astutely managed by assertion and concession to remain king until his death in 1685. In this candid biography, the author portrays Charles as an able manager of his cabinet, Parliament, and his many mistresses.

Subjects: Charles II, King of Great Britain; Great Britain; Group Discussion Books; Kings

Now Try: Jean Plaidy has written a trilogy of novels about the life and reign of Charles II, *The Wandering Prince, A Health Unto His Majesty,* and *Here Lies Our Sovereign Lord.* Charles's enemy, Puritan Oliver Cromwell, is another historical figure who is difficult to judge. Peter Gaunt presents evidence for and against the religious general in the concise biography *Oliver Cromwell* (see chapter 10). Like Charles, Elizabeth I of England spent her youth first as a beloved royal child and then in prison as an endangered contender for the throne. David Starkey focuses on Elizabeth's youth and early years as a monarch in *Elizabeth: The Struggle for the Throne.* French diplomat Charles Maurice de Talleyrand-Périgord was another cunning survivor. As a member of successive French governments under a king, a revolutionary alliance, an emperor, and finally under another king, he constantly changed his loyalties. David Lawday chronicles his astute actions and narrow escapes from death in *Napoleon's Master: A Life of Prince Talleyrand* by (see chapter 10).

Guy, John

Queen of Scots: The True Life of Mary Stuart. Houghton Mifflin, 2004. 581p. ISBN 0618-254110.

Mary, Queen of Scots (1542–1587) led a short but eventful life. At age twenty-five, when she was imprisoned by her cousin Elizabeth I, she had already been queen of France and Scotland, had been married to three husbands, had her son James taken away from her, and had dramatically escaped from a Scottish prison after abdicating the Scottish throne. For eighteen years while she awaited trial, she wrote many secret letters to her allies, seeking deliverance from her plight. When the day of her beheading came, she shocked witnesses with her forthright statements and blood red petticoats. According to historian John Guy, Mary was an astute politician and powerful woman, a person to be admired, not the helpless pawn she is sometimes portrayed to be.

Subjects: Executions; France; Great Britain; Mary, Queen of Scots; Prisoners; Queens; Scotland

Now Try: More about the circumstances that pitted Mary against her cousin Elizabeth is told in *Elizabeth and Mary: Cousins, Rivals, Queens* by Jane Dunn. In the fashion of Mary, French queen Marie Antoinette made a statement with her petticoats at her execution. Her story is told in *Queen of Fashion: What Marie Antoinette Wore to the Revolution* by Caroline Weber (see this chapter). Like Mary, Egyptian queen Cleopatra was denied a throne. Lucy Hughes-Hallett examines many legends about the tragic queen in *Cleopatra: Histories, Dreams and Distortions* (see chapter

5). As first lady in Argentina, the beautiful and evocative Eva Perón was in some respects queenlike, and like Mary was suspected of being involved with spies. Alicia Dujovne Ortiz tells about her tragic life in *Eva Perón: A Biography* (see chapter 6).

Lever, Evelyne

Madame de Pompadour: A Life. Farrar, Straus & Giroux, 2000. 310p. ISBN 0374-113084.

When Madame de Chateauroux died in late 1744, French king Louis XV needed a new official mistress. To be chosen by his advisors, she needed to be attractive, but not politically ambitious. Her relatives, who would benefit from elevated social standing, needed to be closely evaluated, too. The advisors erred in selecting young Jeanne-Antoinette de Pompadour (1721–1764), who stole the king's heart and became a very influential and dangerous person in the court, having close access to the monarch. In this admiring biography, French historian Evelyne Lever claims that this bourgeois girl essentially became a second queen.

> **Subjects:** France; Louis XV, King of France; Mistresses; Pompadour, Jeanne-Antoinette Poisson, Marquis de; Royal Favorites; Women

> **Now Try:** Princess Michael of Kent describes the rivalry of Catherine de' Medici, the queen of France, and Diane of Poitiers, the royal mistress, for the love of Henri II in *The Serpent and the Moon: Two Rivals for the Love of a Renaissance King*. The illegitimate daughter of Pope Julius was a very dangerous woman in Renaissance Rome. Caroline P. Murphy tells how the ambitious woman undermined her own interests by making too many enemies in *The Pope's Daughter: The Extraordinary Life of Felice della Rovere*. Two American first ladies may have had undue influence in the affairs of the American government. Phyllis Lee Levin examines whether Edith Wilson acted as president during her husband's illness in *Edith and Woodrow: The Wilson White House* (see chapter 10). Carl Sferrazza Anthony describes the entertaining of underworld figures in the Harding White House in *Florence Harding: The First Lady, the Jazz Age, and the Death of America's Most Scandalous President* (see chapter 5).

Massie, Robert K.

🏵 *Peter the Great: His Life and World.* Random House, 1980. 909p. ISBN 0394500326. Audiobook available.

When Peter (1672–1725) was born, Russia was a large, isolated country that shunned Europe. Its capital was Moscow, a mostly wooden city without grand buildings. When he died, Russia was a powerful player in European affairs, and its new capital was St. Petersburg, a center of culture, architecture, and naval affairs. As tsar from age ten, the engaging, ambitious ruler embraced the West, importing culture, science, and industry to his impoverished land. In the process he executed some opponents, but he was also generally liberal with pardons. According to Robert K. Massie, Peter the Great earned his name and stands as a positive example of benevolent despots.

> **Subjects:** Peter the Great, Tsar of Russia; Russia; St. Petersburg; Tsars

Awards: ALA Notable Book; Pulitzer Prize for Biography

Now Try: Like St. Petersburg, Washington, D.C., was built on swampy ground on a French design. Scott W. Berg recounts the life and work of architect Pierre Charles L'Enfant, who served in the American Revolution under General George Washington and designed the city named for him, in *Grand Avenues: The Story of the French Visionary Who Designed Washington, D.C.* When Franklin Delano Roosevelt became president, the United States was in the depths of a terrible economic depression. Like Peter the Great, he used his persuasive power to initiate an economic program to provide work and build a modern nation. Jonathan Alter dramatically describes the difficult task in *The Defining Moment: FDR's Hundred Days and the Triumph of Hope* (see chapter 4). In 1852, when Emperor Meiji took the Japanese throne, the country was poised to enter the modern world. Donald Keene chronicles sixty years of change in the epic biography *Emperor of Japan: Meiji and His World, 1852–1912.* Micah D. Halpern does not challenge the benevolence of Peter the Great, but he does expose the bad side of many other omnipotent rulers in *Thugs: How History's Most Notorious Despots Transformed the World Through Terror, Tyranny, and Mass Murder.*

Pinsky, Robert

The Life of David. Nextbook/Schocken, 2005. 209p. <u>Jewish Encounters</u>. ISBN 0805242031.

According to poet Robert Pinsky, a hero is "one who does great deeds and suffers for the good of the community, but in addition the hero must be talked about." He adds that heroes need flaws to seem genuine and worthy of praise for their accomplishments. David, the King of Israel (1037–967 BCE), fits this description. When only a young shepherd he fought the warrior Goliath, whom no others would. For this, Saul, the king of Israel, gave David command of his army and his daughter in marriage. Military victory, rebellion, luxury, adultery, and repentance are part of the story that Pinsky tells about a royal life in biblical times.

Subjects: David, King of Israel; Group Discussion Books; Israel; Kings

Now Try: In the novel *God Knows,* Joseph Heller describes David as more modern and down-to-earth. The elevation of David for killing Goliath resembles the crowning of the young Arthur of the Britons for pulling a sword from a stone. Arthur is one of several legendary figures examined in *In Search of Myths & Heroes: Exploring Four Epic Legends of the World* by Michael Wood. Like Pinsky, Vanessa Collingridge searches through folktales and records of fact to find the truth and meaning behind a legendary character in *Boudica: The Life of Britain's Legendary Warrior Queen* (see chapter 5). Like David, Robert Pinsky is most known for his poetry, including *Jersey Rain* and *Gulf Music,* and for his translation of *The Inferno of Dante.*

Rounding, Virginia

Catherine the Great: Love, Sex, and Power. St. Martin's Press, 2006. 566p. ISBN 9780-312328870.

Catherine II of Russia (1729–1796) was not Russian, having been born in a royal family in a German principality, and she had no claim to the throne once her husband Peter III died, yet she seized control and ruled the country for thirty-four years. During her reign she continued the Westernization of education and foreign relations begun by Peter I and expanded the development of the imperial city of St. Petersburg. She also took many lovers and fought off numerous rebellions. Virginia Rounding incorporates Catherine's many letters to friends and family in this sympathetic and intimate examination of the powerful queen's life.

Subjects: Catherine II, Queen of Russia; Queens; Russia; St. Petersburg

Now Try: Dorothy Schiff intended to let her second husband George Backer, run the *New York Post*, which she had bought, but when he proved ineffective, she seized control. Marilyn Nissenson portrays Schiff as an influential woman eager to control politicians and public policy in *The Lady Upstairs: Dorothy Schiff and the **New York Post*** (see chapter 10). Like Catherine, Indian Prime Minister Indira Gandhi spent her childhood in the home of a national leader, but she was not expected to become a head of state. Katherine Frank describes the education and ascension of Mrs. Gandhi in *Indira: The Life of Indira Nehru Gandhi* (see chapter 10). Boston heiress Isabella Stewart Gardner had many of Catherine's qualities: loving art, architecture, and beautiful dresses, and demanding adherence to her will. Douglass Shand-Tucci describes the art connoisseur's life in *The Art of Scandal: The Life and Times of Isabella Stewart Gardner* (see chapter 8). From her days as the highest paid actress in silent films to her years as a Hollywood producer, Mary Pickford maintained control of her artistic work and bank account. Scott Eyman tells the story of an assertive woman and her career in *Mary Pickford: America's Sweetheart*.

Saul, Nigel

Richard II. Yale University Press, 1999. 514p. English Monarchs. ISBN 03000-70039.

Richard II (1367–1400) was only ten years old when he was put on the British throne in 1377, succeeding his grandfather, who had been king for over fifty years. As a boy king, he submitted to his many advisors, who steered his reign; but by age fourteen he was asserting himself, insisting on pardoning participants of the Great Revolt of 1381. According to historian Saul Nigel in this revisionist text, Richard II was not as terrible a monarch as other scholars have suggested, but a victim of his own disregard of several key nobles, who turned to Henry Plantagenet to restore their influence. In this sympathetic account, Saul gives readers a look at the inner workings of the British royal court in the fourteenth century.

Subjects: England; Kings; Richard II, King of England

Now Try: In the novel *Passage to Pontefract*, Jean Plaidy portrays young King Richard II as doomed for his foolish disregard of his advisors and wasting of the royal treasury. In the mystery novel *The Whyte Harte* by P. C. Doherty, Matthew Jankyn, a petty thief in the employ of the Bishop of Beaufort, seeks to find out whether Richard II has escaped from Henry IV or is really dead. Egyptian pharaoh Tutankhamen was a boy when he inherited his throne and only lived to be about sixteen. Christine El Mahdy reexamines the legends and archeological evidence of the pharaoh's life in *Tutankhamen: The Life and Death of a Boy-King* (see chapter 5). Ann Wroe writes about another young man who claimed that he should be king in *The Perfect Prince: The Mystery of Perkin Warbeck and His Quest for the Throne of England* (see chapter 5).

Skidmore, Chris

Edward VI: The Lost King of England. St. Martin's Press, 2007. 346p. ISBN 9780312351427.

When Henry VIII died and his ten-year-old son Edward VI (1537–1553) succeeded him on the throne, the people of England were ready for happier times. They were tired of religious turmoil and increasingly repressive rule and welcomed a new beginning with the bright young king. Of course, much of the power of the king was vested in his regent, Edward's uncle, the Duke of Somerset, but the young monarch quickly showed talents in diplomacy and expressed an interest in royal affairs. In this sympathetic biography, Chris Skidmore portrays Edward as a promising monarchy who might have brought rival factions together had he not died at age sixteen. Anglophiles and historical novel readers will especially enjoy this royal biography.

> **Subjects:** Edward VI, King of England; Great Britain; Kings
>
> **Now Try:** Edward is the lively and curious prince mistakenly locked out of the castle in Mark Twain's comic satire *The Prince and the Pauper*. Edward's two sisters both became queens of England, ruling before and after his reign. Alison Weir also adds the hapless Lady Jane Grey into the story of *The Children of Henry VIII*, her account of the long partisan struggle for power that followed the death of Henry VIII. Stephen Crane had only begun a promising career as a novelist when he died of consumption (tuberculosis) at age twenty-nine. Linda H. Davis tells his short and tragic story in *Badge of Courage: The Life of Stephen Crane* (see chapter 6). Felix Mendelssohn was young, talented, and well-liked when he died from a stroke at age thirty-eight. Peter Mercer-Taylor describes a career that held great promise in *The Life of Mendelssohn* (see chapter 7).

Stuart, Andrea

The Rose of Martinique: A Life of Napoleon's Josephine. Grove Press, 2003. 455p. ISBN 0802117708.

Born Rose de Tasher on her family's sugar plantation on the Caribbean island of Martinique, Empress Josephine of France (1763–1814) lived a privileged but dangerous life. Widowed when her husband was beheaded in the French Revolution, she survived by living with friends and lovers until she caught the eye of rising military leader Napoleon Bonaparte, who renamed her after his dead brother. She enjoyed the life of luxury and power until her jealous husband, perhaps seeking new alliances and wanting an heir (which Josephine has not produced), divorced her for infidelity. In this biography of a scandalous woman, Andrea Stuart tells a sympathetic story that will please readers who enjoy melodrama.

> **Subjects:** Bonaparte, Napoleon; de Tasher, Rose; Empresses; Josephine, Empress of France; Marriage; Martinique; Women
>
> **Now Try:** Sandra Gulland has Josephine tell her own story through her diary in a trilogy of novels, *The Many Lives and Secret Sorrows of Josephine B.; Tales of Passion, Tales of Woe;* and *The Last Great Dance on Earth.* Jean Plaidy also uses a trilogy of novels to tell the story of a queen disposed of for not producing an heir, Henry VIII's first wife, Catherine of Aragon: *Katharine, the Virgin Widow; The Shadow of the Pomegranate;* and *The King's Secret Matter.* A sense of both romance and tragedy pervades *Natasha: The Biography of Natalie Wood* by Suzanne Finstad (see chapter 8). Like Josephine, Jeannette Jerome of Brooklyn was also brought from the new world to the old to marry into the nobility. Charles Higham describes a woman who was never satisfied with her mansions or her many lovers in *Dark Lady: Winston Churchill's Mother and Her World* (see chapter 8).

Weber, Caroline

Queen of Fashion: What Marie Antoinette Wore to the Revolution. Henry Holt, 2006. 412p. ISBN 9780805079494.

Marie Antoinette (1755–1793) wore a simple chemise over a white under-skirt to her execution. The deposed queen of France had not always shown such good sense in her choice of garb. According to scholar Caroline Weber, the lavish gowns and costly accessories that she wore in the final days of the reign of Louis XVI were not only a reflection of her personality and lifestyle but were also a grave insult to the poor French public. In this unusual cultural biography, the author connects the rise and fall of Marie Antoinette's popularity with public opinion of her wardrobe.

> **Subjects:** Fashion; France; French Revolution; Group Discussion Books; Marie Antoinette, Queen of France; Queens; Teen Reads; Women

> **Now Try:** One of Marie Antoinette's children survived the French Revolution to later become a beloved figure in the restoration of the monarchy. Her story is told in *Marie-Thérèse, Child of Terror: The Fate of Marie Antoinette's Daughter* by Susan Nagel. What Diana, Princess of Wales, wore was a constant topic in the British and international press throughout the 1980s and 1990s, un-til her tragic death in 1997. In his illustrated biography *Diana Style*, fashion writer Colin McDowell chronicles how the princess rose and fell in public opinion based largely on her clothes, hats, and accessories. Coco Chanel brought French fashions to America in the twentieth century. Edmonde Charles-Roux describes her soap-opera-like life in *Chanel: Her Life, Her World, and the Woman Behind the Legend She Herself Created* (see chapter 8). The connection of clothes and disregard for the poor is also present in the story of former first lady of the Philippines Imelda Marcos. Catherine W. Ellison tells how a beautiful young woman was corrupted by power in *Imelda, Steel Butterfly of the Philippines*.

Weintraub, Stanley

Edward the Caresser: The Playboy Prince Who Became Edward VII. Free Press, 2001. 429p. ISBN 0684853183.

Because his mother, Queen Victoria, lived a long life, Edward VII (1841–1910) was stuck being the Prince of Wales for a very long time. What was there to do? Edward took advantage of his large income to seek the pleasures of drink, entertainment, lively company, and beautiful women. Though his mother was displeased with the reports of his behav-ior in newspapers, most of the English public loved him for his bonhomie. Stanley Weintraub chronicles the social life, romantic affairs, and world travels of the gregarious prince in this entertaining biography.

> **Subjects:** Edward VII, King of Great Britain; Edwardian Age; Great Britain; Kings; Princes

> **Now Try:** Christopher Hibbert examines the character of Edward's mother with great depth and sympathy in *Queen Victoria: A Personal History*. Lady Randolph Churchill was a frequent companion of the prince while her son Winston was still young. Edward appears as a character in *Churchill: Young Man in a Hurry* by Ted Morgan. According to Nigel Hamilton, young John Fitzgerald Kennedy was a lover of action, travel, food, women, and cigars. His

exploits are told in *JFK, Reckless Youth* (see chapter 6). Unlike the prince, leading actor Errol Flynn suffered greatly from feeling that he had no real purpose. His hedonistic life was destructive and led him to seek unlikely employment, as described in *Errol Flynn: The Spy That Never Was* by Tony Thomas (see chapter 8).

Weir, Alison

Queen Isabella: Treachery, Adultery, and Murder in Medieval England. Ballantine Books, 2005. 487p. ISBN 0345453190. Audiobook available.

When young Princess Isabella of France (1292–1358) first arrived in England in 1308, her marriage to the royal heir signaled improved relations between the countries. Later, when she invaded England with her lover and French forces in 1326, she deposed her uninterested husband, King Edward II. It is still a mystery whether she had him murdered. In her lively biography of the powerful queen, Alison Weir sympathetically portrays Isabella as a justified woman with scores to settle, but no sense for political survival.

Subjects: Great Britain; Isabella, Queen of England; Queens; Women

Now Try: Italian duchess Lucrecia Borgia, the illegitimate daughter of Pope Alexander VI, married three times, each time gaining more wealth and power in Renaissance Rome. Sarah Bradford examines whether Borgia was really so cruel as to murder her husband in *Lucrezia Borgia: Life, Love and Death in Renaissance Italy*. There is also speculation that Florence Harding had her husband, President Warren G. Harding, murdered. Carl Sferrazza Anthony examines the evidence in *Florence Harding: The First Lady, the Jazz Age, and the Death of America's Most Scandalous President* (see chapter 5). Jiang Qing, widow of Mao Zedong, was a key figure in the Cultural Revolution in China under her husband. After his death, she and her Gang of Four were accused of plotting to take over the country. Ross Terrill portrays the ambitious Chinese woman as evil in *The White-Boned Demon: A Biography of Madame Mao Zedong* (see chapter 5).

Wilson, Derek

Charlemagne. Doubleday, 2006. 226p. ISBN 0385516703.

When Charlemagne (742–814) was born, his father Pepin III was trying to reconstruct Francia, an alliance of French kingdoms that had fallen apart upon the death of his grandfather, Charles Martel. By the time of his death Charlemagne, who had taken the title of emperor, had not only reassembled the alliance but also expanded its boundaries across the European continent, establishing the Holy Roman Empire. According to Derek Wilson, Charlemagne is the historical bridge between ancient and modern history and the embodiment of the idea of a monarch. Although he claimed to have a holy mission to expand the rule of Christianity, he personally increased his royal power with each fiefdom that he conquered. Wilson's lively book concisely chronicles the powerful ruler's life and his historical legacy.

Subjects: Charlemagne, Holy Roman Emperor; Emperors; France; Holy Roman Empire; Kings

Now Try: Thomas Bullfinch collected stories about the French king in *The Age of Chivalry and Legends of Charlemagne*. Richard I of Great Britain is traditionally portrayed as a good king destined to extend Christianity. Frank McLynn examines the evidence of the English king and his brother in *Richard and John: Kings at War*. Like Charlemagne, Tsar Ivan IV of Russia used military force and political ruthlessness to expand his kingdom, but historians have condemned Ivan while forgiving Charlemagne. Isabel De Madariaga chronicles the tsar's violent career in *Ivan the Terrible: First Tsar of Russia* (see chapter 5). French general Napoleon Bonaparte idealized Charlemagne and sought to rebuild his empire. Paul Johnson portrays the general as a military genius without political understanding in *Napoleon* (see chapter 3).

Historical Biography Collections

The books in this section differ from others in this chapter in that they profile multiple historical figures instead of one or two. They are to biography what short stories are to fiction. People with only short periods to devote to reading may enjoy the brief, satisfying biographical narratives, and readers who wish to sample authors or the lives of characters before committing to reading an entire book may also enjoy these collections. Often thematic, these collections also appeal to readers interested in a particular topic or era.

> *Historical Biography Collections* include books that gather profiles of many similar historical characters into a single volume. Authors focus on the key incidents and dominant characteristics in these quick profiles. These works are ideal for more leisurely or interrupted reading.

Brands, H. W.

Masters of Enterprise: Giants of American Business from John Jacob Astor and J. P. Morgan to Bill Gates and Oprah Winfrey. Free Press, 1999. 354p. ISBN 0684854732. Audiobook available.

Whereas the deeds of our political and military leaders have always been widely reported and generally understood, the leaders of commerce have often worked behind the closed doors of board rooms, according to historian H. W. Brands. As a result, contributions by businesspeople to the American way of life have not always been recognized. In this entertaining collective biography, Brands profiles twenty-five individuals whose vision and quest for wealth have given the world railroads, mass manufacturing, soft drinks, television, pop music, home computers, cosmetics, and other products and services vital to modern life.

Subjects: Capitalists; Collective Biography; Industrialists; Wealth

Now Try: Maury Klein tells stories about twenty-six Americans who have become legends on Wall Street and beyond in *The Change Makers: From Carnegie to Gates, How the Great Entrepreneurs Transformed Ideas into Industries*. In a group biography, *Tycoons: How Andrew Carnegie, John D. Rockefeller, Jay Gould, and J. P. Morgan Invented the American Supereconomy*, Charles R. Morris focuses on the men who controlled steel, oil, railroads, and banking during the rapid growth of the country in the latter half of the nineteenth century. Richard S. Tedlow admiringly profiles seven businessmen from different eras in *Giants of Enterprise: Seven Business Innovators and the Empires They Built*.

Brokaw, Tom

Boom! Voices of the Sixties: Personal Reflections on the '60s and Today. Random House, 2007. 662p. ISBN 9781400064571. Audiobook and large print available.

American life changed dramatically in the 1960s, when the assassination of President John F. Kennedy, the civil rights movement, the Vietnam War, drugs, sex, and rock and roll shook the nation's social foundations. In the vein of his popular *The Greatest Generation*, television journalist Tom Brokaw examines the lives of eighty-five individuals who came of age in the turbulent decade, describing their experiences and the directions their lives took. He includes civil rights leaders, politicians, social reformers, and figures from popular culture. Baby boomers and their children will find this work thought-provoking.

> **Subjects:** 1960s; Collective Biography; Group Discussion Books; Social Change

> **Now Try:** Brokaw's *The Greatest Generation* and *The Greatest Generation Speaks: Letters and Reflections* take readers back to World War II. Rosemary Dinnage profiled women in the arts and literature who challenged social conventions in her collective biography *Alone! Alone!: Lives of Some Outsider Women* (see chapter 4). Studs Terkel offers interviews with sixty-eight seniors who "came of age" in the twentieth century in *Coming of Age: The Story of Our Century by Those Who've Lived It* . For its seventy-fifth anniversary, *The New Yorker* editors collected stories on twenty-five of the most interesting people of the twentieth century in *Life Stories: Profiles from* **The New Yorker**.

Roberts, Cokie

Founding Mothers: The Women Who Raised Our Nation. HarperCollins, 2004. 359p. ISBN 0060090251. Audiobook and large print available.

Historians of the revolutionary period often neglect the women. Cokie Roberts points out that it is the women who kept the family, the farm, and the business running when the men were off fighting or attending the Continental Congress. These mothers, wives, and daughters did not always just accept everything the men said and did. They advised and sometimes criticized them. Roberts tells lively and sometimes humorous stories about Deborah Franklin, Abigail Adams, Kitty Greene, Eliza Pinckney, Martha Washington, Mercy Otis Warren, and Mary Wollstonecraft in the time of the American Revolution.

> **Subjects:** Adams, Abigail Smith; American Revolution; Franklin, Deborah Read; Greene, Catharine Littlefield "Kitty"; Group Biography; Group Discussion Books; Pinckney, Eliza Lucas; Warren, Mercy Otis; Washington, Martha; Wollstonecraft, Mary; Women

> **Now Try:** Roberts has continued the story of the women of the American Revolution with the story of the women who witnessed the writing of the U.S. Constitution, ran the presidential mansion, and entertained diplomats at foreign missions, in *Ladies of Liberty: The Women Who Shaped Our Nation*. Bonnie Angelo profiles a diverse collection of women who all raised American presidents in *First Mothers: The Women Who Shaped the Presidents* (see chapter 10). Former first daughter Margaret Truman evaluates twenty-nine presidents' wives in her collective biography *First Ladies: An Intimate Group Portrait of White House Wives*.

Starkey, David

Six Wives: The Queens of Henry VIII. HarperCollins, 2003. 852p. ISBN 069401-043X. Audiobook available.

1

King Henry VIII of England loved women and needed a male heir. For these reasons, he wed three Catherines, two Annes, and a Jane in a series of marriages that grew progressively shorter. According to David Starkey, the story of Henry's six wives is the ultimate soap opera, with elements of romance, intrigue, horror, and tragedy. Using primary sources, including long-forgotten Spanish documents, the author challenges standard portrayals of all six women in this mostly sympathetic collective biography.

2

Subjects: Anne of Cleves; Boleyn, Anne; Catherine of Aragon; Collective Biography; Divorce; England; Henry VIII, King of England; Howard, Catherine; Parr, Catherine; Queens; Seymour, Jane

3

Now Try: Philippa Gregory re-creates life in the court of Henry VIII in *The Other Boleyn Girl: A Novel,* and Jean Plaidy wrote about several of the queens in her books in <u>The Tudor Saga Series</u>. Eleanor of Aquitaine, believed to be the most beautiful woman of the twelfth century, married first Louis VII of France and then Henry II of England. In *Eleanor of Aquitaine: A Life,* royal families historian Alison Weir recounts Eleanor's quest for personal power and thrones for her sons. Louis XIV of France, who reigned for seventy-two years, had only one wife but a series of royal mistresses. Antonia Fraser depicts their lives in *Love and Louis XIV: The Women in the Life of the Sun King.* Celebrity readers can find several books about frequently married characters, including *Elizabeth* by J. Randy Taraborrelli (see chapter 8) and *Jack: The Great Seducer: The Life and Many Loves of Jack Nicholson* by Edward Douglas (see chapter 8).

4

5

6

Waller, Maureen

Sovereign Ladies: Six Reigning Queens of England. St. Martin's Press, 2006. 555p. ISBN 9780312338015.

7

Thanks to the very long reigns of three of its six sovereign queens, Great Britain has been ruled by a female hand for 187 of the past 455 years (1553–2008). According to historian Maureen Waller, the six women faced many of the same challenges, but drew on different strengths to rule. All had to deal with the question of the roles of men in their lives and whether to produce successors. Most of them strengthened the empire. Waller portrays each individually in this intimate collective biography.

8

9

Subjects: Anne, Queen of England; Collective Biography; Elizabeth I, Queen of England; Elizabeth II, Queen of England; Great Britain; Mary I, Queen of England; Mary II, Queen of Great Britain; Queens; Victoria, Queen of Great Britain; Women

10

Now Try: Daughters of monarchs usually were not in line for the throne, so they were often used as pawns in alliances with other nations. Julie P. Gelardi compares the stories of three ruling queens and their unlucky daughters in *In Triumph's Wake: Three Royal Matriarchs, Three Tragic Daughters.* James II of England was forced off the throne by his two Protestant daughters, Mary and Anne, to prevent their Catholic half-brother from becoming heir. Mary then reigned as queen with William of Orange, and Anne became queen after their

11

12

deaths. Maureen Waller tells a story of family discord and religious conflict in ***Ungrateful Daughters: The Stuart Princesses Who Stole Their Father's Crown***. Two British queens and a hapless Lady Jane Grey are characters in the tragic group biography ***Children of Henry VIII*** by Alison Weir. Few books published in English profile any twentieth-century reigning queens other than Queen Elizabeth II of England. An exception is ***Queen Juliana: The Story of the Richest Woman in the World*** by William Hoffman, an entertaining but also sensational and disputed account of the Dutch monarch, who reigned from 1948 to 1980.

Consider Starting With . . .

These well-written Historical Biographies of modest length will appeal to general readers.

- Ball, Edward. *The Sweet Hell Inside: A Family History.*

- Brinkley, Douglas. *Rosa Parks.*

- Coote, Stephen. *Royal Survivor: A Life of Charles II.*

- D'Antonio, Michael. *Hershey: Milton S. Hershey's Extraordinary Life of Wealth, Empire, and Utopian Dreams.*

- Downer, Lesley. *Madame Sadayakko: The Geisha Who Bewitched the West.*

- Gerzina, Gretchen Holbrook. *Mr. and Mrs. Prince: How an Extraordinary Eighteenth-Century Family Moved Out of Slavery and into Legend.*

- Kukla, Jon. *Mr. Jefferson's Women.*

- LaPlante, Eve. *American Jezebel: The Uncommon Life of Anne Hutchinson, the Woman Who Defied the Puritans.*

- Lever, Evelyne. *Madame de Pompadour: A Life.*

- Madsen, Axel. *John Jacob Astor: America's First Multimillionaire.*

- Roberts, Cokie. *Founding Mothers: The Women Who Raised Our Nation.*

- Skidmore, Chris. *Edward VI: The Lost King of England.*

- Smitten, Richard. *Jesse Livermore: World's Greatest Stock Trader.*

- Sobel, Dava. *Galileo's Daughter: A Historical Memoir of Science, Faith, and Love.*

- Weber, Caroline. *Queen of Fashion: What Marie Antoinette Wore to the Revolution.*

- Williams, Juan. *Thurgood Marshall: American Revolutionary.*

Further Reading

Adamson, Lynda G.

Thematic Guide to Popular Nonfiction. Greenwood Press, 2006. 352p. ISBN 0313328552.

    Adamson includes chapters about commerce, family, and race relations in her book about nonfiction topics. Each chapter describes a topic and then presents three lengthy reviews before suggesting other titles.

Cords, Sarah Statz

The Real Story: A Guide to Nonfiction Reading Interests. Libraries Unlimited, 2006. 460p. ISBN 1591582830.

    Cords discusses history in chapter 6 and biography in chapter 7 of her book. She describes the genres and reviews dozens of titles, with further reading recommendations.

Wyatt, Neal

The Readers' Advisory Guide to Nonfiction. American Libraries, 2007. 318p. ISBN 9780838909362.

    Wyatt discusses history and historical biography stories in chapter 10 of her book and includes a generous list of titles to recommend to readers.

Chapter 10

Political Biography

Definition of Political Biography

Politics is the art or science of government. Political Biographies are accounts of the lives of the women and men who lead governments and make decisions that affect the lives of citizens. Many of the most known Political Biographies profile presidents, prime ministers, and other heads of state, but books are also written about their advisors, supporters, rivals, and families.

According to Carl Rollyson in *Biography: A User's Guide* (Ivan R. Dees, 2008), the modern Political Biography is a twentieth-century creation. In nineteenth-century America, biographers were signed by publishers to write positive portraits of leaders as strong virtuous men who were industrializing the nation and moving its borders westward and around the world. In Great Britain the purpose of a Political Biography was to praise monarchs, lords, and military leaders. No biographer of that time questioned the actions or intentions of the subject. That all changed when Lytton Strachey published his unflattering profiles of four leading British figures in his collective biography *Eminent Victorians* (1918).

In today's highly charged political culture, biographies praise, criticize, and even condemn historical statesmen, current leaders, and candidates for political offices. Nearly two years before the 2008 presidential election, books by and about every possible candidate appeared, giving details about their lives and political positions. Many were obviously biased accounts, destined to be forgotten as soon as candidates dropped out of the race. More lasting are the seriously researched accounts of past political figures with which the ephemeral works compete for shelf space in bookstores and libraries. During the same two-year period leading up to the 2008 election, Franklin D. Roosevelt, Thomas Jefferson, John Quincy Adams, James Polk, Aaron Burr, Machiavelli, Milton Friedman, and Richard Nixon were the subjects of popular new Political Biographies, showing that there is still interest in past leaders, their advisors, and their supporters.

Political Biography include accounts of the lives of the women and men who lead governments and make decisions that affect the lives of citizens. Many of the most known Political Biographies profile presidents, prime ministers, and other heads of state, but books are also written about their advisors, supporters, rivals, and families. These biographies feature strong characters in political contests, in which significant governing decisions must be made. Detailed settings are essential to these stories. Readers learn about the characters and the times that they lived in. Quick reads and longer biographies are included in this chapter.

Appeal of the Genre

The appeal of enigmatic characters is perhaps the strongest in Political Biography. Readers already know most of the names of the presidents and other leaders before they choose their books. Many readers may already know stories about them from history classes in school, watching movies and television documentaries, reading previous biographies, or following their careers in the news. People commit to reading these stories again to refresh their knowledge of the political characters, delve deeper into their characters, and perhaps also reevaluate them. This reading urge continually sells books about Thomas Jefferson, Abraham Lincoln, and anyone named Kennedy or Roosevelt.

Political Biography stories always involve a contest of wills and uncertainty about the means politicians will use to prevail, giving the narrative tension. Even when the readers know the outcome from the outset, they read the books to revisit familiar tales and find newly revealed incidents.

Second to character in the appeal of Political Biography is setting or frame. Politics must have a context or setting, just as leaders must have followers in a time and place. Readers often seek out biographies about characters who lived in historical periods that interest them. Reading Political Biographies is an excellent way to learn more about history.

The pacing of Political Biographies varies. A few shorter works tell only the essential stories and qualify as quick reads. Many are longer, slower works that describe characters and events thoroughly, requiring readers to understand the story sequence and remember the many names involved. As mentioned previously, the appeal of learning is also high in Political Biographies. Readers may commit to the time involved in reading big books to learn new facts and different viewpoints about the politicians and time periods that fascinate them.

Organization of the Chapter

The first section in this chapter is "Leadership Stories," which includes biographies of political figures who led their nations in times of crisis. The overall tenor of these books is upbeat, admiring the skills exhibited by these leaders even when the biographers disagree with their politics. President Franklin Roosevelt and Indian Prime Minister Indira Gandhi are joined by Vietnam's Ho Chi Minh and Soviet leader Vladimir Ilyich Lenin in this section.

"Reassessing Reputations" follows. These Political Biographies reexamine the characters of leaders to see if they deserve their reputations. Japan's Emperor Hirohito, Confederate President Jefferson Davis, and Soviet Premier Nikita Khrushchev are among the figures considered in this section.

In the third section, "Practicing Politics," readers will find a collection of biographies about people who successfully shaped the policies of their governments. These figures may have wielded their powers from inside or outside public office, either elected or appointed—perhaps even from behind the scenes. First Lady Dolley Madison, French statesman Charles Maurice de Talleyrand-Périgord, newspaper publisher Dorothy Schiff, and Secretary of State Condoleezza Rice are among the subjects in this section.

The final section is "Political Biography Collections." Readers who enjoy short profiles of political figures that can easily be read in single sittings, and readers who want to sample stories of various individuals before committing to reading a longer work, will appreciate these entertaining collections.

Political Biography is a favorite subgenre with book critics. Many of these books have won awards, as evidenced by the award symbols at the beginning of several entries. (Note: The titles in this chapter are not marked for teen appeal.)

Leadership Stories

Biographies of presidents, prime ministers, and other heads of state are featured in bookstores every publishing season. Biographers find these powerful people interesting subjects about whom to write, and publishers issue countless titles on well-known and often studied characters year after year. Because readers continue to faithfully buy these books, the cycle continues. To match readers' interests, libraries fill shelves with Political Biographies about heads of state.

In this section are biographies of familiar political figures from many eras and nations. Historian Anthony Everitt takes readers back to the ancient world to portray a figure with contemporary ideas and modern political problems in *Cicero: The Life and Times of Rome's Greatest Politician*. William J. Duiker shares little known stories about a charismatic Vietnamese communist leader in *Ho Chi Minh: A Life*. Katherine Frank tells the tragic story of India's first female head of state in *Indira: The Life of Indira Nehru Gandhi*. These characters have name recognition among American readers, who enjoy the stories of how they obtained and used their political power.

Strong characters and great stories abound in these books. In the longer works, settings tend to be well developed, whereas the shorter works focus mostly on personal stories. Most of the books are lengthy and require some reader commitment, but there are several quicker reads, including photobiographies of John F. Kennedy and Nelson Mandela. From all these books, readers learn about the leaders in the context of their time.

> *Leadership Stories* include biographies of political figures who led their nations in times of crisis. The overall tenor of these books is upbeat, admiring the skills exhibited by these leaders even when the biographers disagree with their politics. Most of these titles are detailed studies that require unhurried reading. A couple of photographic biographies are included.

Addison, Paul

Churchill: The Unexpected Hero. Oxford University Press, 2005. 308p. <u>Oxford's Lives and Legacies Series</u>. ISBN 0199279349.

Before the Second World War, Winston Churchill (1874–1965) was an aging British politician who had offended nearly every constituency at some point in his career. Many members of Parliament considered him unreliable, because he suddenly changed sides on issues. Some thought that his ego often overruled his judgment. However, his leadership during the war restored his reputation, earning him high acclaim. In this clever and compact narrative, Paul Addison tells how Churchill's reputation rose and fell during the course of his long public life.

Subjects: Churchill, Winston; Great Britain; Politics and Government; Prime Ministers; Quick Reads

Now Try: Churchill wrote glowingly of his coming-of-age in *My Early Life: A Roving Commission*. Elliott Roosevelt makes Churchill a character in mysteries featuring his mother, Eleanor Roosevelt, in *Murder in the Palace* and *The White House Pantry Murder*. Both Churchill and U.S. President Theodore Roosevelt have been described as having the character of a bulldog. Like Churchill, Roosevelt was a strong head of state able to dictate legislation at the peak of his power. Edmund Morris tells of Roosevelt's active presidency in *Theodore Rex* (see this chapter). Like Churchill, French poet, dramatist, and philosopher Voltaire was a self-assured man of strong opinions, who cared little what his contemporaries thought about him. Roger Pearson describes his long, melodramatic life in *Voltaire Almighty: A Life in Pursuit of Freedom* (see chapter 9).

Dherbier, Yann-Brice, and Pierre-Henri Verlhac

John Fitzgerald Kennedy: A Life in Pictures. Phaidon Press, 2003. 304p. ISBN 0714-843628.

A photographic biography is especially appropriate for John F. Kennedy (1917–1963), whose image helped him narrowly win the presidential election of 1960. Within this big book are photographs of JFK at all ages of his short life. He is shown with his family at Hyannis Port, on the Harvard swim team, on a camel in front of the pyramids, as a young Massachusetts politician campaigning, at his wedding to Jacqueline Bouvier, at work as president of the United States, and in Dallas in November 1963 prior to his assassination. Sometimes pensive, often smiling, overly tanned, and impeccably dressed, JFK's image is a large part of his legacy, which the Yann-Brice Dherbier and Pierre-Henri Verlhac capture in this handsome book.

Subjects: Assassinations; Kennedy, John F.; Photographic Biography; Politics and Government; Presidents

Now Try: Dherbier and Verlhac have published a series of similar photobiographies about Jaqueline Kennedy Onassis, Grace Kelly (see chapter 8), Paul Newman, and Sophia Loren. In the photobiography *Man in the Green Shirt*, Richard Williams shows jazz musician Miles Davis as a confident, risk-taking musician surrounded on stage and off by other great musicians. As a general in the Civil War when photography was new, Ulysses S. Grant was one of the first political figures to have his fame spread through photographic images. William S. McFeely collects many historic photographs and describes Grant's rise to the presidency in *Ulysses S. Grant: An Album* (see chapter 3). Martin Luther King Jr. may have lived in the same era as Kennedy, but his world was far different, as seen in *King: The Photobiography of Martin Luther King, Jr.* by Charles Johnson and Bob Adekman (see chapter 9).

Donald, David Herbert

🎗 *Lincoln.* Simon & Schuster, 1995. 714p. ISBN 0684808463. Audiobook and large print available.

Among the many books on Abraham Lincoln (1809–1865), this substantial biography by David Herbert Donald stands out for its intimacy and readability. Using many letters and other writings by the subject, the author pays particular attention to what Lincoln thought and felt at all the important junctures in his life. The resulting portrait shows a man who wanted to find practical solutions rather than change the world ideologically.

Subjects: Civil War; Illinois; Lincoln, Abraham; Politics and Government; Presidents

Awards: ALA Notable Books

Now Try: In his epic novel *Lincoln*, Gore Vidal presents the president as seen by family, friends, and enemies. Even a big book may not satisfy a reader's thirst for Lincoln stories. A good follow-up title is *Lincoln's Sanctuary: Abraham Lincoln and the Soldiers' Home* by Matthew Pinsker, which looks closely at the three summers that Lincoln spent commuting to the White House from the cottage at the Soldier's Home in suburban Washington. John Brown shared with Lincoln a common dislike of slavery and both have been blamed for starting the American Civil War, but their personalities differed greatly. In *John Brown, Abolitionist: The Man Who Killed Slavery, Sparked the Civil War, and Seeded Civil Rights* (see chapter 9), David S. Reynolds describes a man who claimed that terror was an acceptable means to a just end. Like Lincoln, the Jewish leader Moses brought his people through a difficult time and then died without enjoying the accomplishment. Jonathan Kirsch describes a great leader in his sweeping biography *Moses: A Life*.

Duiker, William J.

Ho Chi Minh: A Life. Hyperion, 2000. 695p. ISBN 0786863870.

Vietnamese revolutionary Ho Chi Minh (1890–1969) is probably the least known of the major twentieth-century Communist leaders. He did not write well-distributed books like Lenin and Mao, he was known by many names, and he spent many years in hiding. As a youth on the run from the French colonial police, he served as a cook on a passenger steamer and studied in London and Paris. Later he attended Communist conferences around the world and slowly took command of the North Vietnamese government. Was he a patriot or a tyrant? The nature of his character mystified Western strategists, who underestimated his political acumen. In this expansive but very readable biography, historian William J. Duiker reveals the life and times of the man who inspired the defeat of the world's most powerful military.

> **Subjects:** Communists; Ho Chi Minh; Revolutionaries; Vietnam

> **Now Try:** *On Revolution: Selected Writings, 1920–1966* highlights the Communist leader's elegant defense of his movement. Shawnee chief Tecumseh was known as a grand orator who traveled from the Gulf of Mexico to Canada with his message of Native American unity. John Sugden portrays Tecumseh as a courageous warrior with a greater understanding of the stakes for Native Americans than others of his time had, in *Tecumseh: A Life* (see chapter 3). Just as Ho Chi Minh outlasted French and U.S. forces in the series of conflicts in Southeast Asia, former slave Toussaint Louverture led poorly equipped rebel forces against the French and the British in eighteenth-century Haiti. Madison Smartt Bell profiles the clever African in *Toussaint Louverture: A Biography* (see chapter 5). Master criminal Joseph Silver was another mysterious figure about whom legends grew. Like Ho Chi Minh, he was well traveled and his crimes were difficult to verify. Charles Van Onselen tells Silver's story in *The Fox and the Flies: The Secret Life of a Grotesque Master Criminal* (see chapter 2).

Everitt, Anthony

Cicero: The Life and Times of Rome's Greatest Politician. Random House, 2001. 359p. ISBN 0375507469. Large print available.

Roman statesman Marcus Tillius Cicero (109–43 BCE) held the state together by suspending rights after the assassination of Julius Caesar. In doing so, he violated the very principles of constitutional law to which he had dedicated his life. As a result, he sacrificed his reputation among his contemporaries but impressed hosts of future kings, queens, and presidents. In his intimate look at the life and thoughts of Cicero, Anthony Everitt draws on the Roman's many speeches, essays, and letters to his friends, including Marcus Junius Brutus and Caius Cassius Longinus, famous as characters in William Shakespeare's play *Julius Caesar*. This modern interpretation of an ancient life will engage contemporary readers.

> **Subjects:** Cicero, Marcus Tillius; Orators; Politics and Government; Rome; Statesmen

> **Now Try:** Cicero wrote about philosophy, politics, rhetoric, and morals in *The Treatises of Cicero*. Taylor Caldwell dramatized Cicero's life as the most noble Roman in the novel *A Pillar of Iron*. Octavius, later known as Augustus, was a member of the Second Triumvirate that condemned Cicero to death after the assassination of Julius Caesar. Anthony Everitt describes this powerful Roman who thwarted the republican cause in Rome in *Augustus: The Life of Rome's First Emperor*. President Franklin D. Roosevelt ignored constitutional limitations to hold the country together during the Great Depression and to manage the defense of the country during World War II. His life is intimately told in *FDR* by Jean Edward Smith (see this chapter). Knowing that he might be the last monarch in Great Britain if he failed to please commoners and nobility alike, King Charles II compromised the traditional powers of the crown when necessary. His life is told in *Royal Survivor: A Life of Charles II* by Stephen Coote (see chapter 9).

Frank, Katherine

Indira: The Life of Indira Nehru Gandhi. Houghton Mifflin, 2002. 567p. ISBN 039573-097X.

As the child of Indian Prime Minister Jawaharlal Nehru, future Prime Minister Indira Gandhi (1917–1984) lived a very public life. As a young woman she attended prestigious schools, traveled the world, and served as her father's hostess. Witness to the violence of the founding of her nation, she worked with Hindus, Sikhs, and Muslims seeking to bring peace to India. Drawing from manuscripts and interviews, biographer Katherine Frank sympathetically depicts how the most powerful woman in India used her political talents to survive many tragedies, only to be assassinated by her bodyguard in 1984.

Subjects: Assassinations; Gandhi, Indira; India; Prime Ministers; Women

Now Try: Much was expected of Gandhi because her father, Jawaharlal Nehru, had been able to bring rival factions together in compromise. Stanley Wolpert chronicles Nehru's life and career in *Nehru: A Tryst with Destiny*. Gandhi's sons died tragically, one in a suspicious plane crash and the other assassinated. Like the Gandhis in India, the Kennedy family in America has suffered many tragedies. Edward Klein chronicles the terrible events across several generations in *The Kennedy Curse: Why Tragedy Has Haunted America's First Family for 150 Years*. Like Indira Gandhi, Pakistani Prime Minister Benazir Bhutto was elected twice, was dogged by charges of corruption in her government, and was assassinated. Her partially autobiographical book about the politics of her region, *Reconciliation: Islam, Democracy, and the West*, has been published posthumously. Gandhi contemporary Prime Minister Golda Meir of Israel also found sticking to her principles difficult once she was in office. Elinor Burkett describes conflict between Meir's political and personal life in *Golda*.

Mandela: The Authorized Portrait. Andrews McMeel Publishing, 2006. 355p. ISBN 9780740755729.

African National Congress leader Nelson Mandela (1918–), the central figure in the history of South Africa in the last half of the twentieth century, was an influential and often photographed figure before his imprisonment in 1964 and after his release from prison in 1990. During his imprisonment, protesters in his country and human rights groups around the world called for his release. With the end of apartheid, his calming presence as president kept South Africa from factional violence. Filled with photos, commentaries, interviews, and documents, this handsome collective work shows the evolution of Mandela from tribal leader to international statesman.

Subjects: African National Congress; Mandela, Nelson; Photographic Biography; Prisoners; Revolutionaries; South Africa

Now Try: Mandela eloquently recounts his childhood, political activism, and years in prison in *Long Walk to Freedom: The Autobiography of Nelson Mandela*. Elizabeth I of England, once a prisoner herself, was able to hold her country together during sectarian strife. David Starkey describes the early years of Elizabeth's monarchy in *Elizabeth: The Struggle for the Throne* (see chapter 6). Like Mandela, Soviet dissident Alexander Solzhenitsyn spent many years in prison while foreign activists lobbied for his release. The story of his long battle for freedom is told in *Alexander Solzhenitsyn: A Century in His Life* by D. M. Thomas (see chapter 9). Readers who enjoy photographic biographies of strong characters in historical settings will also enjoy *Paul Robeson: Artist and Citizen* (see chapter 9).

McCullough, David

🎗 *John Adams.* Simon & Schuster, 2001. 751p. ISBN 0684813637. Audiobook and large print available.

Reading a David McCullough book, one can almost hear his voice, which is familiar to viewers of public television. President John Adams (1735–1826) was a great character on whom to focus for this skilled storyteller. Adams knew and clashed with all the important statesmen in colonial America and the early republic, and his love affair with wife Abigail is legendary. Using many letters from Adams and his correspondents, McCullough tells the intimate story of a life devoted to family and country. Readers of historical fiction will have no trouble moving to nonfiction with this epic biography.

> **Subjects:** Adams, John; American Revolution; Massachusetts; Politics and Government; Presidents

> **Awards:** ALA Notable Books; Pulitzer Prize for Biography

> **Now Try:** Irving Stone dramatizes the long marriage of John and Abigail Adams in the novel *Those Who Love*. John Quincy Adams was temperamentally and politically much like his father. Joseph Wheelan describes in depth the latter part of his life in *Mr. Adams's Last Crusade: John Quincy Adams's Extraordinary Post-Presidential Life in Congress* (see this chapter). Readers wanting more on the Adams family will enjoy *The Adams Chronicles: Four Generations of Greatness* by Jack Shepherd. Like Adams, author E. B. White was a meticulous, no nonsense man who adored and relied on his wife. Like McCullough, Scott Elledge writes warmly about his subject in *E. B. White: A Biography* (see chapter 7). Ronald Reagan advanced from being president of the Screen Actors Guild to California governor and later U.S. president, always encouraged by his wife Nancy. Anne Edwards describes a remarkably close couple with errant children in *The Reagans: Portrait of a Marriage*.

McCullough, David

🎗 *Truman.* Simon & Schuster, 1992. 1117p. ISBN 0671456547. Audiobook available.

Harry Truman (1884–1972) was described by some East Coast commentators as a political unknown from nowhere when he became president after the death of Franklin Roosevelt. Historian David McCullough disagrees, pointing out that the new president came straight from the heart of America. Raised on the Missouri frontier, Truman worked hard at every stage of his life and knew the concerns of the working class. Ascending to the presidency when he did, he made many of the most important decisions of the twentieth century. He authorized use of the atomic bomb, advocated the formation of NATO, and committed the United States to the Cold War with the Soviet Union. McCullough's book on Truman provides readers who like strong characters with a lengthy but compelling narrative.

> **Subjects:** Missouri; Politics and Government; Presidents; Truman, Harry

> **Awards:** ALA Notable Books; Pulitzer Prize for Biography

> **Now Try:** The warm feeling for Truman continues in *Eleanor and Harry: The Correspondence of Eleanor Roosevelt and Harry S. Truman*, a collection of letters between two American icons. *Memoirs: Year of Decisions* and *Memoirs: Years of Trial and Hope*, both written by Truman in the decade after his highly criticized presidency, won him many fans. Raised on a farm in Iowa, oil tycoon Frank Phillips grew up with hard work and crop failures. Like Truman, the Midwesterner diligently worked his way up from poverty to prominence. Michael Wallis tells his success story in *Oil Man: The*

Story of Frank Phillips and the Birth of Phillips Petroleum (see chapter 9). Like Truman, astronaut Neil Armstrong displayed quiet courage throughout his life. His story is told in great detail in *First Man: The Life of Neil A. Armstrong* by James R. Hansen (see chapter 1).

Meacham, Jon

Franklin and Winston: An Intimate Portrait of an Epic Friendship. Random House, 2003. 490p. ISBN 0375505008. Audiobook and large print available.

World War II brought American President Franklin D. Roosevelt (1882–1945) and British Prime Minister Winston Churchill (1874–1965) together. In a five-year period the two powerful heads of state, both hailing from privileged backgrounds, exchanged over 2,000 letters, spoke via international telephone, and met at highly publicized summits. According to Jon Meacham, the two developed a warm relationship, which helped them plan the course of the war. Meacham describes scenes vividly and quotes his subjects heavily in this dramatic dual biography.

Subjects: Churchill, Winston; Friends; Letters; Roosevelt, Franklin D.; World War II

Now Try: The meeting of the two world leaders in Cairo in 1943 provides the setting for *The Sands of Sakkara,* a thriller by novelist Glenn Meade. Max Born and Albert Einstein discussed many personal, professional, and political topics in the forty years that they wrote letters to each other. These warm and discursive letters are collected in *The Born–Einstein Letters: Friendship, Politics and Physics in Uncertain Times 1916 to 1955.* Historian Stephen E. Ambrose pays tribute to friendship among men in his collective biography *Comrades: Brothers, Fathers, Heroes, Sons, Pals* (see chapter 3). The meeting between President Richard M. Nixon and Chinese Communist Party leader Mao Zedong did not lead to friendship, but it did lead to a thawing of American–Chinese relations. Margaret Macmillan profiles the two dangerous men in *Nixon and Mao: The Week That Changed the World.*

Morris, Edmund

🏆 *Theodore Rex.* Random House, 2001. 772p. ISBN 0394555090. Audiobook available.

When Theodore Roosevelt (1858–1919) assumed the office of U.S. president upon the assassination of William McKinley, he arrived with an ample supply of support and energy. Within weeks he began shaking up the establishment by inviting a black man to dinner in the White House, beginning investigations of securities fraud, and sponsoring antitrust legislation. He followed with major domestic and international initiatives that became increasingly populist as his power increased. Though he seemed unstoppable in many ways, he failed to stop lynching and blundered on race issues in the military. In this entertaining sequel to *The Rise of Theodore Roosevelt,* Edmund Morris accounts for seven and a half years of daily speeches, meetings, dinners, travels, and home life of a very active president.

Subjects: Politics and Government; Presidents; Roosevelt, Theodore

Awards: ALA Notable Books; Los Angeles Times Book Prize for Biography

Now Try: Roosevelt, who had been an urbane Easterner, created his outdoorsman image with *Ranch Life and the Hunting Trail*, his memoir of cowboy life in North Dakota. Another great introduction to the life of Theodore Roosevelt, one of the most colorful of American presidents, is *Mornings on Horseback* by David McCullough (Simon & Schuster, 1981). Roosevelt's British contemporary Rudyard Kipling was a man of both literature and adventure. Like Roosevelt, Kipling could "wave a big stick," but he could also be precise in his political assessments. David Gilmour describes a complex man, enthusiastic about the British Empire and yet sympathetic to the colonials in India and South Africa, in *The Long Recessional: The Imperial Life of Rudyard Kipling*. General Douglas MacArthur was another larger than life figure, always eager for a fight. Richard B. Frank concisely describes his career in *MacArthur: A Biography* (see chapter 3). Like Roosevelt, Pope John Paul II was a crusader for causes and busy world traveler. Peggy Noonan tells about the Polish pope in *John Paul the Great: Remembering a Spiritual Father* (see chapter 4).

Service, Robert

Lenin: A Biography. Harvard University Press, 2000. 561p. ISBN 0674003306.

Russian communist Vladimir Ilyich Lenin (1870–1924) used over 160 pseudonyms in his career as a writer, revolutionary, and Communist Party leader, thoroughly confusing Western scholars. According to Russian expert Robert Service, Lenin was the leader most responsible for the rise and development of the Soviet Union, the essential man in the revolution that spread to other nations. Given unparalleled access to Communist Party archives, Service tells how Lenin's upbringing and early experiences radicalized him. The key question that the author answers is whether the Russian leader let his personal desire for power lead him away from Marxist precepts. Service makes Lenin more understandable in this analytical biography.

Subjects: Lenin, Vladimir Ilyich; Revolutionaries; Russia; Soviet Union.

Now Try: Lenin's most important writings are included in *The Essential Works of Lenin: "What Is to Be Done?" and Other Writings*. Che Guevara began his revolutionary career as a academic, well versed in the philosophy of Marx. Jon Lee Anderson portrays El Che as a person who could care for people as a doctor or as president of the Cuba's National Bank, as well as lead guerrillas through the jungle, in *Che Guevara: A Revolutionary Life* (see chapter 3). Like Lenin, abolitionist John Brown was ruthless in the pursuit of his revolutionary goals. Though Brown is responsible for far fewer innocent lives lost, he was as radical and committed to his beliefs. David S. Reynolds tells Brown's story in *John Brown, Abolitionist: The Man Who Killed Slavery, Sparked the Civil War, and Seeded Civil Rights* (see chapter 9). By the time Mikhail Gorbachev became the head of the Communist Party in 1985, the citizens of the Soviet Union were turning away from the party. Gorbachev's reform policies prepared the union for dissolution into many republics. He describes the history of his country and his role in world affairs in *Gorbachev: On My Country and the World*.

Smith, Jean Edward

FDR. Random House, 2007. 858p. ISBN 9781400061211. Audiobook available.

According to Jean Edward Smith, Franklin Delano Roosevelt (1882–1945) was a visionary statesman. Whereas President Hoover and other state governors did little to help the unemployed during the Great Depression, Governor Roosevelt led extensive relief efforts in New York. Although most Americans opposed the country becoming involved in the upcoming European conflict, President Roosevelt prepared the country for war. The author portrays FDR as a confident man who was never afraid to act and make mistakes that could later be corrected. She also examines his complicated personal relationships and political alliances in this in-depth biography.

Subjects: New York; Politics and Government; Presidents; Roosevelt, Franklin D.

Now Try: Elliott Roosevelt describes life with his parents Franklin and Eleanor Roosevelt in two memoirs, *An Untold Story: The Roosevelts of Hyde Park* and *A Rendezvous with Destiny: The Roosevelts in the White House*. Elliott's brother, James Roosevelt, disagrees with some of Elliott's stories in *My Parents: A Differing View*. During his many years in office, Roosevelt helped lift his country out of poverty, as did Russian Tsar Peter the Great. Robert K. Massie describes the Russian monarch's dynamic efforts to modernize his country and improve the lives of his subjects in *Peter the Great: His Life and World* (see chapter 9). Whereas a study of Roosevelt's life reveals all the major political movements in the United States during his time, a study of Albert Einstein reveals the politics of Europe and the world of science as well. His life is entertainingly told by Walter Isaacson in *Einstein: His Life and Universe* (see chapter 11). Herbert Hoover's failure to avert the Great Depression spoiled his reputation as the man who could do wonders. Richard N. Smith describes how Hoover rebounded after his presidency to regain his status as a humanitarian and statesman in *An Uncommon Man: The Triumph of Herbert Hoover*.

Reassessing Reputations

No matter how many books are written, political debates are never settled. Likewise, there is never universal agreement about important historical and contemporary political figures. Biographers with differing viewpoints are always willing to come forward with their evidence and arguments to sway public opinion.

In this section, the Political Biographies continue or resurrect the debates about enigmatic leaders whose lives still interest readers. Historian Herbert P. Bix enters the debate over whether Japanese Emperor Hirohito was directing his country's war effort in World War II or was a figurehead controlled by powerful generals in *Hirohito and the Making of Modern Japan*. In *Machiavelli: Philosopher of Power,* Ross King asks whether Italian statesman Niccolò Machiavelli has been unfairly maligned by historians. William J. Cooper continues the debate about the divisive role of Confederate President Jefferson Davis before, during, and after the Civil War in *Jefferson Davis, American*.

The difference between the Political Biographies in this section and the titles in "Leadership Stories" sections is that the titles in the previous section *portray* character, and this section's titles *question* character. In both sections, however, story remains an important reader appeal. Development of setting varies with the length of the books. Because the narrative includes pros and cons in the arguments about the characters, the pace of these books may be deliberate or unhurried. All of these titles could be book discussion selections.

> *Reassessing Reputations* biographies reexamine the characters of leaders to see if they deserve their good or bad reputations. Leaders from many periods are included. Readers learn about their works and their motives, as well as the societies that they represent. Quick reads and longer biographies are included in this section.

Baker, Jean H.

James Buchanan. Times Books, 2004. 172p. <u>American Presidents</u>. ISBN 0805069461.

Was James Buchanan (1791–1868) the worst U.S. president ever? Could he have averted the American Civil War? According to Jean H. Baker, much was expected of Buchanan when he was elected, because he had been very effective as a congressman, senator, minister to Russia, and secretary of state. Though born in Pennsylvania, he was surprisingly sympathetic to Southern causes, especially the preservation of states' rights. Did putting four strong Southern statesmen in his cabinet hasten the war? Baker lets the reader decide Buchanan's culpability in this quick-reading volume in the popular <u>American Presidents</u> series.

> **Subjects:** Buchanan, James; Politics and Government; Presidents; Quick Reads.

> **Now Try:** The <u>American Presidents</u> series from Henry Holt and Company are concise, highly readable biographies of American presidents written by well-known authors, aimed at students and general readers. The publishers intend to include every president. Books include *Dwight D. Eisenhower* by *New York Times* reporter Tom Wicker and *James Monroe* by former senator Gary Hart. Readers may find more on Buchanan's role in historical context in the third edition of *The Causes of the Civil War*, edited by Kenneth M. Stampp. Like Baker, Michael Fellman has little sympathy for and much criticism of his biographical subject in his exposé, *The Making of Robert E. Lee* (see chapter 5). Like Buchanan, President Andrew Jackson had little interest in the lives of slaves or Native Americans and dedicated his administration to business and expansion. Andrew Burstein explains Jackson's positions in *The Passions of Andrew Jackson*.

Bix, Herbert P.

Hirohito and the Making of Modern Japan. HarperCollins, 2000. 800pp. ISBN 006019314x.

After the Japanese surrender in World War II, world opinion favored indicting Emperor Hirohito (1901–1989) for war crimes. Through skillful diplomacy, however, he became an American ally and continued as supreme monarch of his country. In this character study that also serves as a political history of twentieth-century Japan, Herbert P. Bix dispels the myth that the emperor was a puppet of the Japanese military regime and claims that he was fully in control of the actions of his ruthless generals. This richly detailed and controversial biography will appeal to readers who enjoy epic tales.

> **Subjects:** Emperors; Hirohito, Emperor of Japan; Japan; World War II

> **Awards:** National Book Critics Circle Award for Biography; Pulitzer Prize for Nonfiction

> **Now Try:** In *American Shogun: General Macarthur, Emperor Hirohito, and the Drama of Modern Japan*, Robert Harvey provides a very different, more sympathetic view of the Japanese emperor. No one questions whether German Chancellor Adolf Hitler knew about the atrocities executed in his name. Ian Kershaw chronicles the years of his

control of Germany in *Hitler: 1936–1945: Nemesis*. Likewise, *Mao: The Unknown Story* by Jung Chang (see chapter 5) contends that the chairman of the Chinese Communist Party was directly responsible for millions of deaths. Niall Ferguson examines the causes and results of wars within and between nations, focusing on the murder of citizens, in *War of the World: Twentieth-Century Conflict and the Descent of the West*.

Cooper, William J.

🎗 *Jefferson Davis, American.* Alfred A. Knopf, 2000. 757p. ISBN 039456-9164.

Confederate President Jefferson Davis (1808–1889) is often portrayed as a broken man, one of history's great losers. Some scholars blame his lack of effective leadership during the Civil War for Southern defeat. Southern historian William J. Cooper Jr. disagrees. In this epic biography, he argues that Davis was a very powerful national figure before the war and that the former slave holder and plantation owner regained much of his influence in the South after the war. Although admitting that Davis's ideas are now repugnant and rejected, Cooper holds that they were accepted opinions in both the North and the South during his time. Readers interested in lives placed in historical context will enjoy this detailed account.

Subjects: Civil War; Confederate States of America; Davis, Jefferson; Presidents; Statesmen

Awards: Los Angeles Times Book Prize for Biography

Now Try: Davis defended the attempt by Southern states to secede from the country in *The Rise and Fall of the Confederate Government*. In the decades leading up to the American Civil War, Senator John C. Calhoun was the Southern leader who most often threatened to pull his state out of the union. Irving H. Bartlett examines the life and beliefs of a man whose first loyalty was to the state of South Carolina in *John C. Calhoun: A Biography*. Both Davis and former Vice President Aaron Burr had strong political support while they were still living. In *Fallen Founder: The Life of Aaron Burr* (see this chapter), Nancy Isenberg shows that the reputation of her subject has suffered since his death. Likewise, the eloquence and diplomacy of Shawnee chief Tecumseh have been forgotten over time. John Sugden resurrects his reputation in *Tecumseh: A Life* (see chapter 3).

Ellis, Joseph J.

🎗 *American Sphinx: The Character of Thomas Jefferson.* Knopf, 1997. 365p. ISBN 0679444904. Audiobook and large print available.

It can be maddeningly difficult to pin down the character of our third president, Thomas Jefferson (1743–1826). He declared that all humanity was equal, but still owned slaves. He proposed methods of economy, while spending lavishly. He spoke of limiting government powers, then extended them by buying the Louisiana Territory from the French. He turned a blind eye to the horrors of the French Revolution and purportedly slept with his slave, Sally Hemings. In this psychological biography, historian Joseph J. Ellis weighs the evidence for and against the red-headed founding father whose words and actions are still cited by all sides in current political debates.

Subjects: Jefferson, Thomas; Politics and Government; Presidents; Slavery Debate; Virginia

Awards: National Book Award for Nonfiction

Now Try: *The Life and Selected Writings of Thomas Jefferson* includes selected essays, letters, and a brief autobiography. Jon Kukla updates Jefferson's story with DNA test results in his lively collective biography *Mr. Jefferson's Women* (see chapter 9). Jefferson's peer Robert Carter did free his slaves in 1791. Andrew Levy describes how Carter was able to do what others only contemplated in *First Emancipator: The Forgotten Story of Robert Carter, the Founding Father Who Freed His Slaves*. Like Jefferson, abolitionist minister Henry Ward Beecher did not always practice what he preached. Debby Applegate tells of his fall from grace in *The Most Famous Man in America: The Biography of Henry Ward Beecher* (see this chapter). Political philosopher Karl Marx never had the chance to rule a country, but he still lived a life inconsistent with his writings. Francis Wheen portrays him as an impractical, unfocused academic in *Karl Marx: A Life* (see this chapter).

Gaunt, Peter

Oliver Cromwell. New York University Press, 2004. 144p. <u>British Library Historic Lives</u>. ISBN 0814731643.

Four hundred years after his life, Oliver Cromwell (1599–1658) remains a controversial figure in British history. Was he a hero who extended rights to every citizen of the land, or a tyrant consolidating power to impose his own moral code? Was he a cruel military leader destroying ancient properties and slaying innocent people, or simply doing what needed to be done to defeat Charles I? In this compact narrative, scholar Peter Gaunt lays out the historical evidence in favor of and against the Lord Protector. This attractive volume in the <u>British Library Historic Lives</u> series is colorfully illustrated and includes a helpful chronology.

Subjects: Cromwell, Oliver; England; Generals; Puritan Revolution; Quick Reads

Now Try: Novels have typically treated Cromwell unkindly. *Charles the King* by Evelyn Anthony is no exception, but the author makes the confusing events of the English Civil War understandable. Though less is known about Sir Thomas Malory, the author of *Morte d'Arthur*, than about Cromwell, there may be as many questions about his character. Christina Hardyman presents the evidence for and against his reputation in *Malory: The Knight Who Became King Arthur's Chronicler* (see chapter 5). Like Cromwell, Puritan clergyman Jonathan Edwards believed that the church had the right to impose its faith and precepts on the community. Historian George M. Marsden advises readers not to apply modern standards to historical characters in *Jonathan Edwards: A Life* (see chapter 4). Spanish dictator Francisco Franco justified many of his actions as necessary to rid society of undesirable elements. The story of his harsh rule of Spain is told in *Franco: A Concise Biography* by Gabrielle Ashford Hodges (see chapter 5).

Isenberg, Nancy

Fallen Founder: The Life of Aaron Burr. Viking, 2007. 540p. ISBN 9780670063529. Audiobook available.

Nancy Isenberg rebukes other historians and novelists for failing to check original sources before writing about Aaron Burr (1756–1836). Too many have relied on accounts from Burr's enemies, of whom there were many in the cut-throat political world of the early American republic. In her book the author chronicles Burr's quick rise to prominence, becoming a New York assemblyman at age twenty-eight, U.S. senator at thirty-five, and U.S. vice president at forty-five. In midlife he killed Alexander Hamilton in a duel, fled to the frontier, and was charged with treason, but he survived these controversies and outlived all of his detractors. Isenberg contends Burr was no worse ethically than other historical leaders who are now revered. When he died at age eighty, a respected New York lawyer, he had not yet become a historical outcast. Readers who enjoy historians correcting misconceptions will enjoy this lively biography.

> **Subjects:** Burr, Aaron; Duelists; New York; Politics and Government; Vice Presidents

> **Now Try:** Gore Vidal rewrites history in his entertaining *Burr: A Novel*. Who has a worse reputation than Aaron Burr? How about railroad tycoon Jay Gould, who was famous for hostile takeovers and for manipulating markets for personal gain? Edward J. Renehan Jr. argues that he was not any worse than other corporate executives in *Dark Genius of Wall Street: The Misunderstood Life of Jay Gould, King of the Robber Barons* (see chapter 9). The reputation of President James K. Polk is not so much maligned as neglected, according to Walter R. Borneman, who claims the twelfth U.S. president was more influential than most historians admit in *Polk: The Man Who Transformed the Presidency and America*. American novelist, essayist, and travel writer Washington Irving began his career as a writer for Aaron Burr's newspaper *The Morning Chronicle*. Andrew Burstein profiles Irving as an energetic man attuned to the industry and expansion of his era in *The Original Knickerbocker: The Life of Washington Irving* (see chapter 7).

King, Ross

Machiavelli: Philosopher of Power. Atlas Books, 2007. 244p. <u>Eminent Lives</u>. ISBN 9780060817176. Audiobook available.

Has Italian statesman Niccolò Machiavelli (1469–1527) been maligned by historians? Not according to historian Ross King. He was untrustworthy as a diplomat, unfaithful as a husband, and very cynical as a writer of political philosophy and ribald plays. Many of his contemporaries counted him as an enemy. Can anyone view him sympathetically? King provides evidence for the debates about the infamous Renaissance statesman who rubbed shoulders with tyrants, popes, and artists. Not for gentle readers, this account includes grisly details about executions and quotes Machiavelli's profanity-filled papers.

> **Subjects:** Diplomats; Italy; Machiavelli, Niccolò; Politics and Government

> **Now Try:** *The Prince* and *The Art of War* are Machiavelli's most read books. Tammany Hall politician turned Civil War general Dan Sickles was also untrustworthy, unfaithful, and violent. Thomas Keneally reveals his outlandish crimes in *American Scoundrel: The Life of the Notorious Civil War General Dan Sickles* (see chapter 2). Peter Goodchild never calls physicist Edward Teller evil, but he supplies plenty of evidence for readers to reach that conclusion about the government scientist in *Edward Teller: The Real Dr. Strangelove* (see chapter 11). Samuel F. B. Morse was a sometimes acerbic man who fought with competitors over patents. How his belligerence hampered

his business life is told in *Lightning Man: The Accursed Life of Samuel F. B. Morse* by Kenneth Silverman (*see* chapter 11). In the business of newspapers and media, Australian Rupert Murdoch is a terrible enemy to have. In *Rupert Murdoch: The Untold Story of the World's Greatest Media Wizard* (see chapter 5), Neil Chenoweth portrays the newspaper mogul as solely concerned with his own power and wealth, with no regard for employees or stockholders of the companies he ruins.

Lawday, David

Napoleon's Master: A Life of Prince Talleyrand. Thomas Dunne Books, 2006. 386p. ISBN 9780312372972.

How did an aristocratic French statesman survive the end of the French monarchy, the revolution, the rise and fall of Napoleon, and the reestablishment of the monarchy? The cunning Charles Maurice de Talleyrand-Périgord (1754–1838) lived by his wits, constantly realigning his allegiances and staying ahead of changes in public sentiment. Although historians now portray this defrocked bishop as a fiend who betrayed nearly every ally he ever had, David Lawday writes about Talleyrand sympathetically, admitting that the French statesman served his own interests first, but arguing that he was also the architect of contemporary Anglo–French relations, which stabilized European politics. Lawday's book provides readers with a fascinating account of a much-maligned character.

Subjects: Diplomats; France; French Revolution; Politics and Government; Talleyrand-Périgord, Charles Maurice de

Now Try: Knowing what rivals are scheming is essential for surviving in politically volatile times. The master of secret information in the reign of Queen Elizabeth I was the ruthless Sir Francis Walsingham. Stephen Budiansky recounts how the career diplomat established a ring of spies in *Her Majesty's Spymaster: Elizabeth I, Sir Francis Walsingham, and the Birth of Modern Espionage*. Like Talleyrand, media mogul Rupert Murdoch survives by deducing societal changes and astutely positioning his companies to meet them. He is also ruthless and despised. Neil Chenoweth exposes the newspaper man's backroom deals in *Rupert Murdoch: The Untold Story of the World's Greatest Media Wizard* (see chapter 5). The defrocked monk Giacomo Casanova was less menacing than Talleyrand, but he also risked his life in alliances with royalty and criminal characters. Lydia Flem describes his outlandish life in *Casanova: The Man Who Really Loved Women* (see chapter 5). Whereas Talleyrand is often depicted as cunning and immoral, his contemporary, the Marquis de Lafayette, is described as a noble, selfless man. David A. Clary recounts how Lafayette won the hearts of Americans when he came to their aid during the revolution in *Adopted Son: Washington, Lafayette, and the Friendship That Saved the Revolution.*

Taubman, William

🕯 *Khrushchev: The Man and His Era.* Norton, 2003. 876p. ISBN 0393051447. Audiobook available.

The life of Nikita Khrushchev (1894–1971) mirrors the history of the Soviet Union . Khrushchev led strikes in the Revolution of 1917 and rose through the ranks of the Communist Party. As a faithful confidant of Joseph Stalin, he arrested and condemned old friends. He later denounced Stalin, then led economic reforms that contributed to agricultural shortages and a housing crisis. Though he died long before the demise of the Soviet Union, he initiated the political reforms that later allowed Soviet leaders Mikhail Gorbachev and Boris Yeltsin to rise to power. Historian William Taubman uses Krushchev's memoirs as well as newly available documents and interviews to reexamine the long career of a former metalworker turned world statesman. Readers can decide whether the Soviet leader was a criminal, buffoon, hero, or a mixture of all of these.

Subjects: Communists; Dictators; Khrushchev, Nikita Sergeyevich; Soviet Union

Awards: ALA Notable Books; National Book Critics Circle Award for Biography; Pulitzer Prize for Biography

Now Try: In *Khrushchev Remembers*, the Soviet leader wrote about the years that he served under Stalin, the development of the Cold War, and the Cuban Missile Crisis. General Francisco Franco was the central character in the history of Spain for half a century. Gabrielle Ashford Hodges chronicles his decades of sadistic misrule in *Franco: A Concise Biography* (see chapter 5). Foreign correspondent Georgie Anne Geyer tells a similar story linking the destiny of a country to just one man in *Guerrilla Prince: The Untold Story of Fidel Castro*. Mikhail Gorbachev came of age during the Khrushchev administration. He describes the history of his country and his role in world affairs in *Gorbachev: On My Country and the World*.

Wheelan, Joseph

Mr. Adams's Last Crusade: John Quincy Adams's Extraordinary Post-Presidential Life in Congress. Public Affairs, 2008. 308p. ISBN 9780786720125.

When most presidents leave office, they are expected to gracefully retire. John Quincy Adams (1767–1848) intended to follow suit but was asked by his hometown leaders to run for Congress. Believing he had an obligation, he agreed, won a seat without campaigning, and spent the last seventeen years of his life in the fight to end government support of slavery. Joseph Wheelan portrays Adams as a cranky elder statesman who overcame physical limitations to outlast most of his opponents, but failed to save his country from an eventual civil war. This biography of a virtuous man will appeal to readers who enjoy strong characters.

Subjects: Adams, John Quincy; Congresspersons; Politics and Government; Presidents; Slavery Debate

Now Try: Adams came from a renowned American family about which many books have been written. *John Adams* by David McCullough (see this chapter) and *The Adams Chronicles: Four Generations of Greatness* by Jack Shepherd are excellent books for further reading. John Quincy Adams's hero was the Roman politician Marcus Tillius Cicero, who is admiringly portrayed in *Cicero: The Life and Times of Rome's Greatest Politician* by Anthony Everitt (see this chapter). Senator John C. Calhoun was Adams's arch enemy throughout his years in government, opposing nearly every position that he took. Irving H. Bartlett examines the life and beliefs of a man whose first loyalty was to his state of South Carolina in *John C. Calhoun: A Biography*. William Jennings Bryan was a very religious man. Michael Kazin describes how Bryan, like Adams, applied his faith to his job as a congressman in *A Godly Hero: The Life of William Jennings Bryan* (see this chapter).

Williams, John Hoyt

Sam Houston: A Biography of the Father of Texas. Simon & Schuster, 1993. 448p. ISBN 0671746413. Audiobook available.

For every achievement in his life, Sam Houston (1793–1863) seemed to have a failure. As governor of two states, president of the Republic of Texas, a congressman, a senator, and a commanding general in the Texas victory over Mexican forces under General Santa Anna, he collected enemies and was often criticized for not meeting his obligations. Alcohol, divorce, and other personal problems often disrupted his work. Using quotations by and about Houston to introduce each brief story about him, historian John Hoyt Williams portrays the statesman as a flawed man with a remarkable ability to rebound from personal problems and scandal.

Subjects: Governors; Houston, Sam; Politics and Government; Tennessee; Texas

Now Try: *The Autobiography of Sam Houston* uses passages from his letters to complete the story begun in his memoir about his childhood. Singer Johnny Cash had Houston's lack of personal discipline as well as his ability to rebound from failure. Michael Streissguth chronicles Cash's long and varied career in *Johnny Cash: The Biography*. Houston's life in some ways resembles Aaron Burr's, yet they are remembered very differently centuries later. Nancy Isenberg attempts to restore the reputation of Thomas Jefferson's vice president in *Fallen Founder: The Life of Aaron Burr* (see this chapter). Like Houston, Zachary Taylor came from a time when military men often participated actively in politics. John S. D. Eisenhower describes how Taylor used his success in the U.S. war against Mexico to win the presidency in *Zachary Taylor*.

Wills, Garry

James Madison. Times Books, 2002. 184p. American Presidents. ISBN 0805069054. Audiobook available.

Why was James Madison (1751–1836) so brilliant in the creation of government and the writing of constitutions, and then so mediocre as the head of that same government? Why was he an effective secretary of state, and then as president unable to guide his country safely through an international crisis? Was he just dealt a bad hand in 1809 when he took the presidency, or did he bungle the job? In this volume in the American Presidents series, popular historian Garry Wills methodically examines Madison's presidency, setting out the evidence clearly and concisely, and argues that Madison performed as well as could be expected.

Subjects: Madison, James; Politics and Government; Presidents; Quick Reads; War of 1812

Now Try: With Alexander Hamilton and John Jay, Madison was a coauthor of America's most famous unsigned political essays, *Federalist: A Commentary on the Constitution of the United States*. Madison's strengths were his abilities to think, write, and persuade his contemporaries with his rhetoric. In the next generation, Congressman Henry Clay was the author of many acts that brought together rivals in compromise. Robert V. Remini chronicles the life and career of a key American politician who never became president in *Henry Clay: Statesman for the Union*. American scholar William James thought and wrote in many disciplines and shaped the country's academic traditions. Robert D. Richardson portrays the influential philosopher in *William James: In the Maelstrom of American Modernism* (see chapter 7). Like Madison, General Omar Bradley worked in the shadows of more famous men, including Generals MacArthur, Eisenhower, and Marshall, but his military tactics have had a more lasting impact on the U.S. Army. Alan Axelrod describes the career of the general in *Bradley* (see chapter 3), a quick-reading title in the **Great Generals Series**.

Witcover, Jules

Very Strange Bedfellows: The Short and Unhappy Marriage of Richard Nixon and Spiro Agnew. Public Affairs, 2007. 412p. ISBN 9781586484705.

When the year 1968 began, no one would have guessed that Richard Nixon (1913–1994) and Spiro Agnew (1918–1996) would be running mates in that fall's presidential election. Nixon was far behind candidate George Romney in the preference polls, and few people outside Maryland knew Governor Agnew. Electoral strategies, however, brought the strangers together, and for a short time they enjoyed a good working relationship. Growing distrust eventually led to Nixon's unrealized plot to oust Agnew from the 1972 presidential ticket. Jules Witcover portrays two untrustworthy men in this joint Political Biography.

> **Subjects:** Agnew, Spiro T.; Dual Biography; Nixon, Richard M.; Politics and Government; Presidents; Vice Presidents

> **Now Try:** Agnew offered his story of his years as vice president in *Go Quietly . . . Or Else: His Own Story of the Events Leading to His Resignation*. Nixon defended his part in the Watergate Scandal in *In the Arena: A Memoir of Victory, Defeat, and Renewal*. Artists Vincent Van Gogh and Paul Gauguin came to live together in Arles under an optimistic but ultimately unworkable agreement. Their falling apart is chronicled in *The Yellow House: Van Gogh, Gauguin, and Nine Turbulent Weeks in Arles* by Martin Gayford (see chapter 7). Very similar characters with similar backgrounds, revolutionary Generals George Washington and Benedict Arnold found themselves competing for the same honors and appointments. Washington won, and Arnold defected. Dave R. Palmer examines the differences between the men in *George Washington and Benedict Arnold: A Tale of Two Patriots* (see chapter 3). The loss of friendship during the Spanish Civil War is the story in *Breaking Point: Hemingway, Dos Passos, and the Murder of José Robles* by Stephen Koch (see chapter 3).

Practicing Politics

You don't have to be a head of state or a government administrator to be politically influential. Government and policy may also be shaped by those advising or lobbying governmental leaders in private, working from legislative or judicial offices, or addressing voters from their positions as citizens. The power of these people can be controversial and newsworthy, but in some cases it may not even be recognized in their own time.

Biographies of cabinet members, legislators, judges, first ladies, Washington matrons, and newspaper editors can be found in this section. Many of their names are as well known now as the presidents of the past, such as Dolley Madison, Sandra Day O'Connor, and Alexander Hamilton. Some are less known. Janann Sherman shows how a woman fared among the men as the only female senator in *No Place for a Woman: A Life of Senator Margaret Chase*

Smith. Stacy A. Cordery chronicles the long life of a president's daughter in *Alice: Alice Roosevelt Longworth, from White House Princess to Washington Power Broker.* Lanny Ebenstein shows how the theories of a strong-willed economist and presidential adviser affected public policy in *Milton Friedman: A Biography.*

Stories of distinctive characters fill this section. They are all unlikely, because the subjects followed rather unique paths to attain their political power. Setting is an important appeal factor, because the context in which they lived their lives is well described in these books. Pace varies in these books in which readers learn about people applying political power.

> *Practicing Politics* biographies are about people who successfully shaped the policies of their governments. These distinctive characters may have wielded their powers from inside or outside public office, either elected or appointed—perhaps even from behind the scenes. Readers learn about their methods and motives, as well as the times in which they lived. Quick reads and longer biographies are included in this chapter.

Allgor, Catherine

A Perfect Union: Dolley Madison and the Creation of the American Nation. Henry Holt, 2006. 493p. ISBN 9780805073270. Audiobook available.

When Gilbert Stuart painted twin portraits of Dolley Madison (1768–1849) and her husband James in 1804, the wife of the secretary of state humbly said that the artist had made them look very pretty. Citizens of swampy Washington, D.C., agreed, and invited the gracious young woman to their dinners. She became the city's leading lady, giving her own parties, able to bring cabinet members, senators, and congressmen together socially, and gently helping contentious opponents into compromise. In this admiring biography, historian Catherine Allgor contends that Dolley Madison saved more than a portrait of George Washington when the British burned the city in 1814. Without her political skills, the city would never have recovered.

Subjects: First Ladies; Madison, Dolley; Washington (DC); Women

Now Try: *The Selected Letters of Dolley Payne Madison* portrays both daily life and the workings of politics in the nineteenth century. In *Dolley: A Novel of Dolley Madison in Love and War*, Rita Mae Brown creates a diary for Madison in her novel about the capable first lady. The role of the powerful woman in Washington was created by Madison and continued later by Alice Roosevelt Longworth, the daughter of President Theodore Roosevelt. Stacy A. Cordery chronicles her many years in the U.S. capital in *Alice: Alice Roosevelt Longworth, from White House Princess to Washington Power Broker* (see this chapter). Another entertaining Washington matron turned out to be a Confederate spy with a residence close to the White House. Her bold story is told by Ann Blackman in *Wild Rose: Rose O'Neale Greenhow, Civil War Spy* (see chapter 3). Whereas James Madison relied on his wife to run their social affairs and advise him, President Woodrow Wilson needed his wife Edith to be his personal assistant after he suffered his stroke in 1919. Phyllis Lee Levin describes the close relationship and dependency in *Edith and Woodrow: The Wilson White House* (see this chapter).

Applegate, Debby

🎗 *The Most Famous Man in America: The Biography of Henry Ward Beecher.* Doubleday, 2006. 527p. ISBN 9780385513968.

Staunch abolitionist Henry Ward Beecher (1813–1887) was the man most responsible for the American Civil War, according to some of his critics. His call for reform and message of brotherly love threatened the Southern way of life. When the war ended, he was the leading religious figure in the country, having replaced his fire-and-brimstone father, Lyman Beecher. Within the next decade, however, his public image was soiled, as he admitted committing adultery and reaping unseemly wealth from his lectures and publications. The author notes how Beecher's campaign to rebound from shame has served as a model for troubled twentieth-century public figures. Fans of historical documentary will enjoy this correspondence-filled narrative.

Subjects: Abolitionists; Beecher, Henry Ward; Clergymen

Awards: Pulitzer Prize for Biography

Now Try: Beecher's sister Harriet Beecher Stowe is often credited with sparking the American Civil War with her antislavery novel *Uncle Tom's Cabin*. Joan D. Hedrick tells how Stowe dealt with fame and the obligations to her family in *Harriet Beecher Stowe: A Life* (see chapter 4). In England, Charles Dickens played the role of celebrity author, urging reform through his novels and lectures. Unlike Beecher, he was able to keep his romantic affairs secret. Novelist Jane Smiley mixes the details of Dickens's daily life with analysis of his famous novels in her eloquent biography *Charles Dickens* (see chapter 7). In a later era, Charles Lindbergh, who pioneered flying solo across the Atlantic Ocean, was the most famous man in America. He too lost much of his support, as A. Scott Berg explains in the epic biography *Lindbergh* (see chapter 1). Newspaper publisher Randolph Hearst used his newspapers to lobby the public for his political positions. News of his indiscreet affairs and his attacks on very popular figures eventually tainted his reputation. Ben Proctor tells a fascinating story of a man obsessed with personal power in *William Randolph Hearst: Final Edition, 1911–1951* (see chapter 9).

Biskupic, Joan

Sandra Day O'Connor: How the First Woman on the Supreme Court Became Its Most Influential Justice. CCCO, 2005. 419p. ISBN 9780060590185.

Supreme Court Justice Sandra Day O'Connor (1930–) surprised the American public with the announcement of her retirement in 2005. For twenty-four years she had been in the news, often as the deciding vote in important cases before the court. Appointed by President Ronald Reagan as the first woman ever on the high court because her judicial record was conservative, she moderated her views over time, eventually becoming a target for criticism from the administration of Republican President George W. Bush. In this admiring biography, Supreme Court correspondent Joan Biskupic tells O'Connor's story, from her birth in El Paso, Texas, to her retirement, with an emphasis on her Supreme Court career.

Subjects: Arizona; Judges; O'Connor, Sandra Day; Supreme Court; Women

Now Try: In *Lazy B: Growing Up on a Cattle Ranch in the American Southwest*, O'Connor recounts her childhood in Arizona, and in *Majesty of the Law: Reflections of a Supreme Court Justice*, she tells the history of the Supreme Court and her role as the first female justice. In 1879 Belva Lockwood was the first woman to argue a case before the Supreme Court, long before women could vote, much less sit as justices on the court. Jill Norgren tells the life of a dynamic early activist in the women's rights movement in *Belva Lockwood: The Woman Who Would Be President*. Like O'Connor, shipping heiress Nancy Cunard showed confidence and skill while working with famous men. The story of her transformation from socialite to poet, publisher, reporter of the Spanish Civil War, and humanitarian aid worker is told in *Nancy Cunard: Heiress, Muse, Political Idealist* by Lois Gordon (see chapter 8). Stories of many women of influence are told by Senator Kay Bailey Hutchinson in the collective biographies *American Heroines* and *Leading Ladies: American Trailblazers* (see chapter 4).

Blackman, Ann

Seasons of Her Life: A Biography of Madeleine Korbel Albright. Scribner, 1998. 398p. ISBN 0684845644.

Born in Prague, Madeleine Albright (1937–) was always studious and active politically, even as a mother and homemaker. At the time of her appointment as secretary of state in 1997, she was highly qualified for the position, having experienced world conflict firsthand and served in many foreign policy positions for Presidents Carter and Clinton, including as U.S. Ambassador to the United Nations. In this admiring biography, Ann Blackman tells how Albright escaped both the German Nazis and the Soviet Communists, served as an advisor to Senator Geraldine Ferraro, discovered her Jewish ancestors, and became the leading foreign policy advisor to President Clinton.

Subjects: Albright, Madeleine; Ambassadors; Cabinet Members; Politics and Government; Secretaries of State; Women

Now Try: Albright describes her childhood, life as a mother, and the challenges of her political career in *Madam Secretary: A Memoir*. In an era before women attained political offices, Pearl S. Buck became an unofficial world diplomat, especially interested in Asian–American affairs. Her life as a writer and an advocate for peace is told in *Pearl S. Buck: A Cultural Biography* by Peter Conn (see chapter 4). Albright opened the office of secretary of state to other women. Marcus Mabry assesses the character of the first black woman in the job in *Twice as Good: Condoleezza Rice and Her Path to Power* (see this chapter). Readers interested in Albright's discovery of her Jewish ancestry will enjoy *Identity's Architect: A Biography of Erik H. Erikson* (see chapter 4), in which Lawrence J. Friedman describes the psychoanalyst's search for his heritage.

Brady, Patricia

Martha Washington: An American Life. Viking, 2005. 276p. ISBN 0670034304. Large print available.

After her husband George died, Martha Washington (1731–1802) burned over forty years' worth of letters to and from her husband, destroying what could have been a prime source for biographers. The devoted couple had been parted by war, politics, and business throughout their marriage. While apart, Martha managed the household and planned their moves to wherever George was stationed. While together, she was the general's primary moral support, advising him on social, political, and even military matters. According to historian Patricia Brady, Martha

Washington was beloved in her time, especially by the general's troops. In this admiring biography, the author tells how Martha created the role of first lady and served her country.

Subjects: American Revolution; First Ladies; Virginia; Washington, Martha; Women

Now Try: *Mount Vernon Love Story: A Novel of George and Martha Washington* is the reissuing of *Aspire to Heaven*, Mary Higgins Clark's first novel, a romance that claims that Martha was always George's true love. Martha Washington is one of the women lovingly portrayed in the group biographies *Founding Mothers: The Women Who Raised Our Nation* and *Ladies of Liberty: The Women Who Shaped Our Nation* by Cokie Roberts (see chapter 9). Some women became combatants in the American Revolution. In *Masquerade: The Life and Times of Deborah Sampson, Continental Soldier* (see chapter 5), Alfred F. Young describes the life of Deborah Sampson, who spent seventeen months as a soldier in the Continental Army during the American Revolution. Eleanor Roosevelt expanded the role of the first lady in advocating for social causes. Living a long and active life, Roosevelt wrote her memoirs several times, the last being *Autobiography of Eleanor Roosevelt*, published in the year before her death. She told of her life with Franklin Roosevelt, her years as first lady, and her travels around the world.

Chernow, Ron

Alexander Hamilton. Penguin Press, 2004. 818p. ISBN 1594200092. Audiobook available.

Early American statesman Alexander Hamilton (1757–1804) was a man with many political enemies, including John Adams, Thomas Jefferson, James Madison, and James Monroe. His life was a series of battles over public policy and the shaping of the new America government. After he was fatally shot in a duel by Vice President Aaron Burr, the other founders of the country downplayed his role in the American Revolution and its aftermath. In this epic biography, economic historian Ron Chernow argues that Hamilton was a primary architect of the federal government, as well as the resulting American economy. This political tribute will especially please readers who enjoy dashing, controversial historical figures.

Subjects: American Revolution; Cabinet Members; Hamilton, Alexander; Politics and Government; Secretaries of the Treasury

Awards: ALA Notable Books

Now Try: With James Madison and John Jay, Hamilton was a coauthor of America's most famous unsigned political essays, *Federalist: A Commentary on the Constitution of the United States*. Admiral Stephen Decatur shared Hamilton's temperament and willingness to defend his honor with a duel. His short and dramatic life is told by Leonard F. Guttridge in *Our Country, Right or Wrong: The Life of Stephen Decatur, the U.S. Navy's Most Illustrious Commander* (see chapter 3). Hamilton and John James Audubon were both illegitimate sons of French extraction born on Caribbean islands. Richard Rhodes focuses on the private and family life of the man who became his adopted nation's most famous ornithologist and painter of birds in *John James Audubon: The Making of an American* (see chapter 1). John Jacob Astor is just the type of man for whom Hamilton designed the American economy. He took advantage of every business opportunity and became fabulously wealthy. Axel Madsen tells his rags to riches story in *John Jacob Astor: America's First Multimillionaire* (see chapter 9).

Cordery, Stacy A.

Alice: Alice Roosevelt Longworth, from White House Princess to Washington Power Broker. Viking, 2007. 590p. ISBN 9780670018338.

In the "wedding of the century," Alice Roosevelt (1884–1980) married Nicholas Longworth at the White House in 1905. As daughter of a president and wife of a prominent member of the Republican Party, she used her beauty and wit to become the most influential woman in the nation's capital, a position she retained for many decades, despite her sometimes scandalous behavior. Senators, congressmen, cabinet members, leaders of industry, and foreign leaders attended her social gatherings, at which she lobbied for various causes. Strongly opposed to the League of Nations proposed by Woodrow Wilson and the New Deal policies of her cousins Franklin and Eleanor Roosevelt; and supportive of Richard Nixon's presidency, she fed sharp statements to journalists from Will Rogers to Sally Quinn. According to Stacy A. Cordery, this outrageous woman was the fourth in a quartet of powerful Roosevelts who shaped American politics in the twentieth century.

> **Subjects:** Children of Presidents; Longworth, Alice Roosevelt; Politics and Government; Washington (DC); Women

> **Now Try:** During the Great Depression, Longworth published *Crowded Hours: Reminiscences of Alice Roosevelt Longworth,* a best-selling memoir that told about her parties, travels, and clothes. Being the daughter of a president, Longworth was always in the public eye. In *American Legacy: The Story of John & Caroline Kennedy* (see chapter 6), C. David Heymann describes the constant attention that hounded the young lives of the children of John F. Kennedy. When young Jeanne-Antoinette de Pompadour became the mistress of French king Louis XV, she was expected to be quiet and unnoticed. Instead, she became an influential and dangerous player in French affairs. Evelyne Lever tells her sensational story in *Madame de Pompadour: A Life* (see chapter 9). Like Longworth, art dealer Peggy Guggenheim brought people together and lived a scandalous life. Anton Gill chronicles her romantic travels and affairs in the intimate biography *Art Lover: A Biography of Peggy Guggenheim* (see chapter 7).

Damrosch, Leo

Jean-Jacques Rousseau: Restless Genius. Houghton Mifflin, 2005. 566p. ISBN 97806-18446964.

The life of idealist Jean-Jacques Rousseau (1712–1778) resembles a Dickens novel with a continuously twisting plot. His mother died within weeks of his birth, he was raised by an aunt until age ten, and he was given to a pastor, who later apprenticed him to an engraver, from whom he ran away. He converted to Catholicism, taught music lessons, became a tutor, took a job as the secretary for the French ambassador in Venice, sired five children who were all sent to orphanages, and then wrote a prize-winning essay on the philosophy of science. Then he became famous, and the story becomes even more fantastic. In this complex and convoluted story, Leo Damrosch describes how Rousseau survived a turbulent childhood, rose to prominence, and wrote political treatises, comedies, operas, and novels that sparked riots and ultimately led to his death.

Subjects: France; Philosophers; Rousseau, Jean-Jacques

Now Try: *The Confessions of J. J. Rousseau* is often cited as one of the first truly frank memoirs. Rousseau also wrote the philosophical novel *Emile*, which encouraged the "natural" education of children, harnessing the inborn curiosity of children to excite them with learning. Like Rousseau, pediatrician Dr. Benjamin Spock promoted the care and education of children but was mostly absent from the lives of his own children. Thomas Maier discloses the disturbing contradictions in the man who greatly influenced child psychology in *Dr. Spock: An American Life* (see chapter 5).French author and philosopher Voltaire also lived a fast-paced life just like the plots in his novels. The story of his life and political ideals is told by Roger Pearson in *Voltaire Almighty: A Life in Pursuit of Freedom* (see chapter 9). Artist Marc Chagall became an art commissioner in the early days of the Soviet Union, one of many jobs that he held in his mostly apolitical life. Jonathan Wilson describes his long and varied career in *Marc Chagall* (see chapter 7).

Ebenstein, Lanny

Milton Friedman: A Biography. Palgrave Macmillan, 2007. 286p. ISBN 97814-03976277.

Written before economist Milton Friedman (1912–2006) died, this biography refers to him as living and includes the text of a recent interview. Focusing on the importance of his marriage, his work with presidents and political organizations, and his popular writings, Lanny Ebenstein portrays Friedman as a practical and influential University of Chicago professor always ready to argue for his capitalistic ideals. This assessment of one of the most important economists of the twentieth century is a must read for those interested in the history of public policy.

Subjects: Economists; Friedman, Milton; Libertarianism; Presidential Advisors

Now Try: Friedman and his wife Rose wrote a joint memoir, *Two Lucky People*. Warren Buffett is an astute student of financial markets whose investing is closely watched by others wishing to make similar profits. Roger Lowenstein profiles Buffett as a calm, thoughtful, almost old-fashioned investor who finds good stocks and stays with them, never buying low and selling high, in *Buffett: The Making of an American Capitalist*. Like Friedman, Federal Reserve Board Chairman Alan Greenspan collaborated with as well as clashed with many important Washington figures. His behind-the-scenes memoir is *The Age of Turbulence: Adventures in a New World*. Friedman resembled Secretary of the Treasury Alexander Hamilton in that he had firm ideas about government monetary policies. How Hamilton's ideas clashed with those of Jefferson and other early leaders is discussed in *Alexander Hamilton* by Ron Chernow (see this chapter). The moral use of capital was a theme throughout the writings of Scottish philosopher and economist Adam Smith. James Buchan describes how Smith lived for ideas in *The Authentic Adam Smith: His Life and Ideas*.

Isaacson, Walter

Benjamin Franklin: An American Life. Simon & Schuster, 2003. 590p. ISBN 0684807610. Audiobook available.

Colonial leader Benjamin Franklin (1706–1790) was a talented and ever-evolving man. Franklin the apprentice begat Franklin the printer, who begat the businessman, the scientist, the inventor, the man about town, the statesman, the diplomat, and the author. No matter what his trade, he exhibited a knack for being a central character in the affairs of colonial and revolutionary America. In this lengthy and admiring biography, Walter Isaacson tells how Franklin led his contemporaries to rebel against Great Britain and shaped the diplomacy of the new nation.

> **Subjects:** American Revolution; Diplomats; Franklin, Benjamin; Inventors; Paris; Philadelphia; Printers

> **Now Try:** Relating only the events of his life up to 1731 and never really finished, *The Autobiography of Benjamin Franklin* was used as a model for many inspirational biographies written during the Industrial Revolution of nineteenth-century America. Samuel Adams was one of the first colonists to openly favor breaking the political bond to Great Britain. Mark Puls describes him as a genius of political protest who convinced many to join his cause in *Samuel Adams: Father of the American Revolution*. Leonardo da Vinci was the model for the Renaissance man, the figure who excels in many endeavors. His life is intimately told in *Leonardo da Vinci: Flights of the Mind* by Charles Nicholl (see chapter 11). Like Franklin, English pottery maker Josiah Wedgwood began his career as an apprentice and became a wealthy and prominent citizen who kept company with scientists and statesmen. His rags to riches story is told in *Wedgwood: The First Tycoon* by Brian Dolan (see chapter 9).

Kazin, Michael

A Godly Hero: The Life of William Jennings Bryan. Knopf, 2006. 374p. ISBN 0375-411356.

William Jennings Bryan (1860–1925), a deeply religious man, drew openly from his Christian faith in the conduct of his public life. His interpretation of the Bible led him to champion the welfare of poor farmers and laborers, causes that the liberal wing of the Democratic Party retained throughout the twentieth century. Ironically, he is now most remembered for the populist agendas of his three presidential election losses and for his victory in the John Thomas Scopes evolution trial. Michael Kazin aims to restore the great populist's reputation in this sympathetic biography.

> **Subjects:** Bryan, William Jennings; Democratic Party; Politics and Government; Populism; Presidential Candidates

> **Now Try:** Bryan reviewed his career as a populist politician in *The Memoirs of William Jennings Bryan*, with a chapter about each of his unsuccessful attempts to become president. Suffragette Victoria Woodhull was scorned for her unsuccessful attempt to run for president when she could not even legally vote. Her life of dissent is recounted by Mary Gabriel in *Notorious Victoria: The Life of Victoria Woodhull, Uncensored* (see chapter 4). Congregationalist minister Jonathan Edwards spent his life preparing immortal souls, both his as well as those of the members of his congregations across colonial New England, New York, and New Jersey, for their eventual meeting with their lord. George M. Marsden describes the spiritual and political life of a colonial minister in *Jonathan Edwards: A Life* (see chapter 9). Like Bryan, the abolitionist John Brown felt a call from God to change his society. Unlike Bryan, he tried to fulfill his vision through violent means. David S. Reynolds retells the story of the man who ignited the Civil War in *John Brown, Abolitionist: The Man Who Killed Slavery, Sparked the Civil War, and Seeded Civil Rights* (see chapter 9). Like Bryan, author James Boswell, friend of the essayist, poet, lexicographer, and biographer Samuel Johnson, is sometimes depicted as a foolish man. Adam Sisman portrays Boswell as an alcoholic procrastinator

who pulled himself up to finally complete his great account of Johnson's life, in *Boswell's Presumptuous Task: The Making of the Life of Dr. Johnson* (see chapter 7).

Levin, Phyllis Lee

Edith and Woodrow: The Wilson White House. Scribner, 2001. 606p. ISBN 074-3211588.

How did Edith Bolling Galt (1872–1961) win the heart of the recent widower, President Woodrow Wilson (1856–1924)? After their marriage, how influential did the new Mrs. Wilson become in the White House? Did she become the secret acting president after her husband's stroke in October 1919, as is often charged? How ill was he? How much control did she have over the late president's official biographers, and the script of the Hollywood film *Wilson: The Rise and Fall of an American President*? Using the president's letters, memoirs from cabinet members, and news accounts, journalist Phyllis Lee Levin unravels the mystery in a detailed account of a little understood political couple.

Subjects: Dual Biography; First Ladies; Marriage; Presidents; Wilson, Edith Bolling Galt; Wilson, Woodrow

Now Try: Readers may examine how the romance between the president and the widow developed in *A President in Love: The Courtship Letters of Woodrow Wilson and Edith Bolling Galt*. Like Edith Wilson, Florence Harding is suspected of having great influence over her husband. Carl Sferrazza Anthony investigates the first family relationship in *Florence Harding: The First Lady, the Jazz Age, and the Death of America's Most Scandalous President* (see chapter 5). The marriage of President Ronald Reagan and his second wife Nancy Reagan is usually depicted as supportive. Celebrity biographer Anne Edwards looked for problems between the pair but found only their children to criticize in *The Reagans: Portrait of a Marriage*. Queen Elizabeth II and Prince Philip have also been rather happily married for over sixty years, but their children have had many problems with their spouses. Gyles Brandreth tells family stories bound to interest fans of the British royalty in *Philip and Elizabeth: Portrait of a Royal Marriage* (see chapter 8).

Mabry, Marcus

Twice as Good: Condoleezza Rice and Her Path to Power. Modern Times, 2007. 362p. ISBN 1594863628.

The life of Secretary of State Condoleezza Rice (1954–) could be used to argue that twentieth-century liberal reforms have worked. Born in Alabama, she benefited from desegregated schools, affirmative action, and the women's movement. Ironically, she is now identified with conservative political power. According to Marcus Mabry, her opinions on social issues are unknown, as she has concentrated her career on international affairs. Through stories told by friends and colleagues, Mabry portrays Rice as a person who worked diligently to attain her stature. Readers interested in the success of women in politics will appreciate this admiring profile.

Subjects: African Americans; Cabinet Members; Foreign Policy; Politics and Government; Presidential Advisors; Rice, Condoleezza; Secretaries of State; Women

Now Try: Congresswoman Barbara Jordan attended segregated schools and knew the poverty of the black neighborhoods in Houston as a child and young woman. She described how she took charge of her life by attending Boston University Law School and entering politics in *Barbara Jordan: A Self-Portrait*. All presidents need loyal allies like Rice. For President Jimmy Carter, one of those allies was his chief of staff, Hamilton Jordan. Jordan recounted his time in the White House and his struggle with cancer in *No Such Thing as a Bad Day: A Memoir*. Abraham Lincoln put men who had been his rivals into his cabinet. David Herbert Donald tells about a group of contentious men who served the sixteenth president in *We Are Lincoln Men: Abraham Lincoln and His Friends* (see this chapter). Without tackling policy questions, Bradley H. Patterson examines the workings of the bureaucracy in support of the presidency in *To Serve the President: Continuity and Innovation in the White House Staff*. Like Rice, decorating and entertaining guru Martha Stewart has faced her critics calmly and remains popular with many fans. Lloyd Allen profiles her gently in *Being Martha: The Inside Story of Martha Stewart and Her Amazing Life* (see chapter 8).

Nelson, Craig

Thomas Paine: Enlightenment, Revolution, and the Birth of Modern Nations. Viking, 2006. 396p. ISBN 0670037885. Audiobook available.

Though his writings sparked the American and French Revolutions and reform in his native England, Thomas Paine (1737–1814) was a difficult man to befriend. As soon as he allied himself with a group or cause, he began itemizing its faults. As a result, friends became enemies, and the energetic Paine moved on to new battles. By the time of his death he was well-traveled but mostly friendless. Craig Nelson examines Paine's life and the current lack of recognition for this writer who was an important American founding father.

Subjects: American Revolution; French Revolution; Paine, Thomas; Philosophers; Revolutionaries.

Now Try: *The Collected Writings of Thomas Paine* brings together his essays "Common Sense" and "The Rights of Man" with many other works. After he confessed wrongdoing in the Salem witch trial, Judge Samuel Sewall became an advocate for the rights of all people. Eve LaPlante describes a clergyman who wrote the first abolitionist treatise, argued for better relations with the Indians, and discussed the rights of women, in *Salem Witch Judge: The Life and Repentance of Samuel Sewall* (see chapter 4). British mineralogist James Smithson was another Englishman who actively supported the French Revolution. Heather Ewing describes the life of the adventurous scientist who endowed the Smithsonian Museum in *The Lost World of James Smithson: Science, Revolution, and the Birth of the Smithsonian* (see chapter 11). Because he was as cynical and irreverent offstage as he was onstage, comedian Groucho Marx was a hard man to befriend. In *Groucho: The Life and Times of Julius Henry Marx* (see chapter 8), Stefan Kanfer tells the story of a man who entertained millions of people but could not find happiness. Like Paine, mathematician Paul Erdös lived a nomadic life and often relied on the hospitality of colleagues. Unlike Paine, he was easy to befriend. How he was able to continue a scholarly career while wandering the globe is the story of *The Man Who Loved Only Numbers: The Story of Paul Erdös and the Search for Mathematical Truth* by Paul Hoffman (see chapter 11).

Nissenson, Marilyn

The Lady Upstairs: Dorothy Schiff and the **New York Post.** St. Martin's Press, 2007. 500p. ISBN 9780312313104.

Born into great wealth, Dorothy Schiff (1903–1989) refused to be "just a girl." On a whim, she bought the floundering *New York Post* in 1939 and made her second husband, George Backer, its publisher. When he proved ineffective, she took over the position, involved herself in many aspects of the business, and turned a profit. In the process, she shaped the old newspaper into a strong voice for liberal politics and became friends with many leading politicians, including Franklin and Eleanor Roosevelt, the Kennedy brothers, Lyndon Johnson, and Nelson Rockefeller. Marilyn Nissenson portrays Schiff as an influential woman in this book that will appeal to anyone interested in high society, politics, and twentieth-century events.

Subjects: *New York Post*; Newspaper Publishers; Schiff, Dorothy; Women

Now Try: After her husband's suicide in 1963, Katherine Graham replaced him as publisher of the *Washington Post*. She discusses her over thirty years at the helm of the prestigious newspaper during contentious times in her memoir, *Personal History*. William Randolph Hearst was a more influential publisher in his prime than Schiff, but he wasted his political capital admiring Adolf Hitler and opposing Franklin Roosevelt. His fall from power is told in *William Randolph Hearst: Final Edition, 1911–1951* by Ben Proctor (see chapter 9). While Schiff was trying to control national politics from her newspaper office, Mayor Richard J. Daley was trying to do the same from his office in Chicago. Written while Daley was still in power, *Boss: Richard J. Daley of Chicago* by Mike Royko describes Chicago machine politics and the man who controlled the local party (see chapter 5). Nancy Cunard was another society heiress who decided to do more with her life than attend parties. Lois Gordon tells an admiring tale about a shipping heiress who became a model, poet, publisher, advocate for racial justice, reporter in the Spanish Civil War, and humanitarian aid worker in post–World War II Europe, in *Nancy Cunard: Heiress, Muse, Political Idealist* (see chapter 8).

Russell, Jane Jarboe

Lady Bird: A Biography of Mrs. Johnson. Scribner, 1999. 350p. ISBN 0684814803.

Claudia Alta "Lady Bird" Taylor (1912–2007) eloped with Lyndon Baines Johnson, who proposed to her on their first date. She wore a lavender dress and accepted a $2.50 ring that Lyndon's assistant bought at Sears Roebuck. The presiding minister told witnesses that the marriage would not last, but Lady Bird stuck by her husband through his many indiscretions and public failures until his death in 1973. Considered by many to be one of the most effective first ladies, she was a key figure in the early environmental movement, proud of her beautification campaign and support of wildflower propagation. According to Jane Jarboe Russell, Lady Bird was a tough and resourceful woman worthy of admiration.

Subjects: Environmentalists; First Ladies; Johnson, Lady Bird; Johnson, Lyndon Baines; Presidents; Texas; Women

10

Now Try: Johnson told about her years as first lady in *A White House Diary*. Like Johnson, poet Anne Bradstreet spent most of her life caring for her family and husband. Charlotte Gordon describes her life as the daughter and the wife of early Massachusetts governors in *Mistress Bradstreet: The Untold Life of America's First Poet* (see chapter 7). Like Johnson, Rachel Carson loved being outdoors with the wildflowers and the wildlife. Mark Hamilton Lytle tells how the nature writer turned activist in *The Gentle Subversive: Rachel Carson, Silent Spring, and the Rise of the Environmental Movement* (see chapter 4). John Wesley Powell, who led an expedition down the Grand Canyon, was influential in the beginning of the American park movement. Donald Worster tells his adventurous story in *A River Running West: The Life of John Wesley Powell* (see chapter 1). After being separated from her husband for twenty years, Isabelle Godin left her comfortable home in the Ecuadorian Andes to cross the Amazon rain forest to try to release him from prison. In *The Mapmaker's Wife: A True Tale of Love, Murder, and Survival in the Amazon* (see chapter 1), Robert Whitaker tells a story of extreme devotion.

Sherman, Janann

No Place for a Woman: A Life of Senator Margaret Chase Smith. Rutgers University Press, 2000. 298p. ISBN 0813527228.

In 1964 Margaret Chase Smith (1897–1995), a moderate senator from Maine, ran for the Republican nomination for U.S. president, the first serious woman candidate for the high office. At that point she had served as an influential member of Congress for twenty-four years, the only female senator during much of that time. Though she was not a feminist, she hired mostly young women from her state for her staff and chastised her congressional colleagues for being bad boys when they acted unethically or out of self-interest. A widow who said that she was too busy with national affairs for a family, she faithfully cared for her staff, even sitting in the hospital with a dying aide. Historian Janann Sherman offers an admiring profile of a powerful woman who lived ninety-seven years.

Subjects: Presidential Candidates; Senators; Smith, Margaret Chase; Women

Now Try: In 1950 Smith was one of the first members of Congress to speak out against the House Un-American Activities Committee, saying Americans had the right to dissent and unpopular views. The title of her memoir, *Declaration of Conscience*, came from that speech. In preparation for her 1972 run for the presidency, Congresswoman Shirley Chisholm published her autobiography *Unbought and Unbossed*. Margaret Thatcher was successful in becoming the prime minister of Great Britain. She recounts her eleven years as the leader of her country in *The Downing Street Years*. Like Chase, birth control activist Margaret Sanger tried to avoid being called a feminist. Even after she felt the need to campaign for women's rights, she tailored her appeal for the right to contraception to business and financially conservative interests. Ellen Chesler chronicles her crusade in *Woman of Valor: Margaret Sanger and the Birth Control Movement in America* (see chapter 4).

Wexler, Alice

Emma Goldman: An Intimate Life. Pantheon Books, 1984. 339p. ISBN 0394529758.

By the time the U.S. government deported anarchist Emma Goldman (1869–1940) in 1919 as an undesirable alien, she had spent thirty years in the country advocating labor reform, women's rights, birth control, free love, and pacifism. Called a "monster" and "Red Emma" by many, she drew crowds of supporters and hecklers and sometimes sparked riots. According to Alice Wexler, Goldman was not as tough as she pretended. In this psychological portrait, the author shows that the revolutionary questioned her own work and often sought the reassurance of friends, who sometimes betrayed her.

Subjects: Anarchists; Goldman, Emma; Labor Activists; Revolutionaries; Women

Now Try: *Living My Life* is a recent abridgement of Goldman's two-volume autobiography, recounting her activities as an anarchist, Communist, and feminist. Militant labor activist Mother Jones preceded Goldman as woman sparking riots across the country. Elliott J. Gorn chronicles her life and political activities in *Mother Jones: The Most Dangerous Woman in America* (see chapter 4). British epidemiologist Alice Stewart was either ignored or denounced by the medical establishment for her warnings about the dangers of radiation. Gayle Greene tells another story of a woman disliked for speaking up in *The Woman Who Knew Too Much: Alice Stewart and the Secrets of Radiation* (see chapter 4). In eighteenth-century France, Gabrielle Emilie le Tonnelier de Breteuil, the Marquise Du Chatelet, was an unconventional woman who supported the radical causes of her lover, the philosopher and novelist Voltaire. Judith Zinsser recounts how the marquise left her husband and wrote physics and mathematics treatises in *La Dame d'Esprit: A Biography of the Marquise Du Chatelet* (see chapter 11).

Wheen, Francis

Karl Marx: A Life. Norton, 1999. 431p. ISBN 039304923X.

Karl Marx (1818–1883), a middle-class German philosopher and coauthor of the influential *Communist Manifesto*, tried to free himself of his cultural influences, but never really succeeded. He enjoyed good books, wine, cigars, and evenings playing parlor games with friends and family, contrary to his pronouncement that a man was better off without a family. He wasted much of his time on minor disputes, while his great ideas languished. According to Francis Wheen, Marx was a misunderstood philosopher, who would not have approved of how his ideas were applied in the twentieth century. Wheen's softened image of the political icon may surprise readers.

Subjects: Communists; Germany; London; Marx, Karl; Philosophers

Now Try: Marx is most known for *Capital: A Critique of Political Economy* and *The Communist Manifesto*, which he wrote with Friedrich Engels. With the demise of the Soviet Union and the opening of Russian archives, Dmitrii Antonovich Volkogonov has written a trilogy of biographies about the three men most responsible for the application of Marxist philosophy to government. In *Trotsky: The Eternal Revolutionary, Lenin: A New Biography,* and *Stalin: Triumph and Tragedy,* Volkogonov tells how each allowed radicalism and personal power to suppress true Marxist concern for the citizens. Children's storyteller Hans Christian Andersen was another nineteenth-century author with clearly professed ideas but a complicated life that compromised his beliefs. His story is sympathetically told in *Hans Christian Andersen: A New Life* by Jens Andersen (see chapter 5). Like Marx, novelist and short story writer Nathaniel Hawthorne accomplished little beyond a few masterpieces.

Instead of writing, he wasted much time with unfruitful schemes to get government employment from his political friends. Brenda Wineapple describes him as an unsettled character in *Hawthorne: A Life* (see chapter 7).

White, Richard D.

Kingfish: The Reign of Huey P. Long. Random House, 2006. 361p. ISBN 140006354X. Audiobook available.

Senator Huey P. Long (1893–1935) had just announced his candidacy for U.S. president when he was assassinated. Only forty-two years old at the time, he had taken complete control of Louisiana politics and was aiming to run the country, too. President Franklin Roosevelt had called the former salesman of lard substitute who delivered relief to the poor and found jobs for the unemployed one of the most dangerous men in America. According to Richard D. White, Long was a canny politician whose longing for power threatened the entire democratic process. The danger of charismatic figures is the theme of this biography from the Great Depression.

Subjects: Assassinations; Governors; Long, Huey P.; Louisiana; Politics and Government; Senators

Now Try: Robert Penn Warren used Long as the model for his character Governor Willie Stark in his novel ***All the King's Men***. Venezuelan President Hugo Chávez is a brash and powerful politician in the Long mold. Christino Marcano and Alberto Barrera Tyszka investigate his character in ***Hugo Chávez: The Definitive Biography of Venezuela's Controversial President*** (see chapter 5). Long's control of patronage jobs is compared with that of Boss Tweed, the corrupt mayor of New York, who is portrayed in ***Boss Tweed: The Rise and Fall of the Corrupt Pol Who Conceived the Soul of Modern New York***, by Kenneth D. Ackermann (see chapter 2). In ***Boss: Richard J. Daley of Chicago*** (see chapter 5), written while the mayor was still living, Mike Royko described Daley as a corrupt politician who controlled all the patronage jobs and political offices in Chicago, with control over national politics as his goal.

Political Biography Collections

The books in this section differ from others in this chapter in that they profile many political figures instead of one or two. They are to biography what short stories are to fiction. People with only short periods to devote to reading will find in them biographical narratives, and readers who wish to sample authors or the lives of characters before committing to reading an entire book will also enjoy these collections.

Please note that although titles throughout this chapter are generally available in audio versions but not in large print, titles in this section are an exception. All four of these collections are available in large print, but not in unabridged audio.

Political Collections include books that gather profiles of many similar political characters into a single volume. Authors focus on the key incidents and dominant characteristics in these quick profiles. These works are ideal for more leisurely or interrupted reading.

Angelo, Bonnie

First Mothers: The Women Who Shaped the Presidents. William Morrow, 2000. 451p. ISBN 0688156312. Large print available.

The women in this book are mostly famous for being mothers of someone famous, but they were also strong, talented individuals who guided their sons through childhood to become men of consequence. Lillian Carter was a nurse and a Peace Corps volunteer. Ida Eisenhower was a pacifist, and Hannah Nixon was a Quaker. Dorothy Bush was a tennis champion. Some were single parents. Some of their sons gave them much grief in youth, as well as in adulthood. In this collective biography for general readers, journalist Bonnie Angelo profiles all the presidential mothers from Franklin D. Roosevelt's to Bill Clinton's.

Subjects: Collective Biography; Mothers and Sons; Mothers of Presidents; Women

Now Try: Harold I. Gullen wrote a related book, *First Fathers: The Men Who Inspired Our Presidents*. A similar collective biography is *First Ladies: An Intimate Group Portrait* by first daughter and novelist Margaret Truman. In *A Remarkable Mother*, former President Jimmy Carter turns biographer to tell the story of his mother, Lillian Carter, who was a mother, nurse, Peace Corps volunteer, and leading citizen in Plains, Georgia.

Beschloss, Michael

Presidential Courage: Brave Leaders and How They Changed America 1789–1989. Simon & Schuster, 2007. 430p. ISBN 9780684857053. Large print available.

The White House in Washington, D.C., is the recurring backdrop for dramatic episodes in American history. In the Oval Office, Abraham Lincoln called men into service of the Union, composed the Emancipation Proclamation, and planned the Reconstruction of the South. Harry Truman decided to use the atomic bomb in Japan while in the office, and from there, John F. Kennedy ordered troops to protect black students entering previously all-white colleges. In this collection of compelling stories, Michael Beschloss tells how nine American presidents weighed their options and chose politically dangerous actions for the sake of the nation.

Subjects: Collective Biography; Courage; Politics and Government; Presidents

Now Try: Paul F. Boller Jr. takes a lighter look at White House residents in *Presidential Diversions: Presidents at Play from George Washington to George W. Bush*. H. W. Brands contends that businesspeople have shaped our world as greatly as politicians have. In *Masters of Enterprise: Giants of American Business from John Jacob Astor and J. P. Morgan to Bill Gates and Oprah Winfrey* (see chapter 9), he briefly profiles twenty-five leaders of commerce and tells how they have changed our world. In the world of sports, great courage was shown by the men who integrated major league baseball. Steve Jacobson tells their stories in *Carrying Jackie's Torch: The Players Who Integrated Baseball—and America* (see chapter 4).

Donald, David Herbert

We Are Lincoln Men: Abraham Lincoln and His Friends. Simon & Schuster, 2003. 269p. ISBN 0743254686. Large print available.

President Abraham Lincoln did not have many close friends before or even during his time in office. Historian David Herbert Donald believes that only Joshua Speed, William Herndon, Orville Browning, William Seward, and his private secretaries John Hay and John Nicolay were ever really confidants. In this collective biography, the author describes how each man came to know Lincoln, and the roles that they played in his public career. This quick read is a great choice for readers who enjoy stories from history.

> **Subjects:** Browning, Orville; Collective Biography; Friends; Hay, John; Herndon, William; Lincoln, Abraham; Nicolay, John; Seward, William; Speed, Joshua

> **Now Try:** In *Team of Rivals: The Political Genius of Abraham Lincoln,* Doris Kearns Goodwin describes three politically ambitious men that President Lincoln chose for his cabinet and how he ultimately drew strength from them. Like Lincoln, shipping tycoon Cornelius Vanderbilt surrounded himself with talented people. Louis Auchincloss tells about his family and friends, who at times inhabited the tycoon's mansion, in *The Vanderbilt Era: Profiles of a Gilded Age* (see chapter 8). Jim Henson, creator of the Muppets for *Sesame Street* and other television and movie productions, surrounded himself with dedicated staff. The troop of Muppeteers are described by Christopher Finch in *Jim Henson: The Works* (see chapter 8).

Kennedy, John F.

🏵 *Profiles in Courage.* Harper & Brothers, 1956. 245p. Large print available.

Throughout American history, members of the U.S. Senate have voted as their constituents and their political parties have dictated. Usually this is no problem, because the senators owe their jobs to the voters that elect them and the parties that nominated them, but as Senator John F. Kennedy pointed out in this 1956 book, majority rule is not always ethical. Elected officials sometimes have to vote according to their convictions, risking their political careers. In this best-selling collective biography, Kennedy tells compelling stories of eight senators who broke with the voters of their states and their political parties to vote for the greater good.

> **Subjects:** Collective Biography; Courage; Politics and Government; Senators

> **Awards:** ALA Notable Books; Pulitzer Prize for Biography

> **Now Try:** Michael Beschloss follows the Kennedy model to write about courageous men in the White House in *Presidential Courage: Brave Leaders and How They Changed America 1789–1989* (see this chapter). The story that Kennedy tells about John Quincy Adams's career in the Senate is greatly expanded in *Mr. Adams's Last Crusade: John Quincy Adams's Extraordinary Post-Presidential Life in Congress* by Joseph Wheelan (see this chapter). Throughout the history of the Jewish people, rabbis and scholars have been challenged to protect the tenets of their faith. Elie Wiesel describes Jewish leaders and the lessons of integrity that may be learned from them in *Wise Men and Their Tales: Portraits of Biblical, Talmudic, and Hasidic Masters* (see chapter 4).

Consider Starting With . . .

These well-written Political Biographies of modest length will appeal to general readers.

- Addison, Paul. *Churchill: The Unexpected Hero.*
- Biskupic, Joan. *Sandra Day O'Connor: How the First Woman on the Supreme Court Became Its Most Influential Justice.*
- Donald, David Herbert. *We Are Lincoln Men: Abraham Lincoln and His Friends.*
- Ellis, Joseph J. *American Sphinx: The Character of Thomas Jefferson.*
- Kennedy, John F. *Profiles in Courage.*
- King, Ross. *Machiavelli: Philosopher of Power.*
- Nelson, Craig. *Thomas Paine: Enlightenment, Revolution, and the Birth of Modern Nations.*
- Wheelan, Joseph. *Mr. Adams's Last Crusade: John Quincy Adams's Extraordinary Post-Presidential Life in Congress.*
- White, Richard D. *Kingfish: The Reign of Huey P. Long.*
- Wills, Garry. *James Madison.*

Further Reading

Cords, Sarah Statz

The Real Story: A Guide to Nonfiction Reading Interests. Libraries Unlimited, 2006. 460p. ISBN 1591582830.

Cords includes titles about American presidents and other political leaders in her biography chapter and describes political reporting in her investigative writing chapter.

Rollyson, Carl

Biography: A User's Guide. Ivan R. Dees, 2008. 321p. ISBN 9781566637800.

Rollyson defines and describes political biography at length in his dictionary of biographical topics.

Wyatt, Neal

The Readers' Advisory Guide to Nonfiction. American Libraries, 2007. 318p. ISBN 9780838909362.

Wyatt discusses political stories in chapter 11 of her book and includes a generous list of titles to recommend to readers on pages 209–211.

Chapter 11

Science Biography

Definition of Science Biography

Science Biography includes narratives about the lives of men and women who observe, experiment, and theorize about physical phenomena. They include accounts of mathematicians, physicists, biologists, naturalists, chemists, physicians, astronomers, geologists, inventors, engineers, doctors, scientific researchers, and other students of life, as well as stories about people such as medical patients, whose lives are used to illustrate scientific processes.

Biography has not always been a concern in scientific literature. Throughout ancient and medieval history, people who developed crops, designed tools, studied the stars, and healed the sick remained anonymous. Of course, at the time they were not recognized as scientists, and there was no culture of public reporting to disseminate knowledge of their innovations quickly. Only with Gutenberg's development of the printing press did Western society at large begin to read about scientific discoveries and note the names of the scholars involved.

The identity of history's first scientist is a subject of debate among biographers. In *Newton's Gift: How Sir Isaac Newton Unlocked the Systems of the World* (see this chapter), David Berlinski identifies the seventeenth-century English physicist as the first true scientist, because he laid out the rules of the scientific method. Brian Clegg champions the thirteenth-century Franciscan monk Roger Bacon, who preceded Newton by four centuries; Clegg's *The First Scientist: A Life of Roger Bacon* (see this chapter) claims that nineteenth-century researchers learned that Bacon had used the scientific method when they translated the rediscovered papers of this early astronomer and mathematician. Use of the method was not required as a criterion by Isaac Asimov, who started his chronological reference book *Asimov's Biographical Encyclopedia of Science and Technology* (Doubleday, 1972) with the Egyptian scholar Imhotep, who engineered step pyramids and whose healing skills have been remembered as magical. Because there is an excellent, readily available biography of Bacon, he is the scientist of greatest antiquity in this chapter.

Science Biography includes narratives about the lives of men and women who observe, experiment, and theorize about physical phenomena. In the course of telling stories about these people, biographers may emphasize scientific work and careers more than personal details about the scientists. Readers will learn scientific methods and theories in reading about these professionals. Although some of the biographies take some concentration to read, others are quick reads.

Appeal of the Genre

According to Natalie Angier in *The Canon: The Whirligig Tour of the Beautiful Basics of Science* (Houghton Mifflin, 2007), most people claim that they do not like science. Thinking of science as work in laboratories and complicated calculations, they claim that scientific thought is difficult and beyond their mental abilities. General readers do, however, admire people who are scientifically talented. Those who solve great scientific puzzles or devise new products that improve the lives of many people interest them and thus become famous. Dava Sobel, Simon Winchester, Walter Isaacson, and other popular authors have turned these remarkable lives into best-selling books with scientific appeal factors.

Science Biographies may emphasize character less than some other forms of biography. Little is known about some early scientists, such as the monk Roger Bacon, the anatomist Henry Gray, and the clockmaker John Harrison; surviving documents focus on their work and tell little about their daily lives. Some of the more recent scientists, such as Charles Darwin, have been reluctant to become public figures. In some cases, biographers have to piece together what they can to create plausible lives. Other scientists, however, were important, well-known people about whom much was written during their lives. Albert Einstein, Marie Curie, Sigmund Freud, Thomas Edison, and Richard Feynman were very public figures and remain science icons.

Story plays an important role in Science Biographies, as readers enjoy the tales of great discoveries made by scientists. How did Jonas Salk develop his polio vaccine after so many other scientists had failed? How did Louis Leakey discover hominid remains among the rocks of the Olduvai Gorge in Tanzania? What did Wernher von Braun do to be considered one of the most important figures in aerospace history? All of these people's stories include great challenges, diligent work, and wondrous moments of discovery.

In Science Biographies, settings may be mental landscapes more than time and place, as some of the scientists worked in social isolation, concerned more with science. Gregor Mendel worked with peas in a monastery. Charles Darwin studied his biological specimens at home on his estate. Mathematician John Forbes Nash Jr. was lost in his calculations; it hardly mattered that he was seen wandering on the campus of Princeton University. In other Science Biographies, time and place are more evident. Inventor Robert Fulton became a recognizable character in early nineteenth-century New York City, where he often demonstrated his steamboats and torpedoes. Physicist William Thomson belonged to London clubs, led meetings of scientific societies, and met Queen Victoria. Louis Leakey spent much time with African tribesmen.

Readers inclined toward Science Biographies usually want to understand the discoveries and may be disappointed if authors skip over clarifying details. Thus, the pace can often be slower in these biographies than in others, because there is science to explain. Talented biographers present this science using commonly understood vocabulary without unnecessary jargon. For example, Walter Isaacson is particularly successful in explaining the work of Albert Einstein in a lucid and economical manner in his *Einstein: His Life and Universe.*

Science Biographies rank high in learning and experiencing appeal, for there is always at least some scientific content, such as a description of the geological ages of England, an explanation of gravity, or an account of attempts to split an atom. Readers of *B. F. Skinner: A Life* by Daniel W. Bjork learn all about behavior modification; those of *The Curies: A Biography of the Most Controversial Family in Science* by Denis Brian are introduced to the properties of radiation. Good Science Biographies make this learning more enjoyable than that gained by reading textbook accounts, and they also feature the added drama of discovery and compassion for characters in their stories.

Organization of the Chapter

This chapter is divided into five sections. The first is "Discovery Stories." These detail-filled biographies portray characters who spent their lives examining the large and small forces of nature. In some cases their great scientific discoveries contradicted accepted beliefs, leading to confrontations with scientific, political, or religious authorities. These compelling books reveal the world of working scientists.

The second section, "Medical Stories," focuses on discoveries specifically about the physical and mental health of humans. In this section some of the books tell the stories of medical patients rather than the professionals who studied their illnesses. Readers concerned about their own health and health care may identify with these books more than with others in this chapter.

"Invention Stories" includes biographies of creative people who applied science to make devices to improve human lives. Failure is as much a part of these stories as success, and the motive of profit is also usually present, making these detailed accounts good choices for business and history readers as well as science readers.

Biographies in which the lives of the scientists or entire populations were threatened by their research and how it could be applied are covered in the last section, "Science on the Edge." Because of the dangers, tension and suspense are common to these stories; and some even feature confident and heroic protagonists who display James Bond–like nerves.

Discovery Stories

Humans have always wanted to understand the world and their role in it. Ancient peoples devised myths about supernatural characters that created and sustained the earth, all-powerful gods and goddesses who might grant prosperity to those they favored and destroy those who displeased them. The rising and setting of the sun, the growth of crops, the birth of children, storms, natural disasters, and diseases were all caused by the actions of divine beings. With the rise of education in ancient civilizations, however, the old explanations began to be questioned. Naturalists and philosophers began a process of discovery continued to this day by scientists.

In this section are stories of men and women who took up the challenge to discover the truth about the workings of the universe and its components. These curious people possessed a singularity of purpose that guided them into research that challenged prevailing beliefs of their time. Not all were comfortable with the revolutions that they began. Naturalist Charles Darwin, reluctant to report his findings, retreated to his estate for decades of study of the specimens that he had collected on the voyage of HMS *Beagle*. Botanist Gregor Mendel worried about the reactions of church leaders to his genetic studies. Others, like molecular biologist Frances Crick and astronomer Carl Sagan, seemed to enjoy the criticism, attention, and even ridicule their bold statements generated. Whether secretive or attention seeking, all succeeded in changing the core beliefs in their fields.

These narratives are enjoyable for their adventurous stories of discovery as much as for the tension of conflict underlying them. There is usually at least a modest amount of scientific detail, so few of these works are fast paced, yet the stories are compelling. They are generally best suited for nonfiction readers who value learning as part of their entertainment.

> *Discovery Stories* are detail-filled biographies that portray characters who spent their lives examining the large and small forces of nature. In some cases their great scientific discoveries contradicted accepted beliefs, leading to confrontations with scientific, political, or religious authorities. Readers will learn some science in these compelling books that reveal the world of working scientists.

Berlinski, David

Newton's Gift: How Sir Isaac Newton Unlocked the Systems of the World. Free Press, 2000. 217p. ISBN 0684843927.

English school boy Isaac Newton (1643–1727) was only an average student at the boarding schools that he attended, and later at the University of Cambridge. At one point his mother brought him home and tried to turn him into a farmer. He disliked the work and pleaded to go back to school. In this admiring work, novelist and mathematician David Berlinski tells how the great scientist overcame his scholarly mediocrity and laid the foundation for all future scientific inquiry with his mathematical theories of physical mechanics. This concise biography of a gentleman scientist who never left his native England will appeal to readers who want to understand his life and work without having to know complicated math.

Subjects: Great Britain; Newton, Sir Isaac; Physicists; Quick Reads

Now Try: Some of Newton's treatises, including *Opticks: Or a Treatise of the Reflections, Inflections and Colours of Light* and *Principia: Mathematical Principles of Natural Philosophy*, are considered scientific masterpieces and are available to readers in separate volumes or in Britannica's <u>Great Books of the Western World</u>. Like Newton, young Josiah Wedgwood was an unlikely candidate to become a leading scientist and gentleman. He was a simple potter's son, unable to afford school, but he experimented with glazes and discovered processes that made him famous and rich. Brian Dolan tells the story of the inventor turned industrialist in *Wedgwood: The First Tycoon* (see chapter 9). Another entertaining quick read about a historical Englishman who defined his own field (literature) for future generations is *Chaucer* by Peter Ackroyd (see chapter 7). Scientist and classifier Peter Mark Roget, author of *Roget's Thesaurus*, never struggled with academics, as Newton did; his problem was insanity, which ran in the family. Joshua Kendall tells how keeping lists kept him sane in *The Man Who Made Lists: Love, Death, Madness, and the Creation of Roget's Thesaurus* (see chapter 4). British polymath Thomas Young discovered some failings in Newton's research. Andrew Robinson tells his story in *The Last Man Who Knew Everything: Thomas Young, the Anonymous Genius Who Proved Newton Wrong and Deciphered the Rosetta Stone, Among Other Surprising Feats*.

Henig, Robin Marantz

The Monk in the Garden: The Lost and Found Genius of Gregor Mendel, the Father of Genetics. Houghton Mifflin, 2000. 292p ISBN 0395977657.

Gregor Mendel (1822–1884) began growing peas when his bishop forbade him to breed mice, thinking the latter inappropriate for a monk who had taken a vow of chastity. In 1865 he presented his genetic findings based on his pea experiments in a two-part lecture that was reported by the Brunn Society for the study of Natural Science. Because Darwin had not yet published his theory of evolution, the importance of Mendel's work was not recognized; it was forgotten until Carl Erich Correns rediscovered his papers in 1900. When Mendel died in 1884, his experiments were barely mentioned in his obituaries, which told about his charity, love of gardening, and beekeeping. In this psychological biography, Robin Marantz Henig intimately recounts the monk's education, experiments, correspondence, daily routine, and legacy. Science readers will enjoy this admiring work that tells how Mendel's reputation as a pioneer in genetic studies was restored.

Subjects: Austria; Botanists; Genetics; Mendel, Gregor; Monks

Now Try: Mendel's *Experiments in Plant-Hybridization* has been translated into English and is available in print and on the Internet. Readers who enjoy stories of quietly determined naturalists will find more in *Beatrix Potter: A Life in Nature* by Linda Lear (see chapter 7) and *Chrysalis: Maria Sibylla Merian and the Secrets of Metamorphosis* by Kim Todd (see chapter 1). The suppression of scientific knowledge by religious authorities is also found in *The First Scientist: A Life of Roger Bacon* by Brian Clegg (see this chapter) and *Kepler's Witch: An Astronomer's Discovery of Cosmic Order Amid Religious War, Political Intrigue, and the Heresy Trial of His Mother* by James A. Connor (see this chapter).

Hoffman, Paul

The Man Who Loved Only Numbers: The Story of Paul Erdös and the Search for Mathematical Truth. Hyperion, 1998. 302p. ISBN 0786863625.

Hungarian mathematician Paul Erdös (1913–1996) had no wife, children, job, or home, but he had friends who enjoyed his entertaining banter. He was a scholarly nomad, constantly visiting other mathematicians around the globe and accepting their generous hospitality. With only a few clothes in his battered suitcase and his notebooks in a shopping bag, he would suddenly appear and then be off again in a few days. Remarkably, by collaborating with 485 other mathematicians, he published 1,475 academic papers relating to number and set theories. This book reads like stories told at a wake. In this humorous book for readers who like funny stories, Paul Hoffman traces the physical and mathematical journey of a genius.

> **Subjects:** Erdös, Paul; Hungary; Mathematicians
>
> **Now Try:** Indian mathematician Srinivasa Ramanujan died at age thirty-two, but he left many texts that are still being studied. Robert Kanigel traces his brief career in *Man Who Knew Infinity: A Life of the Genius Ramanujan*. Woody Guthrie was another nomadic character about whom there are many stories from friends. Elizabeth Partridge includes many photographs with the remembrances in *This Land Was Made for You and Me: The Life and Songs of Woody Guthrie* (see chapter 7). Like Erdös, children's author Margaret Wise Brown was a great collaborator. Her melancholic story is told in *Margaret Wise Brown* by Leonard S. Marcus (see chapter 7). *Peter Jennings: A Reporter's Life* is a memorial tribute full of stories told by his friends and acquaintances on an *ABC News Special* after his death from cancer in 2005.

Lindley, David

Degrees Kelvin: A Tale of Genius, Invention, and Tragedy. Joseph Henry Press, 2004. 366p. ISBN 0309090733.

Physicist William Thomson (1824–1907) was only sixteen when he published a paper in the *Cambridge Mathematical Journal* correcting mistakes in an acclaimed textbook. Throughout his youth he exhibited confidence and flamboyance. This scientist dazzled the British science community with clever work, such as inventing a compass for steel-bodied ships and improving underwater telegraph cables. Known as Lord Kelvin after being knighted by Queen Victoria, he failed to keep pace with younger scientists as he aged. According to David Lindley, he isolated himself by denying the existence of atoms and radioactivity and by publicly ridiculing Darwin's theories of evolution. This cautionary tale about an obstinate man who relied too much on past achievements is an appropriate choice for general readers.

> **Subjects:** Great Britain; Inventors; Kelvin, William Thomson, Baron of; Physicists
>
> **Now Try:** Thomson's *Principles of Mechanics and Dynamics* is still studied in engineering programs. Late in Queen Victoria's reign, Italian-born physicist Guglielmo Marconi was the talked-about inventor around London. Erik Larson recounts Marconi's social and business life in *Thunderstruck*, a story of crime and science in 1900s London. The character of Irving Berlin resembles that of Kelvin in that both transformed from innovators to reactionaries as they aged. The songwriter's progression is described in *Irving Berlin: American Troubadour* by Edward Jablonski. In the world of literature, Nathaniel Hawthorne lost his progressive sentiments as he aged. His melancholy life is described in *Salem in My Dwelling Place: A Life of Nathaniel Hawthorne* by Edwin Haviland Miller.

Maddox, Brenda

🏆 *Rosalind Franklin: The Dark Lady of DNA*. HarperCollins, 2002. 380p. ISBN 0060184078.

Despite caustic remarks about her by James Watson in *The Double Helix*, Rosalind Franklin (1920–1958) was a respected microbiologist with many friends in her field. The geneticist's portrayal of Franklin was unfair, for he and Crick relied heavily on her research findings and her photographs of DNA in their work. Award-winning biographer Brenda Maddox claims that they even took some of her data without permission, which Franklin, fighting ovarian cancer, was unable to stop. In this sympathetic account for readers who like stories about heroic women, Maddox restores the reputation of a brilliant scientist and mountain climber who should be acclaimed for her breakthroughs on DNA.

Subjects: DNA; Franklin, Rosalind; Microbiologists; Women

Awards: Marsh Biography Award

Now Try: In *The Double Helix*, James Watson describes his work and life among a community of scientists. Gorge Johnson tells the story of another female science who was denied credit for her important discoveries in *Miss Leavitt's Stars: The Untold Story of the Woman Who Discovered How to Measure the Universe*. Like Franklin, who was a mountain climber, Isabelle Grameson had no fear of difficult journeys. Robert Whitaker describes her terrible journey over the Andes and through the Amazon Basin in search of her husband in *The Mapmaker's Wife: A True Tale of Love, Murder, and Survival in the Amazon* (see chapter 1). Nancy Schoenberger describes a talented novelist whose life was tragically shortened and her accomplishments forgotten in *Dangerous Muse: The Life of Lady Caroline Blackwood* (see chapter 7). The betrayal of a woman is also the theme in a story about the struggle for the English throne in *Queen Isabella: Treachery, Adultery, and Murder in Medieval England* by Alison Weir (see chapter 9).

Morell, Virginia

Ancestral Passions: The Leakey Family and the Quest for Humankind's Beginnings. Simon & Schuster, 1995. 638p. ISBN 0684801922.

Born in Kenya in 1903, Louis S. B. Leakey (1903–1972), the son of missionaries isolated from white society, developed a uniquely African perspective on the land and its history, which he later imparted to his wife Mary and son Richard. Together this trio of anthropologists revolutionized scientific understanding of human origins. In a candid family history, science journalist Virginia Morell tells how the Leakeys survived field work in the Olduvai Gorge in Tanzania, attacks by conservative scientists, and even family fights. A compelling family portrait, this book will likely appeal to general readers.

Subjects: Anthropologists; Family Biography; Fossils; Leakey, Louis; Leakey, Mary; Leakey, Richard; Tanzania

Now Try: The Leakeys wrote many books. Louis Leakey recounted much of their early work in *By the Evidence: Memoirs, 1932–1951*. Mary Leakey's account of the family work is *Disclosing the Past*. Their son Richard tells about his work as conservation minister in Kenya in *Wildlife Wars: My Fight to Save*

Africa's Natural Treasures and about his work as an archeologist in *One Life: An Auto-biography*. Louis Leakey was the champion of two women who wanted to study African primates. Their contrasting stories are told in *The Dark Romance of Dian Fossey* by Harold T. P. Hayes (see chapter 2) and *Jane Goodall: The Woman Who Redefined Man* by Dale Peterson (see chapter 4). In *The Clarks of Cooperstown: Their Singer Sewing Machine Fortune, Their Great and Influential Art Collections, Their Forty-Year Feud* (see chapter 8), Nicholas Fox Weber tells the story of another family that gained renown despite its strong internal disagreements.

Nicholl, Charles

Leonardo da Vinci: Flights of the Mind. Viking, 2004. 623p. ISBN 0670033456.

As a great observer of the natural world, Leonardo da Vinci (1452–1519) is revered as both an artist and a scientist. For Leonardo the vocations were inseparable; he drew everything that he saw and kept copious notes. Human anatomy, botany, astronomy, mechanics, and architecture fascinated him. In this stately and well-illustrated work set in Renaissance Italy, Charles Nicholl draws heavily from Leonardo's notebooks, which provided intimate details of his daily life.

Subjects: Architects; Inventors; Italy; Leonardo da Vinci; Painters; Renaissance; Scientists

Now Try: Like Leonardo, physician Henry Gray was fascinated by the human body. In *The Anatomist: A True Story of Gray's Anatomy* (see this chapter), Bill Hayes reveals the long-lost story of how Gray and his illustrator, Henry Vandyke Carter, wrote the pioneering anatomy text. Few figures in history were as talented in so many ways as Leonardo. In *Benjamin Franklin: An American Life* (see chapter 10), Walter Isaacson makes a case for Franklin, who was a printer, businessman, scientist, inventor, statesman, and diplomat. Artist and inventor Samuel B. Morse was also multitalented, but he lacked business and relationship skills. Kenneth Silverman describes him as a man torn by unrealistic ambitions in *Lightning Man: The Accursed Life of Samuel F. B. Morse* (see this chapter). Ross King shows that Renaissance Italy was a dangerous place for artists in his biography of a Leonardo contemporary, *Michelangelo & the Pope's Ceiling* (see chapter 7).

Poundstone, William

Carl Sagan: A Life in the Cosmos. Henry Holt, 1999. 473p. ISBN 0805057668.

Astronomer Carl Sagan's (1934–1996) success as a popular scientist was based on his ability to inspire public interest in an almost hopeless search for extraterrestrial life. His readers and viewers of his television series cheered his efforts, for they too wanted to learn if humans had company in space. Fascinated by futuristic displays at the 1939 Worlds Fair in New York, Sagan studied astronomy and astrophysics at the University of Chicago, taught at Harvard and Cornell, and worked on many NASA space exploration projects. Though his marriages suffered from his absorption with work, his friendships multiplied. William Poundstone profiles the exobiologist as a passionate man in pursuit of an idea. No scientific background is needed to read this admiring biography.

Subjects: Astronomers; Extraterrestrial Life; Sagan, Carl; Space Exploration

Now Try: Sagan published numerous science books for popular reading, including *Cosmos*, the companion book to his television series with the same name, and *Broca's Brain*, a book about human intelligence. Since Sagan's death in 1996, theoretical physicist Stephen Hawking has held the spotlight in the debate over the shape of the universe. Leonard Susskind presents his view of Hawking and his theories in *Black Hole*

War: My Battle with Stephen Hawking to Make the World Safe for Quantum Mechanics. Hawking presents his views in *A Briefer History of Time* and *The Theory of Everything.* Like Sagan, Walt Disney was a dreamer who asked people to believe in what seemed impossible. The story of his complicated life is told in *Walt Disney: The Triumph of the American Imagination* by Neal Gabler (see chapter 9). As they did for Sagan, popular books, magazines, and television programs have made primatologist Jane Goodall a scientific icon. Dale Peterson describes her as a tireless and inspiring environmental leader in *Jane Goodall: The Woman Who Redefined Man* (see chapter 4).

Quammen, David

The Reluctant Mr. Darwin: An Intimate Portrait of Charles Darwin and the Making of His Theory of Evolution. Norton, 2006. 304p. ISBN: 9780393059816. Audiobook available.

In this intimate biography, David Quammen tells how Charles Darwin (1809-1882) studied and perfected his theory of evolution over many years before ever announcing it to the public. Only the threat of Alfred Russel Wallace reporting his findings first convinced the cautious Darwin to publish. The story starts after Darwin returns from his travels on the *Beagle,* describes his career, explains his theories, and discusses his private life. A little knowledge of evolutionary theory will help when reading this detailed account aimed at the naturalist's admirers.

> **Subjects:** Darwin, Charles; Evolution; Great Britain; Group Discussion Books; Naturalists
>
> **Now Try:** Three of Darwin's books are classics and are readily available: *The Voyage of the Beagle, On the Origin of Species,* and *The Descent of Man.* His *The Autobiography of Charles Darwin* is also in many bookstores and libraries. Irving Stone's *The Origin: A Biographical Novel of Charles Darwin* is strong on characterization but simplistic in explaining evolution. Darwin only published his findings when he learned in a letter from Alfred Russel Wallace that the latter was close to announcing similar conclusions. In *The Heretic in Darwin's Court: The Life of Alfred Russel Wallace,* Ross A. Slotten recounts the life of the scientist who received little of the credit for evolutionary theory. *Monk in the Garden: The Lost and Found Genius of Gregory Mendel, Father of Genetics* by Robin Marantz Henig (see this chapter) is another book about a quiet figure who revolutionized genetics.

Repcheck, Jack

The Man Who Found Time: James Hutton and the Discovery of the Earth's Antiquity. Perseus, 2003. 247p. ISBN 073820692X.

Scottish gentleman farmer James Hutton (1726–1797) is often called "The Father of Geology." His curiosity led him to gather and examine rocks from the Scottish countryside, which he took to meetings with other amateur Enlightenment-era scientists. From their conversations he formulated his theory of geologic time, which, to the chagrin of some, directly challenged biblical accounts of the creation. Charles Darwin later used Hutton's geologic ages in his dating of evolutionary changes. According to science writer Jack Repcheck, Hutton is often forgotten as a giant of his field because his writings are so difficult to read. Happily, this biography is a lively tale bound to please readers.

Subjects: Geologists; Hutton, James; Scotland

Now Try: Hutton was a friend of the economist Adam Smith. James Buchan describes how Smith lived for ideas in *The Authentic Adam Smith: His Life and Ideas*. About forty years after Hutton's death, geologist Charles Lyell used the Scotsman's work to support the theory of advancing and receding glaciers. Edmund Blair Bolles describes how Lyell, Louis Agassiz, and Elisha Kent Kane revealed geological history together in *The Ice Finders: How a Poet, a Professor, and a Politician Discovered the Ice Age*. Readers looking for other gentlemanly characters will find them in *E. B. White: A Biography* by Scott Elledge (see chapter 7) and *Norman Rockwell: A Life* by Laura Claridge (see chapter 7). A more adventurous tale of geologic exploration is told in *A River Running West: The Life of John Wesley Powell* by Donald Worster (see chapter 1).

Ridley, Matt

Francis Crick: Discoverer of the Genetic Code. Atlas Books, 2006. 213p. Eminent Lives. ISBN 9780060823337.

Molecular biologist Francis Crick (1916–2004) did not get along well with his partner, James Watson. Though they discovered the structures of DNA together, they often bickered about how to report their findings. Crick was very unhappy with Watson's book *The Double Helix*, and Watson was in turn upset by Crick's lectures and journal articles. With wit and a talent for simple explanations of scientific principles, Matt Ridley chronicles the long life of an irascible molecular biologist, who as a boy earned mediocre grades in science but as an adult solved one of nature's greatest puzzles.

Subjects: Crick, Francis; Geneticists; Microbiologists; Quick Reads

Now Try: Crick has written a series of books about genetics and the ways scientists work, including the memoir *What Mad Pursuit: A Personal View of Scientific Discovery*. James Watson told his differing version of the team's work on DNA in *The Double Helix*. A third view of the Crick/Watson partnership is found in *Rosalind Franklin: The Dark Lady of DNA* by Brenda Maddox (see this chapter), which charges the men with not crediting Franklin for her important work on DNA. The musical team of W. S. Gilbert and Arthur Sullivan stuck together through terrible disagreements to produce many beloved operettas. Michael Angier describes their working relationship in *Gilbert and Sullivan: A Dual Biography*. Readers will find another dysfunctional professional relationship in the dual biography *Very Strange Bedfellows: The Short and Unhappy Marriage of Richard Nixon and Spiro Agnew* by Jules Witcover (see chapter 10).

Winchester, Simon

The Map That Changed the World: William Smith and the Birth of Modern Geology. HarperCollins, 2001. 329p. ISBN 0060193611. Audiobook and large print available.

Canal engineer William Smith (1769–1839) was a trusting man of modest birth and little income, who shared his ideas freely. Recognizing that fossils identified layers of rock across the island of Great Britain, he drew a map that showed its geological history and suggested where to find coal, oil, and precious minerals. Because he allowed others to view his work as he delayed publication, men of higher rank profited from his work while he landed in debtors' prison. In this novel-like biography for general readers, Simon Winchester tells the sad story of how a working-class scientist struggled for recognition and compensation in a very class-conscious society.

> **Subjects:** Geologists; Great Britain; Group Discussion Books; Smith, William

> **Now Try:** *Longitude: The True Story of a Lone Genius Who Solved the Greatest Scientific Problem of His Time* by Dava Sobel (see this chapter) is another book about British gentlemen scientists failing to recognize the accomplishments of a working-class colleague. For British epidemiologist Alice Stewart, the discrimination was sexual. As the bearer of bad news about the health risks of radiation, she was either ignored or denounced by members of the medical establishment. In *The Woman Who Knew Too Much: Alice Stewart and the Secrets of Radiation* (see chapter 4), Gayle Green tells how time has proven Stewart right. In the United States, the scientific establishment treated Rachel Carson in the same manner. Mark Hamilton Lytle recounts Carson's efforts to alert the nation to the harmful side effects of DDT in *The Gentle Subversive: Rachel Carson, **Silent Spring,** and the Rise of the Environmental Movement* (see chapter 4).

Zinsser, Judith

La Dame d'Esprit: A Biography of the Marquise Du Chatelet. Viking, 2006. 376 pp. ISBN 9780670038008.

> What would you do if you were bored with your marriage? Gabrielle Emilie le Tonnelier de Breteuil (1706–1749), the marquise Du Chatelet, wrote treatises on mathematics and physics, translated Newton's work into French, and started a love affair with the great author Voltaire. She even described the relationship of energy to matter more than 150 years before Albert Einstein! Judith Zinsser recounts the exciting life of an unconventional woman, who has been unfairly portrayed as a sycophant by Voltaire scholars. Readers seeking great stories about women of achievement will enjoy this fascinating book.

> **Subjects:** Du Chatelet, Gabrielle Emilie le Tonnelier de Breteuil, Marquise; France; Mathematicians; Physicists; Women

> **Now Try:** For more on the Du Chatelet/Voltaire relationship, try *Passionate Minds: The Great Love Affair of the Enlightenment, Featuring the Scientist Emilie Du Châtelet, the Poet Voltaire, Sword Fights, Book Burnings, Assorted Kings, Seditious Verse, and the Birth of the Modern World* by David Bodanis. Roger Pearson describes Voltaire as a pioneer of the movement for human rights in his approving biography, *Voltaire Almighty: A Life in Pursuit of Freedom* (see chapter 9). Anarchist Emma Goldman was also deported by a court that judged her seditious. Her causes were labor reform, women's rights, birth control, free love, and pacifism. Alice Wexler describes the personal life of the outspoken woman in *Emma Goldman: An Intimate Life* (see chapter 10). In *Naked in the Marketplace: The Lives of George Sand,* Benita Eisler tells the story of a passionate French woman who rivaled men in literature rather than science.

Medical Stories

In many groups, when generations gather, there is talk about health. Who is expecting babies? Are the children growing as expected? Who has cancer or diabetes? Who needs to lose a few pounds? Although the children may find all the talk rather boring, the adults, who feel the loss of their youthful vitality and have a growing sense of mortality, can hardly help listening and contributing to the discussions. The physical condition of the human body and the mental health of individuals are primary concerns for many people, and books about health and medicine fill bookstores and libraries.

In this section are two subsections. In "Doctors" are books about scientists who observe, theorize, and test phenomena. For example, Jeffrey Kluger describes the rigors of research during a polio epidemic in *Splendid Solution: Jonas Salk and the Conquest of Polio*. Bill Hayes identifies the forgotten nineteenth-century physician Henry Gray in *The Anatomist: A True Story of Gray's Anatomy*. In "Patients" are books about people whose medical conditions illustrate the successes and limitations of medical science. An especially thought-provoking patient story is *Crashing Through: A True Story of Risk, Adventure, and the Man Who Dared to See* by Robert Kurson.

Character and character development as appeal factors in these books vary. The medical patients are common people in uncommon circumstances. The medical scientists, on the other hand, are striking characters who stand out as unique and often heroic individuals. As in other Science Biographies, the level of detail slows the pace but will please readers wanting to learn about health and medicine while reading interesting stories.

Medical Stories focus on the physical and mental health of humans. In this section, some of the books tell the stories of medical patients rather than of the professionals who studied their illnesses. Readers concerned about their own health and health care may identify with these books more than with others in the chapter. Some of the books are quick reads.

Doctors

Bjork, Daniel W.

B. F. Skinner: A Life. Basic Books, 1993. 298p. ISBN 0465006116.
Psychologist B. F. Skinner (1904–1990) upset many people with his books and articles espousing "radical behaviorism." This was the idea that populations can be managed with environmental controls and positive reinforcement to create happy, contented societies. Political conservatives considered his theories, which called for reduced consumerism and the building of utopian communities, a threat to the American way of life. Particularly offended by his observations that they, like rats and dogs, were susceptible to behavioral manipulation, they attacked his reputation, even starting rumors that he raised his daughter in a box. According to historian Daniel W. Bjork, the psychologist continued his studies throughout the controversies and enjoyed a relatively happy family life. In this biography he admiringly tells how Skinner met personal, professional, and public challenges while changing management practices in business and education.

Subjects: Behavioral Scientists; Psychologists; Skinner, B. F.

Now Try: In *Walden Two*, Skinner presents a fictional utopian community that illustrates his vision for behavioral modification. Skinner recounted his life in *A Matter of Consequences* and its sequel, *The Shaping of a Behaviorist*. Ted Geisel, better known as Dr. Seuss, was another uncompromising character with fixed ideas about psychology. The story of his unconventional life is told by Judith Morgan and Neil Morgan in *Dr. Seuss & Mr. Geisel: A Biography* (see chapter 7). Anthropologist Margaret Mead was a contemporary of Skinner who studied preindustrial cultures. She described her life and work in *Blackberry Winter: My Earlier Years*. Unlike Skinner, experimental psychologist Harry Harlow, who studied the effects of isolation on the young, was unable to hold his own life together while he stirred public controversy with his theories about the need for love. His sad story is found in *Love at Goon Park: Harry Harlow and the Science of Affection* by Deborah Blum (see this chapter).

Blum, Deborah

Love at Goon Park: Harry Harlow and the Science of Affection. Perseus, 2002. 336p. ISBN 0738202789.

Personal relations were always difficult for experimental psychologist Harry Harlow (1905–1981) of the University of Wisconsin, who isolated young monkeys in cages to study their need for love. The obsessive professor could not keep graduate students, who inevitably disliked the work. Feeling neglected, his wife and children left him. Ironically, he subsequently became famous as an advocate for familial love and in 1959 appeared on a child development documentary on CBS television. His claim that parents could not spoil children with too much attention drew protests from traditional disciplinarians. Science writer Blum intimately examines the life of a contradictory character in this sympathetic biography.

> **Subjects:** Child Development; Group Discussion Books; Harlow, Harry; Primate Studies; Psychologists

> **Now Try:** In *The Nature of Love*, Harlow reports his findings on the reactions of rhesus monkeys to isolation. Cartoonist Charles Schulz is another character who exhibited great understanding about human nature yet struggled with his own relationships. His melancholy story is told in *Schulz and Peanuts: A Biography* by David Michaelis (see chapter 7). In *Hans Christian Andersen* (see chapter 5), Jens Andersen recounts the life of the author of children's stories who was uncomfortable around children. Author and literary critic Alfred Kazin sacrificed his relationships to his career. Richard M. Cook profiles the unhappy intellectual in *Alfred Kazin: A Biography* (see chapter 7).

Hayes, Bill

The Anatomist: A True Story of Gray's Anatomy. Ballantine Books, 2008. 250p. ISBN 9780345456892.

When Bill Hayes first became interested in *Gray's Anatomy*, the best known of all medical textbooks, he found only a few facts about its author, Henry Gray (1827–1861). At the time of its publication, the anatomist had been highly praised for the textbook, elected a Fellow of the Royal Society, and awarded a teaching position at St. George's Hospital in London. Then at age thirty-four, he suddenly died of smallpox, which he contracted from a patient. Little else seemed to be known about him. But after Hayes identified the textbook's illustrator as Henry Vandyke Carter (often not credited in twentieth-century editions), he located Carter's diaries and letters, containing many details about Gray's life, which he was able to verify through other sources. Readers who enjoy mysteries will enjoy this entertaining, investigative biography.

>   **Subjects:** Carter, Henry Vandyke; Gray, Henry; Great Britain; Physicians

>   **Now Try:** The fortieth edition of Gray's textbook was published in 2008 as *Gray's Anatomy: The Anatomical Basis of Clinical Practice*. As Gray gave his name to a series of textbooks, Amerigo Vespucci gave his name to two continents. Little was known about the explorer until Felipe Fernández-Armesto discovered old records. The author describes a man who rose from being a simple merchant to leading dangerous explorations in *Amerigo: The Man Who Gave His Name to America* (see chapter 1). Artist George Bellows was another young man whose very promising life was cut short by disease. His brief but productive life is described in *George Bellows: An Artist in Action* by Mary Sayre Haverstock. Composer Wolfgang Amadeus Mozart was a man who lived mostly as he pleased and would have done well with just a little more luck. In *Mozart*, Peter Gay describes a genius who wrote a great deal of wonderful music in his short life.

Kluger, Jeffrey

Splendid Solution: Jonas Salk and the Conquest of Polio. G. P. Putnam's Sons, 2004. 373p. ISBN 0399152164. Audiobook and large print available.

When Jonas Salk (1914–1995) was a boy, New York had annual polio outbreaks. His mother, like many others of her time, kept him indoors all summer, away from other children and suspected infection hotspots, such as swimming pools and movie theaters. She was determined to protect him so he could grow up to become a rabbi. He disappointed her by choosing a career in medical research. In this dramatic story, Jeffrey Kluger chronicles the education and work of a headstrong scientist who, by rejecting the methods and conclusions of his older colleagues, developed an effective polio vaccine. Readers will learn much about the history and politics of medical research in this admiring biography.

>   **Subjects:** Physicians; Polio; Polio Vaccine; Salk, Jonas

>   **Now Try:** Salk's books about contemporary issues include *World Population and Human Values: A New Reality* and *Anatomy of Reality: Merging of Intuition and Reason*. German physician Gerhard Domagk lost many patients to bacterial infections in field hospitals in World War I. The story of his development of sulfa drugs, which changed the direction of medicine and helped the Allied effort in World War II, is told in *The Demon Under the Microscope: From Battlefield Hospitals to Nazi Labs, One Doctor's Heroic Search for the World's First Miracle Drug* by Thomas Hager. Readers who enjoy stories about political crises may wish to read *Chasing the Flame: Sergio Vieira de Mello and the Fight to Save the World* by Samantha Power (see chapter 4), which tells about an international diplomat's tense negotiations to end international conflicts. Charles R. Morris takes readers onto the operating floor of a hospital, portraying a group of physicians in *The Surgeons: Life and Death in a Top Heart Center*.

Kramer, Peter D.

Freud: Inventor of the Modern Mind. Atlas Books, 2006. 213p. <u>Eminent Lives</u>. ISBN 9780060598952.

The luster of Sigmund Freud's (1856–1939) reputation has been tarnished in recent decades by psychiatrists turning away from the psychology pioneer's theories and therapies. The quality of his research has also been questioned. In this sympathetic biography, psychiatrist Peter D. Kramer chronicles the Austrian physician's life and career, showing how the learned man's personal experiences colored his research results and interpretations. In the process, Freud is shown to be less a god of psychological science and more a fallible scholar, who still contributed significantly to our understanding of the human condition.

Subjects: Freud, Sigmund; Group Discussion Books; Psychiatry; Quick Reads; Vienna

Now Try: *The Interpretation of Dreams, A General Introduction to Psychoanalysis, Beyond the Pleasure Principle,* and *The Ego and the Id* are just a few of Freud's influential books still readily available. Freud's reputation has survived better than that of psychoanalyst Bruno Bettelheim, whose scientific fraud is exposed in *The Creation of Dr. B: A Biography of Bruno Bettelheim* by Richard Pollak (see chapter 5). David Michaelis, in *Schulz and Peanuts: A Biography* (see chapter 7), tells the story of cartoonist Charles Schulz, who artfully drew from Freud's observations about human motivation in his comic strip *Peanuts,* but who could never straighten out his own life. Like Freud, social scientist and educator William James is esteemed as a philosopher. Robert D. Richardson portrays James as the leading thinker of the late nineteenth century in *William James: In the Maelstrom of American Modernism* (see chapter 7).

Patients

Blake, Rich

The Day Donny Herbert Woke Up: A True Story. Harmony Books, 2007. 246p. ISBN 9780307383167. Audiobook available.

"Where's Linda?" asked Donny Herbert (1962–2006) from his wheelchair at Father Baker Manor in Buffalo, New York. This was remarkable, because the former fireman had been in an unusual vegetative state for over nine years, ever since a snow-covered roof had fallen on him in 1995. During the decade after his brain trauma, his wife Linda insisted physicians try new treatments that might rouse her unresponsive husband, and she had repeatedly taken him on family outings in the wheelchair. Journalist Rich Blake tells the story of Herbert, who suddenly spoke for nineteen hours straight, and then slipped back into a coma. Fans of true life mysteries will likely enjoy this strange story.

Subjects: Comas; Firefighters; Herbert, Donny; Quick Reads; Teen Reads

Now Try: French publisher Phillipe Vigand woke after two months in a coma to find that he was paralyzed and could only blink and move one finger voluntarily. The story of his learning to communicate with his wife and family is told in his memoir, *Only the Eyes Say Yes. French Vogue* editor Jean-Dominique

Bauby could only blink after coming out of his coma. In the memoir *The Diving Bell and the Butterfly*, Bauby describes the frustration of being alert but totally immobile. *Kathy* by Barbara Miller relates the story of a thirteen-year-old girl who spent seven weeks in a coma after an automobile accident. Six months later she ran a marathon. In 1967 Oliver Sacks revived twenty elderly patients with encephalitis lethargica who had been catatonic for forty years by giving them an experimental drug, laevo-dihydroxyphenylaline (L-Dopa). In his book *Awakenings*, he discusses the temporary restoration of lives, which quickly declined after the drug lost its effectiveness.

Colapinto, John

As Nature Made Him: The Boy Who Was Raised as a Girl. HarperCollins, 2000. 278p. ISBN 0060192119. Audiobook available.

Medical journals of the late 1960s reported that a boy whose penis had been damaged and removed in a botched circumcision was being successfully raised as a girl. These reports, never naming the child, were often cited as proving that sexual identity was taught and not instinctive. Then in 1997, medical journals updated the story. In 1972 at age fourteen, doubting that he was female and facing drug and surgical treatment to create his sex organs, David Reimer (1958–) learned his true sexual identity and ended the experiment. Journalist John Colapinto documents the case to tell an unusual tale about a man who continued struggling with his self-image. In the hands of a less sympathetic author, this sad story could have been sensationalized. Instead, Colapinto has written a thoughtful work for general readers.

Subjects: Gender Identity; Group Discussion Books; Reimer, David; Sex Change

Now Try: In the 1950s, when an ex-GI underwent sex change surgery and hormone treatments in Denmark to become female, newspapers reported the story as an outrage against society. Richard F. Docter sympathetically reexamines the case in *Becoming a Woman: A Biography of Christine Jorgensen*. In the memoir *Second Serve: The Renée Richards Story*, Richards recounts her sex change surgery and the storm of protest caused by her participation in women's tennis. A truly disturbing book about a young life sacrificed for medicine and carnival voyeurism is *African Queen: The Real Life of the Hottentot Venus* by Rachel Holmes (see chapter 5), which tells of a young African woman displayed as a medical anomaly against her will in Regency England. Mark Kriegel tells another tragic story, of a son unfairly manipulated, in this case by his overly demanding father, in *Pistol: The Life of Pete Maravich* (see chapter 12).

Kurson, Robert

Crashing Through: A True Story of Risk, Adventure, and the Man Who Dared to See. Random House, c2007. 306p. ISBN 1400063353. Audiobook and large print available.

Mike May (1954–) was blinded by a chemical explosion in his family's garage when he was three. Never the shrinking type and encouraged by his mother, he lead a typical boy's life of climbing trees, playing sports, and, when old enough, dating girls. The title of this work refers to the risks that Mike took to ski downhill at record speeds. He even tried to drive a car, just to say that he had. In this inspiring biography with a large dose of medicine and physiology, Robert Kurson describes May's most dangerous adventure, taking a combination of experimental drugs and undergoing cornea transplant surgery to recover his sight. Although the surgery was successful, May found adjustment to regained sight very difficult. A medical story that teaches readers much about human resilience.

1

> **Subjects:** Blindness; Eye Surgery; Group Discussion Books; May, Mike

> **Now Try:** *A Sense of the World: How a Blind Man Became History's Greatest Traveler* by Jason Roberts (see chapter 1) is another incredible tale about a man who did not let blindness limit his activities. Helen Keller overcame both blindness and deafness to become a writer and world traveler. She tells of her childhood and early accomplishments in *The Story of My Life*, and Joseph P. Lash completes the story in *Helen and Teacher: The Story of Helen Keller and Anne Sullivan Macy* (see chapter 4). Like May, Franklin Delano Roosevelt was a very ambitious man who took great risks with his fragile health. Many stories about the president are included in the epic biography *FDR* by Jean Edward Smith (see chapter 10). Baseball player Jim Abbott was born without a right hand, but overcame his handicap to enjoy a successful major league career. Bob Bernotas describes Abbott's life and career in *Nothing to Prove: The Jim Abbott Story*.

2

3

4

Martin, Russell

5

Beethoven's Hair: An Extraordinary Odyssey and a Scientific Mystery Solved. Broadway Books, 2000. 276p. ISBN 0767903501.

> By the time his coffin lid was secured, German composer Ludwig van Beethoven's (1770–1827) head was nearly shorn of hair, because the fans attending his wake had snipped locks as mementos. Though his later years had been difficult, beset by deafness, ill health, and depression, he still had many devoted followers. In this unusually constructed book, Russell Martin alternates chapters on the history and scientific analysis of one good-sized twist of the composer's hair sold at Sotheby's in 1994 with chapters on his life, death, and legacy.

6

7

> **Subjects:** Beethoven, Ludwig van; Composers; Death; Hair Analysis; Quick Reads; Teen Reads

> **Now Try:** Once he became deaf, Beethoven kept notebooks at hand for conducting written conversations with his visitors. Important portions of these notebooks are incorporated into *Beethoven: Letters, Journals, and Conversations*. Scientific analysis proving that Napoleon was poisoned plays a big part in the nonfiction mystery *Assassination at St. Helena Revisited* by Ben Weider. An analytical biography of a legendarily moody character is *Blake* by Peter Ackroyd (see chapter 7). Writing to help medical examiners, Philip A. Mackowiak revisits eight medical mysteries involving historical figures, including the Egyptian pharaoh Akhenaten, Christopher Columbus, Wolfgang Amadeus Mozart, and Booker T. Washington, in *Post Mortem: Solving History's Great Medical Mysteries*.

8

9

10

Nasar, Sylvia

11

🏵 *A Beautiful Mind: A Biography of John Forbes Nash, Jr., Winner of the Nobel Prize in Economics, 1994.* Simon & Schuster, 1998. 459p. ISBN 0684819066. Audiobook and large print available.

> Nonrational intuition was the source of mathematician John Forbes Nash Jr.'s (1928–) genius. In flashes he saw solutions to complex problems in

12

the fields of game theory, computer architecture, and geometry, becoming a famous MIT professor before he turned thirty. Trusting his flashes, however, turned against him, as he began to imagine extraterrestrials and a messianic mission that would make him a prince of peace, transforming his eccentric behavior into true insanity. In a sympathetic and admiring biography, economics reporter Sylvia Nasar chronicles how Nash woke from a thirty-year delusion to recover his cognitive abilities and win a Nobel Prize in economics.

Subjects: Group Discussion Books; Mathematicians; Nash, John Forbes, Jr.; Paranoia; Schizophrenia; Teen Reads

Awards: ALA Notable Books, National Book Critics Circle Award for Biography

Now Try: Nash's story inspired Rebecca Goldstein to write her philosophical novel *The Mind–Body Problem,* which tells a story similar to Nash's from the mathematician's wife's point of view. In *Love You to Bits and Pieces: Life with David Helfgott,* Gillian Helfgott describes her husband, a talented Australian pianist who after twelve years in hospitals recovered from a stress-induced mental breakdown. Alston Chase tells the story of mathematician Theodore John Kaczynski, whose mental illness became deadly in *Harvard and the Unabomber: The Education of an American Terrorist* (see chapter 2). Popular medical writer Oliver Sacks shares numerous mysterious stories about mental illness in his classic *The Man Who Mistook His Wife for a Hat and Other Clinical Tales.*

Invention Stories

Ever since people shaped sticks, bones, and rocks into tools, they have been fascinated by inventions. Fueled by the desire to work more productively and enjoy comfortable and interesting lives, they have supported innovation through the ages by buying the latest farming tools, personal effects, appliances, and electronic devices. Before the rise of corporations with research centers full of mostly unknown scientists, individuals designed and built most new products with an aim toward their own profit. Some of them, including Wilbur and Orville Wright, became quite rich and famous, qualities that interest many readers.

In this section are biographies of individuals who spent much of their lives tinkering with devices for which they risked their livelihoods and reputations. "Folly" was the word often used to describe Robert Fulton's steamboats and other inventions. Charles Goodyear and Thomas Hancock spent years reworking the processing of natural rubber in hopes of making it useful. Thomas Edison filed hundreds of patent registrations and became an international celebrity. For all of them, failure was more common than success.

Invention biographies might especially appeal to readers who imagine becoming rich and famous by inventing something that everyone wants to buy, but general readers, particularly those who are intellectually curious, enjoy these stories as well. Like other biographies in this chapter, scientific laws that explain the many details of the designing and testing of products may slow the reading pace. The nonfiction appeal of learning is also strong in these biographies.

> *Invention Stories* include biographies of creative people who applied science to make devices to improve human lives. Failure is as much a part of these stories as success, and the motive of profit is also usually present, making these detailed accounts a good choice for business and history readers as well as science readers. Some quick reads are available.

Kemp, Martin

Leonardo. Oxford University Press, 2004. 286p ISBN 0192805460.

Leonardo da Vinci (1452–1519) is the model of the Renaissance man, the figure who excels in many endeavors. Because of his talents as artist, architect, scientist, and engineer, his work was always in demand by wealthy patrons and government officials. He rarely turned down commissions, and as a result was often behind schedule. Leonardo scholar Martin Kemp believes his work was compromised by a lack of focus, but he was still remarkably innovative and influential. In a series of artful and illustrated biographical essays, the author distills the essence of the great man's inventive work and lasting legacy.

> **Subjects:** Architects; Inventors; Italy; Leonardo da Vinci; Scientists
>
> **Now Try:** A light, fact-filled look at Leonardo's career is the entertaining *101 Things You Didn't Know About Da Vinci: The Secrets of the World's Most Eccentric and Innovative Genius Revealed!* by Shana Priwer and Cynthia Phillips. Like Leonardo, physician and polymath Thomas Young was a sort of Renaissance man, talented in many fields. His work advanced the fields of medicine, optics, engineering, and linguistics. Andrew Robinson tells Young's story in *The Last Man Who Knew Everything: Thomas Young, the Anonymous Genius Who Proved Newton Wrong and Deciphered the Rosetta Stone, Among Other Surprising Feats.* Thesaurus writer Peter Mark Roget excelled in many areas but struggled with daily life. Joshua Kendall tells the story of his unusual life in *The Man Who Made Lists: Love, Death, Madness, and the Creation of Roget's Thesaurus* (see chapter 4). Science fiction author Isaac Asimov had a Leonardo-like interest in everything, writing nonfiction books about many topics, including science, religion, and humor. He recounted his career in *It's Been a Good Life.*

Sale, Kirkpatrick

The Fire of His Genius: Robert Fulton and the American Dream. Free Press, 2001. 242p. ISBN 068486715X.

When throngs of New Yorkers crowded the wharves of Manhattan in August 1807, some hoped to see the latest invention of Robert Fulton (1765–1815) explode. Fulton's torpedo demonstration in July of that year had been an entertaining and embarrassing failure, and "Fulton's Folly" was already a familiar phrase on lips and in newsprint. The steamship *North River*, however, performed well at a speedy four miles per hour, and the sometimes ridiculed maritime engineer was proclaimed a hero. According to author Kirkpatrick Sale, Fulton's steamboat played a vital role in American westward expansion, but the contentious inventor failed to protect his patents and died in financial distress. A tragic account of a flawed individual whose life reflected his times.

> **Subjects:** Engineers; Fulton, Robert; Inventors; Steamboats

> **Now Try:** Magician Harry Houdini marketed himself through public display, as did Fulton before him. Like Fulton, his short life was closely followed by the press and fans. William Kalush and Larry Sloman tell the magician's sad story in *The Secret Life of Houdini: The Making of America's First Superhero* (see chapter 5). Jesse Livermore worked his way up from chalkboard boy at Paine Webber in Boston to become a full trader at the New York Stock Exchange. Richard Smitten describes him as a tragically flawed modern man in his novelistic biography *Jesse Livermore: World's Greatest Stock Trader* (see chapter 9). Like Fulton, author Nathaniel Hawthorn had many expectations that he never realized. Brenda Wineapple portrays the author of stories of New England as a maddeningly complex man filled with conflicting values, much like the age in which he lived, in *Hawthorne: A Life* (see chapter 7). Ornithologist and painter John James Audubon was a Fuller contemporary who also lacked business acumen. Richard Rhodes details Audubon's daily life in *John James Audubon: The Making of an American* (see chapter 1).

Silverman, Kenneth

Lightning Man: The Accursed Life of Samuel F. B. Morse. Knopf, 2003. 503p. ISBN 0375401288.

Samuel F. B. Morse (1791–1872) was the son of Jedidiah Morse, a nationally known Congregationalist minister and geographer. Sent to the best schools, the young man was expected to succeed as his father had, which he did as a painter, early photographer, and inventor. His greatest fame came from his development of the telegraph. His problems, however, sprang from his lack of business sense and inability to make and keep friends. He repeatedly found himself in court defending patents and trying to stave off bankruptcy. His name was also often in the news for making offensive statements about immigrants and Roman Catholics. In this candid biography, Kenneth Silverman shows Morse as an advocate of technical progress who exhibited all that was good and bad about society during the Industrial Revolution.

> **Subjects:** Inventors; Morse, Samuel F. B.; Painters; Telegraph

> **Now Try:** Morse was convinced that the Vatican in Rome was plotting an overthrow of the U.S. government and wrote *Foreign Conspiracy Against the Liberties of the United States*. David Lindley tells about another man of science whose prejudices and inability to compromise led to his downfall in *Degrees Kelvin: A Tale of Genius, Invention, and Tragedy* (see this chapter). Charles Revson was a mean-spirited man who had a good sense for the invention of consumer products. Andrew Tobias describes his gossip-filled life in *Fire and Ice: The Story of Charles Revson—the Man Who Built the Revlon Empire* (see chapter 5). Baseball player Joe DiMaggio was another antisocial character, despite his great popularity among fans. Richard Ben Cramer recounts the outfielder's career in *Joe DiMaggio: The Hero's Life* (see chapter 12).

Slack, Charles

Noble Obsession: Charles Goodyear, Thomas Hancock, and the Race to Unlock the Greatest Industrial Secret of the Nineteenth Century. Theia, 2002. 274p. ISBN 0786867892. Audiobook available.

The American Charles Goodyear (1800-1860) and the Englishman Thomas Hancock (1823–1871) could hardly have been more different. Goodyear was a struggling inventor whose financial mistakes had kept his family poor and landed him in jail. Hancock was a successful businessman living well off his inventions. What they shared was an obsession to perfect rubber so that it could be used for many industrial purposes. According to journalist Charles Slack, the discovery of the secret process brought the men into a conflict that resulted in a famous trial on which the fortunes of the rubber industry depended.

Subjects: Dual Biography; Goodyear, Charles; Hancock, Thomas; Inventors; Quick Reads; Rubber

Now Try: Physicists Subrahmanyan Chandrasekhar and Sir Arthur Eddington publicly sparred over the existence of black holes created by the collapse of dying stars, in a rivalry that was colored by the decline of the British Empire. Arthur I. Miller shares an important story about how scientific progress was subverted by the Englishman's need to prevail over the colonial subject in *Empire of the Stars: Obsession, Friendship, and Betrayal in the Quest for Black Holes*. Charles Darwin and Alfred Russel Wallace partook in a competition that was more cordial on the surface, but about which there is still controversy. David Quammen describes their race to explain the evolution of species in *The Reluctant Mr. Darwin: An Intimate Portrait of Charles Darwin and the Making of His Theory of Evolution* (see this chapter). Although the ideal is that cooperation drives scientific advancement, rivalry sometimes exists. Michael White describes some of the bitterest fights in science in *Acid Tongues and Tranquil Dreamers: Eight Scientific Rivalries That Changed the World*. In 1894 the plague broke out in Hong Kong and rival medical researchers sought its source. In *Plague: A Story of Science, Rivalry, and the Scourge That Won't Go Away*, Edward Marriott reveals that the wrong scientist with the wrong answer was praised by public officials for discovering the disease's cause.

Sobel, Dava

Longitude: The True Story of a Lone Genius Who Solved the Greatest Scientific Problem of His Time. Walker, 1995. 184p. ISBN 0802713122. Audiobook and large print available.

As a teenager Carpenter John Harrison (1693–1776) taught himself to make clocks. When he learned that the British Parliament was offering a prize of £20,000 for a device or method to measure meridians of longitude, he took up the challenge. While the jury of peers from Parliament waited for clever devices to locate ships by the stars, Harrison perfected a clock that would keep correct time at sea, unaffected by the motion of waves. Knowing London time and noting noon on the ship, sea captains could calculate their longitude. According to science reporter Dava Sobel, prejudice within the jury toward mechanics and the lower classes kept Harrison from claiming the prize for nearly forty years.

Subjects: Chronometers; Clock and Watch Makers; Great Britain; Group Discussion Books; Harrison, John; Inventors; Longitude; Teen Reads

Now Try: The largest prizes in science come from the Nobel Foundation in Sweden. Medical researcher J. Michael Bishop recounts the institution's history and his own career in *How to Win the Nobel Prize: An Unexpected Life in Science*. Julia Child patiently and persistently applied to culinary schools in France when they only admitted men. Laura Shapiro recounts how Child's efforts paid off in *Julia Child*. Josiah Wedgwood, another self-taught English inventor, was much better rewarded for his work than Harrison was. Brian Dolan tells of his rise from craftsman to industrialist in *Wedgwood: The First Tycoon* (see chapter 9). Author John D. McDonald was a persistent man who continued to write crime stories despite low sales and little recognition. Hugh Merrill tells how McDonald finally won acclaim in *The Red Hot Typewriter: The Life and Times of John D. MacDonald*.

Stross, Randall

The Wizard of Menlo Park: How Thomas Alva Edison Invented the Modern World. Crown, 2007. 376p. ISBN 9781400047628.

Thomas Alva Edison (1847–1931) was not only an important inventor but also a great promoter. He managed to stir up great interest in his inventions and thus earn more attention than most other scientists and inventors. When fame "went to his head," he became an industrialist with a self-defeating inclination to manage his companies alone, dismissing the advice of consultants. According to Randall Stross, Edison made a series of terrible decisions. Some of his products, such as concrete furniture, failed to attract customers; others proved difficult to manufacture in profitable quantities. Nevertheless, he retained celebrity status and made friends with powerful manufacturers Harvey Firestone and Henry Ford. In this candid narrative, Stross tells a fascinating story of genius sometimes wasted.

> **Subjects:** Edison, Thomas Alva; Electrical Engineers; Group Discussion Books; Industrialists; Inventors
>
> **Now Try:** Edison wrote a memoir, *Diary and Sundry Observations of Thomas Alva Edison*. Milton S. Hershey had trouble selling his innovative confections until he turned his attention to chocolate. His rags to riches story is told in *Hershey: Milton S. Hershey's Extraordinary Life of Wealth, Empire, and Utopian Dreams* by Michael D'Antonio. Croatian immigrant Nikola Tesla was one of Edison's main rivals in the contest to develop commercial electricity. His story of failure and injustice is told by Marc Seifer in *Wizard: The Life and Times of Nikola Tesla: Biography of a Genius*. Edison contemporary George Washington Carver also became a celebrity scientist, but Jim Crow Laws kept him from eating at restaurants with the white scientists with whom he met and worked. His story is told in *George Washington Carver: Scientist and Symbol* by Linda O. McMurry.

Tobin, James

To Conquer the Air: The Wright Brothers and the Great Race for Flight. Free Press, 2003. 433p. ISBN 0684856883. Audiobook and large print available.

Aeronautical pioneers Wilbur Wright (1867–1912) and Orville Wright (1871–1948) were not instantly acclaimed the victors in the race to fly mechanically after their very short flights at Kitty Hawk, North Carolina, in 1903. Famous and better-funded men wanted the honor and were unwilling to concede that they had been beaten. The brothers had to defend their claims with public demonstrations, which they did repeatedly until 1910, when they were recognized as first and were awarded the Langley Medal, ironically named for one of their rivals. In this elegantly written biography that will especially please history buffs, James Tobin intimately describes the close but sometimes prickly working relationship of the ambitious brothers in the context of the struggle for scientific achievement.

Subjects: Aeronautics; Dual Biography; Flight; Inventors; Wright, Orville; Wright, Wilbur

Now Try: Late in his life, Orville Wright wrote *How We Invented the Airplane*, a small book about the brothers' efforts to fly. Letters and other writings from both brothers are found in *Published Writings of Wilbur and Orville Wright*. Novelist Louisa May Alcott and her father Bronson Alcott had a more adversarial relationship than the Wright brothers, but the daughter drew much of her insight and drive from her parent. Readers who like family relationship stories will enjoy *Eden's Outcasts: The Story of Louisa May Alcott and Her Father* by John Matteson (see chapter 9). A contest among rivals to solve a scientific problem is also the theme in *Longitude: The True Story of a Lone Genius Who Solved the Greatest Scientific Problem of His Time* by Dava Sobel (see this section). King Richard the Lionhearted and his brother John struggled over the throne of England. Their rivalry is described in *Richard and John: Kings at War* by Frank McLynn.

Science on the Edge

Testing the forces of nature can be dangerous in many ways. Scientists work with volatile materials, powerful equipment, or poisonous plants and animals, and their work may take them to dangerous places. Perhaps the most danger occurs when scientific work offends powerful people who want it suppressed at any cost.

Biographies in which the lives of the scientists or others were threatened by physical, political, or military forces are described in this section. Physicists Marie and Pierre Curie studied deadly radiation; mineralogist James Smithson flew early hot air balloons and aided the French Revolution. Naturalist and astronomer Roger Bacon was charged with sorcery and imprisoned by church authorities. During World War II, German rocket engineer Wernher von Braun worked with volatile fuels within the confines of secretive Nazi laboratories, while others in this section worked in the United States on the Manhattan Project, developing an atomic bomb.

The characters in the biographies in this section were strong individuals who overcame their fears to continue with their work. Some, including physicist Richard Feynman and stockbroker turned secret scientist Alfred Lee Loomis, even exhibited a love for risky behavior. Their stories are filled with dramatic tension in dangerous settings. The pace of some of these books is slow, because the authors explain the science as well as building the suspense. Readers who persevere will learn much about history as well as science.

Science on the Edge stories include biographies in which the lives of the scientists or entire population were threatened by their research and how it could be applied. Because of the dangers, tension and suspense are common to these stories. Consider these books for readers who enjoy suspense and intrigue.

1
2
3
4
5
6
7
8
9
10

11
12

Bird, Kai, and Martin J. Sherwin

🎗 *American Prometheus: The Triumph and Tragedy of J. Robert Oppenheimer.* Knopf, 2005. 721p. ISBN 0375412026. Audiobook available.

After World War II, physicist J. Robert Oppenheimer (1904–1967) had second thoughts about the Manhattan Project, which he expressed in public. He asserted that atomic weapons, which he helped to create, endangered the country and needed to be eliminated. In Cold War America, with J. Edgar Hoover and Senator Joseph McCarthy leading efforts to cleanse the country of "un-American activities," Oppenheimer's honesty proved to be political suicide. Kai Bird and Martin J. Sherwin profile this admirable atomic scientist and policy advisor as a man of conscience in a dark period of American history.

Subjects: Atomic Bomb; Cold War; Oppenheimer, Robert J.; Physicists

Awards: National Book Critics Circle Award for Biography; Pulitzer Prize for Biography

Now Try: Oppenheimer left no memoir, but his letters are available in *Robert Oppenheimer: Letters and Recollections*. Judge Samuel Sewall of Salem in the Massachusetts Bay Colony had second thoughts about his role in the witch trials of 1692. Eve LaPlante tells how the people of New England refused to listen to his confession in *Salem Witch Judge: The Life and Repentance of Samuel Sewall* (see chapter 4). German art dealer Ernst Hanfstaengl, ashamed of his association with Adolf Hitler, defected to the Allies to deliver German military secrets. Peter Conradi tells how he was deported back to a homeland that shunned him after the war in *Hitler's Piano Player: The Rise and Fall of Ernst Hanfstaengl, Confidant of Hitler, Ally of FDR* (see chapter 3). Famed African explorer Henry Morton Stanley felt that he had erred in helping King Leopold of Belgium claim the rubber-rich lands of the Congo. Tim Jeal portrays Stanley as a contrite man in *Stanley: The Impossible Life of Africa's Greatest Explorer* (see chapter 1).

Brian, Denis

The Curies: A Biography of the Most Controversial Family in Science. John Wiley, 2005. 438p. ISBN 9780471273912.

It was difficult for a woman to break into the fraternity of science in nineteenth-century Paris. But when Marie Sklodowska (1867–1934) was invited to a tea party by her physics professor, a fellow Pole, she hoped to find a scientific partner. There she met Pierre Curie, son and grandson of successful physicians. The two worked together, married, and won six Nobel Prizes in physics and chemistry while studying dangerous radiation. Denis Brian tells how Marie, Pierre, and their family, though attacked as communists and financially insecure, achieved world renown in chemistry, physics, mathematics, journalism, and peace advocacy. A fascinating chronicle of the Curie family, and an interesting family saga.

Subjects: Chemists; Curie, Marie; Curie, Pierre; Family Biography; Paris; Physicists

Now Try: Eve Curie wrote an admiring biography of her mother, *Madame Curie: A Biography*, and Marie Curie wrote a tribute to her husband, *Pierre Curie*. Shunned for religious rather than political reasons, members of the Warburg family were German bankers for generations. Their epic story is told by popular business biographer Ron Chernow in *The Warburgs: The Twentieth Century Odyssey of a Remarkable Jewish Family* (see chapter 9). A family saga with racial barriers as the challenge to prosperity is *The Sweet Hell Inside: A Family History* by Edward Ball (see chapter 9). Beatle John Lennon and artist Yoko Ono attracted much controversy about their art and political protests, including their sleep-in to protest the Vietnam War. The staff of *Rolling Stone* assembled articles from the magazine about the couple in the dual biography *The Ballad of John and Yoko.*

Clegg, Brian

The First Scientist: A Life of Roger Bacon. Carroll & Graf, 2003. 244p. ISBN 0786711167.

The life of scientist Roger Bacon (1214–1294) was dangerous. He became a Franciscan monk to assure his livelihood and to gain access to the religious order's library; but his position as a cleric limited his ability to report his findings on nature, mathematics, astronomy, and optics, some of which contradicted church dogma. Brian Clegg describes how Bacon, who should be credited with the development of the scientific method, served ten years in prison for sorcery, and was mostly forgotten until his papers were translated in the nineteenth century. Readers will enjoy this sympathetic account of a man far ahead of his time.

Subjects: Astronomers; Bacon, Roger; Mathematicians; Monks

Now Try: For Jack Repcheck, the man to whom all scientists owe a debt is Nicolaus Copernicus. In *Copernicus' Secret: How the Scientific Revolution Began,* Repcheck credits Georg Joachim Rheticus, a Lutheran minister, for giving Copernicus the final mathematical data he needed to successfully challenge church scholars. In *It Started with Copernicus: How Turning the World Inside Out Led to the Scientific Revolution,* Howard Margolis asserts that accepting that the earth rotated around the sun, in defiance of church teachings, was the key victory of science over religious suppression of knowledge. English statesman Thomas More tried to avoid prison and death by simply not stating his views on controversial topics, but Henry VIII forced him to reveal his opposition to the king's divorce. His tragic story is told in *The Life of Thomas More* by Peter Ackroyd (see chapter 4). Readers who like books that recover stories about mostly forgotten historical figures may enjoy *Malory: The Knight Who Became King Arthur's Chronicler* by Christina Hardyman (see chapter 5).

Conant, Jennet

Tuxedo Park: A Wall Street Tycoon and the Secret Palace of Science That Changed the Course of World War II. Simon & Schuster, 2002. 330p. ISBN 0684872870. Large print available.

The story of Alfred Lee Loomis (1887–1975) sounds like a 1940s Hollywood movie plot, something for a Saturday afternoon matinee. The handsome millionaire stockbroker kept a secret laboratory in his fabulous mansion, where he met with great scientists to invent devices to save the world from the Nazis. When he wasn't at a night club or on his yacht with attractive women, he was meeting with Albert Einstein, Niels Bohr, or Enrico Fermi about designing radar and atomic bombs. According to Jennet Conant, this entertaining and adventurous story about Loomis leading a double life of financial business by day and dangerous science by night is true.

Subjects: Atomic Bomb; Loomis, Alfred Lee; Physicists; Radar; Stockbrokers; Teen Reads; World War II

Now Try: World War I flying ace Eddie Rickenbacker was also able to mix defense of the country with business. H. Paul Jeffers chronicles the pilot's adventures in *Ace of Aces: The Life of Capt. Eddie Rickenbacker* (see chapter 1). Somerset Maugham was a debonair British novelist who traveled the world in the service of his country as a spy. Jeffrey Meyers combines elements of the adventure story with celebrity reporting and psychological insight in his profile of a major literary figure of the first half of the twentieth century in *Somerset Maugham: A Life* (see chapter 7). Shakespeare's contemporary, playwright Christopher Marlowe, was also a spy. His life and death are described in *Christopher Marlowe: Poet & Spy* by Park Honan. Not all of the citizens drawn into the effort to win World War II came from the upper classes. Ben Macintyre describes the life and character of small-time crook Edward Arnold Chapman, who became a double agent for MI5, in *Agent Zigzag: A True Story of Nazi Espionage, Love, and Betrayal* (see chapter 3).

Connor, James A.

Kepler's Witch: An Astronomer's Discovery of Cosmic Order Amid Religious War, Political Intrigue, and the Heresy Trial of His Mother. HarperSanFrancisco, 2004. 402p. ISBN 0060522550.

The astronomer Johannes Kepler (1571–1630) is known for his discovery of the three laws of planetary motion, advances in calculus, and study of the optics of telescopes and cameras. What is not remembered is that he was a man of peace and conscience in a time of religious warfare. His efforts to befriend both Catholics and Protestants led to his eventual marginalization. In this sympathetic biography, religious author James A. Connor takes readers back to the early seventeenth century to follow Kepler's career and to attend his mother's dramatic trial for witchcraft. Knowledge of scientific principles is not needed to enjoy this admiring biography.

Subjects: Astronomers; Germany; Kepler, Johannes; Thirty Years War; Witchcraft

Now Try: In *Galileo's Daughter: A Historical Memoir of Science, Faith, and Love* (see chapter 9), Dava Sobel uses letters from Galileo's daughter Maria Celeste to show how the Italian astronomer tried to faithfully discover scientific truth while being closely watched by religious authorities. In *Salem Witch Judge: The Life and Repentance of Samuel Sewall*, Eve LaPlante (see chapter 4) tells another dramatic story involving religious intolerance and court proceedings. A more modern trial of science in the courts of law and public opinion involved the teaching of evolution in Tennessee schools. Michael Kazin explains the role of populist politician William Jennings Bryan in the highly publicized Scopes trial in *A Godly Hero: The Life of William Jennings Bryan* (see chapter 10). Sir Isaac Newton enjoyed more comfort and security when he studied optics and physics. David Berlinski chronicles the great scientist's achievements in *Newton's Gift: How Sir Isaac Newton Unlocked the Systems of the World* (see this chapter).

Ewing, Heather

The Lost World of James Smithson: Science, Revolution, and the Birth of the Smithsonian. Bloomsbury, 2007. 432p. ISBN 9781596910294.

British mineralogist James Smithson (1765–1829), who left his fortune to the U.S. government to found the Smithsonian Museum, has long been thought to have been a quiet, unsocial man, mostly because there was so little known about him other than the twenty-seven scientific papers that he published. Heather Ewing has unearthed his letters, legal documents, bank accounts, and other papers that dramatically change the story. An illegitimate son known as John Louis Macie until he was thirty-five, Smithson was an adventurous scientist who cheered the French Revolution and flew in early balloons.

Subjects: Macie, John Louis; Mineralogists; Philanthropists; Smithson, James

Now Try: The renowned artist and ornithologist John James Audubon was another adventurous European of suspect parentage who enriched American scientific heritage. Richard Rhodes tells his admiring but somewhat sad story in *John James Audubon: The Making of an American* (see chapter 1). Thomas Paine also fled England, supported the French Revolution, and left a political legacy in the United States. Using newly discovered documents, Craig Nelson recounts the life of a visionary man in *Thomas Paine: Enlightenment, Revolution, and the Birth of Modern Nations* (see chapter 10). British hydrologist and naturalist William Dampier was a pirate who charted ocean currents and described exotic birds when not attacking Spanish treasure ships. Diana Preston and Michael Preston describe him as a man who escaped prosecution for his crimes simply because he was a friend of eminent people, in *A Pirate of Exquisite Mind: Explorer, Naturalist, and Buccaneer: The Life of William Dampier* (see chapter 1). When Smithson left his legacy to the United States, most of the members of Congress had no idea what should be done with the funds to build a museum. Senior Congressman John Quincy Adams led the effort to honor the bequest. Adams's role in the formation of the Smithsonian is told in *Mr. Adams's Last Crusade: John Quincy Adams's Extraordinary Post-Presidential Life in Congress* by Joseph Wheelan (see chapter 10).

Gleick, James

Genius: The Life and Science of Richard Feynman. Pantheon, 1992. 532p. ISBN 9780679408369. Audiobook available.

Physicist Richard Feynman (1918–1988) was a free spirit and an unlikely person to be a member of the Manhattan Project, where secrecy and decorum were necessary. His antics and weird interests disturbed other physicists at Los Alamos, but his knowledge and insight were essential for the development of the atomic bomb. After his wartime work he became a leading researcher in the field of quantum electrodynamics, taught at Caltech, wrote popular books on physics, and was awarded a Nobel Prize in physics. Credited with inventing quantum computing and nanotechnology, he also played bongos and studied throat singing in the remote Asian region of Tuva. James Gleick includes some challenging physics in this entertaining telling of Feynman's life, which will appeal to science buffs and those who enjoy offbeat characters.

Subjects: Atomic Bomb; Feynman, Richard; Physicists; Quantum Physics

Now Try: In *Surely You're Joking, Mr. Feynman: Adventures of a Curious Character* and *What Do You Care What Other People Think: Further Adventures of a Curious Character*, Feynman tells entertaining stories about his life as a physicist working on top secret projects during and after World War II. Another charismatic figure during Feynman's time was astronomer Carl Sagan. William Poundstone profiles Sagan as a passionate man who believed there are other intelligent life forms in the universe in *Carl Sagan: A Life in the Cosmos* (see this chapter). Cartoonist, children's author, and songwriter Shel Silverstein was another energetic free spirit who was praised for his work in many fields. Lisa Rogak describes his nomadic life in *A Boy Named Shel: The Life and Times of Shel Silverstein* (see chapter 7). Like Feynman, naturalist and broadcaster William Beebe had a knack for scientific discovery and entertaining the public through mass media. His adventurous story is told in *The Remarkable Life of William Beebe: Explorer and Naturalist* by Carol Grant Gould (see chapter 1).

Goodchild, Peter

Edward Teller: The Real Dr. Strangelove. Harvard University Press, 2004. 469p. ISBN 0674016696.

Physicist Edward Teller (1908–2003) strongly objected to reporters asking about his resemblance to the evil scientist in Stanley Kubrick's film *Dr. Strangelove*. Understandably disliking the comparisons, he always turned conversations to his grand schemes to use atomic power for electricity and civil engineering projects. Although sympathetic to the discomfort that Teller felt in these situations, journalist Peter Goodchild claims the similarities between fact and fiction were quite striking. In this critical biography, he tells the controversial Hungarian scientist's story and points out that Teller was not the man of peace he purported to be, always opposing test ban treaties and actively planning the next war.

Subjects: Atomic Bomb; Group Discussion Books; Immigrants; Physicists; Teller, Edward

Now Try: Teller wrote many books that would make good book discussions, including *Better a Shield Than a Sword: Perspectives on the Defense and Technology* and *Conversations on the Dark Secrets of Physics*. Teller described his childhood in Hungary, his work on weapons programs, and personal life in *Memoirs: A Twentieth-Century Journey in Science and Politics*. Through his best-selling books and frequent lectures, former president Richard M. Nixon was able to regain some of his stature in the two decades after the Watergate scandal. Anthony Summers reminds readers why the California politician made so many enemies in *The Arrogance of Power: The Secret World of Richard Nixon* (see chapter 5). Railroad baron Jay Gould was another controversial figure whose dishonest actions helped shape our country. Edward J. Renehan Jr. draws a surprisingly sympathetic portrait in *Dark Genius of Wall Street: The Misunderstood Life of Jay Gould, King of the Robber Barons* (see chapter 9).

Isaacson, Walter

🌶 *Einstein: His Life and Universe.* Simon & Schuster, 2007. 675p. ISBN 9780-743264730. Audiobook and large print available.

Albert Einstein (1879–1955) was a key figure in the first half of the twentieth century. Not only did he pose revolutionary theories in physics, he also became involved in many of the public issues of his time. Frequently moving among European countries, he renounced nationalism and claimed to be a citizen of the world. He supported Jewish settlement in Palestine but opposed the formation of a Jewish state. He preached pacifism until the Nazis took control of Germany. A low-paid patent clerk and totally unknown as a scientist in 1905, unable to get an academic appointment, he wrote five brilliant articles that challenged Newtonian physics and became the basis of the science of quantum physics and the concept of relativity. According to Walter Isaacson, Einstein struggled to live an ethical life.

Readers do not have to understand the science to enjoy this epic biography of a great man.

1

> **Subjects:** Einstein, Albert; Group Discussion Books; Immigrants; Jews; Pacifists; Physicists
>
> **Awards:** ALA Notable Books
>
> **Now Try:** Modern Library has published a selective collection of Einstein's writings and speeches as *Ideas and Opinions*. Many hours can be spent reading *The New Quotable Einstein*. When Einstein died, Dr. Thomas Harvey kept his brain for study. Michael Paterniti describes efforts to return the brain to its rightful owner in *Driving Mr. Albert: A Trip Across America with Einstein's Brain*. Readers who enjoy epic biographies of larger-than-life characters may wish to read *Theodore Rex* by Edmund Morris (see chapter 10) or *John Adams* by David McCullough (see chapter 10). Each defines its hero with stories and evocative descriptions. Like Einstein, Sigmund Freud became a symbol of scientific achievement. Peter D. Kramer tells a concise story of his life and legacy in *Freud: Inventor of the Modern Mind* (see this chapter).

2

3

4

Neufeld, Michael J.

Von Braun: Dreamer of Space, Engineer of War. Knopf, 2007. 587p. ISBN 9780-307262929.

5

A 2003 poll of readers of *Aviation Week and Space Technology* named Wernher von Braun (1912–1977) second only to the Wright Brothers in importance in the history of flight. A rocket specialist who designed missiles for the German Army in World War II, von Braun surrendered to U.S. troops at the end of the war and soon became a key figure in the American space program of the 1950s and 1960s, despite his shadowy past. Years after his death in 1977, the public learned about his membership in the Nazi Party and the use of concentration camp labor on his projects. In this thorough telling of the German engineer's life, Michael J. Neufeld weighs the Jekyll and Hyde aspects of von Braun's life.

6

7

> **Subjects:** Astronautical Engineers; Germany; Nazi Party; Rocketry; Von Braun, Wernher
>
> **Now Try:** Early in the U.S. space program, von Braun entertained the American public with his futuristic books *The Exploration of Mars* and *First Men on the Moon*. During his life he published three editions of *The History of Rocketry & Space Travel*. Homer H. Hickam Jr. was a reader of these books. He tells how he and a group of friends from Coalwood, West Virginia, built their own experimental rockets in *Rocket Boys: A Memoir*. When psychoanalyst Bruno Bettelheim escaped the Nazis before the Second World War, he faked many of his credentials to get an American academic appointment. Richard Pollak reveals a life filled with secrets in *The Creation of Dr. B: A Biography of Bruno Bettelheim* (see chapter 5). Another exposé about an important figure in the history of the aerospace industry is *Howard Hughes: The Secret Life* by Charles Higham (see chapter 5).

8

9

10

11

12

Pringle, Peter

The Murder of Nikolai Vavilov: The Story of Stalin's Persecution of One of the Great Scientists of the Twentieth Century. Simon & Schuster, 2008. 368p. ISBN 9780743264983.

Russian plant geneticist Nikolai Vavilov (1887–1943) was already a promising young agricultural scientist when the Russian Revolution overthrew the tsar in 1917. While other scientists abandoned the country to escape the violence and find jobs in Europe and America, Vavilov stayed to work for Vladimir Lenin's agricultural initiative, eventually becoming director of the Bureau of Applied Botany. There he established a seed bank from which he hoped to improve Soviet crop species. According to Peter Pringle, all of Vavilov's progress was lost when Joseph Stalin collectivized private farms and demanded that the geneticist produce bounteous crops immediately. Unable to meet this demand, Vavilov was sent to prison, where he starved to death. Pringle documents a dark time in Soviet history in this admiring biography.

> **Subjects:** Botanists; Plant Breeding; Soviet Union; Vavilov, Nikolai Ivanovich

> **Now Try:** Ray Moseley tells another story about a high-level bureaucrat whose life was ruined by associating with a dictator in *Mussolini's Shadow: The Double Life of Count Galeazzo Ciano* (see chapter 3). Those who enjoy reading about characters involved in dangerous power struggles will appreciate *Machiavelli: Philosopher of Power* by Ross King (see chapter 10). Plasma physicist Roald Z. Sagdeev was a Soviet scientist after the time of Nikolai Vavilov. He tells how cooperation in space led to other fields of Soviet–American cooperation in his autobiography, *Making of a Soviet Scientist: My Adventures in Nuclear Fusion and Space from Stalin to Star Wars*. The reputation of Soviet dictator Joseph Stalin rose and fell in the West over time. Simon Sebag Montefiore tells how he discovered that before Stalin became a leading revolutionary, he had been a notorious gangster, in his exposé *Young Stalin* (see chapter 6).

Consider Starting With . . .

These well-written scientific biographies of modest length will appeal to general readers.

- Berlinski, David. *Newton's Gift: How Sir Isaac Newton Unlocked the Systems of the World.*

- Hayes, Bill. *The Anatomist: A True Story of Gray's Anatomy.*

- Kluger, Jeffrey. *Splendid Solution: Jonas Salk and the Conquest of Polio.*

- Kurson, Robert. *Crashing Through: A True Story of Risk, Adventure, and the Man Who Dared to See.*

- Nasar, Sylvia. *A Beautiful Mind: A Biography of John Forbes Nash, Jr., Winner of the Nobel Prize in Economics, 1994.*

- Quammen, David. *The Reluctant Mr. Darwin: An Intimate Portrait of Charles Darwin and the Making of His Theory of Evolution.*

- Ridley, Matt. *Francis Crick: Discoverer of the Genetic Code.*

- Sobel, Dava. *Longitude: The True Story of a Lone Genius Who Solved the Greatest Scientific Problem of His Time.*

- Winchester, Simon. *The Map That Changed the World: William Smith and the Birth of Modern Geology.*

Further Reading

Adamson, Lynda G.

Thematic Guide to Popular Nonfiction. Greenwood Press, 2006. 352p. ISBN 0313-328552.

Adamson includes chapters about the mind, rocket science, and technology in her book about nonfiction topics. Each chapter describes a topic and then presents three lengthy reviews before suggesting other titles.

Cords, Sarah Statz

The Real Story: A Guide to Nonfiction Reading Interests. Libraries Unlimited, 2006. 460p. ISBN 1591582830.

In chapter 5 Cords covers science and math narratives, describing the genres and reviewing popular titles.

Wyatt, Neal

The Readers' Advisory Guide to Nonfiction. American Libraries, 2007. 318p. ISBN 9780838909362.

Wyatt discusses science, mathematics, and nature in chapter 4 of her book. In her discussions she identifies key authors and includes generous lists of titles to recommend to readers.

1

2

3

4

5

6

7

8

9

10

11

12

Chapter 12

Sports Biography

Definition of Sports Biography

Sports Biographies are stories about people who excel at and are well-known for their participation in athletic games. Athletes who compete and the coaches who direct the play of athletes are often the subjects of these biographies.

The tradition of honoring winning athletes goes back at least as far as the Olympic games in ancient Greece. Victors were given laurels and their names were proclaimed across the city-states of the peninsula. Similar traditions have continued throughout history, from ancient Roman contests in the Coliseum, to tournaments between medieval knights, to today's Super Bowl. However, the names of the ancient Olympic champions, Roman gladiators, medieval knights, and most of the victors since their times are now known only by scholars studying historic cultures. The first athletes to be remembered by many in our culture are the pioneers of professional sports, whose names are repeated often in sports histories and televised sports documentaries.

Professional sports as we now know them arose in the latter half of the nineteenth century, when advances in industry and the economy gave more people leisure time to play sports and to attend games played by local champions. Railroads allowed teams to travel between cities to play other teams, and leagues were formed. Telegraphs allowed scores and game reports to be sent around the country, and some sportsmen became nationally known. Now, with archives of nineteenth- and early twentieth-century newspapers and historical documents digitized and more accessible, biographers may readily reconstruct the lives of these revered sports heroes. Baseball player and manager Connie Mack, football legend Red Grange, and Olympic champion Jim Thorpe are examples of subjects of recent Sports Biographies that may be found in bookstores and libraries along with books about living sports personalities, such as basketball's Michael Jordan and golf's Arnold Palmer.

Sports Biographies are stories about the lives of individuals who compete in athletic games. The authors of these books describe the training of the athletes, the action of the games, and the rewards and trials of being competitors. The love of sports attracts many readers to these books featuring many well-known athletes.

Appeal of the Genre

It's no exaggeration to say that Americans are sports-obsessed. According to Robert Jacobson in *Sports in America: Recreation, Business, Education, and Controversy*, nearly seventy-five million people attended major league baseball games in 2005; sixty-four percent of the American public claim to be fans of professional football; over twenty-five million people golfed in 2004; and nearly $23 billion were spent on sporting goods in 2004. Americans read about sports in their newspapers and magazines, keep up with scores and news on the Internet and on their handheld devices, and watch countless games on television. For many Americans, sports are a daily interest, and a sports book next to the recliner or on the nightstand is a familiar sight.

Sports books in general and Sports Biographies in particular emphasize character. In these books athletes and their coaches always have a challenge to meet, whether in the form of a champion to beat, an opposing team to play, or a record to break. To meet the challenge, they must not only train to get their bodies in shape and their athletic skills honed; they must prepare mentally. In our world of rapid communications and twenty-four-hour news, sports figures have become celebrities with big contracts, fashionable clothes, and many fans. Reporters watch and interview professional athletes and world class amateurs as they train before highly advertised events; then broadcasters and sports analysts are on the sidelines ready to comment as soon as games end. If an athlete performs admirably, he or she is held up as a role model; if he or she breaks the rules, the broadcast world spreads the news with critical commentary. Present and future biographers have a wealth of primary evidence from which to learn about the athletes' desire, drive, doubts, and disappointments.

But Sports Biographies are not just about characters. They include many compelling stories. The authors recount inspiring success stories—how the athletes developed their talent, the hardships they overcame, and the opportunities they recognized when others did not. Included are lively descriptions of the games that they played, accounting for every significant move. And of course, readers can also find heart-rending tragedies in Sports Biography. Even when the reader knows the outcome, the stories are infused with drama.

Setting can be a significant part of the Sports Biography as well. Sports stories are set in fields, stadiums, boxing arenas, golf courses, and racetracks—all public gathering places. The crowd lends drama to the games that would be mere personal contests if unnoticed and unreported. Readers who have attended games may quickly recognize the settings and add their own memories to the emotional content of the stories.

The pace of Sports Biographies varies. Those relying more on the accounts of races and games may be fast paced, whereas those that dwell on the preparation of the individual through training may be unhurried.

In an age when many athletes have been accused of self-absorption, greed, drug use, and cheating, some argue that sports figures should not be held up as role models. Most fans pay no attention to this criticism. Readers continue to read sports books for their lessons on life, knowing that some stories are models to emulate, while others are cautionary tales.

Organization of the Chapter

The first section of this chapter, "Sports Celebrities," is a collection of titles about top athletes who excelled at their sports and garnered extensive public attention. Some of the most recognized names in sports are found in this section, including Babe Ruth, Jack Dempsey, and Michael Jordan.

The second section, "Role Models and Rule-Breakers," focuses on biographies of athletes who are honored for the way they played the game and for their efforts to redress injustice in sports. Baseball outfielder Curt Flood, pioneering bicyclist Marshall Taylor, and football great Red Grange are among the athletes featured in this section.

The third section, "Tragic Figures in Sports," includes biographies of athletes whose character flaws or bad luck led to legendary failures, costing them their careers or their lives. Baseball player Shoeless Joe Jackson and NASCAR driver Dale Earnhardt are among the subjects in this section.

The last section, "Renowned Rivals, Famous Friends," broadens the scope beyond a single athlete. In most cases, the sports discussed are not played alone. Usually competition between rivals is involved. Tennis stars Chris Evert and Martina Navratilova, boxers Joe Louis and Max Schmeling, and baseball players Babe Ruth and Ty Cobb are among the pairings in this section.

Sports Celebrities

In this age of expansive media and Internet access, the lives of star athletes get extensive news coverage, similar to movie stars and fashion models. Top players, such as Michael Jordan or Arnold Palmer, even find their pictures on celebrity pages in newspapers and magazines, and people who care little for sports will attend games or watch for their television appearances just to see them. Newspaper articles quote them after games in which they play; sports radio panels critique their play daily; and fans cheer or jeer them on daily blogs. Every aspect of their lives is reported: sports feats, contracts, nightlife, relationships, and legal problems.

In every age and for every sport, biographical books are written about sport heroes who distinguish themselves far above the common player and capture the admiration of fans. Some athletes set amazing sports records. In *Wilt, 1962: The Night of 100 Points and the Dawn of a New Era*, Gary M. Pomerantz blends the account of Philadelphia Warriors star Wilt Chamberlain scoring 100 points in an early NBA basketball game with the story of his colorful life. Some athletes attract fans by being dominant performers for years. Heavyweight boxer Jack Dempsey held the world boxing title for over seven years after an earlier life as a miner and a hobo. Veteran sportswriter Roger Kahn describes this pioneering athlete who went on to star in Hollywood films in *A Flame of Pure Fire: Jack Dempsey and the Roaring '20s*. Some athletes are noticed because they are physically gifted or have incredible origins. Houston Rocket center Yao Ming represents China as well as his team when he plays in the National Basketball League. Brook Larmer describes the life of this 7 foot, 6 inch athlete, who is also an international ambassador, in *Operation Yao Ming: The Chinese Sports Empire, American Big Business, and the Making of an NBA Superstar*.

Confident and aggressive characters populate these biographies, which are mostly written about retired sports figures. In this section, only baseball star Orlando Hernández and basketball player Yao Ming are active athletes at the time of this writing. Readers may read about retired athletes to revisit stories that they remember and enjoyed in the past or to learn newly revealed details about these stars and the games that they played. Most of these books are longer than other Sports Biographies and require unhurried reading.

> *Sports Celebrities* biographies focus on athletes who distinguish themselves from other athletes by their record setting, consistency over time, or uncommon personal characteristics. With their talents and interesting personalities, these athletes attract the continued attention of reporters and fans who enjoy reading about stars' personal lives as much as their professional achievement. Those wanting to read about familiar characters will enjoy the books in this section.

Cramer, Richard Ben

Joe DiMaggio: The Hero's Life. Simon & Schuster, 2000. 546p. ISBN 0684853914. Audiobook and large print available.

At the awards ceremony of Major League Baseball's centennial dinner in 1969, the Baseball Writers Association of America honored Joe DiMaggio (1914–1999) as the Greatest Living Player. It was a great honor, which the longtime New York Yankee center fielder accepted but did not relish. Though DiMaggio was worshiped by fans, writers, and the baseball establishment, he was indifferent to the attention. His marriages had failed; he was estranged from his brother Dominic; he resented Mickey Mantle, who had replaced him in center field; and he sought more privacy. In this candid account, Richard Ben Cramer chronicles DiMaggio's rise from the sandlots of San Francisco and early days in the Pacific Coast League to stardom in the American League and his long, unhappy retirement.

Subjects: Baseball Players; DiMaggio, Joe; Group Discussion Books; New York Yankees; Retirement; San Francisco

Now Try: Original *New York Times* articles about DiMaggio, as well as many about Babe Ruth, Lou Gehrig, and Mickey Mantle, are collected in *Sultans of Swat: The Four Great Sluggers of the New York Yankees*. DiMaggio's rival, Ted Williams of the Boston Red Sox, was an equally antisocial character, but he had more assertive friends. *The Teammates: A Portrait of Friendship* by David Halberstam (see this chapter) is a happier story about four longtime Red Sox players, including DiMaggio's brother Dominic. Whereas DiMaggio and Williams were to varying degrees antisocial, Ty Cobb, the Detroit Tiger who sharpened his spikes before games, was simply mean. Al Stump tells how Cobb outfought all foes when baseball was a sport for ruffians in *Ty Cobb: The Life and Times of the Meanest Man Who Ever Played Baseball: A Biography*. The band leader Nelson Riddle, another melancholy man, refused to let anyone help him with his emotional problems. Peter J. Levinson tells a sadly sympathetic story in *September in the Rain: The Life of Nelson Riddle* (see chapter 8). Extreme disdain for attention was also a characteristic of short story writer J. D. Salinger. Ian Hamilton describes his encounter with the reclusive author in *In Search of J. D. Salinger: A Biography* by Ian Hamilton (see chapter 5).

Dodson, James

Ben Hogan: An American Life. Doubleday, 2004. 528p. ISBN 0385503121.

Champion golfer Ben Hogan (1912–1997) was once so focused on his own game that he failed to notice his partner's hole-in-one. A serious golfer who practiced his famous swing religiously, young Hogan struggled for years to make the tour before he attained the confidence to be a consistent winner of major tournaments. His popularity reached its peak when he returned to golf after surviving a terrible automobile accident, and it remained high as he became a marketer of golf equipment and author of golfing books. In this admiring biography, James Dodson reveals how Hogan overcame self-doubt and maintained his game far into retirement.

Subjects: Golfers; Hogan, Ben; Self-Confidence

Now Try: The golfing guide *Ben Hogan's Five Lessons: The Modern Fundamentals of Golf* (titled *Five Lessons: The Modern Fundamentals of Golf* in older editions) remains popular in libraries and bookstores. Hogan followed golfer Bobby Jones into the spotlight. In *The Immortal Bobby: Bobby Jones and the Golden Age of Golf*, sportswriter Ron Rapoport describes a man who remained an amateur despite being the world's best golfer in one of its greatest eras. Hogan's self-doubt was more of a problem than his golf swing. Even a psychoanalyst can suffer self-doubt, as revealed by Lawrence J. Friedman in *Identity's Architect: A Biography of Erik H. Erikson* (see chapter 4). Jimmy Stewart appeared to be confident on the screen, but he had been shy as a young actor. Marc Eliot admiringly profiles an actor who overcame self-doubt in *Jimmy Stewart: A Biography* (see chapter 8).

Fainaru, Steve, and Ray Sánchez

The Duke of Havana: Baseball, Cuba, and the Search for the American Dream. Villard Books, 2001. 338p. ISBN 0375503455.

In 1997, as Cubans officially celebrated Christmas for the first time in twenty-eight years, Orlando "El Duque" Hernández (1965?–), the Cuban national baseball team's greatest pitcher, prepared to lie in the bottom of a fishing boat to flee the island country and change his life forever. In the wake of the 1996 Olympics in Atlanta, his brother and teammate, Liván, had already defected and signed a rich contract with the Florida Marlins. Despite money paid in advance to smuggle Hernández safely from the country, the escape proved difficult. Journalists Steve Fainaru and Ray Sánchez's recount the dramatic escape in this in-depth examination of a talented Cuban baseball player's life.

Subjects: Baseball Players; Cuba; Hernández, Orlando; Teen Reads

Now Try: Luis M. Garcia's family left Cuba on a visa in 1971 when he was only twelve. He remembers the indoctrination and the terror of having his father sent to a work camp in *Child of the Revolution: Growing Up in Castro's Cuba*. Marcos Bretón describes the difficulties foreign players have adjusting to

American life in his profile of young Miguel Tejada, *Away Games: The Life and Times of a Latin Baseball Player*. Ballet dancer Rudolf Nureyev recounts the events of his life leading to his dramatic defection from the Soviet Union in *Nureyev: An Autobiography*; in *Baryshnikov: From Russia to the West*, Gennady Smakov describes Mikhail Baryshnikov's early ballet career and his eventual defection. Chinese basketball star Yao Ming did not have to flee his country to become an American sports hero. Brook Larmer explains the deal to bring Yao to the National Basketball Association in *Operation Yao Ming: The Chinese Sports Empire, American Big Business, and the Making of an NBA Superstar* (see this chapter).

Greene, Bob

Hang Time: Days and Dreams with Michael Jordan. Doubleday, 1992. 406p. ISBN 0385425880.

In the 1990s, the face of Michael Jordan became one of the most known sports images. During that decade he led the Chicago Bulls to six National Basketball Association championships. He retired with the third highest total scoring in NBA history and was popularly proclaimed the game's greatest player. Early in the run of championships, *Chicago Tribune* columnist Bob Greene followed Jordan around the court and away from the game and was granted many interviews, during which Jordan discussed his family, teammates, and attitudes toward life. Though Greene does reveal that teammates disliked Jordan's arrogance, *Hang Time* offers a tribute from an obvious fan to a talented player.

Subjects: African Americans; Basketball Players; Chicago Bulls; Jordan, Michael

Now Try: National Public Radio reporter Scott Simon expresses his admiration of Jordan's play in his book about the important presence of sports in his life, *Home & Away: A Memoir of a Fan*. Michael Leahy updates the Jordan story with an account of his three disastrous seasons with the Washington Wizards as team president and then as a player in *When Nothing Else Matters: Michael Jordan's Last Comeback*. Sam Smith has little that is nice to say about Michael Jordan. According to Smith, Jordan sought his own glory, not the good of the team, even in the winning years. The author argues his case in *The Jordan Rules: The Inside Story of a Turbulent Season with Michael Jordan and the Chicago Bulls*. In Jordan-like fashion, singer Michael Jackson dominated the popular music scene in the 1970s and 1980s, scoring hit records and winning millions of devoted fans. Margo Jefferson examines the singer's life and how it reflects American culture in *On Michael Jackson* (see chapter 8). Just as Jordan gave Greene permission to observe his life, Katherine Hepburn let A. Scott Berg into hers. Though he describes her as funny and warm to friends, he also shows that she was a bit arrogant and self-focused in *Kate Remembered* (see chapter 8).

Hauser, Thomas

Arnold Palmer: A Personal Journey. Collins, 1994. 192p. ISBN 0002554682.

Looking at photographs of legendary golfer Arnold Palmer (1929–), one might almost guess that he was a dancer. In his prime, costumed in short sleeves or sweaters, his body was lithe and his movements were fluid and expressive. Each green and landscaped golf course was, of course, a very large stage on which he was surrounded by admiring fans. In the text of this attractive photographic biography, Thomas Hauser describes how with grace Palmer won and lost many important tournaments, endorsed consumer products, and became a popular sportscaster.

Subjects: Golfers; Palmer, Arnold; Photographic Biography

Now Try: Sports heroes often lend themselves to being subjects of oversized photobiographies. Other good choices are *Wayne Gretzky: The Authorized Pictorial Biography* by Jim Taylor, *Favre* by Brett Favre, and *Rare Air: Michael on Michael* by Michael Jordan. Palmer's ability to parlay his name recognition from golf into business and media and create a "brand" resembles the success of home economist Martha Stewart, who is admiringly described in *Being Martha: The Inside Story of Martha Stewart and Her Amazing Life* by Lloyd Allen (see chapter 8). Bing Crosby remained in the public eye for many decades, as has Palmer, and his popularity never wavered. Gary Giddins recounts the singer's great musical career and business success in *Bing Crosby: A Pocketful of Dreams, the Early Years, 1903–1940* (see chapter 8).

Kahn, Roger

A Flame of Pure Fire: Jack Dempsey and the Roaring '20s. Harcourt Brace, 1999. 473p. ISBN 0151002967.

Jack Dempsey (1895–1983) told sportswriter Roger Kahn that he decided at age eleven to become a heavyweight boxing champion. It was a typical boyhood dream, unlikely to be realized by the son of a poor miner in Colorado. Working as a miner and cowboy, and wandering as a hobo, Dempsey fought frequently, often losing, but always learning new moves. In 1919 he defeated Jess Willard to win the heavyweight title, which he held for over seven years. He used his fame to become an actor and businessman. Kahn depicts Dempsey as a man of his times, admirable for both his brutal knockouts and generosity to friends.

Subjects: Boxers; Dempsey, Jack; Group Discussion Books; Rags to Riches Stories

Now Try: Jack Dempsey wrote two autobiographies, both titled *Dempsey*. Like Dempsey, Gene Tunney used boxing fame to enter high society. Jack Cavanaugh recounts the Irish American's rise from the tough neighborhoods of New York in *Boxing's Brainiest Champ and His Upset of the Great Jack Dempsey*. Oil executive Frank Phillips also came from humble beginnings and tried various professions before finding his vocation. Michael Wallis describes the colorful career of a ruthless tycoon who threw great barbecues, met glamorous people, and in the end gave most of his money away, in *Oil Man: The Story of Frank Phillips and the Birth of Phillips Petroleum* (see chapter 9). Like Dempsey, actor John Wayne became a symbol for tough masculinity. Garry Wills examines the meaning of the actor's life in *John Wayne's America: The Politics of Celebrity* (see chapter 8). Sports author Roger Kahn is most famous for his books on baseball, including *The Boys of Summer* and *A Season in the Sun*.

Larmer, Brook

Operation Yao Ming: The Chinese Sports Empire, American Big Business, and the Making of an NBA Superstar. Gotham Books, 2005. 350p. ISBN 159240-0787.

Chinese sports authorities were aware of Yao Ming (1980–) from the day of his birth, because the hospital in which he was born sent them a message that an eleven-pound baby measuring twenty-three inches had been born. The news was not unexpected; his parents were former basketball players, the tallest couple in China, and they had been urged by the sports-crazed communists to marry. In this investigative biography, journalist Brook Larmer recounts Yao's childhood, the training that he received in Chinese sports academies, his play on Chinese national teams, and the complicated negotiations that brought him to the National Basketball Association's Houston Rockets.

Subjects: Basketball Players; China; Group Discussion Books; Houston Rockets; Teen Reads; Yao, Ming

Now Try: In *Yao: A Life in Two Worlds*, Yao describes his childhood and basketball career in a lighthearted and humorous manner. Like Yao, retired basketball star Magic Johnson is modest and likeable. He writes candidly about his career and surviving AIDS in his autobiography, *Magic Johnson: My Life*. The first athlete born in China to win an Olympic medal was Eric Liddell, a missionary's son. David McCasland describes Liddell's track career and life as a missionary in China in *Eric Liddell: Pure Gold*. Baseball was the first American sport to import players from other countries. Nick Wilson tells the story in *Early Latino Ballplayers in the United States: Major, Minor, and Negro Leagues, 1901–1949*. In the nineteenth century, Charles Dickens came to America to entertain the citizens and return home to England with his earnings. The great English author told about the trip in *American Notes: A Journey*, and Nigel Gearing turned the story into a play, *Dickens in America*.

Montville, Leigh

The Big Bam: The Life and Times of Babe Ruth. Doubleday, 2006. 390p. ISBN 9780385514378. Audiobook and large print available.

Why did the parents of Babe Ruth (1895–1948) put him in an orphanage? Was he really an unmanageable seven-year-old? Why was he hospitalized in 1925? Was he in league with gamblers? Did he really call the home run in the 1932 World Series in Wrigley Field? Although there are many books on the Bambino, there are still unanswered questions about his life. Sports columnist Leigh Montville draws on the research of many Ruth biographers in this entertaining account of one of baseball's greatest stars.

Subjects: Baltimore; Baseball Players; Boston Red Sox; New York Yankees; Ruth, Babe

Now Try: Robert W. Creamer, a sportswriter who has spent many years studying the myths of Ruth's career, comes to some different conclusions than Montville did in *Babe: The Legend Comes to Life*. In the 1960s Ruth was still considered a baseball immortal. When Mickey Mantle and Roger Maris threatened to break Ruth's single-season home run record, many Yankee fans rooted for Mantle because they thought Maris was not "a Yankee for life." Longtime sportswriter Maury Allen chronicles the life of a disregarded player in *Roger Maris: A Man for All Seasons*. The controversy over steroid use and self-seeking behavior dampened public excitement about Barry Bonds's quest to break the career home run record. In *Love Me, Hate Me: Barry Bonds and the Making of an Antihero*, Jeff Pearlman tells why fans were lukewarm to Bonds despite his Ruth-like career. W. C. Fields, a Babe Ruth contemporary, was an iconic star of vaudeville and early films and a far different person on stage than off. Like Ruth, he was known in public as a clown. Simon Louvish looks behind the facade in his admiring biography, *Man on the Flying Trapeze: The Life and Times of W. C. Fields* (see chapter 8).

Pomerantz, Gary M.

Wilt, 1962: The Night of 100 Points and the Dawn of a New Era. Crown, 2005. 267p. ISBN 1400051606. Audiobook available.

On a cold winter night in February 1962, in an arena in Hershey, Pennsylvania, basketball star Wilt Chamberlain (1936–1999) scored 100 points in a single game, helping his Philadelphia Warriors beat the New York Knickerbockers 169 to 147. This almost unbelievable record was as flamboyant as Wilt himself and helped draw media attention to the struggling National Basketball Association, which sent its teams touring away from their home cities to find more fans. According to Gary M. Pomerantz, this game also marked a change in the manner of play and helped get more black players into the league. For Chamberlain, it meant the beginning of stardom. By inserting stories about Chamberlain's night life, sexual boasting, and drug use between the quarters of the game, Pomeratz recounts the maverick life of a basketball legend.

Subjects: African Americans; Basketball Players; Chamberlain, Wilt; Group Discussion Books; National Basketball Association; Philadelphia Warriors

Now Try: Baseball's Reggie Jackson had an ego and swagger to compare with Chamberlain's. He describes his headline-making career in *Reggie: The Autobiography*; it is also recounted in *October Men: Reggie Jackson, George Steinbrenner, Billy Martin, and the Yankees' Miraculous Finish in 1978* by Maury Allen. Like Chamberlain, novelist Nelson Algren enjoyed life in rough neighborhoods. Bettina Drew depicts Algren as a free spirit who lived according to his whims and convictions, in *Nelson Algren: A Life on the Wild Side*. Boston Celtics center Bill Russell was always one of the opponents who most tested the talented Chamberlain. In *The Rivalry: Bill Russell, Wilt Chamberlain, and the Golden Age of Basketball*, John Taylor argues that Russell and Chamberlain led a group of black basketball players who quickened the game and increased scoring while elevating the NBA from a weak barnstorming league to a premier sports organization. Early NBA history resembles that of the Negro Baseball Leagues. A good look at those times is found in *Don't Look Back: Satchel Paige in the Shadows of Baseball* by Mark Ribowsky and *I Was Right on Time* by Buck O'Neil.

Role Models and Rule-Breakers

One of the attractions of sports is that they usually have better defined rules than life in general. Athletes who can follow these rules and can perform well in their sport become examples for the general public to follow in their daily lives. Fans see success and its rewards and admire athletes for their stellar qualities, such as dedication, courage, and cooperation with the team. Like the laws of governments, however, the rules of sports may be flawed and may be changed. Some athletes resent rules, especially the unwritten ones—the decrees that have little to do with sports and much to do with discrimination or labor relations. In the past century, professional sports has been one of the most visible battlefields for civil rights. Players of color and women demand to have equal opportunity to prove their athletic ability and reap the rewards of sports achievement.

In this chapter are biographies of players who exhibited commendable qualities of sportsmanship. In *Johnny U: The Life & Times of Johnny Unitas*, Tom Callahan describes the leadership Baltimore Colts quarterback Johnny Unitas showed on the football field and in his neighborhood. Jane Leavy describes Los Angeles Dodgers pitcher Koufax as an uncommon player who balanced his career with his Jewish faith and downplayed his fame, in *Sandy Koufax: A Lefty's Legacy*. Also included are biographies of athletes who challenged managers, owners, and society as a whole by their actions. In *Stepping Up: The Story of Curt Flood and His Fight for Baseball Players' Rights*, Alex Belth tells how Curt Flood challenged Major League Baseball's long-held reserve clause by refusing to be traded to another team. In *Great Time Coming: The Life of Jackie Robinson from Baseball to Birmingham*, David Falkner tells how Jackie Robinson broke the color line in baseball.

All these Sports Biographies feature characters who will long be remembered by readers. Their lively stories, which alternate between sports action and conflict off the field of play, will likely keep readers enthralled. Set in the popular world of sports, these books may attract fans who follow sports in the news and attend games. Many quick reads are included.

Role Models and Rule Breakers biographies focus on athletes who are honored for the way they played the game and for their efforts to redress injustice in sports. Authors write admiringly about these popular figures, who serve as examples for readers to follow in their lives outside sports. Memorable characters and conflict-laden stories attract readers to these compelling books.

Balf, Todd

Major: A Black Athlete, a White Era, and the Fight to Be the World's Fastest Human Being. Crown, 2008. 306p. ISBN 9780307236586.

Bicyclist Marshall Taylor (1878–1932), known as "Major," was America's first dominant black athlete. According to journalist Todd Balf, the confident young cyclist upset many racially minded Americans throughout the 1890s and 1900s by constantly defeating their white champions in what was then the country's hottest sport. Even when banned from a race, he would sneak onto the track behind the starting line, pass the pack, and win. At a time when many African Americans were lynched, Balf was often threatened. In this admiring biography that mixes stories of sports and civil rights, the author describes how Taylor faced the challenges and toured the world as the "world's fastest man."

Subjects: African Americans; Bicycle Racing; Cyclists; Discrimination in Sports; Group Discussion Books; Taylor, Major; Teen Reads

Now Try: Like Taylor, African American boxer Jack Johnson was hated by many whites for challenging their belief in black inferiority. In ***Unforgivable Blackness: The Rise and Fall of Jack Johnson***, Geoffrey C. Ward describes the difficult life of a black champion in Jim Crow America. In the same era as Taylor and Johnson, novelist and playwright Oscar Wilde was hated for his sexual orientation, which became known through his trial for homosexuality. Barbara Belford describes Wilde's incautious life in ***Oscar Wilde: A Certain Genius*** (see chapter 7). Taylor's persistence in joining races uninvited is reminiscent of the civil rights activities of comedian Dick Gregory, who never let threats stop him from demonstrating for civil rights. Gregory wrote about his experiences in *Nigger: An Autobiography* and *Callus on My Soul: A Memoir.*

Belth, Alex

Stepping Up: The Story of Curt Flood and His Fight for Baseball Players' Rights. Persea Books, 2006. 228p. ISBN 0892553219.

When the telephone woke him early one morning, Curt Flood (1938–1997) knew something was wrong. After twelve loyal years with the St. Louis Cardinals, he had been traded to the Philadelphia Phillies. However, instead of accepting the standard transaction, Flood decided to challenge the power structure of major league baseball by refusing to report to the new team. When he lost his case, he lost his career. According to Alex Belth, Flood never felt that his story was as tragic as the media reported. In this candid biography, Belth recounts how the determined Flood rose from the ghetto in Oakland to become a National League All-Star, and then walked away from the game and moved to Europe when he felt he had been mistreated.

> **Subjects:** Activists; African Americans; Baseball Players; Flood, Curt; Labor Activists; St. Louis Cardinals

> **Now Try:** Flood wrote about his career and the case against major league baseball's reserve clause in *The Way It Is*. The Major League Baseball Players Association ultimately was successful in eliminating the reserve clause. Charles P. Korr chronicles the union's activities in *The End of Baseball as We Knew It: The Players Union, 1960–81*. Rayard Rustin was another African American activists ahead of his time. John D'Emilio tells of Rustin serving as an inspiration to the civil rights leaders of the 1950s and 1960s in *Lost Prophet: The Life and Times of Bayard Rustin* (see chapter 4). In the 1950s, African American Chester Himes was an acclaimed crime writer, often compared with Dashiell Hammett and Raymond Chandler, yet he could not get a fair book contract. James Sallis tells how the practical Himes moved to France, where he was more appreciated, in *Chester Himes: A Life* (see chapter 7).

Callahan, Tom

Johnny U: The Life & Times of Johnny Unitas. Crown, 2006. 292p. ISBN 9781400081394.

Through mud, blood, and pain, Baltimore Colts quarterback Johnny Unitas (1933–2002) called the plays that led his team to victory. According to sports author Tom Callahan, Unitas was a working-class hero at a time when football was a players' game, not a chess match run by coaches as it is today. In the off season he worked construction, and he later owned a bar. Callahan's quick read about Unitas is an admiring biography full of gridiron stories that will please sports fans.

> **Subjects:** Baltimore Colts; Football Players; Quick Reads; Unitas, Johnny

> **Now Try:** In 1958 Unitas was on the field in the National Football League championship game that Mark Bowden describes in *Best Game Ever: Giants vs. Colts, 1958, and the Birth of the Modern NFL*. While Unitas was passing

1

2

3

4

5

6

7

8

9

10

11

12

footballs with Baltimore, Mike Ditka was knocking heads with defensive linemen as the tight end of the Chicago Bears. The tough-talking Bear recounts his life as a player and head coach in his entertaining memoir, *Ditka*. In baseball, players whose gritty play reminds fans of the game before large contracts and pampered stars are called "throwbacks." George Castle describes a dozen players who fit the definition in *Throwbacks: Old-School Baseball Players in Today's Game*. Football is often compared with war, and quarterbacks are like field commanders. Larry Alexander describes Major Richard D. Winters and how he led his troops through danger behind German lines in *Biggest Brother: The Life of Major Dick Winters, the Man Who Led the Band of Brothers* (see chapter 3).

Carroll, John M.

Red Grange and the Rise of Modern Football. University of Illinois Press, 1999. 265p. ISBN 0252023846.

To many Americans, Red Grange (1903–1991) was not only a football player but also a hero. Starring as a running back at the University of Illinois in the 1920s, when newspapers were expanding their sports coverage by including photographs and commercial radio was first broadcasting games, Grange became one of the first sports figures known nationally. Joining the Chicago Bears after his college career helped legitimize professional football, and he was able to broker his popularity into contracts for product endorsements and a movie career. After his playing days, he kept his name in the sports pages by becoming a broadcaster and motivational speaker. In a series of biographical essays, sports historian John M. Carroll examines the importance of Red Grange to professional football, broadcast sports, and American culture.

Subjects: Biographical Essays; Chicago Bears; Football Players; Grange, Red; Sports Broadcasters

Now Try: In 1953 Grange published *The Red Grange Story: An Autobiography*. Another key figure in the shaping of professional football was Chicago Bears owner George Halas, who moved the team to Chicago from Canton, Ohio, in 1921 and coached it himself until 1967. Jeff Davis recounts a celebrated life in *Papa Bear: The Life and Legacy of George Halas*. Halas tells his own story in *Halas: An Autobiography*. After sports, Grange's life was in broadcasting. Ed Sullivan was a contemporary who was described as talentless yet seemed to be very successful. James Maguire recounts the life of the man who pioneered celebrity news in newspapers, radio, and television in *Impresario: The Life and Times of Ed Sullivan* (see chapter 8). Like Grange, mystery writer Rex Stout was a man who succeeded in every endeavor. John McAleer shows how being a math prodigy, banker, sailor, and civil libertarian influenced his novels, short stories, and poems in *Rex Stout: A Biography*.

Falkner, David

Great Time Coming: The Life of Jackie Robinson from Baseball to Birmingham. Simon & Schuster, 1995. 382p. ISBN 0671793365. Audiobook available.

When Jackie Robinson (1919–1972) retired from major league baseball, he appeared worn out and older than his years. He had broken the racial barrier and thrilled fans with his aggressive play, but his victories had come at great cost. There had been years of heckling, and the Brooklyn Dodgers star had even been called before the House Un-American Activities Committee for supporting civil rights. In his deferential biography of a sports hero, baseball writer David Falkner tells an intimate story from Robinson's birth in a sharecropper's cabin in Georgia to his work with Martin Luther King Jr. He portrays Robinson as a sensitive man who struggled to succeed.

> **Subjects:** African Americans; Baseball Players; Brooklyn Dodgers; Civil Rights Leaders; Discrimination in Sports; Group Discussion Books; Robinson, Jackie; Teen Reads

> **Now Try:** Robinson wrote a series of autobiographies, of which *I Never Had It Made* is the last and most complete. *First Class Citizenship: The Civil Rights Letters of Jackie Robinson* is also available. Radio announcer Red Barber, who broadcast games for all the New York baseball teams, wrote a colorful account of the year that Robinson debuted, *1947, When All Hell Broke Loose in Baseball*. Cleveland Brown's running back Jim Brown may be the African American player who had the most effect on race relations in the National Football League. Mike Freeman recounts the life of the often volatile player in his respectful but candid biography *Jim Brown: The Fierce Life of an American Hero.* Edward Brooke of Massachusetts, a liberal Republican, was elected to the U.S. Senate in 1967, the first black in the Senate since the Reconstruction Era. He recounts his civil rights work during World War II and as a political leader in *Bridging the Divide: My Life.*

Feinstein, John

Caddy for Life: The Bruce Edwards Story. Little, Brown, 2004. 300p. ISBN 0316777889. Large print available.

Sports columnist John Feinstein had to tell this story. In early 2003 he learned that caddy Bruce Edwards (1954–2004) was diagnosed with amyotrophic lateral sclerosis (ALS), also known as Lou Gehrig's disease, and that Edwards was determined to continue caddying for Tom Watson as long as he could. Edwards, who had known Feinstein for over twenty years, soon asked the columnist to write his life story, which the caddy would be unable to complete himself. Feinstein agreed and shadowed Edwards in his final season. The result is this warm account of a familiar golf professional's career and final year, showing how important a knowledgeable and thoughtful caddy is to a professional golfer.

> **Subjects:** Amyotrophic Lateral Sclerosis; Caddies; Edwards, Bruce; Golfers; Group Discussion Books; Lou Gehrig's Disease; Quick Reads; Watson, Tom

> **Now Try:** Jazz bassist and composer Charles Mingus learned that he had ALS in 1977 and put away his bass forever. Sue Mingus describes how during her husband's physical and mental decline their relationship strengthened, in *Tonight at Noon: A Love Story.* Jonathan Eig explains how New York Yankee first baseman Lou Gehrig became the model for courage during his struggle with his fatal disease in *Luckiest Man: The Life and Death of Lou Gehrig.* Jeannie Morris recounts the story of a brave football player with cancer in *Brian Piccolo: A Short Season.* Sportswriter and humorist Rick Reilly thought he would try caddying for a season. He reports what he learned about the job, his own shortcomings, and the celebrity golfers that he met in *Who's Your Caddy?: Looping for the Great, Near Great, and Reprobates of Golf.* Other Feinstein books about golf include *A Good Walk Spoiled: Days and Nights on the PGA Tour* and *The Majors: In Pursuit of Golf's Holy Grail*; he has also written about baseball, basketball, football, and tennis and penned sports novels for teens, including *Cover-Up* and *Vanishing Act.*

Gray, Frances Clayton, and Yanick Rice Lamb

Born to Win: The Authorized Biography of Althea Gibson. John Wiley, 2004. 244p. ISBN 0471471658.

At five feet, eleven inches tall, tennis player Althea Gibson (1927–2003), a sharecropper's daughter, could only be described as a dominant presence on the tennis court. Between 1942 and 1949 she excelled in the all-black American Tennis Association, but she was ineligible to play in the all-white United States Lawn Tennis Association. In 1950 Gibson applied to play in the U.S. Open. She would have been denied had not revered champion Alice Marble written a public letter calling for Gibson to get her chance. Frances Clayton Gray and Yanick Rice Lamb report that Gibson lost her first USLTA match, but she came back to eventually win championships at the U.S. Open, French Open, and Wimbledon. The authors chronicle the life of an amazing athlete who also played basketball with the Harlem Globetrotters and became a professional golfer.

> **Subjects:** African Americans; Gibson, Althea; Teen Reads; Tennis Players; Women
>
> **Now Try:** Gibson won several doubles championships at Wimbledon. In one of those matches she was paired with a Jewish partner, Angela Buxton. Bruce Schoenfeld reports how the two shunned players became good friends in *The Match: Althea Gibson and Angel Buxton: How Two Outsiders—One Black, the Other Jewish—Forged a Friendship and Made Sports History*. Gibson's presence in professional tennis paved the way for Arthur Ashe, who recounted his career in *Days of Grace: A Memoir*. Congresswoman Barbara Jordan attended segregated schools and knew the poverty of the black neighborhoods in Houston as a child and young woman. She described how she took charge of her life by attending Boston University Law School and entering politics in *Barbara Jordan: A Self-Portrait*. After tennis, Gibson joined the ladies' golf tour. David L. Hudson Jr. recounts the history of the ladies' tour and profiles some key players in *Women in Golf: The Players, the History, and the Future of the Sport*.

Leavy, Jane

Sandy Koufax: A Lefty's Legacy. HarperCollins, 2002. 282p. ISBN 0060195339. Audiobook and large print available.

For five consecutive years (1962–1966), Los Angeles Dodger Sandy Koufax (1935–) led the National League in earned run average and was considered the dominant pitcher in baseball. Then, concerned about the health of his arm and only thirty-one years old, he retired, giving up a high salary, a chance to break more records, and membership on a great team. Sportswriter Jane Leavy contends that Koufax was always an uncommon player, who balanced his career with his Jewish faith and downplayed his fame. She also shows how he has stayed active in retirement, often playing golf. Readers will enjoy this humanizing reassessment of a sometimes deified figure.

> **Subjects:** Baseball Players; Jews; Koufax, Sandy; Los Angeles Dodgers; Quick Reads; Retirement
>
> **Now Try:** Harper Lee stopped writing at a young age, right after publishing *To Kill a Mockingbird*, her only novel. Charles J. Shields examines the life of an author who walked away from success in *Mockingbird: A Portrait of Harper Lee* (see chapter 6). Detroit Tigers slugger Hank Greenberg was one of the first high-profile Jewish players in the major leagues. In *Hank Greenberg: The Story of My Life*, he describes the prejudice that he faced on a daily basis early in his career. In the early days of the twentieth

century, Jewish player Johnny Kling mixed baseball with his billiards career. Gil Bogen recounts his life in *Johnny Kling: A Baseball Biography*. When many athletes retire, they take up golf. When golfers retire from the Pro Tour, they keep playing in the Senior PGA Tour. Mark Shaw describes a year watching the older players in *Diamonds in the Rough: Championship Golf on the Senior PGA Tour*.

Macht, Norman L.

Connie Mack and the Early Years of Baseball. University of Nebraska Press, 2007. 708p. ISBN 9780803232631.

Unlike other major league managers, Philadelphia Athletics skipper Connie Mack (1862–1956) always wore a three-piece suit with high collar and tie in the dugout, lending a bit of dignity to a roughhouse game. Behind the facade, however, Mack was a tough disciplinarian who had been a wily catcher in baseball's mean days of the 1890s, and he was ready to trade or release any player whose performance did not meet his standards. As a result, Mack won many championships. In this well-researched and detailed biography of one of the founders of the American League, baseball historian Norman L. Macht examines the early years of a baseball legend's long career as player, manager, and team owner.

> **Subjects:** Baseball Managers; Baseball Players; Mack, Connie; Philadelphia Athletics
>
> **Now Try:** Connie Mack came from the same era as former player and sporting goods manufacturer Albert Goodwill Spalding. In *Spalding's World Tour: The Epic Adventure That Took Baseball around the Globe and Made It America's Game*, Mark Lamster describes a six-month, around-the-world tour that Spalding led in 1888 to promote baseball to the world. Few managers ever last a decade, much less the fifty years that Mack spent with the Athletics. Most are hired to be fired. In *The Ballad of Billy and George: The Tempestuous Marriage of Billy Martin and George Steinbrenner*, Phil Pepe tells how Steinbrenner fired Manager Billy Martin five times. Proclaiming his love of Dodgers blue, Tommy Lasorda held his job as manager of the Los Angeles Dodgers for twenty-one years. Sportswriter Bill Plaschke profiles the charismatic skipper in *I Live for This!: Baseball's Last True Believer*. Mack's attitudes toward labor and business reflect those of the most successful industrialists of his time, including Andrew Carnegie. David Nasaw tells an equally epic story about the Scottish immigrant who became a tycoon in *Andrew Carnegie* (see chapter 9).

Maraniss, David

Clemente: The Passion and Grace of Baseball's Last Hero. Simon & Schuster, 2006. 401p. ISBN 9780743217811. Audiobook and large print available.

The Brooklyn Dodgers scouting report said that Puerto Rican youth Roberto Clemente (1934–1972) had all the tools necessary to become a major baseball player if he could adjust to life in the United States. In his remarks about the man who would become a folk hero on his island, Dodgers scout Al Campanis said, "Will mature into a big man." David Maraniss explains how true the statement became in his admiring biography of the great Pittsburgh Pirate player, who led his team to two World Series and died while flying aid to earthquake victims in Nicaragua.

Subjects: African Americans; Baseball Players; Clemente, Roberto; Pittsburgh Pirates; Puerto Rico; Teen Reads

Now Try: Franciscan brother and fireman Mychal Judge died on September 11, 2001, trying to save lives at the World Trade Center. Michael Ford lovingly describes a warm, thoughtful spiritual leader who gave his life for others in many ways in *Father Mychal Judge: An Authentic American Hero* (see chapter 4). Clemente's rival, Hank Aaron of the Braves, was another steady, dedicated player who helped open the game for more blacks. Tom Stanton describes Aaron's conquest of Babe Ruth's career home run record in *Hank Aaron and the Home Run That Changed America*. Like Clemente, the end of New York Yankee first baseman Lou Gehrig's career came suddenly. After playing 2,130 consecutive games, he left the game suffering from amyotrophic lateral sclerosis. His courageous fight for life is told in *Luckiest Man: The Life and Death of Lou Gehrig* by Jonathan Eig. Before his death from AIDS, tennis star Arthur Ashe reflected on breaking the color barrier in tennis and his life away from the court in *Days of Grace: A Memoir*.

Maraniss, David

When Pride Still Mattered: A Life of Vince Lombardi. Simon & Schuster, 1999. 541p. ISBN 0684844184. Audiobook and large print available.

In nine years, Coach Vince Lombardi (1913–1970) led the Green Bay Packers to five National Football League championships. After he died of cancer at the relatively young age of fifty-seven, his eloquent statements about the game and life began to be repeated frequently by sports broadcasters and motivational speakers, fostering a legend of Lombardi as genius and saint. In this thorough biography, David Maraniss candidly reexamines the life and career of the coach with the philosophy of "winning at all costs," stripping away the myths, but retaining awe for an accomplished man.

Subjects: Football Coaches; Green Bay Packers; Leaderhip; Lombardi, Vince

Now Try: Like Lombardi, explorer Ernest Shackleton was an inspiring leader who is often quoted. George Plimpton describes the life of a man who caught the imagination of his age in *Ernest Shackleton* (see chapter 1). When East St. Louis High School football coach Bob Shannon drilled his players, there was more at stake than winning and losing games. He was preparing his students for life and helping them get football scholarships so they could attend college. Kevin Horrigan pays tribute to a remarkably successful teacher in a poverty stricken community in *The Right Kind of Heroes: Coach Bob Shannon and the East St. Louis Flyers*. Similarly, at St. Anthony's High School in Jersey City, New Jersey, Bob Hurley coached basketball with the intention of saving directionless boys from misfortune. Adrian Wojnarowski describes the tough but compassionate coach in *The Miracle of St. Anthony: A Season with Coach Bob Hurley and Basketball's Most Improbable Dynasty*. One of the most respected head coaches in college football has been in the same position for over forty years at Penn State. Joe Paterno shares his life and philosophy in *Paterno: By the Book*. More inspiring coach stories from well-known authors, such as Pat Conroy, Francine Prose, and John Irving, can be found in the collection *Coach: 25 Writers Reflect on People Who Made Difference*.

Tragic Figures in Sports

1

Athletes play to win, and for the most part, it is the winners who are remembered through biographies. Some athletes, however, are remembered for the tragic aspects of their lives. Dropped passes, missed shots, and booted plays are usually forgotten in time, but errors of judgment that reveal character flaws and miscalculations that end in death are long remembered. Athletes who made these more serious errors are the subjects of tragic stories.

Authors may either sympathize with or criticize the athletes in these books. Bill Crawford reveals that Olympic star Jim Thorpe was driven by extreme injustice to break the amateur athletics rules by playing professional sports under an assumed name. Readers will sympathize with his story, as told by Bill Crawford in *All American: The Rise and Fall of Jim Thorpe*. On the other hand, Brian McDonald describes how self-destructive baseball star Louis Sockalexis ruined his career and ultimately his life in *Indian Summer: The Forgotten Story of Louis Sockalexis, the First Native American in Major League Baseball*. For NASCAR driver Dale Earnhardt, the danger of driving racing cars at high speeds finally proved fatal, as Leigh Montville explains in *At the Altar of Speed: The Fast Life and Tragic Death of Dale Earnhardt*.

The characters in these biographies are some of the most fascinating in this chapter. Each has much natural talent that has been developed by years of training, but some flaw turns triumph into tragedy. The stories draw readers who want to find out what went wrong. These books also offer detailed descriptions of the eras in which the athletes lived and made their fateful mistakes. Quick reads are included among these compelling books.

Tragic Figures in Sports stories include biographies of athletes whose character flaws or bad luck led to legendary failures, costing them their careers or their lives. Sympathetic and critical accounts are included. Most of the books are quick reads.

Crawford, Bill

All American: The Rise and Fall of Jim Thorpe. John Wiley, 2005. 284p. ISBN 0471557323.

Money was always a problem for young Jim Thorpe (1887–1953), the legendary Sauk Indian athlete who set records in track and field and starred in football and baseball. Being an amateur, he could not be paid for playing games. The situation became tense when Indian agent Horace Johnson denied Thorpe the $100 needed to participate in the Olympic Games in Sweden. Thorpe "found" the funds and won decathlon and pentathlon medals that would later be taken away when it was revealed that he had played professional baseball under an assumed name to raise cash. Although he eventually did become a professional athlete, actor, and president of the National Football League, Thorpe never forgot the embarrassment of his Olympic rebuke. Journalist Bill Crawford's book offers a sympathetic account of the great but mistreated athlete.

> **Subjects:** Discrimination in Sports; Native Americans; Olympics; Quick Reads; Sauk Indians; Teen Reads; Thorpe, Jim; Track and Field Athletes

> **Now Try:** In *Inside Track: My Professional Life in Amateur Track and Field*, Carl Lewis disclosed that violations of amateur athletics financial rules were still rampant in the 1980s. In the same decade, an entire team of boys was hoping that sports would lift them out of poverty. Michael Sokolove tells the story in *The Ticket Out: Darryl Strawberry and the Boys of Crenshaw* (see chapter 6). Winning the event that comes with the boast "world's greatest athlete" at the Olympics is an honor in any era. Bruce Jenner recounts his experiences in *Decathlon Challenge: Bruce Jenner's Story*. Adapting to another culture is never easy. Bill Neeley profiles a Comanche chief who eventually succeeded in white society as a prosperous rancher in *The Last Comanche Chief: The Life and Times of Quanah Parker* (see chapter 9).

Fleitz, David L.

Shoeless: The Life and Times of Joe Jackson. McFarland, 2001. 314p. ISBN 0786409789. Large print available.

Officially, the career of Shoeless Joe Jackson (1888–1951) ended with the 1920 season. The great hitter was suspended and then banned for his part in the 1919 Black Sox scandal, in which players took bribes from gamblers to throw the World Series. Unwilling to adhere to the ruling, Jackson played minor league baseball under assumed names for the next two decades. In this thoughtful biography, which lays out the evidence for restoring Jackson's place in baseball history, David L Fleitz tells how Jackson rose from South Carolina poverty to play the national sport and lived the rest of his life in defiance of the ban.

> **Subjects:** Baseball Players; Chicago White Sox; Jackson, Joe; South Carolina

> **Now Try:** Readers wanting more Shoeless Joe stories will want to read *Say It Ain't So, Joe!* by Donald Gropman. Jackson is a key character in the entertaining and philosophical baseball fantasy *Shoeless Joe* by W. P. Kinsella. The classic account of the Black Sox scandal is *Eight Men Out: The Black Sox and the 1919 World Series* by Eliot Asinof. Both Kinsella's and Asinof's books have been adapted for movies. Shoeless Joe's itinerant life, wandering the country and playing under assumed names, suggests the life of the hobos of the 1930s and the Beat poets in the 1950s. Woody Guthrie road rail cars with the hobos during the Great Depression. Elizabeth Partridge chronicles the constant movement of a man who would not sit still when there were political marches and rallies to attend, in *This Land Was Made for You and Me: The Life and Songs of Woody Guthrie* (see chapter 7). Jack Kerouac and his friends sought pleasure from drugs and alcohol while constantly seeking a better place to be. Kerouac described the Beat life in *On the Road*.

McDonald, Brian

Indian Summer: The Forgotten Story of Louis Sockalexis, the First Native American in Major League Baseball. Rodale, 2003. 244p. ISBN 1579545874.

Baseball historians always describe the forty-two-year life of Louis Sockalexis (1871–1913) as tragic. Brian McDonald agrees. He tells how the Penobscot Indian starred in several sports at Holy Cross College before moving to Notre Dame, where he was expelled for destroying property in a local saloon before he ever played a game. Then Louis joined the ruffians of the Cleveland Spiders of the National Baseball League. He was an almost instant success, hitting well and making spectacular catches in the outfield, but like many other players of his time, he spent his evenings in bars drinking and fighting. His career was short, as was his alcoholic life. Readers learn about the rough world of 1890s baseball and racial prejudice in this heartbreaking biography.

> **Subjects:** Alcoholics; Baseball Players; Cleveland Indians; Native Americans; Penobscot Indians; Quick Reads; Sockalexis, Louis
>
> **Now Try:** The classic book on bad behavior by baseball players is *Ball Four: My Life and Hard Times Throwing the Knuckleball in the Big Leagues* by former Yankees pitcher Jim Bouton. Detroit Tigers pitcher Denny McLain won thirty-one games in 1968, but within two years he was suspended for gambling, dousing reporters with water, and carrying a gun into a clubhouse. He wrote a series of autobiographies, starting with *Nobody's Perfect*. Like Sockalexis, basketball player Dennis Rodman seemed to be bound to cause trouble. Sportswriter Dan Bickley chronicles years of bizarre and antisocial behavior in *No Bull: The Unauthorized Biography of Dennis Rodman*. In the late 1960s, life should have been easy for the highly successful Brian Wilson of the Beach Boys, but musical disagreements, use of drugs, and the intense expectations of his father tormented him. Peter Ames Carlin portrays Wilson as a troubled man who surrendered to depression in *Catch a Wave: The Rise, Fall & Redemption of the Beach Boy's Brian Wilson*.

Montville, Leigh

At the Altar of Speed: The Fast Life and Tragic Death of Dale Earnhardt. Doubleday, 2001. 203p. ISBN 0385503636. Audiobook and large print available.

The death of champion stock car racer Dale Earnhardt (1951–2001) shook the NASCAR world. Though many racers have died over the years, Earnhardt was a fan favorite and a link to the past, when racing was just about speed and less about rules and politics. Many remembered Earnhardt's father on the track and were following his son Dale's blossoming career. Using interviews with friends, family, and competitors, sportswriter Leigh Montville describes the rise and triumph of a racing legend.

> **Subjects:** Earnhardt, Dale; NASCAR; Quick Reads; Race Car Drivers; Racing Accidents; Teen Reads
>
> **Now Try:** Stock car driver Dale Earnhardt Jr. recounted his father's advice and described his own career in *Driver #8*. Like the Earnhardts, the Allisons are a multigenerational stock car racing family with a history of tragic accidents. Peter Golonbeck describes the resilience that Bobby Allison and his family have shown in the NASCAR world in *Miracle: Bobby Allison and the Saga of the Alabama Gang*. Actor James Dean was a reckless young man just becoming a major star in Hollywood when he died in an accident on the open highway. Warren Newton Beath provides an hour-by-hour account of the events leading up to the accident in *The Death of James Dean*. In an era long before NASCAR, World War I pilot Eddie Rickenbacker raced cars. H. Paul Jeffers takes readers back to the 1920s in *Ace of Aces: The Life of Capt. Eddie Rickenbacker* (see chapter 1).

Seymour, Miranda

Bugatti Queen: In Search of a French Racing Legend. Random House, 2004. 323p. ISBN 1400061687.

> After leaving her French village for Paris in 1918, Hellé Nice (1900–1984) earned money as a cabaret dancer, ballerina, and nude model. The rural postmaster's daughter quickly made friends and lovers among men of both high and low social standing. Expressing a desire to be "the fastest woman in the world," she convinced Italian automobile manufacturer Ettore Bugatti to let her drive his racing cars. Throughout the late 1920s and 1930s she drove in Grand Prix races against men in Europe, South America, and Africa. Then an accident and World War II ended her career. During the war she was accused of collaborating with Nazi officials in France. In this candid biography, Miranda Seymour tells the story of a reckless woman who broke the rules of sport and society and died in bitter poverty and shame.

> **Subjects:** France; Nice, Hellé; Race Car Drivers; Women

> **Now Try:** Two decades after Nice raced, young American women bought little European sports cars and began to race them. Todd McCarthy tells about their friendships and rivalries in *Fast Women: The Legendary Ladies of Racing* (see this chapter). Janet Guthrie was the first woman to drive in the Indianapolis 500 and Daytona 500. She recounts her adventurous life, including a stint in astronaut training, in *Janet Guthrie: A Life at Full Throttle*. Like Nice, Evelyn Nesbit arrived in the big city as an unknown and quickly was noticed as a model. Paula Uruburu recounts her short time as a high society girl in New York City in *American Eve: Evelyn Nesbit, Standford White, the Birth of the "It" Girl, and the Crime of the Century* (see chapter 6). Zelda Fitzgerald, wife of novelist F. Scott Fitzgerald, was another reckless woman. Nancy Mitford tells the story of their tragic Jazz Age marriage, Zelda's career as an author, and her mental breakdown in *Zelda: A Biography*

Renowned Rivals, Famous Friends

Sports are competitive, which implies that at least two athletes or two teams must be contending for a prize or victory. The most common and often dramatic contests are head-to-head competitions with one winner and one loser. When athletes find themselves repeatedly pitted against the same opponents, rivalries develop, in which the athletes learn their opponents' strengths and weaknesses. Likewise, in team situations players get to know teammates well over time, learning when to rely on their help.

The biographers included in this section profile two to four athletes in stories of rivalry or alliance. Lewis Erenberg takes readers back to the tense days just before World War II to describe a boxing match that pitted black against white and democracy against Nazism in *The Greatest Fight of Our Generation: Louis vs. Schmeling.* Over the course of sixteen years, tennis stars Chris Evert and Martina Navratilova faced each other in championship matches over sixty times. Johnette Howard describes the frequent opponents and their serious but amiable contests in *The Rivals: Chris Evert vs. Martina Navratilova: Their Epic Duels and Extraordinary Friendship.* Todd McCarthy describes a close circle of women who raced European sports cars in the 1950s in his tribute to forgotten athletes, *Fast Women: The Legendary Ladies of Racing.* In *Teammates: A*

Portrait of Friendship, David Halberstam depicts a quartet of Boston Red Sox players who remained close companions for decades after their playing days.

Relationships are the focus of these character-rich Sports Biographies. The authors chronicle the athletes' careers, describe what happened when rivals met, and assess the state of the relationship when their careers were finished. The stories are set against the backdrop of pennant races, annual tournaments, and championship games. Many readers will find these somewhat intimate biographies especially compelling sports stories.

> *Renowned Rivals, Famous Friends* biographies feature the relationship of two or more athletes who were associated by their sport. Biographers describe how these relationships developed over time as the athletes met repeatedly in competition or alliance. Readers find these somewhat intimate stories especially compelling.

Bascomb, Neal

The Perfect Mile: Three Athletes, One Goal, and Less Than Four Minutes to Achieve It. Houghton Mifflin, 2004. 322p. ISBN 0618391126. Audiobook and large print available.

Breaking long-standing records and achieving what commentators have said was impossible is a great source of drama in sports. In the wake of the Helsinki Olympics of 1952, long distance runners Roger Bannister (1929–) of Great Britain, Wes Santee (1932–) of the United States, and John Landy (1930–) of Australia set their sights on running the first ever four-minute mile in track and field history. From widely varied backgrounds, each man put school, careers, and relationships on hold to train for the highly sought record. In this compelling group biography, journalist Neal Bascomb profiles the three dedicated athletes and recounts their training and head-to-head competitions, which grabbed headlines around the world.

Subjects: Bannister, Roger; Group Biography; Landy, John; Olympics; Rivals; Runners; Santee, Wes; Teen Reads; Track and Field Athletes

Now Try: In 1926 the great challenge was to be the first woman to swim the English Channel. Four well-trained American women declared they were in the race. Gavin Mortimer re-creates the excitement and describes the physical and personal challenges that the women faced in *The Great Swim.* Two years later American promoter C. C. Pyle sponsored a California to New York run to celebrate the opening of Route 66, the first highway across America. Geoff Williams tells the story of the world class athletes and the dreamers who joined them in *C. C. Pyle's Amazing Foot Race: The True Story of the 1928 Coast-to-Coast Run Across America.* For chemists Charles Goodyear and Thomas Hancock, the race was to perfect a process to make rubber a cheap and useful industrial product. Charles Slack describes their rivalry and the resulting court case over patents in *Noble Obsession: Charles Goodyear, Thomas Hancock, and the Race to Unlock the Greatest Industrial Secret of the Nineteenth Century* (see chapter 11). In 1912 Antarctic explorer Robert Falcon Scott wanted desperately to be the first man to reach the South Pole. The trek from base camp to the pole and back had to be planned carefully and executed without a hitch. David Crane describes a man whose obsession cost him his life in *Scott of the Antarctic: A Life of Courage and Tragedy* (see chapter 1).

Erenberg, Lewis

The Greatest Fight of Our Generation: Louis vs. Schmeling. Oxford University Press, 2006. 274p. ISBN 0195177746.

When African American Joe Louis (1914–1981) and German Max Schmeling (1905–2005) boxed in 1938, more than sports glory was at stake. Newspapers around the globe had billed the match as a fight between American democracy and Nazi aggression. For the first time, white Americans were rooting for a black athlete to defend their national pride. The highly publicized bout lasted only about two minutes; and the loser, Schmeling, faced an unhappy Fuhrer. In this respectful dual biography, historian Lewis Erenberg continues the story after the fight and World War II, revealing that in later years Louis and Schmeling became friends. In fact, Schmeling even helped pay for the down-on-his-luck Louis's funeral.

> **Subjects:** African Americans; Boxers; Dual Biography; Germany; Group Discussion Books; Louis, Joe; Schmeling, Max
>
> **Now Try:** At the age of sixty-four, Louis wrote intimately about his boyhood on a farm in Alabama and his most famous matches in *Joe Louis: My Life*. Whereas Louis and Schmeling spoke mainly with their boxing gloves and were relatively reserved during their careers, boxer Muhammad Ali and sports broadcaster Howard Cosell were loud and brash. Different in many ways, Ali and Cosell became friends on and off the television screen. Dave Kindred recounts a warm alliance in *Sound and Fury: Two Powerful Lives, One Fateful Friendship*. David Remnick recounts how boxers Floyd Patterson and Sonny Liston lost to Ali in *King of the World: Muhammad Ali and the Rise of an American Hero* (see chapter 6). In the 1936 Olympics held in Berlin, Adolf Hitler expected the German athletes to outperform athletes from what he considered inferior races. William J. Baker recounts the triumph of an African American at the games in *Jesse Owens: An American Life* (see chapter 4). The race to break the four-minute mile in track was another international contest. Neal Bascomb recounts the story of an American, an Englishman, and an Australian in *The Perfect Mile: Three Athletes, One Goal, and Less Than Four Minutes to Achieve It* (see this chapter).

Feinstein, John

Living on the Black: Two Pitchers, Two Teams, One Season to Remember. Little, Brown, 2008. 525p. ISBN 9780316113915. Audiobook and large print available.

Home plate is white, seventeen inches wide, and outlined with a narrow band of black. According to veteran left-handed pitcher Tom Glavine (1966–) of the New York Mets, throwing the baseball to barely nick the space above the black and none of the white is the key to success. Having played twenty-one seasons when he spoke with sports author John Feinstein, Glavine knew what it took to win, but could not always do so. In his seventeenth season, right-hander Mike Mussina (1968–) of the New York Yankees pitched for another team in a different league, but he too knew the precision and nerve needed to be a successful pitcher in the spotlight of New York baseball. In this dual biography, Feinstein brings readers along as he learns what kinds of players excel as major league pitchers.

Subjects: Baseball Players; Dual Biography; Glavine, Tom; Mussina, Mike; New York Mets; New York Yankees

Now Try: Feinstein originally wanted to profile pitcher David Cone, but veteran sportswriter Roger Angell from *The New Yorker* spoke to Cone first. His book about a player's struggle with injuries in his last season is *Pitcher's Story: Innings with David Cone*. At the end of his long career, fastball pitcher Nolan Ryan wrote about his life in baseball in *Miracle Man: Nolan Ryan, the Autobiography* and about opposing pitchers in *Kings of the Hill: An Irreverent Look at the Men on the Mound*. Joshua Chamberlain of Maine and William Oates of Alabama lived remarkably comparable lives. Both were farmers' sons who fought in the Civil War and survived to become governors of their states. Mark Perry describes their commonality in *Conceived in Liberty: Joshua Chamberlain, William Oates, and the American Civil War* (see chapter 3). Robert E. Lee and Ulysses S. Grant were two of the most successful generals of the American Civil War. Gene Smith examines their leadership in *Lee and Grant: A Dual Biography*. Finding the similarities between two English novelists with different reputations is the premise of *The Same Man: George Orwell and Evelyn Waugh* by David Lebedoff.

Halberstam, David

The Teammates: A Portrait of Friendship. Hyperion, 2003. 217p. ISBN 14013-0057x. Audiobook and large print available.

After Ted Williams (1918–2002) died, David Halberstam sought out the former Boston Red Sox outfielder's closest friends. Among the former Red Sox players whom the author visited were Dominic DiMaggio (1917–), Bobby Doerr (1918–), and Johnny Pesky (1919–), men with whom Williams had been friends for over sixty years. Using the resulting interviews and research he had done for his 1989 book *Summer of '49*, the author wrote this portrait of the quartet, describing their origins, careers, and families. Readers will notice how strongly the author admires the four men and see how DiMaggio, Doerr, and Pesky lent stability to the emotionally explosive Williams.

Subjects: Baseball Players; Boston Red Sox; DiMaggio, Dominic; Doerr, Bobby; Friends; Group Biography; Group Discussion Books; Pesky, Johnny; Quick Reads; Williams, Ted

Now Try: In another of Halberstam's poignant sports books, athletes play the roles of both teammates and rivals. In *The Amateurs,* he reports on four American rowers competing at the Olympic trials in 1984 to represent the country in single sculls. Friendship among men is also the topic of Stephen Ambrose's look at soldiers and explorers, *Comrades: Brothers, Fathers, Heroes, Sons, Pals* (see chapter 3). Christopher Finch tells about the great creativity, accomplishment, and fun of a fellowship of Muppeteers and the genius of a creative leader in *Jim Henson: The Works* (see chapter 7).

Howard, Johnette

The Rivals: Chris Evert vs. Martina Navratilova: Their Epic Duels and Extraordinary Friendship. Broadway Books, 2005. 296p. ISBN 0767918843.

When Martina Navratilova (1956–) first faced Chris Evert (1954–) across the net of a tennis court, she was a sixteen-year-old unknown representing a communist country. Though she was only eighteen, Evert was an international sports star and symbol for women in sports. Over the next sixteen years the two women would play each other eighty times, sixty times in widely-watched title matches, in one of sports' greatest rivalries. However, according to sports journalist Johnette Howard, off the court the women were great friends. In this admiring dual biography set against a backdrop of the sexual revolution, the Cold War, gay rights, invasive journalism, and the rising popularity of women's sports, Howard tells how a friendship withstood the competitive strains of sports.

Subjects: Dual Biography; Evert, Chris; Friends; Homosexuals; Navratilova, Martina; Rivals; Teen Reads; Tennis Players; Women

Now Try: The most sensational rivalry in tennis was a battle of the sexes. Male chauvinist Bobby Riggs accepted the challenge of women's activist Billie Jean King to play in the Astrodome in 1973. Sports journalist Selena Roberts describes the event and its contenders in *A Necessary Spectacle: Billie Jean King, Bobby Riggs, and the Tennis Match That Leveled the Game*. A different type of prejudice brought African American tennis champ Althea Gibson and England's Jewish star Angela Buxton together at the Wimbledon Tennis Championship in 1956. Neither could find a doubles partner among the other women players. Bruce Schoenfeld reports that the two players became good friends and won the women's doubles title, in *The Match: Althea Gibson and Angel Buxton: How Two Outsiders—One Black, the Other Jewish—Forged a Friendship and Made Sports History*. Unlike Evert and Navratilova, tennis rivals John McEnroe and Bill Scanlon never became friends. After McEnroe wrote about his tennis career in *You Cannot Be Serious*, Scanlon wrote *Bad News for McEnroe: Blood, Sweat, and Backhands with John, Jimmy, Ilie, Ivan, Bjorn, and Vitas* to counter McEnroe's stories about their feud.

Joravsky, Ben

Hoop Dreams: A True Story of Hardship and Triumph. Turner, 1995. 301p. ISBN 1570-361533.

Chicago high school basketball stars Arthur Agee (1972–) and William Gates (1972–) will long be remembered as the young men they were in the 1994 documentary film *Hoop Dreams*. Ben Joravsky offers this gritty account of the six years that film crews followed the two talented athletes, who had to cope with the hardships of living in subsidized housing, resisting the temptations of drugs and gangs, and getting through the private school to which they had been recruited after years in Chicago public schools. Much of the story is told through dialogue, giving the book an on-the-spot tone. Although candid, Joravsky is remarkably hopeful that the boys' educations and altered dreams will offer them a better life.

Subjects: African Americans; Agee, Arthur; Basketball Players; Chicago; Dual Biography; Gates, William; Group Discussion Books; Poverty; Teen Reads

Now Try: The bad neighborhoods of Los Angeles have all the same problems as those in Chicago. Michael Sokolove recounts how a group of boys sought their salvation through high school baseball in *The Ticket Out: Darryl Strawberry and the Boys of Crenshaw* (see chapter 6). Jim Thorpe was not able to escape the Indian reservation system without breaking some amateur athletics rules, according to Bill Crawford in *All American: The Rise and Fall of Jim Thorpe* (see this chapter). Like Agee and Gates, the brothers Lafeyette and Pharoah Rivers grew up in public housing in Chicago, amid the drugs and gang warfare. Alex Kotlowitz describes their attempts to survive in *There Are No Children Here: The Story of Two Boys Growing Up in the Other America.* Some inner city children have found the help they need to get a good education. Miles

Corwin describes a year at South-Central High in Los Angeles in *And Still We Rise: The Trials and Triumphs of Twelve Gifted Inner-City Students*

McCarthy, Todd

Fast Women: The Legendary Ladies of Racing. Miramax Books, 2007. 311p. ISBN 1401352022.

When hot little European cars appeared in America after World War II, some sporty women bought them and started challenging men on race-tracks and in cross-country races. Driving Porsches, Jaguars, Ferraris, and MGs, they formed a virtual sorority of racers, who competed across the United States and in the Bahamas in the 1950s. Todd McCarthy profiles Evelyn Mull, Denise McCluggage, Ruth Levy, and their friends in this lively group biography that shows how daring women can be.

> **Subjects:** Friends; Group Biography; Levy, Ruth; McCluggage, Denise; Mull, Evelyn; Race Car Drivers; Women

> **Now Try:** In the 1920s Hellé Nice talked a manufacturer of Italian sports cars into letting her drive his cars in Grand Prix races. Her story is told in *Bugatti Queen: In Search of a French Racing Legend* by Miranda Seymour (see this chapter). Faster than the women in cars were the women in airplanes. In *The Happy Bottom Riding Club: The Life and Times of Pancho Barnes*, Lauren Kessler tells about one of the brave women pilots who flew in the barnstorm-ing circuit of early aviation. Eileen F. Lebow identifies over 100 such women in *Before Amelia: Women Pilots in the Early Days of Aviation*. Downhill skiing also offers an adrenaline rush. Olympic gold and silver medalist Picabo Street describes her "risk everything" life in *Picabo: Nothing to Hide*.

O'Connor, Ian

Arnie & Jack: Palmer, Nicklaus, and Golf's Greatest Rivalry. Houghton Mifflin, 2008. 354p. ISBN 9780618754465.

When they first met at the Athens Country Club in Ohio in 1958, Arnold Palmer (1929–) was almost twenty-nine years old, and Jack Nicklaus (1940–) was only eighteen. The older golfer, already a pro, beat the young amateur that day, but Nicklaus impressed all the veteran players on hand with his powerful drives. In the forty years that followed, Nicklaus won more of their head-to-head contests, but the charming Palmer always had more fans, a disappointment that Nicklaus finally accepted late in his ca-reer. In this dual biography, sports columnist Ian O'Connor claims that an intense rivalry eventually transformed into a warm friendship.

> **Subjects:** Dual Biography; Friends; Golfers; Nicklaus, Jack; Palmer, Arnold; Rivals

> **Now Try:** Palmer has penned several memoirs, the latest being the highly il-lustrated *Arnold Palmer: Memories, Stories, and Memorabilia from a Life On and Off the Course*. Though Nicklaus has collaborated on many golfing books, only in *Jack Nicklaus, My Story* does he discuss in detail his life and career. James Dodson loves writing about golf and golfers because he loves playing the game. In *The Dewsweepers: Seasons of Golf and Friendship*, Dodson de-scribes a summer that he spent recapturing the joy of the game with an elderly

12

group of early morning players. Friendships between world leaders rarely develop across oceans. David Fromkin describes how an English king and a U.S. president became friends in *The King and the Cowboy: Theodore Roosevelt and Edward the Seventh, Secret Partners.*

Stanton, Tom

Ty and the Babe: Baseball's Fiercest Rivals: A Surprising Friendship and the 1941 Has-Beens Golf Championship. Thomas Dunne Books, 2007. 290p. ISBN 978031236-1594.

"Ruth is a freak hitter," said Detroit Tigers hitting champion Ty Cobb (1886–1961) of his rival, Boston Red Sox player Babe Ruth. "Who will not last long," he added in a newspaper article about the big home run hitter. Of course Cobb was very wrong and probably knew it, for he was always jealously aware of Ruth's every accomplishment. Cobb had been the great star when Ruth entered major league baseball, and he did not share the spotlight willingly. In this dual biography, sportswriter Tom Stanton chronicles a great rivalry that became sweeter after retirement, when the athletes turned to golf.

> **Subjects:** Baseball Players; Cobb, Ty; Detroit Tigers; Dual Biography; Friends; Golfers; New York Yankees; Rivals; Ruth, Babe

> **Now Try:** Ty Cobb told his own story in *My Life in Baseball: The True Record.* Between 1951 and 1964 the New York Yankees won twelve pennants; the Chicago White Sox (with the next best overall record in the American League) won only one. The rivalry was fierce, and the game scores were close. At the heart of the teams were Chicago's Minnie Minosa and New York's Mickey Mantle. Bob Vanderberg recounts the rivalry in *Minnie and the Mick: The Go-Go White Sox Challenge the Fabled Yankee Dynasty, 1951–1964.* David Halberstam chronicles a great season, in which rivals Ted Williams and Joe Dimaggio both set hitting records while trying to get their teams to the World Series, in *Summer of '49.* Political differences may be as fierce sports rivalries. Doris Kearns Goodwin describes how President Abraham Lincoln managed to bring fierce political opponents together in his cabinet in *Team of Rivals: The Political Genius of Abraham Lincoln.* It is said that once a war has ended, the opposing soldiers often find that they are very similar. Harold G. Moore and Joseph L. Galloway returned to Vietnam to talk with former enemies in *We Are Soldiers Still: A Journey Back to the Battlefields of Vietnam.*

Consider Starting With . . .

These well-written Sports Biographies of modest length will appeal to general readers.

- Balf, Todd. *Major: A Black Athlete, a White Era, and the Fight to Be the World's Fastest Human Being.*

- Bascomb, Neal. *The Perfect Mile: Three Athletes, One Goal, and Less Than Four Minutes to Achieve It.*

- Callahan, Tom. *Johnny U: The Life & Times of Johnny Unitas.*

- Feinstein, John. *Caddy for Life: The Bruce Edwards Story.*

- Gray, Frances Clayton, and Yanick Rice Lamb. *Born to Win: The Authorized Biography of Althea Gibson.*

- Halberstam, David. *The Teammates: A Portrait of Friendship.*

- Kahn, Roger. *A Flame of Pure Fire: Jack Dempsey and the Roaring '20s.*

- McDonald, Brian. *Indian Summer: The Forgotten Story of Louis Sockalexis, the First Native American in Major League Baseball.*

- Pomerantz, Gary M. *Wilt, 1962: The Night of 100 Points and the Dawn of a New Era.*

Further Reading

Adamson, Lynda G.

Thematic Guide to Popular Nonfiction. Greenwood Press, 2006. 352p. ISBN 0313328552.

Adamson includes a chapter called "Sports Dreams" in her book about nonfiction topics. Each chapter describes a topic and then presents three lengthy reviews before suggesting other titles.

Cords, Sarah Statz

The Real Story: A Guide to Nonfiction Reading Interests. Libraries Unlimited, 2006. 460p. ISBN 1591582830.

Cords includes sections called "Sports Adventure" and "Sports Biographies" in her guide to nonfiction. She identifies titles and recommends further reading.

Jacobson, Robert

Sports in America: Recreation, Business, Education, and Controversy. Information Plus, 2006. 140p. ISBN 9781414407692.

Jacobson defines sports and examines its history and impact on the American people. Professional and amateur athletics of many levels are included.

Wyatt, Neal

The Readers' Advisory Guide to Nonfiction. American Libraries, 2007. 318p. ISBN 9780838909362.

Wyatt discusses sports stories in chapter 6 of her book and includes a generous list of titles to recommend to readers.

Appendix A

Biography Awards

There are many great biographies that, for lack of space, were not included this book, especially if they were older and out of print. One way of identifying them is to scan biographical awards lists. Because these lists are somewhat elusive, I have included here the ones that I identified during my research. Some of these prizes are not strictly biography awards. When the award is broader, I have listed only the books that I consider to be biographies.

ALA Notable Books for Adults

The Notable Books Council of the American Library Association Reference and User Services Association chooses twenty-five best books for adult readers annually, in the categories of fiction, nonfiction, and poetry. Biographies are found in the nonfiction category. The number of biographies included has varied widely since the award was established by the ALA Lending Section of the Division of Public Libraries in 1944.

2008

Einstein: His Life and Universe by Walter Isaacson

Gertrude Bell: Queen of the Desert, Shaper of Nations by Georgina Howell

Zookeeper's Wife: A War Story (about Polish citizen Antonina Zabinska) by Diane Ackerman

2007

James Tiptree, Jr.: The Double Life of Alice B. Sheldon by Julie Phillips

There Is No Me Without You: One Woman's Odyssey to Rescue Africa's Children (about Ethiopian foster parent Haregewoin Teferra) by Melissa Fay Greene

2006

John Brown, Abolitionist: The Man Who Killed Slavery, Sparked the Civil War, and Seeded Civil Rights by David S. Reynolds

The Orientalist: Solving the Mystery of a Strange and Dangerous Life (about author Lev Nussimbaum) by Tom Reiss

2005

> *Alexander Hamilton* by Ron Chernow
>
> *Goya* by Robert Hughes
>
> *The Ticket Out: Darryl Strawberry and the Boys of Crenshaw* by Michael Y. Sokolove

2004

> *Khrushchev: The Man and His Era* by William Taubman
>
> *Michelangelo and the Pope's Ceiling* by Ross King
>
> *Mountains Beyond Mountains* (about medical missionary Paul Farmer) by Tracy Kidder
>
> *Wrapped in Rainbows: The Life of Zora Neale Hurston* by Valerie Boyd

2003

> *Can't Be Satisfied: The Life and Times of Muddy Waters* by Robert Gordon
>
> *Jesse James: Last Rebel of the Civil War* by T. J. Stiles
>
> *Master of the Senate: The Years of Lyndon Johnson* by Robert A. Caro
>
> *Theodore Rex* (about Theodore Roosevelt) by Edmund Morris

2002

> *Grant* by Jean Edward Smith
>
> *John Adams* by David McCullough

2001

> *Bruce Chatwin* by Nicholas Shakespeare

2000

> *A Clearing in the Distance: Frederick Law Olmsted and America in the Nineteenth Century* by Witold Rybczynski
>
> *King of the World: Muhammad Ali and the Rise of an American Hero* by David Remnick
>
> *Vera (Mrs. Vladimir Nabokov)* by Stacy Schiff

1999

> *Beautiful Mind: A Biography of John Forbes Nash, Jr., Winner of the Nobel Prize in Economics, 1994* by Sylvia Nasar
>
> *The Life of Thomas More* by Peter Ackroyd
>
> *Lindbergh* by A. Scott Berg
>
> *Titan: The Life of John D. Rockefeller, Sr.* by Ron Chernow

1998

> *Utopia Parkway: The Life and Work of Joseph Cornell* by Deborah Solomon

1997

> *Sojourner Truth: A Life, a Symbol* by Nell Irvin Painter

1996

Lincoln by David Herbert Donald

Walt Whitman's America by David S. Reynolds

1995

Shot in the Heart (about murderer Gary Gilmour) by Mikal Gilmore

No Ordinary Time: Franklin and Eleanor Roosevelt by Doris Kearns Goodwin

1994

The Warburgs by Ron Chernow

This Little Light of Mine: The Life of Fannie Lou Hamer by Kay Mills

1993

Eleanor Roosevelt: A Life by Blanche Wiesen Cook

Truman. by David McCullough

Lincoln at Gettysburg: The Words That Remade America by Garry Wills

1992

The Jameses: A Family Narrative by R. W. B. Lewis

1991

Small Victories: The Real World of a Teacher, Her Students & Their High School (about teacher Jessica Siegel) by Samuel G. Freedman

1990

Paul Robeson by Martin Duberman

Songs from the Alley (about homeless women named Amanda and Wendy) by Kathleen Hirsch

Among Schoolchildren (about teacher Chris Zajac) by Tracy Kidder

1989

There were no books for this year because the committee changed its dating method.

1988

Oscar Wilde by Richard Ellmann

Freud: A Life for Our Times by Peter Gay

Nora: The Real Life of Maggie Bloom by Brenda Maddox

1987

Look Homeward: The Life of Thomas Wolfe by David Herbert Donald

The Fitzgeralds and the Kennedys by Doris Kearns Goodwin

Sartre: A Life by Ronald Hayman

1986

Margaret Bourke-White: A Biography by Vicki Goldberg

Murrow: His Life and Times by A. M. Sperber

Fidel: A Critical Portrait by Tad Szulc

1985

Chaplin: His Life and Art by David Robinson

Robert Capa: A Biography by Richard Whelan

1984

Diane Arbus: A Biography by Patricia Bosworth

The Nightmare of Reason: A Life of Franz Kafka by Ernst Pawel

Walt Whitman: The Making of a Poet by Paul Zweig

1983

Disraeli by Sarah Bradford

Peron: A Biography by Joseph Page

For the World to See: The Life of Margaret Bourke-White by Jonathan Silverman

1982

The Path to Power: The Years of Lyndon Johnson by Robert A. Caro

Thomas Hardy: A Biography by Michael Millgate

Isak Dinesen: The Life of a Storyteller by Judith Thurman

1981

Waldo Emerson by Gay Wilson Allen

Charles Darwin: A Man of Enlarged Curiosity by Peter Brent

W. H. Auden: A Biography by Humphrey Carpenter

Mornings on Horseback (about Theodore Roosevelt) by David McCullough

The Sage of Monticello (about Thomas Jefferson) by Dumas Malone

William Carlos Williams by Paul Mariani

1980

Walt Whitman: A Life by Justin Kaplan

Helen and Teacher: The Story of Helen Keller and Anne Sullivan Macy by Joseph P. Lash

Peter the Great: His Life and World by Robert K. Massie

Walter Lippmann and the American Century by Ronald Steel

Alice James: A Biography by Jean Strouse

Conrad in the Nineteenth Century by Ian Watt

1979

Streak of Luck (about Thomas A. Edison) by Robert Conot

Royal Charles: Charles II and the Restoration by Antonia Fraser

The Life and Work of Winslow Homer by Gordon Hendricks

Albert Camus: A Biography by Herbert Lottman

The Rise of Theodore Roosevelt by Edmund Morris

The Sitwells: A Family's Biography by John Pearson

1978

Max Perkins: Editor of Genius by A. Scott Berg

Introduction to Rembrandt by Kenneth Clark

The Guggenheims: An American Epic by John H. Davis

Bloody Mary: The Life of Mary Tudor by Carolly Erickson

E. M. Forster: A Life by P. N. Furbank

American Caesar, Douglas McArthur, 1880–1964 by William Manchester

Robert Kennedy and His Times by Arthur M. Schlesinger

1977

Samuel Johnson by Walter Jackson Bate

The Life and Times of Chaucer by John Champlin Gardner

Monet at Giverny by Claire Joyes

1976

Adolf Hitler by John Toland

1975

The House of Medici: Its Rise and Fall by Christopher Hibbert

The Years of MacArthur, Volume 11, 1941–1945 by D. Clayton James

Edith Wharton: A Biography by R. W. B. Lewis

Robert Louis Stevenson by James Pope-Hennessy

The Life of Emily Dickinson by Richard B. Sewall

Samuel Johnson by John Wain

1974

The Ordeal of Thomas Hutchinson by Bernard Bailyn

Aldous Huxley: A Biography by Sybille Bedford

The Power Broker: Robert Moses and the Fall of New York by Robert A. Caro

Paine by David Freeman Hawke

Sir Walter Raleigh by Robert Lacey

Between Me and Life: A Biography of Romaine Brooks by Meryle Secrest

Whistler: A Biography by Stanley Weintraub

1973

Humboldt and the Cosmos by Douglas Botting

Alexander Graham Bell and the Conquest of Solitude by Robert V. Bruce

Macaulay: The Shaping of the Historian by John Clive

FDR: The Beckoning of Destiny, 1882–1928 by Kenneth S. Davis

Cromwell, the Lord Protector by Antonia Fraser

The Death and Life of Malcolm X. by Peter Goldman

Stephen A. Douglas by Robert W. Johannsen

Mahler by Henri-Louis La Grange

H. G. Wells by Norman MacKenzie and Jeanne MacKenzie

George C. Marshall: Organizer of Victory, 1943–45 by Forrest C. Pogue

Bird Lives! The High Life and Hard Times of Charlie (Yardbird) Parker by Ross Russell

O'Neill, Son and Artist by Louis Sheaffer

1972

Virginia Woolf: A Biography by Quentin Bell

Piaf: A Biography by Simone Berteaut

Henry James, the Master: 1901–1916 by Leon Edel

Jackson Pollock: Energy Made Visible by Bernard Harper Friedman

The Clocks of Columbus: The Literary Career of James Thurber by Charles Shiveley Holmes

Eleanor: The Years Alone by Joseph P. Lash

The Unknown Orwell by Peter Stansky and William Miller Abrahams

Queen Victoria: From Her Birth to the Death of the Prince Consort by Cecil Blanche FitzGerald Woodham-Smith

1971

The Compleat Naturalist: A Life of Linnaeus by Wilfred Blunt

William Cullen Bryant by Charles H. Brown

Einstein: The Life and Times by Ronald William Clark

Eleanor and Franklin by Joseph P. Lash

Ibsen: A Biography by Michael Leverson Meyer

Stilwell and the American Experience in China, 1911–1945 by Barbara Tuchman

1970

Norman Rockwell, Artist and Illustrator by Thomas S. Buechner

Roosevelt: The Soldier of Freedom by James MacGregor Burns

Ordeal of Ambition: Jefferson, Hamilton, Burr by Jonathan Daniels

Zelda: A Biography by Nancy Mitford

Cocteau: A Biography by Francis Steegmuller

1969

The Shepherd of the Ocean: An Account of Sir Walter Raleigh and His Times by J. H. Adamson, and H. F. Folland

Mary, Queen of Scotts by Antonia Fraser

Prime Time: The Life of Edward R. Murrow by Alexander Kendrick

Sal Si Puedes: Cesar Chaves and the New American Revolution by Peter Matthiessen,

Darwin and the Beagle by Alan Moorehead

1968

George Washington in the American Revolution, 1775–1783 by James Thomas Flexner

Lytton Strachey: A Critical Biography by Michael Holroyd

Ho Chi Minh by Jean Lacouture

Andrew Wyeth by Richard Meryman

An Artist and the Pope: Based upon the Personal Recollections of Giacomo Manzu by Curtis Bill Pepper

Henry VIII by J. J. Scarisbrick

The Glass House: The Life of Theodore Roethke by Allan Seager

Tolstoy by Henri Troyat

T. H. White: A Biography by Sylvia Warner

1967

Nicholas and Alexandra by Robert Massie

"Old Bruin": Commodore Matthew Perry by Samuel Eliot Morison

Modigliani: A Biography of Amedeo Modigliani by Pierre Sichel

Variety of Men (collective biography of nine twentieth-century men) by Charles Percy Snow

1966

Winslow Homer at Prout's Neck by Philip C. Beam

Gauguin in the South Seas by Bengt Danielsson

Henry Moore: The Life and Work of a Great Sculptor by Donald Hall

Mr. Clemens and Mark Twain by Justin Kaplan

Age of Keynes by Robert Lekachman

J. M. W. Turner: His Life and Work by Jack Lindsay

Prometheus: The Life of Balzac by Andre Maurois

The Sun King by Nancy Mitford

1965

Edith Wharton & Henry James: The Story of Their Friendship by Millicent Bell

The Days of Henry Thoreau by Walter Roy Harding

South African Tragedy: The Life and Times of Jan Hofmeyr by Alan Paton

A Thousand Days: John F. Kennedy in the White House by Arthur Meier Schlesinger

Kennedy by Theodore C. Sorenson

Dreiser by W. A. Swanberg

1964

> *The Life of Lenin* by Louis Fischer
>
> *Marc Chagall* by Franz Meyer
>
> *The Kennedy Years* by the New York Times

1963

> *Eichmann in Jerusalem* by Hannah Arendt
>
> *Francis Bacon: The Temper of a Man* by Catherine Drinker Bowen
>
> *Tutankhamen: Life and Death of a Pharaoh* by Christiane Desroches-Noblecourt
>
> *The Prophet Outcast: Trotsky, 1929–1940* by Isaac Deutscher
>
> *Saint Genet, Actor and Martyr* by Jean Paul Sartre

1962

> *Henry James, Volume 2: The Conquest of London, 1870–1881* by Leon Edel
>
> *John Adams* by Page Smith
>
> *Scott Fitzgerald* by Andrew Turnbull

1961

> *Ishi in Two Worlds: A Biography of the Last Wild Indian in North America* by Theodora Kroeber
>
> *Sinclair Lewis: An American Life* by Mark Schorer
>
> *Citizen Hearst: A Biography of William Randolph Hearst* by W. A. Swanberg

1960

> *Dr. Schweitzer of Lambarene* by Norman Cousins
>
> *The Reluctant Surgeon: A Biography of John Hunter* by John Kobler
>
> *Thomas Wolfe: A Biography* by Elizabeth Nowell
>
> *Queen Mary, 1867–1953* by James Pope-Hennessey
>
> *Lord Burghley and Queen Elizabeth* by Conyers Read
>
> *Robert Frost: The Trial by Existence* by Elizabeth Shepley Sergeant

1959

> *Elizabeth the Great* by Elizabeth Jenkins
>
> *In the Days of McKinley* by Margaret Leech
>
> *John Paul Jones: A Sailor's Biography* by Samuel Eliot Morison
>
> *Age of Roosevelt, Volume 2: The Coming of the New Deal* by Arthur Meier Schlesinger

1958

> *The Private World of Pablo Picasso* by David Douglas Duncan
>
> *Naked to Mine Enemies: The Life of Cardinal Wolsey* by Charles Wright Ferguson
>
> *First Lady of the South: The Life of Mrs. Jefferson Davis* by Ishbel Ross
>
> *The Seven Worlds of Theodore Roosevelt* by Edward Charles Wagenknecht

1957

The Lion and the Throne: The Life and Times of Sir Edward Coke by Catherine Drinker Bowen

Mr. Baruch by Margaret L. Coit

Mighty Stonewall (about Confederate general Stonewall Jackson) by Frank Everson Vandiver

Albert Gallatin: Jeffersonian Financier and Diplomat by Raymond Walter

1956

John Quincy Adams and the Union by Samuel F. Bemis

Helen Keller by Van Wyck Brooks

Roosevelt: The Lion and the Fox by J. M. Burns

Eisenhower: The Inside Story by R. J. Donovan

Bernard Shaw: His Life, Work, and Friends by St. John G. Ervine

Richard the Third by P. M. Kendall

Profiles in Courage (collective biography of U.S. senators) by John F. Kennedy

Olympio: The Life of Victor Hugo by Andre Maurois

Jawaharlal Nehru by F. R. Maoaes

1955

The Solitary Singer (about poet Walt Whitman) by Gay W. Allen

The World of Albert Schweitzer by Erica Anderson

Young Sam Johnson by J. L. Clifford

The Crime of Galileo by George De Santillana

1954

U.S. Grant and the American Military Tradition by Bruce Catton

The Roosevelt Family of Sagamore Hill by Hermann Hagedorn

1953

Willa Cather: A Critical Biography by E. K. Brown

Ben Johnson of Westminster by Marchette Chute

The Life and Work of Sigmund Freud, Volume 1 by Ernest Jones

Lelia: The Life of George Sand by Andre Maurois

Mary Lincoln: Biography of a Marriage by R. P. Randall

Prince of Players: Edwin Booth by Eleanor Ruggles

Until Victory: Horace Mann and Mary Peabody by Louise H. Tharp

1952

Duveen by S. N. Behrman

George Washington, Volume 5: Victory with the Help of France by Douglas Freeman

Hugh Walpole by Rupert Hart-Davis

Abraham Lincoln by Benjamin P. Thomas

Windows for the Crown Prince by Elizabeth Gray Vining

Sam Clemens of Hannibal by Dixon Wecter

1951

George Washington, Volume 3: Planter and Patriot by Douglas Freeman

George Washington, Volume 4: Leader of the Revolution by Douglas Freeman

Life of John Maynard Keynes by Roy F. Harrod

Jefferson and the Rights of Man, Volume 2 by Dumas Malone

Charles Evans Hughes by Merlo J. Pusey

Florence Nightingale by Cecil Woodham-Smith

1950

Berlioz and the Romantic Century by Jacques Barzun

John Adams and the American Revolution by Catherine Bowen

Shakespeare of London by Marchette Gaylord Chute

John C. Calhoun by Margaret L. Coit

Life of Mahatma Gandhi by Louis Fischer

Life of Jesus by Edgar J. Goodspeed

Eleanor of Aquitaine by Amy Ruth Kelly

Captain Sam Grant by Lloyd Lewis

Emergence of Lincoln by Allan Nevins

Mao Tse-Tung by Pierre Stephen Robert Payne

Peabody Sisters of Salem by Louise Hall Tharp

Jane Mecom: The Favorite Sister of Benjamin Franklin by Carl Van Doren

1949

The Great Pierpont Morgan by Frederick Lew Allen

John Quincy Adams and the Foundation of American Foreign Policy by Samuel Flagg Bemis

The Life of Sir Arthur Conan Doyle by John D. Carr

Stalin by Isaac Deutscher

Dickens: His Character, Comedy, and Career by Hesketh Pearson

The Life of Ralph Waldo Emerson by Ralph L. Rusk

Roosevelt and the Russians by Edward R. Stettinius

Nathaniel Hawthorne by Mark Van Doren

1948

George Washington by Douglas S. Freeman

The Africa of Albert Schweitzer by Charles F. Joy and Melvin Arnold

Henry David Thoreau by Joseph W. Krutch

Jefferson and His Time, Volume 1 by Dumas Malone

Roosevelt and Hopkins by Robert Emmet Sherwood

1947

Gandhi and Stalin by Louis Fischer

The James Family by Francis Otto Matthiessen

1946

Geoffrey Chaucer of England by Marchette Gaylord Chute

The Lowells and Their Seven Worlds by Ferris Greenslet

Alexander of Macedon by Harold Lamb

Lafcadio Hearn by Vera McWilliams

1945

A. Woollcott by Samuel H. Adams

Young Jefferson by Claude G. Bowers

The Age of Jackson by Arthur Schlesinger

Tom Paine: America's Godfather by William E. Woodward

1944

Yankee from Olympus: Justice Holmes and His Family by Catherine Drinker Bowen

The World of Washington Irving by Van Wyck Brooks

Good Night, Sweet Prince: The Life and Times of John Barrymore by Gene Fowler

Samuel Johnson by Joseph W. Krutch

Anna and the King of Siam by Margaret Landon

Source: www.ala.org/ala/mgrps/divs/rusa/resources/notablebooks/index.cfm

Bancroft Prize in American History and Diplomacy

Columbia University in New York awards two or more Bancroft Prizes for American History and Diplomacy annually. Biographies are considered in the history category. There was no biography chosen in 2008 and in several previous years.

2007   William James: In the Maelstrom of American Modernism by Robert D. Richardson

2006 *Dwelling Place: A Plantation Epic (about Georgia planter Charles Colcock Jones and his family)* by Erskine Clarke

2004 *Jonathan Edwards: A Life* by George M. Marsden

2001 *The Chief: The Life of William Randolph Hearst* by David Nasaw

1996 *Walt Whitman's America: A Cultural Biography* by David S. Reynolds

1994 *W. E. B. Du Bois: The Biography of Race, 1868–1919* by David Levering Lewis

1993 *Margaret Fuller: An American Romantic Life, Volume 1: The Private Years* by Charles Capper

1992 *The Destructive War: William Tecumseh Sherman, Stonewall Jackson, and the Americans* by Charles Royster

1991 *A Midwife's Tale: The Life of Martha Ballard, Based on Her Diary* by Laurel Thatcher Ulrich

1985 *The Life and Times of Cotton Mather* by Kenneth Silverman

1984 *Booker T. Washington: The Wizard of Tuskegee, 1901–1915* by Louis R. Harlan

1983 *Eugene V. Debs: Citizen and Socialist* by Nick Salvatore

1981 *Walter Lipmann and the American Century* by Ronald Steel; *Alice James: A Biography* by Jean Strouse

1980 *Franklin D. Roosevelt and American Foreign Policy, 1932–1945* by Robert Dallek

1976 *Edith Wharton: A Biography* by R. W. B. Lewis

1974 *Frederick Jackson Turner: Historian Scholar, Teacher* by Ray Allen Billington; *The Devil and John Foster Dulles* by Townsend Hoopes

1973 *Booker T. Washington* by Louis R. Harlan

1972 *The Mathers: Three Generations of Puritan Intellectuals, 1596–1728* by Robert Middlekauff

1971 *Birth Control in America: The Career of Margaret Sanger* by David M. Kennedy

1970 *Charles Wilson Peale* by Charles Coleman Sellers

1969 *Woodrow Wilson and World Politics: America's Response to War and Revolution* by N. Gordon Levin Jr.

1967 *James K. Polk, Continentalist, 1843–1846* by Charles Sellers

1965 *Castlereagh and Adams: England and the United States, 1812–1823* by Bradford Perkins; *Portrait of a General: Sir Henry Clinton in the War of Independence* by William B. Wilcox

1964 *Franklin D. Roosevelt and the New Deal, 1932–1940* by William E. Leuchtenburgh; *The Liberator: William Lloyd Garrison* by John L. Thomas

1963 *John Adams* by Page Smith

1962 *Charles Francis Adams, 1807–1866* by Martin B. Duberman

1961 *Wilson: The Struggle for Neutrality, 1914–1915* by Arthur S. Link

1960 *In the Days of McKinley* by Margaret Leech

1959 *Henry Adams: The Middle Years* by Ernest Samuels

1957 *Wilson: The New Freedom* by Arthur S. Link

1956 *Henry Adams* by Elizabeth Stevenson; *Lincoln the President, Volume 1: The Last Full Measure:* by J. G. Randall and Richard N. Current

1952 *Charles Evans Hughes* by Merlo J. Pusey

1950 *Coronado* by Herbert E. Bolton

1949 *Roosevelt and Hopkins* by Robert E. Sherwood

Source: www.columbia.edu/cu/lweb/eguides/amerihist/bancroft.htm

Best Books for Young Adults

The Young Adult Library Services Association of the American Library Association issues an annual list of best books for teenaged readers, which includes some biographies.

2008

E. E. Cummings by Catherine Reef

The Great Adventure: Theodore Roosevelt and the Rise of Modern America by Albert Marrin

Jane Addams: Champion of Democracy by Judith Bloom Fradin and Dennis Brindell Fradin

Malcolm X: A Graphic Biography by Andrew Helfer

2007

Freedom Riders: John Lewis and Jim Zwerg on the Front Lines of the Civil Rights Movement by Ann Bausum

The Poet Slave of Cuba: A Biography of Juan Francisco Manzano by Margarita Engle and Sean Qualls

Escape!: The Story of the Great Houdini by Sid Fleischman

Something Out of Nothing: Marie Curie and Radium by Carla Killough McClafferty

Robert E. Lee: Virginian Soldier, American Citizen by James I. Robertson Jr.

2006

Maritcha: A Nineteenth Century American Girl by Tonya Bolden

Our Eleanor: A Scrapbook Look at Eleanor Roosevelt's Remarkable Life by Candace Fleming

Good Brother, Bad Brother: The Story of Edwin Booth and John Wilkes Booth by James Cross Giblin

John Lennon: All I Want Is the Truth by Elizabeth Partridge

2005

George Washington, Spymaster: How the Americans Outspied the British and Won the Revolutionary War by Thomas B. Allen

The Voice That Challenged a Nation: Marian Anderson and the Struggle for Equal Rights by Russell Freedman

Andy Warhol: Prince of Pop by Jan Greenberg and Sandra Jordan

Promises to Keep: How Jackie Robinson Changed America by Sharon Robinson

2004

Ben Franklin's Almanac: Being a True Account of the Good Gentleman's Life by Candace Fleming

Fight On! Mary Church Terrell's Battle for Integration by Dennis Brindell Fradin and Judith Bloom Fradin

Runaway Girl: The Artist Louise Bourgeois by Jan Greenberg and Sandra Jordan

The Tree of Life: A Book Depicting the Life of Charles Darwin, Naturalist, Geologist & Thinker by Peter Sis

2003

This Land Was Made For You and Me: The Life & Songs of Woody Guthrie by Elizabeth Partridge

2002

Vincent Van Gogh: Portrait of an Artist by Jan Greenberg and Sandra Jordan

Into a New Country: Eight Remarkable Women of the West by Liza Ketchum

Helen Keller: Rebellious Spirit by Laurie Lawlor

The Greatest: Muhammad Ali by Walter Dean Myers

2001

Ida B. Wells: Mother of the Civil Rights Movement by Dennis Brindell Fradin and Judith Bloom Fradin

Spellbinder: The Life of Harry Houdini by Tom Lalicki

Sitting Bull and His World by Albert Marrin

2000

Babe Didrikson Zaharias: The Making of a Champion by Russell Freedman

The Wild Colorado: The True Adventures of Fred Dellenbaugh, Age 17, on the Second Powell Expedition into the Grand Canyon by Richard Maurer

Restless Spirit: The Life and Work of Dorothea Lange by Elizabeth Partridge

Clara Schumann: Piano Virtuoso by Susanna Reich

Margaret Bourke-White: Her Pictures Were Her Life by Susan Goldman Rubin

1999

Martha Graham: A Dancer's Life by Russell Freedman

Commander-in-Chief: Abraham Lincoln and the Civil War by Albert Marrin

Young, Black, and Determined: A Biography of Lorraine Hansberry by Patricia McKissack

Behind the Mask: The Life of Queen Elizabeth I by Jane Resh Thomas

1998

The Triumphant Spirit: Portraits & Stories of Holocaust Survivors . . . Their Messages of Hope & Compassion by Nick Del Cazo

Jack London: A Biography by Daniel Dyer

Charles A. Lindbergh: A Human Hero by James Cross Giblin

1997

An American Hero: The True Story of Charles A. Lindbergh by Barry Denenberg

The Life and Death of Crazy Horse by Russell Freedman

1996

Abigail Adams: Witness to a Revolution by Natalie Bober

Father Greg & the Homeboys: The Extraordinary Journey of Father Greg Boyle and His Work with the Latino Gangs of East L.A. by Celeste Fremon

Virginia's General: Robert E. Lee and the Civil War by Albert Marrin

Source: www.ala.org/ala/mgrps/divs/yalsa/booklistsawards/bestbooksya/bestbooksyoung.cfm

John H. Dunning Prize

This prize from the American Historical Association honors the best book of the year on any subject pertaining to the history of the United States. A few biographies have won.

2001   *The Education of Laura Bridgman: The First Deaf and Blind Person to Learn Language* by Ernest Freeberg

1990   *A Midwife's Tale: The Life of Martha Ballard, Based on Her Diary* by Laurel Thatcher Ulrich

1989   *The Last of the Fathers: James Madison and the Republican Legacy* by Drew McCoy

1984   *Eugene V. Debs: Citizen and Socialist* by Nick Salvatore

1976   *Burnham of Chicago: Architect and Planner* by Thomas S. Hines

1972   *Mussolini and Fascism: The View from America* by John P. Diggins

1960   *Andrew Johnson and Reconstruction* by Eric L. McKitrick

1948   *Mahan and Sea Power* (about Captain Alfred Thayer Mahan) by William E. Livezey

1944   *Admiral Sims and the Modern American Navy* (about William Sowden Sims) by Elting E. Morison

1940   *Robert Dale Owen* by Richard W. Leopold

1933   *The Mission to Spain of Pierre Soule* by Amos A. Ettinger

1929   *Benjamin H. Hill: Secession and Reconstruction* by Haywood J. Pearce Jr.

Source: www.historians.org/prizes/AWARDED/DunningWinner.htm

Los Angeles Times Book Prize for Biography

This prestigious annual prize for biography was first awarded in 1980.

2007   *Young Stalin* by Simon Sebag Montefiore

2006   *Walt Disney: The Triumph of the American Imagination* by Neal Gabler

2005   *Matisse the Master: A Life of Henri Matisse, the Conquest of Colour, 1909–1954* by Hilary Spurling

2004   *De Kooning: An American Master* by Mark Stevens and Annalyn Swan

2003   *American Empire: Roosevelt's Geographer and the Prelude to Globalization* by Neil Smith

2002   *Master of the Senate: The Years of Lyndon Johnson* by Robert Caro

2001   *Theodore Rex* by Edmund Morris

2000   *Jefferson Davis, American* by William J. Cooper Jr.

1999   *Secrets of the Flesh: A Life of Colette* by Judith Thurman

1998   *Lindbergh* by A. Scott Berg

1997   *Whittaker Chambers: A Biography* by Sam Tanenhaus

1996   *Angela's Ashes: A Memoir* by Frank McCourt

1995   *Under My Skin: Volume One of My Autobiography, to 1949* by Doris Lessing

1994   *Shot in the Heart* (about murderer Gary Gilmour and his family) by Mikal Gilmore

1993   *Daniel Boone: The Life and Legend of an American Pioneer* by John Mack Faragher

1992   *Eleanor Roosevelt: Volume One* by Blanche Wiesen Cook

1991   *Righteous Pilgrim: The Life and Times of Harold L. Ickes, 1874–1952* by T. H. Watkins

1990   *A First-Class Temperament: The Emergence of Franklin Roosevelt* by Geoffrey C. Ward

1989   *This Boy's Life: A Memoir* by Tobias Wolff

1988   *Nora: A Biography of Nora Joyce* by Brenda Maddox

1987   *Hemingway* by Kenneth S. Lynn

1986   *Alexander Pope: A Life* by Maynard Mack

1985   *Solzhenitsyn* by Michael Scammell

1984   *The Nightmare of Reason: A Life of Franz Kafka* by Ernst Pawel

1983   *The Price of Power: Kissinger in the Nixon White House* by Seymour Hersh

1982   *Waldo Emerson: A Biography* by Gay Wilson Allen

1981   *Mornings on Horseback* (about Theodore Roosevelt) by David McCullough

1980   *Walter Lippmann and the American Century* by Ronald Steel

Source: www.latimes.com/extras/bookprizes/winners_byaward.html#biography

Marsh Biography Award

The Marsh Christian Trust of England awards this prize biennially for the best biography by an English author. Many of the books are also published in the United States.

2007   *George Mackay Brown: A Life* by Maggie Fergusson

2005   *My Heart Is My Own: The Life of Mary Queen of Scots* by John Guy

2003   *Rosalind Franklin: The Dark Lady of DNA* by Brenda Maddox

2001   *Mandela: The Authorized Biography* by Anthony Sampson

1999   *Coleridge: Darker Reflections* by Richard Holmes

1997   *Erskine Childers* by Jim Ring

1995   *Evelyn Waugh, a Biography* by Selina Hastings

1993   *The Man Who Wasn't Maigret: A Portrait of Georges Simenon* by Patrick Marnham

1991   *Clever Hearts: Desmond and Molly MacCarthy: A Biography* by Hugh and Mirabel Cecil

1989   *The Last Leopard: A Life of Giuseppe di Lampedusa* by David Gilmour

1987   *Shackleton* by Roland Huntford

Source: www.esu.org/page.asp?p=1836

National Book Award for Nonfiction

Biographies occasionally win this award from the National Book Foundation.

2002   *Master of the Senate: The Years of Lyndon Johnson* by Robert A. Caro

1997   *American Sphinx: The Character of Thomas Jefferson* by Joseph J. Ellis

1990   *House of Morgan: An American Banking Dynasty and the Rise of Modern Finance* by Ron Chernow

1973   *Diderot* by Arthur McCandless Wilson

1971   *Cocteau: A Biography* by Francis Steegmuller

1967   *Mr. Clemens and Mark Twain: A Biography* by Justin Kaplan

1964   *John Keats* by Aileen Ward

1963   *Henry James: A Life* by Leon Edel

1960   *James Joyce* (revised) by Richard Ellmann

1959   *Mistress to an Age: A Life of Madame De Stael* by J. Christopher Herold

1958   *Lion & the Throne: Edward Coke* by Catherine D. Bowen

1951   *Herman Melville* by Newton Arvin

1950   *Life of Ralph Waldo Emerson* by Ralph Rusk

Source: www.nationalbook.org

National Book Critics Circle Award for Biography

The National Book Critics Circle awards prizes for biography every year. The 2008 award will be issued in 2009.

2007   *Stanley: The Impossible Life of Africa's Greatest Explorer* by Tim Jeal

2006   *James Tiptree, Jr.: The Double Life of Alice B. Sheldon* by Julie Phillips

2005   *American Prometheus: The Triumph and Tragedy of J. Robert Oppenheimer* by Kai Bird and Martin J. Sherwin

2004   *De Kooning: An American Master* by Mark Stevens and Annalyn Swan

2003   *Khrushchev: The Man and His Era* by William Taubman

2002   *Charles Darwin: The Power of Place* by Janet Browne

2001   *Boswell's Presumptuous Task: The Making of the Life of Dr. Johnson* by Alan Sisman

2000   *Hirohito and the Making of Modern Japan* by Herbert P. Bix

1999   *The Hairstons: An American Family in Black and White* by Henry Wiencek

1998   *A Beautiful Mind: A Biography of John Forbes Nash, Jr., Winner of the Nobel Prize in Economics, 1994* by Sylvia Nasar

1997   *Ernie Pyle's War* by James Tobin

1996   *Angela's Ashes: A Memoir* by Frank McCourt

1995   *Savage Art: A Biography of Jim Thompson* by Robert Polito

1994   *Shot in the Heart* (about murderer Gary Gilmour and his family) by Mikal Gilmore

1993   *Genet* by Edmund White

1992   *Writing Dangerously: Mary McCarthy and Her World* by Carol Brightman

1991   *Patrimony: A True Story (about the Roth family)* by Philip Roth

1990   *Means of Ascent: The Years of Lyndon Johnson* by Robert Caro

1989   *A First-Class Temperament: The Emergence of Franklin Roosevelt* by Geoffrey C. Ward

1988   *Oscar Wilde* by Richard Ellman

1987   *Chaucer: His Life, His Work, His World* by Donald Howard

1986   *The Life of Langston Hughes, Vol. I: 1902–1941* by Arnold Rampersad

1985   *Henry James: A Life* by Leon Edel

1984   *Dostoevsky: The Years of Ordeal, 1850–59* by Joseph Frank

1983   *Minor Characters: A Young Woman's Coming-of-Age in the Beat Orbit of Jack Kerouac* (a memoir) by Joyce Johnson

Source: www.bookcritics.org/?go=pastAwards

National Book Critics Circle Award for Nonfiction

Biographies occasionally win the award that the National Book Critics Circle issues for nonfiction.

1999   *Time, Love, Memory: A Great Biologist and His Search for the Origins of Behavior* (about geneticist Seymour Benzer) by Jonathan Weiner

1983   *The Price of Power: Kissinger in the Nixon White House* by Seymour M Hersch

1982   *The Path to Power: The Years of Lyndon Johnson* by Robert A. Caro

1975   *Edith Wharton: A Biography* by R. W. B. Lewis

Source: www.bookcritics.org/?go=pastAwards

Pulitzer Prize for Biography or Autobiography

The longest-running prize for biography is given by the Pulitzer Prize Board, which began its annual awards in 1917.

2008 *Eden's Outcasts: The Story of Louisa May Alcott and Her Father* by John Matteson

2007 *The Most Famous Man in America: The Biography of Henry Ward Beecher* by Debby Applegate

2006 *American Prometheus: The Triumph and Tragedy of J. Robert Oppenheimer* by Kai Bird and Martin J. Sherwin

2005 *De Kooning: An American Master* by Mark Stevens and Annalyn Swan

2004 *Khrushchev: The Man and His Era* by William Taubman

2003 *Master of the Senate: The Years of Lyndon Johnson* by Robert A. Caro

2002 *John Adams* by David McCullough

2001 *W. E. B. Du Bois: The Fight for Equality and the American Century, 1919–1963* by David Levering Lewis

2000 *Vera (Mrs. Vladimir Nabokov): A Biography* by Stacy Schiff

1999 *Lindbergh* by A. Scott Berg

1998 *Personal History* by Katharine Graham

1997 *Angela's Ashes: A Memoir* by Frank McCourt

1996 *God: A Biography* by Jack Miles

1995 *Harriet Beecher Stowe: A Life* by Joan D. Hedrick

1994 *W. E. B. Du Bois: Biography of a Race 1868–1919* by David Levering Lewis

1993 *Truman* by David McCullough

1992 *Fortunate Son: The Autobiography of Lewis B. Puller, Jr.* by Lewis B. Puller Jr.

1991 *Jackson Pollock* by Steven Naifeh and Gregory White Smith

1990 *Machiavelli in Hell* by Sebastian de Grazia

1989 *Oscar Wilde* by Richard Ellmann

1988 *Look Homeward: A Life of Thomas Wolfe* by David Herbert Donald

1987 *Bearing the Cross: Martin Luther King Jr. and the Southern Christian Leadership Conference* by David J. Garrow

1986 *Louise Bogan: A Portrait* by Elizabeth Frank

1985 *The Life and Times of Cotton Mather* by Kenneth Silverman

1984 *Booker T. Washington: The Wizard of Tuskegee, 1901–1915* by Louis R. Harlan

1983   *Growing Up* by Russell Baker

1982   *Grant: A Biography* by William McFeely

1981   *Peter the Great: His Life and World* by Robert K. Massie

1980   *The Rise of Theodore Roosevelt* by Edmund Morris

1979   *Days of Sorrow and Pain: Leo Baeck and the Berlin Jews* by Leonard Baker

1978   *Samuel Johnson* by Walter Jackson Bate

1977   *A Prince of Our Disorder: The Life of T. E. Lawrence* by John E. Mack

1976   *Edith Wharton: A Biography* by R. W. B. Lewis

1975   *The Power Broker: Robert Moses and the Fall of New York* by Robert Caro

1974   *O'Neill, Son and Artist* by Louis Sheaffer

1973   *Luce and His Empire* by W. A. Swanberg

1972   *Eleanor and Franklin* by Joseph P. Lash

1971   *Robert Frost: The Years of Triumph, 1915–1938* by Lawrance Thompson

1970   *Huey Long* by T. Harry Williams

1969   *The Man from New York: John Quinn and His Friends* by Benjamin Lawrence Reid

1968   *Memoirs* by George F. Kennan

1967   *Mr. Clemens and Mark Twain* by Justin Kaplan

1966   *A Thousand Days: John F. Kennedy in the White House* by Arthur M. Schlesinger, Jr

1965   *Henry Adams* by Ernest Samuels

1964   *John Keats* by Walter Jackson Bate

1963   *Henry James* by Leon Edel

1962   (No Award)

1961   *Charles Sumner and the Coming of the Civil War* by David Donald

1960   *John Paul Jones* by Samuel Eliot Morison

1959   *Woodrow Wilson, American Prophet* by Arthur Walworth

1958   *George Washington, Volumes I–VI* by Douglas Southall Freeman; *George Washington, Volume VII*, by John Alexander Carroll and Mary Wells Ashworth

1957   *Profiles in Courage* (a collective biography profiling U.S. senators) by John F. Kennedy

1956   *Benjamin Henry Latrobe* by Talbot Faulkner Hamlin

1955   *The Taft Story* by William S. White

1954   *The Spirit of St. Louis* (a memoir) by Charles A. Lindbergh

1953   *Edmund Pendleton, 1721–1803* by David J. Mays

1952   *Charles Evans Hughes* by Merlo J. Pusey

1951   *John C. Calhoun: American Portrait* by Margaret Louise Coit

1950   *John Quincy Adams and the Foundations of American Foreign Policy* by Samuel Flagg Bemis

1949   *Roosevelt and Hopkins* by Robert E. Sherwood

1948   *Forgotten First Citizen: John Bigelow* by Margaret Clapp

1947   *The Autobiography of William Allen White* by William Allen White

1946   *Son of the Wilderness: The Life of John Muir* by Linnie Marsh Wolfe

1945   *George Bancroft: Brahmin Rebel* by Russell Blaine Nye

1944   *The American Leonardo: The Life of Samuel F B. Morse* by Carleton Mabee

1943   *Admiral of the Ocean Sea: A Life of Christopher Columbus* by Samuel Eliot Morison

1942   *Crusader in Crinoline: The Life of Harriet Beecher Stowe* by Forrest Wilson

1941   *Jonathan Edward* by Ola Elizabeth Winslow

1940   *Woodrow Wilson, Life and Letters. Vols. VII and VIII* by Ray Stannard Baker

1939   *Benjamin Franklin* by Carl Van Doren

1938   *Andrew Jackson* by Marquis James; *Pedlar's Progress* by Odell Shepard

1937   *Hamilton Fish* by Allan Nevins

1936   *The Thought and Character of William James* by Ralph Barton Perry

1935   *R. E. Lee* by Douglas S. Freeman

1934   *John Hay* by Tyler Dennett

1933   *Grover Cleveland* by Allan Nevins

1932   *Theodore Roosevelt* by Henry F. Pringle

1931   *Charles W. Eliot* by Henry James

1930   *The Raven: A Biography of Sam Houston* by Marquis James

1929   *The Training of an American: The Earlier Life and Letters of Walter H. Page* by Burton J. Hendrick

1928   *The American Orchestra and Theodore Thomas* by Charles Edward Russell

1927   *Whitman* by Emory Holloway

1926   *The Life of Sir William Osler* by Harvey Cushing

1925   *Barrett Wendell and His Letters* by M. A. Dewolfe Howe

1924   *From Immigrant to Inventor* by Michael Idvorsky Pupin

1923   *The Life and Letters of Walter H. Page* by Burton J. Hendrick

1922   *A Daughter of the Middle Border* by Hamlin Garland

1921   *The Americanization of Edward Bok* by Edward Bok

1920   *The Life of John Marshall* by Albert J. Beveridge

1919   *The Education of Henry Adams* by Henry Adams

1918   *Benjamin Franklin, Self-Revealed* by William Cabell Bruce

1917   *Julia Ward Howe* by Laura E. Richards and Maude Howe Elliott

Source: www.pulitzer.org

Pulitzer Prize for Nonfiction

A biography occasionally wins the prize for nonfiction from the Pulitzer Prize Board.

2001   *Hirohito and the Making of Modern Japan* by Herbert P. Bix

1993   *Lincoln at Gettysburg: The Words That Remade America* by Garry Wills

1980   *Gödel, Escher, Bach: An Eternal Golden Braid* by Douglas R. Hofstadter

1972   *Stilwell and the American Experience in China, 1911–45* by Barbara W. Tuchman

Source: www.pulitzer.org

Whitbread Biography Award (Now Called the Costa Book Award)

The prestigious Whitbread Book Awards were sponsored by the British corporation Whitbread PLC from 1971 to 2005, when sponsorship was transferred to Costa Coffee. The new awards are called Costa Book Awards. These are British awards, but many of the books are subsequently published in the United States and will interest readers who enjoy British culture and history. The 2008 winner will be announced in 2009.

2007   *Young Stalin* by Simon Sebag Montefiore

2006   *Keeping Mum: A Wartime Childhood* by Brian Thompson

2005   *Matisse: The Master* by Hilary Spurling

2004   *My Heart Is My Own: The Life of Mary Queen of Scots* by John Guy

2003   *Orwell: The Life* by D. J. Taylor

2002   *Samuel Pepys: The Unequalled Self* by Claire Tomalin

2001   *Selkirk's Island* by Diana Souhami

2000 *Bad Blood* by Lorna Sage

1999 *Berlioz, Volume 2* by David Cairns

1998 *Georgiana, Duchess of Devonshire* by Amanda Foreman

1997 *Victor Hugo* by Graham Robb

1996 *Thomas Cranmer: A Life* by Diarmaid MacCulloch

1995 *Gladstone* by Roy Jenkins

1994 *D. H. Lawrence: The Married Man* by Brenda Maddox

1993 *Philip Larkin: A Writer's Life* by Andrew Motion

1992 *Trollope* by Victoria Glendinning

1991 *A Life of Picasso* by John Richardson

1990 *A. A. Milne: His Life* by Ann Thwaite

1989 *Coleridge: Early Visions* by Richard Holmes

1988 *Tolstoy* by A. N. Wilson

1987 *Under the Eye of the Clock* by Christopher Nolan

1986 *Gilbert White* by Richard Mabey

1985 *Hugh Dalton* by Ben Pimlott

1984 *T. S. Eliot* by Peter Ackroyd

1983 *Vita: The Life of V. Sackville-West* by Victoria Glendinning; *King George V* by Kenneth Rose

1982 *Bismark* by Edward Crankshaw

1981 *Monty: The Making of a General* (about Field Marshall Bernard Law Montgomery) by Nigel Hamilton

1980 *On the Edge of Paradise: A. C. Benson, the Diarist* by David Newsome

1979 *About Time: An Aspect of Autobiography* by Penelope Mortimer

1978 *Lloyd George: The People's Champion* by John Grigg

1977 *Mary Curzon* by Nigel Nicolson

1976 *Elizabeth Gaskell* by Winifred Gerin

1975 *In Our Infancy: An Autobiography* by Helen Corke

1974 *Poor Dear Brendan: The Quest for Brendan Bracken* by Andrew Boyle

1973 *CB: A Life of Sir Henry Campbell-Bannerman* by John Wilson

1972 *Trollope* by James Pope-Hennessey

1971 *Henrik Ibsen* by Michael Meyer

Source: costabookawards.com

Appendix B

Top Biographers

Most of the titles listed in this book were written by first-time biographers, often historians, journalists, novelists, or others who were inspired enough by the life of a famous person to spend years researching and writing. Reading their introductions, you will learn of their personal journeys to discover the influences and motivations behind the lives that they found meaningful. Many of these authors will never write a biography again.

Other authors are adept at writing biographies and produce a series of books recounting lives of figures that interest them. I call these professionals "top biographers." They either dedicate themselves to biography or return to the genre repeatedly during their writing careers. In either case, they succeed in producing books that find willing readers. Few of these writers are under the age of fifty. Many have come to biography late in their careers. To make identifying biographies by top biographers easy, I have created lists of their titles(listed chronologically by publication date). Readers or librarians may check under an author's name to find unread titles. I have also included under each author the names of other authors who write similar types of books, which may serve as read-alikes. Librarians may consult these lists when selecting, retaining, and promoting biographies.

Ackerman, Kenneth D. (1951–): Attorney who writes detailed historical biographies about flawed political characters.

- *Dark Horse: The Surprise Election and Political Murder of President James A. Garfield* (2003)

- *Boss Tweed: The Rise and Fall of the Corrupt Pol Who Conceived the Soul of Modern New York* (2005)

- *Young J. Edgar: Hoover, the Red Scare, and the Assault on Civil Liberties* (2007)

  Authors to try: Andrew Burstein, Robert A. Caro, David Herbert Donald, Doris Kearns Goodwin, Kenneth Silverman

Ackroyd, Peter (1949–): Poet, novelist, playwright, and critic who writes biographies about historical and literary figures. Many of his novels are also biographical.

- *Ezra Pound and His World* (1981)

- *T. S. Eliot: A Life* (1984)

- *Dickens* (1992)

- *Blake* (1995)

- *The Life of Thomas More* (1998)

- *Chaucer* (2005)

- *Shakespeare: The Biography* (2005)

- *J. M. W. Turner* (2006)

- *Newton* (2006)

- *Poe: A Life Cut Short* (2009)

  Authors to try: Benita Eisler, Paul Johnson, Ross King, John Man, Stanley Weintraub

Ambrose, Stephen E. (1936–2002): Historian who wrote biographies about American military and political figures. His histories also have strong biographical content.

- *Halleck: Lincoln's Chief of Staff* (1962)

- *Upton and the Army* (1964)

- *The Supreme Commander: The War Years of General Dwight D. Eisenhower* (1970)

- *Crazy Horse and Custer: The Parallel Lives of Two American Warriors* (1975)

- *Milton S. Eisenhower: Educational Statesman* (1983)

- *Eisenhower: Soldier, General of the Army, President-elect, 1890–1952* (1983)

- *Eisenhower: The President* (1984)

- *Nixon: The Education of a Politician, 1913–1962* (1987)

- *Nixon: The Triumph of a Politician, 1962–1972* (1989)

- *Nixon: The Ruin and Recovery of a Politician 1973–1990* (1991)

- *Comrades: Brothers, Fathers, Heroes, Sons, Pals* (1999)

  Authors to try: Bruce Catton, Robert Coram, John Keegan, Michael Korda, William S. McFeely, Larry McMurtry, Jean Edward Smith, Evan Thomas

Bego, Mark (n.d.): Prolific biographer who writes enthusiastic biographies of musicians and other celebrities. The following is only a sample of his many titles.

- *Rock Hudson: Public and Private* (1986)

- *I Fall to Pieces: The Music and the Life of Patsy Cline* (1995)

- *Madonna: Blonde Ambition* (2000)

- *Julia Roberts* (2003)

- *Joni Mitchell* (2005)

- *Cher: If You Believe* (2005)

- *Billy Joel: The Biography* (2007)

    Authors to try: Brian J. Robb, Anne Edwards, James Parish, James Spada, J. Randy Taraborrelli

Berg, A. Scott (1949–): Author who writes epic biographies of complex characters whose lives are central to a period of cultural history.

- *Max Perkins: Editor of Genius* (1978)

- *Goldwyn: A* Biography (1989)

- *Lindbergh* (1998)

- *Kate Remembered* (2003)

    Authors to try: Blanche Wiesen Cook, Neal Gabler, Roy Hattersley, Walter Isaacson, Mary S. Lovell, David McCullough, David Nasaw

Bergreen, Laurence (1950–): Biographer whose earlier works focused on cultural figures but who has successfully turned to the great explorers in his latest books.

- *James Agee: A Life* (1984)

- *As Thousands Cheer: The Life of Irving Berlin* (1990)

- *Capone: The Man and the Era* (1994)

- *Louis Armstrong: An Extravagant Life* (1997)

- *Over the Edge of the World: Magellan's Terrifying Circumnavigation of the Globe* (2003)

- *Marco Polo: From Venice to Xanadu* (2007)

    Authors to try: Linda H. Davis, Edward Jablonski, Ben Macintyre, Charles Nicholl, Stanley Weintraub, Simon Winchester

Blackman, Ann (n.d.): Journalist assigned to Washington, D.C., for most of her career. She writes stories associated with the nation's capital city.

- *The Seasons of Her Life: A Biography of Madeleine Korbel Albright* (1998)

- *The Spy Next Door: The Extraordinary Secret Life of Robert Philip Hanssen, the Most Damaging FBI Agent in U.S. History* (2002)

- *Wild Rose: Rose O'Neale Greenhow, Civil War Spy* (2005)

    Authors to try: Katherine Frank, Mary S. Lovell, Brenda Maddox, Claire Tomalin, Margaret Truman

Brands, H. W. (1953–): Historian who has turned to writing biography late in his career.

- *T.R.: The Last Romantic* (1997)

- *Masters of Enterprise: Giants of American Business from John Jacob Astor and J.P. Morgan to Bill Gates and Oprah Winfrey* (1999)

- *The First American: The Life and Times of Benjamin Franklin* (2000)

- *Woodrow Wilson* (2003)

- *Andrew Jackson: A Life and Times* (2005)

- *Traitor to His Class: The Privileged Life and Radical Presidency of Franklin Delano Roosevelt* (2007)

> **Authors to try**: Robert A. Caro, David McCullough, William S. McFeely, Edmund Morris, Robert Remini, Jean Edward Smith

Brinkley, Douglas (1960–): Historian with many interests who is especially known for his biographies of American political figures.

- *Driven Patriot: The Life and Times of James Forrestal* (1992)

- *Dean Acheson: The Cold War Years, 1953–1971* (1992)

- *Jimmy Carter: The Triumph and the Turmoil* (1996)

- *The Unfinished Presidency: Jimmy Carter's Journey beyond the White House* (1998)

- *Rosa Parks* (2000)

- *Wheels for the World: Henry Ford, His Company, and a Century of Progress, 1903-2003* (2003)

- *Tour of Duty: John Kerry and the Vietnam War* (2004)

- *Parish Priest: Father Michael McGivney and the Knights of Columbus* (2006)

- *Gerald R. Ford* (2007)

> **Authors to try**: Robert A. Caro, David Halberstam, Nigel Hamilton, David Maraniss, Garry Wills.

Burstein, Andrew (1952–): Historian who writes lively biographies about nineteenth-century Americans.

- *Inner Jefferson: Portrait of a Grieving Optimist* (1995)

- *The Passions of Andrew Jackson* (2003)

- *Jefferson's Secrets: Death And Desire In Monticello* (2005)

- *The Original Knickerbocker: The Life of Washington Irving* (2007)

> **Authors to try**: H. W. Brands, Joseph J. Ellis, Walter Isaacson, Eve LaPlante, David McCullough, William S. McFeely, Robert Remini, Jean Edward Smith, Brenda Wineapple

Caro, Robert A. (1935–): Investigative reporter who has won numerous literary awards for his political biographies. He is writing a fourth book for his series on Lyndon Johnson.

- *The Power Broker: Robert Moses and the Fall of New York* (1974)

- *The Path to Power: The Years of Lyndon Johnson* (1982)
- *Means of Ascent: The Years of Lyndon Johnson* (1990)
- *Master of the Senate: The Years of Lyndon* Johnson (2002)

    Authors to try: Douglas Brinkley, Robert Dallek, David Herbert Donald, Nigel Hamilton, Edmund Morris, Jean Edward Smith

Chandler, Charlotte (n.d.): Biographer who relies on interviews with friends and colleagues to portray film directors, comedians, and leading ladies.

- *Hello, I Must Be Going: Groucho and His Friends* (1978)
- *I, Fellini* (1995)
- *Nobody's Perfect: Billy Wilder, a Personal Biography* (2002)
- *It's Only a Movie: Alfred Hitchcock, a Personal Biography* (2005)
- *Girl Who Walked Home Alone: Bette Davis, a Personal Biography* (2006)
- *Ingrid: Ingrid Bergman, a Personal Biography* (22007)
- *Not the Girl Next Door* (2008)

    Authors to try: Anne Edwards, Margot Peters, James Spada, David Spoto

Chernow, Ron (1943–): Business journalist who turned into a biographer of bankers and corporate executives. His lengthy but lively books mix descriptions of the financial world with the personal relationships of the subjects.

- *House of Morgan: An American Banking Dynasty and the Rise of Modern Finance* (1990)
- *Warburgs: The Twentieth-Century Odyssey of a Remarkable Jewish Family* (1993)
- *Titan: The Life of John D. Rockefeller, Sr.* (1998)
- *Alexander Hamilton* (2004)

    Authors to try: Peter Collier, Neal Gabler, Walter Isaacson, David Nasaw, Sally Bedall Smith, Jean Strouse

Collier, Peter (1939–): Versatile author of epic family biographies.

- *The Rockefellers: An American Dynasty* (1976)
- *The Kennedys: An American Drama* (1984)
- *The Fords: An American Epic* (1987)
- *The Fondas: A Hollywood Dynasty* (1991)
- *The Roosevelts: An American Saga* (1994)

    Authors to try: Ron Chernow, Neal Gabler, Doris Kearnes Goodwin, Paul C. Nagel, David Nasaw, Jean Strouse

Coote, Stephen (n.d.): English biographer who writes about figures from British and European history. These titles are available in American editions.

- *Royal Survivor: The Life of Charles II* (2000)
- *Samuel Pepys: A Life* (2001)
- *Napoleon and the Hundred Days* (2005)

  Authors to try: Peter Ackroyd, Antonia Fraser, Charles Nicholl, Nigel Saul, John Sugden, Stanley Weintraub

Davis, Linda H. (1953–): Biographer who writes engagingly about literary figures whom other writers have neglected.

- *Onward and Upward: A Biography of Katharine S. White* (1987)
- *Badge of Courage: The Life of Stephen Crane* (1998)
- *Charles Addams: A Cartoonist's Life* (2006)

  Authors to try: Benita Eisler, Jeffrey Meyers, David Michaelis, Diane Wood Middlebrook, Margot Peters

Donald, David Herbert (1920–): A Civil War historian who has written popular biographies about President Lincoln and his associates as well as about novelist Thomas Wolfe.

- *Lincoln's Herndon: A Biography* (1948)
- *Charles Sumner and the Coming of the Civil War* (1960)
- *Charles Sumner and the Rights of Man* (1970)
- *Look Homeward: A Life of Thomas Wolfe* (1987)
- *Lincoln* (1995)
- *"We Are Lincoln Men": Abraham Lincoln and His Friends* (2004)

  Authors to try: Stephen E. Ambrose, Walter Isaacson, Robert K. Massie, William S. McFeely, Paul C. Nagel, Robert Remini, Carl Sandburg, Jean Edward Smith

Edwards, Anne (1927–): Former writer of screenplays and novels who turned to biography after the success of her book on Judy Garland. Most of her celebrity biographies feature women.

- *Judy Garland: A Biography* (1975)
- *Vivien Leigh: A Biography* (1976)
- *Sonya: The Life of Countess Tolstoy* (1981)
- *The Road to Tara: The Life of Margaret Mitchell* (1983)
- *Matriarch: Queen Mary and the House of Windsor* (1984)
- *A Remarkable Woman: A Biography of Katharine Hepburn* (1985)

- *Early Reagan: The Rise to Power* (1987)

- *The De Milles: An American Family* (1988)

- *Shirley Temple: American Princess* (1988)

- *Royal Sisters: Queen Elizabeth and Princess Margaret* (1990)

- *Streisand: A Biography* (1997)

- *Ever After: Diana and the Life She Led* (2000)

- *Maria Callas: An Intimate Biography* (2001)

- *The Reagans: Portrait of a Marriage* (2003)

> **Authors to try**: Fred Lawrence Guiles, C. David Heymann, Charles Higham, Kitty Kelley, Andrew Morton, Tom Santopietro, Sally Bedall Smith, James Spada, J. Randy Taraborrelli

Eisler, Benita (1937–): Author whose distinctive novel-like biographies dramatize artistic lives.

- *O'Keeffe and Stieglitz: An American Romance* (1991)

- *Byron: Child of Passion, Fool of Fame* (1999)

- *Chopin's Funeral* (2003)

- *Naked in the Marketplace: The Lives of George Sand* (2006)

> **Authors to try**: Peter Ackroyd, Linda H. Davis, Thomas Keneally, Sally Bedall Smith, Clairie Tomlin, Anne Wroe

Eliot, Marc (n.d.): Author of enthusiastic music biographies who has turned to serious accounts of Hollywood stars.

- *Death of a Rebel: A Biography of Phil Ochs* (1979)

- *Down Thunder Road: The Making of Bruce Springsteen* (1992)

- *Walt Disney: Hollywood's Dark Prince* (1993)

- *To the Limit: The Untold Story of the Eagles* (1997)

- *Cary Grant: The Biography* (2004)

- *Jimmy Stewart: A Biography* (2006)

- *Reagan: The Hollywood Years* (2008)

> **Authors to try**: Marc Bego, Charlotte Chandler, Charles Higham, Jeffrey Meyers, James Spada, David Spoto

Ellis, Joseph J. (1943–): American historian who writes engaging biographies of revolutionary era figures.

- *The New England Mind in Transition: A Life of Samuel Johnson, 1696–1772* (1973)

- *The Passionate Sage: The Character and Legacy of John Adams* (1993)
- *American Sphinx: The Character of Thomas Jefferson* (1997)
- *Founding Brothers: The Revolutionary Generation* (2000)
- *His Excellency George Washington* (2004)

> **Authors to try**: H. W. Brands, Andrew Burstein, Walter Isaacson, David McCullough, Eve LaPlante, Paul C. Nagel, Robert Remini, Garry Wills, Brenda Wineapple

Frank, Katherine (1949–): Biographer whose interest is in adventurous women who struggle against expectations imposed by their families.

- *A Voyager Out: The Life of Mary Kingsley* (1986)
- *A Chainless Soul: A Life of Emily Bronte* (1990)
- *Passage to Egypt: The Life of Lucie Duff Gordon* (1994)
- *Indira: The Life of Indira Nehru Gandhi* (2002)

> **Authors to try**: Ann Blackman, Benita Eisler, Mary S. Lovell, Diane Wood Middlebrook, Virginia Rounding, Claire Tomalin

Fraser, Antonia (1932): Popular mystery writer who also writes novel-like biographies about British and French monarchs.

- *Mary, Queen of Scotts* (1969)
- *Cromwell: The Lord Protector* (1973)
- *King James VI of Scotland, I of England* (1975)
- *Royal Charles: Charles II and the Restoration* (1979)
- *Warrior Queens* (1989)
- *Wives of Henry VIII* (1992)
- *Marie Antoinette: The Journey* (2001)
- *Love and Louis XIV: The Women in the Life of the Sun King* (2006)

> **Authors to try**: Stephen Coote, Benita Eisler, Robert K. Massie, Nigel Saul, Claire Tomalin, Alison Weir, Derek Wilson

Goodwin, Doris Kearns (1943–): Historian who portrays political figures in the context of their times.

- *Lyndon Johnson and the American Dream* (1976)
- *Fitzgeralds and the Kennedys: An American Saga* (1986)
- *No Ordinary Time: Franklin and Eleanor Roosevelt* (1994)
- *Team of Rivals: The Political Genius of Abraham Lincoln* (2005)

> **Authors to try**: Stephen A. Ambrose, James MacGregor Burns, Peter Collier, Daniel Mark Epstein, David Halberstam, Joseph P. Lash, Jean Strouse

Halberstam, David (1934–2007): Best-selling author interested in characters involved in war, politics, and sports.

- *The Unfinished Odyssey of Robert Kennedy* (1969)
- *Ho* (1971)
- *The Amateurs: The Story of Four Young Men and Their Quest for an Olympic Gold Medal* (1985)
- *Playing for Keeps: Michael Jordan and the World He Made* (1999)
- *Teammates* (2003)
- *Education of a Coach* (2005)

  Authors to try: Douglas Brinkley, Doris Kearns Goodwin, Nigel Hamilton, David Maraniss, Leigh Montville, Garry Wills, Bob Woodward

Hamilton, Nigel (1944–): Biographer who writes lengthy, in-depth books about prominent literary, military, or political figures. He also writes about the history of biography.

- *The Brothers Mann: The Lives of Heinrich and Thomas Mann, 1871–1950 and 1875–1955* (1979)
- *Monty: The Making of a General, 1887–1942* (1981)
- *Master of the Battlefield: Monty's War Years, 1942–1944* (1983)
- *Monty: Final Years of the Field-Marshal, 1944–1976* (1987)
- *JFK: Reckless Youth* (1992)
- *Monty: The Battles of Field Marshal Bernard Montgomery* (1994)
- *Bill Clinton: An American Journey, Great Expectations* (2003)
- *Montgomery: D-Day Commander* (2007)
- *Bill Clinton: Mastering the Presidency* (2007)

  Authors to try: Stephen A. Ambrose, Douglas Brinkley, Robert A. Caro, David Halberstam, David Maraniss, Garry Wills

Hattersley, Roy (1932–): Member of the British Parliament who writes in-depth books about passionate people. These books have been published in the United States.

- *Nelson* (1974)
- *Blood and Fire: William and Catherine Booth and Their Salvation Army* (2000)
- *The Life of John Wesley: A Brand from the Burning* (2003)

  Authors to try: Kenneth D. Ackerman, A. Scott Berg, Ross King, Eve LaPlante, Margot Peters, David S. Reynolds, Brenda Wineapple

Hibbert, Christopher (1924–2008): Prolific biographer who skillfully depicts English and European historical figures.

- *Il Duce* (1962)
- *Garibaldi and His Enemies* (1966)
- *The Making of Charles Dickens* (1967)
- *Charles I* (1968)
- *The Personal History of Samuel Johnson* (1971)
- *Edward: The Uncrowned King* (1972)
- *George IV: Prince of Wales, 1762–1811* (1974)
- *George IV: Regent and King, 1811–1830* (1975)
- *The Royal Victorians: King Edward VII, His Family and Friends* (1976).
- *Gilbert and Sullivan and Their Victorian World* (1976)
- *The Virgin Queen: Elizabeth I, Genius of the Golden Age* (1991)
- *Nelson: A Personal History* (1994)
- *Wellington: A Personal History* (1997)
- *George III: A Personal History* (1998)
- *Queen Victoria: A Personal History* (2000)
- *The Marlboroughs: John and Sarah Churchill, 1650–1744* (2001)
- *Napoleon: His Wives and Women* (2002)
- *Disraeli: The Victorian Dandy Who Became Prime Minister* (2006)
- *Mussolini: The Rise and Fall of Il Duce* (2007)

  Authors to try: Antonia Fraser, Robert K. Massie, Nigel Saul, Alison Weir, Derek Wilson

Higham, Charles (1931–): Poet who tried his hand at biography and never stopped. He has recently turned from Hollywood celebrities to the British upper classes.

- *Ziegfeld* (1972)
- *Cecil B. De Mille: A Biography* (1973)
- *Ava: A Life Story* (1974)
- *Warner Brothers* (1975)
- *Kate: The Life of Katharine Hepburn* (1975)
- *Charles Laughton: An Intimate Biography* (1975)
- *The Adventures of Conan Doyle* (1976)
- *Marlene: The Life of Marlene Dietrich* (1977)
- *Errol Flynn: The Untold Story* (1980)

- *Bette: The Life of Bette Davis* (1981)

- *Princess Merle: The Romantic Life of Merle Oberon* (1983)

- *Audrey: The Life of Audrey Hepburn* (1984)

- *Sisters: The Lives of Olivia de Havilland and Joan Fontaine* (1984)

- *Orson Welles: The Rise and Fall of an American Genius* (1985)

- *Lucy: The Life of Lucille Ball* (1986)

- *The Duchess of Windsor: The Secret Life* (1988)

- *Howard Hughes: The Secret Life* (1993)

- *Merchant of Dreams: Louis B. Mayer, M.G.M., and the Secret Hollywood* (1993)

- *Rose: The Life and Times of Rose Fitzgerald Kennedy* (1995)

- *The Duchess of Windsor: The Secret Life* (2005)

- *Dark Lady: Winston Churchill's Mother and Her World* (2006)

    Authors to try: Anne Edwards, Fred Lawrence Guiles, C. David Heymann, Kitty Kelley, Andrew Morton, Tom Santopietro, Sally Bedall Smith, James Spada, J. Randy Taraborrelli

Isaacson, Walter (1952–): Journalist and network executive who has written acclaimed epic biographies of historic figures.

- *Kissinger: A Biography* (1993)

- *Benjamin Franklin: An American Life* (2003)

- *Einstein: His Life and Universe* (2007)

    Authors to try: A. Scott Berg, Andrew Burstein, Ron Chernow, David Herbert Donald, Joseph J. Ellis, Neal Gabler, Robert K. Massie, David McCullough, Paul C. Nagel, Dava Sobel

Kelley, Kitty (1942–): Journalist who is widely known for unauthorized biographies that reveal unknown stories about prominent people.

- *Jackie Oh!* (1978)

- *Elizabeth Taylor: The Last Star* (1981)

- *His Way: The Unauthorized Biography of Frank Sinatra* (1986)

- *Nancy Reagan: The Unauthorized Biography* (1991)

- *The Royals* (1997)

- *The Family: The Real Story of the Bush Dynasty* (2004)

    Authors to try: Anne Edwards, Fred Lawrence Guiles, C. David Heymann, Charles Higham, Andrew Morton, Tom Santopietro, Sally Bedall Smith, James Spada, J. Randy Taraborrelli

King, Ross (1962–): Historian and novelist who writes biographies of cultural figures in richly detailed settings.

- *Brunelleschi's Dome: How a Renaissance Genius Reinvented Architecture* (2000)
- *Michelangelo and the Pope's Ceiling* (2003)
- *Machiavelli: Philosopher of Power* (2007)

 Authors to try: Peter Ackroyd, Roy Hattersley, Paul Johnson, Charles Nicholl, David S. Reynolds, Nigel Saul, Dava Sobel, Ann Wroe

Lovell, Mary S. (1941–): Versatile British biographer who often writes about brave and adventurous women.

- *Straight on Till Morning: The Biography of Beryl Markham* (1987)
- *The Sound of Wings: The Life of Amelia Earhart* (1989)
- *Cast No Shadow: The Life of the American Spy Who Changed the Course of World War II* (1992)
- *Rebel Heart: The Scandalous Life of Jane Digby* (1995)
- *A Rage to Live: A Biography of Richard and Isabel Burton* (1998)
- *The Sisters: The Saga of the Mitford Family* (2002)
- *Bess of Hardwick: First Lady of Chatsworth, 1527–1608* (2006)

 Authors to try: A. Scott Berg, Ann Blackman, Katherine Frank, Mary S. Lovell, Brenda Maddox, Claire Tomalin

Macintyre, Ben (1963–): Journalist who writes about flamboyant historical characters.

- *Forgotten Fatherland: The Search for Elisabeth Nietzsche* (1992)
- *The Napoleon of Crime: The Life and Times of Adam Worth, Master Thief* (1997)
- *The Englishman's Daughter: A True Story of Love and Betrayal in World War I* (2002)
- *The Man Who Would Be King: The First American in Afghanistan* (2004)
- *Agent Zigzag: A True Story of Nazi Espionage, Love, and Betrayal* (2007)

 Authors to try: Andrew Cook, Laurence Bergreen, Mary S. Lovell, Charles Nicholl, Jack Repcheck, David S. Reynolds, Kenneth Silverman

Maddox, Brenda (1932–): American biographer who writes eloquently about moody British characters.

- *Nora: The Real Life of Molly Bloom* (1988)
- *D. H. Lawrence: The Story of a Marriage* (1994)
- *Yeats's Ghosts: The Secret Life of W. B. Yeats* (1999)
- *Rosalind Franklin: The Dark Lady of DNA* (2002)

- *Freud's Wizard: Ernest Jones and the Transformation of Psychoanalysis* (2007)

  Authors to try: Ann Blackman, Mary S. Lovell, Diane Wood Middlebrook, Margot Peters, Claire Tomalin

Man, John (1941–): Versatile nonfiction author who has recently written biographies of legendary characters from history.

- *Gutenberg: How One Man Remade the World with Words* (2002)
- *Genghis Khan: Life, Death, and Resurrection* (2004)
- *Attila: The Barbarian King Who Challenged Rome* (2006)

  Authors to try: Peter Ackroyd, Philip Freeman, Charles Nicholl, Dava Sobel, Ann Wroe

Maraniss, David (1949–): Journalist who writes perceptively about political and sports figures.

- *First in His Class: A Biography of Bill Clinton* (1995)
- *The Clinton Enigma: A Four-and-a-Half-Minute Speech Reveals This President's Entire Life* (1998)
- *When Pride Still Mattered: A Life of Vince Lombardi* (2000)
- *The Prince of Tennessee: The Rise of Al Gore* (2000)
- *Clemente: The Passion and Grace of Baseball's Last Hero* (2006)

  Authors to try: Douglas Brinkley, Frank Deford, David Halberstam, Nigel Hamilton, Leigh Montville, Garry Wills

Massie, Robert K. (1929–): Journalist turned historian who writes detailed biographies of important figures from Russian history.

- *Nicholas and Alexandra* (1967)
- *Peter the Great: His Life and World* (1980)
- *The Romanovs: The Final Chapter* (1995)

  Authors to try: Andrew Burstein, David Herbert Donald, Antonia Fraser, Walter Isaacson, Virginia Rounding, Alison Weir

McCullough, David (1933–): Historian and narrator for public television documentaries who has written highly popular biographies of American presidents.

- *Mornings on Horseback: The Story of an Extraordinary Family, a Vanished Way of Life, and the Unique Child Who Became Theodore Roosevelt*
- *Brave Companions: Portraits in History* (1992)
- *Truman* (1992)
- *John Adams* (2001)

  Authors to try: A. Scott Berg, Andrew Burstein, Joseph J. Ellis, Walter Isaacson, Edmund Morris, Paul C. Nagel, Robert Remini, Jean Edward Smith

McFeely, William S. (1930–): Historian whose biographies focus on prominent nineteenth-century Americans.

- *Grant: A Biography* (1981)

- *Frederick Douglass* (1991)

- *Ulysses S. Grant: An Album; Warrior, Husband, Traveler, "Emancipator," Writer* (2003)

- *Portrait: A Life of Thomas Eakins* (2006)

  Authors to try: H. W. Brands, Andrew Burstein, David Herbert Donald, Edmund Morris, Robert Remini, Jean Edward Smith, Jean Strouse

Meyers, Jeffrey (1939–): Prolific biographer concerned with making sense of the lives of novelists, actors, and artists.

- *Katherine Mansfield: A Biography* (1980)

- *The Enemy: A Biography of Wyndham Lewis* (1982)

- *Hemingway: A Biography* (1985)

- *Manic Power: Robert Lowell and His Circle* (1987)

- *D.H. Joseph Conrad: A Biography* (1991)

- *Edgar Allan Poe: His Life and Legacy* (1992)

- *Scott Fitzgerald: A Biography* (1994)

- *Edmund Wilson: A Biography* (1995)

- *Robert Frost: A Biography* (1996)

- *Bogart: A Life in Hollywood* (1997)

- *Gary Cooper: American Hero* (1998)

- *Orwell: Wintry Conscience of a Generation* (2000)

- *Inherited Risk: Errol and Sean Flynn in Hollywood and Vietnam* (2002)

- *Somerset Maugham: A Life* (2004)

- *Impressionist Quartet: The Intimate Genius of Manet and Morisot, Degas and Cassatt* (2005)

- *Modigliani: A Life* (2006)

  Authors to try: Linda H. Davis, Marc Eliot, Charles Nicholl, Margot Peters, Carl Rollyson, Stanley Weintraub

Middlebrook, Diane Wood (1939–2007): Biographer praised for her balanced accounts of troubled lives of poets and novelists.

- *Anne Sexton: A Biography* (1991)

- *Suits Me: The Double Life of Billy Tipton* (1998)

- *Her Husband: Hughes and Plath: A Marriage* (2003)

   Authors to try: Benita Eisler, Katherine Frank, Brenda Maddox, Carl Rollyson, Claire Tomalin

Montville, Leigh (n.d.): Sports journalist who writes about the character of top athletes.

- *Manute: The Center of Two Worlds* (1993)

- *At the Altar of Speed: The Fast Life and Tragic Death of Dale Earnhardt* (2001).

- *Ted Williams: The Biography of an American Hero* (2004)

- *The Big Bam: The Life and Times of Babe Ruth* (2006)

- *The Mysterious Montague: A True Tale of Hollywood, Golf, and Armed Robbery* (2008)

   Authors to try: Frank Deford, David Halberstam, Roger Kahn, David Maraniss, Ron Rapoport

Morris, Edmund (1940–): Biographer who won acclaim for his books on Theodore Roosevelt and scorn for making himself a fictional character in his biography of Ronald Reagan.

- *The Rise of Theodore Roosevelt* (1979)

- *Dutch: A Memoir of Ronald Reagan* (1999)

- *Theodore Rex* (2001)

- *Beethoven: The Universal Composer* (2005)

   Authors to try: Robert A. Caro, Nigel Hamilton, Michael Korda, David McCullough, William S. McFeely

Morton, Andrew (1953–): Celebrity biographer who documented the British royal family before turning to American subjects.

- *Andrew, the Playboy Prince* (1983)

- *Duchess: An Intimate Portrait of Sarah, Duchess of York* (1989)

- *Diana's Diary: An Intimate Portrait of the Princess of Wales* (1990)

- *Diana: Her True Story* (1992)

- *Diana: Her New Life* (1994)

- *Diana: Her True Story—In Her Own Words* (1997)

- *Monica's Story* (1999)

- *Madonna* (2001)

- *Tom Cruise* (2008)

   Authors to try: Anne Edwards, Fred Lawrence Guiles, C. David Heymann, Charles Higham, Kitty Kelley, Tom Santopietro, Sally Bedall Smith, James Spada, J. Randy Taraborrelli

Nagel, Paul C. (1926): Author of multigenerational family biographies of the Adamses and the Lees.

- *Descent from Glory: Four Generations of the John Adams Family* (1983)
- *The Adams Women: Abigail and Louisa Adams, Their Sisters and Daughters* (1987)
- *The Lees of Virginia: Seven Generations of an American Family* (1990)
- *John Quincy Adams: A Public Life, a Private Life* (1997)
- *George Caleb Bingham: Missouri's Famed Painter and Forgotten Politician* (2005)

> **Authors to try**: Ron Chernow, Peter Collier, David Herbert Donald, Joseph J. Ellis, Walter Isaacson, David McCullough, Robert Remini

Nicholl, Charles (1950–): Journalist who usually writes about the lives and times of literary figures. The exception is an articulate book about Leonardo and his notebooks.

- *A Cup of News: The Life of Thomas Nashe* (1984)
- *The Reckoning: The Murder of Christopher Marlowe* (1992)
- *Somebody Else: Arthur Rimbaud in Africa, 1880–91* (1997)
- *Leonardo da Vinci: Flights of the Mind* (2004)
- *The Lodger Shakespeare: His Life on Silver Street* (2008)

> **Authors to try:** Peter Ackroyd, Laurence Bergreen, Stephen Coote, Ross King, Jeffrey Meyers, John Man, Ann Wroe

Peters, Margot (1933–): Theater historian who writes about the lives and careers of actors, directors, and playwrights.

- *Unquiet Soul: A Biography of Charlotte Brontë* (1975)
- *Bernard Shaw and the Actresses* (1980)
- *Mrs. Pat: The Life of Mrs. Patrick Campbell* (1984)
- *The House of Barrymore* (1991)
- *May Sarton: A Biography* (1997)
- *Design for Living: Alfred Lunt and Lynn Fontaine: A Biography* (2003)

> **Authors to try**: Linda H. Davis, Benita Eisler, Eve LaPlante, Brenda Maddox, Diane Wood Middlebrook, Stanley Weintraub

Remini, Robert (1921–): Historian who writes in-depth biographies of figures from the Jacksonian era in American history.

- *Andrew Jackson* (1966)
- *Henry Clay: Statesman for the Union* (1991)
- *Daniel Webster: The Man and His Time* (1997)

- *Andrew Jackson and His Indian Wars* (2001)

- *John Quincy Adams* (2002)

- *Joseph Smith* (2002)

    Authors to try: H. W. Brands, Andrew Burstein, David Herbert Donald, David McCullough, William S. McFeely, Jean Edward Smith, Jean Strouse

Reynolds, David S. (1948–): Author of epic biographies of American dissidents. These books are especially rich in cultural detail.

- *George Lippard, Prophet of Protest: Writings of an American Radical* (1986)

- *Walt Whitman's America: A Cultural Biography* (1995)

- *John Brown, Abolitionist: The Man Who Killed Slavery, Sparked the Civil War, and Seeded Civil Rights* (2005)

    Authors to try: Roy Hattersley, Ross King, Ben Macintyre, Kenneth Silverman, Brenda Wineapple

Richardson, John (1924–): Art critic who tells wickedly entertaining stories about the misfits he admires.

- *Manet* (1967)

- *A Life of Picasso: Volume I, Prodigy, 1881–1906* (1991)

- *A Life of Picasso: Volume 2, Cubist Rebel, 1907–1917* (1996)

- *The Sorcerer's Apprentice: Picasso, Provence, and Douglas Cooper* (1999)

- *Sacred Monsters, Sacred Masters: Beaton, Capote, Dali, Picasso, Freud, and More* (2001)

- *A Life of Picasso: Volume 3, The Triumphant Years 1917–1932* (2007)

    Authors to try: Leon Edel, Robert Hughes, Ross King, Carl Rollyson, Simon Schama, Stanley Weintraub

Rollyson, Carl (1948–): Literary critic and editor of literary reference books whose biographies often upset their subjects if they are still living.

- *Marilyn Monroe: A Life of the Actress* (1986)

- *Lillian Hellman: Her Legend and Her Legacy* (1988)

- *Nothing Ever Happens to the Brave: The Story of Martha Gellhorn* (1990)

- *The Lives of Norman Mailer: A Biography* (1991)

- *Pablo Picasso* (1993)

- *Rebecca West: A Life* (1996)

- *Susan Sontag: The Making of an Icon* (2000)

    Authors to try: Anne Edwards, Kitty Kelley, Jeffery Meyers, John Richardson, Sally Bedall Smith

Smith, Jean Edward (1932–): Political scientist who writes comprehensive biographies of important figures in American history.

- *Lucius D. Clay: An American Life* (1990)

- *John Marshall: Definer of a Nation* (1996)

- *Grant* (2001)

- *FDR* (2007)

    Authors to try: H. W. Brands, James MacGregor Burns, David Burstein, Robert A. Caro, David Herbert Donald, David McCullough, William S. McFeely

Smith, Sally Bedall (1948–): Journalist who mixes social history with political history in her biographies about powerful figures.

- *In All His Glory: The Life of William S. Paley, the Legendary Tycoon and His Brilliant Circle* (1991)

- *Reflected Glory: The Life of Pamela Churchill* (1996)

- *Diana in Search of Herself: Portrait of a Troubled Princess* (1999)

- *Grace and Power: The Private World of the Kennedy White House* (2004)

- *For Love of Politics: Bill and Hillary Clinton, the White House Years* (2007)

    Authors to try: Anne Edwards, Fred Lawrence Guiles, C. David Heymann, Charles Higham, Kitty Kelley, Andrew Morton, Tom Santopietro, James Spada, J. Randy Taraborrelli

Spada, James (1950): Celebrity biographer who reveals untold stories about Holly-wood stars. He has added political subjects in recent years.

- *Streisand: The Woman and the Legend* (1981)

- *Monroe: Her Life in Pictures* (1982)

- *Judy and Liza* (1983)

- *Hepburn: Her Life in Pictures* (1984)

- *The Divine Bette Midler* (1984)

- *Fonda: Her Life in Pictures* (1985)

- *Shirley and Warren* (1985)

- *Grace: The Secret Lives of a Princess—An Intimate Biography of Grace Kelly* (1987)

- *Peter Lawford: The Man Who Kept the Secrets* (1991)

- *More Than a Woman: An Intimate Biography of Bette Davis* (1993)

- *Streisand: Her Life* (1995)

- *Jackie: Her Life in Pictures* (2000)

- *Ronald Reagan: His Life in Pictures* (2001)

- *John and Caroline: Their Lives in Pictures* (2001)
- *Julia Roberts: An Intimate Biography* (2004)
- *Bush Family: Four Generations of History in Photographs* (2004)

    Authors to try: Anne Edwards, Fred Lawrence Guiles, C. David Heymann, Charles Higham, Kitty Kelley, Andrew Morton, Sally Bedell Smith, Tom Santopietro, J. Randy Taraborrelli

Spoto, David (1941–): Celebrity biographer interested in film directors, who has recently begun to write about religious figures also.

- *Stanley Kramer, Film Maker* (1978)
- *The Dark Side of Genius: The Life of Alfred Hitchcock* (1983)
- *The Kindness of Strangers: The Life of Tennessee Williams* (1985)
- *Falling in Love Again: Marlene Dietrich* (1985)
- *Lenya: A Life* (1989).
- *Madcap: The Life of Preston Sturges* (1990)
- *Blue Angel: The Life of Marlene Dietrich* (1992)
- *Laurence Olivier: A Biography* (1992)
- *Marilyn Monroe: The Biography* (1993)
- *A Passion for Life: The Biography of Elizabeth Taylor* (1995)
- *Rebel: The Life and Legend of James Dean* (1996)
- *Notorious: The Life of Ingrid Bergman* (1997)
- *Diana: The Last Year* (1997)
- *The Hidden Jesus: A New Life* (1998)
- *Jacqueline Bouvier Kennedy Onassis: A Life* (2000)
- *Reluctant Saint: The Life of Francis of Assisi* (2002)
- *Enchantment: The Life of Audrey Hepburn* (2006)
- *Joan: The Mysterious Life of the Heretic Who Became a Saint* (2007)
- *Spellbound by Beauty: Alfred Hitchcock and His Leading Ladies* (2008)

    Authors to try: Charlotte Chandler, Anne Edwards, Fred Lawrence Guiles, C. David Heymann, Charles Higham, Kitty Kelley, Andrew Morton, Sally Bedell Smith, Tom Santopietro, J. Randy Taraborrelli

Taraborrelli, J. Randy (1956–): Journalist who writes detailed accounts of pop singers, actors, and other public figures, without cooperation from his subjects.

- *Diana* (1985)

- *Cher: A Biography* (1986)
- *Laughing Till It Hurts: The Complete Life and Career of Carol Burnett* (1988)
- *Call Her Miss Ross: The Unauthorized Biography of Diana Ross* (1989)
- *Michael Jackson: The Magic and the Madness* (1991)
- *Roseanne Arnold* (1993)
- *Sinatra: Behind the Legend* (1997)
- *Jackie, Ethel, Joan: Women of Camelot* (2000)
- *Madonna: An Intimate Biography* (2001)
- *Once Upon a Time: Behind the Fairy Tale of Princess Grace and Prince Rainier* (2003)
- *Elizabeth* (2006)
- *Diana Ross: A Biography* (2007)

   Authors to try: Anne Edwards, Fred Lawrence Guiles, C. David Heymann, Charles Higham, Kitty Kelley, Andrew Morton, Tom Santopietro, Sally Bedall Smith, James Spada

Tomalin, Claire (1933–): Author of biographies that focus on private lives of English poets, novelists, and mistresses.

- *The Life and Death of Mary Wollstonecraft* (1974)
- *Shelley and His World* (1980)
- *Katherine Mansfield: A Secret Life* (1987)
- *The Invisible Woman: The Story of Nelly Ternan and Charles Dickens* (1991)
- *Mrs. Jordan's Profession: The Story of a Great Actress and a Future King* (1994)
- *Jane Austen: A Life* (1997)
- *Samuel Pepys: The Unequalled Self,* Knopf (2002)
- *Thomas Hardy: The Time-Torn Man* (2006)

   Authors to try: Katherine Frank, Mary S. Lovell, Brenda Maddox, Virginia Rounding, Stanley Weintraub, Brenda Wineapple

Wayne, Jane Ellen (1936–): Celebrity biographer who focuses on marriages and love lives of actors and actresses.

- *The Life of Robert Taylor* (1973)
- *Stanwyck* (1985)
- *Robert Taylor* (1987)
- *Gable's Women* (1987)
- *Cooper's Women* (1988)

- *Crawford's Men* (1988)

- *Ava's Men: The Private Life of Ava Gardner* (1990)

- *Grace Kelly's Men* (1991)

- *Marilyn's Men: The Private Life of Marilyn Monroe* (1992)

- *Clark Gable: Portrait of a Misfit* (1993)

- *Lana: The Life and Loves of Lana Turner* (1995)

- *The Golden Girls of MGM: Greta Garbo, Joan Crawford, Lana Turner, Judy Garland, Ava Gardner, Grace Kelly, and Others* (2003)

- *The Leading Men of MGM* (2005)

  Authors to try: Charlotte Chandler, Jeffrey Meyers, James Spada, David Spoto, J. Randy Taraborrelli

Weintraub, Stanley (1929–): Versatile author of biographies of cultural and political figures from the Victorian era.

- *Private Shaw and Public Shaw: A Dual Portrait of Lawrence of Arabia and George Bernard Shaw* (1963)

- *Reggie: A Portrait of Reginald Turner* (1965)

- *Beardsley: A Biography* (1967)

- *Journey to Heartbreak: The Crucible Years of Bernard Shaw, 1914–1918* (1972)

- *Whistler: A Biography* (1974)

- *Four Rossettis: A Victorian Biography* (1977)

- *The London Yankees: Portraits of American Writers and Artists in London, 1894–1914* (1979)

- *The Unexpected Shaw: Biographical Approaches to G.B.S. and His Work* (1982)

- *Victoria: An Intimate Biography* (1987)

- *Disraeli: A Biography* (1993)

- *Uncrowned King: The Life of Prince Albert* (1997)

- *The Importance of Being Edward: King in Waiting, 1841–1901* (2000)

- *Edward the Caresser: The Playboy Prince Who Became Edward VII* (2001)

- *Charlotte and Lionel: A Rothschild Love Story* (2003)

- *Fifteen Stars: Intersected Lives: MacArthur, Marshall, Eisenhower* (2007)

  Authors to try: Peter Ackroyd, Laurence Bergreen, Stephen Coote, Jeffrey Meyers, Margot Peters, John Richardson, Claire Tomalin

Weir, Alison (n.d.): Historian who writes richly detailed biographies of British monarchs and their families.

- *The Six Wives of Henry VIII* (1991)
- *The Princes in the Tower* (1994)
- *The Children of Henry VIII* (1996)
- *The Life of Elizabeth I* (1999)
- *Eleanor of Aquitaine* (2000)
- *Henry VIII: The King and His Court* (2001)
- *Mary, Queen of Scots, and the Murder of Lord Darnley* (2003)
- *Queen Isabella: Treachery, Adultery, and Murder in Medieval England* (2005)
- *Mistress of the Monarchy: The Life of Katherine Swynford, Duchess of Lancaster* (2009)

    Authors to try: Antonia Fraser, Christopher Hibbert, Robert K. Massie, Nigel Saul, Derek Wilson

Wills, Garry (1934–): Versatile author who writes about politics, history, culture, and religion. His biographies are insightful and concise.

- *Chesterton: Man and Mask* (1961)
- *Jack Ruby* (1968)
- *John Wayne's America: The Politics of Celebrity* (1997)
- *Saint Augustine* (1999)
- *James Madison* (2002)
- *Henry Adams and the Making of America* (2005)

    Authors to try: Stephen A. Ambrose, H. W. Brands, Douglas Brinkley, David Halberstam, Joseph. J. Ellis, David Maraniss, David Spoto

Wilson, Derek (1935–): English novelist and historian especially known for his books about Tudor England. These biographies have been published in the United States.

- *The World Encompassed: Francis Drake and His Great Voyage* (1977)
- *England in the Age of Thomas More* (1979)
- *Rothschild: The Wealth and Power of a Dynasty* (1988)
- *The Astors: 1763–1992* (1993)
- *The King and the Gentleman: Charles Stuart and Oliver Cromwell* (1999)
- *Charlemagne: Barbarian & Emperor* (2006)
- *Sir Francis Walsingham: A Courtier in an Age of Terror* (2007)
- *Out of the Storm: The Life and Legacy of Martin Luther* (2008)

    Authors to try: Antonia Fraser, Christopher Hibbert, Robert K. Massie, Nigel Saul, Alison Weir

Winchester, Simon (1944–): Journalist interested in the history of science, adventure, and world affairs, who profiles unusual, little-known characters.

- *The Professor and the Madman: A Tale of Murder, Insanity, and the Making of the Oxford English Dictionary* (1998)

- *The Map That Changed the World: William Smith and the Birth of Modern Geology* (2001)

- *The Man Who Loved China: The Fantastic Story of the Eccentric Scientist Who Unlocked the Mysteries of the Middle Kingdom* (2008)

    Authors to try: Laurence Bergreen, Ross King, Ben Macintyre, Jack Repcheck, Dava Sobel

Wroe, Ann (n.d.): Journalist whose eloquent biographies investigate enigmatic historical characters and their deeds.

- *Pontius Pilate* (2000)

- *The Perfect Prince: The Mystery of Perkin Warbeck and His Quest for the Throne of England* (2003)

- *Being Shelley: The Poet's Search for Himself* (2007)

    Authors to try: Benita Eisler, Ross King, John Man, Charles Nicholl, David Spoto

Appendix C

Biography Series

Although books in series are not as prevalent in publishing for adults as they are in publishing for children, there are some distinguished series, especially in biography. Readers often appreciate these series because there is a guaranteed level of similarity in content and style to books that they have already read and enjoyed. The publishing cycles of most series usually do not last long, as publishers turn their attentions to other projects, but some of the books produced during the short period are lasting in appeal.

In this appendix are descriptions of recent biographical series with lists of the titles in them. Most of the titles are introductory biographies that recount the essential events and accomplishments of their subjects. These lists are useful for identifying read-alikes and quick reads. The titles under each series are listed alphabetically.

I have included publisher Web site addresses for some of the lists. Surprisingly, some of the publishers either do not have easily found Web pages for their series or have incomplete listings. I checked all the series in WorldCat (worldcat.org), Amazon (www.amazon.com), and Barnes & Noble (www.bn.com), often finding titles not cited on publisher Web sites.

20th-Century Composers: Well-illustrated biographies of musical figures from Phaidon Press. Most of the subjects come from opera and classical music, but the Beatles and Broadway composers are also included. The publisher is British, but the books are available in the United States. These are ideal for symphony season ticket holders or serious students of music.

- *Alfred Schnittke* by Alexander Ivashkin (1996)
- *Anton von Webern* by Malcolm Hayes (1995)
- *The Beatles* by Allan Kozinn (1995)
- *Béla Bartók* by Kenneth Chalmers (1995)
- *Benjamin Britten* by Michael Oliver (1996)
- *Carl Nielsen* by Jack Lawson (1997)
- *Claude Debussy* by Paul Roberts (2008)
- *Erich Wolfgang Korngold* by Jessica Duchen (1996)
- *Francis Poulenc* by Benjamin Ivry (1996)

- *Gabriel Fauré* by Jessica Duchen (2000)
- *George Gershwin* by Rodney Greenberg (1998)
- *Giacomo Puccini* by Conrad Wilson (1997)
- *Györy Ligeti* by Richard Toop (1999)
- *Igor Stravinsky* by Michael Oliver (1995)
- *Jean Sibelius* by Guy Rickards (1997)
- *Leonard Bernstein* by Paul Myers (1998)
- *Maurice Ravel* by Gerald Larner (1996)
- *Richard Strauss* by Tim Ashley (1999)
- *Sergey Prokofiev* by Daniel Jaffé (1998)

Publisher Web site: http://www.phaidon.com/Default.aspx/Web/Music-And-Performing-Arts-20th-Century-Composers

Ackroyd's Brief Lives: Short biographies from the versatile author Peter Ackroyd, featuring eminent people from British history. Good for readers who enjoy quick reads about historical figures.

- *Chaucer* by Peter Ackroyd (2004)
- *J. M. W. Turner* by Peter Ackroyd (2006)
- *Newton* by Peter Ackroyd (2006)

American Heroes: Compact, nicely written biographies from Forge Books, an imprint of Tom Doherty Associates. Unlike some other series, each volume includes an index and list of sources. All are available in a variety of audiobook formats as well as hardcover and paperback. These would go well in teen or adult collections.

- *Amelia Earhart: The Sky's No Limit* by Lori Van Pelt (2005)
- *Chief Joseph: Guardian of the People* by Candy Moulton (2005)
- *David Crockett: Hero of the Common Man* by William Groneman III (2005)
- *George Washington: First in War, First in Peace* by James A. Crutchfield (2005)
- *John Muir: Magnificent Tramp* by Rod Miller (2005)
- *Mary Edwards Walker: Above and Beyond* by Dale L. Walker (2005)

Publisher Web site (incomplete): http://us.macmillan.com/series/AmericanHeroes

American Presidents: Compact biographies of American presidents written by historians and published by Times Books. Each book focuses on a president's term in office.

- *Andrew Jackson* by Sean Wilentz (2005)
- *Benjamin Harrison* by Charles W. Calhoun (2005)

- *Calvin Coolidge* by David Greenberg (2007)
- *Chester A. Arthur* by Zachary Karabell (2004)
- *George H. W. Bush* by Timothy Naftali (2007)
- *George Washington* by James MacGregor Burns and Susan Dunn (2004)
- *Gerald R. Ford* by Douglas Brinkley (2007)
- *Harry S. Truman* by Robert Dallak (2008)
- *James A. Garfield* by Ira Rutkow (2006)
- *James Buchanan* by Jean H. Baker (2004)
- *James K. Polk* by John Seigenthaler (2003)
- *James Madison* by Garry Wills (2002)
- *Martin Van Buren* by Ted Widmer (2005)
- *Richard M. Nixon* by Elizabeth Drew (2007)
- *Rutherford B. Hayes* by Hans L. Trefousse (2002)
- *Theodore Roosevelt* by Louis Auchincloss (2001)
- *Thomas Jefferson* by Joyce Oldham Appleby (2003)
- *Ulysses S. Grant* by Joseph Bunting III (2004)
- *Warren G. Harding* by John W. Dean (2004)
- *Zachary Taylor* by John S. D. Eisenhower (2008)

Publisher Web site: http://www.americanpresidentsseries.com/booklist.asp

British Library Historic Lives: Compact biographies of major figures from British history. Each features a chronology and full-color illustrations. These titles are intended for general readers.

- *Duke of Wellington* by Matthew Shaw and Arthur Wellesly (2005)
- *George III* by Christopher Wright (2005)
- *Horatio Lord Nelson* by Brian Lavery (2003)
- *Oliver Cromwell* by Peter Gaunt (2004)
- *Queen Elizabeth I* by Susan Doran (2003)
- *Sir Francis Drake* by Peter Whitfield (2004)
- *T.E. Lawrence* by Malcolm Brown (2003)
- *Winston Churchill* by Stuart Ball (2003)

Eminent Lives: A series that claims to be in the tradition of Plutarch's *Lives* and Vasari's *Lives of the Artists*. These compact biographies, like the <u>Penguin Lives</u> before them (see page 490), were written by a variety of eminent scholars. From Atlas Books, an imprint of HarperCollins, these books profile important political, cultural, and scientific figures. <u>Eminent Lives</u> are meant for pleasure reading first and scholarship second.

- *Alexis de Tocqueville: Democracy's Guide* by Joseph Epstein (2006)
- *Beethoven: The Universal Composer* by Edmund Morris (2005)
- *Caravaggio: Painter of Miracles* by Francine Prose (2005)
- *Francis Crick: Discoverer of the Genetic Code* by Matt Ridley
- *George Balanchine: The Ballet Maker* by Robert Gottlieb (2004)
- *George Washington: The Founding Father* by Paul Johnson (2005)
- *Machiavelli: Philosopher of Power* by Ross King (2007)
- *Muhammad: A Prophet for Our Time* by Karen Armstrong (2006)
- *Shakespeare: The World as Stage* by Bill Bryson (2007)
- *Sigmund Freud: Inventor of the Modern Mind* by Peter D. Kramer (2006)
- *Thomas Jefferson: Author of America* by Christopher Hitchens (2005)
- *Ulysses S. Grant: The Unlikely Hero* by Michael Korda (2004)

Publisher Web site: http://atlasandco.com/copublishing-projects/eminent-lives/

English Monarchs: Scholarly biographies based on new research aimed at college level readers. Because of high interest in British monarchs, these books from Yale University Press still make their way into public library collections.

- *Edward I* by Michael Prestwich (1997)
- *Edward IV* by Charles Ross (1998)
- *Edward VI* by Jennifer Loach (1999)
- *George I* by Ragnhild Hatton (2001)
- *George III* by Jeremy Black (2006)
- *George IV* by E. A. Smith (1999)
- *Henry I* by C. Warren Hollister (2001)
- *Henry VI* by Bertram Wolffe (2001)
- *Henry VII* by S. B. Chrimes (1998)
- *James II* by John Miller (2000)
- *Queen Anne* by Edward Gregg (2001)
- *Richard I* by John Gillingham (1999)

- *Richard II* by Nigel Saul (1997)
- *William Rufus* by Frank Barlow (2000)

Publisher Web site: http://yalepress.yale.edu/yupbooks/SeriesPage.asp?Series=64

Great Discoveries: A series highlighting the lives and discoveries of eminent scientists. Noted authors, including novelists, essayists, and historians, explain both scientific concepts and the lives of scientists in these compact and compelling books from Atlas & Company in partnership with W. W. Norton. Suitable for public library collections.

- *The Doctor's Plague: Germs, Childbed Fever, and the Strange Story of Ignác Semmelweis* by Sherwin Nuland (2003)
- *Einstein's Cosmos: How Albert Einstein's Vision Transformed Our Understanding of Space and Time* by Michio Kaku (2004)
- *Everything and More: A Compact History of ∞* by David Foster Wallace (2003)
- *A Force of Nature: The Frontier Genius of Ernest Rutherford* by Richard Reeves (2008)
- *Incompleteness: The Proof and Paradox of Kurt Gödel* by Rebecca Goldstein (2005)
- *Lavoisier in the Year One: The Birth of a New Science in an Age of Revolution* by Madison Smartt Bell (2005)
- *The Man Who Knew Too Much: Alan Turing and the Invention of the Computer* by David Leavitt (2006)
- *Miss Leavitt's Stars: The Untold Story of the Woman Who Discovered How to Measure the Universe* by George Johnson (2005)
- *Obsessive Genius: The Inner World of Marie Curie* by Barbara Goldsmith (2005)
- *The Reluctant Mr. Darwin: An Intimate Portrait of Charles Darwin and the Making of His Theory of Evolution* by David Quammen (2006)
- *Uncentering the Earth: Copernicus and The Revolutions of the Heavenly Spheres* by William T. Vollmann (2006)

Publisher Web site: http://atlasandco.com/copublishing-projects/great-discoveries/

Great Generals Series: Concise biographies of American military leaders. Popular military historians recount generals' personal lives and battle stories. From Palgrave Macmillan, this series is aimed at general readers.

- *Andrew Jackson* by Robert Remini (2008)
- *Bradley* by Alan Axelrod (2007)
- *Eisenhower* by John Wukovits (2006)
- *Grant* by John Mosier (2006)
- *LeMay* by Barrett Tillman (2007)
- *MacArthur* by Richard B Frank (2007)

- *Patton* by Alan Axelrod (2006)

- *Pershing* by Jim Lacey (2008)

- *Sherman* by Stephen E. Woodworth (2009)

- *Stonewall Jackson* by Donald A. Davis (2007)

Publisher Web site (incomplete): http://www.palgrave-usa.com/greatgenerals/

Jewish Encounters: A series on Jewish life and history that includes some biographies of well-known figures. Noted Jewish authors write on a variety of subjects in these quick reads from Nextbook/Schocken.

- *Barney Ross* by Douglas Century (2006)

- *Benjamin Disraeli* by Adam Kirsch (2008)

- *Betraying Spinoza* by Rebecca Goldstein (2006)

- *Emma Lazarus* by Esther Schor (2006)

- *The Life of David* by Robert Pinsky (2005)

- *Maimonides* by Sherwin B. Nuland (2005)

- *Marc Chagall* by Jonathan Wilson (2007)

Publisher Web site: http://www.nextbook.org/bookseries/

Lives and Legacies: Concise biographies intended as introductions to major historical and cultural figures. These books from Oxford University Press are aimed at general readers.

- *Benjamin Franklin* by Edwin S. Gaustad (2005)

- *Churchill: The Unexpected Hero* by Paul Addison (2004)

- *Isaac Newton* by Gail E. Christianson (2005)

- *Mark Twain* by Larzer Ziff (2004)

- *Oliver Wendell Holmes, Jr.* by G. Edward White (2006)

- *Roger Williams* by Edwin S. Gaustad (2005)

- *T. S. Eliot* by Craig Raine (2006)

- *Walt Whitman* by David S. Reynolds (2004)

- *William Faulkner* by Carolyn Porter (2007)

Publisher Web site: http://www.oup.com/us/catalog/general/series/ LivesandLegaciesSeries/ ?view=usa

Men of Faith: Pocket-sized biographies of Christian thinkers from Bethany House Publishers. These books emphasize contributions to religious thought and practice.

- *C. S. Lewis* by Catherine Swift (1990)
- *Charles Finney* by Basil Miller (1969)
- *Charles Spurgeon* by Kathy Triggs (1984)
- *D. L. Moody* by David Malcolm Bennett (1994)
- *Eric Liddell* by Catherine Swift (1990)
- *George Muller* by Basil Miller (1972)
- *John Wesley* by Basil Miller (1973)
- *Jonathan Edwards* by David J. Vaughan (2000)
- *Martin Luther* by Mike Fearon (1993)
- *Samuel Morris* by Lindley Baldwin (1987)
- *William Booth* by David Malcolm Bennett (1994)
- *William Carey* by Basil Miller (1985)

Publisher Web site (incomplete): www.bethanyhouse.com

Musical Lives: Illustrated biographies of composers of classical music. Cambridge University Press describes the books as "organic," saying they describe the composer and his relationship to his music. These profiles are aimed at general readers.

- *The Life of Bach* by Peter Williams (2004)
- *The Life of Beethoven* by David Wyn Jones (1998)
- *The Life of Bellini* by John Rosselli (1997)
- *The Life of Berlioz* by Peter Bloom (1998)
- *The Life of Charles Ives* by Stuart Feder (1999)
- *The Life of Debussy* by Roger Nichols (1998)
- *The Life of Elgar* by Michael Kennedy (2004)
- *The Life of Haydn* by David Wyn Jones (2009)
- *The Life of Mahler* by Peter Franklin (1997)
- *The Life of Mendelssohn* by Peter Mercer-Taylor (2000)
- *The Life of Messiaen* by Christopher Dingle (2007)
- *The Life of Mozart* by John Rosselli (1998)
- *The Life of Mussorgsky* by Caryl Emerson (1999)
- *The Life of Richard Strauss* by Bryan Gilliam (1999)
- *The Life of Schubert* by Christopher H. Gibbs (2000)

- *The Life of Verdi* by John Rosselli (2000)
- *The Life of Webern* by Kathryn Bailey (1998)

Publisher Web site: http://www.cambridge.org/us/series/sSeries.asp?code=ML

Overlook Illustrated Lives: Compact, highly illustrated biographies depicting the lives of popular literary figures. Aimed at readers wanting to know an author's background, these books from Overlook Press focus on each writer's character and career.

- *Ayn Rand* by Jeff Britting (2004)
- *F. Scott Fitzgerald* by Ruth Prigozy (2001)
- *Franz Kafka* by Jeremy Adler (2002)
- *Marcel Proust* by Mary Ann Caws (2003)
- *Samuel Beckett* by Gerry Dukes (2002)
- *Virginia Wolff* by Mary Ann Caws (2002)
- *Vladimir Nabokov* by Jane Grayson (2001)
- *William Faulkner* by M. Thomas Inge (2006)

Publisher Web site: http://www.overlookpress.com/lives.php

Penguin Lives: A distinguished and wide-ranging series of concise biographies by great writers fascinated by their subjects. Some of these titles from Penguin Group USA's now-suspended series are available in audiobook or large print.

- *Andy Warhol* by Wayne Koestenbaum (2001)
- *Buddha* by Karen Armstrong (2001)
- *Charles Dickens* by Jane Smiley (2002)
- *Crazy Horse* by Larry McMurtry (1999)
- *Dante* by R. W. B. Lewis (2001)
- *Elvis Presley* by Bobbie Ann Mason (2002)
- *George Herbert Walker Bush* by Tom Wicker (2004)
- *Herman Melville* by Elizabeth Hardwick (2000)
- *James Joyce* by Edna O'Brien (1999)
- *Jane Austin* by Carol Shields (2001)
- *Joan of Arc* by Mary Gordon (2000)
- *Joseph Smith* by Robert V. Remini (2002)
- *Leonardo da Vinci* by Sherwin Nuland (2000)
- *Mao Zedong* by Jonathan D. Spence (1999)
- *Marcel Proust* by Edmund White (1999)

- *Marlon Brando* by Patricia Bosworth (2001)
- *Martin Luther* by Martin Marty (2004)
- *Martin Luther King, Jr.* by Marshall Frady (2002)
- *Mozart* by Peter Gay (1999)
- *Napoleon* by Paul Johnson (2002)
- *Pope John XXIII* by Thomas Cahill (2002)
- *Robert E. Lee* by Roy Blount, Jr. (2003)
- *Rosa Parks* by Douglas G. Brinkley (2000)
- *Saint Augustine* by Garry Wills (1999)
- *Simone Weil* by Francine du Plessix Gray (2001)
- *Virginia Woolf* by Nigel Nicholson (2000)
- *Winston Churchill* by John Keegan (2002)
- *Woodrow Wilson* by Louis Auchincloss (2000)

Publisher Web site (incomplete): http://us.penguingroup.com/nf/Theme/
ThemePage/0,,634125,00.html

Author/Title Index

Page numbers where the main entries appear are in boldface type.

Subject Index

Chronological Index

The subjects of the biographies reviewed in this book come from 3,500 years of history. For those who enjoy reading about historical periods, this chronological index identifies books in order of the birth year of the biographical subject. (Subtitles are included only where they identify the subject and the main title does not.) All page references are to main entries.

About the Author

Photo by Bonnie Reid.

RICK ROCHE is a librarian who enjoys answering reference question and helping readers at the Thomas Ford Memorial Library in Western Springs, Illinois. A graduate of the Graduate School of Library and Information Science at the University of Texas at Austin, he has worked in a variety of public libraries in Texas, Missouri, and Illinois and spent six years as a stay-at-home-dad, which he thinks helped make him a more client-conscious librarian. He comments on books, movies, technology, and libraries at his Web site, ricklibrarian.blogspot.com.